By the same author

THE DEVELOPMENT OF RELIGIOUS TOLERATION IN ENGLAND

    I From the beginning of the English Reformation to the death of Queen Elizabeth I

   II From the Accession of James I to the Convention of the Long Parliament, 1603-1640

  III From the Convention of the Long Parliament to the Restoration, 1640-1660

  IV Attainment of the Theory and Accommodations in Thought and Institutions, 1640-1660

PHILANTHROPY IN ENGLAND, 1480-1660

THE CHARITIES OF LONDON, 1480-1660

THE CHARITIES OF RURAL ENGLAND, 1480-1660

THE CHRONICLE AND POLITICAL PAPERS OF KING EDWARD VI (*editor*)

EDWARD VI: THE YOUNG KING

EDWARD VI:
THE YOUNG KING

THE PROTECTORSHIP OF THE DUKE OF SOMERSET

BY

W. K. JORDAN

President Emeritus, Radcliffe College
Leroy B. Williams Professor of History and
Political Science, Harvard University

London

GEORGE ALLEN & UNWIN LTD

RUSKIN HOUSE   MUSEUM STREET

PRINTED IN GREAT BRITAIN
in 11 on 12 pt Erhardt type
BY THE ABERDEEN UNIVERSITY PRESS

PREFACE

This is a long work devoted to a relatively short reign. Save for the short initial section, 'The Henrician Background', which is in form and content an introductory essay, the work is an essentially narrative history, in the preparation of which we have attempted at least to consult the relevant secondary materials as well as the principal sources, printed and manuscript. Over a rather long career, we have been occupied with specialized historical problems which, though of some breadth, have none the less been mono-graphic in their method and interest. In this we have conformed to the historical traditions of our generation, though we have always had the somewhat uncomfortable feeling that historical writing over the past generation may have strayed too far from the surely endur-ing canon that it is the ultimate function of the historian to tell the story of a selected interval of time and place. This work has, then, a probably old-fashioned quality, of which, however, we are so far unashamed that we have indulged ourselves even with battles, broils, and death-bed or, more commonly (this being a Tudor history), scaffold scenes.

We are dealing with a short but very important period in the long annal of English history. Strangely enough, the narrative history of this reign has never been extensively done, probably because it is, so to speak, interlarded between the overweening personality and the momentous events of the reign of Henry VIII and the undoubted greatness and glory of the reign of Edward's great sister.

This is not to say, however, that great historians have not lent attention to the whole course of the reign. It was slightly more than a century ago that Froude completed his volume concerned with the reign of Edward VI, forming part of the monumental series that was to deal with most of the Tudor age. This book remains a literary masterpiece; it rests on original research in groups of sources then known or calendared; and it remains of very consider-able value. But it was also perhaps the most faulted of all the numerous volumes comprising the great series, since Froude dealt at once unfairly and inconsistently with the character and policy of Somerset, Edward VI, and Cranmer, while misunderstanding the religious history of the reign and almost ignoring the social and economic crisis of the mid-sixteenth century.

Somewhat more than a generation later (1910) Professor A. F. Pollard dealt judiciously and brilliantly with the history of the reign in an essay of not quite one hundred pages in his notable volume in the Hunt and Poole 'Political History of England' series. This sketch remains, in my view, the best single work on the narrative of the reign, his earlier and youthful *England under the Protector Somerset* (1900) being not well balanced, not always firmly anchored in the sources, and quite uncritical in its estimate of the mind and policy of the Duke of Somerset.

In the course of the two subsequent generations the reign has been carefully considered by a remarkable number of historians whose specialized studies in many of its aspects have greatly assisted, have indeed made possible this more general work. Even more importantly, learned and dedicated bibliographers have charted the way through both the manuscripts and the contemporaneous printed materials, while an eminent group of editors, beginning with Nichols, Pocock, and Tytler, and continuing to the present day, have immensely facilitated the work of students of the period by printing and editing a very large proportion of the important sources. The work of a legion of scholars, then, both present and past, can be no more than generally acknowledged here, though the titles of their works and the distinction of their contribution will be noted as we proceed.

This first volume of our study deals with events during Somerset's tenure of power, which was ended by the *coup d'état* towards the end of 1549. The concluding volume will deal with the narrative of events through the trial and execution of the Duke of Northumberland. It will also include an appraisal of Edwardian thought and culture, an extended treatment of the economic discussions of the period and of the Edwardian view of the state and of history. Certain significant problems and developments, which have seemed to call for unusually detailed study and analysis, have been set directly into the narrative as *Excurses* (they number two in this volume, and there will be two in the second), though they are monographic in form and presentation. Other important matters which had their beginning in the era of Somerset's dominance (notably the expropriation of the chantries, the rise of the charitable impulse, Irish affairs, and diplomatic relations with the Hanse towns) have been set over for full consideration in the second volume, since the 'historical centre of gravity' of these events seems to lie in the period of Northumberland's dominance.

Certain working conventions should be mentioned. It is our

intention to provide a reasonably full and clear bibliographical note on the first reference to a book, only a very brief note thereafter. Manuscript references have not been included in the *Table of Abbreviations*, it being our aim to supply a sufficiently full citation on each reference. After some hesitation, we have decided to break with the habit of a lifetime and accordingly have in this work lightly modernized the spelling, punctuation, and capitalization of material quoted from the sources, though we have left the syntax unaltered.

This work is dedicated to my students—some thousands of undergraduates and some hundreds of graduates—who have taught me much and whose friendship and later achievements have meant much to me. I am indebted to Miss Carolyn Merion and Mr M. R. Pickering who have greatly assisted in the completion of my research on this volume. But my principal debt is to Mrs Sidney Gleason (Madeleine Rowse Gleason) who has worked with me on all my books for almost thirty years and who has mastered a handwriting that rivals even a mid-sixteenth century hand in its illegibility.

March, 1967   W. K. J.
Cambridge, Mass.

CONTENTS

TABLE OF ABBREVIATIONS

A.H.R.	*American Historical Review* [first references to articles in learned journals will include the name of the author and the title; subsequent citations, the name of the author and the journal reference].
A.P.C.	*Acts of the Privy Council of England.* Ed. by J. R. Dasent. New series, vols. II (1547–1550), III (1550–1552), IV (1552–1554), L. 1890–1892.
Cal. Pat. Rolls, Edw. VI	*Calendar of the patent rolls preserved in the Public Record Office.* [Ed. by R. H. Brodie.] 5 vols. and index, L., 1924–1929.
Cal. S.P. Dom., Edw. VI	*Calendar of state papers, domestic series, of the reigns of Edward VI, etc.* Vol. I (1547–1580), ed. by Robert Lemon, L., 1856. Vol. VI (Mar. 1601–Mar. 24, 1603, with addenda, 1547–1565), ed. by Mary A. E. Green, L., 1870.
Cal. S.P. For., Edw. VI	*Calendar of state papers, foreign series, of the reign of Edward VI., 1547–1553, etc.* Ed. by William B. Turnbull, L., 1861.
Cal. S.P. Scotland	*Calendar of the state papers relating to Scotland and Mary, Queen of Scots, 1547–1603, etc.* Vol. I (Feb. 1547–1563), ed. by Joseph Bain, Edinburgh, 1898. [Used entirely from March 11, 1547.]
Cal. S.P. Span.	*Calendar of letters, despatches, and state papers, relating to the negotiations between England and Spain, etc.* Vol. IX (Jan. 29, 1547–Dec. 1549), ed. by M. A. S. Hume and Royall Tyler, L., 1912. Vol. X (1550–1552), ed. by Royall Tyler, L., 1914.
Cal. S.P. Ven.	*Calendar of state papers and manuscripts, relating to English affairs, existing in the archives . . . of Venice, etc.* Ed. by Rawdon Brown. Vols. V (1532–1554), VI, pt. 3

(Nov. 1557–Dec. 24, 1558, with additions, 1363–1557), L., 1873.

Calais Papers	*Cal. S.P. For.*, *Edw. VI*, pp. 292–358.
C.J.	*Commons Journals.*
Dep. Keeper P.R.	*Deputy Keeper of Public Records*, Reports.
DNB	*Dictionary of National Biography.*
Edward VI, *Chronicle*	*The Chronicle and political papers of King Edward VI.* Ed. by W. K. Jordan. L. and Ithaca, 1966.
E.E.T.S.	Early English Text Society publications.
E.H.R.	*English Historical Review.*
Hayward, *Edward VI*	Hayward, John, *The life and reign of King Edward VI.* L., 1630, 1636; used in White Kennett, *A complete history of England, etc.*, II (L., 1719), 273–328.
HMC	Historical Manuscripts Commission publications.
L.J.	*Journals of the House of Lords.*
L. & P., Henry VIII	*Letters and papers, foreign and domestic, of the reign of Henry VIII, etc.* Ed. by J. S. Brewer, James Gairdner, and R. H. Brodie. L., 1862–1932.
S.P. Dom., Edw. VI	P.R.O., State Papers Domestic.
VCH	Victoria County History publications.

I

THE HENRICIAN BACKGROUND

1. *The nature of the Henrician settlement of religion*

The Henrician Reformation was cautious in its progress, limited in its aspirations, and carefully legal in its unfolding. It had little concern with doctrinal matters, for the King's steady preoccupation was with gaining constitutional and administrative control over that body of Christian men and women, who, long embraced by the Church in England, came before the great reign was finished to find themselves, on the whole insensibly, the flock of the Church of England. A true revolution was wrought by Henry VIII and his Parliament over a period of two decades, but so skilfully and slowly was it done, so over-riding the preoccupation with gathering to the crown the totality of constitutional and administrative power, that the government never faced either sustained or widespread opposition from men protesting that the very structure of their faith was being altered. Most Englishmen, including practically all church-men, accepted the course of Henrician change without protest or without any evident violence to conscience, one supposes because it was not clear to men of the generation, including, ironically, the sovereign himself, that an essentially administrative revolution must enlarge itself in time into a reformation of faith. In his superb handling of Parliament, in his faultless sense of timing, and in his subtle appeal to the dominant forces of English life and nationalism Henry VIII wrought in the sphere of politics what can only be described as a Renaissance work of political art; it was not, however, his intent to create a reformed Church of Christ.

Still, as one reflects on these momentous events, the more difficult is it to explain what happened, or to account for the comparative ease with which this translation of faith was made. Professor Powicke has well put the dilemma of an historical explanation when he says: 'The more light is thrown upon the feelings of men at this time, even of the inmates of monasteries, the clearer this incapacity for sustained conviction seems to be ... the general acquiescence is one of the most mysterious things in our history.'[1] In part the explanation surely is that for too long the church had engaged in deeper and deeper accommodation with the civil state, so that when great questions involving the very structure of faith and worship were put, there were no more than heroic and lonely points of opposition springing from conscience, while the great body of men, clergy and laity alike, yielded in successive further accommodations which in their totality severed the church in England from its ancient ties with the Catholic communion. This process of change, of delicately articulated compromises, went forward for twenty years, achieving in the end a revolutionary orientation of the church as a consequence of the inflexible resolution of the sovereign. A few men did raise troubled voices of conscience and were destroyed, but their opposition was in a true sense eccentric and gathered around their martyrdom no considerable body of moral or intellectual support. Royal policy was translated into effective action in statute heaped on statute until the reality of revolutionary change stood complete and men suddenly realized that it could be reversed only by an immense and possibly bloody process of reaction.

The great parliamentary codification of law at the end stood cemented as the unity of the realm, as an important element in the order and peace which the Tudors had imposed on England. The King's laws, the King's justice, ran throughout the realm of England and all but the mad or the dangerous accepted that law as it came down from the Sinai at Westminster. Thus it was that the vicar of South Cerney, when required in 1551 in Hooper's visitation to repeat the Lord's Prayer and prove it from Scripture, could indeed repeat it and declare that he knew it to be the Lord's Prayer '*propterea quod tradita sit a Domino Rege, ac scripta in libro regio de Communi Oracione*'.[2] The formulation and execution of religious policy had become a matter of state, and a system which can only be described as Erastian stood complete.[3]

Imperious, powerful, and persuasive as Henry VIII was, this great revolution in the constitution of the church was not accomplished simply as a consequence of the sovereign's will. The King in fact moved with great caution, by degrees, and with an evident intention of positing his every important action on a consensus of support from the politically dominant classes. This is not to say that a grand design of revolutionary change was in his mind at the

---

[1] Powicke, F. M., *The Reformation in England* (L., 1941), 7.
[2] Gairdner, James, 'Bishop Hooper's visitation of Gloucester', *E.H.R.* XIX (1904), 112.   [3] Powicke, *Reformation in England*, 52–53.

outset, to be unfolded as he prepared English opinion. Henry's early statutes were intended to exert an immense and calculated pressure on Rome, while the later and codifying statutes, rendered necessary after that pressure had failed, were meant to complete the structure of ecclesiastical power. And then towards the end the King was moved to fortify the new settlement against the erosion of power which must follow on his death. In the execution of this policy of careful and graduated change Henry came to a mature and almost intuitive knowledge of the parliamentary skills and to a remarkable and wholly unscrupulous understanding of the supporting forces in English life and thought which he was to exploit with a constantly impressive, and still frightening, skill.

For one thing, when the struggle with Rome opened the King possessed a bench of bishops of considerable administrative and intellectual distinction, almost all of whom were in fact great servants of the crown and few of whom were renowned either for their theological eminence or for the cure of souls. And in the last fifteen years of the reign it is evident that great care was being taken in episcopal appointments and translations in order to strengthen even further the Erastian complexion of the episcopal bench and to introduce new and safe men with at least moderate reforming convictions. It is most significant that of the twenty-seven men who were appointed to sees in the second half of the reign, all save five were drawn from gentle families or from the burgher aristocracy, the two classes which lent the most fervent support to the religious policy of the crown.[1]

Among the forty-six bishops holding office from 1536 to 1551, there was a predominant core of twenty-two men of considerable distinction, half of whom had been educated in the law, all of whom held important administrative, legal, or diplomatic positions in the central government. All these bishops lent full and, one can believe, sincere support to the Henrician ecclesiastical legislation, though they were without exception conservative in sentiment when questions of doctrinal change began to be propounded. Most of these men were really lawyers in training and in temper, thought like lawyers, and acted like them. They tended simply to transfer their allegiance from the Pope to the King, while vigorously opposing any proposal to change the institutional structure of worship. 'The conservatives lacked any great faith in a popular religious revival and

---

[1] Smith, Lacey Baldwin, *Tudor prelates and politics, 1536–1558* (Princeton, 1953), 13–15, 301–305. The discussion in the paragraph following depends heavily on this illuminating study.

their long years in government merely confirmed in them their inbred suspicion of uncontrolled reform.'[1] Further, all save one of this group of prelates, many of whom had been introduced to administrative careers by Cardinal Wolsey, were drawn from the secular clergy, whereas almost the whole of the group of eighteen reforming bishops, men who wished doctrinal as well as constitutional change, were drawn from the regular clergy and had taken their degrees in divinity.[2]

Very nearly half the bench of bishops were, then, in temper, in training, and in the habits of career either servants of the state or lawyers in fact or in disposition. Most of them were worldly, almost all were non-resident, and none of them was really sensitive to the religious implications in the Henrician Settlement. Hence it is hardly surprising that the diplomatic dispatches from Rome of Gardiner, Tunstall, Heath, and Day reveal nothing but contempt for Clement VII both as a man and as a sovereign, with no understanding whatsoever of the fact that he in his office stood as the keystone of the Roman Catholic system of which they were themselves high dignitaries. They were, to put it brutally but accurately, the King's creatures. They lent important and doubtless honest support to royal policy, as they had through their whole careers, even when the King was in fact engaged in the dismantling of the Catholic system. These great officers of church and state, of whom Gardiner and Bonner are the exemplars, assisted the King's cause with their skills and pens only to discover too late that the flood of doctrinal reform was sweeping in on shores from which the bulwarks had been removed, in part by their own efforts. There is tragedy as well as irony in the careers of such men who had late in life to become theologians in order to lend belated defence against a doctrinal revolution whose path they had helped to clear. In the next reign they found themselves helpless and confused under the attacks of the reformers, and quite unable to supply the intellectual and spiritual defence which the ancient faith required. Against all of them may be laid the stricture of Fisher, who alone amongst all the bishops had stood fast, when he spoke against George Day: 'I blame neither Geo. Day nor any other man for favoring the King's cause. But I remember having said, when I heard that he followed neither opinion,

[1] Smith, *Tudor prelates*, 65–66.

[2] They are: Cranmer, Ferrar, Hooper, Latimer, Ridley, Coverdale, Harley, Ponet, Scory, Taylor, Barlow, Bird, Bush, Goodrich, Hilsey, Holbeach, Holgate, and Shaxton. The intellectual and religious position of six bishops may be regarded as either obscure or ambivalent (Chambers, King, Kitchin, Salcot, Wakeman, and Warton).

that I was not pleased with him because he studied to obtain the goodwill of both sides.'[1]

The conservative opposition in the bench of bishops did not begin to coalesce or to offer effective resistance until after Cromwell's fall betrayed the King's own fear of the play of ideas and of the creeping but powerful impetus for doctrinal reform. For the Pilgrimage of Grace and the now strident demands for true reformation had frightened Henry quite as much as the conservative bishops, who now felt strong enough to urge the passage of the Six Articles Act. These severe and rigidly conservative measures replaced the Ten Articles of 1536, which may be regarded as a first effort to find a somewhat hazily defined middle ground on which both parties could stand.

Henry VIII regarded himself through the tempestuous years of revolutionary change as a good and orthodox Catholic and so continued until his death. This was a sincere conviction, and it likewise happens to have lent immense strength to his policy and to the gathering into his own hands of the whole *corpus* of religious power. It is true that he would on occasion tolerate, if he would not encourage, the spread of heretical ideas in order to give himself leverage in his relations with the papacy or in the conduct of his diplomacy. It is also true that his one great miscalculation was that he seems to have believed that on his command thought would stand still and the tide of heresy recede. But he correctly sensed that so long as the central doctrines of the church remained untouched by change, so long as men's habits of worship remained as they had been, so long as the whole texture of religious observance stood to solace and absolve his subjects, his hands were free to effect the revolution in the constitution of the church. He remained, therefore, in this important sense a Catholic because that was what he believed and also because it lent deep support to his policy.

It is noteworthy, however, that, the monarch notwithstanding, early and evangelical Protestantism was spreading in an interesting and most restricted pattern amongst the clergy. Moving out from the universities, and especially from Cambridge, it gained its first and devoted adherents amongst the regular clergy, particularly those who had recently completed their education in the universities. We have seen that in the ranks of the bishops it was on the whole those men who had been nurtured in the monasteries who became the early Protestant partisans. The secular clergy seems to have remained inert in this first crisis of faith just as it did in those that

[1] *L. & P., Henry VIII*, VIII (1535), no. 859, art. 23.

were to follow. These men were with few exceptions ill-educated, without lively intellectual contacts, and were usually drawn from the region in which they served the cure of souls. They were cautious men as well, whose range of interest was confined to their parish, to the more immediate human needs of their flocks, and to the struggle to maintain a usually decaying church fabric. The great crisis of faith in the realm was in fact to be debated, as it was to be decided, principally by royal policy as it was transmuted into law by Parliament, while engaging the minds and concerns of relatively no more than a handful of the clergy of England.

But the power of ideas, the momentum of faith, and the immense advantage of the initiative lay with those who wished not only the utter repudiation of the primacy of Rome, but a considerable measure of reformation in the liturgy and even in the doctrine of the church. Intellectually and perhaps historically the decisive date may be placed between 1531 and 1535, even before the Reformation Parliament had been dissolved. One is tempted to suggest that the shock of Bilney's martyrdom, and the aggregate of evangelical power that flowed from it, was decisive in the sense that moral and intellectual forces were now loosed which could not for long be restrained. In this same year (1531), too, the greatest of the early Protestant propagandists, John Bale, as prior of Doncaster, was preaching overtly Protestant doctrines to his brethren, while three years later he was publicly espousing the new doctrine in his sermons and with his skilled and facile pen. It was in this year too that Barnes published in Wittenberg his summary of Christian devotion with a pronounced Lutheran overtone. These men and others, won over by their eloquence and courage, were protected and to a degree encouraged by Cromwell during his period of power. It is during this short interval that Protestantism rooted itself ineradicably in England. There were to be intervals of brutal repression of these men and of their ideas by a wilful and on the whole an orthodox monarch, but even the Tudors possessed no effective means for the control of thought. There were to be cruel reverses, but now there could be no turning back.

2. THE DEFENCE OF ORTHODOXY (1538–1543)

The religious position as ordained by law at the dissolution of the Reformation Parliament Henry VIII evidently regarded as broadly suitable to his own needs of policy and, as importantly, it matched almost exactly his own religious sentiments. To state the situation in general terms, the constitution of the church had been wholly altered by statute and full powers of administration lay within his hands. The monastic properties were now lodged in the crown and the great abbots and priors had vanished from Convocation and, even more importantly, from the House of Lords. At the same time, however, the official formulation of doctrine and the whole substance and texture of liturgy—of worship—remained essentially unaltered, and the religious habits of men had not been dealt with harshly. But in the years of struggle with Rome, in the ruthless leverage which Henry had brought to bear on the papacy, some measure of calculated freedom had been given to the discussion of doctrinal matters and there was spread through the ranks of the clergy and among far bolder laymen—men who were articulate, courageous, and dedicated—a distinct and now vehemently expressed intention to secure the doctrinal as well as the administrative reformation of the Church of England. The first confrontation with the powerful convictions of Protestantism was at hand in England.

The steady growth of evangelical as well as radical Protestant sentiments in the realm, now articulate as well as bold, frightened Henry VIII and led directly to the passage, on his command, of the Six Articles Act (1539), which may well be regarded as a bulwark of doctrinal orthodoxy thrown across the terrain of faith. There was opposition to the statute, led by the courageous Cranmer and no more than five others amongst the bishops, Cromwell and all the lay lords lending their support to the King. In the end Cranmer and most of his episcopal colleagues withdrew at least their overt opposition, only Shaxton of Salisbury voting against the bill. In the simultaneous debates in Convocation, Cranmer took the advanced view that marriage of priests did not contravene divine law, that the sacraments should be administered in both kinds, and that auricular confession had no other support than that it was 'requisite and expedient'.[1] Cranmer's opposition was courageous, but it was also moderate. In the final session of Parliament he seems to have accepted the full implications of the Act of Supremacy and did not vote against the measure, which was passed by the Lords on June 10th and thereupon immediately submitted to the Commons. Nor did his clear and advanced position lose for him any measure of respect and esteem from the King, who sent a deputation from the Council to express his continuing regard.[2] The deep affection

[1] Ridley, Jasper, *Thomas Cranmer* (Oxford, 1962), 181.
[2] *The acts and monuments of John Foxe, etc.*, ed. by S. R. Cattley (8 vols., L., 1837–1841), V, 265, 398; *ibid.* VIII, 14.

between these two men did not extend to the other articulate opponents of the bill, Latimer and Shaxton shortly being forced to resign their sees.[1]

The Six Articles Act constituted an implacably orthodox and official statement on the central doctrines of the church, laid on by the whip of barbarous penalties.[2] Actually, however, it soon became clear that the sovereign was to exercise a firm control over its enforcement and that his principal concern was political. The King was resolved to damp down dissension springing from religious disputes and he wished to present an orthodox facade towards the Continent.[3] Even during the years of official reaction, progress was being made in securing better catechizing and in insisting on quarterly sermons by the licensed preachers, as well as pressing on with the destruction of superstitious shrines and images. Further, Cranmer, surely with the King's full approbation, was even now engaged in his preliminary work on an English prayer book and on a number of primers designed to prepare the laity for a service in the vernacular.[4] And the King could lash out dangerously if his control and his will were impugned, as was abundantly exhibited when Sir John Gostwick found himself in serious difficulties when in the House of Commons he publicly attacked Cranmer on the charge of having preached heretical sermons in Kent.[5] What the conservative party, both amongst the bishops and in the Council, could not fathom was the extent and the nature of the sovereign's trust in Cranmer.

But the mood of reaction ran deep in England and it was not immediately evident that the King intended to keep it firmly curbed, save as it suited his purpose to release it for specific ends. Continental Protestants were aghast as they read and pondered the doctrinal tenets now by law defined in England.[6] For a moment, too, it seemed that Cranmer might himself be in danger when he gently but courageously reminded the King of the great services which the now doomed Cromwell had rendered to him and to the state. He

[1] Strype, John, *Ecclesiastical memorials . . . of the Church of England, etc.* (3 vols. in 6 parts, Oxford, 1822), I, i, 542–544, for his comments on opposition to the measure.

[2] Fuller, Thomas, *The church history of Britain, etc.*, ed. by J. S. Brewer (6 vols., Oxford, 1845), III, 177, 179–180.   [3] Powicke, *Reformation in England*, 69.

[4] Dickens, A. G., *The English Reformation* (L., [1964]), 181.

[5] Foxe, *Acts and monuments*, VIII, 27; *Narratives of the days of the Reformation, etc.*, ed. by J. G. Nichols (Camden Soc. LXXVII, L., 1859), 251–254.

[6] *Philippi Melanthonis opera*, ed. by C. G. Bretschneider (*Corpus reformatorum*, vol. III, Halle, 1836), 600–601, 796–800; *Original letters relative to the English Reformation . . . chiefly from the archives of Zurich, etc.*, ed. by Hastings Robinson (Parker Soc., 2 vols., Cambridge, 1846–1847), II, 526–530.

was powerless, too, and on this occasion stood mute, when Barnes was done to death by an act of attainder which failed even to specify the heresies which this eminent English Lutheran was supposed to hold. In a grisly and barbarous scene Barnes and two other moderate Protestants together with three Roman Catholic priests were destroyed, all to make it abundantly clear at home and abroad that the sovereign intended to order faith in England as his arrogant whim—and his strangely sensitive personal conscience— should decree. 'Cranmer survived the crisis of the summer of 1540 only because of the protection which Henry always extended to him.'[1] These gruesome and calculated executions suggest that neither faction in the Privy Council could save its adherents, and 'a stranger, standing by, did wonder (as well he might) what religion the king was of, his sword cutting on both sides, protestants for heretics, and papists for traitors'.[2]

The truth is that from 1540 to the end of the reign the religious and political forces in England were skilfully controlled by the King and were maintained by him in a state of delicate equilibrium. This position of balance explains the events of 1543 when the Parr marriage of the King added strength to the Protestant faction and moved the conservative party to a dangerous overreaching of its strength. For more than two years there had been a bitter cleavage in Cranmer's reorganized cathedral chapter at Canterbury, where at least seven of the twelve prebendaries were former monks intensely hostile to the Archbishop and to any preaching of reformed doctrine. These malcontents were unquestionably advised by Stephen Gardiner, now the leading conservative in the Council, and charges of heresy were built up against the Archbishop. This somewhat conspiratorial development appears to have been directly connected with the charges brought by the intemperate and unreliable Canon of Windsor, John London, against four humble men attached to the court at Windsor, of whom three were burned and the fourth, John Marbeck, saved only through the intervention of powerful friends. But far more serious were the accusations laid against Cranmer, which were placed in London's hands in March, 1543. These charges were known to the King in early April, when Cranmer was warned, and it was at this point that the choleric Henry intervened in a dramatic action which saved the Archbishop and which broke the power of the conservative faction whose strength was rooted in the Six Articles Act.

[1] Ridley, *Cranmer*, 212, to which volume the discussion in the two preceding paragraphs owes much.   [2] Fuller, *Church history*, III, 194.

3. THE COUNTER-ATTACK ON REACTION (1539–1547)

English Protestantism, in its various shades of doctrinal opinion, was well established even before the passage of the Six Articles Act and did not submit to the efforts to force it into an Henrician conformity during the bursts of repression that mark the last eight years of the reign. It is true that Latimer was forced out of his bishopric, was for a season in prison, and lived in retirement from 1540 onwards, but the slope of his thought in these years was towards an increasingly radical Protestantism. Such well-known preachers as William Jerome, vicar of Stepney, and Thomas Girard, vicar of another London parish, as protégés of Cromwell, were, with Barnes, done to death even though they had promised to recant. Edward Crome, another famous preacher, saved his life on two occasions (1541 and 1546) by recanting. In London alone 500 persons were endangered by charges of heresy under the act of 1539, to be pardoned by the King—suggesting by the very number involved the now widely based support for Protestantism amongst laity and clergy alike. There were many amongst this early Protestant party who simply conformed until the period of reaction had run its course, but there were many others, whose faith and zeal were knit of tougher stuff, who laid against the Henrician reaction a campaign of well-conceived, implacable, and effective propaganda.

But the more zealous and determined of these Protestant leaders, men who very sensibly had no wish to risk martyrdom, fled abroad to various Protestant centres where their views were matured and seasoned and from which they maintained a drumfire of attack on the halted process of reformation in England. The irony is—as it was to be on a vastly broader scale under Mary—that most of these men fled abroad with relatively unformed and moderate religious views, but after the years of exile and tuition, they were to return after the accession of Edward VI as radical Protestants, principally of Zwinglian persuasion. These were the men who were to assume the intellectual leadership of the Edwardian Reformation.

The counter-attack brought to bear on the Henrician government and steadily intensified was given immense emotional strength by the conscious development of a martyrology for nascent Protestantism. Others participated, but it was John Bale who exploited the limitless possibilities in recounting the few but still brutal executions for heresy in England and who possessed the historical sense and learning to link these judicial murders with the Wyclifite persecutions. The reformed party in England was given a firm basis in the English past; present harsh reality was joined with the past sufferings of saintly Englishmen; and a powerful emotional sentiment came to suffuse English Protestant thought. John Foxe, who knew and admired Bale, was in the next generation to gather these and the all too voluminous Marian materials, with a wonderful artistry and skill, into what may well have been, the Tyndale rendering of the New Testament aside, the most influential book in the English language.

4. THE DECISION FOR PROTESTANTISM

The brutal execution of Anne Askewe in 1546, the tenuous accusations brought against very high ladies in the court, and the somewhat related case leading to Crome's recantations mark the climax of the last wave of reaction in Henry's reign. A well-planned and desperate effort on the part of the conservative faction in the Council and of a now thoroughly frightened group of bishops had failed in the ultimately important sense that the evidence unearthed had been insufficient to divert the sovereign from his control of policy and fell far short of the proofs required to weaken seriously the now rapidly growing power of the reforming group within the King's Council. This failure in a true sense simply re-confirmed the fiasco of the carefully planned attack on Cranmer a few years earlier, which may properly be regarded as the last opportunity given by events to those who were alarmed by the direction in which national policy was moving.

The fact is that at some uncertain date—possibly as early as 1543 and certainly not later than 1545—Henry VIII had made decisions which were in time to make of England a Protestant society, in the terms of doctrine as well as of policy and ecclesiastical constitution. Henry remained a moderately orthodox Roman Catholic and every reason suggests that he would have preferred that the realm to which he had given brilliant and dominating leadership might remain so as well. But his mind, all his blustering and all his choleric rages notwithstanding, was in fact coldly pragmatic, and he sensed correctly that there was a drift in events wholly beyond his control, that forces which he had sought to exploit for no other reason than to bring leverage to bear on the papacy could not for much longer be restrained, and that the mantle of his authority could descend to his son, protecting him for at least a season, only if the nation which he was to rule was moderately Protestant. We should now review in some detail the nature of these forces which were persuading a reluctant monarch that the historical decision must be tipped, so to say, toward Protestantism.

To deal with a relatively minor influence first, the diplomatic situation in Europe from 1545 to the end of the reign gave Henry greater freedom of action and reveals the essential coldness and pragmatism of his religious policy. Thus in late 1545 he was seeking to achieve better relations with the Emperor in order to secure a strong position *vis-à-vis* France, and was accordingly unwilling to yield to Cranmer's recommendations that certain minor superstitions (such as ringing bells on All Hallows, veiling the cross and kneeling before it on Palm Sunday, and creeping to the cross on Good Friday) be abolished. The King had evidently agreed to these reforms, but now he instructed Denny to inform Cranmer that ' "since I spake with him about these matters, I have received letters from my lord of Winchester, now being on the other side of the sea, about the conclusion of a league between us, the emperor, and the French king, and he writeth plainly unto us, that the league will not prosper nor go forward, if we make any other innovations, change, or alteration, either in religion or ceremonies, . . . Wherefore, my lord of Canterbury must take patience herein, and forbear until we may espy a more apt and convenient time for that purpose." '[1]

But some months later, in the summer of 1546, Henry's diplomatic position was stronger and France sent over d'Annebaut with instructions to seek an alliance against the Emperor which would also embrace the German Lutheran princes, with whom Henry was once more in consultation. At the first state dinner for the French envoy, we are told by the always credible Morice, who said he had the information from Cranmer, Henry urged upon the doubtless startled d'Annebaut that his master should abolish the mass and repudiate the papal supremacy as the basis for a tightly knit alliance with England and the Lutheran princes. Cranmer continued, so Morice says, that 'if I should tell what communication between the king's highness and the said ambassador was had, concerning the establishing of sincere religion then, a man would hardly have believed it: nor had I myself thought the king's highness had been so forward in these matters as then appeared'.[2] This may well have

[1] Foxe, *Acts and monuments*, V, 562.

[2] *Ibid.*, 562–564; Wriothesley, Charles, *A chronicle of England during the reigns of the Tudors, etc.*, ed. by W. D. Hamilton (Camden Soc., n.s. XI, XX, L., 1875, 1877), I, 171–173; *Chronicle of the Grey Friars of London*, ed. by J. G. Nichols (Camden Soc. LIII, L., 1852), 51–52.

been one of Henry's heroic gestures, or he may have been probing for the extent of the French envoy's instructions, but it is consistent with the direction of the great sovereign's policy in the closing months of his reign and with the harsh Erastianism which had for many years marked the true content of his religious policy.

As Henry estimated the forces in English life against the day of his own cession of power to his son, he must likewise have brooded on the spiritual change which he knew was occurring in the mind and spirit of the man he trusted most and whom he had saved from 'the ravening wolves' of reaction. Thomas Cranmer was not much at Court or Council for almost a year in 1545–1546, spending most of his time in his diocese and on the liturgical researches which were to bear such rich fruit in the next reign. His mind during these critical months was in rapid motion and was taking on firmly held convictions wholly favourable to the reformed party. It was almost certainly in these months of comparative seclusion that Cranmer repudiated the doctrine of transubstantiation, for in early 1546 he held the conversations with Ridley which he later testified were forever to change his mind.[1] We do not know the exact date of this momentous conversion, and the fact probably is that Cranmer could not himself have given it. Most of the great changes in human convictions come insensibly, or ride in on successive waves of persuasion, which leaves the historian unsatisfied because he insists on the precise ticketing of all his categories. But, be that as it may, the tragic fact remains that Cranmer had now accepted a view of the Holy Eucharist which for years past he had helped to persecute. A recent biographer estimates that Cranmer had had an active role in the burning of at least eleven heretics, ranging from such learned and responsible men as Frith and Barnes to three humble Dutch Anabaptists who were burned in 1538.[2] But he was not at court in the last vicious rage of persecution when Anne Askewe was done to death, Latimer and Shaxton placed in grave danger, and even the Queen brought under suspicion. It is probable that he could not have saved Anne Askewe, but it must be remarked that her heresy in the matter of the Eucharist did not differ substantially from that now entertained by the Archbishop of Canterbury himself.

Nor could Henry have been unaware of the widespread and damaging reaction which was the consequence of the Askewe case. Numerous and courageous Protestant Englishmen spoke out against this brutality and they had succeeded, in a matter of months, in

[1] Ridley, *Cranmer*, 252. [2] *Ibid.*, 253.

creating a Protestant martyrology which was speedily to be diffused amongst all classes of men, particularly in London. Protestantism, even under the lash of persecution, had assumed the offensive in a skilful, a persuasive, and on the whole a successful counter-attack which laid full stress on the absolute political loyalty of the reformed faith and which pictured Henry as entrapped and seduced by conservative men who stood ready to pervert and destroy the royal supremacy. The persuasiveness of this assault on orthodoxy must principally account for the fact that even in remote Yorkshire and Nottinghamshire the testaments of faith contained in wills proved in the period suggest that in 1545-1546 only a fourth of the testators exhibit 'non-traditional' expressions of faith, while in 1547 this proportion had risen dramatically to almost 40 per cent of the whole number.[1]

This mood of change, this rapid rise in the power and confidence of Protestantism, was likewise exhibited in Parliament in 1545 when on November 27th, very early in the session, a bill further to strengthen and implement the Six Articles Act was introduced in the House of Lords. The purpose was declared to be for 'the abolition of heresies and of certain books infected with false opinions'. It was not introduced as a government bill, and after its first perfunctory reading was referred to a commission, including among others Cranmer, Lord Paulet, the Earls of Hertford and Shrewsbury, and the Bishops of Ely, Salisbury, and Worcester.[2] The bill was read five times in the Lords, suggesting almost certainly a bitter difference of opinion, but in the end was passed without recorded opposition and on December 7, 1545, was sent to the Lower House. There it met determined and evidently an organized resistance and in the end was apparently rejected out of hand.[3] Unfortunately our sources on this important event are fragmentary, and the King's views on the proposed measure and its fate are simply unknown. But we do know that Henry VIII was incredibly, almost intuitively, sensitive to the mood and the aspirations of the dominant political classes of his realm, and Parliament, as always expressing the will of these very classes of men, had simply refused to lend further strength to an already attenuated statute, which, however, remained strong enough to destroy Anne Askewe and those who suffered with her.

[1] Dickens, *English Reformation*, 192.   [2] *L.J.* I, 269-271.
[3] Pollard, A. F., *Thomas Cranmer and the English Reformation* (L., 1905,[*1926*]), 177; Froude, J. A., *History of England*, etc. (12 vols., L., 1856-1870), IV, 488; Gairdner, James, *Lollardy and the Reformation in England* (4 vols., L., 1908-1913), II, 422-423.

But one may well believe that the bitterness of the debate which had just occurred may have been in the King's mind when on December 24th he came into the House of Lords to deliver his last and greatest speech, whose theme was Christian charity. It is a justly famous speech, though it is weary and suffused with the sovereign's concern respecting the fate of the child who must in the nature of man's mortality shortly succeed him. Charity, the always imperious monarch declared, was not to be found in any of them. He recalled to them St Paul's statement [Corinthians 13] that 'charity is gentle, charity is not envious'. But what charity was amongst them, he demanded, 'when the one calleth the other heretic and Anabaptist, and he calleth him again papist, hypocrite, and Pharisee'. In part he must blame the clergy, for 'I see and hear daily that you of the clergy preach one against another . . . inveigh one against another'. Some, he declared, 'be too stiff in their old Mumpsimus, other[s] be too busy and curious in their new Sumpsimus'. The spiritual flocks entrusted to them cannot possibly thrive unless correction be made; he must act with dispatch to 'see these divisions extinct, and these enormities corrected'. So too he found the laity at fault in their railing against the bishops and the clergy. He reminded them that by his licence they were permitted to have and read Holy Scriptures in their mother tongue, but only to inform their own consciences and for the instruction of their families, not to feed disputation and divide the realm by brawling dissension. Charity, he continued, was never so faint in the realm. 'I am very sorry to know and hear how unreverently that most precious jewel, the Word of God, is disputed, rhymed, sung, and jangled in every alehouse and tavern, contrary to the true meaning and doctrine of the same.'[1] There runs through the fibre of this moving speech not only a brooding uncertainty, but an almost desperate plea that his realm embrace a moderate faith national in its constitution, gently Protestant in its teachings and worship, and reasonable in its spiritual and intellectual aspirations. There is here, too, a reluctant confession that he had failed in his overweening command that thought itself stand still while he had destroyed, member by member, the fabric of the ancient church in England. Henry VIII, in point of fact, had no choice but to tilt the balance towards Protestantism.

Moreover, in assessing the forces which were in the end to persuade Henry to decide that England was to be Protestant, some

[1] Hall, Edward, *The union of the two noble and illustre famelies of York and Lancaster,* etc. (L., 1542, 1548; Hall's *Chronicle,* ed. by Henry Ellis, L., *1809*; ed. by Charles Whibley, 2 vols., L., 1904), 865-866.

measure of influence was unquestionably in the hands of his last Queen, Catherine Parr. Warm-hearted, mature, evidently at ease with her formidable husband, attractive in her person, and gifted with an almost intuitive understanding of men, the new Queen, who was married to Henry in July, 1543, was on numerous occasions to influence policy when her feelings or sense of justice were aroused. As a girl in Nottinghamshire she had pursued an ambitious curriculum of private studies which fashioned her mind into a sensitive and capable instrument, acquiring an excellent command of Latin and French and no little Greek. It seems certain that well before the time of her marriage she had embraced moderate Protestant views, and she was certainly regarded as deeply sympathetic by such undoubted Protestants as Miles Coverdale and Nicholas Udall. Further, and surely with the King's rather proud consent, she published two devotional tracts over her own name in 1545 and still another in 1547. These are works of real beauty, of dignity, and of power. Works of this sort, happily, are rarely sectarian in temper, but one can say that they are suffused with a moderate and an unsystematic Protestant spirit. Thus on the telling question of justification, she tells us that 'I have certainly no curious learning to defend this matter withal, but a simple zeal and earnest love to the truth, inspired of God, who promised to pour his spirit upon all flesh, which I have by the grace of God . . . felt in myself to be true'. In this and her other tracts the emphasis on justification is at once gentle and strong, while throughout them was a running condemnation of Rome on religious matters, the view being advanced that all questions of belief are to be laid against the clear language of the Scriptures for our determination.[1]

We know too that men of strong Protestant sympathies appealed to the Queen for help with the sovereign, as did Matthew Parker when in 1546 he pleaded that the foundation of Stoke-by-Clare, of which he was governor, should not be dissolved because of the important educational activity which it now bore.[2] It must be recalled, too, that Catherine's personal chaplain after 1543, John Parkhurst, was a strong and an outspoken Protestant, who had

---

[1] Catherine [Parr], Queen, *Prayers sturryng the mynd unto heavenlye meditacions, etc.* (L., 1545), and *The lamentacion of a sinner* (L., *1547*, 1548). The quotation is from the third of these tracts, which was translated into French, possibly by Edward VI's French tutor, John Belmain, a strong Protestant (Royal MS. 16.E.xxviii). Professor J. K. McConica has thoughtful comments on these works (*English humanists and Reformation politics under Henry VIII and Edward VI* (Oxford, 1965), 229).

[2] Parker, Matthew, *Correspondence, etc.*, ed. by John Bruce and T. T. Perowne (Parker Soc., Cambridge, 1853), 31–33.

previously served in the same capacity in the household of that
forthright Protestant, the Duchess of Suffolk.[1] We know, as well,
that on certain occasions she pleaded with the King for victims of
the Six Articles Act, and one supposes, without concrete evidence,
that her influence ran quietly against its rigorous enforcement.
Beyond doubt her greatest contribution was in restoring the royal
household so as to include all three children, and particularly in
extracting from Henry some measure of decency for the two princesses who since Edward's birth had been treated as royal bastards.
All the children were fond of her, responded almost pathetically to
her warm affection, while even Henry under her suasion experienced
something of the paternal joys.

It was in this world of turbulence and danger that Prince Edward,
the long-awaited male heir for the house of Tudor, had been born
on October 12, 1537, the son of Henry VIII and Jane Seymour. It
was to secure this male, and undisputed, heir that Henry had undertaken so much of revolutionary dislocation in the constitution of the
church and had set in train powerful forces which were in due
season to lead to the English Reformation. Tudor the child was
undoubtedly to be—in mind, in disposition, and in his passionate
concern with the realities of power—but his upbringing and his
fate were likewise to be inextricably intertwined with his Seymour
relations, and to their background we should now lend our attention.

Jane Seymour sprang from a family of shadowy Norman ancestry
which had long been established at Wolf Hall in Savernake Forest
in Wiltshire. This ancient royal forest was at the time of the Domes-
day placed in the charge of a Norman, Richard Esturmy, who had
replaced a Saxon warden there. The inheritable feudal post remained for generations vested in the Esturmy family until the line
failed in 1427 when Sir William Esturmy died, the wardenship then
passing through his daughter to her son, John Seymour. On Seymour's death in 1464, he was succeeded by a grandson, Sir John,
who held his post until his death in 1491, having had great difficulty
in protecting the property and the deer herd from armed bands of
poachers, led it would seem by envious gentry of the neighbourhood. This warden was in turn succeeded by his son, also John, who
possessed greater ability than his progenitors and who was to raise
his family to great heights indeed, for this Sir John was the father
of a large family, including Queen Jane, Edward Seymour, Duke of

[1] Read, Evelyn, *My Lady Suffolk, etc.* (N.Y., 1963), 51–52.

Somerset, and the mercurial and ill-starred Thomas, Baron Sudeley.[1] Sir John was literate, though he wrote in a crabbed and almost undecipherable hand. His estate was already considerable and his lineage of some distinction, but both were much enhanced by his marriage to Margery, the daughter of Sir Henry Wentworth of Nettlestead, Suffolk, whose line could be traced by a complex genealogy to Lionel, Duke of Clarence, and thence to Edward III. She bore to Sir John six sons and four daughters, of whom Jane was the eldest.[2] Sir John served with credit in the royal army dispatched in 1497 against the Cornish rebels, having been knighted after the Battle of Blackheath. He likewise served the crown well under Henry VIII, going abroad in the French War and distinguishing himself for gallantry at the Siege of Tournai. He was by that date known to Henry VIII and was respected by him, being in the royal train at the Field of the Cloth of Gold, on Charles V's state visit to England, and on Henry's journey to France in 1532.

Meanwhile, Sir John had introduced his eldest surviving son, Edward, at court, where he served first as a page to Mary Tudor, Queen of France. He then entered Wolsey's service, gaining his first active military experience on Suffolk's expedition to France and being knighted at Roye in November, 1523. His rise as a courtier was thereafter rapid—in 1525 he was appointed Master of the Horse to the Duke of Richmond, and in 1527 he accompanied Wolsey on the state embassy to France.[3] In 1530 Edward Seymour was made an Esquire of the Body to the King, gaining an annuity of 50 marks as well as a modest grant of lands shortly after Wolsey's fall. He attended Henry at the meeting with Francis I in France in 1532,[4] as did his father, Sir John. Seymour was now well established in the royal favour, being vested in 1534–5 with former monastic lands of slight value in Hampshire. It was at about this point that his sister, Jane, first came to the attention of the King, since she became a lady-in-waiting to the new Queen, Anne Boleyn. The first certain date of their meeting, however, was on September 10, 1535, when the King paid a visit to Sir John Seymour at Wolf Hall, an already

[1] Ailesbury, The Marquess of, *A history of Savernake Forest* (n. pl., [1962]). We are deeply indebted to the Marquess of Ailesbury for his hospitality and assistance in our visit to the neighbourhood where Somerset spent his youth.

[2] The genealogical particulars may be found fully presented in Nichols, J. G., ed., *Literary remains of King Edward the Sixth* (Roxburghe Club, 2 vols., L., 1857), I, xxi; The Marquess of Ailesbury, *Savernake Forest*, 32–39; Cokayne, G. E., *Complete peerage, etc.* (Exeter, 1887–1898; ed. by V. Gibbs, 13 vols., L., 1910–1949).

[3] *L. & P., Henry VIII*, III, ii, 3288.

[4] *Ibid.*, IV, iii, 6654 [20], 5406, 6516.

very old, half-timbered manor house of modest size.[1] It was here, too, that Jane Seymour possibly retired in 1536 for a few days before her marriage, a betrothal feast being served in the huge barn, 172 feet in length and 26 feet in breadth.[2]

Henry's passion for Jane Seymour matured rapidly after the first visit to Wolf Hall. His attentions irritated Anne and it was known as early as February, 1536, that he had given Jane expensive presents and favours. It is possible that Anne's somewhat hysterical remonstrances, connected as they doubtless were with a miscarriage early in the year, may have hastened the final estrangement of the King and set in train the events leading to her ruin.[3] During the days before Anne's execution, Jane was placed first in Sir Nicholas Carew's house some seven miles from London, and then in a house on the Thames within a short distance of Whitehall. When the execution was announced to the King, Henry went at once by barge to visit Jane and on the next morning she joined the King at Hampton Court, where in the presence of well-chosen courtiers they were formally betrothed, the marriage taking place ten days later at York Place.[4] Jane was proclaimed Queen on May 29th, and in June when he first met her, the observant Spanish ambassador, Chapuys, found her shy, but intelligent and dignified, and quite unwilling to discuss either politics or religion.[5]

During the difficult and dangerous months before the marriage, Edward Seymour had thrown the mantle of his protection and chaperonage around his sister with great skill and a certain delicacy of touch, but when the marriage had been safely and decently managed, the fortune of the Seymours was made. One brother, Henry, was now knighted, granted lands, and promptly and happily retired to the country where he lived in self-chosen quiet until his

[1] The present-day Wolf Hall is a mixture of sixteenth-, eighteenth-, and nineteenth-century styles and materials, and is now a farm-house. It is almost certainly not on the site of the older Wolf Hall, which was in advanced decay when it was being pulled down by Somerset's son. Its site was probably across the road and to the north of the present structure, where there is a tract of about four acres, never excavated, which suggests levelling and foundation traces.

[2] Jackson, J. E., 'Wulfhall and the Seymours', *Wiltshire Archaeological and Natural History Magazine*, XV (1875), 144, 149, 170–171. The great barn was still standing in Jackson's day. The King was evidently fond of Wolf Hall, though it must have been extremely difficult to house the royal party there. He paid another possibly sentimental visit, almost two years after Jane's death, staying with his court from August 9th through August 12, 1539, when 200 were fed on the first day and 400 on the second, at a total cost to Seymour of £288 19s 10d. The sovereign paid a final visit to Wolf Hall in 1543. The legend that Henry VIII and Jane were married from Wolf Hall, canonized by Jackson, has no basis in fact.   [3] *L. & P., Henry VIII*, X, 282, 495, 601.

[4] *Ibid.* 1000; VCH, *Middlesex*, II, 335.   [5] *Cal. S.P. Span.*, V, ii, 157–158.

death in 1578. The younger brother, Thomas, was also given property and was appointed a Gentleman of the Privy Chamber. But the great favours were extended to Sir Edward Seymour, whose case had been well advanced by his own merits and who had for years enjoyed the confidence and affection of the King. Just a week after his sister's marriage he was created Viscount Beauchamp of Hache (Somerset) and shortly afterwards (June 7th) was granted numerous manors in Wiltshire, which, when added to those he inherited later in the year from his father, made him one of the principal landowners of the county. In May, 1537, he was sworn of the Privy Council and three days after the christening of his nephew, the infant Prince, was created Earl of Hertford.

During the first months of their marriage the King and Queen did not reside at Hampton Court, since work was still in progress on the royal apartments there. Also, the coronation of Jane as Queen was postponed, first because of an outbreak of plague in London, and then in March, 1537, because her pregnancy was at once evident and difficult.[1] In July Parliament acted to vest the succession in Jane's issue, excluding both Mary and Elizabeth. The King now treated her with every consideration, deciding also to cancel his attendance on the recently formed Council of York, since his Queen 'being but a woman, upon some sudden and displeasant rumours and bruits that might by foolish and light persons be allowed abroad in our absence . . . might take . . . such impressions as might endanger no little or displeasure to the infant'.[2] Jane was warm and compliant in her bearing towards the King but did intervene to effect at least a formal reconciliation between him and the Princess Mary, now exiled from the court, and secured better treatment for the now neglected and very young Princess Elizabeth.[3] In September, the renovations being complete, the royal couple removed to Hampton Court to await the birth of the child.[4]

Edward was born, as his parents wished, at Hampton Court by a natural birth, Hayward's story that he was delivered by Caesarian section being without foundation.[5] A formal letter was drawn up, as if from the Queen to the King, announcing the birth of a male heir, which was sent throughout the kingdom, and which may be found today in many manuscript versions.[6] The news of the birth

[1] L. & P., Henry VIII, XII, i, 709.

[2] Ibid. 839; Cotton MSS., Caligula, B, iii, 248.

[3] HMC, 12th rpt., App. IV: Rutland MSS. I, 310; Hume, M. A. S., ed., Chronicle of King Henry VIII of England (L., 1889), 72.

[4] VCH, Middlesex, II, 335.   [5] Hayward, Edward VI, 273.

[6] Among others: Harl. MS. 2131, #7, f. 27; Cotton MSS., Nero, C, x, 1, f. 1b.

of a prince was received with great rejoicing and festivities throughout the realm, but particularly in London where the bells were
rung, 2000 salvos were fired from the Tower, and a high mass was
sung at St Paul's, while ale and wine flowed in the streets for all to
take. Plans were at once drawn, in which the King played an active
role, for the christening of the infant on the third day after birth, a
proclamation being issued dated October 12th, which sternly
forbad access to the court on the baptismal date because of the
plague still epidemic in London. The fear of infection also resulted
in the severe limitation of the list of those who were to participate.[1]
The protocols established for such functions by Margaret Beaufort
were followed, requiring the Queen to receive perhaps as many as
400 guests while she was seated with the King on a state pallet, and
then to observe the procession of the great clergy, the Council, and
the nobles, in that order, as the company moved into the chapel
where Cranmer performed the baptism. Edward was carried by the
Marchioness of Exeter and the train of his robe by the Earl of
Arundel, while Cranmer and Norfolk were godfathers at the font
and Suffolk at the confirmation. Queen Jane, through this long
ordeal, appeared reasonably well, but three days later she was ill
with a very high fever, delirium, and a state of collapse which were
the certain symptoms of almost invariably fatal puerperal fever. On
the 17th a grave medical bulletin was issued, signed by Rutland, the
Bishop of Carlisle, the Queen's chaplains, and her doctors, stating
that on the previous day there had occurred 'an natural laxe by
reason whereof she began to lighten and (as it appeared) to amend,
and so continued till toward night. All this night she hath been very
sick and doth rather appaire(?) than amend. Her confessor hath been
with her grace this morning and hath done that to his office apper-
tains, and even now [at 8 a.m.] is preparing to minister to her grace
the sacrament of unction.'[2] At just before midnight on October
24th the Queen was dead. Henry was deeply grieved, wearing
mourning for a season and advising on the funeral, and then trans-
ferring his immense energy and concern to the care of his son. For
three weeks the Queen lay in state at Hampton Court before the
body was removed to Windsor for burial on November 12th.[3]

Some years later Edward was to describe his infancy tersely and

[1] Harl. MS. 442, #74, f. 149; Egerton MS. 985, f. 33, for the ceremonial of the
christening, as well as Add. MSS. 6113, f. 80; Hall, *Union of the two families*, 825.

[2] Cotton MSS., Nero, C, x, 2, f. 2.

[3] *L. & P., Henry VIII*, XII, ii, 1012; Cotton MSS., Nero, C, x, 3, f. 2b, for the mass
celebrated at St Paul's; Jordan, W. K., *The Chronicle and political papers of King Edward
VI* (L. & Ithaca, N.Y., [1966]),3, for Edward's terse comments on these events .

accurately in his *Chronicle*: 'This child was christened by the Duke of Norfolk, the Duke of Suffolk, and the Archbishop of Canterbury. Afterward [he] was brought up, [un]til he came to six years old, among the women.'[1] The King, shaken by the death of the Prince's mother, personally prescribed almost clinical orders for the protection of the child in his various nurseries.[2] Scrupulous cleanliness was to be observed; the premises were to be scrubbed and swept twice daily; no outsider was to have physical contact with the baby; and every article used by him was to be washed immediately. Henry lavished an almost pathetic personal affection on the child, visiting him at Hampton Court, bringing him to Greenwich for his first Christmas, and then in May, 1538, to the royal hunting lodge at Royston, playing with 'much mirth and joy, dallying with him in his arms a long space, and so holding him in a window to the sight and great comfort' of the townspeople who had gathered round to see their sovereign and their prince.[3]

Shortly after the child's first year the King established him in his own household, initially paying the considerable sum of £6500 into the nursery account for his care. A detailed constitution of the household was prepared under the direct supervision of the sovereign, being addressed to Sir William Sidney, who was to serve as Chamberlain, and to Sir John Cornwallis, who was appointed Steward.[4] The all-important Lady Mistress was Lady Bryan, who had served in the same capacity for the Princesses Mary and Elizabeth.[5] The dry nurse, most immediately responsible for the child's care, was Sybil Penne, a sister-in-law to Sidney, a woman of great warmth and wholly at ease with children, who was remembered by Edward when he was king with a quite special, and somewhat uncharacteristic, affection.[6] These persons, and their numerous helpers and servants, were strictly required to attend and guard the King's and 'the whole

---

[1] Edward VI, *Chronicle*, 3.   [2] *L. & P., Henry VIII*, XII, ii, 894.

[3] *Ibid.*, XIII, i, 1011. Our account of Edward's infancy owes much to Hester W. Chapman, *The last Tudor king, etc.* (L., [1958]), 40–47.

[4] The manor of Michelmersh (Hants) was granted to Sidney in 1543 in consideration of his service as head of the early household of the Prince. (VCH, *Hants*, III, 424; *L. & P., Henry VIII*, XVIII, 623; Pat. 35 H. VIII, pt. 2, no. 10.) Cornwallis died at Ashridge in 1541.

[5] She was the daughter of Lord Berners and the wife of Sir Thomas Bryan. She was a widow at the time of her death in 1551 and was receiving a pension of £7 p.a.

[6] In 1541 the manor of Beamond in Little Missenden (Bucks) was bestowed upon her in consideration of her services 'in the nurture and education of Prince Edward' (*L. & P., Henry VIII*, XVI, 1500 (f. 71b); *A.P.C.* IV, 252). Her husband was David Penne, who died *c.* 1565. The manor was held by the Penne family until 1731 when the male line failed, and then went to Sarah Penn, wife of Sir Nathaniel Curson, and has remained in that family (Lord Howe) until present times.

realm's most precious Jewel . . . and foresee that all dangers and adversaries of malicious persons and casual harms (if any be) shall be vigilantly foreseen and avoided'. They alone were to have access to the person of the Prince, and no one under the degree of knight was to be admitted, and then only under supervision. None of his household was to visit London or any other place in the summer months, when there was danger of plague, and any sick person in the household was to be withdrawn at once.[1]

The infant prince, as we have noted, was kept first at Hampton Court, but as early as September, 1538, was at Havering (Essex) and some time in 1539 was taken to Hunsdon (Herts), and still later, certainly in 1543, to Ashridge.[2] In September, 1538, members of the Council were permitted by Cromwell to visit the Prince, Chancellor Audley reporting that he had never seen so 'godly a child' for his age, for he 'shooteth out in length, and waxeth firm and stiff, and can steadfastly stand', and could doubtless walk were his nurses not resolved to restrain him lest his legs be injured.[3] Possibly in preparation for this visit Mrs Bryan had reported to Cromwell that the Prince was well and merry and had three teeth fully out and another on the way, while when Edward was aged about two she proudly related that recently 'the minstrels played, and His Grace danced and played so wantonly that he could not stand still, and was as full of pretty toys as ever I saw [a] child in my life'. At about the same time (in the spring of 1539), the Cleves embassy, escorted by Gardiner and Essex, paid a state visit, but on this occasion the proud attendants could extract neither interest nor manners from the child who fled into Mrs Penne's capacious arms.[4]

Edward seems to have been singularly free of ill health until 1541, when, while visiting Henry VIII at Hampton Court, he became ill with a quartan fever to which the whole battery of royal physicians lent their full attention and skill. It was late November before he had recovered sufficiently to be taken to Ashridge, where the Princess Mary was then living, with Dr Butts still in attendance and frequently reporting to Edward Seymour on the gradual convalescence of the child.

[1] Cotton MSS., Vitellius, C, i, f. 65.

[2] Both Edward and Elizabeth spent a considerable portion of their childhood at Ashridge. He and the Princess were both living there in 1543 when Mary was brought to stay for the sake of her health (VCH, *Herts*, II, 209). The two younger children likewise spent some time at Hatfield House, which had come into the King's possession from the Bishop of Ely in 1538. When Edward conveyed it to John Dudley in 1548, Elizabeth protested her own affection for the house and it was given to her by Dudley in exchange for compensating lands (*ibid*. III, 92).

[3] *L. & P., Henry VIII*, XIII, ii, 306.   [4] Nichols, *Remains*, I, xxxviii.

At the age of four, just before his illness, the formal education of the Prince had begun, but it lacked clear focus or direction until the complete reorganization of the household in 1544 betokened the end of infancy and the beginning of preparation for adult life. Henry VIII lent careful attention to the critical decisions that had now to be made for his son shortly before he left for his expedition to France in July, 1544. The Prince was to be moved to Hampton Court and his entourage changed or revised, and most of the persons who had directed the nursery household were to be pensioned off. Sir Richard Page was now appointed Chamberlain and Sidney was given the less onerous post as Steward. Sir Jasper Horsey, formerly steward to Anne of Cleves, was made Chief Gentleman of the Privy Chamber, and Richard Cox, who had already been serving as the Prince's tutor, was made his almoner and placed more formally in charge of the child's education.[1]

The decision to appoint Cox, and the supporting appointments which were added in the next two years, was perhaps the most momentous that Henry VIII had ever made and was to have a decisive effect on the history of the realm and its faith. For it was well known that Richard Cox (1500–1581) was quietly but firmly of a moderate Protestant persuasion. Educated at Cambridge, he had for a season held appointment in Wolsey's new foundation at Oxford, but his reformed views had resulted in the loss of the post, though he was shortly named headmaster of Eton. His doctrinal views remained moderate and his ecclesiastical views Erastian, while he enjoyed the steady friendship and support of Cranmer, who almost certainly recommended him for the critical appointment as

---

[1] Cox was later an Elizabethan bishop of decidedly Puritan sympathies. John Leland held him in the highest esteem:

> *Quum fucis adeo laboret orbis*
> *Totus, me rogitas, amice, narrem*
> *Ore ut veridico tibi petenti,*
> *Si dum reppererim, omnibus fidelem*
> *Quem possem numeris virum probare.*
> *Talem me volo repperisse credas :*
> *Albo rarior est ac ille corvo.*
> *Novisti bene Coxium pium illum,*
> *Sacri Evangelii tubam sonoram :*
> *Quem clarus patriae pater Britannus*
> *Dilectuum refovet, suoque nato*
> *Inservire jubet probum tenello.*
> *Is vir judicio omnium piorum*
> *Omni ex parte fidelis integerque.*

(Leland, John, *Collectanea*, ed. by T. Hearne, V (L., 1770), 149.)

tutor for the young Prince. Quite as important, as we shall note, every later addition to the staff of men charged with the teaching of the sensitive and precocious boy ranged from moderately to radically Protestant in their doctrinal views. The decision was, then, deliberately undertaken with the King's full knowledge and it was made in conjunction with other decisions, also in 1543–1544, which in their total consequence were to make England Protestant.[1]

The momentous decision, almost certainly made reluctantly by the King, was made also with reference to the inevitable circumstances which must prevail for his son from the moment of his accession. Edward's very legitimacy and title were safe and unsullied only in a Protestant settlement of faith and ecclesiastical constitution. Moreover, Henry VIII undoubtedly sensed, with that half-intuitive understanding of his people that marked all the great Tudors, that Protestantism possessed the initiative in England, that it enjoyed the support of the best minds of the realm, and was gaining a rapidly expanding loyalty amongst the gentry and the urban mercantile aristocracy. He still felt strong enough to delay if he could not halt this sweep of change; his young son could not do so without endangering the very basis of order in the state. And, finally, he had come to distrust the conservative, the moderately Catholic, faction in his own Council, from whom at the end of his life he withdrew all the instruments of power. England in 1543–1544 might still wonder regarding the future course of reformation in the land; Henry VIII did not.

Also appointed to assist Cox, and actually bearing most of the burden of instruction for the young Prince, was John Cheke, who assumed his post in July, 1544.[2] Perhaps the most brilliant humanist in England, Cheke was only thirty years of age, though he had been superbly successful at Cambridge for the past four years as Regius Professor of Greek. Ascham, in the *Toxophilus*, praised Henry VIII for the appointment of 'this excellent man, full of

---

[1] L. B. Smith, in a most interesting and thoughtful essay, holds that both Cox and Cheke may more accurately be described as Henrician humanists, 'tainted with a touch of heresy', than as known Protestants. The line of distinction is fine, but the evidence known to me suggests that 'moderate Protestants well tainted with Erastianism' may be nearer the mark. (Smith, L. B., 'Henry VIII and the Protestant triumph', *A.H.R.* LXXI (1966), 1245–1247).

[2] Strype, John, *The life of . . . Sir John Cheke, etc.* (Oxford, 1821), 25–27. Strype says that Cheke obtained the post principally on the recommendation of the royal physician, Dr Butts, his closest friend at court. Cheke was at the same time appointed Canon of Christ Church (Oxford), this stipend being augmented by a special annuity of £26 13s 4d p.a. Shortly afterward Cheke married the daughter of Richard Hill, a London wine merchant.

learning, to teach noble Prince Edward, an office full of hope, comfort, and solace to all true hearts of England'. These two gifted men, both Protestant in sympathy, turned now to their task of bringing up the Prince 'in learning of tongues, of the scripture, of philosophy, and all liberal sciences'.[1] They were to be assisted at a slightly later date by an austere and stoutly Calvinist French master, John Belmain, whose exercises set for his royal pupil reflect his religious concern and zeal. There is reason to believe, indeed, that Belmain, who remained in England after Edward's death and who was well rewarded by land grants from him, may directly have influenced the development of strongly held Protestant sentiments in the boy.[2]

These were the men principally responsible for the education and the moulding of the mind of an undoubtedly precocious boy blessed with an immense zest for learning. There were others as well—we do not know all their names—who were on occasion employed for special purposes or reasons. Ascham, the greatest of all sixteenth-century teachers and now the tutor to the Princess Elizabeth, says that on Cheke's request he was often called upon to teach the boy and always found him tractable (and courteous) even after he had become king.[3] Like all his family, Edward was musically gifted, being instructed in the lute by a Fleming, Philip van Wilder, and taking pleasure from the occasions when Thomas Sternhold rendered his great metrical version of the Psalms to him. There has likewise been a persistent tradition that Sir Anthony Cooke was for a time one of the tutors, this rising gentleman having been passionately concerned with the humanistic education of his justly famous daughters. If so—and we have found no certain proofs—the period of his instruction may have been during the interval when Cheke, temporarily out of favour, returned to Cambridge for some months.[4]

We know a great deal regarding the education which this brilliant group of teachers gave to a willing and highly competent student. In a quite full sense it was the curriculum which Erasmus and Vives had so eloquently recommended, varied by the pacing which the precocity of the boy made possible and by the fact that he became a reigning monarch before the process of his education was completed. It was a stern, an exacting, and an inexorable intellectual discipline that was maintained, in which no compromise was made with the still tender age of the child, save as instruction in music, dancing, fencing, and running at the ring offered diversion. One has the

[1] Edward VI, *Chronicle*, 3.   [2] Strype, *Memorials*, II, i, 13–16.
[3] Lansdowne MS. 3, #2: Ascham to Cecil, Sept. 27, 1552.   [4] *Vide post*, 375.

sense on occasion that these teachers felt they were hurrying against
time, for Henry's health failed rapidly after 1543, and it was of
course their aspiration to set on the throne a thoroughly educated
Christian prince. But one is to a degree misled because even as late
as the mid-sixteenth century educational theory and practice made
few concessions to childhood. One can almost say that the reality of
late childhood and what we call adolescence scarcely existed.
Directly the child had grown from babyhood, it was clothed in
exactly the same manner, the style, and the dress of the adult world
of the class to which it belonged.[1] So it was with Edward, as the
early portraits of the child prince so well testify. Edward was, then,
treated as if he were an adult after about the age of seven, and this
assumption all educational theorists of the generation would have
found normal.[2] A half-century later, after spreading education had
had its effect, the horizon of childhood began to be extended and
adolescence came to be considered as a threshold and a transition
to the adult world.

When Cox and his colleagues took the young Prince in hand in
July, 1544, he had of course already been taught to read and write
English. It seems certain that somewhat earlier a special textbook had
been prepared for his use, drawn in part from William Lily's famous
authorized grammar, containing also a formulary of the religious
rudiments, and a closing section with useful reference materials.
This interesting book, bearing the Prince's device and having all the
marks of hard usage, is extant.[3] The grounding had been thorough
and as early as December, 1544, Cox could report to Paget that the
Prince had mastered the rudiments of grammar and was ready to
enter on the reading of Cato and Aesop, having for some unspecified
time past been daily at work on the reading of Solomon's proverbs
in Latin. He had kept Edward's attention by making a game of
learning, particularly in mastering the duller aspects of Latin
grammar, presenting the objectives as military exploits. Cox confessed that the Prince had been wearied by his insistence that the Old
Testament proverbs be mastered, and on at least one occasion he
had thought it wise to resort to mild corporal punishment.[4] It was
at about this point in the Prince's educational progress that the
principal responsibility was turned over to the brilliant Cheke,
though it was Cox, still formally in charge, who reported to Cranmer
in January, 1546, that Edward had mastered Cato, could construe

[1] Aries, Philippe, *Centuries of childhood, etc.* (N.Y., 1962), 50.
[2] *Ibid.*, 411.
[3] In the British Museum (C.21.b.4.(3)).   [4] *L. & P., Henry VIII*, XIX, ii, 726.

and parse well, and was then working on the *Satellitium Vivis* (a popular collection of epigrams) and on Aesop's *Fables*.[1] Cox and Cheke were also training him in Latin composition by suggesting letters to a variety of eminent persons.[2] A letter to Bishop Day (January 25, 1547) is particularly full of classical allusions, suggesting that Edward was at this time using Erasmus' collection of Lucian's *Dialogues* and probably Erasmus' *Copia* as well. By this date the young boy's Latin was very nearly soundly in hand, while some months earlier he had begun his French with Belmain.[3] Just as he became king, Edward was moving into the study of the mature Latin authors,[4] while at about the same date Cheke had begun the study of Greek with him.

Following sound humanistic theory, Cheke and Cox likewise very sensibly arranged that the young Prince, and a little later the young King, should gain experience in humanity by sharing his upbringing and at least some aspects of his education with well-born youths of his own age, at least fourteen of whom may be fairly certainly identified and most of whom were sons of peers of the realm. Later evidence makes it clear, however, that Edward became a close friend of only one of this group, Barnaby Fitzpatrick, son of an obscure Irish peer, with whom to the very end of his life the King spoke with an ease and informality suggesting a strong personal affection. During the period when Barnaby was abroad completing his education in the French Court, the young King addressed to his friend a remarkable series of letters, most of which survive, which are strangely mixed in mood, being 'in part the bubbling confidences of boy to boy and in part the imperious dicta of a Tudor sovereign addressing a subject'.[5] Of the group of youths, carefully chosen to serve as 'henchmen' of the young Prince and King, 'Suffolk and Sidney were the most gifted and intellectual; Barnaby the poorest and most agreeable; and Robert Dudley the most athletic and dashing'.[6] The Prince's household was established in these months before his accession either at Westminster or at Hampton Court,

---

[1] Nichols, *Remains*, I, 3.

[2] Burnet, Gilbert, *The history of the reformation of the Church of England*, ed. by Nicholas Pocock (7 vols., Oxford, 1865), II, 34–35.

[3] Nichols, *Remains*, I, lxxviii. On October 12, 1546, Cox wrote to Paget that the Prince was 'this day' beginning to 'learn French with a great facility even at his first entry'.

[4] Baldwin, T. W., *William Shakspere's small Latine & lesse Greeke* (2 vols., Urbana, 1944), I, 219.   [5] Edward VI, *Chronicle*, xii.

[6] Chapman, *Last Tudor King*, 70. Somewhat reluctantly, we are postponing our discussion of the education of the young King and the gradual translation of power to him to the second volume of this work.

though when plague threatened it was withdrawn to Copt Hall or Ashridge.

Edward was in this period of his education likewise first introduced to the responsibilities of state when in September, 1546, the Admiral of France, Claude d'Annebaut, arrived on a formal visit. At Henry's direction, the young Prince was charged with responsibility for the first reception of the envoy, under the eyes of Cranmer, Hertford, and Huntingdon, and, leading 800 yeomen of the guard, welcomed the French party as it came up the Thames in barges. He then conducted the embassy to their lodgings and made the first address of welcome and distributed the customary gifts of plate to the visitors. Though Edward was still very young indeed the mantle of responsibility, though not of power, was beginning to fall on his shoulders as his fond father watched him perform these ritual acts of royalty with pride and surely a large measure of confidence. One hopes so, for the moment for the translation of power to his son lay but a few months distant in the shrouded future.

During these years of education and preparation of the Prince, there seems to have been relatively little informal contact between him and his maternal uncle, Edward Seymour, who even after the death of Queen Jane rose rapidly in the King's favour and trust. The Earl of Hertford, as he had become shortly after Edward's birth, was in fact much away from London on various administrative tasks and as a gifted military commander in the King's wars. In March, 1539, he had been entrusted with strengthening the defences of Calais and Guînes. During much of 1540, however, he was more frequently in London and for the first time was active in meetings of the Council. In 1542 he was made Warden of the Scottish Marches, while in 1544 he received his first important military command when he was entrusted with the army sent against Scotland from Berwick by sea transport. Brilliant as this foray was, it had no more lasting consequence than to drive Scotland farther into the arms of France.[1]

Hertford, now high in Henry's esteem, was in July, 1544, appointed Lieutenant of the Kingdom during the King's absence in France, subject to the power of regency vested in Queen Catherine (Parr).

[1] HMC, *Report on the manuscripts of the ... Marquess of Bath preserved at Longleat.* Vol. IV: *Seymour papers, 1532–1682.* Ed., with an introduction, by Marjorie Blatcher, who has kindly lent me the corrected page proofs of this important work, which is scheduled for early publication. My references to the volume follow the pagination of the proofs. An interesting group of documents deals with Seymour's experience as Warden of the Marches in 1542, and as Lieutenant-General of the North, March–June, 1544 (pp. 52–78).

In mid-August, however, he joined Henry before Boulogne, being present at its capture. During much of the remainder of the reign he was in France, being entrusted with the command of Guînes and then (January, 1545) of Boulogne where he severely defeated a French assault on the town. From thence he was ordered once more to the Scottish border, throwing a raiding force into Scotland which burned and sacked numerous monasteries before withdrawing. Early in 1546 he was sent once more to Boulogne, where he concluded terms of peace with France, supervised the demolition of fortifications required by the treaty, and then in October, 1546, returned to London where he was deeply involved in the bitter struggle for power which marked the last few months of Henry's life.[1] Hertford's brilliant military exploits, his experience in diplomacy, and his close blood relation to the Prince had by the date of his return from France marked him out as unrivalled in prestige and personal power, save for the Duke of Norfolk and Bishop Gardiner. In Miss Blatcher's apt summary, 'no man could have been better equipped by varied exercise in command to be the head of a caretaker government during a royal minority'.[2]

---

[1] In this brief account we have followed Pollard, A. F., *England under Protector Somerset* (L., 1900), 10–14.

The tangled and unhappy facts relating to Hertford's marriage may be noted here. He first married, before 1527, Katherine, daughter and co-heir of Sir William Fillol of Horton, Dorset. This wife, who died in about 1535, had been repudiated before 1531, and her father's will (May 14, 1527: PCC Porch 33) passes over both her and Seymour, save for an annuity of £40 to be paid to Katherine 'as long as she shall live virtuously and abide in some house of religion of women'. Seymour believed her to have been incontinent and doubted the paternity of his eldest son, John. John Seymour and a second son, Edward (1529–1593), were specifically excluded from the succession to Seymour's title. John Seymour was sent to the Tower with his father in 1551 and died there in the next year. Edward was knighted at Pinkie and by Act of Parliament was restored in blood in 1553 (*Statutes of the realm*, ed. by A. Luders, T. E. Tomlins, J. Raithby, *et al.* (11 vols., L., 1810–1828), IV, i, 160).

Seymour's second marriage, contracted prior to 1535, was with Anne, the daughter of Sir Edward Stanhope and Elizabeth Bourchier, whose lineage on the maternal side could be traced to Edward III (G. E. C[okayne], *Complete Peerage* (13 vols. in 14, L., 1910–1959), XII, i, 64; also *ibid.* II, 246). The first surviving son, also named Edward, in the second family was born in 1539 and bore the courtesy title of Earl of Hertford. He was a schoolmate of King Edward, was sent to France as an hostage in 1550, and in 1551 was much about Court. Following Somerset's execution, he was made a ward, first of Winchester and then of Northumberland, being reduced in rank to a knighthood. He was restored as Earl of Hertford by Queen Elizabeth. The second son, known as Lord Henry Seymour, died without issue after a not very distinguished military career. There was still another son, also Edward by name, who was only four years of age at the time of his father's execution. There were in addition six daughters born to this second marriage. Though Anne Seymour has been somewhat maligned, the fact remains that she was an arrogant and proud woman, whose grasping selfishness and occasional pettiness may well have stemmed from a certain insecurity in relation to her husband's first marriage.   [2] HMC, *Bath MSS.* IV: *Seymour papers*, x.

We have seen that for some years past Henry VIII with great skill and with a kind of petulant pleasure had maintained a carefully poised balance of strength in the Privy Council between the forces of moderate Catholicism and moderate reform. But in fact the conservative position had undergone steady erosion, particularly because all men knew that, from 1544 onwards, the heir to the throne was being educated as a Protestant with the full approbation of his wilful father. The conservative group was led in the Council by Norfolk, a loyal man of great prestige but of indifferent abilities, and by Bishop Gardiner. Further, this party enjoyed the support of the overwhelming majority of the bench of bishops, but this strength was vitiated by the fact that, Gardiner and Tunstall aside, ability and learning amongst the prelates was to be found almost wholly in the reformed minority of the group. It must be emphasized, however, that the conservative party was Catholic only in English terms of reference. For these conservative bishops, to a man, were with respect to the central points of the royal supremacy and the con-stitutional break with Rome as completely Henrician as were such prelates as Cranmer or Holgate. The matchless, and indispensable, leader of the conservative party was Stephen Gardiner, a fine lawyer, a cultivated and urbane councillor, an experienced nego-tiator, and an unscrupulous and highly gifted factional leader. But Gardiner's room for manoeuvre was severely limited in Henry's late years, and in the whole of Edward's reign, by the fact that his great book, *De vera obedientia* (1535), was a brilliant and memorable denunciation of papal power and had laid the intellectual *Grundlagen* for Henrician Erastianism.

Henry VIII was a shrewd judge of men and of their motives, and for a good many years past had clearly shown an essential distrust, a kind of fear, of Gardiner, though the prelate's unmatched skill as a diplomatist had made him invaluable in difficult negotiations. Thus from 1538 to 1540 Gardiner was decidedly out of power, even having the novel experience of residing in his see at Winchester for a short season. But in late 1540 he was recalled and dispatched abroad in search of a diplomatic understanding with Charles V. While in Germany he attended the Diet of Ratisbon, where he met and entered into a controversy with Bucer on various doctrinal matters. He gained from the Emperor the promise of a treaty of friendship and for a time after his return in October, 1541, was once more in the favour of the King and seemed to enjoy a pre-dominant position in the Council. During this interval he worked closely with Seymour, with whom he established an easy friendship that was to survive, and with Paget, while displaying brilliantly his great administrative ability by acting as purveyor to the royal army commanded by Seymour in the Scottish campaign.

During these years, and especially in 1543, Gardiner was exerting every effort to undermine Cranmer's authority and his unique position with the King. The course of reaction, which Gardiner was guiding, reached its climax in the burning of Anne Askewe and over-reached in the thinly disguised and awkwardly handled effort to implicate the Queen herself. Power was now flowing from the monarch to the Protestant party in his Council, and by September, 1546, the imperial envoy in London, Van der Delft, thought Seymour and John Dudley the dominant figures in the government. And then shortly afterwards, Gardiner fell abruptly and disastrously from all favour, he liked to hope because of Henry's wrath when he had raised cautious objections to the exchange by his see of certain lands with the King. He now sought the aid of Paget, who enjoyed Henry's absolute confidence, begging that a conciliatory letter be handed to the King and that he be permitted to present his case in person, since those 'who now come to the Court, were specially sent for',[1] and expressing his regret that his actions were not well taken. This letter, the last of importance that Gardiner was to write to a king whom in many ways he had served all too well, is skilful, suppliant, and pathetic. The great bishop professed his complete loyalty and his full duty, and 'if, for want of circumspection, my doings or sayings be otherwise taken in this matter of land[s]', he humbly craved the royal pardon. But above all, he was troubled and wounded 'because I have no access to your Majesty'.[2]

Nor was he ever to have it again, nor, for that matter, was the conservative faction which he had led. This was a great man, and a great servant of the Crown. His early letters and writings ripple with wit and a pleasant and fragrant earthy quality. He was a highly skilled lawyer and a marvellous advocate, always pouncing on the central weakness of an opponent's position. But his weaknesses were also great, for he was stubborn, contentious, and often unreliable. Above all, his fatal weakness sprang from the fact that he had re- nounced the Church Catholic in a brilliant book and in his invaluable support of the Crown's position in the struggle with Rome, not realizing until it was historically much too late that it was impossible to save the faith which he professed and which very late in his

---

[1] L. & P., Henry VIII, XXI, ii, 488: Dec. 2, 1546.
[2] The Letters of Stephen Gardiner, ed. by J. A. Muller (Cambridge and N.Y., 1933), 247.

career he sought to defend with a theology roughly hewn, since his whole training and instinct lay with the law and not with divinity.

In these days when events were moving rapidly and when momentous decisions were being taken, it was Seymour who stood as the rallying point for the Protestant position, though he remained cautious in the expression of his views. Gardiner's influence was now completely gone, and when in the final weeks the King's intimates amongst the councillors were in consultation with the monarch regarding the royal will which would lay out in law the terms of the succession, we are told by Foxe that the bishop would linger unwanted in the outer chamber, leaving with his colleagues so he would not seem to have been excluded.[1] And when in the final draft Gardiner's name was unmentioned, we are told that his supporter, Sir Anthony Browne, raised the point with the King himself, pretending that it must have been excluded by inadvertence. And then came the reply, freighted with such significance for the future of England: ' "Hold your peace . . . I remembered him well enough, and of good purpose have left him out; for surely, if he were in my testament, and one of you [as an executor], he would cumber you all, and you should never rule him, he is of so troublesome a nature. . . . I myself could use him, and rule him to all manner of purposes, as seemed good unto me; but so shall you never do. . . ." '[2] All that remained of 'bounden duty' for the Bishop of Winchester was to preach the funeral sermon of his royal master.

The final cataclysm for the conservative party came when Norfolk, the other pole of strength, fell in a disaster that was as complete as it was senseless. This was the consequence of the folly of that infinitely gifted juvenile delinquent, the Earl of Surrey, who on December 2, 1546, was arrested on charges of high treason, quickly tried, and brought to a hurried execution on January 19, 1547. Inevitably, the Duke of Norfolk, around whom so much of feudal and popular strength had clustered, was regarded as involved in his son's undoubted treason and was included in the bill of attainder passed by Parliament and given royal approval by a stamped commission on January 27th. In a last rage of energy and power, it was Henry who had launched the terrible charges against Surrey and Norfolk, assisted, because of his legal knowledge, by Wriothesley, himself one of the conservative faction. The ruin of the Howards was complete, and Norfolk escaped execution only because the moment of Henry's

[1] Foxe, *Acts and monuments*, V, 691.
[2] *Ibid*. 691–692. Foxe tells us that the story is on Denny's authority, who so reported it to Cranmer.

death spared him and probably because the royal assent to his attainder by stamp was regarded as incomplete and too informal. With the ruin of the Howards and the eclipse of Gardiner the whole conservative position may be said to have collapsed; it now stood without effective leadership and the balance of power had been tilted irrevocably towards Protestantism.[1]

[1] Pollard, *Somerset*, 16; Froude, *History of England*, IV, 508–509; Egerton MS. 985, f. 65, for the 'disgrading of Thomas Howard, late Duke of Norfolk, and Henry Howard, late Earl of Surrey, his son'.

II

THE ACCESSION OF EDWARD VI AND
THE SETTLEMENT OF POWER

I. THE ACCESSION OF EDWARD VI

Henry VIII died at near midnight on January 28th, competent, and
dangerous, to the end. Even in his last days, when death was very
near, he had been 'loth to hear any mention of death'. It had been
his friend Sir Anthony Denny who had insisted that Cranmer be
summoned to administer the strange last rites when Henry, now
speechless, could only press the Archbishop's hand in token of his
faith in Christ and, one can surely assume, of an affection which had
for many years suffused his relations with Cranmer. While awaiting
the end Seymour and Paget, since 1543 a secretary of state, a
member of the Privy Council, and high in the King's confidence,
paced the long gallery outside the King's chamber and together
reached an informal agreement for the transfer of power. The King's
death was not to be immediately announced; Prince Edward was to
be brought at once to London from Hertford where he was lodged;
and a portion of the royal will, with which they were thoroughly familiar, and which was now in Seymour's possession, was to be for a time
suppressed. In a further conversation the two ministers agreed more
informally that, the will notwithstanding, Seymour was to bear the
power and responsibilities of a protector, it being understood, as
Paget was later to remind Seymour, that Paget was to serve as his
principal adviser.[1]

At about 3 a.m. Seymour, accompanied by Sir Anthony Browne,
the Master of Horse, left to secure the person of the Prince. In the
confusion, however, Seymour had forgotten to leave with Paget the

[1] Strype, *Memorials*, II, i, 17; S.P. Dom., Edw. VI, I, 1; Tytler, P. F., *England under
the reigns of Edward VI, and Mary, etc.* (2 vols., L., 1839), I, 15-16. The authorities have
disagreed on Edward's place of residence at the time of Henry VIII's death, but the
young King clearly states (Edward VI, *Chronicle*, 4) that he was then at Hertford, while
evidence from the State Papers makes it certain that he was there at least in the interval
Jan. 10-25, 1547 (*L. & P., Henry VIII*, XXI, ii, 685, 686, 737, 745).

key to the safe in which the will had been placed. From Hertford
early in the morning of January 29th, Seymour answered a frantic
note from Paget and, in his letter accompanying the needed key,
reminded his friend that for the moment it would be prudent to
keep the will safely in hand until it had been determined how much
of it should be published, adding, 'for divers respects I think it not
convenient to satisfy the world'. He suggested, too, that they meet
again to confirm their understanding so there could be no future
controversy. Somerset pressed on swiftly, bringing Edward first to
Enfield, where the Princess Elizabeth was living, and then 'the death
of his father was first showed him'.[1] No time was wasted, for the
return journey to London from Enfield was made on Monday,
January 31st, the outskirts of London being reached in the early
afternoon. We are credibly informed, too, that on the return journey
Seymour opened his mind to Browne, a Roman Catholic in sympathy, who 'gave his frank assent [in] communication in discourse of
the State, that his Grace should be *Protector*, thinking it . . . both
the surest kind of government, and most fit for that Commonwealth'.[2]

The news of Henry's death had been well kept by the Council,
Parliament actually having been illegally in session on January 29th.
When it was convened on the 31st, the Lord Chancellor, Wriothesley, made the formal announcement of the late King's death and
Paget read the greater part of the royal will. Thus the news was
abroad in London when Edward, accompanied by his uncle, made
his entrance into the City, where the 'nobility of his realm were
ready to receive him, to their great joy and comfort', and where on
his approach to the Tower there 'was great shot of ordnance in all
places there about, as well out of the Tower as out of the ships',
while within the ancient fortress-palace richly hung and garnished
apartments had been prepared for the new King.[3] On this same
morning, before Seymour's return, Paget had met with the Council
and had secured from it agreement that the will should be breached
by the appointment of Seymour as Lord Protector. At mid-morning
the death of the late King was formally announced at Westminster
from a stage of boards set upon hogsheads, followed by the proclamation of the accession of Edward, who, 'being his only son and

[1] Edward VI, *Chronicle*, 4.
[2] Tytler, *England*, I, 169; S.P. Dom., Edw. VI, VII, 8: William Wightman to Cecil,
May 10, 1549.
[3] Nichols, *Remains*, I, lxxxvi–lxxxvii, from Coll. of Arms MSS. I, 7, f. 29; Stow, John,
The annales, or generall chronicle of England, etc. (L., 1565, *1615*), 593; Wriothesley,
Chronicle (Camden Soc., n.s. XI), I, 179.

undoubted heir', is 'now invested and established in the crown imperial of this realm', and who calls upon his subjects for their obedience, and to 'see our peace kept' and laws respected. Later in the morning the same ritual was performed in numerous places in the City, and on the next day warrants were dispatched to all sheriffs ordering the proclamation to be promulgated in their jurisdictions.[1]

Seymour and Paget had moved with speed and self-confidence in this critical period which can be measured in hours rather than in days. They had gained the precious time required by their complete success in keeping secret the news of the King's death. Thus the Earl of Sussex did not inform his wife until the last day of January, when he was at last able to supply the list of the executors of the late King's will, and to ensure his Countess that while lamenting Henry he looked for comfort from the new King. He concluded by saying that the Court was now in the Tower, that the date for the coronation had been set, and that he would shortly send a servant to bring her to London, presumably for the ceremony.[2] It is also evident from the somewhat crestfallen dispatch of the imperial ambassador in London that he had not been informed of the late sovereign's death until arrangements for the transfer of power had been made. He says that the secrecy was complete, 'not the slightest signs of such a thing were to be seen at Court, and even the usual ceremony of bearing in the royal dishes to the sound of trumpets was continued without interruption'. Security measures were now in strict effect, all roads from London being closed. The Secretary Petre had informed him officially and he has learned that Seymour would be the chief Councillor, 'and indeed was in possession of the place before the King died'.[3]

With the leisurely pace of events of an earlier century, condolences drifted in from foreign states and diplomatic speculation was reported on the probable consequences of the death of a great monarch. Thus on February 14th Francis I forwarded a note of probably sincere regret and expressed his hope for continued

[1] Hughes, Paul L., and James F. Larkin, *Tudor royal proclamations*, Vol. I. *The early Tudors (1485–1553)* (New Haven and L., 1964), 381; Rymer, Thomas, *Foedera, etc.*, XV (L., 1728), 123; Strype, *Memorials*, II, i, 20–22; Tanner MSS., 90, #41, f. 143. Instructions to Council of the North respecting proclamations in its jurisdiction, and assuring the Council that the loss would have been greater had not the late King provided 'orders for the government' of the realm during Edward's tender years (signed by Cranmer, Lisle, Paget, Herbert, Hertford, Durham, Thomas Seymour, Wriothesley, Russell, Denny, and North).

[2] Cotton MSS., Titus, B, ii, 25, f. 51: from Ship Lane, Holborn.

[3] *Cal. S.P. Span.*, IX, 6–7.

amicable relations with the new King.[1] The Venetian ambassador accredited to the Emperor sent the news to his government on February 10th, with reports of speculation at the Court of internal revolution in England and the prediction that France would move at once to secure the reduction of Boulogne. But on the next day Mocenigo reported that the English ambassador had told him that the young King would need the support of 'une padre esterno', and that this would in the very nature of things be the Emperor.[2] And from the stronghold of evangelical Protestantism the report went out on March 18th that the young King had succeeded his father, and that the '16 gentlemen' assigned to assist him had promised under oath still to eschew the papacy, even though the bruit had it that Cardinal Pole is about to be dispatched to England on behalf of the Pope.[3]

2. THE ROYAL WILL

We have seen that Henry's will was the governing consideration in the formation of the new government and that Seymour and Paget enjoyed decisive power because they had possession of the document and likewise because their intimate knowledge of the late King's thinking and intentions inevitably carried great weight during a few critical days of decision. The will gained its massive authority from the statute empowering Henry VIII to order the succession by will, and altered the hereditary rights to the throne by the exclusion of the Scottish branch of the Tudor family.[4] The will, consequently, was an extremely important legal and constitutional document, was much in the sovereign's mind, and was kept by him, as it were, in a constant state of revision. The will in its final form was drawn on December 30, 1546, the draft being the revision of an earlier will prepared in 1544 when Henry was preparing for the invasion of France. But the evidence, though circumstantial, suggests that even in late 1546 Henry did not believe that his end was near, being in fact in the midst of elaborate planning for the invasion of Scotland. Hence the ultimate document exhibits no sense of haste or finality, referring to the possibility of other children and of the King's death overseas. Nor do we know certainly whether

---

[1] *Twenty-seventh report* [1866], Dep. Keeper of Public Records, App., 129.

[2] *Venetianische Depeschen vom Kaiserhofe*, ed. by Gustav Turba, II (Vienna, 1892), 171–176.

[3] *Briefwechsel der Brüder Ambrosius und Thomas Blaurer, 1509–1567*, ed. by Traugott Schiess (3 vols., Freiburg i.B., 1908–1912), II, 611: Blaurer to Bullinger.

[4] 28 Henry VIII, c. 7, and 35 Henry VIII, c. 1.

the will was signed when drawn on December 30th or not until January 27th a few hours before the King's death.[1]

The nature of the document, then, suggests that it was meant to be interim in nature. Henry VIII's always vigilant sense of the realities of political power strongly suggests that it was probably signed when death was near at hand, so as to make revision impossible. The will had the effect of proscribing Gardiner and the Howards from the seats of power and of lodging power corporately in the sixteen Councillors who were at the moment fully in Henry's confidence, almost all of whom were either politiques in their religious views or moderately Protestant in persuasion. The two signatures on the document, as most modern authorities have agreed, are certainly the King's, though the date of signing is stated as December 30, 1546. Had there been the slightest doubt regarding the authenticity of the document, we may be certain that Gardiner, Wriothesley, and probably Rich would have raised immediate protest.[2]

---

[1] Smith, L. B., 'The last will and testament of Henry VIII: a question of perspective', *Journal of British Studies*, II (1962), 18–19. This brilliant essay treats the problems connected with the will with great authority; our discussion owes much to it.

[2] Doubt regarding the authenticity of the will was first raised by the excluded Stuart line in 1567 (Burnet, *Reformation*, IV, 533–536). The argument is that beginning in August, 1546, the King had commanded Denny, Gates, and Clerc to relieve him of the fatigue of signing public documents by the use of a dry stamp, or embosser, the signatures impressed then being inked in. All such signatures were to be catalogued monthly and then initialled by the King (*L. & P. Henry VIII*, XXI, i, 1537). But the statutes of 28 Henry VIII, c. 7, and 35 Henry VIII, c. 1, required that the will itself be signed, and it is inconceivable that Henry or the meticulously careful Paget would have employed the stamp on so important a document. Clerc does list the will among the documents placed before the King on January 27th, the group including also Norfolk's attainder, but adds that it bore the date of 'the thirty day of December last ... signed above ... and beneath', and as being then delivered 'in our sights with your own hand' to Seymour (*ibid*. ii, 770). This would tend to suggest that the final signing of the document did occur on January 27th, but by no means suggests that it was done by stamp. Further, an examination of the document by Smith, Pollard, and the present writer reveals no persuasive suggestion of embossing. The will was enrolled by order of the Council on February 14, 1547 (S.P. Dom., Edw. VI, I, 12) and was given into Wriothesley's custody. Shortly after his fall, the Council ordered St John to regain possession and to deliver it into the Exchequer for preservation there. It was returned sealed, was opened and examined, and then once more sealed (*A.P.C.* II, 59).

Some measure of doubt is, however, cast upon the technical validity of the will by the great legal scholar, Edmund Plowden, in a carefully drawn opinion dated from internal evidence in late 1566. Plowden, a firm Catholic but also an incorruptible lawyer, must have been concerned with another legal treatise in Harl. MS. 849, #1, which sought to prove that Mary Queen of Scots was not disabled because of her foreign birth. Plowden says flatly that the will was only stamped, and that he had himself heard Paget state in the House of Commons in 1 Mary that Henry had not signed the document and that this had been confirmed by the evidence of Sir Henry Neville, 'who is still alive' (*ibid*. #2, ff.31d–38). This important document deserves to be edited and published, though even this impressive testimony does not convince me that the will was in fact technically invalid, principally because Wriothesley and Rich would at once have raised objections to its acceptance.

The late King's will, then, bore no legal fault, but it was fatally faulted in its constitutional theory. It was in fact unworkable, arguing still further the thesis that death overcame the King before his mature decision with respect to the nexus of power had been made. It in effect appointed a body of executors, sixteen in number, as a Council of Regency, possessing equal power, bound by the terms of the will, and by implication making it impossible to vest either sovereign or formal power in any one of them. These Councillors were regarded by Henry as executors of his will, and their power was conceived as flowing to them from this curious constitutional document. No clear provision was made for the removal or replacement of the executors, and they were to be guided and advised by a named body of assistant executors whose function was not defined and whose position can only be described as amorphous. Further, this Council of State, so to describe it, possessed no constitutional powers, with the consequence that a constitutional fiction had to be devised which identified the will of the King with that of the Privy Council and which assumed that a child was a man.[1] Then further weakening the position of the named Council of State was a clearly drawn Henrician statute which provided that all laws enacted in the minority of the young King, and all major administrative decisions made by the Privy Council, were subject to repeal on the attainment of his majority, which as we shall see provided a standing-ground during Edward's reign for those opposing religious change.

We shall deal in detail with the composition of the Edwardian Council in a later connection, but a brief comment on the sixteen executors may here be introduced. The Tudor contempt for the old nobility and their confidence in the gentry and the urban commercial aristocracy is suggested by the startling fact that none of the Council bore a title of nobility more than a decade old; they were new men, careerists, who had gained wealth and power in the late years of Henry VIII because of their devotion to the monarchy and because they all accepted without reservation the constitutional implications of the Act of Supremacy. Further, as has been suggested, the overwhelming majority of these men, and of the assistant executors as well, were either overtly Protestant in sympathy or were Henrician Erastians. Among these, Cranmer, Seymour, Russell, Dudley, Denny, and Herbert were undoubted and overt Protestants. Paget, St John, Sir Edward North, and Sir Edward Wotton were politiques

---

[1] Pollard, A. F., *The history of England from the accession of Edward VI to the death of Elizabeth, 1547–1603* (L., 1911), 4.

without strong religious convictions, all in fact lending support to the religious policy of reformation soon to be undertaken. To this group may be added the two judges, Bromley and Montague, who did not often attend meetings of the Council and both of whom were probably Erastians. There were, then, only four of the initial Council who possessed even moderate sympathies with Roman Catholicism, and this support must be further limited by saying that they were 'Henrician Catholics'. These were Wriothesley, the Lord Chancellor, who was soon to be expelled from the reigning junta; Cuthbert Tunstall, Bishop of Durham, now upwards of seventy years of age; Sir Anthony Browne, who died in 1548; and possibly Nicholas Wotton, too well skilled as a diplomatist ever to reveal the roots of his faith.

3. THE SETTLEMENT OF POWER

Over this as yet unorganized body of Councillors of Regency, Seymour and Paget enjoyed an early and a decisive dominance. They had agreed privately on a disposition of power which amounted to a violation of the will; Seymour had brought the young King to London and was his only blood relation among the executors; and both men had in recent months been close to the late King, Paget, indeed, as his most intimate adviser. Further, Paget and Seymour during the last month had been fully entrusted with important diplomatic negotiations with France and with general oversight over the preparations for the intended Scottish invasion. So great was Paget's prestige that, as we shall see, his oral account of the late King's intentions with respect to advances in honour amongst the executors was accepted without the slightest demur.[1] Moreover, on the day before his death Henry and Paget had been known to have talked at great length regarding policy to be followed, and both Paget and Seymour were in attendance at his death. Among the moderate Roman Catholic executors and Erastians both Sir Edward Wotton and Dr Nicholas Wotton were out of the country; Browne, as we have noted, had committed himself to Seymour on the journey back from Enfield; and Tunstall had for many years past been a close friend to Seymour.[2]

At meetings of the executors on January 31st and again on February 1st, therefore, proposals were made and accepted which violated not only the spirit but the letter of the will, but which at the

[1] *Correspondance politique de Odet de Selve, etc.* (Paris, 1888), 184; *A.P.C.* II, 12–22.
[2] Pollard, *Somerset*, 23.

least made it workable. Edward in his *Chronicle* deals briefly but accurately with what transpired: 'The next day, being the [31st] of [January] he [the King] was brought to the Tower of London, where he tarried the space of three weeks; and in the mean season the Council sat every day for the performance of the will. . . .' At length, the King continued, 'they thought best to choose the Duke of Somerset to be Protector of the realm and Governor of the King's person . . . during his minority, to which all the gentlemen and lords did agree, because he was the King's uncle on his mother's side'.[1]

The Acts of the Privy Council set out in great fullness the decisions taken, though not all of the deliberation, by the thirteen executors present in London, as they sought to apply the will to the practical situation in which they found themselves. They solemnly called upon God for aid and swore to 'maintain the said last will and testament of our said master, and every part and article of the same to the uttermost of our powers, wits, and cunnings'. The solemn oaths having been taken, they proceeded almost immediately to break them after the will had been read and Paget had urged the wisdom and necessity for giving Seymour primacy among the group. The formal reasons given for the decision were that in transmitting messages to foreign powers, and for 'sundry other great and urgent things to be presently dispatched within the realm', and because of the large number of executors named with 'like and equal charge', it would be difficult and disorderly to govern unless 'some special man' of their number should be 'preferred in name and place before others'.[2] The tradition that Wriothesley offered some measure of opposition to the decision, stemming from Burnet's account,[3] cannot be substantiated from the sources available, and in any event was not so strongly held as to breach the unanimity with which the executors present acted. All those subscribing declared that in view of the close affinity in blood with the King and his long experience in the conduct of the affairs of the realm, Seymour should be that 'special man', being in name and title 'Protector of all the realms and dominions' of the King and governor of the King's person. It was, however, expressly resolved that the Protector should 'not do any act but with the advice and consent of the rest of the co-executors'. Seymour having agreed to these decisions and conditions, it was voted to postpone the taking of oaths and the formal constitution of a government until the next day, the Lord Chancellor

---

[1] Edward VI, *Chronicle*, 4.   [2] *A.P.C.* II, 4–5.
[3] Burnet, *Reformation*, II, 40.

being instructed in the meantime to make out new patents for the
principal law officers of the realm.[1]

Though it is clear that the executors had made decisions technically violating the instructions of the will from which their own
power flowed, there were ample and sufficient grounds of a pragmatic nature and there were probably legal justifications as well.
Neither the Lord Chancellor nor Judge Montague raised substantial objection, the other judge, Bromley, being absent. The
parliamentary statute which guided Henry's action in devising the
succession, and which also bound the executors, stated clearly that
the guardianship of the minor King should be vested in a Council
to be named by the King. Pollard may well be correct in his view
that under the statute Henry probably could not in fact have
named a Protector,[2] and he notes as well that the will carries no
specific prohibition of the action just taken. And, finally, the will
itself bore an enabling clause which may have been freighted with
sufficient authority: 'We will that our said executors, or the most
part of them, may lawfully do what they shall think convenient for
the execution of our said will, without being troubled by our said
son, or any other, for the same.'[3]

Be the law as it may, the deed was effectively done. On February
1st Seymour and the other executors brought the King from his
state apartments in the Tower into the presence of the assembled
nobility of the realm, who by their several degrees made their
obedience to the King. The will was then read from beginning to
end and the Lord Chancellor made known the fact that all the
executors had agreed that Seymour should be governor of the King's
person and Protector, since 'it was expedient for one to have the
governance of the said young king during his nonage'.[4] The executors
further indicated that they declared their resolution to the King, to
the other Councillors, and to the Lords here assembled, who did
with one voice give 'their consents to the same'.[5] This being done,
the Privy Council moved at once to draft letters to foreign states
announcing the change in government and to dispatch special
envoys to bear these communications. Legal effect for the decision

[1] A.P.C. II, 5–6.   [2] Pollard, Somerset, 27–28.
[3] This interpretation is in general agreement with that advanced by Roskell in a
valuable essay, 'The office and dignity of Protector of England, with special reference to
its origins', E.H.R. LXVIII (1953), 193–233.
[4] Nichols, Remains, I, lxxvii, quoting Coll. of Arms MSS., I, 7, f. 29.
[5] A.P.C. II, 7–8. Possibly for the use of the executors, a single-page list of the kings
of England and their ages had been drawn up, setting out those instances in which pro-
tectors had been appointed (HMC, Salisbury MSS. I, 51).

so carefully taken was secured by gaining from the King a signed commission, which with all the Council's names appended was passed under the Great Seal as a warrant for sovereign power 'until such time as we shall have . . . accomplished the age of eighteen years'. The new government had then been formed and began at once to function.[1]

Through all these critical and decisive events Seymour had acted with speed and with an assurance which secured decisions and carefully ordered constitutional commitments vesting great power in his person. From the hurried trip to gain the person of the child king to the achievement of the Protectorate, there had been nothing of hesitation, no introspective brooding, and no want of a shrewd sense of timing. Never again in his tragic career, in fact, was he to prove himself quite as capable of great decisions; never again was there to be quite the same sureness of touch; never again was he to move so swiftly and surely that opposition did not have the time or the will to form. The explanation surely is, at least in large part, that it was Paget who supplied the momentum, the skill, and the audacity required to bridge the gulf between the two reigns and to deposit an immense aggregate of power in Seymour's hands. Long a friend of Seymour's, and of the same age, Paget had served Henry VIII faithfully in many capacities. During the last three years of the reign, as we have noted, he was of all the advisers to the sovereign the most trusted, as he was certainly the most devoted. The executors knew that of all their number Paget best knew the mind and intentions of the late King, and so immense had been the power and so overweening the personality of Henry VIII, that Paget spoke with great authority and confidence. And he seemed to speak with no thought of his own advancement, for he argued in terms of the well-being of the realm and its young monarch, as he created the edifice of Seymour's power. Only he and the Protector knew that undergirding their relation was the private agreement that Paget would in effect be the first minister to the Lord Protector. It was unfortunate and ruinous to Seymour that this agreement was not maintained.[2]

The prestige and moral authority of Paget in these early days of the new reign was evident to all men, while the rapid diminution of

[1] Nichols, J. G., 'The second patent appointing Edward Duke of Somerset Protector, etc.', *Archaeologia*, XXX (1844), 475-476.

[2] Towards the end, Paget was the principal—often the sole—contact of the King with the Privy Council (Gammon, S. R., *Master of practises. A life of William, Lord Paget of Beaudesert, 1506-1563* (unpubl. Ph.D. thesis, Princeton Univ., 1953)).

his influence remained to a degree hidden. Of all the Edwardian Council, the imperial ambassador, Van der Delft, possessed a high regard for none save Paget. As early as February 10, 1547, he wrote to Mary, the Emperor's sister and his Regent in the Low Countries, that Paget must be kept content, 'for his authority in this country is great'. He further expressed the view that the four key figures in the new government were the two Seymours, Wriothesley, and Paget, and that Wriothesley out of fear and Paget out of affection would continue their support of the Protector, even though he be 'looked down upon by every body as a dry, sour, opinionated man'.[1] Just two days later the ambassador, in a dispatch to the Emperor, reported that in his view Paget was the key minister in the government and that Paget had told him that he had spent the last days closeted with Henry, 'passing entire nights in conversation together'.[2] Nor was Van der Delft easily shaken from his estimate, reporting in the spring of 1547 that Paget continued to carry great weight with the Protector: 'I see that a very close understanding exists between [them] . . . and that one depends upon the other.'[3]

The new government in the first days of its tenure of power proceeded with caution and with no more than necessary business until the old King should be buried and the new King crowned. These matters were the principal problems on its agenda for the meeting on February 2nd, it also being then ordered that formal letters announcing the succession and the structure of the new government should be dispatched to the sheriffs, to the Wardens on the northern borders, to Ireland, and to Calais and Boulogne.[4] A few days later orders were issued to assist the English party holding St Andrew's, upwards of £1000 being sent for emergency needs there,[5] and instructions were forwarded for the payment of arrears to the garrison at Boulogne, at least so far as the £2500 which could be spared from the depleted exchequer would suffice.[6] During these early days, too, the King was endued with knighthood by Somerset, who immediately raised the Lord Mayor of London to that rank, as well as William Portman, one of the judges.[7]

Far more important, and, to the conservative party, more ominous,

---

[1] Cal. S.P. Span. IX, 19–20. [2] Ibid. 30.
[3] Ibid. 111: Van der Delft to Charles V, June 24, 1547. Van der Delft had formed an accurate estimate of the relations of Somerset and Paget in the early months of the new reign. The two men had long been close friends, and during the whole of the first year Paget seems always to have been with the Protector save during the Scottish campaign.
[4] A.P.C. II, 9–11. [5] Ibid. 12.
[6] Ibid. App., 437–439: Feb. 6, 1547.
[7] Stow, Annales, 593; Strype, Memorials, II, i, 24.

was the decision, with Cranmer's approval, that the jurisdiction of
all bishops had terminated with Henry's death. Accordingly, Paget
was instructed by the Council to draw new documents restoring
their spiritual authority.[1] Perhaps few even of the bishops comprehended the significance of this starkly Erastian interpretation of
the Act of Supremacy, but it did not escape the vigilant Gardiner
who protested to the Council in a sharply worded letter addressed
to Paget.[2] Paget in his reply on the following day denied that he
sought to 'nip or snatch' any person or that he wished to usurp any
power not his. Nor would he malign the bishops, though he would
wish that they would so order themselves as to lend more benefit to
the realm. But as to the immediate question, 'Your Lordship will
have your commission in as ample manner as I have authority to
make out the same, and in an ampler manner than you had it
before; which I think you may execute now with less fear of danger
than you have had cause hitherto to do'.[3]

Meanwhile, the slow and complex preparations for the funeral of
Henry VIII and the coronation of his son, which would follow,
were under way. In an almost pathetic, but, as always, a prickly,
letter Bishop Gardiner wrote to Paget on February 5th informing
him that he intended on the following day to celebrate a solemn
dirge and mass for the late King at Southwark. But now he learns
that the Earl of Oxford's players have announced a play in Southwark at the same time 'to try who shall have the most resort, they
in game or I in earnest, which seemeth' a 'marvellous contention,
wherein some shall profess in the name of the commonwealth,
mirth, and some sorrow at the same time'. As for himself, he pro-
poses to remain in mourning until his former master is buried. He
had failed to secure the cancellation of the play by the justice of
the peace in Southwark, and now has no recourse save to appeal to
the Protector.[4] Out of favour though he was towards the end, deliberately excluded from the seats of power as he had been, Stephen
Gardiner, it must be said, never wavered in a deep and an abiding
memory of his duty to 'the old king', as he so often phrased it. And
now the old King 'was buried at Windsor with much solemnity, and
the officers broke their staves, hurling them into the grave. But they
were restored to them again when they came to the Tower.'[5]

[1] *A.P.C.* II, 13–14.
[2] S.P. Dom., Edw. VI, I, 25.
[3] S.P. Dom., Edw. VI, I, 26: Mar. 2, 1547.
[4] *Ibid.* I, 5; slightly faulty text in Tytler, *England*, I, 21–22.
[5] Edward VI, *Chronicle*, 5; S.P. Dom., Edw. VI, I, 17, 18.

4. THE REWARDS OF POWER

Not quite a fortnight had elapsed since the death of the King when 'divers noblemen and others'—to employ the delicately anonymous language of the Privy Council's minute—came forward with claims for honours and lands which they said had been promised by Henry in his late days. Accordingly, the Council called before them Paget, Sir Anthony Denny, and Sir William Herbert, the last two being chief gentlemen of the Privy Chamber to Henry VIII, as Councillors favoured by Henry and much with him in his last illness. Paget, who was most fully informed, dealt at length with the matter, the other witnesses subscribing to his statement as according with their own knowledge.

Paget deposed that at about the time of the arrest of Surrey and Norfolk, Henry, in one of the expansive moods to which he was given, spoke freely with him of grants which he intended to make amongst his servants, since 'the nobility of this realm was greatly decayed, some by attainders, some by their own misgovernance and riotous wasting, and some by sickness and sundry other means'.[1] The King had then indicated several peerages which he meant to bestow, and in the presence of Sir John Gates, a member of the Privy Chamber, had discussed the land distributions with which these promotions in dignity amongst his servants were to be supported. Paget, who was always frank with the King, suggested that the proposed amounts were too little in certain instances and mentioned others who needed lands. On the King's own instruction he had spoken with those under consideration, and found that some did not wish to be advanced in degree and others felt the proposed increases were too small to maintain their needs and port.

The whole subject was reviewed, so Paget's testimony ran, at a slightly later date, when the King indicated that he could not live long and that he was resolved 'to place us all about his son as men whom he trusted and loved above all others specially', setting down promotions and ennoblements ranging downwards from Seymour's advance to a duchy with £800 p.a. of lands, and £300 p.a. from the next bishop's lands that should fall vacant, to six knights who were to be made barons. In addition, Herbert, Denny, Gates, and Carden were not to be raised to the peerage but were to receive lands valued at from 100 marks to 400 marks p.a., while still others, all senior servants of the Crown, were to be rewarded with stewardships and

[1] *A.P.C.* II, 16: Feb. 6 (?), 1547.

other remunerative posts.[1] Paget further deposed that he had once more reviewed the King's intentions with all those involved and 'all were pleased', but before any further step could be taken the King was dead.[2]

There is no reason for doubting the truth of Paget's elaborate, and costly, deposition. For one thing he was an honest and forthright man, and for another his conversations, at the King's command, with at least twenty senior Councillors or servants of the Crown, were within the knowledge of most of those comprising the Edwardian Council. Furthermore, several of those whom Henry had singled out for honours, including Russell, Paulet, Cheyney, and St Leger, formally declined advancement at this time for a variety of reasons. Likewise, in view of the disfavour entertained by most of the Council for Wriothesley, and his impending expulsion from that body, it is hardly conceivable that he would now have been advanced to a richly endowed earldom (Southampton) had not Henry's intentions been well known to those composing the new government. It seems quite clear that Henry at the very end of his life intended a considerable augmentation of the peerage by advancements amongst the executors and the assistant executors of his will and that he hoped thereby to rivet the loyalty and devotion of these experienced servants of the Crown to the safeguarding of his son during the inevitable interval of a minority.[3] But the fact remains that those whom the King undoubtedly meant to reward moved too swiftly, with no more than a thinly disguised rapacity, and with a kind of half-guilty determination to protect themselves, and their reputations, by a surprisingly full minute in the records of the Privy Council. It remains to Paget's great credit that he claimed neither a peerage nor lands for himself under this disclosure.

The testimony and its corroboration having been concluded, the Council with one voice declared themselves resolved to carry out the late King's will and intention, and accordingly ordered the appropriate officers of the Court of Augmentations to draw warrants 'as shall be necessary for the perfection of the same', not doubting that 'our sovereign will when he cometh to the age of knowledge and judgment . . . graciously weigh our considerations, and accept benignly both that we do in this and in all other things during his . . .

---

[1] They were: Sir Philip Hoby, Sir Thomas Paston, Sir Thomas Darcy, Lord Wentworth, Sir William Petre, Sir Richard Southwell, Sir William Goring, and Sir Ralph Vane.   [2] *A.P.C.* II, 15–20, for the full text.

[3] Pollard, *Somerset*, 28–30; Pollard, *Cranmer*, 185; Burnet, *Reformation*, II, 41–43.

minority'.[1] The arrangements were quickly made, it being resolved by the Council on February 15th to confer the following advancements in honours on the next day, though the formalities were in fact delayed until February 17th:

Earl of Hertford (Seymour) to Duke of Somerset
Earl of Essex (Parr) to Marquis of Northampton
Viscount Lisle (Dudley) to Earl of Warwick
Lord Wriothesley to Earl of Southampton
Sir Thomas Seymour to Baron Seymour of Sudeley
Sir Richard Rich to Baron Rich of Leeze (Leighs)
Sir William Willoughby to Baron Willoughby of Parham
Sir Edmund Sheffield to Baron Sheffield.[2]

The ceremony at the Tower, for all the haste in preparation, was elaborate and impressive. Before all the assembled nobility, Edward Seymour was first created a duke, being dressed in an 'inner robe' of honour, with the heralds preceding him, and the Garter next following. Then came the Earl of Shrewsbury carrying a verge (rod) of gold and Oxford carrying the duke's cup and coronet of gold, while Arundel bore the sword. Escorted by the Duke of Suffolk and the Marquis of Dorset, Seymour offered his obedience to the child King sitting in the chair of state, and then knelt before him. Paget read the charter, while at the appropriate point Edward placed the duke's mantle on Seymour, girt him with the sword, put the coronet on his head, gave him the verge of gold, and pronounced him Duke of Somerset. Somerset then stood by the King while the others were ennobled.[3]

5. THE CORONATION

Full of pageantry as these exercises were, they paled indeed when compared with the grave ceremony of the coronation of the King a few days later. It is difficult to remember that England had not witnessed a coronation for almost forty years, with the consequence that the Council devoted much time to working out the arrangements. Their task was further complicated by the fact that the new sovereign was a child, and hence after 'mature and deep deliberation' the Protector and Council determined that the accustomed ceremonies should be drastically amended, in part because of the 'tedious length of the same which should weary and be hurtsome

[1] A.P.C. II, 22.   [2] Ibid. 34–35; S.P. Dom., Edw. VI, I, 11–12, 14: Feb. 15, 1547.
[3] Hargrave MSS. (BM), 497, f. 35 (old number, f. 39); Edward VI, Chronicle, 5; Stow, Annales, 594.

peradventure to the King's majesty, being yet of tender age' and in part because certain of the traditional exercises were deemed popish and not now by law allowable. On February 12th the Council approved a detailed order of the event, which was not particularly elaborate, costing the treasury only £442 10s 0d as compared with the £1039 9s 7d just expended for the funeral of the late sovereign.[1] None the less, so poignant was the coronation of a child king and so strong the cult of monarchy in Tudor England that an extraordinary deposit of manuscript accounts of the exercises remains, leaving one to wonder why some enterprising printer did not bring forth a timely and a certain best-seller.[2]

On Saturday, February 19th, 'all things being prepared for the coronation', Edward, 'being then but nine years old, passed through the City of London . . . as heretofore has been used, and came to the palace of Westminster' in order to be near at hand for the ceremonies of the day following.[3] Escorted by the Protector and Council, followed by the nobility and the upper clergy of the realm, and fondly guarded by several thousand men of arms, the King's journey from the Tower to Westminster was a moving and joyful pageant, the City pouring out its people, its enthusiasm, and its loyalty. The King was dressed in a 'gown of cloth of silver, all over embroidered with damask gold, with a girdle of white velvet wrought with Venice silver, garnished with precious stones, as rubies and diamonds . . . a doublet of white velvet according to the same . . . a white velvet cap, garnished with like stones and pearls; and a pair of buskins of white velvet'.[4] At various points along the route the King was greeted with pageants, with songs, and salutations, but the procession was delayed for some time on reaching the precincts of St Paul's where the King watched enthralled as a Spanish rope-walker, after various acrobatic feats on a cable stretched from the spire to an anchor near the Dean's house, descended the rope on his breast, head first, ' "as it had been an arrow out of a bow " '.[5]

---

[1] A.P.C. II, 29–33, 77.

[2] Among these—and the list is selected—were Lansdowne MSS. 162, #46, f. 236b; ibid. 260, #3, f. 49; Harl. MSS. 169, #12, f. 45b; ibid. 353, #3, f. 2; ibid. 5176, #25; ibid. 6063, #18; Add. MSS. 9069, and ibid. 6307, f. 18, the latter being a later copy; Soc. Antiq. MS. 123, #1, #2; Ashmole MSS. (Oxford), 817; ibid. 863, #21, ff. 185-196; Gonville and Caius MSS. (Cambridge), 665/472, #7, ff. 344-346; and Egerton MS. 3026, probably a contemporary transcript of Coll. of Arms MSS. I, 7, and 18, from which Nichols' account is derived.   [3] Edward VI, Chronicle, 5.

[4] Nichols, Remains, I, xcv; Grey Friars chronicle (Camden Soc. LIII), 53.

[5] The rich pageantry of the procession and coronation and the excitement of London are brilliantly and fully described by Chapman, Last Tudor king, 87–96, and hence our narrative may be terse. Another full account may be found in Strype, John, Memorials of . . . Thomas Cranmer, etc. (2 vols., Oxford, 1840), I, 203–207.

The coronation took place on the following day, Sunday, February 20th, attendance at the Abbey and at Westminster Hall, where the coronation banquet was proffered, being limited to the Court circle, the nobility, and the upper clergy. The nobility were summoned to be in their places not later than 7 a.m., while the King entered through the private stair between 9 and 10. Seated first in King Edward's chair, he then sat in a lighter chair, which, carried by four gentlemen ushers to the four sides of the platform, displayed him to all the assembled gathering, who accepted him with the cry, 'Yea, yea, yea, God save King Edward'. Three crowns were then set on his head, one following the other: King Edward's crown, the imperial crown of England, and then a richly decorated crown made for the occasion. Cranmer, who had presided, then preached briefly, his address being a remarkable vindication of the royal supremacy and a summons to the King to the further reformation of the Church of England. He reminded the King that in his coronation oath he had promised to forsake the devil and all his works and that England must stand inviolate against any intrusion of papal authority. The King, he continued, is by God anointed, 'not in respect of the oil which the bishop useth, but in consideration of their power, which is ordained; of the sword, which is authorized; of their persons, which are elected of God'. The King stands then as God's vicar to see Him 'truly worshipped, and idolatry destroyed; the tyranny of the Bishops of Rome banished from your subjects, and images removed'.[1] And to complete the formal assumption of power, the proclamation went forth on this same day announcing the regnal style of the young monarch: 'the most high, most puissant, most excellent prince and victorious King Edward, by the Grace of God King of England, France, and Ireland, Defender of the Faith, and in earth of the Church of England Supreme Head, and Sovereign of the most noble order of the Garter'.[2]

Much indeed of loyalty, of incipient power, and of responsibility had been vested in a sovereign who was still a very young boy, and a boy who must have been weary by the time the magnificent exercises in the Abbey had been concluded. But his duty for the day was still not done, for now he 'was brought to the hall [Westminster Hall] to dinner . . . where he sat with the crown on his head, with the Archbishop of Canterbury and the Lord Protector, and all the

---

[1] For further accounts of the exercises and Cranmer's sermon, *vide* Strype, *Cranmer*, I, 206; Ridley, *Cranmer*, 262; Hayward, *Edward VI*, 272 [276]; Edward VI, *Chronicle*, 5; Stow, *Annales*, 594.   [2] Coll. of Arms MSS. I, 7, 32.

Lords sat at boards in the hall beneath; and the Lord Marshal's
deputy (for my Lord of Somerset was Lord Marshal) rode about the
hall to make room. Then came in Sir John Dymoke, Champion,[1]
and made his challenge, and so the King drank to him and he had
the cup.' And then finally, mercifully, 'At night the King returned
to his ... palace at Westminster, where there were jousts and
barriers; and afterward order was taken for all his servants being
with his father and [with] him [while] being prince, and the ordinary
and unordinary were appointed'.[2]

It is of course impossible to estimate the impact of such an event
on the public mind and imagination. We have seen that London had
risen to the occasion with displays of excitement, direct participation—and a great deal of ale drinking. There is evidence, too, of a
measure of relaxation now that a great monarch was gone—one
who, though blessed with great popularity, had none the less
fractured the whole *corpus* of English thought and who had reorganized its institutions to his own ends. The chronicles reflect
this mood of relaxation and the portents of a more laxly imposed
sovereignty upon the realm.[3] So too do the ballads, composed for
the occasion and sung as the King made his progress from the
Tower to the Abbey. Perhaps the sentiments expressed by one—
and it was sung throughout the reign—will suffice to exhibit the
mood of the day and the hope of England in the young Prince who
had ascended the throne:

Sing, up heart, sing, up heart, and sing no more down,
But joy in King Edward, that weareth the crown.

King Edward up springeth from puerility,
And toward us bringeth joy and tranquility;
Our hearts may be light and merry cheer,
He shall be of such might, that all the world may him fear.

Ye children of England, for the honour of the same,
Take bow and shaft in hand, learn shootage to frame.
That you another day may so do your parts,
So serve your King as well with hands as with hearts.

---

[1] Dymock was the third member of his family, in direct descent, to serve as King's
Champion. His father, of the same name, had played this role at the coronations of
Richard III, Henry VII, and Henry VIII.
[2] Edward VI, *Chronicle*, 5.
[3] Those already cited, and, as well: Wriothesley, *Chronicle*, I (Camden Soc., n.s. XI),
182–183; *A breuiat cronicle, etc.* (Canterbury, [1551], [*1552*], 1553), no pagin.

Sing, up heart, sing, up heart, and sing no more down,
For joy of King Edward, that weareth the crown.[1]

Indeed, the only jaundiced note in reporting the occasion was that of the coolly professional imperial ambassador in his dispatch to the Regent in Antwerp. The progress from the Tower to Westminster had required four hours. He had walked with Cranmer in the procession, 'who acted the part of a dumb man all the way'. Just before the exercises he had greeted the King in French, but Somerset, standing near, had told him that the King understood Latin better than French, though 'the truth to tell, he seemed to me to understand one just as little as the other'. Van der Delft was piqued because the diplomatic corps had not been invited to the services within the Abbey, he having with offended dignity declined a last-minute invitation from Paget to attend. Nor was he at all pleased with the state dinner that followed, proper tables not having been assigned to the resident diplomatists, so that they were herded with the bishops and the gentry. And shortly before, he felt obliged to report, Paget had been especially assiduous in his entertainment of the French ambassador at a state dinner. All power, he concluded, was now in Somerset's hands, but he was persuaded that the Protector 'acts entirely on the advice and counsel' of Paget.[2]

6. THE FALL OF WRIOTHESLEY

Scarcely was the coronation over and the government settled into the dull routine of policy and administration, than an internal crisis developed which occasioned the first fracture in the group of executors named by Henry VIII, who were also now in effect the Privy Council of the realm. We have already observed that Wriothesley, since 1544 Lord Chancellor, was not only known to be conservative in his religious views but was also an ambitious, an able, and a not wholly reliable man. Further, he was by instinct and sympathy a civilian, preferring them in his service, and was hence suspect to the common lawyers. But most difficult of all, Wriothesley was also an inveterate intriguer who tended to gain support for his position by the employment of the wiles of faction. The astute Sir Richard Morison wrote of him shortly after his death:

[1] Strype, *Memorials*, II, ii, 329–330.   [2] *Cal. S.P. Span.* IX, 46–49.

'I was afraid of a tempest all the while that Wriothesley was able to raise any. I knew he was an earnest follower of whatsoever he took in hand, and did very seldom miss where either wit or travail were able to bring his purposes to pass. Most true it is, I never was able to persuade myself that Wriothesley could be great, but the King's Majesty must be in greatest danger.'[1]

The plain fact was that he was an opinionated and thorny man, and not an easy or trustworthy colleague.[2]

Wriothesley, then, would predictably have been a formidable colleague in the Council even had he maintained the somewhat aloof attitude of a Lord Chancellor presiding over a distracting and time-consuming judicial office. But the problem became critical when it was discovered that he intended, on his own authority, to delegate his responsibilities in the Chancery in order to devote himself fully to the work of the Council. Hence two days before the coronation he had commissioned four well-qualified civil lawyers to hear cases in his absence. There was an immediate and a strong reaction from the common lawyers and the Inns of Court, who complained of manifold abuses in Chancery and more especially of Wriothesley's action which was alleged to be 'to the great hindrance, prejudice and decay of the said common laws'.[3] The Council, after consulting with the judges and the 'best learned men in the laws of this realm', was advised that the Chancellor's commission, issued without warrant, was offensive to the King and that by common law Wriothesley had forfeited his office and had laid himself liable to such fines and imprisonment as the King, on the advice of the Protector and the Council, might determine.[4] Further, a hearing afforded to Wriothesley in the matter revealed that he had menaced those who had advised the Council, had used unfitting words towards the Protector, and could cite no authority for his action. In the end, however, he yielded, asking that 'in respect of his old service he might forgo his office with as little slander and bruit as might be'. The Council thereupon determined that in view of the great prejudice done to the common law and the injury that might come from 'so stout and arrogant a person', the Great Seal should be taken from him and he

[1] Morison to Northampton, Innsbruck, Nov. 18, 1551, *Cal. S.P. For.*, *Edw. VI*, #491.
[2] This was the judgement of Hayward (*Edward VI*, 272[276]), who tended to be Roman Catholic in his sympathy.
[3] The civil lawyers were John Tregonwell, Sir Robert Southwell, John Oliver, and Anthony Bellasis. Froude, *History of England*, V, 11–12; Pollard, *Somerset*, 32.
[4] *A.P.C.* II, 48–59. One of those consulted was Sir Richard Rich, who was shortly to succeed Wriothesley as Chancellor (Harl. MS. 284, #7).

must lie subject to such fines and imprisonment as the King, with the advice of the Council, might impose.[1]

Wriothesley was in fact treated with great magnanimity considering the gravity of what can only be described as a stupid offence. His relations with Somerset remained at least formally friendly, though it must be stated that on every later opportunity until the day of his death Wriothesley intrigued with the Protector's enemies. The former Chancellor was not imprisoned, his fine was remitted, and his bond was apparently later cancelled.[2] Some months later he was quietly re-admitted to the Council, though from this time forward he was rarely in attendance and was without substantial influence, save for a brief moment when as a known Catholic sympathizer he was useful to Warwick in the events connected with Somerset's first fall in 1549. Wriothesley's religious sympathies being well known, his fall greatly disturbed the Regent in the Low Countries, who instructed the imperial ambassador to watch the 'trend of popular opinion' in England in the case. Van der Delft reported in late May that he had recently talked with Wriothesley who maintained that all his troubles sprang from an enmity which Somerset had borne against him and that he had been guilty of no illegality in the matter alleged against him. Somerset had offered him trial either in the courts or before the Council, and he had taken the latter course in order not to excite 'divisions in the realm'.[3]

Thus, less than a month after his creation as Earl of Southampton, Wriothesley had fallen from power and one of the principal opponents of further religious reformation had been removed. None the less the lands, principally in Hampshire and Devonshire, which had been granted in connection with his advancement in the peerage, amounting to an annual value of £339 12s od were in due season

[1] *A.P.C.* II, 56–57; Burnet, *Reformation*, II, 57–58, and see *ibid.* V, 137–139, for the commission and the judges' opinion on it; and Harl. MS. 249, #4, f. 16, for an interesting, though fragmentary, narrative of the handling of the matter. Harl. MS. 249, #4, is clearly a first draft of the final version as printed in the *Acts of the Privy Council*. There is only one substantial difference, the Harleian copy at the end noting that Wriothesley had accepted the judgement 'given and pronounced by us, as the personages having authority to pronounce and give judgement against him in this case', and that he would accept judgement even though the Council did not enjoy competence. This is stricken from the final draft.

Harl. MS. 284, #7, ff. 9–10, is also a preliminary draft of the document printed in *A.P.C.* II, 53–55, and is valuable in revealing that 'the students of the law' who had complained against Wriothesley were Rich, Sir John Baker, Richard [Roger ?] Cholmeley, Thomas Moyle, John Caryll, John Gosnold, and Robert Kellaway—all lawyers of considerable eminence and position.

[2] *Ibid.* 102–104: June 29, 1547.

[3] *Cal. S.P. Span.* IX, 65: Apr. 1, 1547; *ibid.* 91–92.

conveyed to him.[1] He was much concerned with the completion of
his great house at Titchfield, Hampshire, where he spent considerable time during his enforced retirement. But he died on July
31, 1550, at his London house in Holborn and was taken to Titchfield for burial.[2] Ironically, Bishop Hooper of Gloucester, the most
ardent and effective of all the reforming party, was chosen to preach
his funeral sermon.[3] A self-seeking and a somewhat unscrupulous
man, Wriothesley seems to have been guided by no clear principles
and was moved by no deep loyalties.

Despite Wriothesley's allegations to the imperial ambassador
that it was Somerset's enmity which had destroyed him, there is in
fact no evidence that this was the case. The bitter opposition of the
common lawyers, in and out of the Council, had been the precipitating cause, and the decision was made by the unanimous
agreement of the entire Council. As yet, all the evidence seems to
indicate, the Council was earnestly seeking to govern as a body;
attendance was high; and the relation of the Lord Protector to his
colleagues seems unexceptionable.

7. THE CONSOLIDATION OF POWER IN THE LORD PROTECTOR

In the course of the first two months of the reign no problem of
administration or policy had arisen which had not been easily and
legally resolved under the authority of the late King's will or under
Somerset's pre-eminent authority, as unanimously defined by the
executors. Yet questions had been raised in the dispatch of the
Wriothesley case and more particularly in negotiations under way
with Francis I for a defensive alliance which suggested a certain
degree of constitutional ambiguity. This was at least in a measure
clarified when on March 1, 1547, a commission 'for the settling of
the Lord Protector and for choosing of the Privy Council' set out a
list of twenty-six names, with the addition of Somerset. This had
the effect of consolidating the body of executors and assistants into
the Privy Council.[4] But there still remained the question, actively
raised by the French diplomatist, as to whether Somerset and the
Council possessed power to bind the King and, indeed, whether
they derived from the will, or from subsequent action, sufficient

[1] *Cal. Pat. Rolls, Edw. VI*, II, 131.
[2] Edward VI, *Chronicle*, 42.
[3] Wriothesley, *Chronicle*, II (Camden Soc., n.s. XX), 41.
[4] Lansdowne MS. 160, #81, f. 273. The Council as thereby constituted was very
nearly identical with that at the time of Henry VIII's death. Gardiner, Wriothesley, and
Thirlby had been dropped from the list; Southwell and Peckham had been added.

capacity to employ the Great Seal without further commission from the King.

Accordingly, on March 13, 1547, the Privy Council, with, it may be noted, only seven members signing the document,[1] asked for a fresh commission signed in the King's own hand, empowering them to wield full authority during his minority, which, the Privy Council minutes state, was done and a copy thereof delivered to the French envoys to assure them of 'the undoubted power and sufficiency of the . . . Lord Protector and Council to treat and conclude upon any matter wherein they should have to do on his Highness' behalf'.[2] The commission recites that the King, on the advice of his Councillors and divers of his nobles and prelates, having appointed Somerset to be governor of his person and Protector of the realm in the years of his minority, has so done by word of mouth but not by any writing set forth under the Great Seal. This action was formally ratified and he now granted Somerset 'full power and authority' during his minority to transact and conclude all matters 'both private and public, as well in outward and foreign causes and matters' as in domestic affairs. The King continued by naming the Privy Council to aid and advise the Lord Protector in acts of governance, while fully empowering Somerset to add Councillors to the present list, and vesting him with full powers to proceed in matters of state with 'so many of our Privy Council or of our Councillors as he shall think meet to call unto him from time to time'. And, finally, all acts of the Lord Protector and the Council were declared to be 'good, sure, stable, vailable, and effectual', and those so vested with sovereign powers were indemnified for their actions.[3]

By this action the Lord Protector had been cloaked with very substantial powers. Though measured in time by the King's minority, they were in fact regal. The Council might be increased at will, though at no time did he seek to pack it with his adherents; he might act with or without its deliberation and approval; he might convene it as he chose. In legal theory it is not too much to say that the 'trammels that hampered Edward's prerogative were removed, and his uncle seized unfettered the royal power of the Tudors'.[4] This immense lodging of power had proceeded, it must be emphasized, not from any overweening ambition on Somerset's part—and he

[1] Somerset, St John, Russell, Northampton, Cheyney, Browne, and Paget.
[2] A.P.C. II, 63–64.
[3] Ibid. 67–74; Roskell, in E.H.R. LXVIII (1953), 229; Rymer, Foedera, XV, 174–178; Add. MSS. 35838, f. 33 (for a copy of the patent, Mar. 12, 1547, with two dependent patents of July 9 and Nov. 3, 1547); Nichols, in Archaeologia, XXX (1844), 468–469; Burnet, Reformation, V, 140–146.   [4] Pollard, Somerset, 37–38.

employed that power temperately—but rather from the fact that
the conduct of business and the maintenance of order in Tudor
England required such a vast aggregate of power in whoever ruled
the realm that it would have been perilous indeed to have risked its
dispersion. Further, as Professor Bindoff has so admirably shown,
Seymour, even before Henry VIII's death, had amassed a powerful
parliamentary interest in Wiltshire and, to a lesser degree, in other
counties. In the Parliament of 1545 seven members were either of
Seymour blood or bound by service to the King's brother-in-law.
In the first Edwardian Parliament, summoned to convene in November, 1547, the number had been increased to twelve, and one
wonders whether the fifty manors he held in Somerset did not
ensure as well a substantial interest in that neighbouring county.[1]

But despite the great honours and powers which had been bestowed upon him, Somerset was still not content, not so much with
the extent of his authority, as with its structure. He seems to have
felt that he had sufficient power to act on any issue, but he was never
wholly comfortable with the source of the power he wielded. Thus
in May he secured licence to retain two hundred servants beyond
those in his already large household, and on July 9, 1547, his emolu-
ments were set at 8000 marks p.a. so long as he should retain his
high office. But still, either not content or not comfortable with his
position, on the eve of the assembling of Parliament, he secured
letters patent under date of November 3, 1547, which provided for
his place in the Lords. The King decreed that 'our said uncle shall
and do sit alone, and be placed at all times, as well in our presence . . .
as in our absence upon the midst of the bench or stool standing
next on the right hand of our siege reall in our parliament chamber',
and there shall enjoy all the liberties and prerogatives of any protector of the realm in earlier minorities. The document states that
Somerset had first been named 'principal councillor and governor'
by royal word of mouth and that these powers were herewith cancelled, he being now by the new instrument reappointed 'governor
of our person and protector of our realms, dominions, and subjects'.
Further, the Council was re-named and Somerset was declared to
be 'our chief and principal councillor and chiefest of our Privy
Council', with powers to add or remove those now re-appointed.[2]

This elaborate and repetitious document was brought forward for

---

[1] VCH, *Wiltshire*, V, 114–115. The second rising parliamentary interest in Wiltshire
was in the Herbert family, now gaining rapidly in wealth and in power, which supplanted
the Seymour interest for a season following the Protector's fall (*ibid.* 128).

[2] Rymer, *Foedera*, XV, 164–165; *L.J.* I, 293; S.P. Dom., Edw. VI, II, 20.

ratification on December 24, 1547, just prior to the parliamentary Christmas recess, having been signed by the King's sign manual, by all the peers present on that day in Parliament, by those of the Council who were in attendance, by thirteen of the bishops, and by all the principal law officers. It considerably enlarged the base of Somerset's authority and committed every significant element of the governing mechanism to the support of his now quasi-regal powers. But in this restless search of the Duke for full constitutional powers, one important concession was made—probably had to be made—to appease jealousies now appearing in the Council itself. Wherever the earlier patent conferred essentially sovereign authority until the King had attained eighteen years of age, the new document bestowed such powers 'until such time as we shall declare to our said uncle our pleasure to be otherwise by writing signed with our hand and sealed with the Great Seal of England'.[1] This eventuality must have seemed remote indeed in December, 1547, with the King just a few weeks past his tenth birthday and still subject to the direct and rather stern control of an uncle who, though he had many children, so evidently never understood them. The structure of Somerset's constitutional powers stood as complete as legal ingenuity and a marked care for the proprieties could make it. Only one further power was to be added, when in August, 1548, he was vested with the authority of a Captain General who might wage war, hire mercenaries, call out the musters, execute martial law, and treat with foreign powers.[2]

The vast and legally almost unfettered power now lodged in Somerset's hands was well understood and on the whole unquestioned in England and was certainly recognized by the foreign diplomatists of the period resident in England. He possessed authority to withdraw gold and jewels from the King's secret jewel-house for the making of Edward's crown[3]; peers of the realm sought ways to lay petitions and letters before him[4]; and the holder of the oldest peerage in the realm found his romantic attachment to a quite unsuitable lady laid in review before the Lord Protector.[5] All matters of state, of peace and war, of justice and compulsion flowed through his not particularly efficient hands, or—perhaps more accurately—were in the Council subject to his intervention.

[1] Nichols, in *Archaeologia*, XXX (1844), 480–481.
[2] Rymer, *Foedera*, XV, 175; Roskell, in *E.H.R.* LXVIII (1953), 229.
[3] S.P. Dom., Edw. VI, III, 7: Feb. 12, 1548.
[4] *Ibid*. IV, 37: Lord de la Warr to Cecil, Aug. 3, 1548.
[5] *Ibid*. I, 45: Sir Thomas Darcy to ?, regarding the love affair of the Earl of Oxford and Mrs Borothy, June 27, 1547.

As the words of address of a contemporary chronicler suggest, England regarded Somerset as its ruler. Thus Thomas Cooper praised the Protector for his 'affability and clemency', which are 'so great, that all people of every state and degree, as well poor as rich, may at all convenient times have free access to your grace, and have their reasonable suits, complaints, and petitions benignly heard, and according to equity, justice, and good conscience dispatched'.[1] This is in tone and intent an address to royalty, and so it had to be in Tudor England where the centrality and the personality of royal power had by such a firm policy been established by the first two of the Tudor line. There is, indeed, ample reason to believe that this is as the people of England wanted it, particularly as the persuasion that this was the 'good Duke' rooted itself in the realm. The jealousies, the frailties, and the dangers were rather to be found in Somerset's own brooding and hesitant nature, and in factional alienation at the very heart of government, in the Council of State, amongst his closest colleagues. These dangers, too, were in Cooper's mind when he warned Somerset that the most kindly and the best of rulers stood always imperilled by false advisers who would pervert the ends of government and justice to their own selfish purposes and then betray the clement and salutary intentions of the ruler.[2]

As we have suggested, the great lodging of power in the Duke was also observed by the foreign diplomatists resident in London, often with a kind of bewilderment mixed with apprehension. Van der Delft, in May, 1547, again informed the Emperor that all power was now vested in Somerset, 'to such an extent, indeed, that very little mention is made of the King and his Court, and all solicitation and resort are at the Protector's palace, where the Council meet and all business is despatched'. The French ambassador, de Selve, complained to Paget because Somerset was signing dispatches without reference to the King, his excuse being that Edward was only then learning to sign documents in a new hand. So, too, when Vieilleville had been sent by Henry II shortly after his accession to discuss the remaining frictions between the two governments, the ambassador was most struck by the centrality of power which had been lodged in the Duke. It was also his feeling that there was amongst the nobles some resentment because of this great authority, particularly

---

[1] Lanquet, Thomas, *An epitome of cronicles, etc.*, transl. by Thomas Cooper (L., 1549), A ii. Lanquet died in 1545 while working on the chronicle. It was translated and completed by Cooper, who also prepared a famous Latin-English dictionary (1565); he was appointed Bishop of Winchester in 1584.   [2] *Ibid.* A iii.

since it was linked with the wide military powers vested in Thomas Seymour, the ambitious and untrustworthy brother of the Lord Protector. The secretary to the mission, Carloix, related that Lord Cobham, while escorting Vieilleville back to his lodgings after a meeting with Somerset and the King, spoke freely of the unpopularity of the Seymour brothers and dwelt bitterly on their ill-gotten wealth and power, while Vieilleville gained the general impression that there was active discontent amongst the nobility which might in time fatten into revolt.[1]

But these intimations of difficulty, these diplomatic gossipings— some remembered well after the event—do not alter the pragmatic fact of the greatness of power vested in Somerset, first at the moment of the King's accession and then steadily, and legally, enhanced until the structure of that power stood complete in August, 1548. Somerset's position seemed secure so long as he commanded the loyalty of his Council, from which his own strength in the final analysis sprang, and until wholly unpredictable, and to an extent unavoidable, erosions began rapidly to weaken his capacity to lead and command the politically and economically dominant classes of men in the realm. It required revolutionary forces and colossal and tragic mistakes in judgement on the Lord Protector's part to weaken the structure of the power with which he stood seised in late 1548.

[1] *Cal. S.P. Span.* IX, 91; de Selve, *Corr. politique*, 111–112; Petitot, M. (ed.), *Collection complète des mémoires relatifs à l'histoire de France, etc.*, XXVI: *Mémoires de . . . François de Scepeaux, Sire de Vieilleville, etc.* (Paris, 1822), 153–159.

III

THE STRUCTURE OF POWER IN EDWARDIAN ENGLAND

I. THE PRIVY COUNCIL

The Privy Council had taken shape as a recognized and a formally established instrument of administration and government not much more than a decade before the accession of Edward VI. Dr Elton has dealt fully and convincingly with this profoundly important constitutional development, and we need do no more than briefly re-state his conclusions.[1] Long in process of evolution, this inner, or Privy, Council became differentiated from the ancient Great Council shortly after, and in part as a consequence of, Cromwell's administrative reforms of 1534–1536. It was a small body of nine-teen Councillors, with a clerk, with a formally kept record, and with an adequate institutional organization. It is evident that appointments to it were carefully made, with a special emphasis on administrative and diplomatic ability and experience, while the proceedings, recorded in its *Acts*, suggest very wide powers of administrative authority, always subject to the policy and the occasional personal intervention of the King. The Council was in the main comprised of experienced royal servants with a fairly specialized knowledge of particular branches of government, to which were added members with a more ranging interest and competence.[2]

The Henrician Privy Council was also notable for the fact that in the main its membership was comprised of new men, Councillors who had risen from humble beginnings in the service of the Crown. This tendency reflects not only the Tudor suspicion of the nobility but the very evident inclination of Henry VIII to advance promising young men who had enjoyed the benefits of a humanistic education and who, at the least, were pliable in their religious persuasions. It

---

[1] Elton, G. R., *The Tudor revolution in government* (Cambridge, 1953), esp. 317–342.
[2] Elton, G. R., *The Tudor constitution. Documents and commentary* (Cambridge, 1960), 91.

was against such 'base born' men that one of the principal demands
of the Pilgrimage of Grace was levied. The conservative demand in
the north was that the King should expel 'all villain blood from the
King's grace and his Privy Council for the commonwealth, and
restoring of Christ's Church', and that they be replaced by virtuous
and 'well born men'.[1] This persistent and rankling grievance, most
specifically directed against Cromwell, was rebutted principally
by Morison and Starkey, the former arguing that the duty of Christian obedience includes the acceptance of the authority of those
chosen by the King to wield power, and enquiring who can justly
blame the sovereign 'for making them great, that indeed have all
those things which at the beginning of nobility only made them
noble'.[2] The King sets in high places of authority those endowed
with special and needed virtues and capabilities, with the consequence that in a well-ordered state true personal virtue is 'only
to be the way to promotion' and 'in all other things, it little availeth
whose son a man be'.[3] These sentiments were well reflected in the
composition of the Privy Council in 1536–1537, when a fairly
certain and formal list of members may be assembled. Only six of the
nineteen members were of the nobility in the second generation,
though the surprisingly high number of five were bishops (including
Gardiner, then abroad on a diplomatic mission), most of whom
were valued for their diplomatic skill and experience.

The tendency towards vesting great responsibility and power in
new and thrusting men, in men who had proved their devotion to
the monarchy which had raised them to exalted rank, continued
with great force in the later Henrician years, and is most dramatically
reflected in the list of twenty-eight men named as executors or
assistants and who as a body were incorporated into the Edwardian
Privy Council. So too, and even more dramatically, was the tendency towards the increasing secularization of policy, occasioned in
part because younger and extremely able and educated laymen
were now available for diplomatic assignments. Thus when Gardiner
and Thirlby had been removed by the fiat of Henry VIII's will,
additional laymen, and all 'new men', had replaced them in the
persons of Thomas Seymour, Richard Southwell, and Edmund
Peckham. Further, this reigning group possessed important links
with Parliament, since almost every member of the Privy Council

[1] *L. & P., Henry VIII*, XI, 622, 705 (i, ii, iii), 892, 902.
[2] [Morison, Richard], *A lamentation in whiche is shewed what ruyne cometh of seditious
rebellyon* (L., 1536), A iv.
[3] [Morison, Richard], *A remedy for sedition, etc.* ([L.], 1536), A iv–B ii.

not a judge or a peer held a seat in Edward's first Parliament, and another, Sir John Baker, was its Speaker.[1]

The most immediately striking fact regarding the composition of the Edwardian Council at the outset of the reign is its almost wholly

---

[1] The list of Privy Councillors at the outset of the reign follows, with their then offices and titles:

Edward Seymour, Duke of Somerset
William Paulet, Lord St John of Basing, Great Master of the Household
Thomas Cranmer, Archbishop of Canterbury
Sir John Russell, Keeper of the Privy Seal
William Parr, Earl of Essex
John Dudley, Viscount Lisle, Lord Admiral
Henry Fitzalan, 12th Earl of Arundel, Lord Chamberlain of the Household
Sir Thomas Seymour
Cuthbert Tunstall, Bishop of Durham
Thomas Wriothesley, Chancellor, shortly replaced by
    Sir Richard Rich
Sir Thomas Cheyney, Treasurer of the Household
Sir John Gage, Comptroller of the Household
Sir Anthony Browne (d. 1548), Master of the Horse
Sir Anthony Wingfield, Vice-Chamberlain
Sir William Paget, Principal Secretary
Sir William Petre, Principal Secretary
Sir Ralph Sadler, Master of the Wardrobe
Sir John Baker, Speaker of the House of Commons
Dr Nicholas Wotton, Dean of Canterbury and of York
Sir Anthony Denny (d. 1549), Gentleman of the Privy Chamber
Sir William Herbert, Gentleman of the Privy Chamber
Sir Edward North, Chancellor of the Court of Augmentations
Sir Edward Montague, Chief Justice of Common Pleas
Sir Edward Wotton, Treasurer of Calais
Sir Edmund Peckham, Cofferer of the Household
Sir Thomas Bromley, Justice of Common Pleas
Sir Richard Southwell

(*A.P.C.* II, 70-71, with additions; Lansdowne MS. 160, #81, f. 273, for a list dated March 1, 1547, and hence with revisions.)

The membership of the Privy Council remained remarkably stable during the first three years of the reign. The following additions or promotions are noted in Edward's *Chronicle* or in the *A.P.C.* to Apr. 19, 1550.

Paget succeeded Gage as Comptroller of the Household (June 29, 1547).
Sir Thomas Smith, until then a clerk of the Council, was sworn April 17, 1548, though it is not stated that he was then admitted to membership.
Walter Devereux, 3rd Baron Ferrers (cr. Viscount Hereford 1550), sworn Jan. 26, 1549, though he had attended earlier.
Francis Talbot, 5th Earl of Shrewsbury, admitted Mar. 15, 1549.
Dr Nicholas Wotton, appointed Secretary, Oct. 15, 1549, replacing Smith.
Thomas Goodrich, Bishop of Ely, admitted, probably, Nov. 12, 1549.
Henry Grey, 3rd Marquis of Dorset, admitted Nov. 28, 1549.
Sir Thomas Darcy, admitted Jan. 24, 1550.
Lord Wentworth, admitted shortly before his appointment as Lord Chamberlain on the dismissal of Arundel (Feb. 20, 1550).
Sir John Mason, admitted Apr. 19, 1550.

secular complexion. Cranmer attended meetings with a dutiful regularity during the years of Somerset's dominance, but his principal interest was in ecclesiastical affairs and religious policy generally. Tunstall, now aged and normally seated in distant Durham, rarely attended sessions and was principally concerned with his essentially secular responsibilities as President of the Council of the North, being for many months wholly absorbed with border problems during the festering war with Scotland. And finally, there was the professional diplomatist Dr Nicholas Wotton, who, though Dean of both Canterbury and York, was so completely secular in his interests and attitudes that one forgets, as he doubtless did, that he was in holy orders. It is safe to say that never before in the long history of the realm had so overwhelmingly secular a group of advisers and administrators been responsible for the governance of the realm.

The Edwardian Privy Council is also remarkable, even when compared with that of Henry VIII just a decade earlier, for the fact that its complexion is almost exclusively that of new men, of new families, of thrusting men whose fortunes were only now being made. It reflects the decisive change that had occurred during the preceding century when first the Yorkist kings and then the Tudors gradually but inexorably freed England of the menace of the great territorial magnates. The Poles, the Staffords, the Courtenays, and the Percys had been struck down, and then at the very end of Henry's reign the Howards, who stood out as conspicuous survivals, were brought, it seemed, to utter ruin.[1] Of the whole Edwardian Council at the beginning of the reign, only one member, Arundel, was the son of a peer, and he was to be ruined by Northumberland's vaulting ambition before the brief reign was done. For the rest, eleven were the sons of members of the upper gentry and nine of lesser gentry, this predominant group comprising almost three-fourths of the whole body and including both Somerset and Northumberland. Four men were drawn from families which in the time of their youth hovered uncertainly in that ill-defined frontier between the yeomanry and the gentry, while one (Wriothesley) was the son of an official and two (Paget and North) sprang from the rising urban middle class.

The whole social complexion of the Council in terms of origin was, then, middle class, with a heavy preponderance of them drawn upwards from the gentry. So too, the *first* marriage of the twenty-six

[1] MacCaffrey, Wallace T., 'England: the crown and the new aristocracy, 1540-1600', *Past and Present*, no. 30 (April, 1965), 52-53.

who married at all reflected accurately and significantly the social origins of the group. Thomas Seymour, as in all other matters, was an exception, having with impetuous ambition married Catherine Parr, the widow of the late King—a rash action not unconnected with his early and violent disappearance from the scene of affairs. Two of the members, the Earl of Arundel and William Parr, married daughters of noblemen. But the overwhelming proportion of these men contracted their marriages within the class that had bred them, seventeen having married women whose fathers had been of the gentry. Three of the group married within the powerful urban middle class, while one (Sadler) married a woman of distinctly lower urban class. The social status of the wives of two of the Councillors (Cheyney and Peckham) cannot certainly be established.

These high officers of state, entrusted by Henry VIII with sovereign powers during the minority of his son, were, particularly in sixteenth century terms, almost without exception mature in both years and experience. The average age of the group was slightly more than forty-seven years, both Seymour and Dudley, it may be noted, being a few years younger than the average of their colleagues, so to speak. Two of them, Tunstall and Gage, were past seventy as the new reign began, while four men were past sixty years of age. Only three of the Councillors (Parr, Arundel, and Thomas Seymour) were in their thirties, their average age being slightly more than thirty-six years. Perhaps even more important was the fact that amongst these officers of state the really powerful and predominant figures, including Somerset, Dudley, Wriothesley, Paget, and Petre, were at the full tide of their maturity. This, then, was a government of new men, but it was by no means a government of young or inexperienced men.

Almost without exception these Councillors had risen rather slowly in the service of the King, in careers as officers of state rather than as courtiers. Though it is somewhat difficult to date entrance into the royal service in these terms, it seems fairly conservative to suggest that on the average these men had been in the King's service, on a career basis, for 16·7 years at the time of Edward's accession. In other words, they had begun their careers—again in average terms—at about 1530; a number of them had as young men been trained by Cromwell; and they all possessed a deep, an almost habitual loyalty to the Crown and to the royal supremacy. Some of these careers in government had been very long indeed, ranging from Russell's forty-one years, Gage's thirty-four years, Tunstall's thirty-two years, to Seymour and Dudley who had both been servants of the Crown for upwards of twenty years. Further—to support the long and seasoned experience of the Privy Council—there were only four among its members (Cheyney, Herbert, Bromley, and Southwell) who had served for less than a decade, and, perhaps significantly, only one of these was to have any considerable influence in affairs during the course of the reign.[1]

It should be further observed that the Edwardian Council possessed easily discernible and in numerous instances notable specialized competencies, which, unfortunately, were not always fully employed by either Somerset or Northumberland. As one reviews the Henrician careers of these men it becomes clear that sixteen of the number, or well over half, had discharged successfully important administrative responsibilities. Among these were Dudley, Tunstall, Arundel, Rich, Gage, Paget, Petre, North, and Edward Wotton, all of whom had displayed very considerable ability and a capacity for making decisions. Quite as important was the long and often brilliant experience of nine of the Councillors in the conduct of diplomatic negotiations. For good reason such men as Tunstall, Paget, Sadler, Nicholas Wotton, and Somerset himself were well and favourably known abroad, and three of the group rivalled Gardiner himself in experience. Further, another nine had held senior military commands under Henry VIII, though two of them (Russell and Parr) were decidedly unimpressive in commands held in the Edwardian era. Among these Councillors Somerset and Northumberland may be regarded as really gifted generals, while Paulet, Thomas Seymour, Gage (though now too old), and Herbert had displayed capacities in the field of the second order of competence. And, finally, in analysing the specialized competencies available to the new government, six of the Privy Council had been well trained in the law, though only Tunstall, Montague, and Bromley possessed legal abilities of a high order.

In considering the general complexion and competencies of the Council at the opening of the reign, one is likewise deeply impressed by the fact that most of these men had been well and formally educated. It is wholly safe to say that never before had the principal officers of state as a body enjoyed as high a degree of literacy and of

[1] The materials from which conclusions and data are drawn in this and the three preceding paragraphs are as diffuse as they are numerous. The principal sources are the *DNB*, wills (particularly for the fathers of Councillors and their wives), *Inquisitions post mortem*, university matriculations, and other very scattered materials. The birth year for seven of the twenty-eight, including Somerset, is not certainly known and in these instances I have taken the traditional date or one established no more than approximately.

intellectual competence, for the fruits of sixteenth-century humanism in England were beginning to mature. We have also observed that, three members aside, all of the Council were laymen, and their education had been preponderantly secular and humanistic. It is certain that just over half (fifteen) of the Councillors had matriculated in one of the universities or Inns of Court, and it is possible that four more, including Somerset, regarding whom the evidence is very unreliable, should be added to this number. Seven of the principal officers of state (including Northumberland) had not been formally educated,[1] at least beyond grammar school, while we are without any evidence at all in two instances (Browne and Cheyney).

There is about this body of men a complexion of literacy, of interest in ideas, and of respect for knowledge. In a later connection we shall deal in detail with the maturing of English humanism in this generation and with the first great burst of interest in making more generally available the facilities and the opportunities of at least grammar school education. It had become generally agreed in England as early as 1547 that the great servants of the Crown must be literate in the full sense of the term, as were well over half of the Council at its institution. Even more significant, as the reign wore on and as replacements or additions were made in the Council, not only were these men of a slightly younger generation—men like Smith, Mason, Cecil, Hoby, and Cheke—highly educated; they were humanists in the full sense of the term, several in fact being professional scholars.

Evidence, rather casually collected, from the diplomatic sources suggests that at least eight of the original Council, Somerset being one, spoke French with an ease which satisfied even the French ambassador, and at least nine more certainly read and understood the language. And a considerable number of officers of state were cultivated and bookish men. Thus in 1548 Sir Francis Bryant, one of the King's Privy Chamber, translated Antonio de Guevara's, *A disapraise of the life of a courtier*, in a competent and graceful rendering with sensitivity of ear and considerable gifts of phrasing. Bryant tells us in his dedication to Parr that he had determined on the translation when not long before he had seen Northampton reading a French edition of the work.[2] A few years later Morison's

---

[1] Herbert was uneducated and also somewhat uncouth. His deficiencies were so marked in relation to his colleagues that the somewhat acid Van der Delft reported to the Emperor that he knew no language save English, while wrongly adding that Herbert was illiterate (*Cal. S.P. Span.* X, 19: Jan. 31, 1550).

[2] Guevara, Antonio de, *A disapraise of the life of a courtier, etc.* (L., 1548), *Dedic.*

always informal diplomatic dispatches were interwoven with lively remarks regarding Mildred Cecil's polished Greek correspondence, for she was one of the superbly educated daughters of Sir Anthony Cooke[1]; and towards the end of the same year Pickering was writing to Cecil from his embassy in Paris that he was having bound for him 'Euclid with the figures in a small volume, and two discourses, one of Machiavelli, the other of Mons. Long', and assured the Secretary that he knew of only one new work from Italy not already available in England, which he would forward when it came to hand. A few days later he reported that he had found more interesting books for Cecil: a Greek New Testament, notes on Aristotle's *Ethics* in Italian, and *Le Discourse de la Guerre* of Laugnay, which he would forward when they were properly bound.[2] Cecil's interest in new books—and solid books—was continuous, the equally learned Dr Nicholas Wotton being a great joy to him when, as ambassador to France, he assured him that 'if I knew [of] any kind of books here which you like, I would buy them for you, and bring them home with some of my own'. He added that 'here is *Clemens Alexandrinus*, and *Theodoretus* in *Epistolas Pauli* turned into Latin by *Geneyan*. But forbecause I hear that you have *Clemens* . . . in *Greek already*, I suppose you care not for him in Latin'.[3]

This literate and cultivated taste suffused rather more than half of the Privy Council in the Edwardian period and was even more marked amongst junior officers of state and public servants of the second rank. The tone was set by the rapidly forming tastes of the King himself who, according to Bale, gathered a considerable library of manuscripts and books during his short lifetime.[4] Cranmer, more selective and learned in his tastes, left a library of forty-nine valuable manuscripts, and 350 books, most of which came into the possession of the highly literate Earl of Arundel after the Archbishop's execution.[5] Though his whole collection was certainly larger, twenty-two of the books in Sir William Petre's library have been noted,[6] while the one-time professional scholar, Sir Thomas

---

[1] *Cal. S.P., For. Edw. VI*, #287: Morison to Cecil, Augsburg, Feb. 3, 1551.

[2] *Ibid.* #520: Paris, Dec. 15 and 25, 1551. Still later (Dec. 29) Pickering wrote that the Euclid and Machiavelli were so 'buggerly bound' that he had destroyed them both (*ibid.* #522).

[3] HMC, *Salisbury MSS.* I, 123; Haynes, Samuel, *A collection of state papers . . . left by William Cecill Lord Burghley, etc.*, I (L. 1740), 152: Wotton to Cecil, Poissy, June 21, 1553.

[4] Bale, John, *Index Britanniae scriptorum, etc.*, ed. by R. L. Poole and Mary Bateson (Oxford, 1902), 514–516.

[5] Jayne, Sears, *Library catalogues of the English Renaissance* (Berkeley, 1956), 106.

[6] *Ibid.* 104.

Smith, had gathered 406 books in his library at Hill Hall.[1] North-umberland's tastes were not bookish and he rather plaintively confessed, when the King was busily engaged in the reform of the Garter statutes, that his Latin was not competent, but he none the less left a library of at least forty-one manuscripts and books.[2] And, finally, though he was never of the Council, we must include the large library of books devoted to law, grammar, poetry, history, and science left by Henry, first Baron Stafford, the gifted and attractive son of the ill-fated Duke of Buckingham.[3]

The Privy Council, whose composition and complexion we have examined at some length, was then wholly competent in terms of ability and experience to conduct the affairs of state. But the men who comprised it had in the past functioned under the eye and at the direction of an overweening monarch who laid out the lines of policy at will, who was given to unpredictable personal interven-tions, and who in the final analysis kept the reins of power in his own hands. This body had now to adapt itself to new habits of work and to create a new tradition of competence during a legal minority in which, to put it in blunt terms, first Somerset and then North-umberland stood in an ambiguous relation to it. None the less the *Acts*, or the official minutes, of the Council, which unfortunately are incomplete, suggest that it exercised an extensive and highly generalized administrative capacity from the beginning. It was charged with the task of routine administration, with some measure of essentially delegated responsibility from Somerset for the con-duct of diplomacy, with promulgating a large number of proclama-tions on a great variety of matters, with problems of defence, and with a detailed and energetic supervision of religious worship and doctrinal reformation. The Council met normally in or near London, most often at Westminster, and a great deal of its work was actually carried on by its Secretaries, Paget and Petre at the outset, with Smith, Nicholas Wotton, and Cecil later serving as additions or replacements. Theirs was a fairly recent office of state, the Secretary having earlier been a confidential servant of the sovereign, vested with the signet, and in charge of the royal correspondence. But as the office was developed by that superb administrator Cromwell, the post came to have very high prestige indeed. As the adminis-trative routines became more formidable, two Secretaries were appointed in 1540, one of whom seems to have attended the King,

[1] Strype, John, *The life of . . . Sir Thomas Smith, etc.* (Oxford, 1820), 274–281.
[2] Jayne, *Library catalogues*, 104.
[3] *Ibid.* 109.

and the other the Council.[1] The load of correspondence and of
record-keeping, supervised directly by the Secretaries, was in the
main delegated by them to the Clerk of the Council, of which at the
outset of Edward's reign there were three: William Hunning,
Armigill Wade, and Sir Thomas Chaloner, whose salaries were
substantially increased in 1548 so that Hunning was to receive
£50 p.a., Chaloner £40, and Wade 50 marks.[2]

We have suggested that the Privy Council possessed very wide
and important responsibilities during the Edwardian period. In
addition to the administrative and executive competence already
mentioned, there should be added a direct concern, which under
Northumberland became a preoccupation, with the maintenance of
civil order. Its principal instrumentality was the Court of Star
Chamber which in this period, as Pollard suggests, may be regarded
as consisting of the Council as a whole.[3] Through this court it was
concerned with a great variety of matters, including riots, unlawful
assemblies, assaults, and the enforcement of its own proclamations.
In the course of this brief reign the Court of Star Chamber dealt
with upwards of 2500 cases, the great proportion of which were to
arise in the troubled period of Northumberland's government. A
rough curve of the rigour of administration is suggested by Pollard's
estimate that entries of fines imposed by the Council numbered
approximately four-and-one-half per month on the average during
the later reign of Henry VIII, declined drastically to one a month
under Somerset, and then rose abruptly to about eleven a month
under Northumberland.[4]

Some suggestion of the nature of the Council's working habits
and of the focus of power within it may be suggested by an analysis
of its meetings in three selected periods. We have taken three blocks
of thirty-four consecutive recorded meetings, the first of which
extends from February 22, 1547, to May 5, 1547, in the period of
Somerset's complete and unquestioned dominance. This is an
interval in which the Protector kept the reins of executive authority
tightly in his own hands. He had put his personal affairs wholly in
the charge of his trusted friend, Sir John Thynne, in order to lend
full attention to the conduct of state business. So completely did he
dominate foreign affairs, with the assistance of the secretaries of
state, that only a sparse record of discussions and decisions appears
in the *Acts* of the Council, while at the same time he undertook most

[1] Elton, *Tudor constitution*, 118–119.
[2] *A.P.C.* II, 184: Apr. 17, 1548.
[3] Pollard, *Somerset*, 85.   [4] *Ibid.* 87.

of the direct, and often the routine, problems of defence and preparation for war. In this period, too, the Protector was deeply involved in the gradual, and restrained, unfolding of a reformed religious policy; and it is in these months that the groundwork was laid for the policy of social and economic reform which was to be the principal cause of his undoing.

During the period of seventy-three days under review, the Council met very nearly once every other day. Somerset and the always industrious Paulet are recorded as attending every meeting, while Russell, Cranmer, and Anthony Browne were absent only once or twice. Paget, Cheyney, and Northampton were also fairly regular in attendance, all being present more than half the time. Dudley, who was ill for some time in this interval, Wingfield, Denny, and Herbert were not present at more than a third of the meetings, while those other Councillors who attended at all had very irregular records. The average attendance over the whole period was 8·5 members (six constituting a quorum), and the range of attendance at meetings was from 6 to 11. There were in this period 27 members of the Council, and of this number there is no record at all of the attendance of almost half (13), these being principally persons away on diplomatic missions, the law officers, and those with military commands. It should also be observed that during this period Somerset is on occasion listed as present when we know he was absent or away from London, having evidently signed the minutes after his return in a space left blank for the purpose.

We have taken as the second block of time a period of eighty-four days (October 25, 1549–January 16, 1550), in which there were also thirty-four meetings, a period just after Somerset's first fall when Northumberland was securing control of the apparatus of power. In this interval the Privy Council numbered 29 to 30 members and, it is interesting to note, there are only 3 members for whom there is no record of attendance. Further, the average attendance had risen sharply to 11·6 members, while the range of attendance was now from 8 to 15 members. Paulet, that dull but conscientious professional civil servant, once more had a perfect record of attendance, while a longish list of Councillors—Russell, Herbert, Paget, Petre, Rich, Arundel, and Dr Wotton—were almost invariably present, their recorded attendances ranging from 25 to 32 occasions. Still another group of 9 members were present at from a third to half of the recorded meetings, including Dudley who was present at exactly half the occasions. One may conclude, then, that there were 17 members who were either normally or frequently present and whose experience was sufficiently continuous to permit the formulation and execution of policy.

We have taken as our third period the interval extending from November 2, 1551, through December 15, 1551, when there were also thirty-four meetings—a very active period indeed, with meetings recorded on approximately three out of every four days. This was a period of great crisis, when preparations were being made for Somerset's trial which began on December 1st. There were now 33 members of the Council, and of this number only 8 did not attend at all, these being principally judges, diplomatists away from London, and members on active military duty. In this period Paulet faltered, missing one meeting, though for the total of 102 days being analysed his attendance record totalled 101, while Russell, with a perfect attendance for this third interval, was present on 99 of the occasions for the full term. So great was the crisis and so important was full control of the Council, that Northumberland was present on 32 of these occasions, though his record for the whole reign is indifferent, the Duke having confessed that he detested the tedium of Council meetings. The average attendance had again risen sharply to 13·9 members, while the range of attendance was wide: from 8 to 20 Councillors. A long list of 16 members, in addition to Paulet, Russell, and Dudley, may be noted who attended at least half the meetings in this period of great and dramatic crisis.

2. THE ECLIPSE OF THE ANCIENT PEERAGE [*Excursus* I]

England, as we have suggested, was governed during the Edwardian period by a junta of grandees drawn principally from crown servants recently ennobled by Henry VIII. The most effective and powerful of these men, all Privy Councillors, were very rapidly advanced in status and wealth by Somerset, as he sought to create a stable basis for power and administration and then, towards the close of the reign, by Northumberland, as he endeavoured to secure the destruction of Somerset and then to gain all possible support for the revolutionary *coup* which his restless and ruthless mind was framing. As we have said, these were men of new families; men who had proved themselves able and wholly loyal servants of the Crown in the later years of the reign of Henry VIII; men who had made a career of service to the state; and men who, with very few exceptions, were either Protestant in their sympathies or Henrician politiques. We should now examine the structure of the power and wealth of these new peers against the background of the older peerage which they were so completely to replace in power, in wealth, and in favour.[1]

There were a total of fifty-seven noble families in England during the brief Edwardian period. This number was very close to what may be described as the Tudor norm, though it may be noted that Henry VII had permitted the steady erosion of genetic failure and attainder to draw the number down from probably fifty-seven peers early in his reign to forty-four at its close.[2] Henry VIII had been erratic in his creations, but clusters of ennoblement may be observed in the very early years of the reign, at the critical moment of the divorce and the break with Rome, and at the end of the reign as the King raised high in power and favour the group of Crown servants who would, so he hoped, stand as a bulwark during his son's minority. At the moment of Edward's accession, however, the total number of peers stood at no more than forty-eight, if Courtenay, Howard, Northumberland in the Percy line, Dacre of Gilsland, and Grey of Ruthen be not counted because of attainders, abeyances, lapses, and 'suspensions'. The number increased slightly under Edward, the total of the effective peerage, so to say, standing at fifty-six at the moment of his death.

Nor was this relatively small body of peers in any way an entity, since there was a distinct and a rapidly widening cleavage in the Edwardian period between the old noble families and the new, even if one most generously defines the 'old nobility' as those peers who in 1547 were members of families which in direct descent had been ennobled before the accession of Henry VIII in 1509. There were twenty-six such families, but of these only nine were of really considerable antiquity with roots of nobility extending well back into the Middle Ages.[3] It is notable that all of these families were completely excluded from the seats of power in Edwardian England, save intermittently for Henry Fitzalan, twelfth Earl of Arundel (1511?–1581), who was named by Henry VIII as an assistant

[1] The principal sources employed are Collins, Arthur, *The Peerage of England*, ed. by S. E. Brydges (9 vols., L., 1812); G. E. C., *Complete peerage*; 'Creations of peerage, 1483–1646', *Forty-seventh report, Dep. Keeper of Public Records* (1886), App.; Stone, Lawrence, *The crisis of the aristocracy, 1558–1641* (Oxford, 1965); MacCaffrey, in *Past and Present*, no. 30 (Apr., 1965), 52–64; *DNB*; and divers county histories and the *VCH* for numerous counties in which peers were resident or were born.

[2] Professor Stone has reckoned that there were twenty-seven attainders in the Tudor period (*Crisis of the aristocracy*, 398).

[3] These were Berkeley, De Vere (Oxford, 1142), Grey of Wilton (1290), Clifford (Cumberland, 1299), Zouche (1308), Fitzalan (Arundel, 1323), Talbot (Shrewsbury, 1332), Scrope (1371), and Neville (Westmorland, 1397).

executor of his will and who very late in the reign was admitted to the Privy Council and appointed Lord Chamberlain of the Household. Arundel had served with some distinction as Deputy at Calais and in the assault on Boulogne. Conservative in religion, without strongly held political principles, and markedly gullible in nature, Arundel at no time exercised much influence, save in the crisis of 1549 when he lent his full support to Dudley against Somerset, almost certainly in the naive expectation that there would be a reversal in the religious policy of the government. Not many months later he was dismissed from office on outrageous charges of embezzlement, confined to his house, and heavily fined. Shortly released to a precarious freedom, the Earl formed a close friendship with Somerset and was imprisoned in the Tower as an alleged accomplice on the occasion of the Duke's final fall. Northumberland never brought Arundel to trial—there was almost certainly no case against him—but in 1552 compelled him to sign a humiliating confession before the Council and laid on him a crippling fine as the price of his freedom. Shortly afterwards, as the King's health began to fail, Northumberland again sought to use Arundel as a dupe, restoring him to the Council board and remitting his fines. Though he signed the letters patent denying the succession to Mary, Arundel betrayed Northumberland at the first possible moment, and, ironically, it was he who was sent to secure the person of the ruined Duke. Though of great personal charm, of commanding presence and undoubted cultivation, Arundel was in fact a weak and somewhat stupid man to whom the substance of power was steadily denied.

Only one other member of the ancient peerage, William Grey, thirteenth Baron Grey de Wilton, who had succeeded his brother to the title in 1521, played a role of some significance in Edwardian affairs. Without either political interest or ability, Grey was a steady and valiant professional soldier. He had been wounded before Montreuil (1544), and on his recovery was entrusted with first the Calais command and then (1546) Boulogne. He held a high command in Somerset's assault on Scotland (1547), being wounded at Pinkie, and was entrusted with the command of the occupying forces when the Duke returned to England. It was Grey who in 1549 supplied a professional stiffening to Russell's timorous and blundering campaign against the western rebels. An honourable and a valuable soldier, Grey was quite unjustly charged in 1551 with having conspired with Somerset against Northumberland, was kept a close prisoner in the Tower for more than a year and then, on his release in December, 1552, was at once packed out of the country to assume command of the English forces at Guînes. These alone among the really old peerage of England played even secondary roles in governmental and military affairs in the Edwardian period, while none of this group profited substantially from the stream of landed wealth enriching the group in which power was vested.[1]

There was also a slightly larger group of thirteen families, whom we have rather arbitrarily described as 'old peerages', whose ennoblement antedated the accession of Henry VII, all having been raised to the peerage between 1405 and c. 1482. If one may take the median date for these creations (1461), these may be described as families which had been ennobled for not quite a century, most of them being in the third or fourth generation of their original title.[2]

Of these peers, only two may be said to have exercised a considerable influence on affairs, while two others were entrusted with at least slight responsibility by the ruling group. Henry Grey is a rather special case, being descended from Thomas Grey, Lord Ferrers, whose mother in a later marriage was the queen of Edward III. Grey succeeded to his title, third Marquis of Dorset, in 1530 at the age of thirteen, and remained without much more than a decorative role in the courts of Henry VIII and Edward VI. Without the slightest ability or judgement, such influence as he had stemmed from his marriage to Frances, the daughter of Charles Brandon and Mary Tudor, and the fact that he was the father of Lady Jane Grey, the pawn whom Northumberland was to employ in his assault upon the throne. Grey managed to lend his support to every frail and hopeless cause that presented itself throughout his short life: first to the treacherous Sudeley, then to Northumberland, and at the end of Wyatt's rising under Queen Mary. His colleagues took his measure accurately under Edward VI, appointments as the Lord Lieutenant of Leicestershire and Rutland and then in 1551,

---

[1] Stone (*Crisis of the aristocracy*, 760) estimates the gross rentals of these families in 1559—and they were probably not much different in 1547—as being:

Talbot	£5000–£5999
Berkeley	£3000–£3999
Vere	£3000–£3999
Fitzalan	£3000–£3999
Clifford	£2000–£2999
Neville	£2000–£2999
Scrope	£1000–£1999
Zouche	£500–£999
Grey of Wilton	Less than £500 p.a.

[2] These families were: Abergavenny (1450), Audley (1405), Blount (1465), Clinton (1464), Cobham (c. 1443), Dacre of the North (c. 1482), West (de la Warr, 1427), Grey (Dorset and Suffolk, 1475), Devereux (Ferrers, 1461), Hastings (Huntingdon, 1461), Latimer (1432), Ogle (1461), Stourton (1448).

the year in which he was elevated to the Duchy of Suffolk, as Warden of the Scottish Marches being the sum of the responsibilities vested in him.

Far abler and, in terms of the possession of trust, far more important was Edward Fiennes (1512–1585), the ninth Lord Clinton. He enjoyed mild favour in the middle years of Henry VIII, but his opportunity did not come until 1540 when he took naval command under Dudley, then Lord Admiral, and served with distinction against both Scotland and Boulogne. Somewhat later (1545) Clinton was in command of the fleet which lifted the threat of French invasion by repulsing the naval expedition led by the famous admiral, d'Annebaut. Clinton, whose great abilities have never been fully set forward, had over the years acquired high professional competence, to be abundantly demonstrated in the remarkable naval support which he lent to Somerset in the assault on Scotland in 1547. Clinton was appointed governor of Boulogne where he served until May, 1550, when he was deservedly made Lord High Admiral and rich gifts of land were showered on him. Upright, blunt, and loyal, Clinton remained what he was: a highly gifted and dependable naval officer without the desire to hold or to exercise political influence.

Of much slighter influence amongst this group of nobles were George Brooke, Baron Cobham, and William Dacre, the fourth Baron Dacre of the North. Cobham was fifty years of age at the time of Edward's succession and had served without much distinction with Surrey in France and under Seymour in the foray into Scotland in 1546. His only independent command was that of reinforcements sent to Scotland in 1551. An amiable and a rather dull man, Cobham was without political interest or influence. Dacre, known as a sturdy though moderate Roman Catholic, had narrowly escaped a charge of high treason in 1534. He, like Cobham, was without political influence, though he was a soldier of considerable ability, commanding the rear in Scotland in 1547 and serving as Warden of the Scottish Marches for two periods under Edward.

Finally, among the older peerage, there were in addition four families whose ennoblement dated from the very early days of Henry VII when he was paying political debts connected with the circumstances of his accession.[1] The Bridgwater title lapsed in 1548 when Henry Daubney died without heirs. Neither he nor the third and fourth Barons Burgh held any political or military posts and they remain dim and inconsequential figures. Edward Stanley, the

---

[1] These are: Stanley (Derby, 1485), Radcliffe (Sussex, 1485), Daubney (Bridgwater, 1486), Burgh (1487).

third Earl of Derby, who was appointed Lord Lieutenant of Lancashire in 1552, was evidently Roman Catholic in sympathy and was
courageous enough to dissent on the third reading of the act establishing the second *Book of Common Prayer*, but lived quietly, being
notable under Edward VI only for his reckless prodigality and
hospitality.[1] The remaining peer in this undistinguished group was
Henry Radcliffe, second Earl of Sussex, who, though he had had
some military experience in the Henrician period, was now without
influence, being content to share the Lord Lieutenancy of Norfolk,
and bestirring himself only when in 1553 he declared for Mary
Tudor and assumed command of the forces forgathering for her
defence at Framlingham.

It is clear, then, that this group of twenty-six families constituting
the older peerage was barred from the tenure of power by those who
possessed it either because of their religion, because of genetic
deterioration, or because of sheer want of ability. These were not
aggressive men. More than half of them remained shadowy figures
even in their own lifetimes, men who had been passed over in the
contest for power and royal favour quite as ruthlessly by Henry VIII
as by his son. Of the whole group, only Clinton possessed distinguished ability, but his competence was professional, not political. Further, the late sovereign's always shrewd and hard estimate
of the ability and loyalty of these families had been unremitting
in its harshness. The acid test was the appointment of the executors
and assistant executors in his will, the group in which he sought to
vest the wholeness of power during the minority of his son. Not
one of these men was named an executor, and only Arundel was
designated an assistant. Moreover, only four of the old peerage
were ever at any time admitted to the Privy Council through the
whole course of the Edwardian era, and none of them was significant in either his attendance or his counsels. The true seats of
power were reserved for a governing group drawn almost wholly
from the new, the reconstituted, peerage of Henry VIII and Edward
VI.

The old peerage was, then, set apart, neither trusted nor employed, and was isolated from the realities of power and from the
thrust of historical movement in our period. This insularity is in
part further demonstrated by the fact that of the twenty-nine first
marriages made by these peers or by their eldest sons during our
period, twelve were with women who were themselves of this small

---

[1] VCH, *Lancashire*, III, 161; *L.J.* I, 421; Stone (*Crisis of the aristocracy*, 760) reckons
his gross rentals in 1559 in the range of £4000–£4999.

and contracting society. Only four marriages were concluded with members of the more recent and dominant peerage; five of the 'old peers' were venturesome enough to enter into marriages with daughters of the gentry, one with a very rich merchant family; and the remainder of the matches were with women of uncertain social status. Their insularity and perhaps their general incapacity is further attested by the fact that in an era when power was being entrusted increasingly to educated men, only one of the group (Arundel) had attended a university, though two more (Clinton and Henry Grey) may have attended for short periods.

Rather surprisingly, it must be said that the religious convictions of the 'old peerage' do not appear to have been as overwhelmingly conservative as has sometimes been supposed. Only seven of these families may be set down as intransigently Roman Catholic, while almost as many (five) were regarded as Protestant in sympathy at least by the close of the reign. For the rest, neither their wills nor their votes in the House of Lords suggest more than that another seven were contentedly Henrician politiques, men who were quite willing to follow governmental policy whether under Edward, Mary, or Elizabeth. All the rest seem either to have been quite unclear regarding their own sentiments or cautiously mute. In this respect the 'old peers' do not seem to differ greatly from the whole of the realm of England.

The isolation of the old peerage, the almost contemptuous neglect of it by both Somerset and Northumberland, is, of course, most effectively demonstrated by the fact that only a tiny proportion of crown lands bestowed during the reign, whether by sale or by gift, served for the enhancement of the port and fortunes of this group. This decisive matter we shall shortly analyse in some detail, but we may here point out that the political and economic significance of this deliberate discrimination can be emphasized in another way by employing Professor Stone's estimates of the gross rentals supporting this social group in 1559.[1] Excluding the great Howard estates—for the Howard fortune was in ruins throughout the Edwardian period—the total value of the estates of the older peerage would seem to have been something like £56,750 p.a. in the Edwardian period, or a capital worth of about £1,135,000. If this be so, we may say with some confidence that royal bounty did not enhance the capital value of the estates of the older peerage by more than 2·53 per cent during the whole of the Edwardian era.

In most decided contrast stands the group we have described as

---

[1] Stone, *Crisis of the aristocracy*, 760.

the 'new peerage' of England, those of Henrician or Edwardian creation. In all there were thirty-one noble families constituting this group, though, as we know, certain of these families did not survive the ruthless struggle for power which marked the whole of Edward's brief reign and the convulsions which attended its close. But this was the group in which political power was centred, the violent struggle for dominance—and survival—being, with the one exception of Arundel, amongst its members.

There were, however, very sharp and well-defined cleavages within the ranks of the new peerage. Ten of these families had been ennobled in the first half of Henry VIII's reign (1509–1529), and it is interesting to note that none of these families possessed considerable power or influence at any time during the Edwardian era. The nobles of this group were, say in 1550, in the main the sons or grandsons of men who had been translated to the peerage in what was historically a very different age, when different values and different loyalties found royal favour. Further, it must be said, these families were in the second and third generation a not particularly impressive or effective group.[1]

It is also significant that none of this group of Henrician peers was named as an executor or even as an assistant executor of the King's will; none was admitted to the Council in the Edwardian period; and only two were called upon to render much more than nominal services in the whole course of the reign. Bray, the son of the famous treasury expert of Henry VII, was inactive under Edward save for an ornamental role in the mission sent to confer the Garter on Henry II of France. The third Baron Conyers served inconspicuously in the war against Scotland and for a season as Warden of the Western Marches, but was never entrusted with independent responsibility. Lord Morley, educated as a humanist, and by far the most gifted of this group of peers, was inactive throughout the reign, in part perhaps as a consequence of the infirmities of age. Thomas Stanley, second Baron Mounteagle and grandson of the first Earl of Derby, had served Henry with some distinction on military and diplomatic assignments and knew Somerset intimately, but was wholly inactive in public life after 1544. Henry Manners, second Earl of Rutland, held independent military commands in the Scottish war and, with almost every other peer who could be corralled, was a member of Northampton's diplo-

---

[1] These families were: Conyers (1509), Somerset (Worcester, 1510), Manners (Rutland, 1512), Mounteagle (1514), Morley (1518), Sandys of the Vyne (1523), Vaux of Harrowden (1528), Bray (1529), Wentworth (1529), Windsor (1529).

matic mission to France in 1551, but was excluded from the seats of power despite his known sympathy with the religious policy of the government and his affable and reliable nature.[1] Thomas Sandys, second Lord Sandys of the Vyne, remains a shadowy figure in these years, while the activities of the second Baron Windsor, highly educated and trained as a lawyer, were limited to raising forces in Buckinghamshire for the support of Mary in the great crisis at the close of the reign. Thomas Vaux, second Baron Vaux (1510–1556), was in age, in education, and in taste similar to many of the ruling group, but he was never entrusted with power, contentedly writing poetry of considerable merit through these exciting years.

Of this whole group of early Henrician peers, only two assumed tasks or commands of even secondary importance. Thus the first Baron Wentworth, a cousin to Somerset, had served with honour in a variety of military tasks under Henry VIII and in the summer of 1549 held commission under Northampton in the bootless campaign against the Norfolk rebels. In October, 1549, he was one of the six lords designated to lend personal attendance on the King, and in February, 1550, he was appointed Lord Chamberlain of the Household, but died a few months later, just as it seemed his star might be rising. Wentworth, it should be noted, was the single peer amongst this group to receive a substantial gift of crown lands in this period. He was succeeded by his son, also Thomas Wentworth, well educated at Cambridge, more articulate than his father, and in all respects gifted. But the second Baron was only twenty-six years of age when he succeeded—too young and inexperienced to render much more of public service than a joint tenure of the important Lord Lieutenancy of Suffolk.

There were also two Earls of Worcester during this brief reign, Henry Somerset, the second Earl, being wholly inactive until his death in 1549, though he had rendered many military and diplomatic services, always of the second importance, to Henry VIII. The third Earl was young when he succeeded, though earlier he had served ably with Somerset before Boulogne. But there is no record of considerable public service under Edward save for his inclusion

---

[1] Rutland desperately wanted lucrative assignments. In 1547 his mother was petitioning for relief from a debt of £316 15s 6d owed to the Crown, incurred in part for setting her son forward in the King's service. In late December of the same year Rutland's agent was seeking chantry properties or ecclesiastical properties if the bishops should 'forsake their temporalties', as close as might be to the seat at Belvoir Castle or to Rutland's manor at Eagle. (HMC, *Twelfth rpt.*, App. IV: *Rutland MSS.*, I, 31–33.) The search was in vain, for Rutland's properties were not to be greatly enhanced by the Crown.

4

in that 'pageant of English nobility' which was the embassy of Northampton to France in 1551.

One is puzzled in seeking to explain the almost complete exclusion from the substance of power of this group of early Henrician peers. Four of these men were well educated; five or six seem uncommonly able; four, possibly five, were confirmed Protestants, while none, save possibly Windsor, was an intransigent Catholic. In large part the explanation may well be that, recent as these peerages were, these families had fused too completely in blood, in point of view, and in customary attitudes with the old peerage. It is significant that of thirteen *first* marriages contracted by this group of peers or their heirs, six were with the old nobility, one with the Scottish nobility, two with the recent nobility, and the remainder with the gentry. These men were already too far removed from the gentry, from which almost all of them had sprung, and in which the Tudors by a sort of steady intuition vested the real substance of power. Their exclusion from power and ultimate favour was very nearly complete, since by the stern and telling test of crown land grants these ten families received no more than £4930 16s 0d in capital value, of which the £3884 awarded to Wentworth accounts for almost the whole sum.

The second group of recent peers—and very recent indeed they were—were those raised to the nobility in the later years of Henry VIII's reign (1532–1547). There were twelve of these families, all singled out for high favour after the course of the Reformation was well under way. These were men who had exhibited complete loyalty to the monarchy in trying times, and rather more than half of them were regarded as Protestant in conviction in the closing years of the reign. It was from this group that Henry drew heavily as he named his executors: these men were in fact his political heirs.[1] All but two (Cromwell and Eure) of these men so ennobled were alive and active at the time of Edward's succession. It is significant that of the twelve all save two had been raised to the peerage directly from the gentry, though several of them did have at least remote familial connections with the older nobility. These, then, were truly the 'new men', nurtured in the period of the great struggle with Rome, with brilliant careers well established in 1547, and enjoying the confidence of a shrewd and determined sovereign. Most of them had already profited greatly, two hugely, from the monastic expropriations out of which their estates had been formed. It was from this small group of peers that the government of Edward VI was to be

[1] MacCaffrey, in *Past and Present*, no. 30 (Apr., 1965), 55.

constituted and among them, with the addition of those ennobled by the young monarch, that the whole structure of power was to be shared. In fact, the centre of gravity of Edwardian power may be found squarely and almost exclusively in six of these men and their families.

For various reasons, then, six of these families did not share in the substance of authority in the Edwardian era. Thus Gregory Cromwell, created second Baron Cromwell despite his father's attainder, though he had married Seymour's sister, lived quietly and inconspicuously until his death in 1551, as did the third Baron, who remained a shadowy and poverty-stricken figure until his death in 1592. The second Lord Eure, who had succeeded his grandfather to the title, was a minor through most of the reign and hence without the possibility of public influence. The first Baron Mordaunt, on the other hand, was aged and infirm when the reign opened and took no part in public life. So too, the first Baron Parr of Horton, the uncle of Catherine Parr, who had served Henry well in many military and diplomatic missions, was aged in 1547 and died a few months after Edward's accession, the title becoming extinct. Age or youth, then, excluded four of the group of recently created peers from the possibility of public service and the power that flowed from it. But this does not explain the exclusion of Thomas, first Baron Wharton, from the circle of power. He had been a reliable and reasonably competent soldier and administrator in the North and in the Marches for a full generation and in 1545, a year after his elevation to the peerage, had been named to the Council of the North, where he served reliably throughout Edward's reign. Though he did receive modest grants of land, Wharton was never really in full favour, perhaps because of his irascible and occasionally churlish nature and because Somerset, with some justice, never quite believed in his military capabilities.[1]

Also excluded from the inner circle of power was John Bourchier, second Earl of Bath. This peerage was revived in 1536 for Bourchier's father, the second Earl succeeding in 1539. Though he too received gifts of land with the slender capital value of £474 in 1552 and was admitted to the Privy Council by Northumberland in his search for support, Bourchier held no important administrative or military post and remains a dim and inconsequential figure.

But the remaining six peers (Russell, Parr, John Dudley, Edward Seymour, Wriothesley, and Paulet—to employ their family names) were all to be important members of the governing body of the

---

[1] *Vide post*, 255ff., for further comments on Wharton's career.

realm, received huge gifts of crown lands, and were directly concerned with the whole mechanism of power and its administration.

There remain nine creations in the peerage during the reign of Edward VI. Four of these may be dismissed as relatively unimportant for the history of the period. Darcy of Aston, son of the attainted Lord Darcy, was restored in blood and created first Baron Darcy in 1548 and lived quietly throughout the reign. Henry Stafford, the son of the ill-fated and ill-used Duke of Buckingham, was restored in blood and created Baron Stafford in December 1547, but eschewed any political interests despite his great ability. Edmund Sheffield, a young, vigorous, and promising peer, created Baron Sheffield in February, 1547, was killed in action in the streets of Norwich in the campaign against Kett; his heir was a minor through the rest of the reign. William Willoughby had also been raised to a barony in 1547. An experienced and skilful soldier, he played an active part in the suppression of the Norfolk rising and was then sent abroad for two years as Deputy of Calais, closing his Edwardian career on his return as Chief Steward of the Duchy of Calais. Thorny in personality, devoted to country pleasures as well as martial pursuits, Willoughby of Parham was never admitted to the inner circle of power and gained no considerable gift of crown lands for a career of at least modest distinction.

The remaining five of the Edwardian creations were men of very considerable public stature, all of whom were to share, at least for a season, in the responsibilities and fruits of power. Thomas Seymour, created Baron Seymour of Sudeley in 1547, gained great estates and gathered a considerable and dangerous aggregate of conspiratorial power before actions which can only be attributed to an unbalanced mind brought about his own destruction. Darcy of Chiche was created a Baron in 1551, receiving considerable gifts of crown property with which to establish his port. A courtier by temperament, Thomas Darcy had served as Vice-Chamberlain to the King for a year before being designated Lord Chamberlain of the Household in 1551 and admitted to the Privy Council. Richard Rich, created a Baron in 1547, had served Henry VIII as a lawyer and administrator for many years and was appointed Lord Chancellor in the first year of the new reign, his estates being augmented by very large royal grants.

Far more important in the Edwardian government was William Herbert, sprung from a gentle family in Herefordshire, but whose father had been the illegitimate son of William Herbert, the Earl of Pembroke of the first creation. Herbert's fortune had been made when his wife's sister, Catherine Parr, became Queen. Long in Henry VIII's service, he enjoyed the King's complete confidence and was named an executor of the will. At first a warm supporter of Somerset, his loyalty was lost during the Western Rising of 1549, which he helped to put down with troops from his now very large Welsh estates. From this time forward he was to lend his full support to Dudley, and was rewarded in 1551 with the titles Baron Herbert of Cardiff and Earl of Pembroke. A member of the Council throughout the reign, he was a steady and shrewd politician and a not inconsiderable military expert, though at times he moved rather awkwardly and hesitantly amongst his more highly educated and intellectually more sophisticated colleagues. Herbert had built his fortune from nothing, beginning with rich lands granted in 1542–1546 by Henry VIII from the dissolved Abbey of Wilton, while in 1546 Cardiff Castle and supporting estates in Wales were granted to him by the King. The great fortune was completed by gifts of crown lands in the Edwardian period with a capital worth of £32,165, including a total of fifty-three manors in Wales, nine in Wiltshire, five in Gloucestershire, two in Sussex, and one each in Middlesex, Hertfordshire, and Devonshire. With the sole exception of Northumberland, no subject was more richly rewarded than the staunchly Protestant Earl of Pembroke.

Finally, among the new peers, we must note briefly the career of Sir William Paget, who was created Baron Paget of Beaudesert in December, 1549. Born of a modest London family, Paget had been well educated at St Paul's School and at Cambridge, and although already a Protestant in sympathy gained his diplomatic experience first in the household of the redoubtable Bishop Gardiner. He was knighted in 1537, and in 1541, after a brilliant diplomatic mission to France, was made a member of the Privy Council as Secretary of State. We have spoken of his closeness to the King during the last months of Henry's life and of his decisive role in placing power in Somerset's hands. He served in the Edwardian government in several important capacities. Possibly the most able and certainly the most gifted of all the members of the government, Paget could not bring himself wholly to betray Somerset and was in 1551 arrested on insubstantial charges of conspiracy against Dudley, was degraded from the Order of the Garter (1552) because of his base lineage, and was heavily fined and excluded from office for the remainder of the reign. Paget received his one substantial crown grant early in the new reign (May 30, 1547), consisting of property with a net capital worth of £3160 and including three manors in

Middlesex, two in Buckinghamshire, and one each in Kent and Shropshire.[1]

To recapitulate, we have seen that in the Edwardian age power was almost wholly concentrated in a small group of very recently ennobled families. Only Arundel and Grey of Wilton among the really ancient peerage were to play any important role in governmental affairs and neither was ever at the centre of power. Of the peerage created in the fifteenth century before the accession of the Tudors, only Grey (Suffolk) because of his genetic convenience and Fiennes (Clinton) because of his superb military skill were to make any substantial contribution to governance. So too, amongst the families ennobled in the first half of the reign of Henry VIII, only two—Wentworth and the Earl of Worcester—may be regarded as even within the precincts of power. Leadership and power, then, were lodged almost wholly within families raised to the peerage in the late years of Henry VIII or ennobled under Edward for services rendered to his own or to his father's government.

This ruling group—and we are discussing only those of the ruling caste who were peers—possesses several interesting and probably important characteristics which set it clearly apart from the rest of the nobility. We have already observed that almost without exception these men had been drawn from the ranks of the gentry, had married within that class, and, being of very recent ennoblement, had not cast off the organic ties with the great class in which much of the wealth, ability, and strength was concentrated in Tudor England.[2] We have seen, too, that these were on balance educated men, just as they were preponderantly, though moderately, Protestant in their sympathies. They were new men, but they were also on the whole extraordinarily able men who assumed the grave task of government at a particularly perilous time with an almost reckless confidence.

Finally, these were men who had not profited greatly from the Henrician distribution of monastic property, being (Russell aside) too young and at too modest a stage in the development of their careers. They accordingly proceeded with a rapacious haste to carve out estates which would support their new dignity from crown lands, mostly derived from monastic and chantry sources,

[1] The survey in S.P. Dom., 10/19 yields a net worth of £5040, the probably more reliable description from P.R.,I, 45-47, yielding the total given above. In addition, in 1548, on the direct command of the King, Veysey, the aged and irascible Bishop of Exeter, was compelled to grant to Paget his great London town house, Exeter Place.

[2] Vide ante, 78ff, where these matters are discussed in the context of the Privy Council, dominated by these men.

formally and legally disposed by gift to them by the young King, actually divided amongst themselves by the sanction of their own action. We have seen that the old nobility profited only modestly from this re-distribution of wealth; the same may be said for the new nobility unless they were likewise members of the governing hierarchy in the new reign. In all, as we shall shortly note in detail, crown lands with a total worth of £166,151 were vested in the new nobility of England by gift in the Edwardian years, and of this amount slightly more than £159,000 found its way in distributions to the ruling junta. In view of the slender fortunes of most of these men in 1547, this may not in fact be excessive for the endowment of those who bore great responsibilities and great reputations. What these men in effect took from the Crown does not amount to more than 5.89 per cent, if we may translate it into capital values, of the total landed fortune of the peerage of England a decade later as Professor Stone reckons it.[1] This was in fact the only way in which the state in the sixteenth century could reward its great servants. But still the action of these men must stand condemned. The indecent swiftness with which they acted, the all too obvious rapacity of about half the group, and the parlous state of their sovereign's fiscal affairs make it difficult to condone their blatant greed. They were men who seemed to the realm at large to be rising too rapidly and to be founding that swift rise on the substance of wealth which belonged to the Crown and hence to the nation at large. Almost 40 per cent (38.92 per cent) of all the crown gifts made in these seven years were vested in this group of peers. To the larger problems of the vast re-distribution of crown wealth during this brief interval, of which this is only part, we should now turn in some detail. For in this process is to be observed not only the reckless policy of the governing group but a true and irretrievable wasting of the resources of the Crown.

3. THE EROSION OF THE FINANCIAL RESOURCES OF THE CROWN [*Excursus* II]

The re-distribution of ecclesiastical wealth on a vast scale, well advanced under Henry VIII, continued throughout the reign of Edward VI. Occasioned in part by the greed of the King's own servants, it was in larger part compelled by the financial crisis in which the government found itself and by the hesitation of the ruling

---

[1] The proportion would of course be substantially increased if the rise in land values in the decade could be accurately assessed.

junta to lay its needs fully and honestly before Parliament. Thus the sale of crown lands, mostly derived from the older monastic expropriations and now from the chantry confiscations, continued as the government pieced out its revenues by the sale of capital assets. At the same time, there was a steady and a substantial distribution of crown lands as gifts, not only, as we have observed, to the great servants of the King, but to other groups and for other purposes as well. These processes of erosion we should now examine with some care.[1]

A. *Sales of crown lands*

(1) *The structure of sales.* We have counted 444 separate sales transactions in the Edwardian period, involving 668 individual purchasers, the multiple purchasers usually being relatives or partners in a purchasing syndicate. The value of the average transaction was £955 4s 0d, while the median amount was £712 5s 0d; and the average amount paid by the individual purchasers was £634 18s 0d (assuming all syndicate partners to have supplied equal shares of capital). The Crown received in total £424,109 15s 0d from the sale of its lands, the income value of the lands thus conveyed being £21,121 8s 0d p.a. This works out to a true interest rate of 4·98 per cent and hence it has been thought appropriate for purposes of this analysis to assume that the Crown sold at prices which would establish a 5 per cent yield rate on land capital.

There were, however, wide differences in the values which the Crown was able to negotiate in these sales. Chantry properties in general, which tended to be scattered, to consist of tiny tracts, and

---

[1] The principal sources employed in this survey are complex but very full. The whole volume in the State Papers catalogued as S.P. Dom., 10/19, evidently prepared early in Mary's reign with some thought of recoveries in mind, contains a detailed list of the sales, gifts, exchanges, and fee farm grants chronologically arranged. Included are a fair number of exchanges improperly listed as gifts, gifts listed as fee farm grants, and other errors which tend to swell the total beyond the true facts. The Patent Rolls for the period are complete and on the whole are accurate, and have been compared with the entries in the S.P. Dom. volume. The relevant records of the Court of Augmentations have been consulted, while a number of grants not elsewhere noted have been found in the *Acts of the Privy Council* and in scattered entries in the *State Papers Domestic*.

A few notes on method should also be set down. Pence have been rounded off to the nearest shilling, sixpences being alternately rounded off forward and backward. The 'old nobility' has been somewhat arbitrarily (and generously) defined as families which were ennobled prior to 1509; the 'new nobility' are those of a later date of creation.

The statistical details for most of our discussion are fully set out in the Composite Table at p. 118–119, to which further specific reference will not be made. We shall also refer frequently to the table setting out the 'Distribution of Crown Manors', which may be found at p. 117.

were often bundled up for sale in such wise that they were spread over several counties, in total sold at prices yielding an interest rate of 5·16 per cent. Monastic lands, on the contrary, which tended to consist of larger land units, were more sensibly aggregated, and usually lay within one or two counties, brought the very low interest rate of 4·69 per cent. Putting the facts together somewhat differently, all rural properties sold brought an interest rate of only 4·72 per cent, suggesting not only the continuing demand for farming and pasture land, but also that these properties were on the whole better aggregated, in larger tracts, and comprised a larger propor-tion of monastic lands. Urban properties, usually made up of bits and pieces of former chantry endowments, were much more difficult to sell and hence, on the whole, brought the surprisingly high interest rate of 5·86 per cent. These striking differences are also accounted for by the sharp distinction in market value between well-aggregated property (whether urban or rural) and non-aggregated. Truly aggregated holdings were uncommon and such property brought a very low yield value (4·30 per cent), this being demonstrated in another fashion by the fact that all property lots sold which included one or more manors brought an interest return of 4·42 per cent. On the other hand, non-aggregated property, whether rural or urban, was sold at a yield of 5·42 per cent.

It should also be observed that these crown properties were not being fed out more rapidly by the Court of Augmentations than the market could absorb them. The yield curve remains practically flat throughout the reign. The only suggestion of difficulty occurred when widely scattered chantry properties, sometimes in as many as ten to fourteen counties, always in tiny tracts, were being dis-posed of in large lots. Here very real price concessions had to be made, though even so one wonders how the purchasers could pos-sibly have profited when the difficulties of administration or sale are taken into account. These crown properties were not sold at an even rate through the reign, the rate of sale clearly being keyed closely to the fiscal needs of the Crown and the political exigencies of the moment.

The reign was begun with a conservative financial policy and the sales of crown lands were sharply lower than they had ever been since the expropriation of the monasteries. Nor were they really very heavy in 1548, despite the increased outlay for military needs and the support of a difficult foreign policy. Then came the spate of sales in 1549 connected quite as much with Northumberland's search for support for his policy against Somerset as with the heavy costs for suppressing a dangerous internal uprising. Even more impressive is the evident attempt (dramatic in 1551) to stanch the wasting of royal resources by a strenuous effort at economy. And then came the deluge of sales in the half-year of 1553, when Northumberland was casting about desperately at once for supporters and for the means to finance his machinations. It may be remarked that almost two-thirds of all sales occurred in the two critical years 1549 and 1553, and that sales in the latter year were at the annual rate of almost £290,000.

(2) *Status analysis of purchasers.* Of the total of 668 individual purchasers, 77 (11·53 per cent) were intimately identified with the court or government and purchased crown lands with a total value of £81,714 18s od (19·27 per cent of the total value of the property sold). There is no evidence whatsoever that these purchasers were given special concessions, save possibly for the fact that proportionately they did buy properties with slightly more manors in the purchase package. Among these officials and courtiers nineteen were members of the government, officers of the Privy Council, or executors or assistant executors of Henry VIII's will. These men bought in total property for which they paid £29,024 7s od (6·84 per cent of the whole), the average transaction being rather high: £1527 11s od. Then there was a much larger group comprising forty-eight men who served the Crown as judges, ambassadors, heads of governmental departments, or in other positions of relatively high trust. These men laid out £46,097 4s. od in purchases (10·87 per cent of the whole), with an average outlay of £960 7s od, this being very close to the average for all purchasers. Finally, there was a small group of courtiers, grooms, servants, and others who served the Crown in less important capacities in and about the household who expended £6593 7s od for land (1·55 per cent of the whole), with an average outlay of £659 6s od.

These special groups are in turn included in our analysis of land purchases by the several classes of men, which is very revealing for what it says about the social structure, the viable wealth, and the dynamic economic and social forces in Tudor England. Land purchase by the nobility, whether new or old, was insubstantial, though, as will be observed, this class was to secure a substantial share of the lands granted by the Crown. The two classes of gentry together comprised more than half of all purchasers and likewise laid out well over half of all the wealth required to accomplish this re-distribution of landed wealth. Included amongst the lower

gentry are a few large buyers of several lots, who were apparently
acting as speculators or brokers, but further evidence suggests
that when they in turn sold all or portions of the property just acquired
they were likely to sell within this same class. One is interested too
in the number and liquid wealth disposed by yeoman purchasers
and wonders how they could possibly have possessed the knowledge or contacts requisite for this sophisticated kind of buying. The
numerous merchant purchasers, among whom there are a fair number
acting as speculators and brokers, bought nearly 20 per cent of the
whole of the land available. When added to the purchases of the
two linked classes of gentry, this accounts for over three-fourths
(77·77 per cent) of all the land offered. There appear to have been
some brokers and speculators also among the rather small proportion of purchasers of uncertain status, most of whom are described as of London but who cannot be certainly identified as
merchants.

The men best equipped to assess the value of the offered lands,
especially the chantry properties, were of course the Chantry Commissioners themselves. They were drawn almost wholly from the
ranks of the gentry; they tended to serve in counties in which they
already owned property; and they had just completed a searching
and responsible task in their famous survey. About a fifth (22·17 per
cent) of their number purchased land with an outlay of £41,416 8s od,
which amounts to 9·76 per cent of the value of all crown lands sold.
No special favours, save that of access, seem to have been extended
to these purchasers, since they paid in total capital sums suggesting
an interest rate of 4·77 per cent which is just as it should be, since
their purchases included a considerable number of manors and in
almost all instances were well aggregated. Their exploitation of
special and local knowledge is suggested by the fact that of the
fifty-nine transactions in which commissioners were involved,
forty-one were in the county in which they lived or had conducted
their survey.

(3) *Manorial analysis.* Among the lands sold, 263 manors were
conveyed to 188 individual purchasers, the largest number (104)
being disposed of in the last regnal year. In the very nature of the
case there were among the chantry endowments relatively few
manors. As the *Composite Table* suggests, the great proportion were
monastic manors remaining in crown hands, with a considerable
number gained by the Crown through attainder. These manors
were scattered all over England: at least one was found in every

county save for Bedfordshire, Cumberland, Huntingdonshire, Staffordshire, Westmorland, and Cheshire.[1] It is interesting to note that the largest concentration was around London itself— thirty having been sold in Kent and twenty-four in Essex, both prime counties for investment and both commanding high land prices. There were also substantial numbers sold in Gloucestershire, Wiltshire, Yorkshire, Somerset, and Northamptonshire. It seems certain, however, that of all the manors in any given county in England or Wales not more than about 3 per cent were sold in the reign, so there could have been little social or economic dislocation in consequence. Further, as has already been suggested, most sales were to gentry already of the county, gentry who were in the process of strengthening and enlarging their estates. Of the 263 manors involved, 127 (48 per cent) were bought by residents of the county in which they were situated. In all, ninety-one were bought by London residents, by merchants seeking prudent investments or about to make the translation into the gentry, or by brokers in search of a quick profit.

The social status of the 188 manorial purchasers is instructive. Numerous buyers were engaged in really large land purchases. Far more than half of the purchasers were of the gentry and rather more than two-thirds of all the manors disposed found their way into the hands of men already possessed of at least one manor. The process of aggregation and of strengthening of status was thus well advanced.[2]

(4) *Place of residence of purchasers.* Not only were the crown lands sold distributed rather evenly over the realm, but the purchasers themselves represent an interesting geographical cross-section of the realm at large. As the table opposite will suggest, every county in England is represented amongst the buyers and all but ten counties have five or more purchasers, usually, as has been shown, of lands within the county of their residence.

At the same time there are significant concentrations of these purchasers, for somewhat more than half (50.74 per cent) were residents of London, Essex, Kent, Norfolk, Wiltshire, or Yorkshire. By far the largest proportion was in London—which suggests at once the very large aggregates of liquid and speculative capital in

---

[1] See the Table of Distribution of Crown Manors, *post.*

[2] The social status of the purchasers of manors was: Old and New Nobility, 11; Upper Gentry, 38; Lower Gentry, 90; Yeomen, 10; Professional, 14; Merchants, 20; Other or Unknown, 5.

the City and also the fact that London was the locus of the negotiations and of payments. Essex and Kent together, with 9·88 per cent of all purchasers, reflect not only a considerable spill-over of London wealth already settled in those counties but the equally important fact that landed investment in the two counties was much prized and that properties for sale there carried a premium value. Norfolk wealth was great, but it was insular—the 25 purchasers from that county, with only two exceptions, limiting their purchases

Place of residence of purchasers of crown lands

Bedfordshire	4	London	195 (29·19%)
Berkshire	7	Middlesex	6
Bristol	3	Norfolk	25 (3·74%)
Buckinghamshire	6	Northamptonshire	9
Cambridgeshire	5	Northumberland	7
Cheshire	2	Nottinghamshire	11
Cornwall	5	Oxford	6
Cumberland	3	Rutland	1
Derbyshire	6	Shropshire	4
Devonshire	14	Somerset	19
Dorsetshire	6	Staffordshire	5
Durham	2	Suffolk	12
Essex	40 (5·99%)	Surrey	14
Gloucestershire	16	Sussex	8
Hampshire	6	Warwickshire	14
Hereford	8	Westmorland	2
Hertfordshire	8	Wiltshire	19 (2·84%)
Huntingdonshire	2	Worcestershire	3
Kent	26 (3·89%)	Yorkshire	34 (5·09%)
Lancashire	9		
Leicestershire	9	Wales	3
Lincolnshire	11		
		Uncertain	73 (10·93%)
			668

to lots in which the properties disposed were wholly or principally within the narrowly defined area of Norfolk and Suffolk. The Yorkshire buyers, who, rather surprisingly, accounted for 5·09 per cent of all purchasers, were especially interested in monastic and chantry properties largely in five northern counties, though there was a far greater disposition to buy quite distant properties than is exhibited by purchasers from Norfolk.

(5) *Public and charitable uses.* The Crown was disposed to grant very favourable terms to municipalities which wished to acquire

chantry or monastic lands, normally within the borough limits, for charitable or general municipal uses. In all, however, the £2309 12s od so disposed, representing only 0·54 per cent of the value of all crown lands sold, must be regarded as a most cautious outlay considering the opportunities at least briefly presented. Ten municipalities made such purchases, ranging in amount from £51 paid by Bristol to acquire title to an important bridge to £980 9s od paid by London for a variety of municipal and charitable purposes.

(6) *Sources of crown lands disposed.* The properties offered for sale by the Crown were of several kinds and frequently contained lands which had come into its possession by quite different ways, as indicated by the *Composite Table.*[1] It will immediately be observed that a large proportion of all lands sold were chantry properties expropriated early in the reign. The flow of sales began in April, 1548, reaching a climax in 1549–1550; chantry lands were not sold in great volume in 1551 and 1552, though this was of course the case with crown lands generally. But there was a great burst of selling in 1553, though it is apparent that by the close of the reign relatively few desirable lots were left, chantry lands usually being mixed with monastic properties to make the 'packages' more attractive. In addition to the sales of these properties, totalling £272,858 8s od, chantry lands with a capital worth of £47,317 had been given to various recipients, suggesting that in all £320,175 8s od of capital worth had been disposed.[2] Very little remained save the debris, the bits and pieces which were not immediately saleable.[3] There were, of course, very few chantry properties sold during the reign of Queen Mary, while those sold in a straggling fashion by

[1] It should be stated that the figures for the value of the various sorts of crown lands sold and given are in part estimated, though the grand total can be accurately figured. The estimates occur when a lot of crown land, consisting of more than one kind of crown property, was sold or given, making it quite impossible to ferret out the value of individual lots, particularly when the properties were in bits and pieces. But it is believed that the error is small, very probably resulting mostly in a slight over-valuing of chantry and obit lands.

[2] We are reserving for the second volume of this study a full discussion of the chantry expropriations.

[3] We must add that these lands had been sold in a most imprudent fashion, since the Crown had assumed liberal pension amounts for the dispossessed chantry priests. It is true that in average terms these pensioners were fairly advanced in years and also that a considerable number found other employment, but none the less the pension obligations of the government in 1549 amounted to £11,147 14s 1d p.a., which at a yield of 5 per cent would have required probably as much as £139,381 to fund, if one may assume an average age for the dispossessed chantry clergy of 45·2 years. (The average age is calculated from the rather casual statements of the Chantry Commissioners. The actuarial calculation is based on the Carlisle Mortality Table of 1815).

Elizabeth were for the most part properties with disputed titles or, more commonly, properties which had been concealed from the Commissioners.

The second great source of properties sold derived from the monastic expropriation. Steady as the alienations under Henry VIII had been, it must be remembered that something like 40 per cent of the great total remained in the hands of the Crown on the accession of Edward VI, or a capital resource not far off from £1,102,732. During his reign monastic properties were sold with a total capital worth of £104,739 6s od, this representing 24.70 per cent of the worth of all crown lands so disposed and perhaps a tenth of the monastic wealth which remained in crown hands at the death of Henry VIII.[1]

Chantry lands and monastic lands when taken together account for slightly more than 89 per cent of all the lands sold. In addition a considerable source was lands gained by the Crown, principally in the reigns of Henry VII and Henry VIII, by the inexorable process of attainder, which realized £33,725 14s od. It will be observed that no more than really insubstantial amounts were derived from crown lands of all other sorts. It must also be noted that, imprudent as the financial policy of the government undoubtedly was, rapacious as some of its members indubitably were, the old landed wealth of the Crown (as it was in 1509) remained sacrosanct.

B. *The structure of crown gifts*

Far more important than the sales of crown lands, in terms of the weakening of Royal resources, were the numerous and substantial gifts made by the Crown in this period to a variety of persons and for a variety of reasons. Before turning to an examination of the structure of such gifts, it should be said that all stated income values have once more been translated into capital terms by applying a multiplier of 20, thus assuming, for the reasons already indicated, an interest rate of 5 per cent. It should also be noted that deductions have been made of reserved rents and sums paid in, in order to establish in each instance the true value to the Crown. Also, there are a fair number of conveyances labelled as gifts which were in fact not so at all, being verification or clarification of titles already conveyed or the capitalization by a land grant of a pension already outstanding, normally from the reign of Henry VIII, in terms of years or lives.

---

[1] These values were not greatly affected by the inflation under way, since relatively little increase in rentals had been carried forward by the Court of Augmentations after the expropriation values had been determined.

Such grants are not included in our analysis. Finally, there were large gifts of land to the Princess Mary and the Princess Elizabeth, with which their households were sustained, which have been regarded simply as transfers within the crown account, as it were, and have therefore been ignored, particularly since these dispositions were in time rejoined to the Crown.

The true gifts of the Crown to its subjects in the course of the Edwardian period consisted of lands possessing a capital worth of £408,489, only slightly less, it will be observed, than the total of sales. There were 240 separate conveyances by which these lands were disposed, with a resulting rather high average of £1702 worth for each transaction. But since especially favoured recipients often received several grants, the number of individual recipients is markedly lower, there being 189 individual grantees on whom the very high average of about £2161 of land was conferred.

These grants were by no means evenly distributed over the seven calendar years involved, somewhat more than half the total (51·62 per cent) being conveyed in two critical years, 1547 and 1550. In the earlier year, when lands with a capital value of £107,712 were given, large grants were being made to the principal ministers of state, thereby carrying out what was declared to have been the intention of Henry VIII to provide these great officials, usually only recently ennobled or now greatly advanced in the peerage, with estates consonant with their dignities. After the modest outlays of 1548 and 1549 another great spate of gifts flowed out from Augmentations, this total of £103,138 reflecting the vast enhancement of Northumberland's estate and his effort to form a party which would permanently exclude the Duke of Somerset from power. Crown grants continued at a fairly high level during the next two years and then rose abruptly to the £66,234 conferred in the six months of 1553 when Northumberland was seeking by every desperate means at his disposal to prepare for his *coup d'état*.

(1) *Status analysis of the grantees.* As has been suggested, a very large and a disproportionate amount of the grants of land made were to the great officers of state: members of the Privy Council and the executors and assistant executors of Henry VIII's will. To nineteen of these officials lands were conveyed as gifts with a total capital value of £176,304, this amounting to 43·16 per cent of the whole value granted in the course of the reign. Other important officers of the Crown gained lands with a worth of £61,275, or 15 per cent of the whole sum. These two very small and conspicuously favoured

groups together, therefore, gained 58·16 per cent of the worth of the great total granted. Minor officials were given lands worth only £5419 (1·33 per cent of the whole), usually in grants valued at under £200 capital worth.

These specially favoured groups may be considered in another way: with respect to the social class in which they were placed at the time of the gifts made by the Crown. Rather surprisingly, there were in all twenty individual members of the old peerage, representing twelve families, who received land grants with a total value of £28,741, or a quite low average of £1437 for each grant. But if the large gifts made to Lord Clinton (£6356) and one other moderately large gift are excluded, the median gift for this group as a whole— the remnant of the old aristocracy—is no more than £1023. This suggests that something closely akin to largesse was being distributed by the government to a social group which it held in contempt. Further, it should be noted that a large proportion of gifts made to the old nobility occurred in late 1549 and early 1550 when Dudley was casting about for allies for a coalition which he deliberately and harshly fragmented directly he had attained power. And it may also be observed that fourteen families of the old nobility gained precisely nothing from this lavish and imprudent re-distribution of national wealth.

It was, of course, the new nobility, raised up in the Henrician and the Edwardian periods, which was so generously and conspicuously favoured. This was the inner group which dominated the Council throughout the reign. Sixteen of these men, representing fifteen families, gained by gift the huge total of £166,151 in crown lands; but, even so, it must again be stressed that they account for no more than half of the recent nobility of England. The other families of this group—those who favoured the ancient faith, those who for whatever reason took no part in governmental or military affairs, or who were regarded as sympathetic to Somerset—were almost entirely cut off from the very substantial gifts now in process of distribution, gaining no more than £3256 in lands.

The upper gentry were also well served by the policy of grants now under way. There were forty-five of these recipients, at least a third of whom represented families which had also gained monastic lands in the reign of Henry VIII. A considerable number of these grantees were governmental officers of the first or second rank, while a larger number were heads of powerful families in the provinces whose support the government wished to retain and whose loyalty Northumberland in particular was seeking to secure.

This relatively small group of men gained lands worth £102,937, representing about a fourth of the whole land value disposed, and greatly exceeding the amount they deployed (£72,429 10s 0d) for land purchases. Quite clearly, these families, combined with those so generously favoured among the new aristocracy, formed an élite from which the structure of power and service were constituted.

These, then, were the favoured classes, for the combined gifts to the new nobility and to the upper gentry account for almost two-thirds of the great wealth conferred by the government. It seems strange that the most thrusting and perhaps the most important social class in the England of the age—the lower gentry—which had laid out the huge total of £173,036 17s 0d in land purchases (40·80 per cent of the whole amount so disposed), received in land grants no more than £14,652 (3·59 per cent) in capital value. This was a land-hungry class, an expanding class, and a class which bore heavy responsibilities and wielded great authority across the length and breadth of England. There must have been deep resentment in this class at a policy of government which was limiting an almost prodigal generosity to its own members and to a limited number of the upper gentry. The lower gentry, all too clearly, had to buy its way forward.

So, too, though hardly so remarkably, the merchant class received no more than £10,647 in capital gifts, this representing but 2·61 per cent of the whole. It will be recalled that members of the group had laid out the large capital sum of £84,371 19s 0d in land purchases in these same years, this being almost a fifth of the whole. All other classes of men, including, it may be noted, the lawyers, received in all only 1·45 per cent of the worth of the lands being disposed by gift.

There remains a substantial total of crown lands, £79,441, given for various charitable uses. Of this large and useful sum the largest total, £45,813, was devoted to the strengthening of the resources of five dioceses, four of which, it might be said parenthetically, had been seriously weakened by crown takings. A considerable total of £12,097 was granted by the Crown for various schemes of social rehabilitation, by far the largest amounts being those dedicated towards the close of the reign to the founding or reorganization of the royal hospitals in London. In addition, capital to the value of £11,396 was given towards the founding of grammar schools or to the reorganization and secularization of twenty-two institutions in all parts of England. These grants benefited Bath, Birmingham, Bruton (Soms), Bury St Edmunds, Chelmsford, Crediton (Devon),

Giggleswick (Yorks), Grantham (Lincs), Guildford, Louth, Ludlow, Macclesfield (Cheshire), Morpeth (Northumb), Norwich, Nuneaton (Warw), East Retford (Notts), Sedbergh (Yorks), Sherborne (Dorset), Shrewsbury, Spilsbury (Lincs), Stourbridge (Worcs), and Stratford-upon-Avon. To these foundations should possibly be added two more: those at Maidstone (Kent) and at Marlborough (Wilts), where the Crown permitted purchases on favourable terms of chantry lands recently expropriated with the understanding that schools would be founded by the municipalities in question.[1]

In all, grants were given to forty-nine communities and institutions in the realm for a considerable variety of charitable purposes. In addition to those already mentioned, we may recite capital assets of £5506 given for alms and almshouses, £1644 for municipal uses, £785 for the universities, and £2200 for the support of parochial worship in one or another form.

(2) *Manorial analysis.* The crown land gifts tended to be relatively large, and they were designed as well to lend support to the social and political status of the recipient. Consequently far more manors were alienated by the Crown by gift than by sale of crown lands. There were in all 660 crown manors bestowed by gift, as compared with the 263 which we have reckoned as conveyed by sale. These manors were disposed in 135 actual transactions, suggesting at once that certain of these gifts were very large indeed.

It is interesting to observe that, in the sharpest contrast to manors sold, there was little relation between the residence of the recipient and the locus of the manor given. Thus, only 141 manors, or 21·36 per cent, were awarded to grantees certainly of the county in which the manor was to be found. Moreover, nearly half of the total number (318) were given to persons whose residence is known to be London or Middlesex, which is to a degree misleading since a large proportion of the recipients were officers of state. As the following table will suggest, seventeen individuals received very large gifts, including five or more manors, always of course with other lands and properties, and of these fifteen were great or lesser officers of state. It is staggering to realize that this small group of most favoured men received in total 414 manors, or almost two-thirds (62·73 per cent) of the whole number.

As the *Composite Table* suggests, the Crown had derived these manors (and other lands) from very different sources than those

which were sold, there being proportionately a much higher number
which had been gained by attainder, by takings from the bishoprics,
and from manors regarded as part of the royal domain in the
Henrician period. The social and economic effects of this considerable redistribution of manors can best be examined by reference to
the following table analysing the geographical distribution of all
crown manors granted, whether by gift or by sale.[1] In all, it will be

Northumberland	88	Sir John Gates	13
Somerset	63	Cheke	12
Pembroke	51	Farmer (London merchant,	
Thomas Seymour	48	restoration of attaint)	11
Paulet	28	Parr	8
Darcy	18	Cecil	8
Jobson (Master of Jewels)	17	Rich	8
Russell	15	Paget	7
Clinton	13	Wriothesley	6

414

noted, 923 manors found their way into private hands in the course
of the reign, a number approximately equal to the total number of
manors in the three counties of Buckinghamshire, Huntingdonshire,
and Warwickshire. We are dealing here, it need scarcely be said,
with a considerable aggregation of wealth and prestige, though it
must be borne in mind that the total probably does not account for
more than 5 per cent to 6 per cent of the whole number of manors
in the realm. But this re-distribution tended to be quite heavily
concentrated in certain counties. Thus, in the eight counties of
Essex, Gloucestershire, Kent, Norfolk, Somerset, Wiltshire, Yorkshire and Wales there were 475 manors conveyed from royal to
private hands, this amounting to more than half (51·46 per cent)
of the whole number. In these counties it seems quite certain that
something like 10 per cent of all manors changed hands in a
very brief period, and this, as the table on the source for crown
ownership will suggest, was compounded by the fact that a large
proportion of the manors in question had been in crown hands for
less than a generation before the final distribution was made.

(3) *Sources of crown lands given.* It is interesting to observe that
crown lands given were on the whole drawn from quite different
sources than those disposed by sale.[2] The important fact is, of course,

[1] See table, p. 117.
[2] *Vide ante,* 110, for reservations which also apply to this 'partly estimated' analysis.

Distribution of crown manors changing ownership, 1547–1553

County	By gift	By sale	By exchange	Total
Bedfordshire	7	0	6	13
Berkshire	11	3	16	30
Buckinghamshire	16	5	6	27
Cambridgeshire	2	4	3	9
Cheshire	1	0	1	2
Cornwall	14	1	0	15
Cumberland	0	0	2	2
Derbyshire	1	1	10	12
Devonshire	14	8	32	54
Dorsetshire	31	10	8	49
Durham	3	1	0	4
Essex	43	24	27	94
Gloucestershire	40	27	25	92
Hampshire	24	4	23	51
Herefordshire	7	3	3	13
Hertfordshire	9	6	8	23
Huntingdonshire	3	0	2	5
Kent	23	30	41	94
Lancashire	2	7	1	10
Leicestershire	4	5	6	15
Lincolnshire	15	5	44	64
Middlesex	23	1	11	35
Norfolk	37	9	17	63
Northamptonshire	11	12	11	34
Northumberland	27	2	12	41
Nottinghamshire	3	2	13	18
Oxfordshire	10	2	27	39
Rutland	4	2	1	7
Shropshire	8	1	4	13
Somerset	42	16	63	121
Staffordshire	3	0	10	13
Suffolk	23	7	15	45
Surrey	7	5	18	30
Sussex	23	6	9	38
Warwickshire	15	8	29	52
Westmorland	0	0	0	0
Wiltshire	47	21	18	86
Worcestershire	15	1	24	40
Yorkshire	45	21	52	118
Wales	47	3	17	67
	660	263	615	1538

COMPOSITE TABLE

	PURCHASERS Number—%	NUMBER of MANORS Sold—Given	SALES Total—%	GIFTS Total—%	SALES and GIFTS Total—%
1. By years					
1547			£4,313 1s 0d (1·02%)	£107,712	£112,025 1s 0d (13·45%)
1548			61,774 16s 0d (14·57%)	5,148	66,922 16s 0d (8·04%)
1549			127,670 18s 0d (30·10%)	7,645	135,315 18s 0d (16·25%)
1550			64,789 19s 0d (15·28%)	103,138	167,927 19s 0d (20·17%)
1551			5,364 17s 0d (1·26%)	54,603	59,967 17s 0d (7·20%)
1552			15,936 16s 0d (3·76%)	64,009	79,945 16s 0d (9·60%)
1553			144,259 8s 0d (34·01%)	66,234	210,493 8s 0d (25·28%)
			£424,109 15s 0d	£408,489	£832,598 15s 0d
2. By social status					
Old Nobility	11 (1·65%)		£13,158 18s 0d (3·10%)	£28,741 (7·04%)	£41,899 18s 0d (5·03%)
New Nobility	12 (1·80%)		10,887 5s 0d (2·57%)	166,151 (40·67%)	177,038 5s 0d (21·26%)
Upper Gentry	82 (12·28%)		72,429 10s 0d (17·08%)	102,937 (25·20%)	175,366 10s 0d (21·06%)
Lower Gentry	309 (46·26%)		173,036 17s 0d (40·80%)	14,652 (3·59%)	187,688 17s 0d (22·54%)
Yeomen	28 (4·19%)		11,425 5s 0d (2·69%)		11,425 5s 0d (1·37%)
Professional	35 (5·24%)		26,166 0s 0d (6·17%)		26,166 0s 0d (3·14%)

2. By social status—continued

		£424,109 15s od	£408,489	£832,598 15s od
Merchants	122 (18·26%)	84,371 19s od (19·89%)	10,647 (2·61%)	95,018 19s od (11·41%)
Tradesmen	16 (2·39%)	7,659 5s od (1·81%)		7,659 5s od (0·92%)
Other	2 (0·30%)	892 12s od (0·21%)	4,902 (1·20%)	5,794 12s od (0·70%)
Unknown	41 (6·14%)	21,772 12s od (5·13%)	1,018 (0·25%)	22,790 12s od (2·74%)
Charitable and public uses	10 (1·50%)	2,309 12s od (0·54%)	79,441 (19·45%)	81,750 12s od (9·82%)
	668	£424,109 15s od	£408,489	£832,598 15s od

3. By source

			£424,109 15s od	£408,489	£832,598 15s od
Chantry lands	39	3	£272,858 8s od (64·34%)	£47,317 (11·58%)	£320,175 8s od (38·45%)
Monastic lands	141	227	104,739 6s od (24·70%)	150,245 (36·78%)	254,984 6s od (30·63%)
Attainders and felonies	51	218	33,725 14s od (7·95%)	100,108 (24·51%)	133,833 14s od (16·07%)
Episcopal lands	5	95	3,239 17s od (0·76%)	51,521 (12·61%)	54,760 17s od (6·58%)
Recent crown lands	9	56	3,714 10s od (0·88%)	24,785 (6·07%)	28,499 10s od (3·42%)
Crown jointures	14	38	3,268 6s od (0·77%)	17,755 (4·35%)	21,023 6s od (2·52%)
Escheats, forfeits, fines	2	16	1,761 6s od (0·41%)	13,881 (3·40%)	15,642 6s od (1·88%)
Old crown lands (pre-1509)	2	7	802 8s od (0·19%)	2,877 (0·70%)	3,679 8s od (0·44%)
	263	660	£424,109 15s od	£408,489	£832,598 15s od

that a heavy proportion (61·29 per cent) of the lands given by the Crown had been gained by the monastic expropriation and by the grimly effective means of attainder. In contrast, it will be recalled that an even greater proportion (64·34 per cent) of the lands sold had been gained in the expropriation of the chantries, monastic lands having been used to make sales packages more attractive and to provide, usually by the inclusion of a manor, at least one substantial land entity which would give some measure of aggregation to the always dispersed chantry lands. Monastic lands and attainted lands were evidently principally used in crown gift grants because they were normally more valuable and were in their very nature likely to be aggregated and hence very desirable land units.

C. *Remarks on the whole of the dispositions*

Lands were given and they were sold for somewhat different reasons, to somewhat different classes of men, and with a somewhat different chronological pattern in the seven calendar years with which we are concerned. But, whether sold or given, the institutional consequences were the same, for the most viable and valued of the Crown's independent financial resources had been permanently lessened and wasted. In all, the Crown disposed of landed properties with a net capital value of £832,598 15s od during the reign of Edward VI. This dispersal of royal resources was a consequence of the weakness of policy in the reign—roughly half the total being sold to finance current needs and to meet current crises and the other half, in effect, to raise up in status the principal officers of state; to pay, as it were, the current costs of government and administration, and to buy support (with the coin of regal strength) for whichever faction was seeking to secure its grip on the reality of power. The great officers of state and their subordinates gained in all—if gifts and sales are combined—£319,293 18s od, or well over a third (38·35 per cent) of the crown wealth disposed.

The great total of royal resources expended, moreover, was spread amongst the classes which had to be reckoned with in the manipulation of power. Nearly two-thirds (64·86 per cent) of the whole great sum went to the classes in which power was seated and on whose favour the tenure of power depended. This is the clear meaning of the figures. The whole brutal process of the quest for power is relieved only by the fact that a social conscience was quietly and effectively beginning to assert itself in this strange period. One wishes it were more, but it remains true that this great outflowing wealth was, as it were, tithed for the benefit of the realm in the

£81,750 12s od laid out for the various charitable causes. We have elsewhere shown that for the two decades 1541–1560 a total of £227,032 1s od was provided for the various charitable uses which were so greatly and so quickly to improve the lot of mankind. This total represents, we believe, a sampling which includes about half that for the whole of England. If so, a weak and harassed government must have provided from its strained resources approximately 18 per cent of this fruitful sum; never before, certainly, and not again until our own generation, has a government ever intervened with as much vigour and enlightenment to secure the social and cultural advance of its own citizens with charitable dispositions of its own.

When we combine the capital values of sales and gifts in order more accurately to measure the process of the deterioration of royal resources, we find a flatter curve of the erosion of crown resources than those previously projected and one that is perhaps more meaningful, since it does suggest the continuous nature of the pressures to which the government was subject. At the same time, it must be stressed that the huge wastage occurred in the half-year 1553 when royal wealth was drawn down at the rate of about £421,000 p.a. (£35,000 per month). It was in these months that Northumberland pushed his bold plans forward with remorseless energy, and he financed them with the substance of his sovereign's wealth.

Crown resources were sharply drawn down during these years, but the depredations were by no means ruinous and may easily be exaggerated unless they are kept in scale. The £832,598 15s od of crown lands disposed by sale and gift represents, for example, wealth equivalent to approximately three-fourths of the whole value of wealth remaining in royal hands from the expropriated monastic properties; however, the ancient crown lands, re-gathered by Henry VII, were really left untouched. To put it another way, these dispositions equalled the whole value of the expropriated chantry lands, which may be regarded as a windfall which doubtless should have been liquidated quickly for reasons of religious policy, plus roughly a fifth of a million pounds more, taken from other and more plentiful pockets of royal resources. The wealth remained by which more prudent and wiser successors could more than restore that fund of capital credit with which the sovereign was for about another century to seek to live on his own.

Further, in estimating the weakening of crown resources by the sales and gifts made in the Edwardian period, it must be recalled that the Tudors constantly employed the dread device of attainder and crippling fine to reduce the fortunes of the over-mighty subject and to accomplish the ruin of the great minister whose policy had failed. Our total for gifts and sales is in this broader context a substantial overstatement of the true drain on crown resources, since the fall of great men like Edward Seymour, Thomas Seymour, and Arundel, and the heavy penalties laid against the estates of servants of the second rank like Sharington, Paget, and Thynne recovered for the Crown—in the main for re-granting to others now more favoured —a total of upwards of £112,838, or something like 13 per cent of the whole of the wealth so recklessly bestowed. Further—if we may extend this process of recovery through the first year of Mary's reign—the expiation of Northumberland and his faction recovered to the Crown upwards of £52,000 additionally of Edwardian and Henrician generosity.

In concluding our remarks on Edwardian sales and grants of crown lands (we are ignoring a small number of fee-farm grants in which the Crown reserved the full value of the then revenues), we must comment on a considerable number of formal exchanges of landed property arranged between the Crown and individual or corporate owners. There were 78 of these exchange transactions in which 54 individuals or institutions were involved. The following table sets out the anatomy of these transactions:

Individuals	Transactions	Identity	
5	23	Great officers of state	
11	11	Lesser crown officials	
8	13	Dioceses	
4	4	Other ecclesiastical institutions	
2	3	Members of royal family	
24	24	Individuals: Old nobility,	4
—	—	Upper gentry,	7
54	78	Lower gentry,	10
		Merchants,	3

The worth of these exchanged properties was substantial, running to £3707 13s 9d p.a. for the Crown, of which, however, rents in the amount of £590 10s 7d were reserved. Thus the net value to the Crown of the lands conveyed was £3117 3s 2d p.a., or a capital worth of about £62,343. Generally it is quite evident that the motive behind these exchanges—especially those in which the principal officers of state were involved—was the strong urge of the owner to consolidate his holdings, often by yielding back to the Crown grants received earlier from the King. There is, however, no clear pattern of motive on the part of the Crown.

By every test that can be applied it would seem on balance that the Crown received from private owners just a little less than a fair exchange. It is equally certain that in the episcopal exchanges the pressure came from the Crown, which got much the better of the bargain. It is equally evident in several cases that in its negotiations with the great officers of state the transactions ran heavily against the interests of the Crown—so much so that in two or three instances we may well be dealing with concealed gifts. But in all other cases the exchanges seem to have been quite fairly constituted. We have accordingly concluded that taken together the exchanges were neutral in their effect on crown resources.

But in another sense these exchanges may have had very important historical consequences, since a total of 615 manors changed hands, spread over almost every county in England, even though we have excluded the fairly large transactions within the royal family in which Mary and Elizabeth were involved. There were 342 manors formerly the property of the Crown—though many had not been held for long—which passed to new owners, almost all of whom were non-resident and few of whom could have known personally the lands which they had acquired. At the same time 273 manors formerly in private hands passed by these transactions into crown hands. These changes in manorial ownership must of course, if the social and cultural consequences are to be estimated, be joined with the 923 manors which, as we have already seen, had passed from crown to private hands as a result of the sales and gifts of the period.

In all, then, 1538 manors in England and Wales, as a consequence of crown policy, or, to speak more accurately, of crown necessity, changed ownership in a very short interval of seven years. This means that something like 8 per cent to 9 per cent of all the manors in the realm were caught up in a most disrupting process of change, for we are dealing with a society still largely manorial in its organization and structure. An incomplete study on which we are engaged suggests that when external forces were not at work changes in manorial ownership occurred only very slowly and then ordinarily within the county itself. But in a large number of manors the weakness of the Crown had introduced a profoundly dislocating influence into the structure of rural life and organization. We may be sure that few of the new and great owners ever lived on the manors they had acquired; few could even have visited them, but simply counted them as building-blocks in the landed fortunes which they were in process of acquiring. In more than half the counties of England as many as thirty manors found new owners as a consequence of royal necessity or prodigality. And it is especially noteworthy that these disturbing changes were heavily concentrated in twelve counties in which 938 manors came into new and thrusting hands.[1] We believe it no coincidence that some considerable political and economic disturbance will be found to have occurred in eleven of these twelve counties in the course of this reign. This was perhaps the greatest of the impairments which the ruling junta was to lay against the substance of sovereignty in England.

[1] The counties are Devonshire, Dorset, Essex, Gloucestershire, Hampshire, Kent, Lincolnshire, Norfolk, Somerset, Warwickshire, Wiltshire, Yorkshire.

IV

RELIGIOUS POLICY: THE TRIAL OF TOLERATION (1547)

1. THE RELIGIOUS VIEWS OF THE PROTECTOR AND THE COUNCIL

We have observed that Henry VIII had decisively tipped the balance of power in his Council, and by the selection of the executors of his will, towards a Protestant settlement of faith. Above all, he must have sensed that Seymour had long been Protestant in his sympathies and the structure of the faith of the young King was assured by the education which had been carefully arranged for him. In the new government, formed with such speed and sureness of touch by Seymour and Paget, the power vested in the Lord Protector was very great and included—almost all men of whatever complexion of faith would have agreed—the ordering of the church, the settling of doctrine, and the extirpation of error. The question of the personal faith of the Protector and his own inclination with respect to the governing of the church were then matters of the greatest moment to the whole of the realm.

Somerset was an undoubted Protestant of moderate and Erastian persuasion. Without any particular interest in theological matters and in no way disposed towards precision of doctrinal definition, either for the church or for himself, his views were probably very close to those of Cranmer, though his thinking was more directly influenced by Calvinism than was that of the Archbishop. The always astute merchant observer Richard Hilles,[1] who had despaired of any true reformation in England as late as April 30, 1546,[2] wrote to Bullinger shortly after the accession of Edward VI to express his

[1] Hilles was an early and an ardent reformer, leaving England before 1540 because of his then heretical views. He settled in Strassburg, conducting a successful cloth business there, served by a London office which he visited from time to time. In the late Henrician years Hilles served English Protestantism by the many and close contacts which he maintained both in England and on the Continent, not to mention his financial help to the Henrician exiles.

[2] Hilles to Bullinger; Robinson, *Original letters*, I, 254.

high hopes in Seymour and Catherine Parr, both of whom were known to be friendly to the cause of reform, adding in his next letter that Seymour was 'a great enemy to the pope of Rome'.[1] Calvin for a season regarded Somerset as a co-religionist, writing long and imperious letters in which the Protector's duty towards the Church of God was set out in detail. But of these the essentially non-theological Somerset soon visibly tired. Some months later, after Somerset's first fall from power, John Knox was to castigate him for having been 'cold in hearing God's word', preferring on a Sunday to visit his masons then raising up his great London house, to hearing the Scriptures preached. But the quiet and moderate nature of his faith, so irksome to the radical reformers, none the less encompassed a deep and devout personal piety. Shortly after his first imprisonment, he wrote that he had found 'great comfort, and an inward and godly working power' in a beautifully drawn manual of devotion which Coverdale had recently translated.[2] His deep and very Protestant piety was finally attested and sealed in the touching devotional writing and meditations in the Tower when he knew that death was at hand.[3] This steady and unemotional lay Protestantism of Somerset was to set the tone and pace of policy during the first and critical years of the new reign. But this want of rigour and precision in religious policy could be both vexing and confusing to extremists in both theological camps. It particularly troubled the imperial ambassador, who again and again broached the question of religious policy. Somerset patiently explained that crosses had been taken down in churches because they entrapped the poor and simple in superstition, while assuring him that the mass was privately still celebrated in the King's chapel, though Van der Delft added that his private intelligence had it that mass was no longer sung in the homes of Thomas Seymour, Dudley, and the Lord Protector.[4]

But there is a deeper and more important explanation of Somerset's moderation and apparent diffidence in matters of faith. Though he was personally devout, though he was undoubtedly and steadily Protestant in faith, he was also a most tolerant man who simply did not believe that force was a proper or a useful instrument in religious policy. The consequence was that during the period of not quite

[1] Hilles to Bullinger, June 26, 1547, and Feb. 25, 1547: Robinson, *Original letters*, I, 256, 258.

[2] Werdmueller, Otto, *A spyrytuall and moost precyouse pearle, etc.*, transl. by Miles Coverdale with a preface by Somerset (L., *1550*; Frankfurt, 1555).

[3] Stowe MS. 1066.

[4] *Cal. S.P. Span.* IX, 219, 221: Van der Delft to the Emperor, Dec. 5, 1547.

three years when his own influence was dominant in governmental affairs, England was to undertake a precocious and perhaps a naive trial of a policy of unofficially announced religious toleration. During this period no one was destroyed for heresy; the power applied against a now re-forming Catholicism was moderate and carefully restrained; and the completion of the conversion of the English people to the reformed church was declared to be the task of a preaching clergy and of the working of God's spirit through His Word, now freely available for all men to read and to ponder. During this interval, too, thought and discussion in England were free, so long as the civil order was not too violently disturbed. This policy was to fail and was to fall with the strange man, the somewhat inarticulate idealist, who was its author. It is sad to reflect, but there may be substance in the view that 'Somerset's tolerance had been individual and was little in touch with the ideals of the great mass of the population always inclined to welcome the use of force as the sign of strong rule'.[1]

These attitudes, so alien to the mid-sixteenth century, were reflected in a moderation and circumspection of policy which made it appear to the radical reformers as if the Church of England was only 'creeping towards reform'. In general it is evident that on questions of policy his views were very close to Cranmer's, though the Archbishop's thought was in motion while Somerset's was not. The Protector was wholly content with the formulation of the first *Book of Common Prayer*, which seems to have expressed fully and accurately his own preferences for doctrine and ritual.[2] He kept change and reform wholly within the grasp of the Privy Council, proceeding by cautious steps towards moderate reform by successive proclamations, while his various ecclesiastical commissions were dominated by laymen, always with a heavy weighting of common lawyers. He wrote rather plaintively to Gardiner, whose bristly friendship he kept, that he was seeking to follow a *via media*. For there are those who 'can abide no old abuses to be reformed, but think every reformation to be a capital enterprise against all religion and good order', just as there are those who press too hard

[1] Einstein, Lewis, *Tudor ideals* (N.Y., 1921), 212. The first assessment of Somerset's policy of toleration was made by an unknown writer, probably in the period of the Restoration (Sloane MS. 5009 (now listed as Cotton Appendix, XLVIII), 61 ff.). In his view, Somerset's policy was richly rewarded by religious peace during the reign, being brought to ruin by what he declared to be the calamitous use of force by Mary and Elizabeth. In the Edwardian period, he argued, a clear separation was maintained between punishment for treason and for religious opinion.

[2] Morris, Christopher, *The Tudors* (L., [1955]), 123; Ridley, *Cranmer*, 261.

and too unquietly for change. He submitted that 'the magistrate's duty is betwixt these, so in a mean to . . . provide, that old doting should not take further or deeper rust [root?] in the common-wealth, neither ancient error overcome the seen and tried truth, nor long abuse, for the age and space of time only, still be suffered: and yet all these with quietness and gentleness, and without all con-tention, if it were possible, to be reformed'.[1]

The government, then, was to move very slowly along the path of reform, in part because this was precisely Somerset's intention, and in part because all counsels of prudence so commanded. In the nation at large, and particularly in London, this policy was to nurture a powerful and highly articulate Protestantism, already complaining that the pace was too slow. The earliest actions taken consequently were to impose restraints on those who wished to move too swiftly. Both Somerset and Cranmer were resolved to proceed 'by slow and safe degrees, not hazarding too much at once'.[2] These cautious moves towards reformation met with little articulate resistance from the lower clergy or from the great and, on the whole, quite inert mass of lay thought. But every move was opposed skil-fully and tenaciously by Gardiner and the more conservative of the bishops, who maintained in effect that Somerset was guilty of a breach of trust and that no considerable innovation should be undertaken during the minority of the King. This contention Somerset rejected absolutely and in his resolution he had the com-plete support of the Council. The fact was that it was his steady intention to answer for England burning questions which the late monarch had either evaded or answered erroneously. The course of policy was firmly and clearly set within a few weeks: England was to be a Protestant realm.[3]

We have already observed that the complexion of the new govern-ment was overwhelmingly Protestant or politique as a consequence of the shrewd care with which Henry VIII had named his successors in power.[4] Within the Privy Council Somerset, Cranmer, Dudley, Russell, Denny, and Herbert were strongly Protestant in their sentiments, and the clear *locus* of policy and power with respect to religious change was lodged in the first three of these men and was not at any time seriously questioned by the others.[5]

The religious policy which Somerset and Cranmer now sought to

---

[1] Foxe, *Acts and monuments*, VI, 28, 30.   [2] Burnet, *Reformation*, II, 70–71.
[3] Pollard, *Somerset*, 97.   [4] *Vide ante*, 56–57.
[5] For other estimates of the religious complexion of the Council in 1547, see Gairdner, *Lollardy*, III, 12; Froude, *History of England*, IV, 529; Pollard, *History of England*, 3–4.

implement, then, had strong support from a majority of the Council and was actively opposed by none. Quite as important, as we shall later note in detail, among the rising young men soon to hold important governmental posts and a number of whom were in due season to be admitted to the Council, there was very strong, often evangelical, Protestant sympathy. Further, such men as Cheke, Cooke, Hales, Thomas Smith, Ascham, Cecil, Morison, and Hoby—to name only the more articulate of the group—were or were to become intimately associated with the King, whose first evidences of maturity were to be expressed in his warm support, indeed, demand, for the hastening and completion of the process of reformation. These men, all humanists, were at once deeply Protestant in their own religious views and almost frighteningly secular in their conception of the control which the state should exercise in religion. Thus Sir Philip Hoby could write in intimate terms to Somerset from the Emperor's court that the 'ruin' of Germany had been occasioned by the princely power and estate of the great German bishops. All sincere German Protestants accordingly pray that Edward will allow to his bishops no more than 'an honest and competent living', sufficient only for their maintenance. Then they will devote themselves without distraction to their preaching, while the expropriated episcopal properties can be employed for raising a professional body of horse for defence and for the 'maintenance of poor gentlemen'.[1] Great influence flowed from these thrusting and perhaps overly ambitious young men, most of whom did not

---

[1] Cotton MSS., Galba, B, xii, 4, ff. 16b–19; Harl. MS. 523, 6, #7, f. 16: Jan. 19, [1548]. Born in 1505, Hoby was as early as 1538 employed in diplomatic missions. He was named ambassador to the Emperor in 1548 and was later admitted to the Privy Council. His much younger brother, Sir Thomas, in 1558 married one of the famous Cooke sisters and was hence the brother-in-law of Cecil.

This manuscript is also printed *verbatim* by Strype (*Memorials*, II, i, 138–139). Typically, there are small errors of transcription, ambiguity as to the dating, and an apparent disregard for the context. But Strype has been too much maligned. He printed and examined an enormous body of manuscript material in his several great works, including some sources not now available in any other form. He was careless in transcription, but none the less the sense of the document is almost invariably accurately set out. His difficulties and weaknesses stemmed from a strange kind of intellectual arrogance which was mixed with secretiveness regarding his materials. Very revealing are Wharton's complaints to Chiswell (Oct. 28, 1693) that though he has in hand Strype's proofs of the *Cranmer*, he was not prepared to proceed because Strype was 'unwilling that the publick correcting his errors should proceed from any but himself'. He had found Strype 'not over-willing to own his obligations', and has at least in the case of the 'Registers of Christ Church, Canterbury and of K. Edward's Councill-book, pretended to have lighted on those registers which he never saw' (*Catalogue of MSS. in Univ. of Cambridge Library*, V, 45, from Baumgartner papers, Strype correspondence, III, i, #27).

5

lend their support to Somerset, who had made them, in the dangerous days of October, 1549. That wonderfully courageous woman, Katherine, Duchess of Suffolk, so earthy in her view of life and so salty of tongue, was to remind the greatest of them that these young advisers had not stood by Somerset, had indeed distracted him from the course of reformation he had set for England. Much later she wrote to Cecil, 'The Duke lost all he sought to keep, with his head to boot, and his counsellors slipped their collars, turned their coats, and have served since to play their part in other matters'.[1]

2. THE CLERGY AT THE OUTSET OF THE REIGN

We have earlier dealt in some detail with the complexion of the bench of bishops during the second half of Henry VIII's reign, and may now summarize the situation as it stood in the early months of the Edwardian period.[2] At the moment of Edward's accession there were ten bishops who by their actions or expressed sentiments were orthodox in their religious views, though by no means all of their number opposed every reform ordered by the government in the months to come. Rather these were men who were disposed to lend grudging support to modest reformation, but who had some sticking-point of conscience beyond which they could not go.[3] Three of this group (Gardiner, Bonner, and Tunstall) were men of considerable force of mind and personality. But none, it is fair to say, was eminent as a theologian or was really adequately equipped to offer detailed and persuasive opposition to the course of the Reformation. Almost as many, nine, were favourable to further doctrinal and ritualistic reformation,[4] and it was in this group that the thrust of intellectual and theological distinction was to be found, as well as the immense advantage of a coherent and an aggressive policy of reform. The remaining eight of the Edwardian bishops may be dismissed as unimportant because they were undecided or as opportunists who desired above all else to hold their sees.[5] Some measure of the relative moderation and tolerance of the reign may be suggested by the fact that only six of all the bishops were to be deprived, Rugg having died, and that even at the time of Edward's death there remained four bishops who were known to be

[1] Quoted by Read, Conyers, *Mr. Secretary Cecil and Queen Elizabeth* (L., [1955]), 43.

[2] *Vide ante*, 19–21.

[3] They were Gardiner, Bonner, Tunstall, Heath, Day, Aldrich, Thirlby, Rugg, Veysey, and King.

[4] Cranmer, Ridley, Holgate, Goodrich, Holbeach, Barlow, Ferrar, Bird, and Bush (with reservations).

[5] Skip, Sampson, Chambers, Salcot, Wakeman, Kitchin, Warton, and Bulkeley.

opposed to the doctrinal and liturgical revolution that had occurred.[1] Under the King's father, we may be sure, these bishops might easily have lost their sees, or even their heads.[2]

One must lend great sympathy to the plight of the conservative bishops under Somerset, far more under Northumberland. These men were all Henricians; they had all lent full support to his partial reformation; and Gardiner had vindicated it in the most effective and persuasive of all the works which sought to vest that reformation in the terms of political theory. All of these men were faced with an extremely difficult decision when the religious temper and intentions of Somerset's government became clear not many months after Henry's death. Most of them had been educated as humanists, all had held important governmental posts, and all had given an almost instinctive, and unstinting support to the Tudor regime. Now they were obliged to re-think their position quickly and under very heavy pressure from that state which they had served so well and loyally; now, to put it bluntly, they had either to learn or to re-learn their theology. Their difficulties, moral as well as intellectual, sprang from the fact that they had accepted, as they had helped to gain, the renunciation of the papal supremacy, only to discover, historically far too late, that they could not renounce the whole system of worship and doctrine of the church in which they had grown up and to which they now lent a belated but courageous devotion.[3]

The real difficulty of the Edwardian government in its course of reform, however, was to be with the lower clergy rather than with the bishops. It is difficult for us to bear in mind the immense gulf which separated the bishops, the upper cathedral clergy, and certain of the collegiate clergy, from their brethren, the thousands of parochial clergy who sought—uneducated, unassisted, and with a very low income—to maintain the cure of souls in the parishes of rural England. These men were in the main drawn from the social class which they served. Moreover, thousands of them had to be

---

[1] The total is more accurately five—Veysey, now aged, being induced to resign on terms which sadly depleted his see.

[2] This discussion owes much to Messenger, E. C., *The Reformation the mass and the priesthood* (2 vols., L., 1936–1937), I, 330–339; Dugmore, C. W., *The mass and the English reformers* (L., 1958), 108–112; and Smith, *Tudor prelates*, 139–158.

[3] Smith, *Tudor prelates*, 159–163. One's sympathies are particularly enlisted by Tunstall's plight. Now aged, he was named an executor of the will, and was a personal friend of Somerset. Moderate and conciliatory in his views, he was prepared to yield much, and his experience in administration, especially in the north, was greatly valued by the Council. It remained for Northumberland to resolve his dilemma by a particularly brutal exercise of the prerogative power.

content with the wholly inadequate income left after monastic
impropriators had skimmed off the cream of parochial tithes; most
of them were uneducated in any meaningful sense of the term; and
almost all of them were uninformed and almost completely insulated
from the centres of thought and culture. Moreover, many benefices
were now held by former monks without any parish experience, men
who were seeking at least a slightly better income than the pensions
which they had been assigned.[1] The great body of the clergy was in
fact intellectually inert, concerned almost wholly with local problems and crises, and probably really unaware of the great events and
decisions at Westminster. The secular clergy had with few exceptions accepted the Henrician Settlement of the Church as they did
the far more radical Edwardian settlement, but without either
understanding or deep spiritual commitment. This was not a
preaching clergy, it was not an informed clergy, and it was not a
clergy in which thought was in motion. At the same time, however,
the intellectual cast of the parochial clergy of most of the realm was
instinctively conservative, perhaps in large part because ignorance
is of itself an immensely conservative force. These were men who,
with their parishes, wanted no change from the comfortable routines
they had known, from the services in which their fathers had been
born, had worshipped, and had died. Though offering little formal
resistance to the course of reform, this clergy was the despair of
active and evangelical bishops, of whom Hooper is only the most
famous, as they came to realize that the Reformation could root
itself and prosper only if an educated, as well as a Protestant, clergy
could be installed in England.

The root of the problem was to be found in the wholly inadequate
stipends afforded to the parochial clergy, particularly in the thousands
of parishes ravaged first in the Middle Ages by the monastic impropriators and in the second half of the sixteenth century by lay
impropriators. In fertile stretches of Lincolnshire in this period
only one-seventh of the livings yielded as much as £10–£19 p.a.,
while about three-quarters of them were in the range of £4 10s od–
£10 p.a. The cultural and intellectual effects were simply catas-
trophic, only one priest in seven in the Diocese of Lincoln leaving
books in his estate a few years before our period, whereas by the
close of the Elizabethan era almost every clergyman left books and
seems to have possessed a study.[2] So too, a random group of

---

[1] Burnet, *Reformation*, II, 22.
[2] Brooks, F. W., 'The social position of the parson in the sixteenth century', *Brit.
Archaeol. Assoc. Jour.*, ser. 3, X (1945–1947), 25, 32.

clerical inventories in this diocese for the years 1530–1540 yields an average worth of £28 11s od, which means that in economic terms these priests were not much better off than the husbandmen in their parishes, whereas after a half-century of persistent effort to raise their status, the average worth of the clergy in the region had risen to £120 8s od.[1]

Similar evidence is yielded by samplings in any part of England in the period 1535–1555. The average stipend designated in deeds of gift establishing chantry endowments in the years before they were declared illegal was £6 3s 9d p.a., and there is no proof that such posts were difficult to fill with stipendiary priests.[2] Evidence cited by Professor Dickens suggests that the *Valor Ecclesiasticus* (1535) reveals in the Diocese of Coventry and Lichfield that well over half the livings were valued at £10 or under, while 87 per cent were worth less than £20 p.a.[3] Similarly, in the relatively rich Archdeanery of Leicester in 1535, slightly more than half the clergy had as much as £10 p.a., and only 14 per cent had as much as £20 p.a., though here too there was to be a vast improvement during the Elizabethan period when the value of benefices in rural parishes increased about fourfold.[4] In Gloucestershire, where the curse of monastic impropriations had been especially widespread, clerical incomes were in average terms even lower, which is surely closely connected with the fact that in this county the clergy were particularly ignorant, inert, and cautious. The evidence suggests that only one priest in the diocese offered resistance to the Act of Supremacy, though his deposition was made on apparently sufficient grounds of faulty appointment.[5] In the Edwardian era, as we shall note in detail, the great Hooper sought zealously but perhaps too rapidly to reform his clergy, but even in his episcopate the disciplinary actions were evoked rather by ignorance, real superstition, and immaturity than by theological conservatism. Here, too, as in so many other counties, in Mary's reign the doctrinal scrutiny of the clergy noted only one clergyman, Hooper and his chaplains aside, all the rest having resumed the ancient service without resistance—some, one supposes, gladly, and others grudgingly.[6]

This is not a pleasant picture of the rural clergy of England, comprising as they did something like nine-tenths of the whole number.

[1] *Brit. Archaeol. Assoc. Jour.*, ser. 3, X (1945–1947), 35–37.

[2] Jordan, W. K., *Philanthropy in England, 1480–1660, etc.* (L., 1959), 307–308.

[3] Dickens, *English Reformation*, 48–49.

[4] Hoskins, W. G., *Essays in Leicestershire history* (Liverpool, 1950), 1–2, 16.

[5] Baskerville, Geoffrey, 'Elections to convocation in the Diocese of Gloucester under Bishop Hooper', *E.H.R.*, XLIV (1929), 7.   [6] *Ibid.* 11.

Nor were conditions of stipend, education, and doctrinal awareness improved much even when a great and fervent bishop like Hooper threw the whole weight of his immense energy into the task of reform and betterment. The gloom of our recital is, however, somewhat relieved by the progress made in London where at the moment of Edward's death sixty-three of the eighty-seven known incumbents were educated men with university degrees in divinity. The quality and the conviction of these men, in the sharpest possible contrast to the generality of the rural clergy, is attested by the fact that of the total number of the Edwardian clergy who were deprived or who fled under Mary they amounted to approximately a third of the whole number.[1] Only beginnings, then, could be made in this short reign in the improvement of the quality, the status, and the doctrinal conviction of the clergy. The time was too short and the resources too few. But a start had been made and far higher standards of qualification were being imposed. The great task was resumed with more of vigour and sureness of touch under Queen Elizabeth so that in 1577 Harrison could boast, certainly with some exaggeration, that it was accounted a fault if the clergy did not know both Greek and Hebrew, while few had been appointed in the past twelve to fourteen years who did not have a working command of Latin.[2]

3. EVIDENCE OF ADVANCED PROTESTANT SENTIMENTS

A. *The evidence of thought*

Into this inert mass of the clergy of England the leaven of a vigorous, an insistent, and a powerfully evangelical Protestantism was to be not only released but encouraged only a few weeks after the accession of Edward VI. We have observed that English Protestantism was well and probably ineradicably rooted even before 1547, but we have also observed that its leaders and most of its spokesmen were in exile and hence gravely handicapped in their work of preaching and propaganda. Almost immediately these leaders began to drift back to England and to be fitted into important and strategic appointments which gave maximum thrust to the stoutly Protestant doctrines and convictions with which they returned from the Continent. To name only a few of the principal at this

---

[1] Mullins, E. L. C., 'The effects of the Marian and Elizabethan religious settlements upon the clergy of London, etc.', *Bull. Inst. Hist. Research*, 22 (1949), 172–175.

[2] Harrison, William, *An historical description of the iland of Britaine, etc.* (L., 1577; Book II, ed. by F. J. Furnivall (New Shakespere Soc., ser. 6, pt. i, L., *1877*)), 111.

point: Coverdale was named as a chaplain to the King; William Turner was made physician and chaplain to Somerset; the immensely formidable Bale was given a living in Hampshire and then a bishopric in Ireland; Rogers gained an important London parish; and Hooper, one of the greatest of all English preachers, was first employed in preaching to huge congregations in London and then was appointed to the see of Gloucester.

There was already strong Protestant sentiment to which encouragement and leadership were now given, particularly in the south of England and in most of the seaport and industrial towns, with the centre of its qualitative strength in London. We shall now endeavour to examine the evidences of early and advanced Edwardian Protestant thought, dealing first with a sampling of relatively minor writers who may reflect more accurately the violence as well as the confusion of thought in an essentially revolutionary era than do the leading Protestant thinkers.[1] Our first group of titles will be rather haphazardly drawn from a considerable body of literature published at the very close of the Henrician regime or in the first year of the Edwardian era. These are in the main fugitive pieces, hastily composed and often crudely printed. Further, almost all are weakened by the intensity and bitterness of their attack on Rome and all its works, with the result that it is much easier to say what these men were against than to describe the *corpus* of their thought.

All of these slender works were violently and often obsessively anti-papal. The progressive spiritual decay of the Church of Christ over the centuries has been the consequence of its bondage to Rome and the false teachings with which it had been corrupted.[2] Most of these authors were likewise bitterly anti-prelatical, it being argued that the bishops have for generations been fellow conspirators with the papacy in the enslavement of mankind and the perversion of the church. This sustained attack centred particularly on Gardiner, who as Joye describes him was a persecutor and a burner of godly men under false accusations of heresy. Joye bitterly taunted Gardiner with the inconsistency of his own career, for he had known him at Cambridge before he entered Wolsey's service, where he 'defended the truth [in the matter of good works] against this papistry which you now maintain'.[3] Gardiner, like so many other bishops, has

[1] Their thought will be considered in the concluding volume of this work.

[2] *A supplycacion to our moste soveraigne Lorde Kinge Henry the Eight, etc.* (L., 1544), in *Four supplications, 1529–1553,* ed. by F. J. Furnivall and J. M. Cowper (E.E.T.S., extra ser., XIII (1871)), 22–25. This tract may have been written by Brinkelow.

[3] Joye, George, *The refutation of the byshop of Winchesters derke declaration, etc.* (L. 1546), 81. Joye, a native of Bedfordshire, was graduated from Cambridge in 1513.

betrayed the truth he once held, the associations he once nurtured, in his steady quest for power and favour. And such men corrupt and weaken the church as bishops, since they appoint unqualified men to benefices, inevitably favouring mute clergy who had no capacity for preaching or for the cure of souls. For too long, indeed, the Crown has rewarded its own servants and councillors with bishoprics, with the result that the nobility has moved in to fill ecclesiastical vacancies and livings with their own retainers.[1] The bishops have in fact become wholly dissociated from their spiritual functions: they are rich and lordly men who know not the needs either of the church they are supposed to serve or of their flocks. This strong anti-prelatism animated too the scurrilous attack on Rugg of Norwich, who resigned in 1549, for his spoliation of his see, his lordly life, and his want of spiritual concern.[2]

This drumfire of attack on the bishops included as well an overt anti-clericalism which was a strong and abiding part of English Protestantism. This is an episcopal caste, it was alleged, which has fattened on tithes and other revenues of the church properties which were originally meant for the care of the poor and for the building of a true Christian community. Not only was this wealth absorbed for the worldly uses of the clergy, but they duped the laity of the realm into building for them 'goodly churches with high steeples, and great bells to ring our pence into their purses, when our friends' lay dead. The whole priestly apparatus of masses, prayers for the dead, images, and pilgrimages was deliberately and wickedly foisted on the laity to ensure their spiritual and economic bondage.[3] These were the sentiments, too, which either very late in the Henrician period or early in that of his son inspired the 'commons' to petition the King to demand from the bishops 'a true and plain declaration of the laws of God and holy church' on the legality and decency of such spiritual practices as buying and selling for gain, holding temporal offices, and indulging in pluralism and non-residence.[4]

A steady and effectively eroding attack was also maintained by

Complaints were lodged against him as early as 1527 for his certainly heretical views. He fled abroad and was for a season associated with Tyndale. He engaged Gardiner in a violent dispute growing out of the burning of Barnes.

[1] *Supplycacion to our moste soveraigne Lorde*, in *Four supplications*, 30–31, 34, 35.
[2] Camb. Univ. MSS., Mm, iii, 12.
[3] *A supplication of the poore commons* (L.,[1546?]), in *Four supplications*, 72–74.
[4] Cotton MSS., Cleopatra, F., ii, 70, f. 257. We have been unable more precisely to date this interesting petition. It resulted in no legislation, but it does mirror the pervading anti-clericalism of the House of Commons.

these polemicists against the doctrinal and liturgical position of the Roman church. The true and simple faith of Christ has been slandered and perverted by its idolatry and the raising up of indifferent liturgical practices into fundamentals of belief.[1] This desperate devotion to teachings and practices has driven the Roman church and its minions to embrace persecution as their weapon: 'it is your devillish drift, and wicked counsel to thrust God's holy eternal word of salvation out ... persecuting it so cruelly with sword and fire, so mercilessly burning the innocent lambs of Christ for professing Christ and his holy word'.[2] So too, the Romish priesthood has entrapped men in the doctrine of purgatory, instilling in them 'vain hope in the prayers of priests to be made ... when they be dead', whereas in truth men who have experienced the saving faith of Christ stand in no need 'of such strange succour and help of men'.[3] The priestly caste has laboured long and with consummate skill, so a ballad writer complained, to confine all religion, indeed Christ Himself, in the sacraments which they control, and above all in the mass. But now:

> ... Some there be that say,
> That Christ cannot all day
> Be kept within a box,
> Nor yet set in the stocks,
> Nor hidden like a fox,
> ....
> Nor can no more be slain,
> Nor offered up again.

The priestly caste has been full of wiles, as the net of doctrinal superstition and trickery has been employed to seduce and subvert the laity.[4]

The whole weight of the reformed Protestant attack came rapidly to bear on the nature of the mass. The discussion was by no means decorous and both Cranmer and the Council took steps in 1547 to try at least to stay the flood of ballads and libels against this central doctrine. Thus one writer pointed out that the principal argument of the Romanists was that the mass was an ancient practice,

> Although none of the Gospels
> No mention maketh or tells.

[1] A compendvois treatyse of sclaudre, etc. (L., [1545?]).   [2] Joye, Refutation, 30-31.
[3] Supplycacion to our moste soveraigne Lorde, in Four supplications, 43.
[4] A pore help, etc., printed by Strype (Memorials, II, ii, 333-337), 335. No date is given, though internal evidence suggests 1545-1549, with 1547 as a very probable date

The mass has no grounding in Holy Scripture, to which the papist counters:

> Ye think nothing but Scripture
> Is only clean and pure.
> Yes, yes, I you ensure
> The mass shall be here better
> As light as ye do set her.

For the Roman priesthood has made of the mass a gay, a pretty, and a jolly thing:

> With goodly candlesticks
> And many proper tricks,
> With cruets gilt, and chalice,
> Whereat some men have malice.

Moreover, all things are claimed for the mass: it will cure our illnesses, will bring rain, make the wind blow, and do all things required for all men. It is, in fact, a priestly trick and a perversion of true faith.[1]

Such tracts undoubtedly constituted immensely effective propaganda. They were brilliant, witty, and often scurrilous in their attack on the ancient church and on the conservative position, while they were so fugitive and essentially disordered that they could not be answered. But their thrust was in the main negative. What these writers were against is certainly luminously evident; what they believed and what they wanted the doctrine of the true church to be is far less clear. All of them, with the exception of the ballads, were in general tone intensely moral, and most of them tended to mix religious with social grievances. They also were marred by a biblical literalism which connects them generically with English Puritanism in the next generation. Joye, for example, devoted a solid and unbelievably dull book principally to an analysis of the Book of Daniel, in which there were intimations of the millenarianism which was to plague England a century later.[2] In still another of his works he stoutly held that the Mosaic Code had not been abrogated by the gospel, advancing a long, tedious, and learned argument that adultery should

---

[1] *The up cheringe of the messe* (L., [1547]), A i–A iii. This extremely rare ballad possesses great power. It is bitterly anti-Catholic, is at points sacrilegious, and is in its general argument almost irreligious. It is, in fact, an intensely secular document.

[2] Joye, George, *The exposycion of Daniel the prophete, etc.* (L., 1545, 1550, *1550*).

be punished with death. In this matter, 'if the magistrates be negligent and cease from their office, should not the public ministers of the Word exhort and warn them of their duty', he enquired.[1]

In 1547, Somerset and Cranmer were proceeding with great caution on the course of reformation, both wishing first to clear away relatively minor and non-essential Romish survivals and indifferent but, as they thought, entrapping matters of liturgy, before turning to the ultimately important question of defining the doctrines of the Church of England. There was, therefore, no leadership in the essential matters of faith among the now powerfully placed sympathizers with Protestantism, and the obscure writers whose thought we have been analysing supplied very little. During the Lenten season of 1547 John Harley, educated at Magdalen College, Oxford, where he was later a schoolmaster, did preach a violent anti-Romanist sermon at St Peter's (Oxford), in which he powerfully urged 'justification by faith alone'. The frightened vice-chancellor cited him for heresy and he was sent up to London where he was speedily cleared, possibly by the intervention of the King, whose favour he later enjoyed, for he was appointed tutor to Warwick's son and in 1553 was made Bishop of Hereford.[2] Such actions were symptomatic of the way the doctrinal winds were gathering, but the first months of the new reign were marked by an extreme, an almost frightened, caution.

There appeared during these early months only one bold and unequivocal Protestant statement of doctrinal position and it, unfortunately, is uncertain in authorship and origin. The prologue of *A brefe and faythfulle declaration of the true fayth of Christ* seems to suggest that this was an attempt of some suspected group to make clear the articles of their faith because they lay under the shadow of possible charges of heresy. There follows a profession of faith, clearly and fully expressed, with an impressive learned interlarding of supporting scriptural quotations. On the central question of the eucharist, the statement simply is that it 'is a memorial of the suffering and death of Christ'. Christ has described his body and his blood as bread and wine only that we thereby shall remember him. Christ will abide with us forever, but not in bread, in wine, or in any other temporal thing. The author of this clearly Zwinglian confession speaks of the blindness of the common people of England,

---

[1] Joye, George, *A contrarye (to a certayne manis) consultacion, etc.* (L., [1549]), F iv–F iv[v].

[2] Edward VI, *Chronicle*, 101, 179; Fuller, Thomas, *The history of the worthies of England, etc.*, ed. by P. A. Nuttall (3 vols., L., 1840), I, 198.

who have been confused and misled in the Roman past and who cannot be expected to find their way without help.[1] This help was near
at hand as Cranmer and Somerset prepared their minds for that
formulation of faith and worship which is the first *Book of Common
Prayer*.

There was tremendous vitality and power in the surge of strong
and uninhibited Protestant thought which we have been examining.
Its general tone was radical; it was bitterly anti-Catholic; it was
highly nationalistic in argument and conviction; and it was on the
whole unsystematic and imprecise in its statement of doctrinal
persuasion. As we have noted, the government was as yet giving no
clear lead with respect to the official canons of faith, with the
consequence that the early Protestant literature was extraordinarily
centripetal in its nature and doubtless in its effect. But within a
year—if we may examine briefly a second sample of fairly obscure
writings, most of which certainly date from 1548—greater solidity
and sureness, and a far greater applicability to the English scene may
be observed in Protestant propaganda. The naive confidence that
all reasonable and devout men would arrive at the same general
position in matters of doctrine was already being dispelled by the
visible anarchy which characterizes Protestant tractarian writing in
1547. It had come to be seen, as Philip Nicolls put it, that truth is
not easily advanced even under conditions of freedom. He reflected
in 1548 'what a number of books there be abroad in every man's
hand of divers and sundry matters which are very greedily devoured',
though, alas, people do not always read good books and reject the
bad, seeming on the whole to prefer 'trifling matters, finely handled'.[2]
It was his own wish that more of the unlearned 'which never wrote
before, should also set themselves to work bestowing the talent that
God hath lent them to the most advantage', particularly when 'it is
not lawful for any man (as yet) to preach in an open audience'.[3]
This is in effect, of course, a call for a full and a free lay consideration and resolution of questions which had for many centuries been
almost wholly within the province of an educated and a professional
clerical caste. And this was precisely what was to occur in England
in the course of the next century.

---

[1] This document evidently enjoyed a considerable audience, for it went through three
printings in 1547. The third printing (STC 14540a) contains additional and useful
prefatory matter.
[2] Nicolls, Philip, *Here begyneth a godly newe story, etc.* (L., 1548), A3ᵛ-A4. Little is
known about this strongly Protestant controversialist, who in 1547 had clashed with
Richard Crispyne, a prebend at Exeter.   [3] *Ibid.* A4ᵛ.

Protestant propaganda in 1548 followed in the main the lines of attack and consideration already observed, but was marked by a noticeable moderation of its earlier, and doubtless frightened, scurrility. But the enemy was still the Pope and his prelates, who had perverted faith and who had held the laity of the church in terror because of the instruments of persecution which they wielded. Thus, in an anonymous treatise, Barnes, the Protestant, and Powell, the Catholic, who had been put to death at the same time by Henry as a lesson to all extremists, meet in paradise; Barnes in the dialogue complains of the poor men, the little men, the 'silly souls', who have for so long been ruled by terror when they sought to find saving truth:

> For the truth's sake
> Some they did make
> Their gods to forsake.
> Some were exiled clean;
> Many they did spill,
> Banish, burn, and kill.[1]

Nicolls too pursued this theme, reflecting that men of his age were at last within sight of the promised land of true faith. For too long they have been bludgeoned and enslaved by these modern pharaohs, the Popes: 'Many a poor soul hath suffered under them most cruel torments. Many a one have they put to death that could not be suffered to answer for themselves; many a one have they put to death the cause whereof was never known. Many a one have they murdered in prison secretly lest their outrageous cruel manslaughter should be openly known.'[2] And even now, under a godly regime, England had not been wholly delivered from the evil courses of her lordly prelates, who have been the papal minions. These were men who subverted the state with their arrogant power, who corrupted the people with the magic of their masses and holy water, and who exhibited 'no mercy upon a poor wretch that once opened his mouth against them, but cried out heretic, heretic, burn, burn, fagots, fire'. These were the men, Christians must not forget, who hid the Bible from the generality of Christian men and who stoutly opposed every effort to make it fully available in the English tongue.[3]

These advanced reformers in 1548 trained their heaviest fire on the central doctrine of the mass, as if to bring all possible pressure

---

[1] *The metynge of Doctor Barons and Doctor Powell at Paradise gate, etc.* ([L.], 1548]), no pagin.

[2] Nicolls, *Here begyneth, etc.*, B6.   [3] *Ibid.*, E1.

to bear on Cranmer whose own thinking on the question was also in rapid motion during these decisive months. There are upwards of thirty tracts dating from this single year in which the mass was assailed by these now bold and highly articulate reformers. Intimately connected with this assault, too, was the almost feverish translation into English and the publication of the principal works of all the leading continental reformers: Luther, Calvin, Zwingli, Melanchthon, Bullinger, and Osiander—to name only the most influential. By the close of the year the whole *corpus* of reformed thought was fully available to English readers, not to mention such more popular and polemical works as Roy's translation from the 'duche tongue' of *A true beliefe in Christ and his sacraments*, a Lutheran work which the printer hoped would be widely read instead of the 'feigned stories of Robin Hood, Clem of the Cloghe, with such like to pass the time withal',[1] or an effective Lutheran propaganda piece, translated by Anthony Scoloker, under the title, *A goodly dysputacion betwene a Christen shomaker, and a popyshe parson, etc.* (1548).

This fruitful spread of ideas, under conditions of almost complete tolerance, is reflected in the sampling of still other tracts which deny absolutely the central Roman Catholic teaching on the mass. John Ramsey, formerly prior of Merton Abbey (Surrey), who had adopted reformed views before the expropriation of the monasteries, also lashed out bitterly against the orthodox clergy who, he says, pretend to be 'godmakers' in their teaching of transubstantiation:

> Then gloria in excelsis for joy doth he sing
> More for his fat living, than for devotion,
> And many there be that remember another thing
> Which sing not with merry heart for lack of promotion.
> Thus some be merry, some be sorry, according to their portion,
> Then forth cometh Collects, bound up in a pack
> Of this saint and that saint, for sickness and extortion,
> But gup godmakers beware your gulled back.[2]

The doctrine of transubstantiation was flatly denounced as being from the devil, being one of his many shifts to ensnare simple and unthinking people and lead them to their own destruction. It is a

[1] Printed in 1550 and dedicated to Anna, Duchess of Somerset, by Walter Lynne, who says he does not know the identity of the author or of the translator; STC 14576. Roy's translation of the Latin version was published in Strassburg in 1526 as *A lytle treatous or dialoge very necessary for all Christen men to learne and to knowe*. (*DNB*: 'Lynne, Walter'; 'Roy, William'.)

[2] Ramsey, John, *A plaister for a galled horse, etc.* (L., *1548*, 1548(?)), no pagin.

fabrication of the 'great clerks, bishops, and of other spiritual pastors . . . that by such teachers and high powers the people might be led and taught to trust' by the mystery of a pretended miracle.[1] Even now, it was complained, in London the majority of the aldermen were leagued with the 'false prophets the bishops' and other 'sturdy priests of Baal' to maintain this enslavement.[2] The formidable Richard Tracy, layman though he was, published a solid and sustained attack on the mass, basing his work principally on the writings of Augustine. In the teaching of transubstantiation, he held, the clergy have fallen into a deep and pagan error, have strayed far from the Bible, and have adopted a doctrine unknown to the primitive church. The mass, he held, got established simply because it was sung in an unknown tongue, and had it not been so, common reason would have dispelled the superstition. The Roman Catholic ministration is simply superstitious, being a kind of parody on the Lord's Supper as defined by Scripture. This is an extremely serious, a crucial, matter, for 'all the learning of religion and of the truth is converted and overthrown if that which is spiritually commanded be not faithfully observed and kept'. Therefore the clergy ought to be reformed by the King and Council so they claim no spiritual power which they do not possess. The sacrament of the mass is simply not Christian and is wholly arrogated and contrived by priestly power.[3]

These works, and we are presenting little more than a tithe of the whole, were pitched in tone and learning at the generality of men: men confused and as yet uncertain regarding the lead of the government in matters of faith. They evidently provoked wide discussion, occasioned puzzled reading of the Scriptures for the controversial passages, and caused a general stretching of the lay mind in England. One shaft of light on this process of discussion and decision is afforded in the autobiography of Edward Underhill, of a Warwickshire gentle family, a soldier who had served the King well and was with the Earl of Huntingdon in the defence of Boulogne in 1549. There, in Huntingdon's lodgings, he would play the lute for his

[1] Tracy, Richard, *A most godly enstruction and very necessarie lesson to be learned, etc.* (L., 1548), no pagin. Tracy was a member of a prominent Gloucestershire gentle family, his father being William Tracy, sheriff of Gloucestershire, whose Lutheran will led to his exhumation and burning at the stake. The son was a member of the Reformation Parliament and as early as 1533 was known as an advanced reformer. His writings were ordered burned in 1546, but he was evidently never in any real danger from Henry VIII. Tracy was one of the commissioners for the Gloucestershire chantry survey but was imprisoned for a season in 1551–1552 for an attack on Northumberland.

[2] *The lamentacyon*, in Gasquet and Bishop, *Edward VI*, 123.

[3] Tracy, Richard, *A bryef and short declaracyon made, etc.* (L., 1548), no pagin.

commander's pleasure and argue theology with Huntingdon's brother Sir Edward Hastings, recently made Master of the Horse. Hastings would 'be very hot when I did overlay him with the texts of the Scripture concerning the natural presence of Christ in the sacrament of the altar, and would swear great oaths, specially "by the Lord's foot", that after the words spoken by the priest there remained no bread, but the natural body that Mary bore'.[1] Under-hill tells us that he would drive Hastings from point to point, main-taining that the clear words of Scripture and common reason must take precedence over the sophistications of the doctors.

Underhill was accurately described in his own generation as a 'hot Gospeller', and among clergy and laity alike their number was growing very rapidly during the first tolerant months of the new regime, before moderate restraints were applied by a nervous and on the whole a cautious government. Most of these obscure writers whom we have been discussing were of this persuasion, and their appeal—and it could be as powerful as it was moving—was to the Bible as the sole authority in all religious matters. And it could also be unimaginative and incredibly dull, as witness Thomas Knell's effort to codify pious sentiments and axioms with copious supporting scriptural references in his margins.[2] So too, a pseudonymous author argued, after careful scriptural examination, that there was to be found in the gospels no authorization whatsoever for the observance of Lent, which he denounced as a formal and meaningless custom. Fasting should rather be self-imposed as a spiritual exercise and obligation: 'If you shall know where is an impotent creature, which lacketh necessary clothing; give him of your superfluous gar-ments, . . . If there be any [that] are harbourless, lead them into your superfluous farms . . . and let them have dwelling there that they may labour the earth and live.'[3]

The principal evil of Roman Catholicism was, so these early Protestant writers all agreed, that the Gospel had been repudiated and perverted by a priestly caste concerned only with the arrogation of power to itself. The Gospel, in all its transcendent glory and effi-cacy, must be restored to all those who seek their own salvation and who would follow the revealed will of Christ. It had been Henry VIII, one writer maintained, who had delivered England from this

[1] Nichols, *Narratives of the Reformation* (Camden Soc., LXXVII), 133–137. Later, when, under Mary, Underhill was in prison on charges of circulating an anti-papal ballad, he asked his wife to send him 'my night gown, my Bible, and my lute' (*ibid.* 146).

[2] Knell, Thomas, *An a b c to the christen congregacion, etc.* (L., [1550?]), s.sh.

[3] *The recantacio of Jacke Lent, etc.* ([L.], 1548), A5v.

dead bondage. But the prelatical and priestly class still uses every endeavour to restrain men's freedom in their search for gospel truth by laying charges of heresy against them.[1] None the less, the gates of Gospel freedom stand open, and the faithful may render thanks that the young King and his worthy Council have 'their consciences pure in all their proceedings, permitting us (the poor subjects) the liberty of Christ's Gospel, and the heavenly word of his Godhead'.[2] The paralysis of a former subjection must now be thrown off; men must move with a quicker boldness and zeal. The faint of heart argue that England must proceed with caution lest a Catholic crusade be launched against her, lest 'great hosts and great armies of men will invade us'. This is no more than a blasphemous argument which denies both God's will and the certainty of His protection. England must press towards the attainment of full Gospel freedom, reflecting that 'if your conscience be clear and ye seek nothing but the only glory of God (though it were with the loss of all your goods if it pleased God so to bring it to pass) . . . why stay ye. Are ye afraid of the number of men', who may be raised up against the realm when it is God's truth that is to be advanced, His commandment that is to be undertaken.[3]

B. *The evidence of action*

We have examined briefly a considerable body of radical Protestant thought which demanded a thorough reformation of religion in England, which wished to proceed much more rapidly than a cautious government desired, and which evidently represented the general religious position of a probably small, but none the less highly articulate and aggressive party of reform. This body of resolute and radical Protestantism was particularly strong, and was growing very rapidly, in London, where it was centred amongst the merchants and tradesmen and their apprentices. The religious sentiments of this confident and highly evangelical group tended to be expressed not so much in writing, in the spiritual warfare of ideas now under way in England, but in overt and often violent actions against the symbols of the old Roman Catholic liturgy and worship, which was not altered in many important particulars until Parliament met in November, 1547. A tolerant government had no wish to repress this group, with which it in fact had considerable

[1] Nicolls, *Here begyneth, etc.*, B6v–B7.
[2] Ramsey, John, *A corosyfe to be layed hard unto the heartes of all faythfull professours of Christes Gospel, etc.* ([L., 1548]), no pagin.
[3] Nicolls, *Here begyneth, etc.*, C5v, C7.

sympathy; but it was soon alarmed by illegal actions committed and by evidences of civil turbulence, which were almost obsessively feared by all Tudor governments. Some instances of these violently Protestant actions we should now examine, first in London and then in the provinces.

Even before Edward's coronation the Privy Council was disturbed by the action of the wardens and the clergyman of St Martin's in Ironmongers' Lane who without authority from the bishop or the Lord Mayor had simply taken out the crucifix and the images, placing the royal arms where the crucifix had stood, and adorning the now bare walls with texts of Scripture, 'whereof some were perversely translated'. When haled before the Council the wardens most unconvincingly explained that their church roof was unsafe; that the old images and crucifix were so rotten that they fell to powder while the roof was being examined and repaired; and that the roof repairs had been so expensive that they were quite unable to replace the images, which in any event had been idolatrously worshipped by certain simple people of the parish. These representations were readily accepted by the Council which only required the wardens, under bond, to restore the crucifix to its usual place before Lent, making no mention of the images.[1] This scarcely restrained recognition of the advanced Protestant sentiments of many in London was dourly observed by the imperial ambassador, who reported that the religious situation in the capital had deteriorated markedly in a few weeks, the common people being openly hostile to Catholicism, 'of which they make all sorts of farces and pastimes, above all of the good bishops'. Further, he was already persuaded, this religious radicalism enjoyed the strong favour of the Council and he expressed grave alarm because there was 'preaching every day before the King, and the preachers seem to vie with each other as to who can abuse most strongly the old religion'.[2]

Events were moving swiftly, for in April Stow reports that the complin was first sung in English in the King's chapel, while from the great pulpit at Paul's Cross Dr Glasier preached that abstinence from meat during Lent was in no sense an ordinance of God but was rather a matter of state policy to secure certain economic benefits.[3] The excitement and tension of these early weeks were greatly heightened by the first burst of radical publishing, some of which

---

[1] *A.P.C.* II, 25–26: Feb. 10, 1547; Burnet, *Reformation*, II, 45–46; *Cal. S.P. Span.* IX, 45: M. de Chantonnay (Perrennot) to the Emperor, Mar. 7, 1547.

[2] *Ibid.* 50: Van der Delft to Queen Dowager, Mar. 7, 1547.

[3] Stow, *Annales*, 594.

we have examined, and particularly by the profound reaction to
Bale's consummate propaganda in his annal of the martyrdom of
Anne Askewe.[1] These excesses frightened Cranmer, and when
Thomas Dobb, a Cambridge graduate, was brought before him for
an outrageous interruption of the service of the mass at St Paul's
and a violent denunciation of the adoration of the Host, the Archbishop imprisoned him in the Compter where Dobb died before
Somerset's pardon could reach him.[2] But at the same time mild
pressure was also maintained on intransigent conservatism, for in
May Dr Richard Smith, the Regius Professor of Divinity at Oxford,
who, had his character been firmer, might have been the foremost
defender of Catholicism in this period, recanted publicly at Paul's
Cross, denouncing his own former writings and teachings. And just
a month later a clergyman named Peren recanted at St Andrew
Undershaft, where a few weeks earlier he had maintained from the
pulpit that it 'was good to worship the pictures of God and of
saints'.[3]

So strong was the spirit of iconoclasm in London during these
early months that one is led to wonder how the Council and Cranmer restrained it as successfully as they did. Some of it was the work
of 'hot gospellers' acting on their own initiative; more, it seems
certain, was by the agreement of churchwardens in parishes now
fairly solidly Protestant. Of the first sort, surely, was Underhill,
aspects of whose career have already been noted,[4] who proudly
confessed that he was known as a 'hoote gospeller' in his parish at
Stratford-on-the-Bow (Stepney). He tells us that he had personally
taken the pix off the altar in the presence of the curate and a popish
magistrate, an action which so outraged the magistrate's wife and
other women of the parish that Underhill declared they sought to
murder him.[5]

In early September, 1547, the imperial ambassador wrote that
images were then being removed from churches all over London, so
completely, indeed, that 'they will not even leave room for them in
the glass'. In many churches, too, some of the lessons in the matin
service had been suppressed and the reading of scriptural lessons
substituted. None the less, mass was still being celebrated, though
no longer for the dead, and the 'Holy Sacrament is held in all

---

[1] *Vide ante*, 27, 30. [2] I follow Ridley, *Cranmer*, 264.
[3] Stow, *Annales*, 594, for both episodes. [4] *Vide ante*, 143–144.
[5] Nichols, *Narratives of the Reformation* (Camden Soc., LXXVII), 159. In fear,
Underhill says, he left the district, taking a 'little house in a secret corner' in London
(*ibid.* 161).

reverence, and the Confession is observed'. It was his judgement, indeed, that the course of reform was being restrained by the government, not moving as rapidly as popular opinion demanded, particularly in London where the populace were much attached to sects and 'clamour for novelties of all sorts'.[1] The report is substantially accurate, for it was in September that wholesale inconoclasm erupted throughout London, surely with the approval of both the clergy and the churchwardens.[2] Again, popular opinion was in advance of governmental policy, for St John wrote for the Council on September 18th, admonishing the Lord Mayor that all images and paintings to which no offerings or prayers were addressed should 'stand still for garnishing of the churches' and should be restored in the event they had been removed without the express command of the priest. A few days later (September 22nd) it was resolved that every alderman should make a secret check of the churches in his ward, accompanied by the parson and two or three responsible parishioners, to make a list of images which had been removed and to note misdemeanors which had occurred in taking them down. But the harassed Council just four days later in effect withdrew its cautious opposition, it now being felt that to force a restoration of images would arouse contention among the people, and determined to delay any further consideration of the problem until Somerset had returned from Scotland.[3] Then, less than two months later, the Council capitulated, determining to remove all remaining images in London churches, though the order to take them down in the realm at large was not given until February, 1548.[4] When on November 17, 1547, the great rood at St Paul's, with all the images, was pulled down at night, two of the workmen were killed and others badly injured, thus sadly closing this whole troublesome episode in which, certainly, Protestant sentiment in London ranged far ahead of the thinking and policy of the Council.

The mood for change and reform was strong, seeming to spring from widespread urban sentiment. In part there was sincere and powerful religious conviction undergirding these largely symbolic actions. But in part, too, there is evidence of turbulence and rowdyism. This the troubled Council understood, observing on November 12, 1547, that there had been many disorders amongst serving-men 'and other young and light persons and apprentices of London' towards priests and those wearing scholars' gowns that resembled

---

[1] *Cal. S.P. Span.* IX, 148: Van der Delft to Queen Dowager, Sept. 6, 1547.
[2] VCH, *London*, I, 289; *Grey Friars Chronicle* (Camden Soc., LIII), 54.
[3] *A.P.C.* II, App., 518: Sept. 26, 1547.   [4] VCH, *London*, I, 289.

the priestly habits. Great offence and scandal had been occasioned which could no longer be tolerated, it being commanded that no such persons should hereafter use 'such insolence and evil demeanour towards priests, as reviling, tossing of them, taking violently their caps and tippets from them' under pain of imprisonment or corporal punishment.[1] This is one of those revealing commentaries on events, coming all too rarely to the hands of the historian, and it most convincingly suggests an almost dangerous unrest which the Council could hardly effectively repress without suppressing the spread of Protestant sentiment.

The evidence for strong and aggressive Protestant conviction, running ahead of governmental policy, is sparser when we move out of London to the provinces. It would seem clear, too, that there radical Protestant strength was concentrated in the towns and cities except where it enjoyed the support of powerful lay figures in the countryside. One of the most important of these last certainly was that remarkable woman Katherine Willoughby, the second wife and, while still a very young woman, the widow of the Duke of Suffolk. The Duke died a moderate Catholic, his will specifying the customary masses, but there is persuasive evidence that the Duchess had for some time past been an ardent Protestant. Following the death of Henry VIII Katherine Willoughby (Brandon) retired to her great house at Grimsthorpe, Lincolnshire, where she assumed an active role in advancing the cause of reform, for some time entertaining the great Latimer in her household while he preached some of his most famous sermons at Grimsthorpe. Her two handsome and precocious sons were given a rigorously humanistic as well as a soundly Protestant education by Thomas Wilson, author of the *Art of Rhetoric*, and a friend to Cheke and Ascham, before the boys were placed in St John's College, Cambridge, in the autumn of 1549.[2] A highly intelligent, witty, and earthy woman, the Duchess wielded great influence in Lincolnshire and East Anglia, always directed towards the advancement of Protestantism, though she could hardly have been responsible for a particularly sacrilegious assault on the symbols of the ancient faith which occurred at St Ives in May, 1549.[3] Radical Protestant sentiment was, it seems evident, already deeply rooted in East Anglia, for at St Neots, in the

---

[1] Harl. MS. 352, f. 47ᵛ; Hughes and Larkin, *Tudor proclamations*, I, 407–408.
[2] Strype, *Memorials*, II, i, 202; Goff, Lady Cecilie, *A woman of the Tudor age* (L., [1930]), 181–182. Her rambling but always pungent and revealing letters to her close friend William Cecil enliven the state papers of the period.
[3] S.P. Dom., Edw. VI, VII, 21.

autumn of 1547, numerous parishioners had on their own authority removed 'images of abuse' from the church and then resisted the command of nearby gentlemen to restore them. A tumult followed which was settled on behalf of the parishioners by the Lord Protector himself as he passed through the town on his victorious return from Scotland, the full weight of the Privy Council being required to force the conservative gentry of the region to accept the action of the parishioners.[1]

In Essex, too, with strong and radical centres of Protestant strength even during the reign of Henry VIII, both sentiment and action were far out-running the policy of cautious reformation being administered by the Council. Throughout 1547 images were being broken or removed in numerous parishes, stained glass was being taken out and interiors whitewashed, many months before the general visitation of the diocese in the autumn of 1547. Also, even farther ahead of governmental policy, church ornaments were being sold with parish consent, in Dovercourt and Dedham, apparently somewhat before the late King's death. A rash of parochial expropriations and sales swept the county, ranging downwards from nearly £100 in Saffron Walden, where the money was used for the support of the free school, care of the poor, and other charitable uses, to £1 9s 2d received at Great Warley and dedicated to the repair of the fabric. These premature sales, inspired at once by strong Protestant views and by an informed guess that an expropriation of church goods might become governmental policy in the near future, produced heavy and general sales across Essex, the proceeds being used for church repairs, roads, the care of soldiers, and the sustenance of the poor.[2] In most instances when appeals were taken to the Privy Council, the government was disposed to support as yet illegal removal of images and other iconoclastic actions, in one case at least causing a protesting Catholic parishioner in Buckinghamshire, who had spoken and acted 'inconveniently', to be imprisoned for a short period in the Fleet and given his discharge only on condition that he openly acknowledge his fault in his native parish.[3]

One of these instances of iconoclasm, at Portsmouth, occurred in the Diocese of Winchester, involving the thorny and wholly

[1] *A.P.C.* II, 140–141: Oct. 23, 1547.
[2] VCH, *Essex*, II, 26–27. The situation in Essex was so out of hand that in 1548 the Council ordered Bishop Bonner to prepare a list of the churches where sales and possible embezzlements had occurred (S.P. Dom., Edw. VI, V, 19).
[3] *A.P.C.* II, 147: Nov. 29, 1547.

courageous Gardiner, who sought to create from the episode a protest against the whole direction of the government's religious policy.
As early as February, 1547, Gardiner had written to Ridley denouncing the latter's wholesale condemnation of images in a sermon before
the Court. Images are of great antiquity, and to maintain, as Ridley
had, that, because 'idolum' once meant images, all images were
idols, was without foundation. At the very least images may be
borne with, just as in many Lutheran churches in Germany, where
Gardiner had observed that they still stood without offence. Nor
could he believe that even the simplest laymen were confused or
spiritually misled by the veneration of images, which he declared to
be a useful aid to true worship.[1] He suggested, indeed, that the
doctrinal and legal position of the Church of England on the matter
was admirably set out in the *King's Book*, with which he declared
he 'was not privy . . . till it was done'.

A few weeks later events played again into Gardiner's hands when
images were broken in Portsmouth churches. He wrote immediately to the mayor and to Captain Vaughan, commander of the
military base there, demanding to know the facts, to have an estimate of the religious temper of the town, and enquiring whether it
would be useful for him to preach in Portsmouth on the next
Sunday, though 'to a multitude persuaded in that opinion of destruction of images, I would never preach'. For this would be truly
casting pearls before swine, such people being Lollards. In this
letter, evidently designed for the eye of Somerset rather than for the
simple Captain Vaughan, Gardiner continued that image-breaking
was a conspiracy to subvert the state and an assault on true religion,
for to destroy images, pictures, and monuments would be to deprive
the unlettered of a fruitful means of instruction. If Vaughan thought
good would be done by preaching, he would so do his duty; otherwise the matter was of such gravity that he must lay it before the
Lord Protector.[2] And the matter was speedily laid before Somerset
and the Council, the Lord Protector refusing to take the incident
seriously or to engage the bishop in theological controversy.

Somerset's cool Protestantism and his evident unwillingness to
join the issue provoked from Gardiner a careful protest against the
further toleration of the evidences of radical Protestant sentiment
which we have been examining. In a letter dated May 21, 1547, he
complained bitterly because Lutheran books were being freely

[1] *Gardiner letters*, 256–257.
[2] *Ibid.* 273–276: May 3, 1547; Strype, *Memorials*, II, i, 53–54; Burnet, *Reformation*, II, 49.

imported and because Bale's eloquent extolling of the virtues of
Anne Askewe, as Gardiner shrewdly sensed, had sought to elevate
a certainly heretical woman to a kind of Protestant sainthood. He
was troubled too by the popular ballads attacking the fundamentals
of the Catholic faith and by the general attitude of contempt towards
the customary Lenten observances. And, in concluding, he warned
Somerset that the principal danger to his own position and policy,
and, for that matter, to England, lay in unbridled religious innovations.[1]

One further, and most revealing, evidence of widespread and
militant Protestant sentiment, running far ahead of governmental
policy and of Somerset's disposition at the least to tolerate such
extreme views, is supplied by the autobiography of Thomas Hancock, a graduate of Oxford, who had been suspended from his
living at Amport, Hampshire, on charges of Zwinglian heresies
under the Six Articles Act.[2] During Edward's first regnal year
Hancock was an effective but violent preacher against the mass,
also being given to interrupting orthodox services to inveigh against
transubstantiation. Such an episode at Salisbury resulted in a
hearing before the mayor when Hancock was bound over to the
assize; bond was provided, significantly, by a woollen dyer, who
boasted that 'a hundred of them would be bound in an hundred
pounds for me'. The impetuous and zealous Hancock rode at once
to Syon where he gained an audience with the easily accessible
Somerset, who released him from his bond. Shortly afterwards,
however, Somerset forbad Hancock to preach at Southampton, in
Gardiner's diocese, since it 'was a haven town, and . . . if I should
teach such doctrine as I taught at Sarum the town would be divided, and so should it be a way or a gap for the enemy to enter in'.
Hancock was as stubborn as he was arrogant, but yielded and,
instead, attended divine services there, at which Somerset was also
present and, on Hancock's testimony, upbraided the priest who 'did
suffer the images in the church, the idol hanging in a string over the
altar, candlesticks and tapers on them upon the altar, and the people
honoring the idol, contrary to law'.[3]

Later in 1547 Hancock gained the living at Poole, a parish in
which there was already militant Protestant sentiment. In an early

[1] *Gardiner letters*, 277–283; Foxe, *Acts and monuments*, VI, 30–34.
[2] Nichols, *Narratives of the Reformation* (Camden Soc., LXXVII), 71–84. The
manuscript (Harl. MS. 425, #29, ff. 124–130) has been examined but adds nothing to
Nichols' excellent rendering.
[3] *Ibid.*, 75–76.

sermon there he preached strongly against transubstantiation, whereupon a rich merchant with a former mayor of the town walked out, denouncing Hancock for teaching a devilish doctrine. Shortly afterwards these two worthies, accompanied by still another former mayor, requested Hancock to say a dirge on All Souls Day, which he flatly declined to do. Consequently there was an unseemly disturbance at the service on that day when 'did they all as it were with one mouth call me knave and my wife strumpet, some of them threatening me that they would make me draw my guts after me'. The then mayor intervened by pulling Hancock into the choir, then commanding those present to keep the peace and dismissing the congregation forthwith.[1] Once more the persistent and tiresome Hancock appealed for protection to Somerset, who this time referred the matter to Cecil, who contented himself with demanding peace and quiet in the parish.

We have been concerned with the evidences of early and militant Protestant sentiment, possibly emphasizing too heavily the violent and sometimes almost bizarre insistence of an already strongly rooted minority that the reformation of Christ's Church proceed at once with a thorough cleansing of an official doctrine and liturgy which were in the essentials Catholic. Many of the instances cited were connected with the threat of a turbulence so severe or with actions so flagrantly illegal that they have found their way into the official records of a government beleaguered from both the left and the right. But more important, and in the end more powerful, was the quiet conviction of many thousands of Englishmen, especially those with urban backgrounds, who in their own way and with a prudent circumspection had embraced Protestant teaching during the time of danger when 'the King that dead is' had held his imperious sway. One of these instances is the remarkable narrative, supposedly written in 1620 in her eighty-fifth year, by Mrs Rose Throckmorton. She was first the wife of Anthony Hickman, a rich London mercer, who had entertained Henry VIII in his house, was knighted, and held office as sheriff. Rose records the memory of her father's stories of buying Protestant books for Queen Anne Boleyn on his journeys overseas, while her mother had early been converted to Protestantism by English books imported from abroad by her husband's factors. Hickman traded with his wife's elder brother as a partner, venturing on several voyages and building for their service the famous *Mary Rose*, named for Mrs Hickman and her brother's

[1] Nichols, *Narratives of the Reformation* (Camden Soc., LXXVII), 78. There is also a full and fairly accurate account in Strype, *Memorials*, II, i, 114–117.

wife. It is perfectly clear that her own and her husband's family were staunchly but discreetly Protestant in the late years of Henry's reign, while under Edward they gave 'entertainment to Bishop Hooper, Mr Foxe, Mr Knox, and divers other godly preachers'.[1] These families—and there were many like them—remained quiet but steadfast Protestants in the evil days of Queen Mary, holding informal services in their own houses, until forced to flee abroad as the severity of the Marian policy began to take its dreadful toll. It was amongst this quieter sort, in London and across the whole of the realm, that Protestantism was taking ineradicable root in the first year of Edward's reign.

[1] The narrative is printed in Stark, Adam, *The history and antiquities of Gainsburgh*, *etc.* (2nd ed., L., 1843), 452–458; the original manuscript is now in Add. MS. 43,827A, and a copy with variations in Add. MS. 43,827B (*Brit. Mus. Quarterly*, IX (1934–1935), 74–76).

V

THE COURSE OF MODERATE REFORM
BY PREROGATIVE ACTION (1547-1548)

I. THE CAUTION OF THE EARLY MONTHS AND THE
DIALOGUE WITH GARDINER

As we have already suggested, the government proceeded with
great circumspection and moderation during the early months of
the new regime. Parliament was not to meet for eight months, but
the Protector and Council possessed sufficient power under the
prerogative and, more particularly, under the Act of Supremacy to
effect any reformation which they wished, short of a transformation
of the doctrine of the church or of its constitutional structure. But
this great aggregate of power was in fact to be used most modestly
for almost two years, during which time no more than piecemeal
reforms were introduced, though it is important to observe that
every change was in the direction of Protestantism. The new temper
of policy was, however, amply demonstrated by the fact that all the
Lenten preachers were Protestants—Bishop Barlow, then of St
David's, a known and ardent Protestant since at least 1535, giving
particular offence to the conservative clergy by his stern summons to
a thorough cleansing of the church.

The conservative party on the whole stood mute during these
early and decisive months, entrusting its whole case to the skilful
advocacy of Bishop Gardiner, who enjoyed the friendship of the
Protector and who was wanting neither in courage nor in ingenuity.
We have already noted his interventions on specific matters of
sacrilege on occasions when Protestants had given offence not only
to him but to the government and to moderate Protestants as well.
He sought, in fact, to find some measure of common ground and to
bring restraining pressure to bear on the Protector and on as many
of the bishops as possible. In his mild controversy with Ridley in
February, 1547, he had frankly admitted that 'there has been
between you and me no familiarity, but, contrariwise, a little disagreement (which I did not hide from you)'. But he none the less

wrote personally in order clearly to present his views and to further
the cause of unity.[1]

Gardiner professed himself to be greatly troubled by Barlow's
sermon, protesting directly to Somerset that the innovations urged
by the Lenten preacher would 'disorder this realm' in a time when
unity was required. If Barlow or others have 'any new platform',
he would wish that during Edward's minority they would be content to study and prepare their proposals, but not to upset both
church and state by radical change. He declared it the Protector's
duty to hand on to the King in due season religion, laws, lands, and
decrees as he found them, thereby preserving unity and avoiding
partisan dissension. He likewise ventured to counsel Somerset to
preserve peace: 'any peace, whatsoever it were', including the
abandonment of the war which Henry had meant to launch against
the Scots; 'for a time let Scots be Scots'. In a vein invoking the
nostalgia of an old friendship, he wished he might commune with
Somerset as he had in earlier days when they were together in
Brussels, 'devising of the world at large'.[2] One cannot fail to admire
the great skill of this man or to be persuaded by his candour and
good sense in this early effort to gain back some measure of influence in the affairs of state. Gardiner had much to offer, particularly in the realm of foreign policy, but one sees why Henry
VIII thought he would devour his colleagues were he entrusted with
power during Edward's minority.

Gardiner also pleaded with Paget, with whom he had once been
very close, that his voice might be heard. He is called a persecutor,
which Paget knows he never was, and he knows that his own
position is as perilous as it is weak.[3] Some months later, in one of
the last of the letters to Somerset that is personal in tone, he reviewed
the whole range of issues that troubled him. He protested the
shifting of the service into the English tongue, formed not more
than two centuries before and still immature, when Latin and Greek
had served religion well for the past 1500 years. The government's
toleration of image-breaking he regarded as at once sacrilegious and
conducive to civil disorder. He insisted again that the *status quo*
should simply be maintained during the King's minority. Law, he
seems to say, is a better guide for the state than the counsels of
those who prate of the clear commandment of Scripture in matters
of worship and ceremony. Any other policy would serve only to
subject the realm to alterations in religion with each change of its

[1] *Gardiner letters*, 262.   [2] *Ibid.* 265–267: Feb. 28, 1547.
[3] *Ibid.* 270–271: Mar. 1, 1547.

governors. Nor does he like the wavering of Catholic spokesmen, such as Dr Smith, for 'I neither liked his tractation of unwritten verities, nor yet his retraction'. He pleaded, in brief, for a period of stability and quiet in England, for the preaching of religion as it was defined in the *King's Book*, lest both church and state be caught up in a maelstrom of change. And he assured Somerset of his loyalty and obedience, for 'I am even as well learned to live in the place of obedience as I was in the place of direction in our late sovereign Lord's life'.[1]

These views command some measure of respect, and they proceed quite as much from long experience in the affairs of state as from the Catholicism in doctrine and usage which the Bishop of Winchester found himself belatedly defending. His central argument, adopted by Bonner, Tunstall, and probably by Thirlby as well, was that since the King was personally the undoubted supreme head of the church this authority was in abeyance during his minority. He therefore urged that a kind of 'stand-still' position be taken in religion as well as in foreign policy. This not very impressive theoretical argument was undercut by the fact that Gardiner and all his episcopal colleagues had in fact been obliged to accept new licences from the sovereign at the outset of the reign; their own jurisdiction was consequently linked with the plenary competence of the civil power. In Pollard's astute phrase, 'It was impossible to set up a distinction between the Supreme Head's power to confer ecclesiastical jurisdiction and his power to effect ecclesiastical changes: if the one could be exercised in his minority, so could the other'.[2] In a much broader sense, there was no constitutional or legal precedent for holding that the regal power was in any wise diminished during the minority of a king. Any other view would have resulted in political and legal anarchy. This, of course, Gardiner fully understood, and it must not be forgotten that his own brilliant treatise made an important contribution to the whole doctrine of the royal supremacy. He had left himself very little room for manoeuvre, but such room as he had he exploited with great skill and ingenuity. We may be sure that he realized full well that the moment of his own defeat would be at hand when the Council or a statute of the new government required from him obedience and conformity under the vast authority imposed by the Act of Supremacy.

[1] *Gardiner letters*, 287–295: June 6, 1547.
[2] Pollard, *Cranmer*, 191.

2. THE BEGINNINGS OF CHANGE (1547)

But even as Gardiner wrote, the process of gradual change was under way, prompted by the spiritual policy unfolding in Cranmer's mind and by the pressure of Protestant sentiment now strongly reflected in the Council. In the spring of 1547 all episcopal authority was suspended until a general royal visitation could be arranged, which was to occur in the autumn just prior to the convention of Parliament. Under authority of injunctions promulgated in July, to which we shall recur, important, though cautious, actions were taken when Erasmus' *Paraphrases* and Cranmer's *Book of Homilies* were ordered set up in all parish churches in the realm.

The work of completing and translating Erasmus' *Paraphrases* was already well under way under the general direction of Nicholas Udall, though the *Preface* makes it clear that only the translation of Luke was specifically from his hand. The translation of Mark was done by Thomas Key of Oxford, while the essentially conservative character of the whole text is suggested by the fact that on the urging of Catherine Parr the Princess Mary had well advanced the rendering of the Gospel according to St John, though it was completed by Dr Mallett. The Gospels were not completed until 1548, when they were published as the first volume of the whole work; the second, published in 1549, was also the work of several hands, including Coverdale, who signed the dedicatory preface to the King.[1] Cranmer had sought to associate Gardiner with this venture, as well as with the preparation of the *Homilies*, but the suspicious and stubborn bishop instead bitterly attacked the *Paraphrases* as full of errors, ignorantly translated, and in any event representative of Erasmus' thought long before his final views were formed. Further, he protested that placing the work in every church would lay a financial charge of at least £20,000 on the realm. Gardiner, now in the Fleet, refused to yield even when brought before the Council, where he added a final objection that the work was being issued in the name of the King who knew nothing of it and pointed out that Somerset, only then returned from Scotland, could not possibly have had leisure for its study.[2] None the less, the work was put in hand, and it is safe to say that by late 1551 most parish churches across the realm possessed and used copies of this beautiful book.

---

[1] We here principally follow McConica, *English humanists*, 240–245.

[2] Strype, *Cranmer*, I, 215–217; Dixon, R. W., *History of the Church of England from the abolition of the Roman jurisdiction* (6 vols., L., 1878–1902), II, 424.

More directly important was the *Book of Homilies*, a collection of twelve sermons on key topics and doctrines, designed to be read in order each Sunday by a non-preaching clergy and hence to be regarded as the most effective of all instruments available for the teaching of the people. This work was largely from Cranmer's own hand and its preparation commanded his complete attention for several months. He endeavoured vainly to secure the approval of the conservative group of bishops by seeking Gardiner's endorsement of the text. Gardiner rejected the *Homilies* before he had even seen them, on the unimpressive ground that their publication was unnecessary because of the recent issue of the *King's Book* (1543) and because no changes of moment should be made in church during the King's minority.[1]

It must be borne in mind that in the preparation and promulgation of this work Cranmer for the first time in his life had a free hand, the doctrinal position subsumed in the work being exactly as he wished it in mid-1547. These sermons lend little support to the entire sacramental system, there being no mention at all of the mass and only by inference to baptism. The first section includes a moving statement regarding the authority of the Word of God and the absolute necessity that our faith be founded on it. It is not enough that we listen to the reading of the Bible; we must read it ourselves, even if we be not learned, for God has made His revealed truth clear for our guidance. 'The Scripture is full, as well of low valleys, plain ways, and easy for every man to use and to walk in, as also of high hills and mountains, which few men can ascend unto.'[2] The whole work is simple, is drafted in memorable prose, and successfully seeks a moderate and uncontroversial tone. There are three sermons which together develop a clearly Protestant teaching on the doctrine of justification, and these may fairly certainly be attributed to Cranmer himself. He cites Hilary and Ambrose in support of his statement that 'he which believeth in Christ should be saved without works, by faith only', while stressing the point that good works flow naturally and inevitably from a lively faith. The doctrine here taught was Protestant, and these

---

[1] Ridley, *Cranmer*, 265–266. This work of Cranmer was by no means precipitate, for it had been begun as early as 1539 (*L. & P., Henry VIII*, XIV, i, 466), and certain of the sermons had been laid before Convocation in 1543, though no action had been taken.

[2] *Certayne sermons, or homilies, appoynted by the Kynges Maiestie, to bee declared and redde, etc.* (L., July 31, 1547), B iii (STC #13639). A fairly extensive collation with the numerous later Edwardian homilies suggests that the text remained almost unaltered during the entire reign, save for unimportant differences in the prefatory matter.

sermons, and the others as well, bring the whole Roman Catholic system of worship under direct attack: 'an attack not (this time) on particular abuses in institutions and practices, but upon the institutions and practices as such—which are now condemned . . . irreformable therefore, and to be destroyed utterly, once and for all.'[1] The tone of the whole work can only be described as stalwartly Protestant. But it is not shrill, and it is magnanimous. Cranmer was no zealot and he was troubled by the controversies already dividing men in England. Accordingly, in the closing sermon on contentions he sought to damp down fanaticism and hot controversy. 'If we be good and quiet Christian men, let it appear in our speech and tongues. If we have forsaken the devil, let us use no more devilish tongues. He that hath been a railing scolder, now let him be a sober counselor.'[2]

Despite the beauty and dignity of style which mark the *Homilies* and the moderation of its tone, it must be concluded that it was undeniably Protestant. Such apparatus of worship as beads, girdles, relics, holy bread and water, palms and candles is denounced as superstitious or papistical, though they were not legally repressed for some six months more.[3] It is scarcely to be wondered, then, that Gardiner placed himself in implacable opposition to the *Homilies*, even though Tunstall found them acceptable. But Gardiner had not done Cranmer the courtesy of reading the text before his rolling denunciation began. Gardiner's appeal was to Somerset, on the ground that Cranmer was giving effect to homilies discussed in Convocation in 1542 but never authorized, and that the Archbishop proposed to set in train a process of change which he could not control.[4] A few days later he wrote at great length to Cranmer, accusing him of now repudiating the *King's Book* which he had accepted and enforced in the late years of Henry's life. The proposed work enjoys no statutory sanction, but more important it will be divisive and raise contention during the minority of the King, when every effort should be made to restrain conflict. He insisted, too, that Cranmer was opening the bulwarks of orthodoxy and order to forces which he and no one else could restrain once they were loosed. There is in this remarkable and revealing letter an engaging sophistication and scepticism, which was always deep in Gardiner's thought. The generality of men, he says, are led to the good life by simple imitation; they really have no idea what a

---

[1] Hughes, Philip, *The Reformation in England*, II (N.Y., 1954), 99.
[2] *Certayne sermons, or homilies*, Z iii.   [3] Ridley, *Cranmer*, 267.
[4] *Gardiner letters*, 296–297: June 10, 1547; *ibid*. 297–298 (shortly after June 12, 1547).

preacher has said in a sermon, which they invariably report to have been good, very good, or 'wondrous good'. Still another sort think they have knowledge far beyond their understanding and become completely and invincibly confused. And there is a third group who 'will not be troubled . . . till learned men agree better'. Of such men most of the realm is composed, and they 'will as patiently suffer' the eight years of the King's minority as they had the past eight years. There may well be faults and imperfections in the church as it is constituted, but these he would bear with in the youth of the King. Hence he would not have homilies read; he would give no encouragement to preachers; in any event, 'it is contrary to the inclination of us Englishmen to be long in the state of hearers'.[1]

These urbane and subtly persuasive arguments of the Bishop of Winchester were without effect, for the *Homilies* were published on July 31st and the *Injunctions* of 1547 ordered all preachers in the realm to read a sermon each Sunday and charged the bishops to enforce the policy. Gardiner now faced the first crisis of his opposition, for he was now confronted with the Act of Supremacy and with the reality of sovereign power. In two letters addressed to the Council he first argued that the *Homilies* were heretical in their teachings on justification and that a doctrinal statement of this importance could not be issued without the approval of Convocation.[2] The second argument was narrowly, and speciously, legal. Gardiner now maintained that the injunctions themselves were illegal since they contravened statutes as yet unrepealed by Parliament and that to obey them would lay him open to the charge of *praemunire*. He could not believe that the King, the Parliament, and the bishops were all deluded in that legal statement of faith which was the *King's Book*, and he angrily declined to order the reading of the *Homilies*.[3] The confrontation with this powerful and irascible man, which both Cranmer and Somerset had patiently sought to avoid, was now at hand.

The *Injunctions*, dated July 31, 1547, against which Gardiner protested so vehemently, were not of themselves in any way radical.

---

[1] *Gardiner letters*, 299–316 (shortly after June 12, 1547). Gardiner restated this argument, again at great length, in still another letter to Cranmer written shortly after July 1, 1547 (*ibid*. 318–359, from Add. MSS. 29, 546, ff. 9–24).

[2] *Gardiner letters*, 361–368 (shortly before Aug. 30, 1547).

[3] *Ibid*. 369–373: Aug. 30, 1547. More specifically, his formal refusal was addressed to Sir John Mason, one of those commissioned to visit the diocese. He declared the *Homilies* and the *Injunctions* to be contrary to unrepealed law (34 and 35 Henry VIII, c. 1), to which he appealed, and he would accordingly seek to prevent the carrying out of the injunctions by the clergy of his diocese (*ibid*. 373–375).

6

They followed closely those of 1536 and 1538, set out in the Crom-
wellian era, and were in the main concerned with the reformation
of church ceremonies rather than with doctrine. All relics of superstition were to be denounced, all images were to be destroyed, and
no torches or candles to be displayed before pictures or images.
The number of candles on the high altar on the occasion of the mass
was to be strictly limited to two. The section ordering the celebration of the Holy Eucharist was extremely cautious and conservative,
the mass being declared 'of the very body and blood of Christ'.[1]
But at the same time each parish should remove and destroy all
shrines, candles, wax, and other symbols of idolatry and superstition, and provide a 'comely and honest pulpit . . . for the preaching of God's Word'.[2] The only innovations ordered in the conduct
of divine service were to forbid all processions around the churchyard or the church when mass was celebrated, to require the priest
and congregation to kneel in the midst of the church for its reception, and to order the rendering of the litany in English. It was
further provided that every parish must within three months
possess the whole Bible in English and within a year must own
Erasmus' *Paraphrases*, which were to be freely available to the
laity, while the clergy must exhort their flocks to read and ponder
these works, 'the special food of man's soul'.[3] And, finally, it was
required that a sermon be preached each quarter, and when there
was no sermon the priest must recite the Lord's Prayer, the Creed,
and the Ten Commandments in English. On each Sunday, too, a
chapter of the New Testament was to be read at morning service
and of the Old at evensong.

Careful and moderate as the *Injunctions* were, there was in their
very texture a pervading Protestant temper, just as there was within
them an impetus which would almost predictably lead to more
substantial innovations, particularly when the realm-wide reading
of the *Homilies* began to have its full effect. There was also a very
explicit morality expressed in the stern admonition to parents to
bring up their children and servants 'either to learning or to some
honest exercise, occupation, or husbandry', in order to equip youth
with required competences. It was declared that there was now too
much idleness and poverty, which might be directly blamed on the
failure of parents to afford to children the tuition which would

---

[1] *Iniunccions geuen by the most excellent prince, Edward the sixte . . . to all and singular
his lovying subiectes, etc.* (L., 1547), #24. Also to be found in Cardwell, Edward, *Documentary annals of the reformed Church of England, etc.* (2 vols., Oxford, 1844), I, 4–31.
[2] *Ibid.* 17 (#28).   [3] *Ibid.* 9 (#7).

'have profited as well themselves, as divers other persons, to the great commodity and ornament of the commonwealth'.[1]

Injunctions were at the same time given to the cathedral churches which differentiated their worship and responsibilities in only a few important particulars. Within a year each cathedral church was to assemble a working patristic library, including the writings of such fathers as Augustine, Basil, Gregory, Jerome, Ambrose, Chrysostom, Cyprian, and, interestingly, Erasmus. Each cathedral was also to provide for the clergy and the laity at least four English Bibles in the large format. The duty of the cathedral chapters towards learning was further emphasized by the fiat that cathedral churches having no free grammar schools were to found them and to maintain them as a charge on the revenues of the chapter—the master to have 20 marks p.a. and his house, and the usher £6 13s 4d p.a. and his chamber.[2]

Even more forthright was the opposition offered somewhat later by Bishop Bonner (London) to the new religious policy now unfolding. When the visitors presented themselves at St Paul's, Bonner demanded to see their commission and, when handed the *Injunctions* and the *Homilies*, received them with the protestation that 'I will observe them, if they be not contrary and repugnant to God's law and the statutes and ordinances of the Church'. He was forthwith haled before the outraged Privy Council where he was obliged to make the unequivocal and formal renunciation of his protestation and in addition on September 18th was committed to the Fleet for two months. This done, the new order of service was introduced at St Paul's and a little later the clearing out of the images in the great church, then literally filled with chapels, altars, and monuments, was undertaken. Before the reign was done both Gardiner and Bonner were to suffer much for their courage and their convictions, but theirs was to be a tempered punishment never really designed to break their wills. In assessing the moderation of ecclesiastical policy in the reign of Edward VI, it must be remembered that both these men might well have lost their heads under Henry VIII and, had they been as obdurately Protestant, would have been burned under Mary Tudor.

The general visitation of the church (1547), which was to order the enforcement of the actions already taken with the *Injunctions*,

[1] Cardwell, *Documentary annals*, I, 7–8 (#5).
[2] *Injunctions given by ... Edward the Sixth ... in every cathedral church*, etc. (L., 1547). We have used the text printed in Frere, W. H., *Visitation articles and injunctions of the period of the Reformation* (3 vols., L., 1910), II, 135–139.

the systematic reading of the *Paraphrases* and of the *Book of Homilies*, and the imposition by prerogative power of certain other minor reforms, was carefully planned and executed. The realm was divided into six circuits, each containing from four to six dioceses, four to six commissioners being named for each circuit by Cranmer and the Privy Council. The commission for each circuit included a preacher and a registrar, but the complexion of the whole body of visitors was heavily secular and, in so far as we have been able to determine, all those appointed were staunchly Protestant or, as for example in the case of Sir John Mason and Sir James Hales, completely Erastian in their views.[1] The commissioners proceeded in each of the circuits by summoning the bishops and the cathedral clergy before them and requiring a formal renunciation of the Bishop of Rome and an unequivocal acknowledgment of the Royal Supremacy. The articles of inquiry were then read and the cathedral clergy were sworn to their performance, whereupon the *Injunctions* and the *Book of Homilies* were delivered into the hands of the bishop and archdeacon with the charge, under pain, of carrying them fully into execution amongst the clergy of the diocese.[2]

The *Articles* relating to the parochial clergy inquire whether the bishop lightly calls persons before him *ex officio*; whether he has personally preached in any of the parish churches of his diocese; and then more specifically whether each incumbent preached against the Bishop of Rome, whether images and shrines continued to be used superstitiously, and whether the articles of faith were regularly expounded in English. The commissioners further wished to know whether the clergy preached at all, and how frequently, and 'whether they have moved the people to read and hear the Scripture in English, and have not discouraged them from reading and hearing of the same'. An omen of future interest was suggested by a question asking specifically whether the chantry priests connected with parish churches lent aid to the clergyman in the conduct of the services and whether they in fact performed such deeds of charity as were required by the deeds of trust.[3]

The visitation, carefully and rather slowly conducted, was accepted by all the bishops and was enforced, save, as we have stressed, for the intransigent opposition of Gardiner and of Bonner, both of whom shortly found themselves in the Fleet. Both were

---

[1] Cotton MSS., Titus, B, ii, 45, f. 89: May 4, 1547; addressed to the Archbishop of York; Stowe MS. 153, f. 2, for appointments to the circuits.

[2] Strype, *Cranmer*, I, 210.

[3] *Articles to be enquired of*, in the *Kynges Maiesties visitacion* (L., [1547]), no pagin.; Frere, *Visitation articles*, II, 103–113.

bishops of populous and very important sees in which Protestantism was in fact already firmly rooted. For the moment the general visitation itself had replaced episcopal power, while by the time of its completion both these conservative champions had been suspended from their spiritual offices. The commissioners sat at St Paul's in September to reform the remaining superstitious practices there, while just a week later the litany was sung in English in the cathedral church, 'between the choir and the high altar, the singers kneeling half on the one side and half on the other side', and the epistle and gospel were read in English during the celebration of the high mass.[1] In Essex, also within Bonner's great diocese of London, the injunctions of the commissioners were carried out with a rapidity and zeal which betoken the sentiments of this probably the most Protestant rural county in the realm in 1547. In at least fifteen parishes the churchwardens were prompt in removing images and saints' pictures in the windows, the whitewashing of the church interiors, and, their accounts suggest, buying copies of the Bible and the *Paraphrases*.[2]

The care and thoroughness of the commissioners is suggested by other evidences in various sees. At Wells the visitors, having first forbidden the further wearing of black copes and other popish habits at Exeter, now commanded the cathedral clergy to abide by the same injunction. They were also to command all the churches in the diocese to give up the practice of church ales, to ring no more than one bell when a person was regarded as mortally ill, and to desist from what was declared to be the 'unmeasurable ringing' of bells at burials.[3] In Yorkshire, where a particularly careful visitation was conducted, the commissioners suggested, among other reforms, the joining of numerous parishes within the decaying City of York, to which a statutory approval was shortly lent.[4] One of the royal visitors to the Diocese of St David's was Robert Ferrar, who had been compelled to recant his Lutheran teachings as early as 1528 and who was in 1547 known as one of the most ardent of the Gospellers. So completely entrenched was the Catholic cathedral chapter in its control that reformation had been blocked at every turn. Ferrar undertook to break this control when he was appointed bishop in 1548 upon Barlow's translation to Bath and Wells. Ferrar alleged that the chapter had despoiled the diocese by the conversion

[1] Stow, *Annales*, 594.
[2] Oxley, James E., *The Reformation in Essex to the death of Mary* (Manchester, [1965]), 151–152.   [3] HMC, *Tenth report*, App. III: *Wells Cathedral MSS.*, 235.
[4] Add. MSS. 33,595, ff. 15, 17; *Statutes of the realm*, IV, i, 14–15.

to private use of property to the value of 500 marks. But his intransigent chapter defied him and then ruined him when it was discovered that the commission for a visitation of this diocese was improperly drawn, 'for it ran in the old popish form, and so the King's supremacy [was] not sufficiently acknowledged therein'. The case dragged on in the courts until Mary's accession when far more serious charges of heresy were brought against Ferrar, leading to his execution by burning in the next year.[1]

The measures thus far taken by prerogative power to secure the reformation of the church had been carefully restrained. All dealt with matters external to the doctrines of the church, with what were regarded as popish and superstitious survivals in the ritual and worship which misled simple men and simple priests, who improperly regarded them as part of the necessary fabric of belief in the administration of the sacraments. The great central doctrine of the mass remained wholly untouched by these modest reforms, and only in Cranmer's carefully composed exposition of the doctrine of justification in the *Homilies* had the course of doctrinal change been advanced. But what had been changed—and that dramatically and abruptly—were the comfortable habits of worship, the routines which had become engrained, and the powerful inertia of custom. And here there was real risk and an explosive danger to a government which was not yet surely seated.

In slow and ordered stages, then, Somerset had brought the Church of England well on the road towards Protestantism in its worship, if not in its doctrine, in the months intervening between his accession to power and the opening of Edward's first Parliament on November 4, 1547. These reformations, no one of which was in itself revolutionary in effect, were in their totality considerable, especially since all were weighted on the side of the reformed faith. These changes, moreover, had flowed out from the prerogative powers, as broadly defined by the Act of Supremacy and other of the Reformation statutes. They had been accomplished in a period when a remarkable atmosphere of free discussion, free preaching, and free writing afforded to the realm its first trial of religious toleration maintained and ordered by administrative policy. The time had now come to lay this policy before Parliament and to extend and deepen it by measures which the government wished to codify as statutory law as it took its next larger step in the transformation of the Church of England into a reformed church whose organic ties would be with Continental Protestantism.

[1] Strype, *Cranmer*, I, 262–263.

VI

REFORMATION IN CHURCH AND STATE: THE FIRST SESSION OF PARLIAMENT
(November 4, 1547–December 24, 1547)

I. THE MAJOR MEASURES, SPIRITUAL AND SECULAR

Parliament was convened for its first session on November 4, the King and the members first attending divine services at the Abbey Church, where Ridley preached and where for the first time the principal parts of the mass were sung in English.[1] After the service the members adjourned to the Parliament chamber in Westminster Palace for the formal opening at which both Houses were present, before the Commons took their places in their quarters in the chapter house of the Abbey Church—for it was not until after the expropriation of the chantries that St Stephen's Chapel, in Westminster Palace, was made available to the Lower House. During the joint session of both Houses, the King, 'sitting in person in the parliament chamber, with the Lords on both sides and the Commons standing beneath the bar, commanded the clerk of the Parliament to read the King's commission' (letters patent) by which, as we have already noted, the Lord Protector was assigned his special seat where he should 'sit alone, both in our presence and when we are absent, in the middle of the bench next on the right of our royal seat in our parliament chamber'.[2]

The sources for Edward's first Parliament are very meagre, being confined principally to the unofficial journals of the House of Lords, which begin in 1509, and of the House of Commons, which have their beginning with this Parliament. The Lords' Journal, in the main very incomplete during its first sixty years, is fortunately complete for the Edwardian period, though it is at once terse and uninformative.[3] The Commons' Journal is even briefer and less

---

[1] Wriothesley, *Chronicle*, I (Camden Soc., n.s. XI), 187; Stow, *Annales*, 594–595; Edward VI, *Chronicle*, 8.

[2] Add. MS. 5758, f. 37 (renumbered); S.P. Dom., Edw. VI, II, 20; *vide ante.*, 162. The first MS. cited is incomplete.

[3] Pollard, A. F., 'The authenticity of the "Lords' Journals" in the sixteenth century', *Trans. Royal Hist. Soc.*, ser. 3, VIII (1914), esp. 20–28.

instructive, being little more than a calendar of legislation considered, with no details of debates and few hints of procedure. Happily, we need be little concerned with comments on the details of procedure and the structure of the organization of the House of Commons, since Sir John Neale's classical study of the Elizabethan Commons reaches back at all critical points to embrace the Edwardian background.[1]

There are, however, reasonably full unofficial, often almost incidental, materials which tell us a great deal about this Parliament and the important legislation which it was to pass in its several sessions. It seems certain that Somerset stood in no fear of Parliament and that he had no wish to limit its debate or competence. Divisions occurred on more than half the bills introduced, and on several occasions members of the Privy Council itself voted against government bills without subsequent criticism or reprisal. In later sessions of this Parliament, but in the period of Somerset's hegemony, at least three bills which he wished passed were defeated in the Commons, again with no apparent fear of reprisal. Pollard has well pointed out that there seems to be no instance of the withholding of royal assent to any measure passed by Parliament under Somerset.[2] Further, the Protector took the view that really important matters relating to foreign policy should be referred to Parliament for ultimate approval, suggesting to Paget (July 4, 1549) that a proposed treaty with the Emperor must be so ratified.[3] We shall also notice that the great chantry legislation was passed only after vigorous opposition in both Houses, not gaining approval, indeed, until the measure was re-drafted and important concessions made to interested groups in the House of Commons.[4] Nor is there any evidence that Somerset and the Council sought to influence the election of members to this predictably important Parliament, save for a rather clumsy effort, renounced when opposition was encountered from the electors, to secure the return of Sir John Baker as a county member from Kent. Baker, a member of the Council and Chancellor of the Exchequer, who was to be Speaker of the House in this Parliament, instead found a seat from Huntingdonshire.[5]

Parliament seems, then, to have enjoyed relatively great freedom during this reign and, as we shall observe, debated and legislated across the whole spectrum of problems with which England was

---

[1] Neale, J. E., The Elizabethan House of Commons (L., [1949]).
[2] Pollard, Somerset, 73.
[3] Here too I follow Pollard (73–74), who cites Cal. S.P. For., Edw. VI, #180.
[4] In the second volume of this work.   [5] A.P.C. II, App., 516–519.

concerned at mid-century. Seven new boroughs were added by Somerset in 1547, of which five (Wigan, Liverpool, Peterborough, Retford, and Westminster) long since merited representation because of increasing population or commercial importance. Not so much can be said for the ten new boroughs created by Northumberland for the second Edwardian Parliament, which were chiefly in Cornwall and which were certainly chosen in the hope of securing a more compliant House. With the addition of Somerset's fourteen seats the total number for the House stood at something like 355, and at 375 at the end of the reign.[1] It is noteworthy that almost every Privy Councillor not a peer held a seat in the Commons, while a fair number of senior civil servants, an essential part of the governmental apparatus, were also returned. Unfortunately, the available lists of the returns of members for this first Parliament are incomplete, only 192 of the total number being fully or partially identifiable.[2] Hence any comparison with the last Henrician Parliament, the returns for which are also not complete, is exceedingly difficult. But in so far as comparisons can be made, it would seem that approximately 60 per cent of the members were new to Parliament, which is not very far off the Tudor norm. If an even more hazardous estimate may be ventured, it is certain that of the 192 names available, fifty-seven were drawn from the upper gentry and about twenty-six from the lower gentry, but this analysis seriously distorts the true composition since we have ventured no identification at all of ninety-two of the members, a very large proportion of whom were certainly of the gentry. Eight of the members were certainly lawyers, seven were London or provincial merchants, while one is listed as an inn-keeper and another as a yeoman.[3] A study of the proceedings suggests that Rich, having been named Lord Chancellor only a few days before the session opened, was the principal government spokesman in the Lords. He guided some of the most important governmental measures through Parliament, working amongst others on the great repealer, on the bill for the decay of houses and tillage and the bill providing the sacrament in both kinds.[4] In the Lower House several of the Council were active in the presentation of bills, in service on committees, and doubtless in the guiding of debate. But of these Cecil and Petre were almost

---

[1] Neale, *Elizabethan House of Commons*, 140.

[2] HMC, *Salisbury MSS*. I, 51; 'Members of Parliament. Part I: Parliaments of England, 1213–1702', in *Parl. Papers*, 1878, LXII, 375–377.

[3] Any mature or helpful discussion of the social composition of the Edwardian Parliaments must await Professor Bindoff's volume in the *History of Parliament* series.

[4] *L.J.* I, 296, 298, 304, 308.

certainly the most skilful as they were the most continuously
engaged.

Probably in preparation for the convention of Parliament, a commission was appointed some weeks earlier consisting of St John
(Master of the Household), Petre, Sir Walter Mildmay, and Robert
Kellaway (Surveyor of Liveries) to examine the various revenue
courts in order to know their state and to call before them all
officers who could be of help to determine all rents, profits, and
revenues due Henry VIII towards the close of his life and to ascertain
what sums were due to him at the time of his death. They were
further to determine what revenues were payable to Edward VI
and what amounts remained unpaid, with particular attention to
the Court of Augmentations and the Duchy of Lancaster where an accounting should be taken of those properties remaining in the King's
possession from the expropriated monastic lands. The commission
was instructed to proceed at once to its task and to report as soon as
possible, probably to arm the Councillors in Parliament with some
measure of information respecting the disordered state of the royal
revenues, already weakened by large grants and sales.[1] This undertaking may also be regarded as the first in a series of studies of the
revenues and the revenue courts which towards the close of the reign
were to lead to an important attempt at administrative reforms.[2]

Convocation was convened the day following the opening of
Parliament and in its discussion was to consider an extremely interesting set of petitions brought forward in the Lower House and laid
before Cranmer and 'the residue of the prelates of the higher house'.
Unfortunately, the records of the sessions are not fully available,
but enough does survive to afford us an extraordinary and helpful
insight into the thinking and the temper of the lower clergy, who, as
we have seen, were separated by a great gulf of status and power
from their episcopal brethren. First, it was asked that the commission, authorized by 35 Henry VIII for the codification of
ecclesiastical laws, be established and carry out its task so that
proceedings under canon law 'may be without danger and peril'.
This recommendation, long urged by Cranmer, was in fact instituted
by royal commission on February 10, 1552, though the report was
never carried into law because of Northumberland's opposition.
Another of the articles dealt with the perennial problem of the hard-
ships incurred in the first year of appointment to a benefice because

---

[1] S.P. Dom., Edw. VI, II, 9. The date is obscured by stain and is uncertain, though
30 September, 1547, as suggested on the dorse, seems probably correct.
[2] Edward VI, *Chronicle*, xxviii–xxx.

of the necessary payment of first fruits. More important was a rather obscurely worded request that 'certain books' already believed prepared by learned men and certain prelates for the worship of the church be laid before the lower clergy 'for a better expedition of divine service'. The concern here expressed suggests that there was widespread knowledge, magnified by rumour, that a codification of the reforms of the service was at hand, though the draft of the first *Book of Common Prayer* was in fact not to be laid before Parliament until its second session. The final and most interesting of the articles proposed that in accordance with 'the ancient custom of this realm' either the lower clergy might be represented in the House of Commons, or all matters of religion and causes ecclesiastical 'may not pass without the sight and assent of the said clergy'.[1] And in this connection the lower clergy asked as well for assurance that in the present Convocation they might speak their minds without danger of statute law. These important matters were again addressed to the Upper House of Convocation in what appears to be a second draft, doubtless preliminary to consideration, in which the right of representation is more strongly urged, in terms actually 'of this present parliament', while it is requested that all matters concerning religion which are disputable 'may be quietly and in good order reasoned and disputed amongst them', so that the truth will appear and men be more fully persuaded in their consciences.[2]

We do not know what action, if any, the Upper House of Convocation took with respect to these remarkable proposals, but it does seem certain that they were never formally presented in Parliament. They reveal a gnawing fear of the penalties of *praemunire* and of the Six Articles Act, as well as a restless concern with novel and important changes which the lower clergy sensed were at hand even in this session of Parliament. Though the language is carefully discreet, this petition seems to reveal a strong, though moderate, Protestant temper amongst these representatives of the parochial clergy of the realm. This conclusion is further documented by the unanimous endorsement of the action of the bishops in recommending communion in both kinds and by the strong majority of thirty-five to fourteen by which the lower clergy endorsed the bill, not to pass in this session, permitting marriage of the clergy.[3]

[1] Burnet, *Reformation*, V, 171, citing Lambeth MS. 1108, f. 2. The last instance of such representation in the House of Commons was in 1295.

[2] Burnet, *Reformation*, V, 172–173, citing Lambeth MS. 1108, f. 3; Wilkins, David, *Concilia Magnae Britanniae et Hiberniae, etc.* (4 vols., L., 1737), IV, 15–16; Cardwell, Edward, *Synodalia, etc.* (2 vols., Oxford, 1842), II, 419.

[3] Burnet, *Reformation*, II, 108.

We may now turn to an analysis of the legislative history of this fruitful session of Parliament, first discussing the major measures passed and then the lesser, with mention as well of public bills proposed which failed of passage. However, discussion of the Chantries Act (1 Edward VI, c. 14) will be reserved for detailed consideration [as an *Excursus*] in the second volume of this study. The full spiritual impact of the expropriation of the chantries was not felt for a year or more after the passage of the act and, as importantly, its institutional and charitable consequences were not fully comprehended until well after Somerset's fall from power.

Historically, the Chantries Act aside, by far the most important of the numerous statutes passed by this Parliament was the famous act *For the repeal of certain statutes concerning treasons, felonies, etc.* (1 Edward VI, c. 12), deliberately designed to dismember the whole edifice of what can only be described as tyranny with which Henry VIII had sought to define his powers in the closing years of his reign. It seems almost certain that Somerset personally drafted at least the effective outlines of the bill, while with Rich he oversaw its passage through Parliament. It may, indeed, be regarded as a prime document for the study and spirit of this remarkable and magnanimous man. Even before Parliament was convened, Somerset had confided to the imperial envoy his intention 'to abolish and to modify several . . . laws which at present were too severe, and to give to the subjects a little more reasonable liberty, without in any way releasing them from the restraints of proper order and obedience'. A little later, in the early days of the Parliament, he had further stressed his resolve to modify or abolish laws 'almost iniquitous in their severity', though he realized that any ill consequences would be laid against him.[1]

The long preamble to this statute sets out a theory of government breaking sharply with the Henrician past and attuned to Somerset's essential tolerance, his conviction that the reins of authority should bear lightly on men, and his persistent belief in the innate goodness of men. It is, perhaps, the soliloquy of a dreamer and idealist rather than of a statesman. It poses the major premise that nothing is more to be wished than the abatement of naked force in the relation of a monarch to his subjects. The subject should be moved to obedience by love rather than by terror, though at times the insolence of unruly men must be restrained by a 'harder bridle'. This, it is apologetically explained, Henry VIII felt obliged

[1] *Cal. S.P. Span.* IX, 197: Nov. 9, 1547; Van der Delft to Emperor, Nov. 15, 1547, *ibid.* 205–206.

to do, passing laws which appeared to men of other realms and to Englishmen too as 'very strait sore extreme and terrible'. 'But as in tempest or winter one course and garment is convenient, in calm or warm weather a more liberal rase [?] or lighter garment both may and ought to be followed and used'. Thus the stern laws of one sovereign may be mitigated in the 'calm and quiet reign' of another. Accordingly, the King, in his tender years, is content that the severity of certain laws be lessened in the hope that his subjects will be bound more closely to him in love.[1]

The bill was introduced in the Lords, probably on November 10th, was on second reading referred to committee, and then proceeded rapidly through two more readings before it appeared in the House of Commons on November 21st. Further changes were then incorporated in this 'omnibus statute', which on November 30th was considered as a 'new bill' and received its third and final reading in the Commons on December 12th. Differences of detail in the versions before the two Houses were resolved by conference on December 16, 1547, and the bill was passed on December 21st.

This statute was, then, under active consideration during almost the whole of the session. It swept away the Treasons Acts of Henry VIII, restoring the carefully defined statute of 25 Edward III, save against those coining false money, counterfeiting the King's sign manual, or attempting to alter the succession as defined by Henry VIII's will. Further, there was encompassed within treason the overt denial of the royal supremacy, now defined as by 'writing, printing, or other overt act', it being no longer treasonable until the third offence to hold by preaching, express words, or sayings that the King was not Supreme Head. The statute thus made it perfectly clear that levying war on the King was treasonable, but was by no means specific with respect to riots and conspiracies to raise riots not aimed directly against the sovereign—a major defect severely cured by 3–4 Edward VI, c. 5, which was passed shortly after the great stirs of 1549.[2] The great repealer also swept away all new felonies defined by statute since 1 Henry VIII; all statutes 'concerning religion', including those of 5 Richard II and 2 Henry V for the punishment of heretics; the Henrician prohibition on the printing, selling, and reading of certain English books; and the two Henrician statutes which together were commonly known as the Six Articles. These clauses in the act, it is not too much to say, had the effect of establishing a large area of religious freedom in

[1] *Statutes of the realm*, IV, i, 18.
[2] Holdsworth, W. S., *A history of English law*, IV (L., [1924]), 495–497.

England, in no wise curtailed until the passage of the first Act of Uniformity ordering the use of the *Book of Common Prayer*, save for the one important exception of the retention of the Act of Supremacy, which was, however, regarded more nearly as a constitutional than as a spiritual matter.[1] This great measure also repealed the two Henrician statutes which had declared royal proclamations to be quite as valid and binding as Acts of Parliament. The evident intention here was at once to mitigate the heavy penalties with which Henrician proclamations were buttressed and to posit the effective power of proclamations on more nearly acceptable constitutional grounds, for, as we shall note, the use of proclamations actually increased considerably in the Edwardian era.[2] And, finally, this great repealer carefully ordained that all prosecutions for 'treason by open preaching or words' must be instituted within thirty days after the offence, the accusation being laid before a member of the Council, a judge, or two justices of the peace within the county where the offence was committed. Finally, it was provided that no man might be adjudged guilty of treason unless he was accused by two sufficient and lawful witnesses, or unless he should 'without violence confess the same'.[3]

In this complex and bold statute Somerset, probably with the encouragement of Cranmer, seems not only to be groping towards a workable formula of religious toleration, but also to be searching for a definition of political freedom, which involved the sweeping away of the whole apparatus of Henrician repression. This is more—far more—than a return to the old law; it is rather a somewhat fumbling but none the less a determined attempt to create new law which would provide a measured but an extended ambit of freedom. This conviction and this intention is nobly set out in the amazing preamble which we have considered; one wishes that it were possible certainly to identify the author. The sentiments are those of Somerset, but the language is not his. It is the language of the Commonwealth Men, and the vocabulary, the thrust of the prose, and the internal evidence would suggest that Hales, Smith, or Cheke could thus have recorded the bill's intent.

Somerset was here codifying a liberality of policy already well advanced before Parliament was convened. To take only one area, the North: the Council had months earlier written to Archbishop Holgate, as president of the Council of the North, that it understood that divers persons were held there in prison under the Six Articles

---

[1] Pollard, *Somerset*, 65.   [2] *Vide post*, 348ff.   [3] *Statutes of the realm*, IV, i, 22.

Act and other similar statutes. Such persons may claim the pardon of the King and should at once be released. And then, just a year later, the Council instructed Holgate to revoke all inhibitions against preaching in the same region.[1] This was, then, a notable extension of freedom, deliberately made without the slightest evidence of pressure; or, perhaps more accurately, this was a deliberate dismantling of the Henrician apparatus of terror. It has been suggested that the great repealer fatally weakened Somerset's aggregate of power and hence led to the disasters which befell him. This was indeed the later and contemplative view of one of his associates, a completely Erastian civil servant and diplomatist, Sir John Mason. ' "In all other countries" ', Mason wrote, ' "speeches are at liberty, for such are the people's natures, as when they have talked they have done. In our country it is otherwise, for there talking is preparatory to doing; and the worst act that ever was done in our time was the general abolishing of the Act of Words by the Duke of Somerset" '.[2] But this is hardly a valid appraisal. Somerset still stood vested with immense statutory powers and was ringed about with associates who in the crisis of the reign were wholly prepared to wield them in his name. His difficulty, exhibited in the Act of Repeals, was that he was imbued with a high view of the nature of man and shrank back, with indecision and fatal compromises, when mankind failed him.

A somewhat related act (1 Edward VI, c. 11), of considerable significance, was also in form a repealer. The act is formally entitled *For the repeal of a certain statute made [28 Henry VIII, c. 17] . . . for revoking of acts of Parliament.* It recited that this act empowered the King on his own initiative to repeal by letters patent all statutes made before he reached the age of twenty-four. Since the King is a minor, the effect has been that good laws have not been passed and laws that should be repealed have been retained, leaving the King's subjects 'to adjudge and think themselves to live for that time under no . . . assurance of any positive law or statute'. The act was accordingly declared repealed in order to provide a stable basis for government and likewise, without any doubt, to cut away the ground of constitutional opposition of Gardiner and other conservative bishops who were pleading that no statutory change in religion should be made during the King's minority.[3]

---

[1] Pocock, Nicholas, 'Papers of Archbishop Holgate', *E.H.R.* IX (1894), 542–548.

[2] Mason to the Privy Council (temp. Mary ?), as quoted by Froude (*History of England*, V, 64), citing MS. Germany, Bundle 16, Mary, State Paper Office—a document which we have not found.   [3] *Statutes of the realm*, IV, i, 17–18.

This statute has an obvious bearing on 1 Edward VI, c. 1, the only important legislation affecting religion to be passed in this session. This act 'against such as shall unreverently speak against the sacrament of the body and blood of Christ . . . and for the receiving thereof in both kinds' was in general tone and effect cautious, and it was doctrinally conservative, being designed to inhibit the ballad and libel writers who had for months been savagely inveighing against the mass with little or no restraint. The initial discussion was probably in the Upper House of Convocation, where it was deemed advisable to secure a specific exemption from the Six Articles Act from the King before proceeding.[1] The bill has a somewhat tangled procedural history, appearing for first reading in the Lords on November 12th and not being delivered to the Commons until after a fourth reading on December 10, 1547. In its early form the bill was entitled 'for the sacrament of the altar, it was substantially revised during debate and finally enacted by the Lords on December 20th, with five conservative bishops opposed. The measure had easy and probably unopposed passage in the House of Commons, where it received the *judicium* on December 17th.[2] None the less, it did not meet the hopes of a small but ardently Protestant group in the Lower House, where Traheron, so Hilles reported to Bullinger, fought manfully for a Zwinglian statement of creed with respect to the eucharist, 'but it was not in his power to bring over his old fellow-citizens to his views'.[3]

The measure regretted that all men did not do their duty to God and the commonwealth from love rather than fear, yet amongst the multitude of men there are those who must be bridled. Though the institution of the sacrament of the altar is from God, there are those who hold it in contempt, revile it, and profane it in 'preachings, readings, lectures . . . talks, rhymes, songs, plays, or gests'. Hence anyone, after May 1, 1548, so reviling the sacrament shall suffer fine and imprisonment at the King's pleasure after trial following on complaint of two persons to the justices of the peace. This conservative purpose having been achieved, the statute then briefly and simply enacted the restoration of the sacrament in both kinds, thereby, so it was said, restoring the practice of the church in its first five hundred years.[4]

[1] Parker, Matthew, *De antiquitate Britannicae ecclesiae, etc.* (L., 1605), 339.
[2] *L.J.* I, 296; *C.J.* I, 2–3; Dixon, *Church of England*, II, 458.
[3] Robinson, *Original letters*, I, 266: June 4, 1549.
[4] *Statutes of the realm*, IV, i, 2–3. The Council forwarded official instructions to the bishops on March 15, 1548, for putting the changes in the service of the mass into full effect. An order of service, for the participation by the laity in both kinds, was enclosed

When we reflect on the steady sympathy of Somerset for the poor and indigent and the undoubted magnanimity of his whole social policy, it is difficult to fathom the thinking which underlay an hysterical and really vicious statute (1 Edward VI, c. 3) 'for the punishment of vagabonds and for the relief of the poor and impotent persons'. Though the history of the measure is not fully revealed in the *Journals*, it does seem clear that it was rushed through both Houses in the short period of sixteen days of intermittent considera-tion, presumably incorporating in final form still another Commons' bill, first introduced on November 17th, 'against Egyptians and vagrants', which also had its final reading on December 19th. In another work we have dealt rather fully with the *corpus* of legislation seeking to deal with the different, though organically connected, problems of vagrancy and poverty in the early Tudor period.[1] Even in the enlightened Henrician statute of 1536 there persisted the stubborn conviction that there were no genuinely unemployed persons, save for the sick, aged, and orphaned, and that beggary and vagrancy, tinged as they were with criminality, could be exorcised from the realm by the harsh application of criminal law. The Edwardian statute under consideration draws, so to speak, the final false inference from these persuasions.

The statute, which is very long, recites that vagabondage and idleness are the root of all social evils and persist in England despite numerous earlier laws against beggary which because of 'foolish pity and mercy' have simply not been enforced. It was accordingly enacted that all loitering or wandering persons, who were not impotent or who were not seeking work, should be deemed vaga-bonds. Such persons who refused work and whose idleness was proved by two competent witnesses before two justices were to be branded on the chest and adjudged slaves of a master for two years and forced to work. If such a slave should run away, he should on capture be branded on the cheek and remain for his lifetime the slave of the master, while he should be punished as a felon with death for running away again. Children of such vagrant persons should be taken from their parents and bound to masters until

and the bishops were enjoined to instruct the clergy in the new ritual before Easter. They must remember 'the crafty work of the devil, who does not rest to hinder all godliness, and considering that many curates, either for lack of knowledge cannot or want of good mind will not' be ready to carry out the required service, they were accordingly to instruct all their clergy and through them the laity before the effective date of the statute. (S.P. Dom., Edw. VI, IV, 2.)

[1] Jordan, *Philanthropy in England*, 83–86.

adulthood for the learning of honest occupations. The statute struck too, and harshly, against the mobility of truly aged and impotent persons who 'making a number doth fill the streets or highways of divers cities, towns, markets and fairs' as beggars, who might and should be nourished in their home communities. Mayors and other local officials were required each month to apprehend and sort out such beggars and return them to their home parishes, 'there to be relieved and cured by the devotion of the good people' of the community. Such properly settled impotent persons were to be permitted to beg, whilst those able to work were to be provided with common work and the whole burden of such relief was to be defrayed by weekly collections in each church of the realm.[1]

So far as the concern was with the central problem of the relief of poverty, this statute may be regarded as making its due contribution to the slow development of a sense of national responsibility for the poor which the great *corpus* of Elizabethan legislation resolved to a fair degree at the close of the century by imposing the taxing power. But in so far as it was concerned with the riddance from the realm of the able-bodied, and often criminal, vagabond, this must be regarded as impossibly harsh and misbegotten. Just two years later Parliament confessed that the rigour of the new law outran public sentiment, for, though 'wholesome' in its intent, it had not been enforced because of its 'extremity'.[2] So far as our knowledge extends, no judicial finding of 'slavery' was made in the months when this vicious statute was in force.

2. LESSER MEASURES AND THE COMPLEXION OF PARLIAMENTARY CONCERNS

Certain other enactments of this Parliament may be mentioned, though they were relatively of minor significance. A starkly Erastian statute (1 Edward VI, c. 2) ended the ancient pretence that bishops were elected and declared the gift of such offices to be wholly in the King by simple letters patent.[3] After long and detailed consideration an act was also passed (1 Edward VI, c. 7) providing for the continuance of cases in trial notwithstanding the death of the King and establishing the long overdue provision that assizes should not be discontinued on the death of a judge, but 'shall stand good and effectual in the law'.[4] And, finally, in the usual act granting the subsidy of tonnage and poundage to the King for life, a proviso was

---

[1] *Statutes of the realm*, IV, i, 5–8.
[2] 3 and 4 Edward VI, c. 16.
[3] *Statutes of the realm*, IV, i, 3–4.
[4] *Ibid.* 12–13.

added confirming the special privileges and exemptions of the Hanse merchants to the end of the present Parliament, though these economic privileges were to become in the course of the reign a matter of serious economic consequence and a festering diplomatic problem.[1]

In the Edwardian period, until Northumberland's terror laid heavy inhibitions on freedom of parliamentary discussion, almost as much is revealed with respect to the sentiments and preoccupations of the politically dominant classes of the realm by a consideration of bills failing of passage by Parliament as of those which became statute law. There were in all forty-eight bills relating to public matters introduced in this Parliament—mostly, it should be stressed, in the House of Commons—which failed of passage for one reason or another. Of these, twenty-three—almost half—disappeared after their first reading; ten enjoyed a second reading; thirteen had a third reading but still failed to become law; and two were actually read four times but were still to fail. To arrange the procedural facts another way, a total of nine of these unsuccessful bills were given final approval in the Commons, but failed of passage in the Lords, though it seems almost certain that three of them were in effect absorbed or joined in committee with measures which did become law. We shall observe in our analysis of the legislative work of subsequent sessions of the first Parliament that when the House of Commons was deeply concerned with a needed reform or felt that a grievance wanted correction, measures that had failed would be introduced in a later session, often apparently after a re-drafting and a slight change of title, and would then prevail. One notable instance was the bill permitting clerical marriages, introduced at the very close (December 19th) of the first session and then rushed through three readings to a *judicium* in two days. This measure, as we shall later note, was introduced once more in the second session and was then passed into law.

It is also important to observe that the thrust of interest, in this and later sessions of the House of Commons, in bills that failed of passage suggests a very different complexion of legislative concern than do the measures enacted into law, most, if not all, of the latter either being government bills or at least enjoying governmental approval. Thus of the forty-eight failing bills, almost half (23) were concerned with economic problems or needed reforms, whereas only a fifth of the measures passed display this preoccupation.

[1] *Statutes of the realm*, IV, i, 22–24. We shall discuss the matter in the concluding volume of this work.

Conversely, only three of the failing measures (about 6 per cent) dealt with religious questions, whereas about a quarter of the statutes were so concerned. For the rest, seven of the failing bills dealt with legal questions, six with social reforms, five with borough privileges and benefits, two with constitutional issues of a minor sort, and two with administrative reforms.

We may close our discussion of the legislative achievements of the first session of Edward's first Parliament by a brief analysis of the reforming proposals connected with the economy of the realm. There were in all, even in the first session, a large number of such measures, all centering around the three interlocking heads of enclosures, sheep, and care of the poor. The most important of these measures was, as we have observed, the act for the punishment of vagabonds and for the relief of the impotent poor which, despite its harsh injunctions for dealing with vagabondage, represents the first serious effort to deal within the parish with the care of the poor and the fate of poor children. But there were other measures in this session failing of enactment which display the same social and economic concern. The very first bill introduced in Commons in this session was 'for bringing up of poor men's children' (first read on November 8th and for a second time on November 24th), which one would suppose was then subsumed in 1 Edward VI, c. 2, as fairly certainly was the bill establishing a 'felony against Egyptians and vagrants'. Divers measures were launched for the better regulation of the cloth trade, as for example the bill 'for wools of Devon and Cornwall', with its first reading on November 25th and its third on December 21st, but never gaining *judicium*. Another for the regulation of clothmaking in Norfolk, Suffolk, and Essex had one reading and then disappears, while still another 'for buying of wools in the most shires of the realm' by staplers and clothiers failed after a second reading, but was presumably re-introduced on December 10th under a somewhat different title when it gained no more than a first reading. One wishes he knew far more regarding the bill introduced on December 15th 'for nursing of children in Wales', which gained its third reading and passage by the Commons towards the end of the session, but failed of enactment. Also closely related in its concern was a bill 'for alms for prisoners, and poor men lame or maimed', which gained its only reading on December 23rd, as Parliament rose for this session, not to be called back into its second session for almost a year.

The body of legislation passed by Parliament in this first session was, then, relatively slight, but a willingness to grapple with critical social and economic problems was evident both in the enactments and in the far larger body of measures at least considered. Most notable was the cautious and modest approach to the whole range of problems bearing on a religious settlement, the only legislation of consequence having gone no farther than to establish communion in both kinds, while leaving intact the Roman doctrine and usage of the mass. This reflects the restraint and caution of both Somerset and Cranmer, both of whom were by the close of 1547 personally advanced Protestants, but who for the sake of civil and religious order wished the reformation to proceed in reasoned and surmountable stages. But as we shall now observe, the Reformation in a true sense was at hand in England and every move, every impulse, was to be along the path which Parliament, and more particularly the House of Commons, had demonstrated the politically dominant classes of England were prepared to follow. The prospect of Zion lay just ahead for England.

VII

THE TRIAL OF IDEAS AND THE RECEPTION OF THE RELIGIOUS REFUGEES

I. THE REMOVAL OF IMAGES

The immense solidarity and power vested by the Act of Supremacy is attested by the patience with which now deeply committed English Protestants awaited the course of reformation, which in their view was scarcely advanced at all in the session of Parliament which rose just as the first regnal year was coming to a close. And for some weeks thereafter the cautious and conservative mood of the Protector and Council continues to be reflected in their policy and official actions. Thus on January 16, 1548, a long and carefully composed proclamation defended the traditional observance of fast days and Lent. The King is declared to wish the continuance of the practice, not only for the spiritual benefit which may accrue but for compelling reasons of 'worldly and civil policy'. England is a realm 'environed with the seas', from which many of the King's subjects gain their living in 'uttering and selling such meats as the sea and fresh water doth minister unto us'. Hence the traditional fast days were to be strictly observed under pain of an undefined royal indignation.[1] Even sterner in tone and certainly more disheartening to the 'gospellers' was another proclamation in early February, 1548, seeking to end the growing practice of private innovations in the worship of the church. The realm was assured that careful attention was being disposed by those in authority on a godly and scriptural settlement of the church. Meanwhile the realm was sorely troubled by those who seek to cling to old and accustomed ritual as well as by those who seek to bring in 'new and strange orders, every one in their church, according to their fantasies'. The result having been confusion and disorder, no further departures from the worship and ritual proclaimed by law were to be permitted under pain of imprisonment, and the justices of the peace and the

[1] Hughes and Larkin, *Tudor proclamations*, I, 413–415.

churchwardens were declared responsible for the enforcement of the proclamation.[1]

In no other respect was there more of private innovation and violent controversy than in the sacrament of the eucharist, with all its elaborate ritual and its central position in the doctrinal edifice of the church. We have seen that Parliament had ordered communion in both kinds, while it left unquestioned the doctrine of transubstantiation and sought to damp down controversy as the learned men of the church gave further thought to an official pronouncement of doctrine. This position the Council sought valiantly to re-enforce by a proclamation promulgated a few days after the statute providing communion in both kinds had passed. In this new proclamation it was urged that Parliament had taken a sufficient course in the matter. Yet men are not content with the words of Christ 'that the body and blood of Jesus Christ is there, which is our comfort', but continue 'to move contentions and superstitious questions . . . entering rashly into the discussing of the high mystery thereof'. Then, flatly stating that the doctrine of transubstantiation remained unchanged, the Council hinted that this central teaching was under consideration, though meanwhile contentious discussion must be curbed. At the same time, however, it was emphasized that quiet discussion and personal search for truth were in no way proscribed.[2] To this whole troubled question the Council returned in March, 1548, being concerned lest the introduction of holy communion in both kinds should itself occasion 'every man fantasying and devising a sundry way by himself in the use of this most Blessed Sacrament of unity', thereby further increasing division. The realm was assured that the King would 'from time to time' further accomplish the work of reformation and set orders to advance God's glory, but meanwhile his subjects, under pain, were to 'stay and quiet themselves with this our direction'.[3]

Almost as incendiary and disrupting was the whole range of problems connected with the place of images in the worship of the church, which, as we have seen, the Council itself had not finally defined. Even in the late Henrician days discreet efforts had been made to remove images which clearly tended to inculcate idolatry, and this the Edwardian Council assumed as its position with, however, a much more sweeping definition of what constituted image worship. The difficulty was that in the final analysis the judgement of

[1] Hughes and Larkin, *Tudor proclamations*, I, 416–417: Feb. 6, 1548.
[2] *Ibid.* 410–412: Dec. 27, 1547.
[3] *Ibid.* 417–418.

the clergymen and churchwardens of each parish church had to be taken and this was an automatic corollary of their personal religious persuasion. The Council consequently tended to support local representations and wishes in the matter for the present.

The Council took the final step on February 11, 1548, when on its own authority, but doubtless after full consultation with Cranmer, a scant quorum (6) enjoined the Archbishop to instruct the bishops to proceed to the removal of all images in the churches and chapels of the entire realm. The Council recalled the earlier policy under which images which prompted superstitious abuses were to be taken down, which in many parts of the kingdom had been faithfully done, but in other areas nothing had been done or superstitious images had even been restored. The fact was that 'almost in no places of the realm is any sure quietness, but where all images be wholly taken away and pulled down already'. Hence to the intent that controversy and abuses be quieted, all are to be removed so that 'the lively images of Christ should not contend' with the dead images of superstition. Cranmer accordingly issued a *mandatum* for all bishops to proceed to the complete removal of images.[1] Though relatively unimportant in any substantive sense, the removal of images and pictures now enjoined and gradually carried out was of very great symbolic importance. The familiar configuration, the habits of worship, perhaps half superstitious, and the richness and satisfaction of the background of piety were thereby cut away, and the scar left on the edifice of worship was in a true sense also a scar on the faith of many thousands of humble and unlettered men. This, and associated reforms of abuses, were certainly more unsettling to worship and to civil quiet than were the great doctrinal changes shortly to be introduced.

The removal of images in the churches of the kingdom proceeded at a pace which may be quite directly associated with the degree of conservatism and zeal exhibited by the clergyman and his churchwardens in the individual parishes. Some images were simply destroyed and broken, though the mandate required no more than that they be removed, with the result that hundreds of images reappeared from barns and lumber rooms on the accession of Queen Mary. In London, as we have already noted, Protestant pressure was so intense that the work of removal had been all but completed months before the full authorization was issued. This clearing had proceeded far in most parishes well before Bishop Barlow, in a

[1] Burnet, *Reformation*, V, 191–192; Foxe, *Acts and monuments*, V, 717–718; Inner Temple MS. 538, #45, f. 407; Wilkins, *Concilia*, IV, 22–23.

dramatic sermon at Paul's Cross on November 27th, exhibited to his great congregation an image made with movable joints which could be made to turn its head and bless with its hand. The sermon was a vigorous denunciation of idolatry and popery, and, we are told, after the sermon, 'the boys broke the idols in pieces'.[1] Not many days later the imperial ambassador sorrowfully reported that not an image or a crucifix was left (in London?), and that though the mass was still celebrated, the common people were beginning to sing psalms 'in their own language in the churches' of the City.[2]

But the remote and normally far more conservative rural parishes of the realm are at once more interesting and more revealing as one seeks to study the creeping impact of this dramatic and abrupt change in the habits and texture of worship. From many such sources where we have at least partial knowledge of the reaction to the unequivocal order of the Council and the Archbishop, we may mention a few, in some cases including as well reactions to later and more stringent injunctions with respect to the cleansing of the service. Even in Cornwall the parish of Stratton responded quickly and fully to the changes now enjoined. In 1547 the image of St George was taken down, and in the next year the horse, on which the image had been mounted, was removed. At the same time the rood was taken away, while in 1549 outlays are recorded for the purchase of the first *Book of Common Prayer* and books with music, the words being in English, for matins and evensong.[3] The church-wardens of Bishop's Stortford, uncertain regarding the extent of the cleansing required, hired a man to ride to London ' "for to view and see other churches there" ', and upon his report spent two days in removing images and for prudent good measure sold the church's silver and vestments. Somewhat later these enterprising churchwardens bought two copies of the *Prayer Book*, while at the same time, with the vicar's consent, they undertook to render the service in their old Latin books into the English language.[4]

The course of the Edwardian Reformation is sensitively reflected in the accounts of the churchwardens of St Michael's in Bedwardine, Worcester, a quite rich parish lying next the cathedral. There in 1547 the King's *Injunctions* and the required *Homilies* had been purchased, and the images were removed in 1548 and the empty

[1] Wriothesley, *Chronicle*, II (Camden Soc., n.s. XX), 1.

[2] *Cal. S.P. Span.*, IX, 222: Dec. 5, 1547.

[3] Peacock, Edward, 'On the churchwardens' accounts of the parish of Stratton, in the county of Cornwall', *Archaeologia*, XLVI (1880), 220–221.

[4] VCH, *Hertfordshire*, IV, 314.

areas whitewashed. In the same year the *Paraphrases* were purchased at a cost of 11s, all the walls were whitened and scriptural
verses were painted for the edification of the congregation. Further,
the three altars were now removed, and a communion table was provided.[1] In another cathedral city, Salisbury, the churchwardens of
St Thomas's parish were evidently more conservative. There it
was not until the royal commissioners visited the diocese that the
images were defaced and removed, and not until 1549–1550 that
the new and authorized communion books were purchased. The rood
was evidently not taken down until the Elizabethan period, nor
were Erasmus' *Paraphrases* purchased until 1560–1561. In still
another Salisbury church, St Edmund's, however, the churchwardens were more immediately and obediently sensitive to the
course of the Edwardian Reformation.[2]

The progress of reform could be very slow indeed in a small
rural parish where spiritual leadership was vested in a conservative
priest and in a body of churchwardens who were Catholic, or at
least traditional, in their convictions. This is well illustrated in the
narrative of Robert Parkyn, the curate of Adwick-le-Street in
southern Yorkshire, written in *c.* 1555, some years after the fact.
Here he notes every official change in the ritual with deep resentment, particularly the changes in the communion service in 1548
when the priest must in the ritual provided proceed 'immediately ...
unto the holy mass', and in both kinds at that. Later in this year
Parkyn bitterly lamented that at Rogation Days 'no procession was
made about the fields, but cruel tyrants did cast down all crosses
standing in open ways'. He and his parish evidently were able to retain
the images in the church until 1550 when both images and altars had
to be removed, 'and a little board to be set in midst of the choir,
called the Lord's Board or Table'. This sacrilege, he confidently
suggests, resulted in God's vengeance as witnessed by the great
dearth and the epidemic of sweating sickness in the whole of the
realm in the next year.[3]

But, deeply as Parkyn, and doubtless hundreds of clergy like
him, may have felt, there was little overt resistance, for that, one
supposes, all men would have agreed was treason. There could be
no other course for such men than delaying and grudging resistance

[1] *The churchwardens' accounts of St Michael's in Bedwardine, etc.*, ed. by John Amphlett
(Worcester Hist. Soc., 1896), xiii–xiv, xviii, xx, 19–25.
[2] VCH, *Wiltshire*, VI, 149, 153.
[3] Parkyn, Robert, *Narrative of the Reformation*, ed. by A. G. Dickens, *E.H.R.* LXII
(1947), 67–72.

leading ultimately to acceptance of the law of the realm. All over the kingdom the images that had adorned the churches, which had been part of the whole experience of worship and which almost certainly did lend themselves to superstition, came down, often finding their way to seaport towns for sale abroad. The epitaph for them is recorded in the cool report of Mason, then serving in France, to the Council in September, 1550, when he casually mentions that three or four ships had arrived from England laden with images which had been eagerly purchased by ignorant people. There had been much of talk, and he implies criticism, in France, all of which could have been avoided had the images been defaced as had been ordered.[1]

2. RESTRAINTS ON PREACHING (APRIL, 1548)

Governmental policy was now under attack from both the right and the left, so to speak, from conservative men who were fearful because of the steady drift towards Protestantism and from the evangelical radicals, particularly powerful and articulate in London, who were becoming bitterly critical of the extreme caution of Somerset's religious policy. Almost all restraints on free discussion and freedom of the press had been lifted for many months, with the consequence that debate and discussion had been intensified and was now focusing on the central and much disputed doctrinal meaning of the Holy Eucharist. The controversy was particularly acute and envenomed amongst the clergy, whose pulpits were still the most effective instrumentality of propaganda, even in the face of the rapidly expanding power of the printed word. Somerset, like all early adherents of the reformed faith—and Cranmer to a more chastened degree—was deeply convinced that the free reading, contemplation, and discussion of the Gospels must inevitably lead to a spiritual consensus in England, and he was hence most reluctant to impose restrictions on free but quiet debate. But it was rapidly becoming evident by early 1548 that no such consensus was evolving, that freedom of debate had rather opened the gates of contention, and that some measure of restraint must be imposed to secure a period of calm in which to prepare the way for the promised doctrinal and liturgical reformation, now being drafted by Cranmer, which we know as the first *Book of Common Prayer*.

Accordingly, on April 24, 1548, the Council issued a sternly worded proclamation, inspired by the determination to quiet

[1] *Cal. S.P. For., Edw. VI*, #237.

controversy and also to check possible ill effects of the scandal of the Northampton divorce case.[1] The Council recited that, despite its command that a godly conformity be preserved in the realm, 'divers unlearned and indiscreet' priests have encouraged stubborn disobedience and have spread malicious rumours: that the King will lay new and strange exaction on the occasion of marriages, christenings, and burials, thereby inspiring disorder and even rebellion; that a man may forsake one wife for another, or 'have two wives or more at once'; or that the sanctity of marriage is preserved only by the Pope's law and not by God's law. In order to quiet these dissensions, all preaching throughout the realm was prohibited save by such clergy as might be expressly licensed by the King, the Lord Protector, or the Archbishop of Canterbury, the licence to be exhibited to the parson and two honest men of the parish before a sermon could be delivered.[2]

The list of licensed preachers, including such great and valued evangels of Protestantism as Grindal, Latimer, Cox, Knox, and Pilkington, seems at the outset to have numbered eighty, of whom seventeen are described as Bachelors of Divinity, nine as Doctors, two as Professors of Divinity, and twenty-one as Masters of Arts.[3] The rather harsh wording of the proclamation was explained about a month later by instructions forwarded by the Council to the licensed preachers. The intent was to avoid destructive controversy and to permit time for the *Homilies*, being read every Sunday, to 'sink into' men's hearts. There was no other wish than that 'rash, contentious, hot, and undiscreet preachers should be stopped'. But at the same time godly and responsible preaching under licence was much desired as an aid to legal order, lest 'every man should run before their heads hath appointed them what to do', and every man should choose his own way in religion. They were accordingly required to avoid controversial subjects, to preach against the Romish survivals, and to wait on the constituted authority for further changes in worship and reformation.[4]

But violent discussion and controversy, especially regarding the mass, could not be stilled by fiat, and even the licensed clergy declined to be restrained by the guidelines laid down somewhat naively by the Council. There was disorder in St Paul's every

[1] *Vide post*, 365-367, for a discussion of this unsavoury case.
[2] Hughes and Larkin, *Tudor proclamations*, I, 421-423.
[3] S.P. Dom., Edw. VI, II, 34 (the date of the document is uncertain). This privileged list was steadily expanded, sometimes on private petition.
[4] Text in Burnet, *Reformation*, V, 193-196 (May 23rd), from Lambeth MS. XXXI, 9.3(8); Cardwell, *Documentary annals*, I, 63 ff., dates it May 13th.

Sunday, inspired by a now almost fanatical demand that the mass be disowned. Bawdy and sacrilegious ballads were circulated, bitterly attacking the teaching of transubstantiation, and the irrepressible Cardmaker and another unnamed preacher at Paul's laid before their congregation a starkly Zwinglian interpretation of the eucharist. At about the same time Ferrar, the newly appointed Bishop of St David's, not known for restraint, preached a violent sermon against the mass, altars, vestments, and copes, speaking in the simple garb of a priest rather than in his episcopal vestments.[1]

The weary and now somewhat disillusioned Council moved reluctantly to its final action on September 23, 1548, noting that even the licensed clergy had abused their privilege and had stirred up contention. Even now 'certain bishops and notable learned men . . . are congregate' by the King's command to draw up shortly 'one uniform order' of service which will end all controversy in matters of faith. Until that time all preaching was prohibited, while the *Homilies* were instead to be read and all men enjoined to pray for the King and his spiritual advisers.[2] The Council now saw its task as holding intact some measure of order and spiritual quiet until the first *Book of Common Prayer* could be promulgated for the establishment of a reformed and a godly church.

3. FERTILIZATION FROM ABROAD (1547–OCTOBER, 1549)

Yet even as the Council strove manfully to quiet dissension and to maintain stability until a uniform worship could be announced for the realm, several of its number, and particularly Cranmer and Somerset, were opening wide the doors of national hospitality for religious refugees from abroad. And more than that—for Cranmer was over a period of years to urge almost all the leaders of Continental Protestantism to settle in England, to accept key posts in the universities, or at the least to make an evangelical visit which would assist in the settlement of the true faith in the realm. In part, as we shall see, Cranmer's purpose was irenic, for he bore steadily in mind the spiritual goal of associated Protestant churches, of which the English would be but one, united in the profession of a common faith and worship. He was likewise moved in his extraordinary policy of seeking the fellowship and help of Protestant leaders from the Continent, men of diverse persuasions, by the fact

[1] *Grey Friars chronicle* (Camden Soc., LIII), 56–57.
[2] Hughes and Larkin, *Tudor proclamations*, I, 432–433; Wriothesley, *Chronicle*, II (Camden Soc., n.s. XX), 6.

that England lacked a preaching clergy; that much had to be done, and that quickly, to raise the intellectual level of those who professed Protestantism; and that these eminent divines to whom he was steadily addressing attractive invitations would greatly assist him in this intention. And, finally, Cranmer reacted quickly and generously to political developments on the Continent which were for a season gravely to threaten Protestantism in Germany and the imperial dominions generally.

Luther had died in February, 1546. Though infirm in his last year, the power of his personality had held Lutheranism intact and had lent a considerable measure of strength to its defence so long as the Protestant princes remained united. But the Emperor invaded Germany with his Spanish infantry shortly after Luther's death and won at Mühlberg in April, 1547, a great victory in which John Frederick of Saxony was taken prisoner and Germany for the first time in Charles' long reign lay prostrate before his power. The Emperor drove first to construct a religious settlement which was moderate in its provisions and which was proclaimed by the Diet of 1548 (May 15th) as the Augsburg *Interim*. The *Interim* bore heavily on the Lutheran conscience, though important concessions had been made, and in the numerous cities which would not accept the decree, including Augsburg, Nürnberg, Tübingen, Strassburg, and Constance, the Lutheran clergy forthwith were driven from their pulpits into banishment. In all, something like 400 were thus deprived, among them such famous preachers and theologians as Alber, Musculus, Brenz, Osiander, Bucer, Fagius, and Blaurer. It was from these Protestant leaders particularly that evangelical strength and learning were drawn to England on Cranmer's invitation. Thus Blaurer, who in 1547 had confided to Bullinger the fear that religion was dead in England, wrote to the great Swiss divine in July, 1548, of the glory of the reformation proceeding there—an attraction so great that he feared 'the kingdom of God will be taken from Germany'.[1] And at about the same date Bucer was writing to Cranmer regarding his thickening troubles at Strassburg because of the *Interim*. He expected shortly to be driven from his ministry, and when the moment came he indicated his joy in accepting Cranmer's invitation to find a spiritual home in England.[2]

During the years 1547–1553 upwards of forty foreign Protestant divines settled in England, most of whom held ecclesiastical or university appointments within the gift of the state or church. Of

---

[1] *Blaurer Briefwechsel*, II, 603, 720.
[2] Robinson, *Original letters*, II, 531–532, 534: Sept. 3 and Dec. 23, 1548.

these; three—Bucer, Martyr, and Ochino, famous at once for their preaching and their learning—may be described as Continental reformers of the second rank when compared with Calvin, Melanchthon, or Bullinger. Another group of perhaps twelve were scholars, humanists, or preachers of the third rank, but none the less of considerable reputation. The remainder were steadfast Protestants, experienced preachers, and men of learning who also supplied a notable addition to the ranks of the Protestant clergy and certainly a fruitful variety of spiritual conviction at a time when the national faith was in process of definition. We shall comment briefly on the first and second groups of these divines, limiting ourselves at this point to the activities and contribution of the refugee clergy from the outset of the reign to Somerset's first fall in the autumn of 1549.

The great Italian Protestant, Peter Martyr (Pietro Martire Vermigli), was of all the refugee clergy probably to have the most telling effect on the spiritual history of England and the diffusion of staunchly Protestant doctrine. An Augustinian monk, an abbot of Spoleto in 1530 and prior of St Peter's in Naples in 1533, Martyr seems certainly to have embraced reformed views as early as 1531 and was shortly in difficulties with the ecclesiastical authorities. In 1541 he was transferred to the priory of his own order in Lucca where his espousal of scriptural and linguistic studies, with a marked reformed bias, again brought him under direct charges of heresy from which he fled, first to Switzerland and then to Bucer at Strassburg where he taught theology for five years.

In 1547 Martyr, with Ochino and Tremellius, both of whom had been associated with him at Lucca, was officially invited by Cranmer to come to England, where he and Ochino arrived in December.[1] Theirs was truly a journey of learned men, the total cost of £126 7s 6d, which was met by the Crown, including freight charges on both men's libraries, as well as books purchased by Ochino at Basel to the cost of £40 7s 0d, and Martyr's outlay of £13 8s 1d for the works of certain of the early fathers.[2] Both men stayed with Cranmer for some time, engaging in intimate and fruitful doctrinal discussions, until in late March, 1548, Martyr was appointed Regius Professor of Divinity at Oxford, to succeed Richard Smith, with whom he was shortly to engage in formal disputation. Martyr was deeply

[1] *Blaurer Briefwechsel*, II, 685: Feb. 17, 1548. It was reported to Blaurer that Bucer and Fagius had also been invited, but that 'the condition of our church' did not permit their acceptance.

[2] Ashmole MSS. (Oxford), 826, #3, ff. 3–4: Dec. 20, 1547 (done by Gorham, *Gleanings*, 38–40); printed in Nicolas, N. H., 'The bill of the expences . . . [of] Martyr and . . . Ochin', *Archaeologia*, XXI (1827), 471–473.

persuaded that Protestant teachings on the eucharist must be clearly and unequivocally defined, here departing from Bucer who was prepared to compromise in order to secure peace in the church.[1] These views were set forward in his lectures at Oxford where he contended that the papal doctrine of transubstantiation enjoys no support in Scripture, is of relatively late origin, and was unknown to the early fathers. But at the same time Martyr's own teaching was on the whole conservative, since he was persuaded that the real Presence is reserved for those who take the sacrament with faith—a view not greatly separated from that of Luther. His denunciation of the 'Romish error' was, however, unmitigated, though gently stated in a wholly dispassionate style and marked by a profound biblical learning and an enviable knowledge of the fathers.[2] There is little evidence that Martyr was successful in changing the conservative theological cast of Oxford in this period,[3] but his influence on the course of the English Reformation was very considerable, since Cranmer held his theological learning in high esteem and was in constant consultation with him. Martyr's own thought on the question of the eucharist was, like Cranmer's, now in rapid motion, the whole inclination of his thinking being in a Zwinglian direction, which one authority believed he had embraced by the close of his English stay.[4]

Martyr's friend and associate, Bernardino Ochino (1487–1564), was one of the greatest preachers of the Reformation era, whose reformed views had occasioned difficulties with the Neapolitan ecclesiastical authorities as early as 1536. His preaching became steadily more radically Protestant and he was one of the first to be cited before the newly formed Inquisition in 1542. Ochino fled first to Geneva and then in 1545 to Augsburg where he was pastor of a reformed Italian church, escaping to Constance in early 1547 and then joining Martyr for the journey to England. Ochino remained as an honoured guest in Cranmer's household for four months before being appointed a prebendary of Canterbury for life without obligation of residence, to which the King added a pension of 40

[1] Strype, *Memorials*, II, i, 189–190.

[2] The lectures were published under the title, *A discourse or traitise ... concernynge the Sacrament of the Lordes Supper*, etc. (L., 1550?).

[3] Protestantism had been nearly rooted out at Oxford in the late Henrician period. Stumphius wrote to Bullinger in late 1550 that the Oxonians 'are still ... pertinaciously sticking' in their popery, and that in opposing them the university authorities too much favoured Fabian tactics (Robinson, *Original letters*, II, 467–468).

[4] Smyth, C. H., *Cranmer and the Reformation under Edward VI* (Cambridge, 1926), 125–133.

marks p.a.[1] The famous Italian preacher at once attained a position of considerable favour and influence, the learned Ann Cooke translating his principal sermons and the Princess Elizabeth turning one of his books from Italian into Latin. Ochino's activities in England were in the main devoted to his own writing, these years, when, according to Dryander, he worked with more energy and dedication than ever before, being perhaps the most fruitful of his long career.[2] So feared were Ochino's sharp wit and his gift of eloquence that the Emperor registered with Wotton a diplomatic protest concerning his activities in England.[3] The imperial ambassador watched him with some care, reporting gleefully, if inaccurately, in February, 1548, that Ochino had lost his great powers as a preacher, and a few months later that Ochino and Martyr were 'the pet children' of Cranmer, over whom they wielded great influence. Van der Delft concluded with the gloomy judgement that the situation in England was most confused, the people being wholly unbridled since the Lord Protector had been 'so assiduous in pleasing them and pandering to their whims that he has almost lost the authority over them which he had thought to gain by this means'.[4]

The third, and most famous, of the refugee scholars so warmly received in England was Martin Bucer (1491–1551), an early associate of Luther and since 1523 a renowned preacher at Strassburg, which under his intellectual and moral dominance became one of the centres of Protestant strength on the Continent. Bucer had patiently but vainly sought for years to bring about a doctrinal compromise between the Zwinglian and Lutheran parties. For almost a decade, too, he was the principal spokesman for the reformed faith in negotiations with the Emperor which bogged down finally in the Colloquy of Ratisbon in 1546.[5] On the death of Luther, Bucer was left as the principal Protestant leader, and as the Emperor's political strength increased, he became more uncompromising in his assertion of the Protestant position. Matters came to an ultimate crisis with the promulgation of the *Interim*. For almost a year, and with great skill, he opposed the City Council at Strassburg, which was prepared to make concessions in order to save the city, but this delaying action was finally abandoned when in March, 1549, the Council voted that he and Fagius, the implacably Protestant

[1] *Cal. Pat. Rolls, Edw. VI*, I, 265–266.
[2] Benrath, Karl, *Bernardino Ochino von Siena* (Braunschweig, 1892), 177; 'Francisci Dryandri, Hispani, epistolae quinquaginta', ed. by E. Boehmer, *Zeitschrift f. d. hist. Theologie*, XL (Gotha, 1870), 429–430: *Ep.* xlvi, Dec. 3, 1549.
[3] *Cal. S.P. Span.*, X, 349.   [4] *Ibid.* IX, 253, 266.
[5] Eells, Hastings, *Martin Bucer* (New Haven, 1931), 373–383.

7

leaders of the clergy, must leave the city with their possessions and a yearly pension.[1]

Long before his expulsion, in December, 1547, Bucer had been invited by Cranmer to come to England to lend his assistance to the reformation there, a second letter being sent by Cranmer in October, 1548, assuring him that 'to you . . . our kingdom will be a most safe harbour, in which, by the blessing of God, the seeds of true doctrine have happily begun to be sown'.[2] Martyr, already in England, added his voice a few weeks later, urging him in view of the personal danger to which he stood exposed to repair to England to carry on his ministry.[3] Bucer, in fact, had numerous invitations: from Calvin, from Melanchthon, and from the University of Copenhagen. But when the moment for decision came, Fagius left for England on March 24, 1549, and Bucer a few days later.[4] Both men were warmly received by Cranmer, the King, and many of the nobility, and for the time being remained at Croydon as the personal guests of the Archbishop.[5] Bucer and Fagius in a joint letter to the ministers of Strassburg informed their former colleagues that they had been received 'as brethren, not as dependents', and that in Cranmer's house they had found Martyr, Tremellius, Dryander, and certain godly Frenchmen. Their first judgement was that the doctrine and rites of the English church left little to be desired, but that preaching was very weak. Though there had been politic concessions to the past in the preservation of vestments, candles, and the commemoration of the dead, it is affirmed that 'there is no superstition in these things, and that they are only to be retained for a time, lest the people, not having yet learned Christ, should be deterred by too extensive innovations from embracing his religion, and that rather they may be won over'.[6] The incumbent, Madew, having resigned in his favour, Bucer was forthwith appointed Regius Professor of Divinity at Cambridge, with a generous annual stipend of £100.[7]

In spite of his inclinations and best judgement, Bucer was quickly drawn into the doctrinal warfare raging in England with respect to the meaning of the Holy Eucharist. Both he and Martyr were all but

[1] Eells, *Bucer*, 397–399.
[2] Robinson, *Original letters*, I, 20.
[3] *Ibid.* II, 475–476; *ibid.* 472, for another letter in the same vein.
[4] *Blaurer Briefwechsel*, III, 23.
[5] *Ibid.* 42: Johannes Marbach to Thomas Blaurer.
[6] Robinson, *Original letters*, II, 535–536: Apr. 26, 1549.
[7] Before his arrival he had on December 4, 1548, by royal mandate, been appointed a Divinity Reader at Cambridge (Add. MS. 5842, f. 376; *ibid.* 5843, f. 425). The patent for Bucer's professorship was signed on Dec. 4, 1549.

compelled to enter the lists in the formal disputations arranged at both universities. While reserving to a later consideration the contributions of both theologians to the development of English religious thought in this critical interval, we should at least note briefly Bucer's initial writings, which have about them the persuasive quality of modesty. Shortly after his arrival Sir Thomas Hoby translated a skilful and hopeful essay in which the German divine expressed his joy to be in England where the Bible may now be freely read and where the public faith will be founded on its precepts. Already it may be said that 'there is not one realm that hath more well learned and godly men in authority, nor none wherein bishops excel in so much of doctrine and purity of life'.[1] But the main body of the work was a continuation of his long-standing vendetta with Bishop Gardiner, and a defence of the reformed teaching that the clergy not only might but should marry. In particular, he lashed out at Gardiner's argument that marriage would distract the clergy from their pastoral duties, reminding his readers that Gardiner's own career had always been concerned with 'worldly business and functions which pertained not to a bishop'.[2]

Martyr, deeply embroiled in controversy at Oxford with the conservative theologians, asked Bucer to comment critically on his own treatise of the Lord's Supper, which he was now drawing into publishable form. Bucer, always conciliatory and always somewhat diffuse in his own position on this central doctrine, was courteous and on the whole well-disposed, but held strongly to the view that Martyr should lay clear and greater emphasis on the point that the elements were far more than empty symbols. Bucer himself advanced a view which may fairly be described as a doctrine of the real presence, depending utterly, however, on the faith of the communicant. In his own estimate, his views lay between those of Luther and of Zwingli, and he had devoted much time and patience in seeking to develop this middle ground on which, he trusted, Protestantism might find agreement.[3] The difficulty was, and had always been, that his own views were not precisely defined and were confused by his conciliatory instincts. But on one point he never wavered: that Christ is in the sacrament in a spiritual sense as a consequence of the faith of the believer. Nothing whatever is changed in the bread and wine, and the ritual of administration is only a sign, an earthly thing, while the partaking of Christ is a heavenly thing,

---

[1] Bucer, Martin, *The gratulation of the mooste famous clerke M. Martin Bucer, etc.* (L., [1549]), K8.   [2] *Ibid.* E6.
[3] Hopf, Constantin, *Martin Bucer and the English Reformation* (Oxford, 1946), 43.

'to be laid hold upon only by faith'.[1] This stout devotion to his own
middle position extended to Bucer's criticism of the first *Book of
Common Prayer*, just coming into use at the time of his arrival. On
all other doctrinal matters he found it acceptable, but on the teaching of the Lord's Supper, he would have agreed with Dryander that
the 'book speaks very obscurely, and however you may try to explain
it . . . you cannot avoid great absurdity', simply because the disagreement amongst the bishops was so great that they could not agree
whether or no to reject the doctrine of transubstantiation.[2] Shortly
afterwards, Bucer was asked to submit his criticisms in conjunction
with the consideration being given to a revision of the *Prayer Book*,
which was in its ultimate form to be far more radical than he could
have accepted.

It is not too much to say that the Council was with one arm of
policy seeking to quiet debate while doctrinal decisions were being
taken, while with the other it was encouraging free and sharp controversy with respect to the central dogma of the church. The writing
and preaching, as well as the intimate discourse with Cranmer, of all
the refugee theologians was wholly untrammelled and added new
and complex theological views to the ferment of ideas in England in
the critical period 1547–1549. Perhaps fortunately, none of the
great refugee divines could preach in the English language, but
these men were sufficiently effective, particularly when they spoke
in Latin in the universities. It was reported to Dryander that Bucer
demanded that the clergy be more ardent and preach the cause of
reformation with more effective zeal. At the same time in his
sermons, delivered to large congregations, he thundered constantly
against the remaining usages of what he described as the 'old hypo-
critical religion' and called the people to penance and reformation.[3]
This was precisely the impetus which both Somerset and Cranmer
wished to supply to the reformation, and it was in preaching zeal
and ability that they found the English clergy both weak and inert.

In addition to the great luminaries, whose fertilizing influence on
the English Reformation we have been discussing, numerous
additional scholars and divines of considerable European reputation
were to be warmly received in England and also to make their due
contributions. Paul Fagius, an eminent Hebraist, who had arrived
with Bucer, had stayed on as Cranmer's guest at Croydon until an

---

[1] Strype, *Cranmer*, II, 864–868; S.P. Dom., Edw. VI, VII, 47: June?, 1549.

[2] Robinson, *Original letters*, I, 351.

[3] Hollweg, Walter, *Heinrich Bullingers Hausbuch, etc. (Beiträge zur Geschcihte und Lehre der reformierten Kirche*, VIII, Giessen, 1956), 146.

appropriate academic appointment could be arranged for him. He reported that he had been warmly received by the Lord Protector and the nobility, as well as by the King himself who, 'though he is still very young, and very handsome, . . . gives for his age such wonderful proofs of his piety, as that the whole kingdom and all godly persons entertain the greatest hopes of him'.[1] Appointed Reader in Hebrew at Cambridge, Fagius had no more than sketched out his intended lectures on Isaiah when death overtook him in November, 1549. He was succeeded at Cambridge by Emmanuel Tremellius (1510–1580), an Italian Jew who had been converted in 1540, probably by Pole, and who in 1541 had embraced Protestant opinions while teaching Hebrew under Martyr's tutelage at Lucca. He arrived in England with Martyr and gained a considerable reputation at Cambridge for his Hebrew scholarship, while winning the warm and enduring friendship of Cranmer, Parker, and Cecil. His great work, begun at Cambridge, but completed after he had fled from England on the accession of Mary, was the translation of the Bible directly from the Hebrew and Syriac into Latin.[2]

Among these refugee divines, too, was the French theologian, Peter Alexander of Arles, whose 'clear head, and great industry' made him much respected by Cranmer with whom he lived for some years until he was made a prebendary of Canterbury and rector of All Hallows, Lombard Street (London). On Cranmer's suggestion he made a careful study of the views of the early fathers on all the doctrinal issues in dispute, which he laid finished before the Archbishop in April, 1550.[3] Drawn from France, too, was the King's staunchly Protestant tutor, John Belmain, whose influence on the young monarch's religious views has probably been underestimated.[4] Also from France had come Valérand Poulain, who in 1547 was serving as pastor of a small congregation of Walloon refugees and arrived in London in 1548 with other Strassburg Protestants. It was not until 1551 that full employment was found for this brilliant but temperamental preacher, when he was named pastor of the refugee congregation which Somerset had gathered at Glastonbury.[5]

Another considerable figure amongst the refugees was a close friend of Poulain, John Utenhove, a native of Ghent, whence he had fled in 1544 after embracing advanced reformed opinions. He had settled at Strassburg, which he left in the summer of 1548 on

---

[1] Robinson, *Original letters*, I, 333–334: May 7, 1549.
[2] Strype, *Memorials*, II, i, 323; *DNB*.
[3] Benrath, *Ochino*, 191; Strype, *Memorials*, II, i, 321–322.   [4] *Vide ante*, 42.
[5] Hessels, J. H., *Epistolae et tractatus, etc.*, II (Cambridge, 1889), 20–21.

Cranmer's invitation, remaining for a season at Canterbury where
he assisted in the organization of a refugee congregation. Probably late
in 1549 he removed to London where he did yeoman service in
assembling the large Dutch and Walloon church under Lasco's
direction. Greatly admired by no less a reformer than Hooper,
Utenhove made great contribution to the settling and organization
of the hundreds of lay refugees now streaming into England.[1]
Closely associated with him in the ministry at Canterbury was
François de la Rivière, a native of Orléans, who had been a Fran-
ciscan but who had embraced Protestant teachings as early as 1542.
He fled to Geneva where Calvin admitted him to the ministry of
the reformed church. He came to England at an uncertain date, but
not later than the summer of 1548, and for some time preached to
the refugee congregation at Canterbury. In 1550 he was called to
London as a minister to the reformed refugee church there. Likewise closely connected with Utenhove was Martin Micronius (de
Cleyne was his family name), who was also a native of Ghent and
an early Protestant convert. Fleeing the repression in the Low
Countries, Micronius settled first in Strassburg and then in Switzerland, where he met Hooper, with whom he came to England in
1549. In 1550 he was appointed to the clergy of the refugee church
in London, fleeing from England to Denmark with Utenhove and
Lasco in 1553.[2]

Of far greater intellectual stature than the clergy we have just
mentioned was Francis Dryander. Born in Burgos in Spain in 1520
of a rich noble family, he was sent to the Netherlands, where his
family had connections, and in 1539 was studying at Louvain, though
probably already a Protestant. In 1541 he removed to Wittenberg
to study with Melanchthon, living in his house and there completing the translation of the New Testament from Greek to Spanish.
He returned to Antwerp to oversee the publication of his work,
which he actually presented in person to the Emperor, who on the
advice of his confessor threw the young reformer into prison, from
which he escaped in 1543. After several stages he made his way to
Switzerland where he learned that two of his brothers had been
burned for heresy in Rome. On the warm recommendation of
Melanchthon, Cranmer invited Dryander to assume the professorship of Greek at Cambridge in 1547. Restless in nature, Dryander
returned to Basel in late 1549 to arrange for the publication of

---

[1] Cross, Francis W., *History of the Walloon and Huguenot church at Canterbury*
(Huguenot Soc. Publ., XV, 1898), 4–6; Hessels, *Epistolae*, II, 4–5, 16, 21–22, 24.
[2] *Ibid.* 12.

certain of his Spanish works, later settling in Strassburg, where he died in 1552. Though only briefly in England, he had expressed great satisfaction with his work at Cambridge and with the progress of the Reformation, to which, he reported to Bullinger, the refugee clergy were making a strong and an important contribution. He found pleasure, too, in the organization of the refugee church in London, which he declared had been vested by the authorities with complete freedom of worship and discipline. An attractive, immensely learned, and vivacious figure, Dryander made little direct contribution to the English Reformation because of the shortness of his stay.[1]

The excitement and the hope of the first two Edwardian years, when it was widely known that the formal statement of faith and ritual was under preparation, reached far beyond the bounds of the realm to embrace all of the reformed world abroad. Amongst the reformers there was much hope and much concern for England, particularly after the *Interim* began to be imposed in one German state after another. It was fully realized that only the triumph of a godly and militant faith in England would, so to say, restore the spiritual, as well as the diplomatic, balance of power. The connections of the English leaders and reformers with the Continent became organic and very close in 1547 and so they were to remain for the whole of this brief reign, especially since the refugee scholars and preachers, for the most part quickly absorbed into the English religious establishment, maintained an excited and certainly voluminous correspondence with friends and colleagues abroad.

The most notable of all the Continental Protestants, following the death of Luther, was of course Melanchthon, to whom Cranmer offered every inducement of flattery and every argument of spiritual duty in his long effort to persuade him to come to England. Melanchthon shared Cranmer's hope that some substantial measure of spiritual unity might be secured amongst the reformed churches. But he had become sceptical of colloquia; he sensed the iron resolution in Calvin's assurance of dogmatic correctness; and with age he had become exceedingly cautious. His duty seemed to him to lie in Germany, and, perhaps most important of all, he was very tired. None the less, his relations with Cranmer remained intimate, and he kept himself closely informed on English religious developments by his correspondence with refugee scholars. He had

[1] *Bibliotheca Wiffeniana, etc.*, ed. by Edward Boehmer, I (Strassburg and London, 1874), 136–153; *Corpus Reformatorum*, VI, 779–780: *Lib.* III, *Ep.* 43; *Zeitschrift f. d. hist. Theologie*, XL (1870), 424, 425–426, 429.

recommended Dryander to Cranmer in unstinting terms,[1] and a few weeks later thanked the Archbishop for his friendly reception of his associate Justin Jonas (the younger), while urging the English primate to confer with learned men and then to move moderately in the matter of the eucharist. He would wish that all matters in dispute amongst the Protestant communions could be resolved in 'a summary of necessary doctrine', publicly set forth after the deliberation of pious and learned men in order to clear away ambiguities and to lay the basis for a common faith.[2] Not many weeks later, knowing that the drafting of the *Prayer Book* was under way, he expressed the hope that Cranmer would issue as well a confession of faith covering the whole body of doctrine. He would assume that such a statement would not differ greatly from the Lutheran, but even in the Lutheran community he would wish to see doctrine more clearly treated.[3] He further assured Cranmer of his personal assistance if a general statement of Protestant (and English) doctrine were to be propounded, though when Cranmer sought later to bring him to England for precisely this purpose the great, but always somewhat diffident, German once more declined.[4]

Somewhat later, after the *Prayer Book* had been ordained as statute law, Cranmer again assured Melanchthon of his abiding irenic interest, for it was the intent to found a godly church in England, and later to set out articles of faith on which all pious Protestants could agree. To help in this great cause, 'many pious and learned men have come over to us', but Melanchthon's own help and presence were sorely needed.[5] Above all, Cranmer confessed in a later letter, he was disturbed by the dissension amongst the Protestant communion on the eucharist, and urged the need for a general meeting of Protestant leaders to find a common ground on this central doctrine of faith, for which purpose he offered the resources and hospitality of England with the King's personal approval.[6] The difficulties were great, such efforts on a smaller scale had failed before, but one still wonders whether after the significance of the *Interim* and the mounting pressure of the Council

---

[1] *Corpus Reformatorum*, VI, 779–780: *Lib.* III, *Ep.* 43, Jan. 13, 1548.

[2] *Ibid.* 801–802: *Lib.* III, *Ep.* 42, *c.* April, 1548.

[3] *Ibid.* 894–895: *Lib.* I, *Ep.* 66, May 1, 1548.

[4] Cranmer, Thomas, *Works*, ed. by J. E. Cox (2 vols., Parker Soc., Cambridge, 1844–1846), II, 425.

[5] Robinson, *Original letters*, I, 21–22: Feb. 10, 1549.

[6] *Ibid.* 26: Mar. 27, 1552; and see Melanchthon's letter to the King (Jan. 13, 1549) commending the irenic interest of the English leaders and urging moderation in religious policy (Strype, *Memorials*, II, i, 188–189).

of Trent had had their effect, such a conference, held in England in
1549, might not have had profoundly important results, had
Melanchthon and Calvin persuaded themselves to accept Cranmer's
urgent and repeated invitations.

There was resilience and a warm desire for understanding in
Melanchthon, whereas in Calvin there was a deep rigidity born of
complete self-assurance in matters of faith. Though Calvin, too,
was urged repeatedly to attend an irenic assembly, his interest seems
never to have been more than polite, though he was well informed
and deeply absorbed in the course of events in England. Though
his correspondents included both the King and Cranmer, Calvin
tended to address himself to the source of power, the Duke of
Somerset, in letters which were meant to be warm but which were
in fact lectures on policy. One of these will perhaps suffice to illus-
trate the point. In October, 1548, he expressed to the Protector his
thanks to God for the work of reformation now under way in
England. He referred to the civil disturbances of the summer of
1548, which he understood sprang from two sources: the intransigent Papists and the fanatics who 'under colour of the Gospel,
would throw everything into confusion'. Both these groups must be
firmly repressed. First the realm must be brought to good order
and then true religion may be established by the careful instruction
of the people. Here, too, however, there is weakness, since he
understands 'there is very little lively preaching' in England where
'most ministers recite as if reading a lecture'. This must be remedied
as soon as may be, as must the want of a single and carefully composed Catechism which would firmly instil the chief points of true
doctrine. So too, the government must move with much greater
vigour to the weeding out of remaining popish superstitions, for
the policy of moderation thus far pursued was self-defeating. The
completion of the reformation in doctrine must be speedily accomplished, which can then only be imposed by the laying on of a
godly discipline which will secure a moral reformation in England.[1]
This harshly clear and assured homily, incredible if one remembers
that it was addressed to a head of state, exhibits at once the immense
power and self-assurance of Calvinism and its inherent inability to
compromise on spiritual matters, whether essential or indifferent.
It displays, too, little understanding of Somerset's tolerant mind or
of the moderate and gradual process of reform by which he and
Cranmer were trying to create and give spiritual meaning to the
Church of England.

[1] Gorham, *Gleanings*, 55–71: Oct. 22, 1548.

The lively concern of Continental Protestant leaders, great and obscure, might be further exhibited by many instances,[1] but we should turn to the Swiss reformer Bullinger, who without doubt was to follow more closely and to influence more directly the course of the English Reformation than any other foreign divine. Bullinger, the foremost exponent of the Zwinglian legacy of radical reformation in our period, was, so to speak, the communications centre of the Protestant Reformation in Europe. We have seen, almost incidentally, that a number of the refugee clergy finding ultimate haven in England had first passed through his surely institutionalized household, just as had so many of the Henrician English exiles. So great was the learned fervour and the force of personality of this remarkable man that no one ever talked or supped with him without being to a degree affected. Further, Bullinger served as a clearing-house for information and ideas, the volume of his correspondence being suggested by the staggering fact that when the last count was made (1932) there were nearly 12,000 letters known to have been extant in his vast letter files.[2] It is accordingly not surprising that this correspondence is a principal source for the English Reformation, hundreds of letters having been addressed to him by refugee clergy, sympathetic English merchants, and high officers of church and state such as Cranmer, Haddon, and Cheke.[3] Bullinger's great influence was further enhanced by his close and enduring friendship with Hooper, who, as we shall see, had long lived in his house and whose own strong and on the whole radical ideals of reform owe much to this great Swiss divine.

Moreover, Bullinger played a more direct and a powerful role in the shaping of the English Reformation, since ten of his writings were translated and published in England in the course of our period. Most of these works, it may be observed, were homiletic

---

[1] Thus Vadian at St Gallen maintained a steady concern (*Vadianische Briefsammlung*, VI, pt. 2 (1546–1551), ed. by Emil Arbenz and Hermann Wartmann (*Mitteilungen zur vaterländischen Geschichte*, XXX, St Gallen, 1908), 660–661, 672, 695–697, 789–790, 800–801), while the Lutheran Aepin, in dedicating his book *De purgatorio* (1548) to the young Edward, proclaimed his enduring absorption with the course of reformation in England (Mönckeberg, 'Aepin's Reise nach England', *Zeitschrift des Vereines für hamburgische Geschichte*, III (1851), 187).

[2] Bouvier, André, *Henri Bullinger . . . le successeur de Zwingli, etc.* (Neuchâtel and Paris, 1940), 35.

[3] The richness and variety of Bullinger's correspondence, and the amazing extent of his knowledge of events, may be demonstrated by a tiny segment of his letters: those to and from Blaurer (*Blaurer Briefwechsel*, II, 566, 603, 611, 618, 637, 639, 643, 645, 650, 661, 663, *etc.*)—and these relate only to English affairs.

rather than learned in tone and all rested on a deep-seated morality which was really broadly Christian rather than sectarian in temper. The huge *corpus* of his works constituted a kind of quarry of sober and sensitive teachings quickly and easily absorbed into the stream of English intellectual and institutional life. There was nothing novel about his writings, which tend to be conventional, but his arguments and his presentation were characterized by a most persuasive practicality and sensibility which gave them, and deservedly, very great appeal.

The reception of the refugee clergy from the Continent, almost all of whom were men conspicuous in ability and nearly half of whom were scholars or preachers of eminence, was to have fruitful consequences. We shall observe that their direct effect on the course of doctrinal reform was slight, but what they had done was to open wide the windows of English thought and discussion, to link England by close ties with Continental Protestant thought, and to establish England very quickly as a haven for Protestants fleeing from a now worsening religious repression. Nor was this movement of men and ideas limited to the clergy, to the courageous leaders of Continental Protestant thought. From the beginning of Edward's reign a small but steady stream of Protestant laity was also being welcomed into England as the grip of repression grew tighter in many parts of Europe. These men and women, often emigrating for mixed economic and religious reasons—and it is impossible to distinguish between them—were drawn principally from Lower Germany, from the Low Countries, and from France.[1] It seems probable that the French Protestant community at Canterbury was originally formed from converted French prisoners of war then working on the city walls, gradual additions being made by later emigrations.[2] At Rye (Sussex) a similar, though larger, refugee community was formed on the foundations of an alien group which dated back at least to 1523 and which included a number of Scots.[3] Though the evidence is fragmentary, it seems probable that there were by 1549 refugee concentrations in Essex, Norfolk, Kent, Sussex, Gloucestershire, and above all in London, in addition to those we have noted.

For London (and Southwark) the evidence is much clearer, though one must take into account the statistical exaggeration so

---

[1] As an example—as early as August, 1547, a correspondent recommended an Italian, 'Mr Silvester', to Lord Cobham as a tutor for his son, adding that this Protestant had been compelled to flee from Italy and was willing 'to take his refuge in England' (Harl. MS. 284, #18, f. 24).

[2] Cross, *Walloon and Huguenot church at Canterbury*, 9.   [3] VCH, *Sussex*, II, 192.

characteristic at once of the sixteenth century and of exilic groups in any age. Even in late December, 1548, Ochino, in his unsuccessful effort to urge Wolfgang Musculus to settle in England, stated that there were in London alone 'more than five thousand Germans, to whom you may preach and administer the sacraments'.[1] Some months later, Bucer in a letter to the pastor of the Lutheran Church at Emden, stressed the need for a zealous and an evangelical preacher for the German community in London, 'almost all natives of Lower Germany', adding that the needed pastor should be of sound conviction in the matter of the eucharist.[2] At about the same time Dryander estimated the number of 'Germans' in London at about 4000, and commented with great enthusiasm on the complete freedom of worship being permitted to the refugee congregation then being organized.[3] Though these estimates were almost certainly high when made, the stream of refugees both widened and deepened after mid-1549, when the full effects of the *Interim* began to be felt and when a more active and far more rigorous persecution was instituted in the Low Countries. With the religious accommodation of these laymen, settling principally in London, and with their contributions to English thought and to the English economy, we shall be concerned in a later connection.

Enlivening the English scene, too, though not in most instances religious refugees, were a considerable number of students from abroad who were now matriculating in the universities and giving to Oxford and Cambridge an international complexion which they had scarcely possessed since the high Middle Ages. A casual and certainly an incomplete count suggests that in the Edwardian period there were upwards of twenty German students matriculated at Oxford or Cambridge. Among this latter group was a medical student from Constance, Alexander Schmutz, who gained a fellowship and did not leave England until 1553; Christopher Froschover, a nephew of the famous printer; and the ineffable John ab Ulmis who came to England with no visible assets other than a letter from the always kindly Bullinger. A born climber, a pension grabber, and an irresponsible reporter of news, ab Ulmis none the less retained the confidence of Bullinger and with his support did extremely

[1] Robinson, *Original letters*, I, 336; and cf. *ibid.* 337, for the same figure given by Musculus in a letter to Bullinger.

[2] Bucer, Martin, *Scripta Anglicana fere omnia a contr., etc.* (Basel, 1577), 863: Oct. 22, 1549. Bucer wished the pastor to be not 'so over scrupulous as to deny the presence of Christ' in the eucharist.

[3] Robinson, *Original letters*, I, 352: June 5, 1549; also in *Zeitschrift f. d. hist. Theologie*, XL (1870), 425–426.

well for himself, though he seems to have been much more frequently in London than at the University. He urged his friends at
home to come, citing in a letter to Ambrose Blaurer, the gift of 20
crowns annually he had recently wheedled from one English noble
and the fact that William Parr (Northampton), being 'not so
generous, addressed me in Latin and promised his support . . . among
other things. I am writing this', he concluded, 'in order to convince
you that you could live here very well and very comfortably, if such is
the case for someone as humble as me.'[1] And so the harvest of talent
came to England: partly men of great learning and prestige; partly
preachers and teachers of deep piety and unflinching Protestantism;
partly laymen, moved at once by spiritual and economic persuasions;
or gay and irresponsible adventurers who sensed that there were
plums to be picked by those who could represent themselves as
Protestant refugees and seekers after truth. But, however inspired,
this stream of humanity now flowing into England was to fertilize
English spiritual and intellectual life.

[1] *Blaurer Briefwechsel*, III, 44.

VIII

MODERATION TOWARDS DISSENT
(1547–October, 1549)

I. THE CASE OF THE PRINCESS MARY: THE EARLY PHASE

The mild courses of the Protector Somerset in religion occasioned
no considerable flight of religious refugees from England and bore
very lightly on the Roman Catholic conscience even after the Act
of Uniformity establishing the first *Book of Common Prayer* went
into effect in May, 1549. So long as Somerset retained power, this
was true even for the Princess Mary, already known as an ardent
and intractable Catholic; indeed, for a period of rather more than
two years the Princess, who had been scorned and buffeted by her
father, enjoyed more of peace and amiability than she had ever
known during her mature lifetime. Both Somerset and the young
King were kind to her and she was well and comfortably settled in
her principal residences at New Hall (Essex), Kenninghall (Norfolk), Hunsdon (Hertfordshire), and Mendham Hall (Suffolk), with
a wholly sufficient income of about £3400 p.a. net.[1] She moved
from residence to residence, depending on mood, weather, and her
hypochondriacal notions of her own health, always surrounded by
a considerable household of her own selection for which the prime
criterion was deep commitment to the ancient faith.

Somerset was an old acquaintance, who always bore himself
with dignity and kindliness in his relations with her, while the
Duchess of Somerset seems certainly to have been an intimate
friend, indeed one of the few this extremely difficult and imperious
woman had. The closeness and warmth of the relation is suggested
by a petition from Mary directly to the Duchess in April, 1547, for
the assistance of certain pensioners. Addressing the Duchess as
'my good gossip' and later in the letter calling her 'Nann', the
Princess asked for help for an old servant of her mother's, asking the
Duchess to intercede with her husband, since 'it is in manner

[1] Add. MS. 24, 124; Madden, Frederick, *Privy purse expenses of the Princess Mary,
etc.* (L., 1831), *Intro.* cv–cvii.

impossible for him to remember all such matters, having a heap of business as he hath', and referring to earlier and successful suits of a similar nature. Later in the year she wrote easily and informally to the Protector himself, thanking him for the favours he had extended to her petitions and now raising the question of governmental support for certain of her own household—the earlier requests having all been for her mother's servants—who were without portion and 'whose years be so far passed that I fear they shall not enjoy it long'.[1]

At about the same time, the King himself wrote to Mary, in a quasi-official letter, signed also by seven members of the Council, inviting her to spend the Christmas holidays with him at Court, particularly since Elizabeth was to be present: 'so we would be glad, and should think us very well accompanied, if we might have you also with us [at] the same time'. The King concluded with the suggestion that if his sister's health were not good, she might wish to postpone her visit until a more convenient season.[2]

Nor were the informal and friendly relations between the Protector and the Princess injured by Mary's protest, in the autumn of 1547, against the cautious changes already being made in her father's religious settlement, which historical circumstances, ironically enough, almost compelled her to embrace.[3] Somerset replied, in easy and moderate terms, that the government sought nothing more than peace and order within the realm and the 'true glory of God' in all its actions. Further, he wrote, Mary was wholly mistaken in her argument that order and tranquillity prevailed in the later days of her father, and he must remind her 'what great labours, travails, and pains, his grace had, before he could reform some of those stiff-necked Romanists or papists: yea, and did not they cause his subjects to rise and rebel against him?' The truth is, Somerset continued, Henry did not survive long enough to complete the work of reformation on which he was determined. That he would have completed this work and that he would have established religion in the realm had he lived, the Protector and others who knew him can well testify.[4]

For well over two years Mary lived quietly in her household with no further religious protestations, the elaborate ritual of the mass

---

[1] S.P. Dom., Edw. VI, I, 38: Apr. 24, 1547; ibid. II, 24, 28: Dec. 28, 1547.

[2] Strype, *Memorials*, II, i, 92.

[3] Strype (*ibid*. 92–93), without citing evidence, believed that Mary's protestation was inspired by Gardiner.

[4] Cotton MSS., Faustin, C, ii, 13, ff. 64–65, as quoted in Burnet, *Reformation*, V, 169.

being conducted by her chaplains without any violation of the law
as it then stood. Numerous marriage negotiations were begun,
though never carried far, and these and her fragile health seem to
have been her principal concerns. But the accustomed worship in
her household became illegal and the religion established for the
entire realm by the Act of Uniformity became in her view heretical
when the statute went into effect in May, 1549. Yet there was no
hint of fear or protest in her letter to the Emperor in March, when
she contented herself with courtesies, nor in her note commending
William Paget who was leaving London on a diplomatic mission to
the empire.[1] None the less, Charles, probably on his own initiative,
had a little earlier instructed Van der Delft to convey his concern to
the Lord Protector and to make it clear that he could suffer no
pressure to be brought to bear on his cousin to make her conform to
any new regulations respecting her faith.[2] Mary was evidently in
consultation, without restriction, with the imperial ambassador,
referring to his visit in a letter dated April 3rd, in which she asked
Charles for his protection against the laws shortly to go into effect
and expressing her resolution to 'continue to live in the ancient
faith, and in peace with my conscience'.[3] Then, as the critical
month of May arrived, Charles instructed his envoy to convey to
the Protector a statement of the diplomatic difficulties raised by the
changes in faith in England and finally to ask from Somerset a
written assurance 'in definite, suitable and permanent form', that,
the laws notwithstanding, Mary would be permitted to 'live in the
observance of our ancient religion'.[4]

The conference between Somerset and Van der Delft on the issue
was amiable and on the whole satisfactory. The Protector pointed
out that the religious changes had been made by Act of Parliament
on the advice of the bishops and other learned men in order to
quiet dissension and to bring the church into accord with the mandate of God's Word. As to Mary, it was simply not in his power to
act against a statute, while she, as the named successor to the throne,
must conform to the law established lest dangerous dissensions be
bred. He had no intention of inquiring into the worship of her
household and in this respect she might do as she would until the
King came of age, but he would not and could not grant the desired
assurances by letters patent.[5] But in the Privy Council Protestant
sentiment was strong, and thus it was resolved on June 16th that

---

[1] HMC, *Salisbury MSS.*, I, 73, 74; *Cal. S.P. Span.* IX, 388, 394.
[2] *Ibid.* 330: Jan. 25, 1549.   [3] *Ibid.* 361.
[4] *Ibid.* 375: May 10, 1549.   [5] *Ibid.* 381–382: May 28, 1549.

Mary might not freely celebrate the mass in her household in open violation of the proceedings of the King, her brother. It was accordingly resolved to send her written word that she must conform to law, must discontinue the celebration of the mass, and must send to them her chaplains and comptroller for a fuller elucidation of the Council's requirements.[1]

Mary then wrote in great heat directly to Somerset, insisting in angry confusion that she had broken no law, 'unless it be a late law of your own making, for the altering of matters in religion', and reminding him that the executors had sworn to uphold the Henrician settlement of religion. By this settlement she intended to live and worship until her brother became of mature years.[2] Somerset, now struggling with rebellion in East Anglia and in the West, somewhat wearily indicated his own wish to tolerate Mary's private worship, if she would only 'do as she pleases quietly and without scandal'.[3] Understanding Mary as no other member of his government did, his own solution was to extend a dispensation for her and her household to participate in the ancient service of the mass in private worship held in her own chamber.[4] Beyond this, surely, he could not possibly go in law or in conscience. In this action, significantly, he was bitterly opposed by Warwick in the Council, who was now the spokesman for zealous and intransigent Protestantism.

2. THE CONTUMACY OF BISHOP GARDINER: THE FIRST PHASE

Far more formidable intellectually and legally than Mary's striving to retain the solace of a faith to which she was devoted with every fibre of her being, was the continued, the courageous, and the ever-shifting opposition of the Bishop of Winchester to every stage of change in the teachings and ritual of the church. We have already treated the early phases of that resistance, which may be described as meddlesome rather than frontal, centering as it had on the introduction of the *Homilies*, the *Paraphrases*, and the royal *Injunctions*. Somerset was disposed to be at once lenient and long-suffering as Gardiner bombarded him and the Council with letter after letter of protest. But patience wore thin and on September 25, 1547, not long before Parliament was to meet, the Council ordered the bishop

---

[1] *A.P.C.* II, 291–292: June 16, 1549. [2] Foxe, *Acts and monuments*, VI, 7–8.
[3] *Cal. S.P. Span.* IX, 406–408: July 19, 1549.
[4] S.P. Dom., Edw. VI, VIII, 51 (the text is much mutilated but may be read in an approximately accurate copy, *ibid.* 53).

to the Fleet quite explicitly for having refused to set forth the
Injunctions and *Homilies* in his diocese.[1] Loosely restrained in a
kind of honourable captivity, the bishop devoted himself to the
composition of still another of his extremely able letters to Somerset,
to a degree justifying Fuller's famous stricture on him: 'His malice
was like what is commonly said of white powder, which surely discharged the bullet, yet made no report.'[2]

In this important statement Gardiner protested that the *Injunctions*, which he had declined to implement in his own diocese, prescribed the *Homilies* and Erasmus' *Paraphrases*, though these two
books 'strive one against another directly' on important matters of
faith.[3] And both works contain matters heretical under the law.
He had presented his views to the Council while Somerset was still in
Scotland, believing that matters of great moment were being
hastened in his absence.[4] He had taken his position squarely on the
law [the Six Articles], on the all-embracing power of an Act of
Parliament, for no one had more experience of the meaning and
danger of *praemunire* than did he. Hence when summoned before
the Council, he could only reply that he would carry out the injunctions so far as God's law and the King's law permitted. He had laid
his case before Cranmer as well, but the Archbishop would 'overcome me that am called the sophister, by sophistry'. He insisted,
in concluding, that the Council was opening up an extremely
dangerous precedent in proceeding with matters of law and doctrine
without the full weight of Parliament behind them.[5]

There was for the moment an impressive merit in Gardiner's
position, though it was to be entirely swept away just a few weeks
later by the great repealer statute of Edward's first Parliament,
whereupon Gardiner shifted his ground. It is important to remember
that the Council's charge against Gardiner (and Bonner) was not
heresy but disobedience. The Council took the view that the
bishops now exercised their spiritual jurisdiction by virtue of royal
licence, and that the licence recently issued bound them to the
crown and its supremacy in crystal-clear terms. To this Gardiner
rejoined that if his authority stemmed wholly from the crown's
commission he would run the risk of exceeding it or contravening
it and would hence find himself under *praemunire*. This argument

---

[1] *A.P.C.* II, 131–132; Edward VI, *Chronicle*, 8.   [2] Fuller, *Worthies*, III, 169.
[3] Muller has collated four texts: Harl. MS. 417, ff. 84–89; Cotton MSS., Vespasian,
D, xviii, ff. 138–145; Bibl. Nat., Latin, 6051, ff. 46v–47; and Foxe, *Acts and monuments*,
VI, 42–46.
[4] *Gardiner letters*, 382–389: Oct. 14, 1547.   [5] *Ibid.* 394–399.

he extended by maintaining that he might find himself under a *praemunire* for violating an Act of Parliament even if he pleaded the King's consent or, he almost says, the King's instruction. Every subtlety of law and every constitutional uncertainty was pleaded by Gardiner until 1 Edward VI, c. 11 and c. 12, compelled him to embrace a wholly different and a decidedly contradictory position.[1]

Gardiner's appeal was still directly to Somerset when he wrote some days later to hint that Cranmer in their last meeting (October 7th) had laid open the possibility that he might be brought back to the Council if he would yield his position. This seems doubtful on the face of it, and if such a veiled offer had in fact been made, Gardiner would have been most ill-advised to have revealed it at this juncture.[2] The bishop continued that he had now given more study to the *Paraphrases*, and though in the past he had 'favored Erasmus name as much as any other', he now realized that from his thought had sprung the monstrous heresies of this later age. So too, upon careful study, he found the *Homilies* to err on the doctrine of justification. But, though he could not accept the *Injunctions*, he had entered no faction against the Council and had lent no support to Wriothesley. He blamed Cranmer wholly for the misfortunes that had befallen him, his hatred of the Archbishop suffusing his cry that Cranmer had borrowed 'of your authority the Fleet . . . wherewith to cause men to agree to that it pleaseth him to call truth in religion'.[3]

The responsibility was not Cranmer's, but that of the whole Council, deeply outraged and a little nervous before Gardiner's stalwart and deepening contumacy. In the Council, it seems quite clear, only Somerset, Cranmer, and Paget were protecting him from strait imprisonment or deprivation. And he was as difficult as he was petulant, the letters of complaint streaming in to the Protector.[4] On the day Parliament was convened he demanded his

---

[1] For fuller discussion of the legal issues, *vide* Elton, *Tudor constitution*, 24–25; Muller, J. A., *Stephen Gardiner and the Tudor reaction* (N.Y., 1926), *passim*; Powicke, *Reformation*, 76–78.

[2] *Gardiner letters*, 403. The source is Foxe, *Acts and monuments*, VI, 46–50.

[3] *Gardiner letters*, 405.

[4] Both Paget and Somerset regarded themselves as personal friends of Gardiner. When on October 23rd Van der Delft expressed his sorrow at Gardiner's treatment, Paget replied that he doubted if there was 'any man living who is more grieved than I am myself' at his misfortune, 'and I have many good reasons for my sorrow. I have had several long discussions with him, as his friend, to persuade him, or at least to mitigate his attitude. But he is quite intractable, and entirely different from what he used to be.' (*Cal. S.P. Span.* IX, 187.)

release so he might take his seat in the Lords; about a week later he required a physician and opportunity for exercise; he blasted the *Paraphrases* as poorly translated and full of errors; and at about the same time he complained once more of the closeness of his imprisonment.[1] The unbroken flow of these letters continued—there were three more addressed to Somerset in November—all defending his stand against the *Injunctions*; and then the tone became harsher when in late November he demanded a personal interview with the Lord Protector and complained once more of his exclusion from Parliament. Cranmer, he said, maintains that in religion Henry was seduced by his Councillors; 'it is possible that your Grace may be seduced also; and therefore it is good for your Grace to heare and to hear in time'.[2] And then, probably in early December, he imperiously complained because Somerset would not hear him, and continued to blame all his sufferings on Cranmer, who feared him—though whosoever feared him 'must fear only truth'.[3]

The Parliament which by its repeal of the Six Articles Act destroyed completely Gardiner's fragile legal case also passed a general amnesty act which, almost certainly by Somerset's decision, did not exclude him. He was accordingly released from the Fleet on January 7, 1548, and was brought before the Council on the following day and required to say whether he would obey the King's *Injunctions* and 'such other doctrine as should be set forth from time to time'. Certain articles touching justification being laid before him, Gardiner answered that he would conform to the *Injunctions* as other bishops did; but with respect to the heads of doctrine he asked for, and was granted, a brief period for their study.[4] He was confined to his London house while that study was under way, while Ridley, Thomas Smith, and Cecil—the latter in the process of moving from his position as Secretary to the Protector to the powerful post of Secretary to the Council—frequently waited on him in what proved to be a vain effort to persuade him to sign the visitation articles and the doctrinal articles laid before him.[5] None the less, the Council, one must say with amazing magnanimity, instructed him to return to Winchester, perhaps hoping to insulate him in diocesan duties. But the experiment was in vain, for within a few weeks there were religious disturbances there, in part caused, so

---

[1] *Gardiner letters*, 410–411: *c*. Nov. 4, 1547; *ibid*., 411–413: Nov. 12, 1547; *ibid*. 413–414: *c*. Nov. 14, 1547.   [2] *Ibid*. 424–425: *c*. Nov. 20, 1547.
[3] *Ibid*. 426–428: *c*. Dec. 4, 1547.   [4] *A.P.C.* II, 157–158: Jan. 8, 1549.
[5] Add. MSS. 28,571, ff. 15–16 and ff. 9–10; Dewar, Mary, *Sir Thomas Smith. A Tudor intellectual in office* (L., 1964), 43–44.

the Council believed, by Gardiner's own servants 'who have not had such due respect in kindling up of the people's minds against things set forth by the King's Majesty's authority' as they should. Accordingly, Gardiner was ordered to repair within about a fortnight to his London house and there to remain.[1]

Gardiner was haled before the Council several times in a wholly unsuccessful effort to secure his unequivocal acceptance of the Council's authority and of the changes in religion thus far made. Though he pleaded illness, he was once more before the Council in May when it was thought that some measure of conformity had been obtained, since he had agreed to offer his views in a public sermon at Paul's Cross, dealing with certain heads prescribed by the Council. Somerset seems to have been wholly responsible for these patient and moderate courses, there being serious misgivings amongst his colleagues with respect to the Protector's leniency. Reflecting these views, Warwick wrote to Cecil on June 14th: 'Being desirous to hear whether my Lord hath proceeded with the arrogant bishop according to his deservings or not . . . I rather fear that his accustomed wiliness, with the persuasion of some of his dear friends, and assured brethren, shall be the cause that the fox shall yet again deceive the lion.'[2] And deceive the lion, Gardiner certainly did, for in the famous sermon at Paul's Cross he expressed only very generally his duty of obedience to the recent religious legislation, pointedly maintained the doctrine of the real presence, and yielded no authority over himself or over religion to the Privy Council.[3]

This was too much, even for the always tolerantly disposed Somerset. Gardiner's offence had been public, dramatic, and calculated and, had it gone unpunished, would have destroyed the very basis of the authority of the government. The wonder is, indeed, that the Council did not proceed instantly to Gardiner's deprivation. It did meet on the matter the following day (June 30, 1548) and recorded a careful and full minute on the whole history of the case. It was recited that the *Injunctions* had been issued with full authority to reform abuses and secure quiet in the realm and save for the refusal of the Bishop of Winchester had been generally received and enforced. For his contumacy he had been committed to the Fleet where he was 'as much at his ease as if he had been in his own

---

[1] *A.P.C.* II, App., 550–551: Apr. 1, 1548.   [2] S.P. Dom., Edw. VI, IV, 17.

[3] All the accounts of this dramatic event stem from that of Foxe (*Acts and monuments*, VI, 87–93). There was a huge audience in attendance, including Somerset and the entire Council, and many prominent civil servants.

house'. On pretending to conform he had been set at liberty and sent to his see where immediately he began to create strife and dissension, of which there had been more 'in that one small city and shire than was almost in the whole realm'. When godly preachers were sent down to quiet the diocese, he barred them from pulpits by his own presence and warned his people to embrace no doctrine save that which he taught. On a second promise to lend obedience, from his London house, he none the less began 'to ruffle and meddle' in matters in which he possessed no authority. And, finally, having promised in a public sermon to state his conformity and obedience, he deliberately, and in the presence of the King and Council, spoke of matters contrary to an express understanding and command, in a manner likely 'to have stirred a great tumult, and in certain great matters touching the policy of the realm handled himself so colorably as therein he showed himself an open great offender and a very seditious man'.[1] It was accordingly resolved to commit Gardiner to the Tower,[2] where he remained until Mary's accession. But it should be noted that deprivation proceedings were not launched against him until after Somerset's fall from power in late 1549. In fact, though there was in the bench of bishops a hard core of determined conservative opposition to the measures of reform thus far taken, none of these men, of whom Gardiner and Bonner were the most articulate and powerful, was deprived during the moderate and tolerant regime of the Duke of Somerset.

3. THE CASE OF BISHOP BONNER (1547-1553)

Overt opposition to the course of reform in Hampshire was difficult enough, but in London, where dominant lay thought ran far ahead of the government's policy in religion and where the whole nexus of power was to be found, it could not safely be ignored. Bishop Bonner, translated to London from Hereford in 1540, had served Henry VIII as a diplomatist; was, like Gardiner, a champion of the Act of Supremacy and the Henrician settlement generally; and, so far as our information extends, seems to have had very little to do with the actual administration of his diocese. Bonner's personal religious views were known to be conservative, though he had never

---

[1] *A.P.C.* II, 208–211: June 30, 1548. Froude has noted that Russell must have signed this minute some months after the event.

[2] Edward VI, *Chronicle*, 10. The Council regarded this as an important action. On the next day a detailed explanation, following the argument of the Council minute closely, was sent to all English ambassadors abroad (S.P. Dom., Edw. VI, IV, 20).

at any time expressed himself formally on theological matters; he had in fact been an effective and certainly a compliant civil servant until exclusion from power and influence by the Edwardian government left him directly responsible for the administration of his see.

But when the royal commissioners entered his diocese in 1547 to carry out the King's *Injunctions* and to introduce the *Paraphrases* and the *Homilies*, Sir Anthony Cooke and his colleagues were met with what they thought was arrogance mixed with contempt. The bishop would receive the *Injunctions* only with a formal protestation 'that I will observe them if they be not contrary and repugnant to God's law and the statutes and ordinances of this church'. This being reported, Bonner was haled before the Council where he first contended that his words had been misunderstood and sought to give evasive replies to the flat question of whether he would stand on his protestation or revoke it. Under pressure, in the end he signed a formal revocation of his contumacious words and craved the pardon of the King. None the less, the Council sent him to the Fleet for a short period while the commissioners proceeded to carry out their visitation of the diocese and to introduce the required measures.[1]

Though closely watched, during the next two years Bonner offered no further overt resistance to the measures of reformation undertaken in the realm, until after the passage of the first Act of Uniformity he began to evade the intent of the law by permitting the celebration of special masses at St Paul's in the private chapels there. The Council accordingly, on June 24, 1549, specifically commanded him to forbid such private masses in any part of the cathedral church, ordering that only 'the holy blessed communion' was to be ministered in the form by law prescribed, and that only at the high altar. These instructions Bonner transmitted without comment to the Dean and Chapter two days later. Bonner was evidently seeking to avoid Gardiner's troubles and he was likewise much more reluctant to place himself in flat contravention with respect to the Act of Supremacy and the whole weight of statute law. But he was deeply disturbed by the radical sentiment so rife in his diocese, both in London and in Essex, later writing that in the Edwardian era subtle heresy and schism were spread in clever and divers ways: 'sometimes by the proceeding [of] preachers' sermons, sometimes by their printed treatises, sugared all over with loose liberty . . . sometimes by reading, playing, singing, and other like means, and new devises.' The result, he believed, was spiritual

---

[1] *A.P.C.* II, 126–127: Aug. 12, 1547; Burnet, *Reformation*, V, 162.

confusion leading to spiritual anarchy.[1] And this he was slowly persuaded he must oppose, though he was long uncertain regarding what would be the sticking-point for his conscience.

That sticking-point was not the introduction of the *Prayer Book* and the accompanying regulations which became legally effective in May, 1549, for when in July of that year the Council enjoined Bonner to make certain that the new service was followed throughout his diocese and to give good example in his own conduct, he straitly directed the Dean and Chapter to heed the *Injunctions* and expressed himself as 'right well willing and desiring' that obedience be lent to the Council's command.[2] Still suspicious of Bonner and now sorely troubled by the evidence of Catholic support of the rebellion then raging in the west, the Council in August once more called the bishop before it and enjoined him vigorously to reform his diocese and by his personal example to see to it that the people did not absent themselves from common prayer and the Holy Communion.[3] They likewise informed him that many still haunted illegal rites and masses in London, and, finally, required him to preach at St Paul's three weeks hence, and quarterly thereafter, setting forth articles thereupon handed to him.[4] They further stipulated that Bonner was to celebrate the communion in person according to the new rites on every major feast of the church, and throughout his diocese to 'see one only order used . . . according to our said book, and none other'.[5]

Unless there had been provocation, about which we know nothing, these strict and quite outrageous stipulations could only have meant to Bonner that the Council had determined either to suspend him from his authority or even to deprive him. The heads which he was ordered to deal with in his sermon on September 1st were principally to declare the sinfulness of the risings, to make clear

---

[1] Bonner, E., *A profitable and necessarye doctryne, with certayne homelies adioyned, etc.* (L., 1555), *Preface.* This, like all of Bonner's writings, is a solid, unimpressive, and rather dull book. In the same year, too, he published a Catechism under the title, *An honest godly instruction . . . for bringing up of children, etc.*, by which he hoped to correct the ungodly Catechism of 1547, which he had unhappily admitted to his diocese, and on which the youth of 1555 had, as he said, been so badly nourished.

[2] Foxe, *Acts and monuments*, V, 726–767: July 26, 1549; Cardwell, *Documentary annals*, I, 78–80. Save as otherwise noted, we have followed Foxe's account in our discussion of the troubles of Bishop Bonner, this being not only the principal but the sole source for much of the narrative. Though Foxe forever, if somewhat unjustly, blackened Bonner's reputation for his persecutions in the Marian period, there is no evidence of any special animus in his treatment of these earlier years.

[3] S.P. Dom., Edw. VI, VIII, 36: Aug. 2, 1549.

[4] *Ibid.* 37: Aug. 10?, 1549, for the heads of the sermons ordered.

[5] Foxe, *Acts and monuments*, V, 729–730.

that the rites and usages of the church might be ordered by the magistrate, and to preach explicitly that the regal power of a king remained unimpaired during his minority. This was for Bonner the sticking-point of conscience. In his sermon, preached before a large congregation at Paul's Cross, he deliberately evaded his instructions, dealing only in passing with the sin of rebellion, spending most of his time on a staunchly orthodox statement of the doctrine of transubstantiation, and ignoring completely the central point of the King's authority during his youth. Among those present were Latimer and Hooper, who immediately denounced Bonner in a letter addressed to the King. The Council, acting in the King's name, with an almost suspicious promptness, on September 8th commissioned Cranmer and Ridley, Petre and Smith from the Council, and May, Dean of St Paul's, to hear evidence, and vested them with full powers of decision.[1]

The hearings on the case were begun on September 10th and extended, in several sessions, to September 23rd, in a period of great stress when Somerset was losing his grip on power and when Warwick was fusing the coalition that was to bring about his fall. There was an evident intention to press the case hard and an almost ruthless determination to secure judgement against Bonner, inspired in part perhaps by the desire to appease London opinion. Bonner's defence was as skilful as it was intransigent. He vigorously attacked his principal accusers: ' "As for this merchant Latimer, I know him very well, and have borne with him, and winked at his doings a great while..... But as touching this other merchant Hooper, I have not seen him before, howbeit I have heard much of his naughty preaching." '[2] He insisted that, whatever the formal charges might be, it was his orthodox view of the mass that was being assailed, while he taunted Cranmer with his own vacillations on the doctrine. But now the formal articles of accusation were handed in against him, centering on his failure unequivocally to denounce the rebellion and to lend support to the fullness of regal power during the King's minority.[3] Bonner strove desperately and with great skill to focus the discussion on the doctrine of the mass and on his vicious attacks on Hooper and Latimer as heretics, hence not to be accepted as reliable accusers. But he was finally driven to explain that though his chaplain had provided him with material

[1] S.P. Dom., Edw. VI, VIII, 57 (and cf. ibid. 36, 37); Foxe, Acts and monuments, V, 746–749; Gairdner, James, The English church in the sixteenth century . . . to the death of Mary (L., 1902), 271.   [2] Foxe, Acts and monuments, V, 752.
[3] S.P. Dom., Edw. VI, VIII, 58: Sept. 13, 1547.

respecting the King's minority, ' "at the time of my sermon, I did fail, or have default of memory" '.[1]

At the fourth session (September 18th) Bonner marshalled all his defences and legal objections: the irregularity of the proceedings, the informal and confused questioning, the obscurity of the articles laid against him, and Smith's part in the proceedings. Cranmer, usually mild and courteous, was driven to a bitter denunciation of Bonner for his contemptuous attitude and for having ' "given to the multitude an intolerable example of disobedience" '.[2] But Bonner had shaken the Council by his stated objections to its procedures, and that body re-cast the articles alleged against him to centre them solely on his failure to deal with the question of the King's minority. Thereupon, the legal trap having been closed, Bonner refused to testify and appealed to the King on the ground that he was a properly constituted bishop who had always done his duty and lived within the laws.[3] He was now committed to the Marshalsea and was formally declared deprived. In late October he appealed to the King against the sentence, alleging malice and hatred on the part of four of his judges, but the Council, sitting in Star Chamber, confirmed the sentence and returned him to prison, where he was to remain until the accession of Mary Tudor.[4]

Difficult, thorny, and devious as Bonner certainly was, his case merits considerable sympathy, particularly when it is compared with the careful slowness of the process against Gardiner, who was not adjudged deprived until April, 1552. Gardiner had provoked and troubled the Council, literally from the first week of the new reign, by an aggressive and hostile opposition to every cautious move in the direction of reform. He assumed the offensive with immense vigour and power, and it is clear that the Protector would have accepted a quiet compromise on his part at several stages of the controversy. Bonner, on the other hand, had shown himself to be reluctantly compliant, had yielded on point after point, until the Council, one believes deliberately, drove him past that point where pride must combine with conviction. There can be little doubt that the Council thought the diocese of London too important and too deeply committed to the reformed faith to be entrusted to Bonner's charge. The Council wanted Ridley in that seat, and Ridley, then Bishop of Rochester, was one of the commission that tried this unhappy, obstinate, and wholly dull man.

[1] Foxe, *Acts and monuments*, V, 768.
[2] *Ibid.* 775–776.   [3] *Ibid.* 778–789.
[4] Wriothesley, *Chronicle*, II (Camden Soc., n.s. XX), 34.

4. MODERATE TREATMENT OF ROMAN CATHOLIC DISSENT
(1547-1549)

Throughout the period of Somerset's dominance in affairs of state it may be said that Roman Catholic dissent was treated with a consistent moderation so long as it remained essentially Henrician and, above all, so long as it did not deny the corner-stone of ecclesiastical policy, the Act of Supremacy. Though, as we have seen, there was a powerful conservative group of bishops, none, save in the certainly special cases of Gardiner and Bonner, had been subjected to any undue pressure and all felt free to express their opposition in the House of Lords by their voices and their votes, as the measures for effecting a reformed church were taken in the first and second sessions of Parliament. Somerset and Cranmer understood that men's sentiments and habits change but slowly, that effective preachers were few, and that great patience and restraint must be exercised. Both were persuaded that the free reading of the Bible, the reformed service in the English language, and the gently applied pressure of governmental persuasion must in due season result in a reformed and godly community of men in England. And both, Somerset particularly, were content to wait.

Further, during these three amazing years there was almost no formal restraint on thought and discussion so long as civil order was not evidently endangered. We have seen that Richard Smith, the professor of divinity at Oxford, not only engaged in disputations with respect to the doctrine of the mass, but seems to have published freely until his own unstable nature and probably exaggerated fears took him into exile.[1] During these years, too, a considerable number of devotional works composed by Catholic authors abroad were translated and freely published in England, though their content was of course not controversial or sectarian in temper. It was possible, too, to publish and distribute in London a work on the doctrine of purgatory wholly Catholic in tone. The book recites that the pain of the soul in purgatory:

> Is hot burning fire that nothing may bate
> But alms deeds, masses and prayer
> That of friends, for them been done here
> To abate that fire, though these been best,
> For they bring soon man's soul to rest.[2]

[1] *Vide ante*, 157; *et vide* Pollard, *Somerset*, 119; McConica, *English humanists*, 266; Edward VI, *Chronicle*, 6.

[2] *Here begynneth a lytell boke, that speketh of Purgatorye, etc.* (L.,[1550?]), B ii.

Pressure for change was being steadily but moderately applied, and quiet evasion or resistance was rarely even challenged. It was probably in late 1549 that expenses were incurred at Winchester for 'repairing and soldering Joseph, sixpence; for cleaning and anointing the Holy Ghost, sixpence; for repairing the Virgin Mary behind and before and making a new Child, four shillings and eightpence; for screwing the nose on the Devil's face, putting a new hair on his head and gluing a bit on his tail, five shillings and sixpence'.[1] In another cathedral city (Exeter) Professor MacCaffrey has shown that the religious fissure ran deeply through the merchant oligarchy which did, however, unite in the face of siege and possible internal rebellion in the interests of Tudor law and order. As late as 1552 only four of the numerous Exeter parishes had provided an English Bible, while only three or four had purchased the *Book of Common Prayer* and Erasmus' *Paraphrases*. But strong as was the conservative sentiment, it is significant to note that no city priest lent support to the great rebellion of 1549, though in a nearby parish a priest was hanged for complicity.[2]

A fairly extensive review of materials available suggests that not more than a score of Roman Catholic priests or scholars were under sustained pressure to yield conformity during the first three years of the reign or felt sufficiently endangered or outraged to go into exile. Among these was Bonner's chaplain, John Harpsfield, an older brother of the more famous Nicholas, who resigned his fellowship at Oxford in 1551 and probably retired abroad, as his brother certainly had in 1550.[3] Another ardent Catholic at Oxford was George Etherege, an excellent scholar in various branches of knowledge, who was actually appointed Regius Professor of Greek early in the Edwardian period but who was deprived of his chair in late 1550, without, so far as we can determine, going abroad.[4] So too, John Morwen, of a landed Devonshire family, educated at Corpus Christi College (Oxford), where he was graduated B.A. in 1538 and M.A. in 1543, was known as a staunch Roman Catholic, but none the less was prized for his abilities in Greek, being appointed a reader in the language in his college. There is no evidence that he was seriously disturbed in the Edwardian period, for he proceeded B.D. in 1552, though he soon found himself in serious trouble on the accession of Queen Elizabeth, having served Bonner as secretary

[1] Chapman, *Last Tudor king*, 159 (quoting from a Winchester Cathedral MS. in Miss Chapman's possession).
[2] MacCaffrey, Wallace T., *Exeter, 1540–1640, etc.* (Cambridge, Mass., 1958), 190–192.
[3] *DNB*.   [4] McConica, *English humanists*, 266–267.

in numerous heresy trials under Queen Mary.[1] Similarly, Henry Cole, warden of New College and a civil lawyer of some eminence at Oxford, was very properly regarded as a Romanist, the university visitors being instructed to examine and deprive him in November, 1550, if he would not submit. But Cole was able to satisfy the visitors and evidently remained in quiet opposition, without further difficulties, until on the accession of Mary Tudor he blossomed forth as an important and zealous Catholic.[2]

Not escaping so lightly was Thomas Watson, of Cambridge, where he had been elected a fellow of St John's College in 1535 and where for several years he was preacher and dean. A brilliant humanist, and in earlier years a fast friend of both Cheke and Ascham, Watson made considerable contribution to the revival of classical learning in his university. Preferment came in 1545 when Gardiner made him his secretary, and there can be no doubt that he prepared many of the papers and arguments with which Gardiner defended himself in the long proceedings which we have already sketched. Watson was committed to the Fleet in late 1550, but seems to have been free a year later (December, 1551) when he was engaged in private doctrinal controversy at Sir Richard Morison's house. In any event, he emerged early in Mary's reign as one of the most effective of the Roman Catholic controversialists, being created Bishop of Lincoln in 1556, only to fall into really serious trouble under Queen Elizabeth.[3] Another of Gardiner's chaplains, John Seton, also of Cambridge, was well known for his publication of a formidable work of logic in 1545. A man of quiet courage, Seton gave evidence for Gardiner in the bishop's trial and was among those present at the disputation conducted by Martyr at Oxford in 1550. There is no evidence that he was seriously molested in the Edwardian period, though he also quickly found himself in prison under Elizabeth.[4]

In many ways the most formidable of these conservative preachers and scholars was the eminent civilian John Story, the first Regius Professor (1544) of civil law at Oxford, who was returned as a member of the House of Commons in 1547 and who seemed for a time disposed to support the measures of reformation. But Story opposed the first Act of Uniformity with such violence in the House that he was briefly imprisoned by order of the Commons until he had made submission for his contempt. Shortly afterwards he went

[1] DNB.
[2] Sander[s], Nicolas, *Rise and growth of the Anglican schism*, ed. by David Lewis (L., 1877), 199.   [3] DNB.   [4] McConica, *English humanists*, 268.

into exile to Louvain, returning to become a principal persecutor of leading Protestants during the reign of Mary and falling afoul the law of treason under Queen Elizabeth.[1] And, finally, we must mention one of the ablest, as he was also the oldest, of this group of Roman Catholic partisans, Ralph Baynes, also educated at St John's College, Cambridge. Always known as a conservative in religious matters, Baynes was a fervent public opponent of Latimer at Cambridge. One of the early Hebraists in England, Baynes went abroad to France where he was appointed professor of Hebrew at Paris and there served until on Mary's accession he was made Bishop of Lichfield and Coventry, taking a leading role in the Marian persecutions and being promptly deprived by Queen Elizabeth.

These were the principal of the forthright and deeply convinced Roman Catholic clergy and scholars who declined to make their submission to the reformation under Edward. There are another eight or possibly nine of somewhat lesser stature, whose histories we need not review, and this would seem to complete the roster. Of the roughly twenty men in the whole group, none, it must be emphasized, was done to death, very few were imprisoned even for a short season, and the rest suffered no more than serious personal inconvenience or deprivation. It should also be stated that, Gardiner and Bonner aside, none of the whole group of ardent and deeply persuaded Roman Catholics was of the first rank either in public estimation or in theological learning. It is not too much to say that Protestantism had by 1553 absorbed into itself the main stream of humanistic learning in England and was thereby to gain immense intellectual impetus and power.

If the government, especially that of Somerset, was disposed to treat with moderation overt Roman Catholic sympathy and even modest literary defence of the Roman Catholic faith amongst the fairly well-known and intellectually sophisticated clergy and scholars, it is no wonder that it moved cautiously and tolerantly with the great mass of the parochial clergy, who, as we have previously noted, were on the whole simply inert and quite prepared to lend at least grudging support to the measures of reformation required by the King and Parliament. The evidence for serious molestation or disciplining of the parish clergy under Edward VI is slight, one can say confidently, because there was very little formal opposition among these simple and generally unsophisticated men. Moreover, it is clear in most known instances that the Council

---

[1] Pollard, *Somerset*, 117–118.

was moved by concern more for public order than for full propriety of belief. We shall present such evidence as we have found of punitive pressure on the parochial clergy, postponing the discussion of the special situation in southwestern England which engendered, at least in part, the great rising there in 1549.[1]

As early as May, 1547, the Council addressed an obscurely worded order to the Council of the North to locate a priest named William Craforth and presumably to send him up to London, for the Council wished to 'speak with' him. Holgate and his colleagues were first to get the priest in their hands and then to prohibit the reading in churches of the book called *Exoneratorium Curatorum*, and also to call in all copies of the book to be found in their area of jurisdiction.[2] There is no record of further action in the case, though, hazily framed as the order was, it seems clear that Craforth was in difficulties because of ardent Roman Catholic views.

Cranmer in his own diocese dealt gently with offences of the conservative clergy so long as civil order was not threatened. At Stepney the vicar was the former abbot of Tower Hill, London, and known in 1547 as an overt and intransigent Catholic. He would deliberately disrupt services in his own church when an appointed preacher took the pulpit by having all the bells rung during the service, by having the choir burst into song in the midst of the service, or by interrupting personally. The parish itself was Protestant in sympathy but could do nothing until one of its members was successful in getting the vicar cited before Cranmer, who however would take no more stringent action than to rebuke the recalcitrant priest, holding that this was by law the limit of his authority and that in any event clemency might accomplish more than rigour.[3]

Earlier in the same year (1547) the Council had intervened at Beccles, Suffolk, on the complaint of two nearby gentlemen of tumult in the parish because of the rival claims of two priests to the benefice. They were instructed to do no more than impress on the 'discreet and honest men of the parish' the danger in such agitation and to bind the priests under penalty against further unseemly disorders.[4] Nor is there any persuasive suggestion of doctrinal concern in the case of the priest at Helmingham (Suffolk) who had been brought before the Privy Council for questioning. The Council thought him of 'no great wit and less learning', and his unstated offence was remitted on condition that before his congregation he should declare that he had been apprehended because of his 'naughty

[1] *Vide post*, 439ff.   [2] Pocock, in *E.H.R.* IX (1894), 545.
[3] Strype, *Cranmer*, I, 246–247.   [4] *A.P.C.* II, 35–36: Feb. 15, 1547.

and lewd words'.[1] More certainly involving Roman Catholic sentiments was the case of Dr Cotes of Chester who was commanded to
appear before the Council, while letters of inquiry were forwarded
to unnamed persons of his city for additional information regarding
his 'lewd behaviour' in sundry of his sermons, though it does not
appear that further action was taken in the case.[2] Concern was also
expressed by the Council in June, 1547, when it was learned that
certain Carthusian pensioners were making their way out of England,
'retaining still in their hearts their old supersitition and popish
monkery', while illegally arranging that friends in England should
collect their pensions. No bar was placed against such emigration,
but measures were ordered for the tightening of pension payments
by requiring more positive identifications.[3] Rather more than a year
later, and after the passage of the first Act of Uniformity, the
Earl of Warwick forwarded to Cecil and the Council a complaint
against the views and Romanist activities of a priest serving
as chaplain to the undoubtedly, though quietly, Catholic Lord
Windsor.[4]

There are other scattered evidences of concern with Roman
Catholic views held by the lower clergy, but none involving greater
severity than in the cases just rehearsed. Even after the adoption of
the first *Book of Common Prayer* there was as yet no wish to lay
formal emphasis on the fracture of faith which had in part already
occurred. Very wisely, the policy adopted was almost by insensible
degrees to incorporate the parochial clergy within the generous
bounds of the church in England. There was no persecution of the
lower clergy in England during the Edwardian period. Nor, so long
as no threat was offered to the civil order, was any considerable
pressure brought to bear on the laity, a large proportion of whom
were undoubtedly Romanist in sentiment, habit, and instinct. One
such instance was a case which came up to the Council from Sandon
(Herts) in December, 1547, involving John Newport, a gentleman
of the region, who had openly reviled the curate in his pulpit, calling
him a whoremonger and other evil names, and forcing him to stop
his preaching, as well as illegally extorting tax payments from the
parishioners. After a season in the Fleet, Newport was released on
condition that he publicly confess his fault in the parish church,
restore the sums taken as taxes, and thereafter comport himself
quietly.[5] There lies against this reign, then, and most especially

---

[1] *A.P.C.* II, App., 465: Mar. 30, 1547.   [2] *Ibid.* App., 483.
[3] *Ibid.* 97–98.   [4] S.P. Dom., Edw. VI, IV, 32: July 21, 1548.
[5] *A.P.C.* II, 150: Dec. 8, 1547.

against the policy of Somerset, nothing that can be called persecution. Perhaps the summary of John Foxe is not far from the mark:
'amongst the whole number of the popish sort, of whom some privily
did steal out of the realm, many were crafty dissemblers, some were
open and manifest adversaries; yet, of all that multitude, there was
not one man that lost his life. In sum, during the whole time of the
six years of this king, much tranquillity, and, as it were, a breathing-
time, was granted to the whole church of England.'[1]

5. THE PROBLEM OF PROTESTANT HERESY (1547–1549)

The term heresy has very little meaning in mid-sixteenth century Europe unless it be remembered that it is the appellation
applied to those who maintained doctrinal beliefs or practices of
worship proscribed by those who possessed power in state and
church. Historically, therefore, after the passage of the first Act of
Uniformity, some areas of Roman Catholic doctrine and considerable areas of Roman Catholic worship were in legal fact heretical,
though they were not in truth so to be treated under the law. The
authorities were, however, to be more sorely troubled by strange
and stubbornly held doctrinal errors of the 'Protestant left', so to
say, which even in this early period suggest the fractionating tendencies implicit in Protestantism. The responsible reformers, those
charged with the administration of a church organically linked with
the state, were deeply alarmed by these centripetal tendencies in
Protestantism, and their theological respectability was outraged and
sorely tried by these zealous extremists, some of whom were undoubtedly mad. For one thing, Lollard convictions and teachings
had survived into the sixteenth century, becoming absorbed in a
strange amalgam with the in-flowing and far more powerful Lutheran
teachings in the first decade of the English Reformation. And a new
and frightening strain of heresy was added by the influx of Anabaptist heresies, a confusing and almost generic term describing
varying and highly individualistic heretical beliefs. After the
terrifying excesses of the Anabaptists in Germany, the term became for more than a half-century an opprobrious accusation to lay
against any Protestant heresy and a convenient abusive term which
the Catholics, wholly inexactly, employed for the denunciation of
Protestantism generally. We shall use the term because it has
become historically fixed, remembering that it is most loosely and
always opprobriously used.

[1] Foxe, *Acts and monuments*, V, 704.

Some time after the fall of Münster (June, 1535), English Anabaptists attended a clandestine meeting at Bocholt (near Wesel)
which sought to rally the now shattered sect and to seek a common
ground of belief in a communion already spiritually weakened by its
almost anarchical individualism. It also seems possible that the
burden of expense for the Bocholt conference was assumed by an
unnamed English Anabaptist, probably a merchant.[1] It is almost
certain that even before 1535 there were numerous Dutch and
Flemish Anabaptists living in England, most of whom were connected with the cloth trade, who were forming close ties with the
Lollard centres of strength, also, and for many years past, closely
associated with that trade. Thus as early as 1532–1534 six English
subjects and two Flemings had been arrested for importing and
distributing an Anabaptist confession of faith, the examination
revealing that the Anabaptists were holding meetings in London,
that they were ministered to by spiritual preachers and leaders, and
that there were also English Anabaptists in Amsterdam and in
Flanders. Some of these were undoubtedly amongst the twenty-five
'Dutch Anabaptists' apprehended in London in 1535, of whom
fourteen were burned.[2] The problem of repression was greatly increased for the English authorities by the flight of Anabaptists
after the fall of Münster, Henry VIII being warned by both Philip
of Hesse and John Frederick that Continental Anabaptists were
moving surreptitiously into English port towns. Two proclamations
were accordingly issued demanding the immediate departure of
such refugee persons and prohibiting the possession of Anabaptist
books,[3] while three more of the sect were burned in the autumn of
1538. In the burst of repression attending the passage of the Six
Articles Act, particular attention was centred on the Anabaptists, a
French groom of the Queen, and an Englishman named Collins
being burned in the spring of 1540, while two Flemish members of
the sect were put to death shortly afterwards.[4]

But these severe measures had no other effect than to drive the
sectarian movement under ground, there being no other way to
enforce an embargo on ideas than to embargo the cloth trade itself.
Somerset's policy of extending almost complete freedom of religion, the welcome given to religious refugees generally, and the

---

[1] I follow the treatment of my colleague, George H. Williams (*The radical reformation*,
Phila., 1962), for the whole of this paragraph.

[2] Williams, *Radical reformation*, 401–402.

[3] Hughes and Larkin, *Tudor proclamations*, I, 270–276: Nov. 16, 1538; *ibid.* 278–280:
Feb. 26, 1539.   [4] Williams, *Radical reformation*, 403.

special bulwark of liberty to be constituted for the Strangers' Church in London, gave radical sectarianism sufficient time to root itself securely in the realm and fostered its rapid development. The movement which resulted was—if we may trust the hostile evidence on which we are almost wholly dependent—highly individualistic in nature, but probably interconnected with an embracing Lollardy, Anabaptism, Libertinism, and anti-Trinitarianism. This development the imperial ambassador watched with fascinated horror, informing his master that he had warned both Somerset and Paget that spiritual freedom in England was resulting in the rapid increase of Zwinglian and other radical tenets and must shortly lead to disorder.[1]

Possibly more affected by Zwinglian than by radical sectarian views was Thomas Dobb, of St John's College, Cambridge, who strongly advocated clerical marriage and who rose in St Paul's during the celebration of the mass to denounce the mass completely and to explicate the errors involved to the congregation. He was committed to the Compter, where he died shortly before Somerset's pardon could release him.[2] Also in 1547, John Hume, a servant to a foreign merchant, was reported for having completely denied the efficacy of the mass and for stating that he would be damned before he would hear it sung. Foxe tells us that Cranmer was informed of the offence, but he knew of no action taken in the case.[3] One of the most troublesome of the extreme sectaries in the early Edwardian period was Robert Cooke, who had served as keeper of the royal wine cellar and who was a man of some education, with a passionate love of music. Cooke denounced infant baptism and the doctrine of original sin, while for good measure he held extremely radical views on the eucharist. Evidently an aggressive, as he was probably a boring, man, he used his position to engage such eminent persons at court as Coverdale and Parkhurst in theological disputation, though he was never in serious difficulties and fled abroad under Mary.[4]

In 1548 Cranmer personally questioned one John Champneys, of Stratford-on-the-Bow, who apparently held an extraordinary *mélange* of radical heresies: that regenerate men cannot sin, that from the apostles' time the true gospel has been so persecuted that a godly man may not profess it, and that God intends the necessaries of life for the use of his elect. These, and other, heretical views

---

[1] *Cal. S.P. Span.*, IX, 111: June 24, 1547.
[2] Foxe, *Acts and monuments*, V, 704–705.
[3] *Ibid.* 705.   [4] Strype, *Memorials*, II, i, 111–112.

Champneys admitted he had held, preached, and taught. Under pressure from the Archbishop the accused man abjured, was sentenced to bear a faggot at Paul's Cross, and was bound to good behaviour.[1] At the same time a clergyman, John Assheton, possibly of Shillington, Bedfordshire, was forced to abjure undoubted Socinian opinions, having taught that the Holy Ghost is not God, 'but only a certain power of the Father', that Christ was no more than 'a holy prophet . . . beloved of God', and that He did no more than reveal God's will and purposes by His testament.[2] So too, in the following year, Michael Thombe, a London butcher, recanted the Anabaptist teachings on baptism and the view that Christ took no flesh from the virgin.[3]

The gathering evidences of radical heresy, obviously concentrated in and around London, alarmed the Council, as well as the lenient Cranmer, particularly when it was learned that there were organized groups of heretical persons, holding at least occasional services and winning converts in Kent, Sussex, and Essex. Accordingly on April 12, 1549, a formidable commission comprising Cranmer and six other bishops, members of the Council, and others was appointed to search out all heretics and contemners of the *Book of Common Prayer*, with full power to reclaim such heretics, to excommunicate and imprison, or to hand over to the secular power for further action.[4] In May (1549) several Londoners were haled before the commission and forced to abjure a variety of Anabaptist and Socinian opinions, all yielding save for Joan Bocher, the ultimate and tragic history of whose case, together with that of George van Parris, will be more appropriately considered in a later discussion.[5] Evidence was also gathered against an Anabaptist group in Faversham, Kent, which in addition to the usual opinions of these sectaries held that predestination was meeter for devils than for Christian men and that there was no one who could not damn himself.[6] One of those accused in the Faversham group, who were in due course released, was Henry Harte, who was already advocating separation from the Church of England, but whose two tracts, *A godly newe short treatyse* (1548) and *A godlie exhortation* (1549), display no particularly incendiary views. The latter work is

---

[1] Wilkins, *Concilia*, IV, 39–40; Strype, *Cranmer*, I, 254–255; Lansdowne MS. 980, #59, f. 70.   [2] Strype, *Cranmer*, I, 256–257; Wilkins, *Concilia*, IV, 41.

[3] Strype, *Cranmer*, I, 257; Wilkins, *Concilia*, IV, 42; Lansdowne MS. 980, #69, f. 80. The name is variously rendered: Tombe, Thornbe, being other spellings. Williams (*Radical reformation*, 779) regards Thombe as a Melchiorite Anabaptist.

[4] Burnet, *Reformation*, II, 203.

[5] In the concluding volume of this study.   [6] Lansdowne MS. 980, #73, f. 82.

especially impressive, being a treatise of piety, almost devotional in nature and cast roughly in the form of a sermon. Cranmer's moderate and careful dealing with undoubted heresy in 1549 disclosed far more of heresy than it cured, and on Hooper's strident demand, after Somerset had fallen from power, was to lead in 1550 to a renewed and far more vigorous effort to rid the realm of these 'pestiferous' heretics and to provoke a mood of reaction which had as its dreadful fruit the burning of the two heretics, Bocher and Parris, whose cases had been opened but not determined in the years when Somerset's quiet but deeply rooted policy of toleration prevailed.

IX

THE POSTURE OF EMPIRE: FOREIGN AFFAIRS (1547–1549)

I. DIPLOMATIC RELATIONS AT THE OUTSET

William Paget, the most gifted and after Gardiner the most experienced of the late Henrician diplomatists, for his own instruction and possibly for the eyes of his colleagues in the Privy Council, drafted a remarkable statement of England's diplomatic position only a few months before his master's death.[1] The analysis is coldly realistic and not a little gloomy, as Paget sought to project policy and to assess the diplomatic dangers which England faced. France will be moved by motives of revenge to regain Boulogne, recently won by Henry VIII, and policy must be plotted with this fact steadily in mind. So too, the Emperor may not be regarded as trustworthy, being influenced by the implacable resolution of the papacy to recover its 'usurped power and tyranny over this realm', as well as by old grudges. Hence neither France nor the Emperor can be regarded as a certain ally, though a steady effort must be maintained to exploit the enmity between them. One possible source of strength would be a cultivation of relations with Venice, fearful as that state is of the possibility of imperial hegemony. The various Protestant states of Germany and the Baltic are directly endangered by imperial power and clamour for aid, but to ally with them would predictably lead to an alliance of France with the Empire against England. On balance—and the field of choice is at once narrow and risky—the best course would appear to be to seek some basis of agreement between the Emperor and the Protestant powers, and to prevail upon Charles to lend such aid as might be necessary in the

---

[1] Cotton MSS., Titus, B, ii, 47, ff. 79–81. The manuscript is dated August, 1546. Strype's summary of the document (*Memorials*, II, i, 87–90) is faulty and should not be used; he also mis-dates it as August, 1547. Paget had to a large degree been entrusted with the conduct of foreign affairs in the last years of Henry VIII's reign. He drafted most of the dispatches to ambassadors, and their home contact was with him. He also utterly charmed the imperial ambassador, Van der Delft, appointed in 1544, and began to exploit the relationship well before the reign of Edward began. (Gammon, *Master of practises*, 118–119.)

event of a French assault on Boulogne. He recommended that
negotiations for a closer alliance with the Emperor be undertaken,
buttressed by a strong effort to find an accommodation between
him and the German Protestant states. Meanwhile, however, Paget
would also seek to increase German Protestant power, by land and
sea, to provide a possible basis of alliance if the Emperor should reject
the English advances. But the foundations of English policy must
be to build her own domestic strength, to establish unanimity within
the realm, and to gather resources 'by knitting to us the surest and
most sincere friends we can get'.

This cool analysis states concisely the foreign situation at the
accession of Edward VI and it lays out in broad outlines the policy
which Somerset's government sought to follow, in part no doubt
because in this period Paget exercised a considerable influence on
decisions. But Paget, quite inexplicably, made no mention of
Scotland, against which Henry in the last months of his life was
preparing still another invading army. And it was as a consequence
of the new government's Scottish policy that peace with France was
to be disrupted and England subject to great foreign dangers.

The situation at the outset of the reign, then, was fraught with
difficult diplomatic problems and with very real dangers. The
papacy was sullenly hostile; Charles was restrained from an overtly
anti-English policy only by the festering problems which required
all his attention in Germany. Moreover, Charles had in recent
months made considerable progress towards restoring the imperial
hegemony, quite as much by diplomacy as by power of arms, and it
was with a kind of horror that England watched the melting of
strength of the German Protestant states. But England was at peace
with the empire and came gradually to realize that Charles stood in
desperate need of time for his twin concerns: Germany and the
Council of Trent, which for the first two years of Edward's reign
absorbed the whole of his time and resources.[1] So too, England was
at peace with France under the recently concluded Treaty of
Campe (June 7, 1546) by whose terms she had gained Boulogne
for a period of eight years, when the town was to be restored on payment by France of a huge indemnity of 2,000,000 crowns in gold.
Scotland was also to be included in the peace on condition she
honoured the earlier treaty of peace (1543), by whose terms Mary
Stuart was to marry Edward VI. England also enjoyed some measure
of protection against France by virtue of earlier treaties with the
Emperor, involving also his Flemish self-interest, which could be

[1] Wernham, R. B., *Before the Armada, etc.* (L., and N.Y., 1966), 165.

invoked by any French assault on Calais and its hinterland—'the Old Conquest', as it came to be called—a military guarantee so menacing to France that when war broke out with England in 1549, France gave formal assurances that Calais would not be assaulted.[1]

England was on the whole well served by its diplomatists during this period. Both Somerset and Northumberland preferred relatively young and humanistically educated laymen rather than the ecclesiastics, men like Gardiner, Bonner, and Tunstall, whom Henry VIII was inclined to employ. It seems certain that all the resident ambassadors appointed were fluent in Latin, in which Paget preferred to converse and write since his French was inadequate.[2] Morison, excellent though his Latin was, knew very little French, though his Italian was fluent and his German evidently passable. Bishop Thirlby, who had recently served under Henry as ambassador in Germany, seems to have had some proficiency in German, while Ascham, when serving with Morison at the Emperor's court, tried to learn the language, though he confessed, 'surely I drink Dutch better than I speak Dutch'.[3]

The ablest and most experienced of all the English diplomatists of the period was Nicholas Wotton, who served in France as resident ambassador from 1546 to 1549, and who was accredited to the Emperor in 1551. His career we have already briefly noted.[4] Sir John Mason, of lowly origin, but well educated and experienced in the royal service, was in France in 1550–1551, and exhibited all the qualities of a highly capable career diplomatist. At ease in French, not to be beguiled, careful in his judgements and skilled in making contacts, his dispatches were uniformly clear and straightforward and precise in their advice. Sir William Pickering, who succeeded Mason in France, was less experienced and observing, but his dispatches were terse, intelligent, and couched in the setting of an expert knowledge of English affairs. The more famous and gifted Sir Richard Morison, accredited to the Emperor in 1550–1553, was none the less a failure in that sensitive post. His sources were often unreliable, he was confessedly lazy, and his reports are rambling, padded out, shockingly thin in content, and sprawl all over Europe in their coverage. He loved to indulge in the universal view, adding nothing to information more expertly forwarded to

[1] *Cal. S.P. Span.*, IX, *Intro.*, xii.

[2] Meyer, A. O., *Die englische Diplomatie in Deutschland zur Zeit Eduards VI., und Mariens* (Breslau, [1900]), 7.

[3] Ascham, Roger, *The whole works, etc.*, ed. by Rev. Dr Giles (3 vols. in 4, L., 1864–1865), I, ii, 285.   [4] *Vide ante*, 81.

the Council by other resident ambassadors. Further, his dispatches strive to be literature, were suffused with a strained and somewhat artificial sense of humour, with Greek sprinkled inappropriately through his letters, more than half of which, incidentally, deal with his need for funds. Far more competent professionally was Sir Thomas Chamberlain, who had served for a time as president of the guild of merchants trading in Flanders, a post resembling that of a modern consul. He was accredited, with Sir Thomas Smith, to try to smooth out Anglo-Flemish relations in January, 1548, and was later made ambassador to the Regent in Brussels. His principal concern was for commercial relations with Flanders, on which he was really expert, and his numerous dispatches were dry, prompt, and useful. The Italian-born Peter Vannes, who had however lived in England since 1513, serving Wolsey and Henry VIII in numerous secretarial and diplomatic capacities, was in the first months of the reign the Latin Secretary to the Council, but was in 1550 appointed ambassador to Venice. His dispatches were usually reliable, though gossipy and discursive, but much of what he wrote was scarcely apposite to English affairs.

These were the principal of the accredited ambassadors of our period, all being men of considerable ability and of complete fidelity. It was still assumed that these were posts of high honour and dignity, which in the preceding generation had usually been held by great nobles or bishops, whose estates were expected to defray most of the heavy charges. But almost all of Edward's resident envoys were in fact career officers without substantial means, and almost to a man they grumbled bitterly and justifiably that they were being ruined by the port they were expected to maintain. They were supposed to keep a large house and a considerable staff; they travelled expensively when the court to which they were accredited moved; and they frequently complained that their houses were regarded as hostels for Englishmen passing through. Pickering and Mason received approximately 37s a day for their maintenance in France, which defrayed little more than their rent and charges for horses. Their stipends were due quarterly, but were almost steadily in arrears, and most of these men had really to beg for additional and outright gifts from the Crown in order to function at all. Morison, who was, however, both independent and inexact in financial matters, was quite unable to meet his creditors when he left Augsburg, having to resort to money-lenders. All of these men displayed considerable skill in developing contacts in the courts to which they were appointed, and a number of them, oddly enough, were especially friendly with the papal nuncios assigned to the same courts. All of them, too, employed spies, usually unreliable, from whose reports they sought to follow policy by collation with information gained in official interviews and from their informal court contacts.[1]

The great weakness of English diplomacy lay not with the ambassadors who, under great difficulty, were able to keep the home government reasonably well and certainly fairly promptly informed. The weakness was in London, where the concern was with domestic affairs. An examination of the records of the Privy Council and of the State Papers clearly reveals that there was no careful group consideration of foreign policy by the Council, decisions of great diplomatic moment being taken without full knowledge or discussion. Nor was there a steady flow of information or even clear instructions given to ambassadors abroad who came to feel more and more remote from the centre of power and decision. Thus at the outset of the reign it was almost five months before Harvell, then ambassador to Venice, was officially informed of the succession of the new King and of his coronation, 'through forgetfulness amongst so many other urgent affairs'; the Council now asked its envoy to inform the Venetian government of the succession, blaming the slowness of the posts, or delay in Antwerp, for an outrageous administrative neglect.[2] During the first two years of the reign, Paget sought vainly to keep some ordered control over diplomatic policy, but the Protector tended increasingly to retain sole responsibility and then to neglect his duty. And later in the reign Northumberland was both impatient and inexpert in diplomatic affairs, the principal burden for maintaining contacts falling on Cecil, still young and inexperienced, to whom the ambassadors came gradually to address dispatches which they now knew would not receive due consideration by the whole body of the Council or even by the head of state.

But, if Somerset was an indifferent and often a confused diplomatist, he was a highly gifted and experienced professional soldier who took immediate steps to strengthen English defences against the diplomatic uncertainties. The proficient Sir Hugh Paulet and Sir John Harrington were sent to make a thorough survey of the defences of Calais and its hinterland and their recommendations were gradually implemented. Orders were forwarded to meet at least part of the arrears of the Boulogne garrison, while the work of

---

[1] Meyer, *Englische Diplomatie*, 11–12, 23–24, 25–29,
[2] *A.P.C.* II, App., 489–490: May 8, 1547,

fortification at Boulogne and at Newhaven was to be hastened by employing the troops on the work at extra pay.[1] The urgent recommendation of Paulet and Harrington that storage facilities must be provided at Newhaven was met with orders that the garrison be moved into tents and thus quartered until adequate provision for stores could be arranged.[2] The morale and efficiency of troops on garrison and field duty was improved when 10,000 marks in full payment of arrears was forwarded to pay the army in Ireland and £10,000 was sent for the soldiers at Boulogne, as well as £2000 for the labourers employed there on the fortifications.[3] At the same time, troops were levied in three counties for strengthening the defences of Portsmouth, where repairs were also undertaken on the neglected fortifications and additional ordnance mounted.[4] While these defensive measures were being prosecuted with considerable vigour, Andrew Dudley, now appointed Admiral of the Fleet, was ordered to sea in the *Pauncy* on patrol off the English and Scottish coasts, shortly engaging and capturing the *Lion*, one of the principal ships in the somewhat tattered Scottish fleet.[5]

These actions were of course set principally against France which the Council was persuaded might strike quickly while the new government was still unsettled. Lord Grey, in command at Boulogne, had warned the Council that French military preparations were under way and he was confident that Bolougne would be attacked.[6] He was in fact totally in error since Francis I, weary, ill, and fearful of the Emperor, earnestly desired a period of settled peace with England and the removal of remaining frictions by the final delineation of the Boulogne enclave. This wish was clearly intimated to Somerset by Odet de Selve, resident ambassador in London from July, 1546, to December, 1548, and on March 4th Somerset appointed Russell, Warwick, Seymour, and Paget to negotiate in London, Antoine Escalin des Aymars coming over on a special mission to assist de Selve in the settlement.[7] The discussions proceeded smoothly and amicably, while both Somerset and Paget assured the always nervous Van der Delft that any understanding reached would offer no threat to the Emperor.[8] At the same time St Mauris in Paris reported to Granvelle that Francis I was much

[1] *A.P.C.* II, 23–24: Feb. 7, 1547; *ibid.* App., 437–439: Feb. 6, 1547.
[2] *Ibid.* App., 482–483: Apr. 17, 1547.   [3] *Ibid.* 92–93: May 19 and 25, 1547.
[4] S.P. Dom., Edw. VI, I, 20, 21, 23.
[5] Edward VI, *Chronicle*, 5–6; S.P. Dom., Edw. VI, I, 23: Feb. 23, 1547.
[6] *Cal. S.P. For., Edw. VI*, #29.
[7] *A.P.C.* II, 47–48: Mar. 4, 1547; *Cal. S.P. For., Edw. VI*, #22.
[8] *Cal. S.P. Span.* IX, 58: Mar. 18, 1547.

irritated by English improvements on the Boulogne defences, which
had been protested to England.[1] The text of the treaty pledging
amity and arranging for the settling of the disputed Boulogne
boundaries was quickly concluded in agreed draft,[2] and was forwarded on April 1, 1547, by the Council to Wotton in Paris, who
was to arrange promptly for ratification and to receive Francis'
formal oath of observance.[3] The Council did not know that on the
preceding day Francis I had died, with incalculable consequences
for England and for Scotland. His wisdom, tolerance, and breadth
of vision gave way to the bigotry and unpredictable violence of
Henry II.

Just a week after Francis' death Wotton forwarded from Paris a
brilliant dispatch which clearly and accurately forecast the difficulties that lay ahead for England as a consequence of the accession
of Henry II. Already all of the old ministers had been swept from
office, with the one exception of Olivier, the chancellor. He expressed the fear that the direction of policy would be lodged in the
hands of the Constable Montmorency, a man always distrusted by
the old king. Finding that all his former contacts were gone, Wotton
suggested it might be well if he were recalled.[4] The new king.
Wotton might have added, had long been the leader of the anti-
English party in France and now came almost immediately under
the dominance of the Guise faction, as well as being deeply under
the influence of his mistress, Diane de Poitiers, twenty years his
senior. Henry II also had strong martial ambitions, the humiliation
of Boulogne rankling from the outset. It speedily became clear that
his policy would be directed towards the conquest of Boulogne and,
what England most feared, the full support of Scotland. For a
season, Boulogne and Scotland were at the centre of French foreign
policy, in place of the concentration on Italy which had marked the
policy of Francis I.[5]

The Council reacted quickly to Wotton's appraisal of French
policy, which their own estimate confirmed. On April 12th they
warned Tunstall at Durham that the new government in France
might quickly pick some quarrel with England and accordingly
ordered him to go north to prepare against possible Scottish diversionary raids.[6] A few days later Somerset expressed at least the
hope that France would not launch war against a child king, but

---

[1] Cal. S.P. Span. IX, 64: Mar. 21, 1547.
[2] Rymer, Foedera, XV, 126; draft in Bibl. Nat., Latin MS. 5120, ff. 95–102, et cf.
ibid. ff. 85–93.   [3] Cal. S.P. For., Edw. VI, #48.
[4] Ibid. #51.   [5] Wernham, Before the Armada, 168.   [6] A.P.C. II, App., 475.

admitted that after Milan it was Boulogne that most 'pricked' the French.[1] The Council was concerned because of the complaint of the French ambassador that English forces had felled timber in the Forest of Guiines on disputed ground and warned Cobham to avoid all incidents and, shortly afterwards, that a French attack might at any time be mounted on Calais.[2] Even greater anxiety was displayed in similar warnings sent to him in July, instructing him in the event of attack to withdraw all outlying forces into the great fortifications at Calais.[3]

It is evident that Somerset thought a major French attack might be launched against Calais and that he was preparing to invoke the imperial commitments with respect to the 'Old Conquest' if this should occur. The French had meanwhile refused to conclude the treaty with respect to the Boulogne frontiers because of work proceeding there on the fortifications, which again suggested to the Protector that an attack there might be imminent.[4] About a month later he informed the imperial envoy that the Scots had mobilized 18,000 men 'with seven thousand savages in addition', and were harassing the frontier, while French galleys were entering the Firth of Forth leading to Edinburgh. He announced as well his intention to move against Scotland, which was disowning its treaty obligations, before French domination there became complete, even though this might lead to war with France.[5] A few days later Somerset learned from Wotton that the French would refuse to honour the annual indemnity due for Boulogne, while St Mauris in Paris reported to Prince Philip that 4000 French troops had been embarked for Scotland.[6] Van der Delft in mid-August was wholly unable to gain access to Somerset, who was away from London putting the English army in the field for the invasion of Scotland,[7] but did see Paget, who indicated that negotiations were still under way with France, though it was assumed that war was near at hand. Van der Delft remained deeply impressed by Paget, since 'everything here goes through his hands, and . . . there is not one of them who can excel him in the management of affairs'.[8] War was indeed at hand with both Scotland and France.

The Emperor during these early months of the Edwardian regime found himself somewhat reluctantly cast in the role of the protector

[1] Cal. S.P. Span. IX, 86: May 4, 1547.
[2] A.P.C. II, App. 488, 489, 509: May 6 and June 13, 1547.
[3] Ibid. 513–514: July 17, 1547.
[4] Cal. S.P. Span. IX, 106–107: Van der Delft to Emperor, June 17, 1547.
[5] Ibid. 126–127: July 24, 1547.   [6] Ibid. 128–130.
[7] Ibid. 133.   [8] Ibid. 145–146: Van der Delft to Emperor, Sept. 2, 1547.

of England, as he watched the deterioration of relations with both France and Scotland following on the accession of Henry II. Above all else, Charles wanted peace abroad in order to devote himself to the chastening of the German princes, the settlement of the Lutheran problem, and the exercise of moderating influences on the Council of Trent. He had at first been concerned respecting the security of the faith of Mary Tudor, his near relation, but, as we have observed, for about two years Somerset permitted her the free private exercise of her religion and, as the next heir to the throne, she was treated generously by the King. The Venetian envoy to Charles had reported a papal plan to be laid before the Emperor for the 'catholicization of England', if he would lead a war in Mary Tudor's support. To this the Emperor wearily replied that he would not take up arms against 'the weakest man in the world', far less against a strong kingdom with which he wished to maintain bonds of friendship. He had further told the papal nuncio, who had broached this hare-brained scheme, that the Pope would like nothing better than to see him involved in war in order further to delay the meeting of the Council.[1] When, some weeks later, further representations were made to him by Cardinal Pole, the Emperor replied categorically that he would not intervene against a friendly power and that he had no wish ever again to have the Pope as an ally.[2]

Relations during the first year, then, were friendly and Van der Delft believed that both Somerset and Paget regarded peace with the Emperor as the cornerstone of their policy. He did, however, find the Privy Council obdurate in refusing to restore property taken from imperial subjects at the time Boulogne had fallen, and when he submitted the usual list of Flemish commercial grievances, the English promptly countered with a list of their own involving English merchants in Spain.[3] Van der Delft continued his friendly but bootless negotiations with Paget, who was finally authorized to adjudicate the Flemish merchant claims, and he was at last able to see the Protector and to discuss with him a wide range of problems.[4] Somerset agreed in principle to the restoration of property taken at Boulogne from imperial subjects. The Protector complained that the Emperor had spoken disparagingly of England as a land without religion, which Van der Delft denied could have been gained from

[1] *Venetianische Depeschen*, II, 202–203: Mar. 21, 547; *et vide* Druffel, August von, ed., *Beiträge zur Reichsgeschichte, 1546–1551 (Briefe und Akten zur Geschichte des sechzehnten Jahrhunderts, etc.*, vol. I, Munich, 1873), 51–52.

[2] *Venetianische Depeschen*, II, 298–302: July 2, 1547.

[3] *Cal. S.P. Span.*, IX, 69–72: Apr. 2, 1547.

[4] *Ibid.* 104–106: June 16, 1547; *ibid.* 109–110: June 24, 1547.

his own reports, save that just after Henry's death he had written that 'nothing was heard but preachers on every side, some to proclaim their opinions and others to inculcate and enforce their fallacies'. The Protector further informed the ambassador that the Scots were mobilizing against England, but stated his belief that Boulogne was now so strongly defended that the French could not carry it.[1]

During the invasion of Scotland and the occupation of the strong points there in the autumn of 1547, Van der Delft's reports on developments were prompt and on the whole accurate and in tone decidedly pro-English.[2] Meanwhile he maintained moderate pressure to secure the settlement of the imperial commercial claims. The Emperor, in one of his own rare diplomatic dispatches, on August 24th expressed himself as content with the agreement reached with respect to the Boulogne claims.[3] But the Regent in Flanders was not so complacent with respect to the claims of the Flemish merchants, holding as well that new and she thought illegal duties were being laid against exports to England. She expressed her wish for a new commercial treaty with England and her view that any inclusion of the Empire in a settlement between England and France should be subject to satisfaction for these claims.[4] Mary was pertinacious, a fortnight later laying before the English envoy a formal memorandum from the Flemish Council of State pointing out that the great commercial towns of Haarlem, Delft, and Leyden had for many years depended in their trade on draperies, fleeces, and wools bought from the Staple at Calais. Now, she indicated, because the English sought to monopolize the trade for themselves, refusing to sell any save the 'residue of the fleeces . . . so poor and thin as to be almost useless', this commerce had been greatly injured and her subjects had suffered. Van der Delft was to represent that there had been deliberate violation of friendship as well as the disruption of settled habits of trade.[5]

Charles often found his sister tiresome; Van der Delft knew her to be both formidable and unrelenting. His dispatches regarding political and military events were excited, full, and just a little disgruntled. He was tired of dealing only with fleeces. He confessed to the Regent on November 9, 1547, that he simply did not know how to restore to the Dutch merchants continued access to the Calais

[1] *Cal. S.P. Span.* IX, 120–122: July 10, 1547.
[2] *Ibid.* 135–136 (Aug. 18, 1547), 142–143 (Aug. 25, 1547), 147–148 (Sept. 6, 1547), 151–152 (Sept. 19, 1547), 161–162 (Sept. 22, 1547), 177–178 (Oct. 18, 1547), 181–182 (Oct. 21, 1547). [3] *Ibid.* 138: Aug. 24, 1547.
[4] *Ibid.* 163 and 165: Oct. 1 and 2, 1547. [5] *Ibid.* 183.

Staple, since in the present Parliament the Staple might well be entirely abolished on the vociferous demand of English merchants. He had complained to Somerset himself that the Boulogne claims remained unsettled, only to have him say again that the frictions would be removed if the Dowager would only submit a detailed memorandum of the losses with a certification that the property involved was really Flemish.[1] A few days later the harassed envoy addressed a letter to the Emperor's Council of State, suggesting that he was too much employed in advancing these Flemish claims in London, many of which he believed to be unwarranted. Only the preceding day, he said, Paget, in whom Van der Delft still had absolute confidence, had chided him as 'too ready to give easy credence to the merchants and other claimants who came to me with their tales'. England had settled some claims directly when the facts were clear, but all others should be prosecuted in the ordinary courts, whether in England or in Flanders.[2] Paget's magic had done its work, for the imperial ambassador now identified himself with English policy. One wonders that he was not recalled in November, 1547, as the first phase of Edwardian foreign policy ends.

Political circumstances and probably inclination too compelled England in the early Edwardian period to depend heavily on diplomatic support from the Emperor, now seeking with all his resources to establish his authority in Germany and to impose the *Interim*. Despite the importunities of the German Protestant states and their desperate need for funds and military help, England could do no more than hear the case of a stream of German diplomatic agents, pleading for an assistance which they must have known England was at once too weak and too prudent to give. At least a few instances of these diplomatic approaches in 1547–1548 may be noted.

Immediately after Henry VIII's death the Duke of Cleves-Jülich dispatched Conrad Heresbach to London as his envoy, in close association with the Saxon Chancellor, Burckhard, to plead for funds to permit the continued prosecution of the Schmalkaldic War. The Duke knew that his much buffeted sister enjoyed friendly relations with Somerset, who received the envoy pleasantly and on April 11, 1547, presented him formally to the King. Heresbach also visited Anne of Cleves, comfortably ensconced at Hever, but gained nothing more than a gift of 80 gold crowns for himself. Nor was a later embassy in 1549 more successful, even with respect to the allowances to Anne, the envoy on this occasion being pleasantly

[1] *Cal. S.P. Span.* IX, 195.
[2] *Ibid.* 200-201: Nov. 12, 1547; *et vide ibid.* 204: Nov. 15, 1547.

received by the King with whom converse was carried on in Latin. But all suggestions of diplomatic or military aid were simply evaded.[1]

Not so easily evaded were the representations laid before the English government in early 1547 by Burckhard and two colleagues, who had just failed to gain help from France, regarding the dire straits of Protestantism in Germany, and more especially the desperate needs of John Frederick of Saxony, the principal Protestant prince in Germany, whose defeat and capture in the great battle of Mühlberg seemed for a time to have wrecked the Protestant cause.[2] The Council could not dismiss this appeal with pleasantries, instructing Paget to inform the Saxon envoy that if his state remained in league with Bremen, Lübeck, and Hamburg through the coming summer (1547) and the need remained, 50,000 crowns would be advanced to meet John Frederick's requests, in the form of a loan, payable to the Steelyard merchants in London against further deliveries of naval stores. At the same time, absolute secrecy with respect to the understanding must be maintained.[3] But this diplomatically dangerous commitment England was never called upon to honour; a few weeks later John Frederick was the close prisoner of the Emperor, the Schmalkaldic League in ruins.

2. THE DETERIORATION OF RELATIONS WITH SCOTLAND
(1543–1547)

The disastrous defeat of Scotland at Solway Moss, involving as it did the death of James V, had placed the northern realm in great peril. The Scottish Reformation was now setting in and inevitably disposed the growing Protestant faction towards close political relations with England. The Queen being an infant, the next heir to the throne, the Earl of Arran, was proclaimed Regent. Henry VIII, having just destroyed Scottish military power, began immediately to apply heavy pressure to secure a binding treaty of marriage alliance between his son, then six years of age, and Mary Stuart, then a few months old. This obsessive diplomatic concern of the

[1] Bouterwek, K. W., 'Anna von Cleve, Gemahlin Heinrichs viij. Königs von England', *Zeitschrift des Bergischen Geschichtsvereins*, VI (1869), 141–142, 143.
[2] Mentz, Georg, *Johann Friedrich der Grossmütige, 1503–1554* (*Beiträge zur neueren Geschichte Thüringens*, vol. I, Jena, 1908), pt. iii, 72, 222, for detailed references to the documents; *Politisches Archiv des Landgrafen Philipp des Grossmütigen von Hessen*, ed. by Fr. Küch, I (*Publikationen aus den Königl. Preussischen Staatsarchiven*, vol. 78, Leipzig, 1904), 578.   [3] *A.P.C.* II, 60–61: Mar. 10, 1547.

old King had, it must be said, much to commend it, since its ultimate intention was to secure the union of the two realms. Sir Ralph Sadler was sent north with detailed instructions for the furtherance of the design, while the Scottish Estates on March 12, 1543, appointed representatives to negotiate the treaty.[1] The diplomatic discussions were carried forward at Greenwich, where on July 1st the terms of the marriage treaty were concluded, including the provision that the Kingdom of Scotland should retain its names, laws, and rightful liberties.[2] But in Scotland Arran's policy was most violently assailed by Cardinal Beaton and the whole force of the church, by the Guise Queen Mother, and by most of the peers, supported by French diplomacy and gold as well as by a fleet cruising in Scottish waters in June, 1543. Arran was not strong enough, or perhaps determined enough, to prevent the repudiation of the marriage treaty by Parliament in December, 1543.[3]

These swift reverses threw Henry, who had for once sought to deal gently and with a certain degree of idealism in his foreign policy, into one of the most choleric of the rages for which he was noted. He immediately declared war on Scotland, though some months were to elapse before a punitive expedition could be set forward. Meanwhile, conversations were held with Lennox, Angus, Glencairn, and other pro-English peers who were persuaded to call for English aid against Beaton.[4] A strong English force was then dispatched under the command of Seymour, then Earl of Hertford, which soon took Leith and Edinburgh, laid waste the countryside around the capital, and then fell back by land and sea to the English frontier. Heavy English troop concentrations lay for months along the border, throwing strong raiding parties across the frontier, until February, 1545, when Arran and Angus trapped Sir Ralph Eure and his small army near Jedburgh, mauling the English force considerably and killing Eure. Scottish resolution was also stiffened in August by the arrival of a French force of about 3000 men, but so weak was Scottish policy and governance that no tactical plan could be devised or problems of command determined before the predictable English counter-move was made.[5] Henry VIII

[1] Cotton MSS., Caligula, B, vii, 159, f. 304.

[2] Rymer, *Foedera*, XIV (L., 1728), 786–797.

[3] Brown, P. Hume, *History of Scotland* (3 vols., Cambridge, 1899–1909), II, 8–10. This remains the standard history of Scotland for our period.

[4] *Calendar of the state papers relating to Scotland, etc.*, ed. by M. J. Thorpe (2 vols., L., 1858), I, 46, 47 (VII: ##6–10, 17, 20, 21). This calendar is used for events prior to March 11, 1547.

[5] *Ibid.* 51–54 (VIII: ##29, 34, 35–38, 43, 44, 46, 47, 53–59).

countered by sending a powerful force across the border, once more under the redoubtable Hertford, which systematically laid waste a large area, including some of the most fertile and populous regions of Scotland. The name of Seymour was not soon to be forgotten in Scotland.

But these savage forays accomplished little else than to stiffen Scottish resistance and to obscure English intentions. Some symbol, some binding force for the advancement of English policy, was required, and that was to be supplied by the brutal destruction of George Wishart, the most notable of the early Scottish reformers, by Beaton's decision and in his presence. This terrible event provided precisely the catalyst needed and lent at least some slight moral basis for the schemes which, with English knowledge and encouragement, had for months past been forming to assassinate the Cardinal. Feared and distrusted by all Protestants, detested even by many of the Catholic nobility, Beaton sensed the plots gathering against him and sought protection by taking up residence in the heavily guarded castle of St Andrew's. But on May 26, 1546, an armed band of men, animated by diverse motives—religious, personal and political—gained entrance and, moving straight to the Cardinal's lodging, cut him down.[1]

The murder of Beaton, as should have been predictable, led to a confusion close to anarchy in Scottish politics rather than to a fusion of the pro-English parties. The Queen Dowager, Mary of Lorraine, was capable and courageous, being able slowly to rally Scottish sentiment and fanatically denouncing both England and Protestantism. When the nobility met in the Convention of Stirling, the covenanted marriage of Mary with Edward was formally renounced, while on June 10th a national levy was ordered to besiege the murderers of Beaton and their supporters, still in full possession of the great castle where the Cardinal had been done to death.[2] Meanwhile, English command of the sea afforded access to St Andrew's, with which Henry VIII was in steady communication and which William Tyrell with a fleet of six vessels was ordered to victual and strengthen in October, 1546.[3] So weak was the Scottish power that Arran was unable to breach the great fortifications, being obliged in December to reach an ignominious truce with the rebels, who made it clear to

[1] Haynes, *State papers*, I, 43–54; *Cal. S.P. Scotland* (ed. Thorpe), I, 56–57 (VIII: ##79, 80, 82, 85, 86, 91). John Knox's famous account of this brutal episode is a classic; he was Wishart's close friend and disciple; *vide ibid.* 58 (IX: 1–3), for various intelligence reports to the English government on the event.

[2] Lang, Andrew, *A History of Scotland, etc.* (3 vols., N.Y., 1902), II, 2–3.

[3] *Cal. S.P. Scotland* (ed. Thorpe), I, 59 (IX: 9–10).

Henry VIII that they were playing for time in which to revictual and gather more support.[1]

This was the confused and incredibly dangerous situation which the new government inherited from Henry VIII, who had all but determined on throwing another powerful raiding force into Scotland in an effort to resolve, or perhaps one should say to save, the English position. The fact is that English support in Scotland had been steadily weakened since 1543, as Henry sought by main force to impose his policy on Scotland. The only hope in 1547 was in a gradual rebuilding of English strength amongst the many dissident elements in Scotland; the steady but discreet furthering of the Reformation, now spreading rapidly through the Lowlands; and the gaining of a free hand by coming to terms with France, which would certainly have meant the cession of Boulogne on honourable conditions. But none of these courses seems seriously to have been considered by Somerset, who sought instead to implement a manifestly bankrupt Henrician policy.

Somerset turned at once to a strengthening of the border defences, building up a force which all Scots knew was intended to be punitive. Wharton, Warden of the West Marches, was ordered better to arm his troops and to strengthen his fortifications;[2] munitions and stores were dispatched by sea to Newcastle;[3] while Lord Eure, in the East March, was mounting day and night patrols and retaliating when harassing Scottish raiders crossed the frontier.[4] Wharton was using gold and persuasion to soften the Scottish borderers, while fairly large raiding patrols penetrated as deep as fourteen miles beyond the frontier.[5] Always nervous and never skilled in sifting his intelligence reports, he was certain in June that a heavy Scottish attack was imminent along the Western March, which would have as its tactical purpose the destruction of his principal fortified point, Langholm.[6] On the more important Eastern March, with its great staging centre at Berwick, Eure reported in early July that the walls there required substantial strengthening, while the bridge leading into Scotland had been damaged by the crossing of heavy ordnance.[7] His spies were reporting that the 'power of Scotland' was assembling,[8] and some days later he was greatly exercised when a French force of twenty galleys, with a course set for Scotland, was sighted off Holy Island.[9]

[1] Cal. S. P. Scotland (ed. Thorpe), I, 60 (IX: 17, 21); Brown, History of Scotland, II, 26–29.   [2] Cal. S.P. Dom., Edw. VI, VI, 320.   [3] Ibid. 321–322.
[4] Ibid. 322.   [5] Ibid. 323.   [6] Ibid. 325–326: June 29, 1547.
[7] Ibid. 326 (Addenda, I:19).   [8] Ibid. 326 (Addenda, I:21): July 6, 1547.
[9] Ibid. 327–328: July 13, 1547. This was Strozzi's fleet; vide post, 245.

Wharton, meanwhile, had called out levies under Cumberland and Dacre, was laying in supplies at Carlisle, but despaired of completing the fortified works at Langholm, because of the nature of the soil.[1]

Meanwhile, St Andrew's having been revictualled, the rebel forces, as was predictable, found loopholes in the papal absolution, and the desultory siege was resumed. In April, John Knox entered the Castle as Protestant chaplain to the garrison, the farce of the siege being suggested by the fact that at the same time he preached freely in the city and at the university. Somerset was in direct communication with the rebel force, with whom he concluded an agreement for carrying out the marriage treaty, while refraining from laying any claim to English suzerainty.[2] In early February funds totalling upwards of £1000 were forwarded for the needs of the Castle party, while somewhat later payments of £336 were sent for the pay of the garrison of eighty men, and £224 for the charge of forty horse 'appointed to keep abroad for the more surety of the said Castle', with appropriate further bribes for those of the nobility and gentry who still lent support to the covenanted marriage treaty.[3] Arran sought to relieve English pressure on St Andrew's by a diversionary raid on Langholm, to be executed by a considerable army, but was summoned back to lend support to a powerful French force under the command of the famous mercenary general Leo Strozzi, which was landed in late June from the French galleys that had successfully evaded the small English fleet lying in the harbour. The castle was immediately invested, great pieces of French ordnance were mounted, and a breach, which could not be closed, was opened on the night of July 29th, the castle surrendering on the last day of July. Favourable terms of surrender had, it seems, been negotiated, but the French none the less packed off the garrison as prisoners to France, a fair number, including Knox, being condemned to the galleys.[4]

Strozzi's brilliant exploit had been so swiftly executed that no direct English intervention, or even any substantial diversionary assault along the border, was possible, which was without doubt to cost England heavily in terms of Scottish support for the great invasion soon to be launched. But there did remain a hard core of the Scottish nobility linked with the English cause by religion,

[1] *Cal. S.P. Dom., Edw. VI*, VI, 326: July 7, 1547.
[2] Rymer, *Foedera*, XV, 131–135, 142–143, 144–145.
[3] *A.P.C.* II, 12–13: Feb. 6, 1547; *ibid.*, 89–90: May 4, 1547.
[4] Stow, *Annales*, 594; Froude, *History of England*, V, 43; Wernham, *Before the Armada*, 169.

ambition, or the inducements of gold. Among them Lord Gray had
pledged his services to Edward VI and had undertaken to deliver
Broughty Castle on demand, as well as to assist in the surrender of
his own town of St Johnston.[1] The irreconcilable Glencairn had
also personally pledged himself to Somerset, offering to go into
Scotland and to raise a diversionary force, while urging the Protector to fortify a strong position that would control the Clyde.[2]
Lennox, though a Catholic, was moved only by his hatred of the
Hamiltons. He gave his complete loyalty to Somerset and held a
command in the west during the English invasion in the east. These
were but the principal of the nobility who remained committed to
England, the list running to two hundred of nobility and gentry, as
Arran well knew from documents that had fallen into his hands
when St Andrew's capitulated.[3] Arran could do no more than
inform his Council that a powerful English invasion must be expected at harvest-time and ask that body to summon the whole of
the nobility to the defence of the realm and to authorize a general
muster of the nation on summary notice.[4]

3. THE FAILURE TO ISOLATE SCOTLAND (1547)

We have discussed the rapidly worsening relations of England and
France after the accession of Henry II, who held as central policy
the intention to recover Boulogne and to maintain the long-standing
commitments to Scotland. We have seen, too, that the treaty arranging for the delimiting of the Boulogne borders, negotiated at the
very end of Francis I's life, was in effect repudiated by his successor, with implications which were all too plain to England. It
likewise early became clear that Henry was bent not so much on
assistance to Scotland as on achieving domination there. It was true
that a new joint commission was appointed to discuss again the
delimitation of the Boulogne boundaries, but the French members
were privately instructed to avoid any agreement. Both sides were
by this date also loosing their privateers, while Scottish marauders
were afforded refuge in French ports.[5] The visit of a special French
envoy, François de Scepeaux, Sieur de Vieilleville, in May, was as
perfunctory as it was fruitless, though he carried back to France an

---

[1] *Cal. S.P. Scotland*, I, 2. From this point the Bain edition, as described in the *Table
of Abbreviations*, will be cited.
[2] *Ibid.* 10; [July, 1547].   [3] Lang, *Scotland*, II, 8.
[4] *The register of the Privy Council of Scotland*, I (1545–1569), ed. by J. H. Burton
(Edinburgh, 1877), 75.   [5] *Cal. S.P. For., Edw. VI*, #48: Apr. 1, 1547.

elegant letter in the young King's hand hoping 'above all other things in this world' for the establishment of a 'good and perfect friendship' between the two countries.[1]

We have observed that Somerset had ordered extensive strengthening of the Calais-Boulogne defences in the early months of his tenure of power.[2] Then, with the accession of Henry II and the steady deterioration of relations with both France and Scotland, more intensive measures were undertaken, the principal being the augmentation of the Calais garrison, an ambitious renovation of the Newhaven fortifications, and considerable improvements in Boulogne harbour, which the French contended were hostile fortifications and the English that they were simply needed harbour renovations.[3] There was also a decided increase in English intelligence activities, agents being set in both Calais and Boulogne to interview English and French merchants passing through from France in order to appraise French troop movements towards Scotland as well as to the fortified enclaves. As early as April 8th Cobham, whose dispatches are reliable, was reporting troop movements around Calais, though his relations with his French counterpart remained most amiable, both men sharing a taste for hunting.[4] Deliberate provocations by the French on the Calais border were, as both Cobham and Somerset believed, in the nature of diversions, since Henry II's central preoccupation was with Boulogne. None the less, Cobham believed that Calais would also be attacked, adding an urgent appeal to the Council for at least 4000 reinforcements over the next half-year and asking that arrangements be made for the evacuation of women and children in the event of an assault.[5] The imperial ambassador in Paris, whose contacts were trustworthy, was persuaded in July that the controversy over the sea-wall being built in Boulogne harbour would be seized upon by France as the pretext for war, and just a month later he informed the Emperor unequivocally that so serious had the deterioration of relations become that France would declare war directly the Emperor's neutrality was assured.[6]

Somerset's preoccupation with Scottish affairs and his attitude of almost personal outrage at the revocation of the marriage treaty was obsessive, and it is clear that he was determined on war even as it

---

[1] Edward VI to Henry II, May 21, 1547 (MS. owned by Goodspeed's, Boston, Mass., as of Feb. 2, 1966).   [2] Vide ante, 234ff.
[3] Calais Papers, 1547–1552, in Cal. S.P. For., Edw. VI, 292–358; vide 329–330, 334–338: Apr. 14, Apr. 18–May 6, 1547.
[4] Lennel, F., Histoire de Calais, etc. (2 vols., Calais, 1910), II, 240.   [5] Ibid. 242.
[6] Cal. S.P. Span. IX, 505–506, 510–511: St Mauris to Emperor, June 30 and July 27, 1547.

became evident that to move troops across the Tweed in force would predictably lead to French intervention. Andrew Dudley had for some time past been at sea, harassing Scottish shipping and lying across the lines of communication with France.[1] The Council was evidently seeking to build a case of overt provocation when on March 24th it instructed Lord Wharton on the West March to render two reports on a recent Scottish border raid, one to inform them accurately of the damage done, while in the other he was to report the number of invading Scots as 700, to say that three or four border villages had been burned, and that they withdrew into Scotland with prisoners and cattle, 'with such other aggravations of that their raid as his wisdom in that behalf could set forth'.[2]

This outrageous act of duplicity probably dates rather accurately the decision of Somerset and the Council to prosecute the war, the whole edifice of general preparation being built stone by stone thereafter. In early April letters were dispatched to the affected counties warning that Scottish and French ships were harassing shipping, and ordering that coastal watches be instituted.[3] A few days later instructions were posted to Bowes in the north, ordering a constant watch on the border, and suggesting that it would be well if all corn were brought in and threshed at once.[4] The muster commissioners were in mid-April required to render a report on military stores available in every county and to order all persons obligated for cavalry service to be in readiness not later than May 20th.[5] Wharton, who was already on alert patrol,[6] was expressing his usual dour doubts regarding his own strength, but was specifically ordered to hold Langholm until it was brought under actual siege, while the Council pointed out to him that heavy siege ordnance could scarcely be moved over Scottish roads at this early season.[7] The Council reiterated its orders on May 16th, making it clear to Wharton that if the Scots moved against him it wanted a clear and evident provocation and a breach of the uneasy peace.

Bishop Tunstall, who had been ordered north in April to assume general charge of military preparations there, was at Bishop Auckland in May, complaining that there was a shortage of bows in the whole region and that such purchases as he could make were in competition with those of royal agents from the south.[8] So absurd

---

[1] S.P. Dom., Edw. VI, I, 29: Mar. 12, 1547.   [2] A.P.C. II, App., 461.
[3] Ibid. 471: Apr. 7, 1547.   [4] Ibid. 473–474: Apr. 12, 1547.
[5] S.P. Dom., Edw. VI, I, 36: Apr. 16, 1547; Add. MSS. 28,212, f. 52.
[6] Vide ante, 244.   [7] A.P.C. II, App., 485–486: Apr. 29, 1547.
[8] Add. MSS. 32, 657, #1, f. 2: May 30, 1547.

was the situation, in fact, that if an archer broke his bow on the
northern border another must be procured from London.[1] The
City of York, as well as other commercial centres, were warned that
a call would shortly be made for 'well expert mariners about our
service upon the seas', and a few weeks later the Council ordered the
City to prepare a complete muster of available manpower and
armament.[2] All over England these militant preparations were
under way, of which the orders from the Earl of Shrewsbury to the
commissioners of Shropshire may be taken as typical. The county
was called on to levy 200 foot 'well furnished with harness and
weapons', over and above an earlier levy, among whom there were
to be skilled hackbutters. Though good troops were wanted, the
commissioners should arrange 'that such idle men and others as
the country may best spare be chosen out' for this force, which was
to present itself at Newcastle not later than June 2nd, while the
county's main force of horse and foot should be warned to stand
ready for the next call.[3]

The mobilization of forces and the gathering of armament and
supplies was, then, well advanced by the end of May, and England
stood poised for intervention in the north. But there came a pause
of a full month, as if during June Somerset were reconsidering or,
more probably, as if he had determined on one more effort to persuade Scotland to bind itself again to the terms of the marriage compact of 1543. In all the official sources for June there are only a thin
sheaf of instructions or actions in which there is any suggestion of
warlike intent. This pause lasted until Strozzi's brilliant reduction of
St Andrew's took the whole of the initiative from Somerset. Then in
July the evidences of formidable preparations and of policy commitments recur as England forced an imprudent and essentially bootless war. One more forlorn effort was made to secure peace when
Tunstall and Sir Robert Bowes were dispatched to meet with the
Scottish commissioners on the border in August, with instructions
to waive all other issues in dispute if the marriage treaty were
honoured, while Somerset hinted to France that Boulogne might be
restored in advance of the treaty date if he were permitted a free

[1] *The Hamilton papers. Letters and papers illustrating the political relations of England
and Scotland in the XVIth century formerly in the possession of the Dukes of Hamilton, etc.*,
ed. by Joseph Bain (2 vols., Edinburgh, 1892), II, 596.

[2] *York civic records*, ed. by Angelo Raine, vol. IV (Yorkshire Archaeol. Soc., Record
series CVIII, York, 1945), 152–153, 153–155.

[3] Shropshire was one of the seven counties for which Shrewsbury was responsible
(Lodge, Edmund, *Illustrations of British history, etc.* (3 vols., L., 1791, *1838*), I, 141–
143, quoting Talbot papers, B, f. 9.

hand in Scotland.[1] At the same time Tunstall was required to search the records at Durham for further medieval proofs of the English claim of sovereignty in Scotland, while prayers were ordered throughout the realm for general peace and for God's blessing on the covenanted marriage between Edward VI and Mary.[2] Correct and salving as these last dramatic moves may have been, the momentum and the commitments of policy were too great: England was at war.

4. PREPARATIONS FOR THE INVASION OF SCOTLAND

The preparations for the great military expedition which Somerset was to launch against Scotland taxed severely the administrative and economic resources of the state. The army assembled was a mixture of three elements: the traditional feudal array; a stiffening of professional mercenary troops of fair quality; and a large contingent of almost wholly untrained conscript troops gathered from the realm at large. Planning for the assembly, the transport, and the victualling and supply of a large striking force of approximately 18,000 men had occupied the government for months, and the problems which arose almost certainly delayed for some weeks its military plans. A careful memorandum had been prepared of cost of setting down an army of 15,000 foot in the Firth of Forth by sea, excluding any costs 'for furniture by sea', which worked out to a total charge of £23,810, save that the various items listed actually total £22,810—a not untypical example of Tudor statistical imprecision. In comparison, it was reckoned that to move 14,000 foot and 4000 horse by land would cost £24,113 6s 8d (if a slight correction in addition may be made), both estimates including conduct money, wages for twenty-eight days, and, in the event of a sea-passage, £2000 for the hire of 9000 tons of shipping. Victualling costs were estimated at between £5000 and £6000, while no figure was provided for the strictly military stores which must be assembled and transported. All calculations, it should be noted, were based on a campaign of twenty-eight to thirty days, suggesting one reason for Somerset's certainly over-hasty withdrawal of his main force from Scotland. Both the cost and the great difficulty of supplying the army were too great to be borne for longer than a month. The final

---

[1] Cotton MSS., Caligula, B, vii, 163, f. 317; *ibid.* 164, f. 320, and another copy, *ibid.* 165, f. 321. Scotland declined to meet the English commissioners.
[2] S.P. Dom., Edw. VI, II, 6.

recommendation was that the army should move by land, the bulk of the supplies by sea.[1]

The government, then, was harassed by very difficult problems of supply, since the northern counties could not provision a large force, and as much as two months could be required for moving supplies north by sea from London to Berwick if the weather were inclement. Moreover, the forwarding of victuals and war stores north from the great staging centre at Berwick was hampered by a shortage of carts and draft animals in its hinterland. The provisions for the army, in this and other Scottish wars of the era, were drawn principally from East Anglia for grain, Suffolk for dairy products, and flesh from cattle driven from the Midlands to the slaughter-houses maintained at Berwick.[2] The weak link in the line of supply to Somerset's army remained to the north of Berwick, since the required number of carts simply could not be found, while later during the occupation the condition of the roads and fords made it quite impossible to move heavy tonnages during the wet seasons of the year. But even so the preparations for the invasion of 1547 were on the whole carried out with amazing efficiency, and fair speed, with the result that the army gathered at Berwick was able to move out promptly to the north and the whole campaign was marked by a quite proficient co-ordination of land and sea transport. The signal was given when Lord Eure reported from Berwick on August 28th that the Marches were in a state of readiness, that he had ordered carts to be gathered in Berwick, and that for the East March upwards of 1000 troops were already at their stations.[3]

Preparations seem to have been completed by about August 2nd when Somerset forwarded orders to the muster commissioners to assemble the county levies and to join him at Newcastle on the 28th.[4] Shrewsbury, charged with gathering levies from seven western and northern counties, had dispatched his forces by about the 18th and was ordered to join Somerset at the staging centre at Berwick, being also entrusted with a command in the invasion force.[5] At about the same time commissions were granted to Northampton,

[1] S.P. Dom., Edw. VI, III, 22. The date of the document is uncertain, but should probably be placed in April or May, 1547.

[2] Davies, C. S. L., 'Provisions for armies, 1509–50, etc.', Econ. Hist. Rev., ser. 2, XVII (Dec., 1964), 236. The remainder of this paragraph depends heavily on this excellent article.

[3] Cal. S.P. Dom., Edw. VI, VI, 329: Eure to Somerset, Berwick, Aug. 28, 1547.

[4] Somerset to Shrewsbury (Lodge, Illustrations, III, Appendix: 'Papers . . . in the Talbot Collection', 9, following Talbot papers, B, f. 1.)

[5] Lodge, Illustrations, I, 144–145, following Talbot papers, B, f. 3.

Arundel, Sudeley, Warwick, and Sir Thomas Cheyney to levy troops in the other counties, men 'being able and meet for the wars', and to array and arm them as circumstances might require.[1] Simultaneously the fleet was ordered to sea, from which was assembled a striking and scouting force of formidable tonnage under the competent command of Lord Clinton. The Lord Protector having assumed the high command, his brother, the Lord Admiral, was placed in military command in the south, while a commission including Cranmer, St John, Russell, Northampton, and Paget, was appointed with special responsibilities in the Council.[2] The extent of the dispositions ordered is suggested by the fact that between August 24 and September 9, 1547, warrants totalling upwards of £31,000 were authorized by the Council.[3] Somerset had meanwhile gone north, stopping briefly at Newcastle on August 27th and arriving in Berwick three days later, somewhat in advance of the forces now moving towards this military centre.

In the meanwhile, the last futile efforts at negotiation and moral explanations were undertaken as, so to speak, ritual actions. The imperial ambassador reported on August 18th that Warwick was already in the field and that Somerset had been detained in London only for the sifting of reports that the French were massing near the Boulogne defences.[4] Just a week later he wrote that Somerset was proceeding north, the English being certain that Boulogne was sufficiently garrisoned and provisioned to withstand siege or assault.[5] Just on the eve of the invasion Paget informed Van der Delft that negotiations were continuing with the French, though Paget thought them hopeless, while a few days later the imperial envoy expressed grudging admiration for the English propaganda which was justifying the war in terms of its proposal for fashioning an island kingdom uniting England and Scotland in one polity.[6] For shortly after his arrival at Berwick, Somerset issued what was in form a proclamation, though without mention of either King or Council, to the people of Scotland, again reciting the marriage compact of 1543 and movingly calling to mind that the two nations shared 'one descent of blood, and of one language, and by the main seas separated from all other nations'. This was the compelling reason for the marriage, it being for the common good of both realms. Hence his force has 'come into their land', in no wise as the enemy of the Queen or of her realm. We are come, he continued, 'in this manner,

---

[1] *A.P.C.* II, 118–119: Aug. 12–17, 1547.   [2] *Ibid.* 115–118.
[3] *Ibid.* 119–123.   [4] *Cal. S.P. Span.* IX, 135.   [5] *Ibid.* 143: Aug. 25, 1547.
[6] *Ibid.* 145–146, 148: Sept. 2 and 6, 1547.

which pretendeth a force in appearance (but not in deed) only to defend and maintain the honor of both the princes and realms' and to punish those who thwart this godly purpose. He invited all Scots who would support his purpose freely to join his camp. He intended now to enter the realm of Scotland, but in so far as possible to pass amicably through it, doing the least hurt that he could, 'saving somewhat in forage, which cannot be avoided when an army marches'.[1] Somerset issued no formal declaration of war, but rather took his position on this apology and exhortation. He was without doubt moved by sincere and noble motives, for he did see clearly the infinite advantages of union and sensed, at least dimly, its historical inevitability. But the scourge shortly to be visited on the realm of Scotland by this complex and brooding man laid waste even the historical possibility of union for another half-century. He moved impetuously where patience was required; he moved with great force where persuasion was needed; and he moved with the apparatus of military power when even in 1547 it was becoming evident that the guarantee of union lay with the Protestant Reformation which it was in his power to cherish and to nurture. We are, therefore, about to chronicle a dreadful and an avoidable failure of policy.

5. THE INVASION OF SCOTLAND

Even before his proclamation to the people of Scotland was issued, Somerset had on August 31st, with a strong scouting party of horse, crossed the border into Scotland, spending the night of September 1st at Eyemouth, while on the following day Clinton put out to sea from Berwick with the whole of his powerful naval force. And on September 4th the main force moved out from Berwick, organized in three divisions, reaching Reston (Berwick on the Eye), a march of six miles, on that day. It was a considerable force of about 16,000 men which Somerset commanded, and it was by mid-sixteenth-century standards a powerful army because of its heavy concentration of horse and ordnance. In all, there were somewhat more than 4000 horse, including a heavily armed mercenary band commanded by the experienced Italian mercenary officer, Malatesta; a force of about 500 cavalry recently brought back from the Boulogne garrison; a troop of heavy cavalry, outfitted with fire-arms and commanded by the Spanish mercenary captain, Pedro de Gamboa; a

---

[1] *To Scotland concerning the projected marriage* [Sept. 4, 1547], STC 7811; Wernham's comments on the document are interesting (*Before the Armada*, 167).

picked English force of gentleman pensioners, comprising most of the royal bodyguard; and the full complement of lightly mounted, somewhat undisciplined, border cavalry, which knew the terrain and which was most useful in scouting well ahead of the rapidly moving army. The main body of about 12,000 foot was not professional, being largely comprised of levies gathered from the counties by the muster commissioners, and, save for a small picked force bearing fire-arms, was armed with bows, bills, and pikes. The foot had not been thoroughly trained, but had been under reasonably effective discipline before it reached Berwick.[1] As has been suggested, the victualling was based on Berwick, where in August stores had been gathered for a force of 18,000, rations being set generously at two pounds of meat per day, a pound of bread, and a bottle of wine for drink.[2] Transport, by no means at ideal strength, was to be served with 900 carts and many additional wagons, while fifteen great pieces of ordnance and more of smaller bore were moved with the army in a remarkable exhibition of co-ordinated organization, considering the rapid movement of the whole striking force.[3]

The naval force, under Clinton, which was to victual and supply the army at points on its march, to clear the sea approaches to Edinburgh, and to join in the final battle, included twenty-four to thirty men-of-war ('tall ships'), or about half the royal naval vessels fit for sea duty,[4] besides a great concourse of merchantmen, barges, and small vessels employed for the transport of men and supplies.[5] In all, this formidable and brilliantly commanded flotilla comprised about eighty vessels with complements of 9222 sailors and soldiers.[6] In addition to these overwhelming forces assaulting Scotland

---

[1] Oman, Sir Charles W., 'The battle of Pinkie, Sept. 10, 1547', *Archaeol. Journal*, XC (1933), 6–7; Oman, Sir Charles, *A history of the art of war in the sixteenth century* (L., [1937]), 359. The battle of Pinkie is brilliantly described in this work, supplemented by Oman's article in *Archaeol. Journal*. Hence we shall deal only briefly with the action, following Sir Charles save as indicated by footnote references. There have been various estimates of the size of the invading force: Hayward (*Edward VI*, 279) sets the total at 16,100–17,100; *Grafton's chronicle : or, history of England, etc.*, ed. by Henry Ellis (2 vols., L., *1809*), from *A chronicle at large, and meere history of the affayres of England, etc.* (L., 1568, 1569), II, 502–503, at 18,100; Oman (*Archaeol. Journal*, XC (1933), 6) at about 14,000, but revised (*Art of War*, 359) to 16,000; and Harl. MS. 540, #33, ff. 70–71, flatly at 18,000. The King, certainly writing well after the event and with official information at hand, puts the figure at 13,000 foot and 5000 horse (Edward VI, *Chronicle*, 7).   [2] S.P. Dom., Edw. VI, III, 22.

[3] Holinshed, Raphaell, *Chronicles, etc.* (L., 1577, 1587; ed. by Henry Ellis, 6 vols. L., *1807–1808*), III, 868.

[4] 'List of the King's ships as of 5 Jan. 1547 [/48]', *Archaeologia*, VI, i (1782), Appendix IV; VCH, *Hampshire*, V, 374–375, for the same list.   [5] *Grafton's chronicle*, II, 500.

[6] *Cal. S.P. Scotland*, I, 11–13; HMC, *Salisbury MSS.*, I, 52; VCH, *Hampshire*, II, 1; Wernham, *Before the Armada*, 170. The estimates differ slightly from source to source.

along her east coast, Wharton and Lennox had called out the full strength of the western array and on September 9th crossed the frontier with a striking force of 2000 foot and 500 horse, of which 200 were Scots in the English service. Moving rapidly, this heavy raiding and diversionary force was on the next day sixteen miles deep in Scotland, and at Annan on September 11th, where after a brisk action the town surrendered and was then fired. This small army forayed in western Scotland for not quite a week until the always cautious Wharton fell back to his base at Carlisle, burning and pillaging as he withdrew. On the same day he wrote to Somerset that he possessed sufficient strength to take Dumfries, if that were desired, though his borderers were reluctant to engage in more than overnight raids (of the classical border pattern) unless they were paid.[1]

Against this powerful army, with its attending naval power, commanded by generals with the long professional experience of Somerset and Wharton, Arran could do no more than call out the motley and undisciplined force which was the Scottish national array. On August 21st Eure had reported to Somerset that Arran had issued the summons.[2] But even as Somerset was crossing the Tweed, it was reported that Arran could not hold his army, assembled near Edinburgh, if action were long delayed,[3] while on the next day Glencairn informed Lennox and Wharton that few in the west had heeded Arran's summons to join his national army, now in the field with sixteen days of victuals.[4] In the end, however, most of the Scottish nobility did appear with their retainers, the force mobilized totalling approximately 20,000 infantry, almost wholly armed with pikes, save for the wild and undisciplined Highland bowmen commanded by Argyle, who were thought by the English to be Irish mercenaries. There were in addition something like 1500 lightly armed and mounted Scottish horse, most of whom were borderers far more efficient on cattle raids and forays by night than in the line of battle. Even weaker was the Scottish ordnance, which was neither well-manned nor provisioned at any moment during the campaign.

Meanwhile, the English army was in motion, following the coastal road from Berwick towards Edinburgh, and in the three separate entities of command 'usual in civil wars', with Warwick leading the van, Somerset the main force, and Dacre of the North the

[1] *Cal. S.P. Scotland*, I, 19–20.
[2] *Cal. S.P. Dom., Edw. VI*, VI, 329: Eure to Protector and Council, Berwick, Aug. 21, 1547.
[3] *Cal. S.P. Scotland*, I, 17–18: Sept. 2, 1547.   [4] *Ibid.* 18–19: Sept. 3, 1547.

rear-guard.[1] The traitor Ormiston had informed Somerset that Arran would make a strong stand at the Pease, which the English army reached the second day after leaving Berwick. The position was, in fact, very nearly impregnable, since a deep ravine several miles in length cut at right angles across the road in an area where cavalry would have been almost useless. Trenches, we are told, had been prepared, but were only lightly defended as the English army approached. A precautionary decision was made to camp for the night near Cockburnspath, where the coastal road is tightly cramped by jutting spurs from the Lammermuir Hills. That night Dunglass Castle surrendered and early the next morning was razed.[2] On the day following, two other smaller castles (Innerwick and Thornton) were surrendered without more than token resistance, the main force pressing on and camping for the night at Linton Bridge, not far from the outskirts of Dunbar. On September 7th Dunbar was deliberately by-passed, the main force now leaving the coastal road and moving towards Haddington. The English train was brought under fire, in a heavy mist, from the small castle of Hailes (on the Tyne), and Warwick with a cavalry detachment in seeking to clear the line of march was set upon by 300 Scottish pickets, who, after a sharp engagement, were beaten off, disappearing into the fog. Despite inclement weather and delaying opposition the English army advanced about nine miles during the course of the day, camping for the night near the coast at Long Niddry. Meanwhile, Clinton had moved his naval forces deep into the Firth, and landing

---

[1] Harl MS. 540, #33, ff. 70–71. This valuable source, found in Stow's manuscript collection (vol. IV) is important for the history of the campaign. It seems certainly to have been written by an eye-witness, a member of the invading force who returned to England with Somerset. The handwriting resembles that of no known member of the expedition. It covers the narrative fully and is most useful, though at points confuses the chronology of events. This source supplements the account of William Patten (*The expedicion into Scotlande, etc.*, L., 1548), a full narrative which is our principal source. Patten, the son of a London clothworker, was also in the expeditionary force and, with William Cecil, took day by day notes on events. In his *Preface* Patten indicates that he had made full use of Cecil's jottings. Patten's account is largely used by Holinshed, while Hayward really transposes it into his history. A third, and less useful, source is Berteville, Le Sieur de, *Récit de l'expedition en Écosse l'an 1546 [sic], et de la battayle de Muscleburgh*. A retainer of Warwick, the author, who was also in the expedition, has left us a confusing account, very often quite wrong in details. Berteville, a French Protestant, also seems to have made the pictorial representation of the battle of Pinkie to be found in Cotton MSS., Cleopatra, A, xi (Crookshank, C. de W., 'A further note on the battle of Pinkie', *Archaeol. Journal*, XC (1933), 18–25).

[2] This area of 'cumbersome passage' had been held by a son of Lord Home, who had no more than twenty-one in his force. Harl. MS. 540, #33; Patten, *Expedicion*, Sept. 5th–6th (this work will be cited by date); Holinshed, *Chronicles*, III, 869; Oman, in *Archaeol. Journal*, XC (1933), 7–8.

for a conference with Somerset, was ordered to lie off Musselburgh, it being known from Clinton's naval scouting that the Scots had occupied and were feverishly strengthening the passage of the Esk between the sea and a swamp to the south. On September 8th, therefore, Somerset advanced slowly with the main force along the coastal road, beating off minor harassing attacks from the hills delivered by about 600 Scottish horse. He sent scouting parties ahead which reported that the Esk was fordable, though very strongly held, and that the swamp to the south made any effort to turn the Scottish flank too hazardous to contemplate. On the following day (September 9th) the army made no move, being within two miles of the heavily held Scottish lines, while Somerset scouted his position. In probing the possibility of flanking the Scots to the south and in order to test the terrain, he sent a strong cavalry force towards Dalkeith, which was countered by nearly the whole of the Scottish cavalry, numbering about 1500 men, who were badly defeated by an English frontal assault, co-ordinated with two flanking attacks. The result was that the already weak and surely weary Scottish cavalry force was almost eliminated from the great battle now so near at hand.[1] Somerset and his commanders were then able to scout from overlooking hills, observing the Scottish array barring the passage of the Esk and lying athwart the approaches to Edinburgh. The events of this day were concluded when Somerset sent through the lines a formal offer of peace to Arran on condition that the marriage treaty be accepted, which was refused as was a Scottish offer of trial by combat.

The military conclusion which Somerset and his staff had drawn was that a frontal assault must be risked against an extremely strong and well occupied Scottish position. As described by Patten:

'The plot where they lay [was] so chosen for strength, as in all that country some thought not a better; safe on the south by a great marsh, and on the north by the Firth, which side also they fenced with two field pieces . . . under a turf wall; Edinburgh on the west at their backs and eastward between us and them, strongly defended by the course of a river called Esk running north into the Firth. . . .'

and the one bridge across the Esk commanded by Scottish ordnance.[2]

---

[1] The English estimate of 1300 Scots killed must be greatly exaggerated. This is the figure as given by Patten (Sept. 9th), and followed by Holinshed. The more conservative Harl. M.S. 540, #33, places the Scottish losses at 800 killed and captured, while reckoning the English killed at about 100.

[2] Patten, *Expedicion*, Sept. 9th; and see Harl. MS. 540, #33: Sept. 10th.

Somerset's field plan was to soften the enemy front with a sustained artillery bombardment, bearing also on the flanks, and then to deliver frontally a combined cavalry and infantry attack. In his view the key position for his battle plan was the steep hill on which Inveresk church stands, with the arc of the river almost encompassing it. This knoll he was determined to occupy in order to mount his heavy artillery there for the battering of the Scottish left, whilst he had ordered the fleet to sail in as close as possible to bring enfilading fire to bear on the Scottish position.[1]

Early on the morning of September 10th, before eight Patten tells us, Somerset set his army in motion, his right wing moving towards the Esk to storm the Scottish line, while the other wings were to shift towards the right in order to give the flank the protection of the Firth and Clinton's naval guns. This difficult and somewhat dangerous manoeuvre was completely misunderstood by Arran, who was immediately convinced that Somerset had decided not to risk an engagement and was placing his army on the coastal road, while he thought Clinton was moving inshore in order to embark much of the English force. As was so often to occur in Scottish military history, a very strong position was impetuously abandoned in order to join battle. Arran accordingly commanded an immediate attack from his prepared defensive positions, though at least Angus, amongst his junior commanders, protested the decision. The Scottish army which was now moved forward to attack frontally, as it thought to flank the entire English force, was in three roughly defined wings. Huntly's left wing of about 8000, including all the lightly armed Highland bowmen, lay near the sea and a little to the rear; Angus commanded the right with perhaps 8000 foot and 400 cavalry, while Arran commanded the centre, composed mostly of 'inland men' and most of the artillery.[2]

This rash move by Arran instantly changed Somerset's battle plan, creating automatically another which was ideal for him, if the English army could be instantly halted and formed for battle in the minutes remaining while the Scots were descending to cross the Esk. 'We could not devise what to make of their meaning', says Patten, and so much 'the stranger as it was quite beside our expectation or doubt that they would ever forsake their strength to meet us in field'. But, though Patten did not know the Scottish chivalry, Somerset did. His army was halted, did form in battle array, while

[1] Oman, *Art of war*, 361.
[2] Patten, *Expedicion*, Sept. 10th; Harl. MS. 540, #33: Sept. 10th; Holinshed, *Chronicles*, III, 878.

Clinton's broadsides pounded much of the advancing Scottish army, completely breaking up the Highland bowmen, who fled the scene, and making it impossible for the already gravely weakened cavalry to engage effectively. 'The whole Scottish army then became one enormous mass of pikes, with its flanks wholly uncovered, since the Highlanders had disappeared and the cavalry was keeping at a great distance.'[1] This enabled Somerset to deliver repeated and heavy cavalry assaults in order to slow the Scottish advance, while steady artillery and hand-gun fire opened great gaps in the fearsome phalanx of pikes. Huntly was obliged to shift to his right at the river to escape Clinton's fire, thereby disorganizing units of Arran's centre which had already crossed the Esk. The first massed English cavalry charge was delivered by Grey straight into Huntly's pike-men, who were disorganized but stood firm, leaving many English dead and many wounded horses. This action was immediately followed by another cavalry assault on Arran, employing the re-doubtable 'Bullen horse' and most of the royal bodyguard. Again the bristling wall of pikes was unbroken, and English losses were sub-stantial.

But the Scottish advance had been slowed and was then checked by heavy artillery fire, by the hand-guns, and then by arrow fire from the now advancing English infantry. At this moment Arran's centre broke ranks and fell back to the river and beyond, a mass neither under discipline nor with any rear-guard fire-power. This retreat unhinged Angus, who alone of the Scottish commanders dis-played competence; he ordered his wing to fall back beyond artillery range, but his force, under steady English pressure, was never able to re-form. For at this moment the effective Scottish line of battle simply dissolved under the impact of the English infantry and still another slaughtering cavalry attack mounted by Grey.

The battle immediately degenerated into a senseless slaughter, as the routed Scots fled towards Edinburgh across terrain affording no protection for a broken army. The English losses had been approxi-mately 250 killed mostly among the heavy horse. The Scottish losses have been subject to what can only be described as heroic exaggeration, though they were disastrously heavy. We have one reliable figure of 1500 prisoners which suggests that quarter was given at least by troops under discipline, and that probably means the cavalry. Patten tells us that the English pursuit was pressed to the gates of Edinburgh and Leith, and that over this space of five miles 'the dead bodies lay as thick as a man may note cattle grazing'

[1] Oman, in *Archaeol. Journal*, XC (1933), 13.

in a pasture. It was his estimate that 13,000 Scots were slain on this bloody day.[1] It was not until 5 p.m., according to Holinshed, who estimated the Scottish killed at from 10,000 to 14,000, that Somerset brought his army under discipline and ordered the wanton killing stopped. The estimates do range widely and wildly, trained French observers present at the action setting the number of Scottish dead at from 6000 to 7000, which is almost certainly low.[2] Edward VI, writing some time after the event and certainly with full access to Somerset's own estimate, sets the total at 10,000 dead, though the royal diarist crossed out in his *Chronicle* the fairly accurate total of 23,000 in the Scottish army to supply a wildly heroic figure of 36,000.[3] Hayward follows Edward's estimate of 10,000 killed, as do the leading modern Scottish historians.[4] The impressively accurate and objective account of the unknown eye-witness, upon whose narrative we have relied heavily, sets the total killed very precisely at 10,400, while raising the number taken prisoner to 2000.[5] Paget, in London before September 19th, in describing the action to the imperial ambassador, fixed the total at something like 13,500, if the prisoners taken numbered 1500.[6] Some weeks later the careful imperial ambassador revised his first estimate as received from Paget, men who had been at Pinkie having told him that the dead totalled 9000–10,000.[7] Van der Delft noted in the same dispatch that though the English dead had been officially set at 200, private sources suggested that the number was more nearly 500–600. And, to complete this dreary recital, Stow and Grafton both estimated the Scottish dead at the very high total of 14,000.[8]

The news of the great victory at Pinkie was received in London on September 17th, the Council at once forwarding instructions to all bishops to cause a sermon to be preached and a *Te Deum* sung, the Latin to be rendered in the English tongue.[9] Wriothesley seems to have attended the services at St Paul's (September 20th?) where

---

[1] Patten, *Expedicion*, Sept. 10th (L6).

[2] de Selve, *Corr. politique*, 218; *et vide* 220, 242, 288–289, 317, 323, 362, 368.

[3] Edward VI, *Chronicle*, 7, 8, 9.

[4] Hayward, *Edward VI*, 286; Brown, *History of Scotland*, II, 31; Lang sets the total at upwards of 10,000 (*Scotland*, II, 11).   [5] Harl. MS. 540, #33: Sept. 10th.

[6] *Cal. S.P. Span.* IX, 151–152.   [7] *Ibid.* 188: Oct. 23, 1547.

[8] Stow, *Annales*, 594; *Grafton's chronicle*, II, 502. Oman, very wisely, does not venture an estimate, though he notes that the earlier estimates, ranging from 10,000 to 14,000, are probably exaggerated (*Archaeol. Journal* XC (1933), 17). Our own instinct in the matter is to accept the most probably reliable estimates which range from Van der Delft's revised total of 9,000–10,000, Edward's 10,000, to the Harl. MS. total of 10,400, with a guess of not more than 9,000 dead. If the Scottish force numbered about 21,500, as seems probable, it is incredible that the killed and captured could have numbered more than 50 per cent of those engaged.   [9] *A.P.C.* II, App., 517.

the sermon was preached in the presence of the Lord Mayor and the aldermen, while that night 'great fires were made in every street' and the citizenry with great joy celebrated this shattering triumph of English arms.[1] The King, in his own hand, on the 18th dispatched a warm note of congratulation to Somerset and to 'all the other of the noble men, gentlemen, and others that have served in this journey' to the overwhelming of Scottish arms.[2] And overwhelming it did seem, the Earl of Huntly, now a prisoner, gloomily reckoning that an English force of 2000 cavalry could move at will anywhere in the realm of Scotland.

With Pinkie, the military campaign was for the time being at an end because there was no organized Scottish force which could be put in the field even for harassing actions. Somerset accordingly moved almost at will to secure such strong points as he might wish to garrison for a possible military occupation of the northern kingdom. Edinburgh Castle was not assaulted and the city was purposely not exposed to the ravaging of a victorious army, for the Protector now wished to resume his diplomatic efforts which alone could give some meaning to his military intervention. On the day after Pinkie he occupied undefended Leith with his main force, and the town was burned and pillaged by an army still not restored to discipline after a heady victory. Somerset remained at Leith for about a week, receiving the submission of Bothwell and a shadowy commitment from at least a faction of the Scottish government to treat at Berwick with Warwick as his deputy. Meanwhile, in the course of about three weeks Inchcolm and Blackness, controlling the Firth of Forth, were occupied and garrisoned, Broughty Castle with its formidable fortifications in the Firth of Tay was taken, while Roxburgh and Home in the eastern Lowlands were seized and lightly garrisoned. Dundee was to be occupied a few weeks later, while the English commanders in the North—Wharton, Grey, and Andrew Dudley—rapidly threw out lines of communication linking the whole pattern of occupied points on Haddington with its very strong defences and its overweening location. Meanwhile, in the west, Wharton and Lennox moved almost at will, reducing strong point after strong point until almost the whole of Annandale lay within their power.[3]

[1] Wriothesley, *Chronicle*, I (Camden Soc., n.s. XI), 186. Wriothesley, be it noted in passing, sets the Scottish dead at 15,000, the captured at 2000.

[2] Lansdowne MS. 1236, f. 16, as quoted in Ellis, *Original letters*, ser. 1, II, 149.

[3] Harl. MS. 540, #33: Sept. 11–18, 1547; *Cal. S.P. Scotland*, I, 19–20; Brown, *History of Scotland*, II, 31; Wernham, *Before the Armada*, 170–171.

These provisions having been made or set in train, Somerset, somewhat inexplicably, suddenly began his return to England with his main force on September 18th, only a week after his great victory had been won. Moving rapidly, the Protector crossed the Tweed near Kelso and camped near Roxburgh Castle, where he left Sir Ralph Bulmer as commander after dubbing thirty knights for conspicuous valour and service at Pinkie. On the last day of the month he crossed the frontier, and then moving on ahead of the army, reached London on October 8th, being welcomed at Finsbury Field by the Lord Mayor and aldermen. On the next day he was with the King at Hampton Court.[1] There was certainly a compulsive haste involved in this precipitate return of the Lord Protector, who seems never to have explained his reasons fully even to the Council. If one may conjecture, the need to make final plans for the Parliament about to be assembled for its first session must have been much in his mind. Then too, he certainly feared a French assault on the south coast of England and he had been disturbed as well by evidences of disaffection and turbulence in the west of England. He did suggest that his army was provisioned for only a month, and we do know that he was troubled by the intransigence and arrogance of his brother, Lord Sudeley. Perhaps, too, he was moved by the realization that there was little more that he could do in Scotland, when no army was disposed against English power. He had dealt a mighty blow with his power, and aside from his occupation of all useful strong points little more could in fact be done in the field. The whole English case must now be submitted to the slow and tedious courses of diplomacy. Somewhere in this complex of reasons, or possibly in the total persuasion of all of them, are to be found the explanations for the sudden withdrawal of English power.[2] Van der Delft, in puzzling over the question, could only conclude that some

<hr />

[1] Harl. MS. 540, #33; Wriothesley, *Chronicle*, I (Camden Soc., n.s. XI), 186; Holinshed, *Chronicles*, III, 888–889.

[2] As always, too, the waging of war had cost far more than had been so carefully estimated by the professional experts, even though Somerset's quick descent on Scotland had in fact been no more than an incursion on an overwhelming scale. The total cost of the expedition into Scotland, when the accounts were audited through November 20, 1547, was, so Sadler, the Treasurer of the Army reported, £45,912 13s 0d, quite exclusive of the considerable direct outlay for Clinton's great naval force (*The state papers and letters of Sir Ralph Sadler, etc.*, ed. by Arthur Clifford (3 vols., Edinburgh, 1809), I, 355–364). This total was very nearly twice that which had been estimated and fell on a government not yet ready to lay its financial needs before Parliament and on an economy already subject to inflationary strains. Much of the cost of the expedition and the very heavy charges for the garrisoning of the strong points still held in Scotland were accordingly to be borne by the eroding of royal resources, by the sale of chantry and monastic lands now in crown hands.

secret agreement had been reached with Scotland which he could not ferret out from Paget, who upbraided him for want of faith in contending that England had negotiated without imperial knowledge or inclusion in any understanding reached in Scotland.[1]

6. THE OCCUPATION OF SCOTLAND
(SEPTEMBER, 1547–DECEMBER 29, 1547)

Though Scotland was for some months without military power, her diplomatic position remained more intransigent than ever. The staggering defeat just incurred seemed for a brief season to unite most most of the nobility and to halt the centripetal forces in national policy. The infant queen was removed to a secure hiding, while the government immediately laid before France an urgent request for full-scale military intervention; was disposed, indeed, to place completely in professional French hands the prosecution of a war to secure the expulsion of the English occupation forces. These developments greatly discouraged Somerset who had naively assumed that only a decisive military defeat would be required to persuade Scotland of the virtues of the Treaty of Greenwich, and who now unhappily confided to the imperial ambassador that the Scots showed no disposition to treat and that further military pressure might have to be applied.[2]

Somerset's only recourse, therefore, was to begin once more the slow building of a party in Scotland, linked to the rapidly spreading course of the Reformation in the Lowlands. Huntly, now a restive prisoner of war, had pressed for release in order to serve the English cause, but the Protector, quite correctly, was suspicious of him and declined to risk English policy in his capricious hands.[3] So too, Bothwell remained in touch with Somerset, offering to support the English cause if an English wife of high estate could be provided for him and a hundred men subsidized with English gold, on which the crusty Warwick drily commented, 'he wanted the men more than leave to see the ladies'.[4] As was predictable, the irresponsible Sir George Douglas was offering his services to Grey of Wilton, in command at Norham, if England would over-match the pensions he had from the Queen and from France. To this proffer of support Somerset angrily retorted that he had always found Douglas full of deceit and that he must first prove his loyalty by actions.[5] Once

[1] Cal. S.P. Span. IX, 177–178, 182, 185–186: Oct. 18 and 23, 1547.
[2] Ibid. 196–197.   [3] Ibid. 220–221: Dec. 5, 1547.
[4] Cal. S.P. Scotland, I, 22: Warwick to Somerset, Berwick, Sept. 30, 1547.
[5] Ibid. 25–26, 28–29, 31–32: Oct. 9, 20, and 26, 1547.

more the fragile policy of building strength in Scotland on treason
and on purchasable aristocratic support was unfolding, whereas the
only sure basis for winning reliable and steady strength was to
link the powerful force of the Reformation, already strong in the
most populous and prosperous areas of Scotland, as tightly and
organically as might be with English support. A union of churches,
so to speak, would in due season lead to a union of states.

Somerset's victory at Pinkie had caught the French quite unawares
and for a season lent some measure of strength and security to
English policy. But not for long. We have earlier noted that the
English had given diplomatic offence by works undertaken in
Boulogne harbour, to which the French countered with fortifications across the river designed to dominate the Lower Town. Both
sides were also indulging in privateering on a considerable scale,
while the English in the spring and summer of 1547 complained
loudly and bitterly of the military stores and 'observers' being set
down in Scotland by the French, often under naval convoy. But
now pressure was relaxed as France soberly considered the extent
to which it was prepared to involve its military and naval strength
in Scotland. A clear-cut agreement was accordingly reached to
suppress privateering, prizes were to be restored, and full commerce
was to be resumed after October 30th, while a rather cloudy and
desultory discussion was instituted respecting terms of ransom for
Boulogne.[1] Somerset, who was for the moment negotiating from
strength, on November 16th proposed implausible terms under
which Boulogne would be restored in return for the retention of
Ambleteuse and Guînes and the cession of Marquise and Fiennes,
to be supplemented by a French undertaking to support the proposed marriage of Edward with Mary Stuart. To this cavalier
proposal Henry II countered by offering support for the desired
marriage in return for the cession of Calais, Guînes, and Boulogne,
which Somerset denounced as an insult to his royal master. The
negotiations, never really seriously undertaken, were wearing thin,
and Somerset learned that a contingent of French officers and
engineers was about to leave for Scotland to inspect the English
fortifications there as a probable prelude to intervention.[2] Somerset's
final, and reasonable, offer was then made for the immediate
cession of Boulogne on the treaty terms in exchange for French
support of the projected marriage treaty, to which Henry replied by
a strong raid into the Boulogne precincts in December in which a

---

[1] Hughes and Larkin, *Tudor proclamations*, I, 405–406.
[2] *Cal. S.P. Span.* IX, 225: Dec. 12, 1547; Wernham, *Before the Armada*, 171–172.

considerable number of the English were killed. Somerset was most anxious to avoid war and strictly forbad any move of reprisal, but by the close of 1547 any serious negotiation was at an end. The Protector now fully understood that war in France, as well as in Scotland, was restrained only by the Emperor's brilliant successes in Germany and by the danger which France faced of a renewal of the war in Italy. English policy had come to rest, in point of fact, on the disposition and the unrevealed intentions of Charles V. At the end of December, 1547, Sir Ralph Bulmer, at Roxburgh, reported to Somerset that fifty French officers had been landed in Scotland and that it was rumoured that a powerful French expeditionary force would follow.[1]

The English commands in Scotland were centred in Grey in the east, usually at Berwick or forward at Norham, who after winning great distinction as a cavalry leader at Pinkie was left in the north as governor of Berwick, Warden of the East Marches, and 'general of the northern parts'. But in administrative fact he shared the responsibilities of high command with Wharton in the west, both men tending to communicate directly with Somerset and all too frequently ignoring each other in the field and on questions of supply. The competent Sir Andrew Dudley was left in command of the most exposed of the English fortified positions, Broughty Castle. Sir John Luttrell was in command at Inchcolm, Bulmer was at Roxburgh, and Grey seems to have retained direct command at the key base of Haddington until it was brought under siege. Clinton, while still in formal command of the naval forces in northern waters, had in fact delegated responsibility to the superbly qualified Wyndham. There were grave weaknesses in this linked system of commands, since the individual officers were not sternly discouraged from directing their reports and appeals immediately to Somerset, rather than to Berwick, with resulting confusion, delay, and waste. Somerset was perhaps too much the professional soldier readily to relinquish the details of command and was himself responsible for this serious flaw in operations. Thus, he thought it not inappropriate that ship captains should report to him from Newcastle that the fleet suffered from foul winter weather, that the King's beer was being lost by leakage, or that all money and victuals had been consumed.[2]

During the remainder of 1547, the English commanders were engaged in fortifying their holding position in Scotland, warding

[1] *Cal. S.P. Scotland*, I, 55.
[2] S.P. Dom., Edw. VI, II, 22, 23: Dec. 12 and 14, 1547.

off orders which would have depleted their own garrisons and supplies for use at other points, and seeking to establish friendly relations with the countryside in order to gain intelligence reports and to keep open local sources of supply. In this period Broughty was by far the most exposed and important of all the commands. It had surrendered to Clinton on demand, but he could not supply Dudley with more than six weeks of victual, detailing three small ships with which sea communications and supply might be maintained. Both he and Dudley regarded the existing fortifications as worthless, repairs being at once taken in hand, though the surrounding towns and country were friendly and well disposed.[1] The nearby town of Dundee made its submission to Dudley in late October, offering provisions at a fair price and, significantly, requesting Protestant preachers, Bibles, and testaments. Dudley none the less thought his force so small and weakened by disease and exposure as to be insufficient to hold in the event of a determined assault.[2] In late November precisely this did occur, when Broughty was brought under heavy siege by a large force of Scots, which after repeated skirmishes lay entrenched against its walls. But in a beautifully co-ordinated effort Wyndham brought in supplies and reinforcements from Holy Island, to find the siege lifted as the Scots withdrew before the reports of his approach.[3] Wyndham, unable to put out of the Firth in winter seas without storm gear, for some days worked up the Tay for several miles, the tides limiting his operations to two hours, and assisted in securing the second capitulation of Dundee, though he could spare only three hundred men for the up-Tay landings which he planned.[4]

Instead, Somerset, by direct orders, called Wyndham home, leaving but one ship for Dudley's needs—an order which both Dudley and Wyndham protested would leave English supporters in the Dundee area quite defenceless—while Dudley wrote that 'this is of no little grief to me, deprived of strength at most need, in a weak house beaten and shaken at the siege, and all our work . . . only rotten sandy turf and shingle, falling down daily'.[5] From Grey, too, Somerset received a letter of protest, arguing vehemently that from Broughty as a base Dundee could be held, St Andrew's threatened or immobilized, and the whole hinterland won over or

[1] *Cal. S.P. Scotland*, I, 21, 24: Sept. 24 and Oct. 8, 1547.
[2] *Ibid.* 35: Nov. 1, 1547.
[3] *Ibid.* 45–46, 48–49: Nov. 30 and Dec. 18, 1547.
[4] *Ibid.* 51: Dec. 22, 1547.
[5] *Ibid.* 53–54: Dec. 27, 1547; Edward VI, *Chronicle*, 8.

controlled.[1] And then a few days later (January 3, 1548) Dudley reported to Somerset that he was trying to fortify Dundee against an expected siege by Argyle, that he desperately needed money and two thousand men, his garrison force being 170, and confirming the dread rumour that French officers had arrived in Scotland, presumably to arrange for the transport and quartering of their troops which were to follow.[2]

In part Somerset's peremptory order for Wyndham's withdrawal from the Tay and his steady refusal to move substantial reinforcements to Dudley arose as a consequence of his decision to make of Haddington an extremely strong, heavily garrisoned, and advanced centre of English occupying power which would not only command the approaches to Edinburgh but would immobilize whatever forces Arran could muster. He accordingly commanded Grey carefully to survey the Haddington area and to make a quick feinting thrust towards Edinburgh, while Wharton was to ravage Annandale. Meanwhile Haddington was heavily garrisoned and work was begun on its defences. Some measure of the importance attached by Somerset to the retention of the place may be gained from an inventory of the victuals laid in by Sadler, probably early in 1548. These included 573 quarters of bread grain, upwards of 16,000 pieces of brined beef, 197 live oxen, and great stores of butter.[3] Somerset's tactical judgement was wholly confirmed, as we shall note, when the necessity for eliminating this centre of English power so near the capital was for many months to tie down almost all the combined Scottish and French military resources in the siege of Haddington.

The remaining English force exerting the pressure of occupation on Scotland was that on the Western Marches, commanded by the experienced, if somewhat pedestrian, Lord Wharton. After Somerset's withdrawal from the Pinkie campaign, when Wharton had moved deep into Scotland in a diversionary raid, the Warden's force was reduced to about 1000 men, based on Carlisle.[4] His destructive raids across the border into Annandale were continued almost at will, and so formidable was his strength that he could report in October that 2700 Scottish foot and horse had now given their oaths to his service, while a few days later he could speak with justifiable pride of the arc of his power which extended out for forty

[1] *Cal. S.P. Scotland*, I, 54: Dec. 30, 1547.
[2] *Ibid.* 56–57.
[3] Lodge, *Illustrations*, I, 150–151, citing Talbot MS. B, f. 31.
[4] *Cal. S.P. Dom.*, *Edw VI*, VI, 329–330.

miles beyond Carlisle.[1] In the course of the autumn his burning raids were pressed ever deeper into Scotland, one on October 19th striking to Kirkcudbright, twenty-four miles beyond Dumfries, as he sought to prevent the rebuilding of Arran's military strength.[2] With persuasive arguments Wharton also proposed a forward strong point at Dumfries, a Haddington of the west, so to say, which would greatly extend the area of English power and which could be largely supplied from the surrounding countryside.[3] He vigorously propagated the English interest in the whole border area, reckoning in mid-November that there were then 6000 Scots under English commitment, from whom he could draw as many as 1500 for military service on command. He none the less stood in grave need of more English troops for striking and garrison duty. But this must remain a dream until his present forces were paid, for towards obligations totalling almost £12,000 for the past three months he had received no more than £3000 with the promise of another payment in the same amount.[4] Wharton had lent good service, and the steady hammering of his raids on an almost defenceless countryside had helped immeasurably in relieving pressure in the central area of concern in the east where now French intervention and French leadership were to produce a crisis in English policy.

7. SCOTTISH AFFAIRS: THE INTERVENTION OF FRANCE (JANUARY–JULY, 1548)

Somerset, the 'hammer of the Scots', now sought to lay the English case, or more accurately the case of empire, before the Scots in what was foredoomed to be a naive and a vain move of propaganda. He was a lenient and a pacific man, a man moved by abstractions, whose history had been really tragically cast in the role of a highly gifted professional soldier. The case for the marriage treaty he thought just and a matter of covenanted honour, while to his brooding and capacious vision it offered as well a surcease to the generations of friction and war between two related peoples. We have seen that almost as he crossed the border in 1547 he had issued a proclamation to the people of Scotland in which he tried to say that he wished to bring peace, not war—whereupon, with a dreadful

---

[1] Cal. S.P. Dom., Edw. VI, VI, 331–332, 333: Oct. 12 and 17, 1547.

[2] Ibid. 335–337: Oct. 23, 1547.

[3] Ibid. 338–340; and see ibid. 340–341, where he recommends even more northerly Kirkcudbright for this purpose.   [4] Ibid. 344–346: Nov. 5 and 12, 1547.

inconsistency, he had destroyed the Scottish army. Now he sought to try again, employing the leverage gained by having left in Scotland occupying garrisons in scattered but strategically placed strong points.

Accordingly, early in 1548, when the weather had imposed a restless armistice in Scotland, he addressed to the people of Scotland 'An Epistle or Exhortation', which in February was given wide circulation north of the Tweed. He submitted that England had won a decisive victory in the field and now controlled most of Scotland. But this, he pleaded, settled nothing, for on five occasions English arms had prevailed in the north without bringing peace and concord. For many dark years the history of Anglo-Scottish relations had, he argued, been dreary, bloody, and disastrous. This was an annal of a kind of civil war among a people 'united together in one language, in one island', similar in culture and government, and in past history. Thus the covenanted marriage should be regarded as a God-given opportunity to join the two kingdoms in one dynasty and destiny. The names of both countries should be abolished, to take 'the indifferent old name of Britaines again', while Scotland would be left with her own laws and customs, and trade would be free one part with another.[1]

There is every reason for believing that this eloquent and moving proposal reflected precisely Somerset's own thinking and a conception of empire which he stood ready to implement, which would have brought peace and greater prosperity for the 'Britain' which he envisioned. He sketched, indeed, the ultimate terms of union with an amazing prescience. But the union which he proposed would also have ended the power of a turbulent nobility in Scotland which wanted no taming. And it would predictably, and shortly, have furthered the course of a spreading reformation which was anathema to the Guise Queen Mother and most of the nobility who advised her. Hence the proposal evoked no considerable response.

Examining in greater detail the benefits of union was another book by one John Harrison, a Scot who as early as July, 1547, wrote to Somerset, offering his services and proposing a plan for the military reduction of the north. Several later unsolicited letters followed with naive judgements on the Scottish people and the military situation in Scotland, accompanied always by pleas for a pension or some other

---

[1] [Seymour, Edward], *Epistola exhortatoria ad pacem ... missa ab ... Protectore Angliae ... ad ... populum regni Scotiae* (L., 1548); published in translation, *An epistle or exhortacion, to unitie and peace, sent from the Lorde Protector, etc.* (L., 1548). The Latin text is a beautiful example of composition and printing.

preferment.[1] In his treatise Harrison stated that he wished for union in order to end the savage wars which had sprung from an unnatural division of a single island. In an excursion into the past he sought to prove by mythological sources that the two nations had once been a single kingdom, which the Treaty of Greenwich did no more than seek to restore. The betrayal of this solemn treaty had been accomplished by French diplomacy and gold and by the treasonable propaganda of the priesthood in Scotland. He proposed more concretely that the union be effected by a restoration of the primitive and reformed church throughout the island, the encouragement of intermarriage amongst the nobility, and binding the Scottish gentry to the Crown by pensions and favours. But even more importantly, the condition of the Scottish poor should be radically reformed, their rights in land guaranteed, and the military slavery which now bound them to the nobility abolished. Further, a great programme of social reformation should be undertaken, establishing almshouses in every parish, founding schools, and reforming the universities. He would also seek to lift the pall of Scottish poverty by state subsidies for fishing fleets, the better training of craftsmen, and the cutting of a canal from east to west. These benefits accomplished, 'the labouring man might safely till his ground, and as safely gather in the profits and fruits thereof; the merchant might without fear go abroad, and bring in foreign commodities', and peace and better governance would lift up the whole nation. Once these things were done, the fruits of union would be manifest, and 'those hateful terms of Scots and Englishmen shall be abolished and blotted out forever, and . . . we shall all agree in the only title and name of Britons'.[2] Harrison was undoubtedly a little fey, and his thought wanted in a sense of practicality. But there was in his proposals a passionate sense of the need for far-ranging reforms as well as Reformation in the north, which he was persuaded could come only when the destructive frictions of the two states could be absolved in union. The thought of Harrison and of Somerset have, indeed, much in common.

Military operations were most limited during the early months of 1548 as cold gripped the north, though Grey from Berwick and Wharton from Carlisle disposed at least 10,000 men in their areas of command. The Queen Mother, Mary of Lorraine, stood steadfast against any military or diplomatic compromise, and with

---

[1] He was called, indifferently, Harrison, Herrison, and Henrison.

[2] Harrison, James, *An exhortacion to the Scottes*, etc. (L., 1547), no pagin.; in variant form, under the title, *The godly and golden book*.

considerable skill sought to secure from France a substantial commitment of military support, a French mission of officers, as we have
noted, having arrived in order to estimate the number of the forces required to place an effective army in the field.[1] The English for their
part were seeking by gold, pensions, and renewed favours to win
back the pro-English faction in the nobility, among whom Lennox,
Glencairn, and Bothwell were counted as reliable supporters. But
now even Argyle, salved by liberal grants of land, declared for the
marriage treaty, and the Governor's brother, John Hamilton, was
known to be well disposed. The powerful Angus was now also
inclined towards the English interest, while Huntly, still in London
as a prisoner of war, was empowered to negotiate marriage terms
unless France forthwith offered full aid and a formal declaration of
war. It is not too much to say that the Scottish nobility were for
sale to the highest bidder, and now the full pressure of French
diplomacy was brought to bear to save a rapidly deteriorating position in Scotland.[2] Discussions were begun in January for a marriage
treaty between the infant queen and the Dauphin, supported by the
insistent pressure of the Queen Dowager; French gold and French
titles began to flow; and the weakness of at least some of the strong
points held by England was demonstrated when Blackness and
Inchcolm were recovered.

Grey at Berwick was harassed during these months by the
insistent demands of the commanders of the occupied points for
reinforcements, by the orders from London to deal lightly with the
lands and houses of nobles who might be won to the English
interest, and by the pressure he was ordered to maintain with
sorties in force. He complained that Wharton was spoiling Angus'
land and cattle without permission, while he had, as instructed,
burned the town of Buccleuch, but could not carry Buccleuch's
house at Newark.[3] Late in January the three English commanders
in the north—Grey, Wharton, and Bowes—met to determine
whether joint operations from the three Marches could be mounted
in mid-winter, reporting to London that for want of victual nothing
more could be done than to carry out diversionary raids in the west
and to occupy Haddington in force when that was desired.[4] And
Grey was troubled because Wyndham had been unable to provide
sorely needed naval support and revictualling to Dudley at Broughty,
in consequence of which Dundee had been lost by negligence.[5]

It was in this season that French diplomacy was securing the

[1] *Cal. S.P. Span.* IX, 245: Jan. 22, 1548.   [2] de Selve, *Corr. politique*, 224, 226–227.
[3] *Cal. S.P. Scotland*, I, 59, 60.   [4] *Ibid.* 66.   [5] *Ibid.* 69.

fragile loyalty of Angus, Douglas, and Cassilis with handsome bribes. Huntly and Argyle were awarded the Order of St Michael, and the wavering Arran was restored in loyalty to the Queen Mother by the grandiloquent title of Duke of Châtelherault on February 8, 1548. Somerset was following these French countermoves nervously and unhappily from distant London and lashed out not a little unfairly at Grey, complaining that heavy outlays over the past months had brought no fruitful results and pointedly upbraiding him for his timid expedition against Buccleuch when he might have burned and raided beyond Edinburgh with 200 horse, as both he and Warwick had done in the past. To this Grey bitterly replied that 'your grace must remember that the enemy is further off than when you, and after, my lord Warwick lay here, and not so readily to be "fetched" ', while asking to be relieved of his command.[1] In England, meanwhile, there was strong sentiment for mounting still another great assault on Scotland in the coming spring, muster rolls being ordered in unusual detail and thoroughness,[2] while a survey was undertaken of ships in port-towns which might be brought into the King's service.[3] These ominous stirrings of English strength and evident firmness of policy were not lost on Chapelle, head of the French mission in Edinburgh, who reported in March that the Scots were still paralysed by the extent and completeness of the English triumph at Pinkie. There was little will for resistance, and he had found few resources on which he might build. Grey and Wharton were raiding across the border almost at will with heavy forces, and the French intelligence suggested that another full-scale invasion might be impending. It was, accordingly, his considered judgement that a full military commitment must be made by his government if Scotland were to be preserved.[4] This and subsequent reports fully persuaded Henry II that larger military commitments must be made. Thirlby reported to the English Privy Council just a month later that the redoubtable Peter Strozzi was in motion with 4000 Italian mercenaries for service in Scotland, and declared his own judgement that the English position there must be held, 'for the bruit of one fort recovered [in Scotland], would be sent abroad in the world, as though all were lost of our side'.[5]

The English position in Scotland had been difficult in the winter of 1548 in part because the weather had been unusually severe,

[1] Cal. S.P. Scotland, I, 73–74.
[2] S.P. Dom., Edw. VI, III, 8–19: Feb.–Mar., 1548.   [3] Ibid. 20–21.
[4] Teulet, Alexandre, Rélations politiques de la France et de l'Espagne avec l'Écosse au XVIᵉ siecle, etc., vol. I (Paris, 1862), 160–162: M. de la Chapelle to Duc d'Aumale, Mar. 22, 1548.   [5] Tytler, England, I, 88–90.

making overland communications and supply almost impossible and driving in the naval force because of dangerous seas. In late March, however, Wyndham was able to bring the fleet in to Newcastle, posting to Somerset a detailed account of illness, need for refitting, and his most urgent plea for 200 more men.[1] He had been in the Tay a short time earlier with his small force of four vessels, his crews unpaid, his ships without cables and other gear, and, so he reported, in need of three more warships with two large landing craft, if his force were to be made effective.[2] It was not until May that the main body of the fleet was able to sail for the north under Clinton, absorbing Wyndham's command, with orders to put in to the Firth of Forth, which he was to clear and fortify in order to sever communications with France and to prevent the landing of an expected French army and its supplies.[3] Grey was instructed to counter by placing a strong force in Haddington and staging raids in force towards Edinburgh. But Clinton and Wyndham were unable to stay the French fleet, so long rumoured, which Lord Grey sighted on June 12th standing off Dunbar and consisting by his eye count of three great men-of-war, a brigantine, sixteen galleys, and a great number of smaller vessels carrying troops and supplies.[4] The French caught a favourable wind two days later and on June 18th Grey reported to Somerset, from Berwick, that the French had landed at Leith to the number of 10,000 troops.[5] The expeditionary force actually numbered approximately 6000 under the command of the formidable André de Montalembert, Sieur d'Essé, and was composed of veteran troops of French, German, and Italian nationality, d'Andelot commanding the French foot, Strozzi the Italians, and Dunow the artillery. To this force, well provisioned and heavily armed, Arran added 8000 Scottish levies of indifferent quality and little training. Even in the preliminary council of war it was agreed that the first and essential objective must be to drive the English from Haddington, the forward English staging-point from which a strong raiding party of horse had burned to within sight of Edinburgh a few days before the French arrived.[6]

Of the strong-points on which the occupation of Scotland had been based, a number had been abandoned during the winter months of 1548 as too difficult to supply; others were lightly held and of no great strategic importance; while two—Haddington and

---

[1] S.P. Dom., Edw. VI, IV, 4.   [2] *Cal. S.P. Scotland*, I, 84: Feb. 25, 1548.
[3] S.P. Dom., Edw. VI, IV, 9: May ?, 1548.   [4] *Cal. S.P. Scotland*, I, 119, 120, 121.
[5] *Ibid.* 121–122; Holinshed, *Chronicles*, III, 891; *Cal. S.P. Span.* IX, 274: June 21, 1548. The landing occurred on June 16th.
[6] *Ibid.* 271: Van der Delft to Emperor, June 13, 1548.

Broughty—were very strongly held and sufficed, so long as English sea power was dominant, to give to England effective military and economic control of eastern Scotland. These two strongholds were gradually strengthened on orders from Somerset during the months prior to the arrival of the French expeditionary force, which was dispatched in large part because Scottish military power was wholly inadequate to deal with these foci of English strength.

In his withdrawal from Scotland Somerset had left a light holding force at Haddington, which was further strengthened in late January, 1548, when Grey reported to Somerset that he could defend the town unless artillery were ranged against the walls.[1] A month later Grey infuriated Somerset by withdrawing most of his force to Berwick on a rumour of Wharton's defeat in the west, suggesting the timidity which always possessed Grey until he was actually in the field.[2] Grey recommended indeed—and sea power and better communications did support him—that Dunbar would constitute a more advantageous forward base than Haddington, but was ordered in no uncertain terms to restore the Haddington garrison. Grey was skirmishing and spoiling from the base towards Edinburgh in March, receiving instructions to proceed with the fortification of the town and to provide it with supplies for a two months' siege, presumably as a forward point for the heavy force which Somerset then contemplated sending into Scotland in the spring.[3] Grey, under orders, moved his own headquarters forward to Haddington, after the passage in the Pease had been secured and entrenched. He wrote to Somerset on April 28th that he had laid out plans for the completion of the fortifications, 'wherein the substance of all the town and fair houses is contained, sufficient for any garrison'. He was at last persuaded that he could command the whole countryside around Haddington, and recommended either Wilford, who was appointed, or Holcroft for the garrison command.[4]

The Privy Council attached ever-increasing importance to the secure holding of Haddington, dispatching John Brende with orders to Grey to exercise his general command from that base as long as possible, to complete the fortifications at full speed, and to work out a better system of mutual support with Wharton.[5] Grey was raiding

---

[1] *Cal. S.P. Scotland*, I, 64: Grey to Somerset, Jan. 24, 1548.

[2] *Ibid.* 85–86. The report was brought to Grey—or so he claimed—by Wharton's son who had commanded the light horse in Wharton's striking force.

[3] *Ibid.* 105.   [4] *Ibid.* 110–111.

[5] *Ibid.* 114: May 21, 1548. Brende had earlier been employed on a mission to the Hanseatic cities to enjoin them not to send naval supplies to Scotland (*Cal. S.P. For., Edw. VI*, #64; *Cal. S.P. Scotland*, I, 93–96; *A.P.C.*, II, 151).

and burning around Leith and Dalkeith in early June, while pressing
to complete his fortifications and victualling before the rumoured
French expeditionary force should arrive.[1] A strong raid was
mounted a few days later on Musselburgh, which with several
nearby villages was burned, though Grey complained of the want
of discipline of his garrison troops, who if they found a cow or horse
simply wandered off with their loot, and asked permission to
recruit steadier Yorkshiremen in their place.[2] Leaving the brilliant,
if irresponsible, Palmer in command, Grey led a troop of horse on
June 10th to scout the coast near Dunbar, for the rumoured French
fleet, which, as we have seen, he reported having observed two days
later. Grey immediately called upon Wharton for 700 horse to add
weight to his striking and scouting force, but the crusty Warden of
the Western Marches would offer no more than as many 'simple
foot'.[3] Without direct orders to do so, Grey fell back with his main
force to Berwick while the landing of the French army at Leith was
under way (he was in Berwick on June 12th). Palmer meanwhile
demolished Haddington church and several houses which lay within
the lines of fire of his ordnance.[4] The importance lent to Haddington
by the French survey party in Scotland during the past winter was
fully confirmed by d'Essé, who even before his artillery was un-
loaded ordered a field manœuvre of the English fortifications there;
he decided immediately to reduce the English garrison, by siege if
need be, since no freedom of movement could be gained until it was
in French hands.[5] The reconnaissance had correctly estimated that
the English garrison numbered about 2000 and that their fortifications were so strongly made that siege ordnance would be required to carry the place.[6] The Queen Dowager enthusiastically lent
her support to plans for a full-scale effort before Haddington,
though asking of the Duc d'Aumale and the Cardinal de Guise
formal assurances that French troops would not be withdrawn until
Scotland had won its full security.[7]

Meanwhile Lord Grey from the somewhat remote safety of
Berwick was reporting to London that heavy French ordnance was
being moved from Edinburgh towards Haddington, eighteen miles
distant, and that Wharton's foot had joined him. He assured the
Protector that he would scout the French movement as closely as

---

[1] *Cal. S.P. Dom., Edw. VI*, VI, 386; *Cal. S.P. Scotland*, I, 115–116.
[2] *Ibid.* 118: Grey to Somerset, June 9, 1548.
[3] *Ibid.* 122: Grey to Somerset, June 18, 1548.
[4] *Ibid.* 123–124; Teulet, *Relations*, I, 164–165.
[5] *Ibid.* 165–166: d'Oysel to Duc d'Aumale, June 18, 1548.
[6] *Ibid.* 169–170.   [7] *Ibid.* 174–175.

possible, but asked urgently for 1000 horse from Shrewsbury's large contingent of reinforcements now marching northwards.[1] This letter must have passed Thomas Fisher, Somerset's private secretary, who on June 26th was sent north with general orders. Reports were to be spread abroad of a large English invading army which would be commanded by the Protector in person. Haddington was to be strongly held and supplied from Berwick. The fleet under Clinton was to blockade the Scottish coast and to set down as many diversionary landings as possible in order to relieve pressure on Haddington. If communications between Berwick and Haddington were endangered, a strong force would immediately attack Dunbar. These orders, with their purposely implanted exaggerations, being delivered to Grey and Shrewsbury, Fisher was to proceed to Broughty and discuss with Luttrell the measures required for its defence and to secure the loyalty of Lord Gray and, if possible, that of Argyle.[2] Grey, meanwhile, on June 28th reported to Somerset that he had sent in a hundred of Gamboa's veteran Spanish mercenaries expressly for the stiffening of the Haddington garrison, advancing the view that to hold the place would be to win Scotland.[3] But when Gamboa's force arrived before Haddington on June 30th they found the town invested and could not gain entrance, though as yet only three siege pieces had been brought to bear.[4] Sir James Wilford, having relieved Palmer, reported cheerfully on July 2nd that the Franco-Scottish army had besieged him, though all their artillery was not in position. On the preceding night he had sallied out and killed more than thirty French; with 2000 more horse he would drive out the French army.[5] From Berwick, Palmer expressed confidence that the fortifications would hold, that the garrison of 200 men was well commanded and in high fettle, and that he doubted not that God would 'reward their travail with immortal fame'.[6] The always restrained and long experienced d'Essé was more cautious in his estimate. Heavy artillery fire, much sapping and trenching, and the containment of sharp and bloody English sallies would be required to effect his purpose, while always in the background was the certainty that Grey would strike him with a swift moving and heavily armed relieving force.[7] But he intended

---

[1] *Cal. S.P. Scotland*, I, 126–127: June 26, 1548.

[2] *Ibid.* 129–131: June 27, 1548. Fisher, of humble origin, had long served both Dudley and Seymour, while building up a landed fortune of his own from monastic properties which he gained on favourable terms. He remains a somewhat misty figure.

[3] *Ibid.* 131.   [4] *Ibid.* 132–133.

[5] *Hamilton papers*, II, 597.   [6] *Cal. S.P. Scotland*, I, 133.

[7] Teulet, *Relations*, I, 182–183: M. d'Essé to Duc d'Aumale, July 6, 1548.

to take Haddington before launching a war of movement. Perhaps the most famous siege in English history was under way.

The second English strong-point, under Sir Andrew Dudley, which had immobilized Scottish resistance and recovery, was Broughty Crag. It commanded the mouth of the Tay, controlled Dundee and the Tay valley, provided a useful haven for the fleet, and dominated the considerable area in which the lands and influence of Lord Gray and of Argyle were centred.[1] But Dudley's position was not without difficulties, particularly when the strong naval squadron in the Tay was withdrawn, since he had neither the manpower nor the materials with which properly to fortify his position and since he was left hostage to the unreliable temperament of the Earl of Argyle. He was troubled and testy, complaining in mid-January of the poor quality of reinforcements sent to him by Grey, many of whom were Scots of dubious loyalty. He could get no help on his projected fortifications, since the sailors stayed on board and his soldiers would not labour. As for Grey's charge that he had asked for enough strength to hold Calais, he could only reply that 'this is another Calais'.[2] At last Somerset intervened personally, sending north the experienced military engineer, Sir Thomas Palmer, with funds for the completion of the work at Broughty and for raising a citadel to secure better control of Dundee.[3] Argyle took the field against him shortly afterwards in an effort to free Dundee, again precariously in English hands, a dubious compromise being reached by which the town was to be neutralized.[4] Palmer, on his arrival, found Broughty only weakly fortified and was aghast at what Dudley was expected to do with an effective garrison force of not more than 150 men, sharply augmented now by a contingent of 300 soldiers and 80 mariners dispatched by Grey from Newcastle at the end of January.[5] Palmer also found himself in agreement that the pebbly terrain of Broughty simply could not bear strong fortifications, and had ordered fortified instead a commanding hill about 2000 feet distant when further reinforcements should arrive.[6] Lord Gray and Argyle were again placated with pensions and gifts, and Palmer on a second visit of inspection in mid-February found the fortifications on the new site well advanced, while a month later he could report to Somerset that the major work would be completed within four days and that ordnance could then be sited.[7] Meanwhile, Sir John Luttrell was

---

[1] *Vide ante*, 265 ff.   [2] *Cal. S.P. Scotland*, I, 62.
[3] *A.P.C.* II, 161.   [4] *Cal. S.P. Scotland*, I, 63, 64, 67–68.
[5] *Ibid.* 66, 68.   [6] *Cal. S.P. Span.*, IX, 251.   [7] *Cal. S.P. Scotland*, I, 89–90.

ordered to raze the works at Incholm and to join Dudley in the command at Broughty, while an Italian mercenary officer was placed in charge of the light ordnance now in position.[1]

In the early spring (1548) it was believed in Berwick that both Broughty and Haddington were sufficiently strengthened, and for a season supplies and manpower were diverted to Sir Robert Bowes, who was seeking to fortify and to hold Lauder in the central Lowlands, though Lord Gray had warned both him and Grey that at least 3000–4000 troops would be required to withstand the probable military reaction from Arran who could hardly tolerate the rupture of his east-west communications.[2] This distraction, for which Grey seems to have been responsible, spread limited English supplies too thinly and disrupted the work still uncompleted on the Broughty bulwarks. At the end of April Luttrell, no fearful commander, complained bitterly to Somerset that he had only a hundred well men, his walls were weak, and he needed shot and powder. He had just been harried by a large force of Scots, stiffened with two troops of French horse, which had tried to overrun communications between the Old Castle and his new hill fort. He concluded that he would rather 'trail a pike' again as a soldier than bear such a neglected command as he had at Broughty.[3] But further supplies and troops could not be spared in view of the arrival of the French and the concentration of the English command on holding Haddington. Luttrell was unjustly upbraided and was warned that he must seek to hold Broughty with the fewest possible troops.[4] This decision Luttrell accepted, a week later writing much more cheerfully after he had beaten off with the guns of the hill fort an attack by a French naval squadron. He reported, too, that he was now in effect lightly besieged, since he was daily harassed by 500–600 horse and 'the country foot' levied by Arran from the Tay valley.[5] But he thought he could hold, and hold he did as the occupying force in Scotland settled down in siege positions at Haddington and Broughty, which as the months extended were to drain off and contain almost the whole of the force and of the supplies which Henry II had sent for the succour of Scotland.

The third important element in the English forces of occupation

[1] *Cal. S.P. Scotland I*, 98: Mar. 19, 1548; *ibid.* 99–100.
[2] *Ibid.* 101, 108, 109.
[3] *Ibid.* 109–110, 112–113: Apr. 11, and 30, 1548.
[4] *The Scottish correspondence of Mary of Lorraine . . . 1542-3 to 15th May 1560*, ed. by A. I. Cameron (Publ. Scot. Hist. Soc., ser. 3, X, Edinburgh, 1927), 247–248: Somerset and Council to Luttrell, June 12, 1548.
[5] *Cal. S.P. Scotland*, I, 124–125: Luttrell to Somerset, June 20, 1548.

in Scotland, which as the events of the first months of 1548 demonstrated could not be checkmated, much less expelled, was Wharton's highly mobile spoiling force based on Carlisle. His lightly held outposts lay in an arc with a radius of about forty miles from Carlisle, while the whole countryside was constantly ravaged by his border horse.[1] Wharton was jealous of Grey, co-operated on his own terms in the few joint strikes undertaken, and constantly complained that he could not lay waste Scottish soil and then be expected to victual his forward garrisons from the countryside.[2] Nor were his communications with London satisfactory, for in February a package of 260 books to be distributed in western Scotland[3] took nine days in transit, though they were posted with the imperative, 'for life, for life'.[4] And then in late February, under pressure from London, he mounted a full-scale raid into Scotland, in conjunction with Grey, with a force of 3000 infantry and all his horse. Angus attacked and scattered the English horse, which was evidently out of close communication with the main force under Wharton, and then assaulted the foot which suffered heavy losses, in part because of the defection of pledged Scots making up part of Wharton's force.[5] The first lurid account of the defeat, from Wharton's excited son, was greatly exaggerated, but it so shook English confidence and disrupted English strategy that a general muster was ordered in the border counties. Wharton was badly shaken, complaining that his army would not have been defeated had his orders been obeyed, and then in the same dispatch contending that his force had been too weak for so ambitious an enterprise. His whole strong position in Annandale and along the border had vanished and he seemed incapable of making any decision without express orders from London.[6] Wharton should, in fact, have been replaced forthwith, but his position as a territorial magnate in the west was too strong and there was no one available who possessed his toughness and ferocity. His dislike of Grey had festered into hatred and the enmity between the two men accounts principally for the failure of what was planned as a general offensive deep into Scotland.[7]

Wharton nursed his wounds and his vanity at Carlisle, meanwhile with an incredible brutality hanging six (possibly ten) hostages from border families which had defected during his recent foray.

[1] *Cal. S.P. Dom., Edw. VI*, VI, 355–356: Jan. 20, 1548.   [2] *Ibid.* 358–359.
[3] Very possibly copies of Somerset's appeal to the Scottish people.
[4] *Ibid.* 360: Feb. 18, 1548.
[5] *Ibid.* 361–362: Sir Thomas Wharton to Somerset, Feb. 23, 1548.
[6] *Ibid.* 363–364, 366–367: Mar. 2 and 8, 1548.
[7] James, M. E., *Change and continuity in the Tudor North, etc.* (York, [1965]), 38–39.

Somerset was furious because of his defeat, demanding an exact recital of events and of losses which, however, Wharton so skilfully
evaded as to leave the episode quite unclear.[1] The Protector thereupon sent the capable Sir Thomas Holcroft north with full powers of
investigation, who all but charged that Wharton had lost his nerve,
that at least 400 of his force had been captured, and that Carlisle was
weak and poorly located as a base. He recommended that the
staging-point should be set forward to some easily defensible border
town, with which Wharton reluctantly agreed just as full-scale French
intervention changed the whole plan of operation for England.[2]

The central English preoccupation in foreign affairs during the
first half of 1548 was, then, with Scotland and the avoidance, if
possible, of a breach with France. We have seen that Henry II
was determined on regaining Boulogne and hence furthered, ultimately at the price of intervention, in every possible way the distraction of English diplomacy and military commitments in Scotland.
But he moved with great caution not only because Pinkie had deeply
shocked French sentiment but because the great English victory
forced on him a complete revision of his estimate of English military
and naval power. And he set forward his policy and commitment
slowly, too, because he remained quite uncertain of imperial
intentions, fearing an attack in northern Italy and the dangerous
possibility of a war on two widely divided fronts. Hence a ragged
and distracted peace was at least formally maintained with the
English during these months.

But in February and March French pressure on Boulogne was
greatly increased, batteries being installed to dominate the mole
recently constructed by the English, while Somerset's spies reported
that a fleet was being gathered for the feared intervention in Scotland.[3] Wotton, the English ambassador in Paris, maintained a steady
flow of warnings of French preparations for war, describing heavy
troop movements towards Brittany which might be destined for
Scotland or for an assault on Boulogne.[4] The Council was gravely
concerned by a later report from Wotton that the formidable
Châtillon was in command of forces 'practising an enterprise upon
Boulogne', including the development of contacts with traitors in
the garrison whom he expected would deliver the fort within a
month.[5] Carefully chosen troops, drawn from the Home Counties,

[1] Cal. S.P. Dom., Edw. VI, VI, 374–375: Mar. 25, 1548.
[2] Ibid. 381–382: Apr. 16, 1548; ibid. 385.   [3] Venetianische Depeschen, II, 400.
[4] Tytler, England, I, 78–79, 79–80, 87–88: Mar. 7–Apr. 10, 1548.
[5] Cal. S.P. For., Edw. VI, #87: Apr. 20, 1548.

were accordingly moved to Calais, Van der Delft estimating in mid-
April, with considerable exaggeration, that 900 men were about to
be dispatched. The imperial ambassador also predicted that English
policy in Scotland during the coming summer would be cautiously
defensive, and that troops now on the border would be withdrawn
for the defence of Boulogne.[1]

As spring approached, the commanders both at Calais and at
Boulogne reported that the defences of their outlying fortifications
were very weak and laid urgent requests before the government
for both stores and men. In mid-May the military council at Boulogne
confirmed that formidable French forces lay on their borders and
that they were persuaded that a frontal assault on their whole
position was intended, to be launched under the personal command
of the French king.[2] Somerset, and perhaps other members of the
Council, considerably discounted the reports of their field commanders, one of whom, Sir John Bridges, at Boulogne, wrote
directly to protest that, Somerset's opinion notwithstanding, three
of the important outworks there were simply not strong enough in
fabric, munitions, or men to withstand vigorous assault.[3]

Somerset held to his own appraisal of French intentions at least
for the near term. In his view the main assault of the considerable
military and naval power being gathered would be directed against
the English in Scotland, while no more than harassing attacks
would for the time being be launched against him at Boulogne or
Calais. On May 22nd, not long before the French expeditionary
force was sighted off Dunbar, he gave to Van der Delft his own
estimate of the English position. He felt that the strong-points in
Scotland were certain to give the French great difficulties, particularly Haddington where he disposed 5000 men in or near the
town. But he had none the less asked the Emperor to permit him
to recruit 2000 German foot, which Charles had formally declined
because of French sensitivities, while privately instructing his sister
to wink at such recruitments in Germany and the Netherlands.
And Somerset trusted above all in England's friendship with the
Emperor, hinting indeed that he might need assistance in the holding
of Boulogne which was the sticking-point in all his negotiations
with the French.[4] But meanwhile, as the French expeditionary
force approached Scotland, the Privy Council as a precautionary
measure ordered watches set and beacons readied against the

[1] *Cal. S.P. Span.* IX, 262, 263.
[2] *Calais papers*, in *Cal. S.P. For., Edw. VI*, 342, 344.
[3] *Ibid.* 346–347: May 26, 1548.   [4] *Cal. S.P. Span.* IX, 267–270: May 25, 1548.

possibility of a French invasion, while gentlemen were notified to remain in their homes in order to command their counties in the event of emergency.[1] But the issue was now to be joined at Hadding-ton, not at Boulogne; in Scotland, not on the coast of England.

Meanwhile, as certain knowledge reached Somerset of the military preparations in France, the expected pressure for permission to recruit imperial mercenaries developed. Thirlby had an audience with the Emperor on the matter in May, 1548, Charles indicating that there would be political as well as diplomatic difficulties, referred him to Granvelle who made it clear that such aid could only be managed informally by the Regent in Flanders.[2] These negotiations were further advanced when Sir Philip Hoby was sent out as ambassador to the Emperor, recommended by Van der Delft as one who had won the favour of the late King by his great skill in languages and who enjoyed the complete confidence of the Lord Protector.[3] Hoby's instructions were handed to him by the Council in mid-April,[4] and when in early June he and Thirlby laid the English case before Charles they were assured of his full sym-pathy. But he pointed out that it would place him in violation of treaty obligations to France if he directly permitted the recruitment of mercenaries, while informally indicating that his sister in the Netherlands would assist in every possible way.[5] Shortly after-wards Sir Thomas Smith was dispatched to Brussels to prepare the way for the employment of mercenary troops and, needless to say, to lay out possible lines of compromise for curing the chronic difficulties regarding the Antwerp market.[6] Though by no means all problems had been settled with respect to mercenary recruit-ments in the imperial dominions, Somerset felt not only reasonably confident of the Emperor's sympathy with his position but fairly certain as well that if France should without overt provocation attack either Calais or Boulogne, some military assistance would be placed in his hands. He accordingly committed heavy military strength in Scotland for the second half of 1548 with reasonable equanimity.

[1] S.P. Dom., Edw. VI, IV, 12, 12i, 13: June 5, 1548.
[2] Cal. S.P. For., Edw. VI, #91: May 16, 1548; Venetianische Depeschen, II, 418.
[3] Cal. S.P. Span. IX, 254.
[4] Cal. S.P. For., Edw. VI, #82.
[5] Ibid. #99, #100: June 5 and 11, 1548.
[6] Ibid. #102, #103: July 8 and 19, 1548.

8. ENGLAND ON THE DEFENSIVE: THE SIEGE OF THE STRONG POINTS (JULY–DECEMBER, 1548)

We have already observed that d'Essé moved quickly and with full power to the investment of Haddington after his forces had been landed at Leith, summoning a large Scottish force to join him in what was to be a long siege and one which was to pin the French and Scots down to a primarily static warfare for well over a year. But at the same time, and dramatically, within the siege lines at Haddington diplomatic conversations were begun between Scotland and France to exact full tribute for the help which France pledged herself to lend to Scotland. By the terms of the Convention of Haddington, d'Oysel, the French ambassador, proposed to the assembled Estates on July 7th that the infant Mary be sent to France for safety and that a marriage treaty be arranged under whose terms she would in due season be married to the Dauphin, the two crowns being joined, with Scotland retaining her own laws and liberties. These terms were unanimously accepted at Haddington, France pledging her full military support. In late July Mary was spirited out of the realm to France, where she was to be educated, to marry the Dauphin, and from whence she was not to return for a full thirteen years.

The conclusion of this treaty and the departure of Mary were for Somerset a bitter blow, representing the ruin of his diplomatic policy *vis-à-vis* Scotland and constituting in effect a French parody on the terms of the Treaty of Greenwich. Though he continued stubbornly to press, with what grounds for hope one cannot see, for the restoration of the English marriage treaty, the basis for his claim on Scotland now shifted to a revival of the medieval claims of suzerainty. Tunstall at Durham forwarded all the documents from his archives citing the homage paid to the crown of England by earlier Scottish sovereigns,[1] while two deeds were produced purporting to prove the title of the King of England (Edward I) to the sovereignty of Scotland.[2] Sir John Mason was also set by Somerset on the task of searching the Exchequer records for proofs of the sovereignty of the English crown over Scotland,[3] while a not especially skilful semi-official propaganda piece was published to advance the English claims.[4]

[1] Cotton MSS., Caligula, B, vii, 169, ff. 329ff., with endorsement.
[2] *Ibid.* 166, f. 322.   [3] Add. MS. 6128.
[4] Under the title, *An epitome of the title that the King's maiestie of England hath to the sovereigntie of Scotland, etc.* (E.E.T.S., extra ser., XVII–XVIII, 247–256).

But the trial was now one of war rather than of diplomacy. Military policy for many months was to be concentrated on the defence of Haddington, the siege of which was to create great excitement in England and which was to evoke European attention. Both England and the Franco-Scottish allies made substantial commitments of power and supplies to the siege and, perhaps as importantly, considerable dedications of prestige. The command in England was really kept in his own hands by Somerset, to whom reports were directly made by the field commanders and by the observers sent north to lend a more objective appraisal of events and of military requirements. Thus, in the interval of about six months after July 9, 1548, there are to be found twenty-six such reports, all but two addressed to Somerset.[1] In broader terms, too, Somerset was attempting to lend direction to the whole of foreign policy, as well as to most phases of domestic policy. Perhaps his greatest weakness—his inability to delegate—was beginning to overtake him, for it was simply impossible to give wise direction from London to the defence of Boulogne or to sorties from Haddington. A brilliant field commander was now miring himself in duties and decisions which should and could have been delegated.

We have seen that d'Essé had moved with all force available to the investment of Haddington in late June, 1548.[2] On July 1st there was a sharp skirmish as the English sallied out, and on the following day Palmer and Holcroft at Berwick, who had incredibly enough asked for hourly reports from Haddington, indicated that the French were entrenched and were mounting sixteen pieces of siege ordnance against the walls of Haddington.[3] For some days, however, the French limited the bombardment to a few cannon, the walls being repaired daily by the garrison from materials in hand. The rate of fire was, however, gradually increased, until six pieces were said to have fired 340 shot in a single day, while the entrenchments of the enemy were rapidly pushed to the foundations of the wall. On July 3rd d'Essé and Arran were very nearly killed by a burst of concentrated artillery fire from the town, several of their party being slain while they were engaged in reconnaissance.[4] Reliable estimates were by this date gathered from spies which set the strength of the besiegers at 5000 French foot, 500 horse, and about 4000 Scots, with more arriving each day. A few days later sapping

---

[1] In Add. MSS., 32,657, with transcripts in Add. MSS. 33,256, ff. 104–133. Some of these have been printed in the second volume of the *Hamilton papers*.

[2] *Vide ante*, 275.   [3] *Cal. S.P. Scotland*, I, 134, 135–136; *Cal. S.P. Span.* IX, 277.

[4] Hayward, *Edward VI*, 291; *Cal. S.P. Scotland*, I, 138.

operations were begun and it was believed in the garrison that a frontal assault was being prepared.[1] Both men and supplies were now badly needed in Haddington, and on July 7th Grey and Hol-croft were in the field near the Pease, the plan being for Grey to remain there with the whole of the foot, while a force of 2000 horse would attempt to put 400 reinforcements into the beleaguered town, each man carrying in a bag of powder and needed matches. This hazardous feat was successfully accomplished under Palmer's command, who while in the town advised Wilford on the further strengthening of his walls and the better siting of his ordnance.[2]

But in the judgement of both Grey and Palmer at least another 1000 men would be required for the defence of Haddington. Palmer in the meantime was preparing to relieve pressure by a diversionary raid with 3000 troops available to him, though he warned that light raids would never suffice: 'The Frenchmen have there as good men of war as any be counted in Christendom. . . . They remain not at this siege for naught. . . .'[3] The Privy Council took this field adviser seriously, on July 11th ordering Shrewsbury to move at once to Newcastle in support with 3000–4000 of his best troops and in-forming him that 2000 German mercenaries 'exceedingly well in order' were on shipboard for dispatch to him with the first favour-able winds.[4] Meanwhile, the French kept Haddington under heavy bombardment, until it seemed in mid-July that an assault might be made against the walls before further reinforcement could be undertaken. Grey, perhaps against his better judgement, thereupon agreed to mount Palmer's diversionary raid, while he once more remained at the Pease with the infantry.

Bowes and Palmer were charged with the command of the strik-ing force. Palmer, always impatient and foolhardy, determined to scout the Haddington area in passing, only to be set upon by a large French force which could not be thrown back until costly help had been supplied from the beleaguered garrison itself. The broken diversionary force was pursued for eight miles before it could be restored to discipline. Bowes and Palmer were both captured, and there were heavy losses, though Brende's original gloomy estimate of 700–800 slain or captured may be reduced to something short of 200. So, Brende reported in a confidential dispatch to Somerset, 'with victory in our hand, this mischance

[1] Cal. S.P. Scotland, I, 138, 139.
[2] Hamilton papers, II, 598–599: Palmer to Somerset, July 9, 1548.
[3] Ibid., 602: July 10, 1548; Holinshed, Chronicles, III, 892.
[4] Cal. S.P. Scotland, I, 146.

has altered things, discouraged and weakened the town by the number that issued on horseback', and had drawn pointlessly on the limited powder and stores of the garrison.[1] Nor was this all. The impetuous Palmer had deliberately disobeyed Bowes' order to 'venture nothing', and the fault was clearly his. Palmer surely should have been court-martialed for the fiasco which his own recklessness had occasioned. But Somerset's anger troubled Paget, his closest and most loyal adviser. Some blame, Paget suggested, must be borne by Somerset himself, who had 'provoked him so much forward, with letters accusing his stillness, slackness, and sleeping without doing anything'. He therefore pleaded that Somerset, who stood in the 'place of a king' should thereafter be restrained in 'every letter, every word, every countenance'. He must on his own part 'remember by times past how the words of a king or cardinal [the reference is to Wolsey] might have moved you and so think yours move other men'. Paget declared that he found this painful to write, but did so because he was 'desirous to tell you the truth because I believe you trust me'. Here in this brooding uncertainty in Paget's letter is revealed the growing impatience and imperiousness of the Lord Protector. As for Palmer, he never forgave Somerset whom he now hated and whom at the first opportunity he would basely betray.[2]

Only a 'royal force', Brende had concluded in his letter to Somerset, could now retrieve the situation at Haddington. And a truly 'royal force' under Shrewsbury was, even as he wrote, moving up towards Berwick, step by step with Clinton's naval and supply fleet. This army, numbering at the least 15,000, of which 3000 were German foot, was under simple orders to relieve and supply Haddington, engaging Arran and d'Essé in pitched battle if the opportunity should offer itself.[3] Shrewsbury had reached Berwick on July 19th, while Grey still lay in the Pease in order to keep open

---

[1] *Cal. S.P. Scotland*, I, 148; Stow, *Annales*, 595; Edward VI, *Chronicle*, 9–10; Teulet, *Relations*, I, 183–184; *Hamilton papers*, II, 615: Gamboa to Somerset, July 23, 1548. This veteran mercenary captain complained bitterly that Palmer had not handled his force properly and had left Gamboa frontally exposed with no more than forty men. See also *Cal. S.P. Span.*, IX, 286; S.P. Dom., Edw. VI, IV, 38 (Aug. 6), in which Somerset placed the number killed at 60 (about 140 were taken prisoner), and correctly predicted that Bowes and Palmer would soon be exchanged by their Scottish captors.

[2] Cotton MSS., Titus, F, iii, 28, ff. 273–276, quoted by Gammon, *Master of practises*, 217–218.

[3] Edward VI (*Chronicle*, 10) greatly exaggerated its size as 22,000; Burnet (*Reformation*, II, 161) placed the figure at 17,000, including 3000 horse; Hayward (*Edward VI*, 291) at 15,000; and Shrewsbury, writing from York on July 12th (*Cal. S.P. Dom.*, Edw. VI, VI, 389), at 11,000 before all levies had joined him.

the lines of communication with Haddington and to have a seasoned striking force, of about 5000 men, which could quickly thrust forward when required. Meanwhile, the imperturbable and wholly competent Wilford, aghast at Palmer's fiasco, urged Grey to risk no battle, assuring him that his force was much stronger than when the siege began, his only needs being powder, shot, and working tools.[1] At Berwick Shrewsbury was striving to replace the recent losses in light horse, occasioned by Palmer's failure, after which the horse from the Western March had simply gone home. He was waiting, too, for Clinton to arrive at Holy Island, where on July 26th–27th the fleet put in to victual and to take on board one thousand troops, and then to sail for the Firth of Forth, seeking a decisive engagement with the French if they could be brought to battle.[2]

Clinton sailed on July 30th, setting off troops at Tynemouth, and, missing the evading French fleet, put into the Firth of Forth where on August 10th he reported that he had burned twelve French supply ships found at anchor and had wholly stopped the normal reception of stores and troops from France at Leith Roads.[3] Shrewsbury delayed his march north from Berwick until his roster of light scouting horse was further augmented. An effort to move powder, shot, and other supplies into Haddington had failed. But Wilford got out a message to Grey urging him to risk no action until Shrewsbury's main force could strike with full weight: ' "rather put me to defend this town with the pike and bill only," than come till you are strong.'[4] But the steady pressure, now heightened, of the French on Haddington had in truth greatly reduced Wilford's stores, for by August 11th he was driven to report that his supply situation was critical. At last the overly cautious Shrewsbury was prodded into moving even before all his light horse had reached him, probably crossing the frontier on August 17th with a battle force of 11,412 foot, 1800 horse, and with a 'floating reserve' still in Clinton's transports.[5] As he pressed north and west the besieging force at Haddington, fully apprised of the formidable strength of Shrewsbury and afraid of being outflanked, broke off the siege and fell back until the principal allied force was on August 23rd encamped at Musselburgh, while the English lay at Long Niddry.[6] Shrewsbury, his principal mission of relieving Haddington accomplished, sought vainly to draw the Franco-Scottish army out of its

---

[1] *Cal. S.P. Scotland*, I, 149: July 22 and 23, 1548.
[2] *Ibid.* 149–150, 150–151; *Cal. S.P. Dom., Edw. VI*, VI, 391: Shrewsbury to Somerset, July 20, 1548.
[3] *Cal. S.P. Scotland*, I, 152–153, 155, 158.   [4] *Ibid.* 157: Aug. 3, 1548.
[5] *Ibid.* 159, 160, 161.   [6] Teulet, *Relations*, I, 185–186.

camp screening Edinburgh, and then, lacking victuals, fell back, burning Dunbar, to the staging point at Berwick, while Grey raided deep towards Liddesdale.[1]

Shrewsbury's withdrawal of this powerful army was by the command of Somerset, who evidently regarded this large and painfully gathered force as not much more than a relief expedition for the momentary raising of the siege of Haddington. On August 5th, well before Shrewsbury had left Berwick, the Protector had asked that 2000 to 3000 of the army be discharged in order to save expenses.[2] And in early September he severely rebuked Shrewsbury for holding his army intact when it was serving no function save to secure the Pease.[3] Wilford, much strengthened and provisioned, was again invested by d'Essé, and before Shrewsbury's force had melted away, as troops were paid and discharged, the situation was much as before. One can say with some certainty that half of Shrewsbury's army could have relieved Haddington; the whole, had it been maintained in the field with the support afforded by Clinton's domination of the sea approaches, could probably have driven the French from Scotland. But Somerset, distracted by insoluble problems of finance, fearful of a French assault on Boulogne, and disturbed by the agrarian stirs of that summer, was in no mood to take even prudent risks on a pitched engagement. Grey, disillusioned and not a little embittered, in late August again asked to be relieved of a command which he had served with diligence and no little skill.[4]

The allies in Edinburgh were likewise having their difficulties. Shrewsbury's relief of Haddington, which had carried him to within sight of Edinburgh, had concentrated large masses of French and Scottish troops in and near the capital, which could not immediately be restored to discipline or disposed until it was clear that the English force had fallen back to the border.[5] During these weeks of uncertainty Scottish and French troops clashed in the streets of Edinburgh. As the disorders spread, bloody rioting broke out between the French and the civilian population, which was with difficulty repressed and shook the confidence and the authority of the commanding French officers. These riots were followed with great interest by the English government through its spies in Scotland, with, inevitably, a considerable exaggeration of the troubles in which the French found themselves.[6] Discipline was in fact rather

[1] Holinshed, *Chronicles*, III, 905; Hayward, *Edward VI*, 291.
[2] *Cal. S.P. Scotland*, I, 157–158.   [3] *Ibid.* 164: Sept. 8, 1548.
[4] *Ibid.* 163: Aug. 29, 1548.   [5] Teulet, *Relations*, I, 185–186.
[6] Cotton MSS., Caligula, B, vii, 168 ff., 325 ff.: Fisher to Somerset, Oct. 15, 1548; *ibid.* 170, f. 333: report of Mason (?), Oct. 17, 1548.

quickly restored in both the French and the Scottish commands when Haddington was once more placed under siege and fairly elaborate fortifications were begun on an arc around Edinburgh, but with particular attention to Leith and Dunbar.[1] The allies were assisted too by the early withdrawal of Clinton's overweening naval force, which towards the end of September had found itself in dangerously dirty weather and sailed south.[2]

Though Shrewsbury had strengthened Haddington with generous stores and had greatly increased its garrison with two thousand foot and two hundred light scouting horse, its dangers were by no means over once the main force had retired to Berwick.[3] D'Essé in early October withdrew his full command from riotous Edinburgh and without preliminary scouting or bombardment hurled his whole force against Haddington in a surprise attack which very nearly prevailed. The English sentries were killed or driven in, the French forcing an entrance before the great gates could be closed or the whole garrison aroused to duty. The fortress was saved when a cannon loaded with grape shot was fired point blank at the French attackers within the walls, and was then reloaded and fired again while the gates were being secured. The slaughter within the base court was terrible, 300 French being killed, while d'Essé failed in three more assaults designed to breach or scale the walls. His force was badly hurt, and he was himself shortly recalled, but Wilford's brilliant defence had only won time. Haddington was again under strait siege.[4]

The war in Scotland, on all besieged points as well as along the border, suddenly quieted after d'Essé's failure to carry Haddington by storm. Both sides had taken substantial losses; both were now war-weary; and particularly vile weather made communications difficult and supply-trains impossible. As early as mid-October English troops, including the mercenary forces, had been distributed to various points south of the border,[5] while the imperial ambassador in Paris reported to Charles V that the French were most unhappy with the small success gained in Scotland at such great cost.[6] Wilford, who rarely complained, warned Somerset as autumn set in that his garrison was gravely weakened by an epidemic of the plague, that he was without resources for caring for his sick,

[1] Teulet, *Relations*, I, 185–186, 187–189: Sept. 1 and 25, 1548.
[2] *Cal. S.P. Span.* IX, 298: Oct. 4, 1548.
[3] *Ibid.* 291–292: Van der Delft to Emperor, Sept. 7, 1548.
[4] Holinshed, *Chronicles*, III, 905–906; Hayward, *Edward VI*, 291; Ellis, *Original letters*, ser. 3, III, 292–300: Fisher to Somerset.
[5] *Cal. S.P. Span.* IX, 299: Du Bois to Flemish Council.   [6] *Ibid.* 304.

and that he could not bring more than one thousand men to the walls.[1] A small contingent of German horse was sent to him, but these troops he found overbearing and undisciplined, while he had sustained a serious loss of thirty light horse who were ambushed while bringing in convoys.[2] Somerset, a month later, harshly disregarded Wilford's cool appraisal of his need and duty by ordering him to confine his strength to the holding of Haddington, to refrain from forays, and warned him that he could expect no more reinforcements for the winter.[3] The Lord Protector had quite failed to answer Wilford's point that his position was made especially weak by the fact that he must bring in supplies by convoy. Wilford could only conclude that he had been abandoned.

A general review of the situation in the north was dispatched by John Brende to the Protector in mid-November, when Wilford's petition must have been before him as well. At Berwick he had felt obliged to put the numerous sick, weak, and unwilling troops in special musters. Grey, who had twice asked to be relieved, he regarded as an honourable and able man, but 'too gentle for this country'. The various commands at Berwick Brende found to be undisciplined, and 'there is better order among the Tartars than in this town', where whatever can be taken is promptly stolen. The sick of Haddington were dying untended in the streets. In the north generally he would regard only Wilford, Dudley, Willoughby, and Gower as suitable and wholly professional commanders.[4] But nothing was done by the Protector, save belatedly in January, 1549, when he called out levies from two northern counties to provide Berwick with greater staging strength, and ordered Haddington and Broughty to be victualled for six months.[5] The war in Scotland was simply at a standstill for the winter.

If Wilford at Haddington felt neglected by both London and Berwick, Luttrell, who had replaced Dudley in command, must have felt completely abandoned at Broughty. There was, it is true, very little activity at this second strong-point during the last six months of 1548, the French fearing to commit substantial forces in the Tay so long as Haddington remained unreduced and fearing as well that a close investment of Broughty would surely bring in Clinton's naval force. After some discussion Clinton had set in on the Forth rather than on the Tay when he moved north in support of Shrewsbury, but did send in fifty needed reinforcements and

---

[1] Cal. S.P. Scotland, I, 166: Nov. 1, 1548.   [2] Ibid. 167: Nov. 11, 1548.
[3] Ibid. 170: Dec. 11, 1548.   [4] Cal. S.P. Dom., Edw. VI, VI, 394: Nov. 14, 1548.
[5] Ibid. 395: Jan. 8, 1549.

victuals for Broughty.[1] Otherwise, no reinforcements were supplied
until the early autumn, though there had been little military activity.
In mid-November Luttrell at last lodged a strong remonstrance
with Somerset as he sought to prepare himself for the winter. He
declared himself to be without money, bread, or beer. He had only
fifty horse, which were essential to him in controlling supplies
coming in to Dundee, now well garrisoned against him. His own
fortifications were weak and would crumble from the fire of a
single battery. He declared, indeed, that he was immobilized from
weakness, whereas some addition of strength and supplies would
permit him to lay waste and re-establish control over an area with
a radius of twenty miles. The chilling reply from the Protector and
Council was to recall the small unit of German foot in his command,
to order him to hold on with a garrison reduced to 130–200 men,
and to promise that he would shortly be victualled for six months.[2]

So too, there had been very little military activity in the west, as
the grudging Wharton was compelled by direct order to give up
cavalry contingents to supply Shrewsbury's needs. There continued
nothing more than a dreary chronicle of raids and counter-raids
along the Western March in these months. But Wharton's militancy
had been greatly chastened by his own recent defeat. He complained
to Somerset in August that he had never been so weak, having just
given up four hundred of his horse to the needs of Berwick.[3] Weak
he really was, in part because of the want of discipline amongst his
own borderers, and then with the coming of the autumn as a
consequence of Somerset's severe contraction of funds and troops
in the whole northern region. Involved though Somerset's pride
and prestige were, the war in Scotland was perforce nearly at an end
at the beginning of 1549.

During the later months of 1548, however, despite Henry II's
impetuosity and Somerset's stubborn pride, formal relations between England and France were reasonably correct and restrained.
Both nations were expending substantial resources and not a little
blood in what was proving to be a bootless struggle in Scotland, and
neither wished to enlarge hostilities into a general war over Boulogne.
These developments followed closely the predictions of the Emperor
himself to his sister, when in March 1548 he stated his conviction
that the commitment in Scotland would be extremely burdensome
and distracting to France.[4] The Emperor's attitude even to this

---

[1] *Cal. S.P. Scotland*, I, 156, 159: Aug. 6 and 10, 1548.

[2] *Scottish correspondence of Mary of Lorraine* (Scot. Hist. Soc., ser. 3, X), 275–278,
282–283.   [3] *Cal. S.P. Dom.*, *Edw. VI*, VI, 392–393: Aug. 14, 1548.

[4] Druffel, *Beiträge* (*Briefe und Akten*, I), 103, 172.

limited war troubled the French, who were convinced that he was lending secret aid to England and that the English were acting with some assurance of imperial intervention in the event of urgent need.[1]

The early summer passed uneventfully until August when Palmer's defeat in Scotland and the gathering of Shrewsbury's powerful army of relief for Haddington caused the French to essay a diversion at Boulogne. Châtillon, long complaining of the mole extending into the harbour of Boulogne, began the building of a strong fort on Mount Bernard, which at the least would dominate the harbour and the Old Town which lay on it. In the first days of August heavy ordnance fire was also directed at the English mole, but without serious damage, though the French continued to hold 'that they do not break the peace in doing this, but only annoy us for further enlarging the pier'.[2] These provocations were taken seriously by the Council, Somerset addressing a detailed letter to his brother, who was as usual at Sudeley, recounting his concern. The French, he said, were prepared to accept the mole as simply an harbour improvement if a flanker were moved together with ordnance which the English contended was provided only to protect workmen. The altercation led to French artillery fire which was being countered by English fire.[3] The French had also been making light raids into the English pale, with some loss of life. Even more ominous was clear evidence of a stepping up of French privateering, some eight or nine English vessels having recently been taken with their crews. As a counter-measure, West Country ships had been told that they might intercept the French Newfoundland fishing fleet, due soon, and this order Seymour, as Admiral, was to implement, employing only Devonshire and Cornish vessels. These instructions Seymour, who loved privateering, immediately placed in effect, forwarding the detailed secret instructions laid down by the Council.[4]

Châtillon's carefully graduated pressure on Boulogne was continued through the whole of August. Somerset countered with hints to the French ambassador that any frontal attack on Ambleteuse or Bolemberg might well result in open war and the handing over of Boulogne to the Emperor. At the Council's meeting on October 3rd

[1] Druffel, *Beiträge (Briefe und Akten)*, I), 161–162: Marillac to Henry II, Sept. 28, 1548; *ibid.* 172: Montmorency to Marillac, Oct. 24, 1548.

[2] S.P. Dom., Edw. VI, IV, 38: Somerset to Thomas Seymour, Aug. 6, 1548.

[3] *Calais papers*, in *Cal. S.P. For., Edw. VI*, 352: Somerset and Council to Governor and Council of Boulogne, Aug. 10, 1548.

[4] S.P. Dom., Edw. VI, IV, 39, 41: Aug. 7 and 11, 1548; *ibid.* 44: Aug. 13, 1548: Russell's comments on the Boulogne and Scottish situations.

a declaration of war was debated, but more prudent considerations prevailed, it being pointed out that a war could hardly be prosecuted on two widely separated fronts, without assurances of the Emperor's intervention. The Council was heartened, too, by news from France that a peasant rising had broken out in the Bordeaux area, which was, however, rather quickly and certainly sternly repressed. The Council was constrained, too, because the inexorable requirements of continuous war in Scotland had resulted in the weakening of defences both in the Boulogne-Calais area and at home. Thus a professional survey of the Boulogne fortifications in August, 1548, suggested grave deficiencies which could not be corrected until November when a commission inspected the troops at Calais and Boulogne, weeding out the padding in the muster rolls and ordering the removal of women and children from the forts.[1] Even more alarming was the state of the coastal defences of England on which Henry VIII had spent large sums and a great deal of labour. They were now ill-fitted, weakly garrisoned, and rapidly mouldering since the government simply did not have the funds for their full support.[2]

By early autumn (1548) it was clear that prudence still restrained both governments, and normal relations, with only minor frictions, were reported on the Calais and Boulogne frontiers. Privateering was also slackening, especially since both countries were now arming merchant vessels, though sales of captured craft and their cargoes were continuing in England.[3] But diplomatic pressure was heightened on both sides, the French complaining bitterly to St Mauris of the Emperor's covert indulgence in permitting England to raise troops in Germany, and especially horse in Cleves.[4] This protest Somerset countered by solemnly laying before the French ambassadors the proof of the English claim to suzerainty in Scotland, which the Council had for some time been gathering. Copies of these papers from the 'national records and documents' were forwarded by Somerset to Wotton in Paris with instructions to lay them before the King in a personal audience.[5] These claims Henry II rejected out of hand, asserting that he was himself the King of Scotland, in consequence of his son's marriage to the Scottish Queen

---

[1] *Calais papers*, in *Cal. S.P. For.*, *Edw. VI*, 352–353, 353–354.

[2] Camber Castle, Sussex, may be cited as an example. VCH, *Sussex*, I, 516; *ibid.* IX, 185, with notes.

[3] Anderson, R. C., ed., *Letters of the fifteenth and sixteenth centuries, from the archives of Southampton* (Southampton Rec. Soc. Publ., Southampton, 1921), 53.

[4] *Cal. S.P. Span. IX*, 317: Nov. 22, 1548.

[5] *Cal. S.P. For.*, *Edw. VI*, #112: [Dec. 13, 1548]; *Cal. S.P. Scotland*, I, 170–171.

and confirming St Mauris' impression that he was under heavy pressure from the Guise faction to intervene with decisive strength in Scotland.[1] It was with these harmless diplomatic posturings that the year ended—a year in which outright war between the two powers had almost miraculously been avoided.

During the last months of 1548 the Emperor gave no direct aid to England, but it was his overweening power which had been the principal factor in restraining French action and confining it to Scotland. Somerset's relations with Charles during these six months were amiable and, as we have seen, the problem of the Lady Mary's household masses had not provoked serious friction. The emperor had winked at the English agents who were recruiting mercenary foot in Germany during these months, but he had declined a request that heavy horse be recruited on the grounds that this could only lead to a French demand for the same privilege and pointing out that in any case it was too late in the year to employ such troops effectively in Scotland.[2] This provoked from Somerset a piqued complaint and still another scarcely concealed threat to settle all with France by the cession of Boulogne for an indemnity of £200,000.[3] But Charles V disposed sufficient power to regard the English protestation as of little consequence. In fact he stood at the moment at the climax of his power.

English policy and diplomacy were during these months so harried and fearful that the quest for allies and aid was extended well beyond the normal channels. The English blockade of Scotland and almost uninhibited privateering were wreaking considerable injury on both Danish and Swedish shipping. The Council replied to Danish objections with an investigation which declared the complaints to be too general and wanting in detailed proof of injury.[4] Good relations with this Protestant state were, however, carefully cultivated, Sir John Borthwick being sent out in November as ambassador to ask for aid and to make a somewhat ambiguous proffer of the Princess Elizabeth's hand in marriage to the Danish prince.[5] Gustavus I of Sweden also protested vehemently against the shipping losses his merchants had sustained from both sides in the war and called upon the Protector to make restitution.[6] He too was answered with general denials and with a certainly forlorn plea for aid

[1] Cal. S.P. Span. IX, 322–323: Dec. 17, 1548.   [2] Ibid. 279–282: Aug. 3, 1548.
[3] Ibid. 284–286: Aug. 21, 1548.
[4] Regesta diplomatica historiae Danicae . . . ad annum 1660, ser. 2, vol. II (Copenhagen, 1907), 159, 163.   [5] Ibid. 164.
[6] Twenty-seventh rpt., Dep. Keeper Public Records [1866], App., 129.

against a Romish enemy. England was in these months seeking
help wherever and however she could gain it.

9. THE COLLAPSE OF ENGLISH FOREIGN POLICY
(JANUARY–OCTOBER, 1549)

English diplomacy shows every evidence of war-weariness
throughout 1549 until a complete paralysis ensued because of the
great civil crisis provoked during the summer by risings which
speedily waxed into rebellions and by the *coup d'état* which accomplished Somerset's ruin in the early autumn. Even at the outset of
the year resolution was shaken and warlike preparation postponed
because of the shattering revelations in January which led to the trial
and execution of Thomas Seymour, the King's uncle and the Lord
High Admiral, for undoubted treasonable actions.[1] And during these
distracted days, when all attention was on domestic affairs, Brende
reported from Berwick that the Scots were already stirring, a large
force being employed for the fortification of Musselburgh and
preparations being made for an assault on Dunglass. He was
obliged to depend on intelligence reports, since his light horse was
so weak and poorly commanded that he did not dare send them
north from Berwick on scouting forays.[2]

French diplomacy reacted immediately, too, to the crisis precipitated by Sudeley's arrest and trial, a special envoy being
dispatched to inform de Selve in London that the King believed
this development would greatly advance his policy in Scotland and
instructing him to use all possible means to foment a civil war in
England, if Sudeley was followed by any considerable faction.
The envoy was likewise to ascertain what forces England meant to
deploy in Scotland during the coming months and whether English
relations with the Emperor remained as amicable as was claimed.[3]
These relations were in fact much more friendly than Henry II
hoped, for a copy of the document just cited was actually handed to
Sir Thomas Gresham by the Regent in the Netherlands. Shortly
afterwards the Council had from Wotton in Paris a long report
suggesting that 2000 additional French troops were to be sent to
Scotland in March and recounting the rumour that the great base at
Berwick was to be assailed.[4] These were, indeed, the French plans,
particularly if stirs could be provoked following Sudeley's execution,

---

[1] *Vide post*, 368–362.   [2] *Hamilton papers*, II, 623: Jan. 17, 1549.
[3] HMC, *Salisbury MSS*. I, 63–64.
[4] *Cal. S.P. For.*, *Edw. VI*, #122: Feb. 23, 1549.

but the French were also war-weary and the demands of the Scots inexhaustible. The French were outraged because Scotland would undertake no portion of the cost of French aid, and so fragile was the alliance that the Scottish nobility could be kept in loyalty only by bribes and pensions. It was common talk in Paris that Henry 'is not far from regretting that he made the alliance, as it is costing him a great deal', while the English ambassador confided to St Mauris the belief that a truce could now be arranged on the Boulogne frontier.[1]

Meanwhile, the Council was considering a general replacement of the commands on the border, which was given effect on May 1, 1549. Henry Manners, second Earl of Rutland, an engaging but very young man, was appointed Warden of the Eastern March, replacing Grey who, as we have seen, had asked to be relieved.[2] Somerset and the Council were almost apologetic in advising Holcroft, Harrington, and other northern field commanders of Rutland's commission. The Warden, it was suggested, should possess 'nobility of blood, courage, and good cultivation', which the Earl did, but he was young and without experience in wars, and the older commanders should counsel him and above all see to it that the troops were brought under better discipline.[3] Wharton was also dismissed, his bitter enmity thereafter fastening upon Somerset, and was replaced by Lord Dacre, against whom Wharton had plotted since the days of the Pilgrimage of Grace.[4] Furthermore, it was agreed that still another striking force would be formed to invade Scotland, August 1st being tentatively set, and that it would be led by Warwick, who while in the field would for the time absorb the commissions of the Wardens.[5]

Rutland's instructions on assuming his charge were personally to inspect at once all troops under his command and to bring under discipline the Northumbrian captains who had for years had the habit of going home with their troops at their own mood and convenience. From Haddington he was advised by the veteran Sir James Croft, as if he were writing to a schoolboy, to issue no orders unless they could be carried out, to deal humanely with his troops, and to take counsel only from those experienced in war.[6] The Council also chided Rutland on his recommendation that mercenary

---

[1] *Cal. S.P. Span.* IX, 361, 366: St Mauris to Emperor, Apr. 5 and 13, 1549.
[2] *Vide ante*, 288.   [3] S.P. Dom., Addenda, III, 27.
[4] Edward VI, *Chronicle*, 12, for certain of these changes.
[5] This force, partially mobilized, was instead to be employed in the suppression of the Norfolk rising.   [6] HMC, *12th report*, App. IV: *Rutland MSS.* I, 35.

troops be paid by the month in advance, since such troops would be tempted to desert, while asking for the names of 120 English soldiers from Cheshire and Lancashire who had recently deserted.[1] In late May Rutland completed the inspection of his command, his report listing a total of 5450 men, of whom 1700 were Germans under Courtpenny, 350 Spaniards, and 150 Italians, garrison troops under siege beyond the border not being included.[2]

The plans being developed for the summer campaign gradually became more ambitious, a general levy of troops being ordered at Berwick not later than May 20th and including heavy drafts from the northern counties.[3] As part of the reorganization of the command along the northern border, moreover, Shrewsbury, who had spent most of his adult life in border commands and who had recently led the force relieving Haddington, was appointed Lord President of the Council of the North, with £1000 p.a. for his own diet and that of his councillors, who were to dine at his table. The Council, among whom were such powerful figures as Westmorland, Cumberland, Dacre, Tunstall, and Wharton, was enjoined to maintain order, to punish rioters, to put in better force the religious policy of the government, and to see to it that wrongful enclosures, which were troublesome in the north, should be ended.[4]

By early June Rutland and Holcroft began to raid deep into Scotland,[5] though without sufficient power or victual to risk decisive action. Broughty had been victualled, but not substantially reinforced, in the early spring, so Wyndham was ordered to employ his detached naval squadron in or near the Tay, since Somerset expected a tightening of the siege of Broughty, if not a frontal assault.[6] But Somerset rejected Luttrell's frantic request for more troops and supplies with the comment that his resources had not been properly managed, which simply happened to be untrue. Luttrell, one of the ablest of the field commanders, held on until early summer when he wrote directly to Somerset to say flatly that his troops were unpaid and without proper clothing, and that his men were worn out from long duty and 'long continuance of salt meat'. He accordingly asked to be relieved of his command on grounds of his own infirmity, a request which Somerset, who well knew Luttrell's tenacity under pressure, categorically refused.[7]

[1] HMC, *12th report*, App. IV: *Rutland MSS.* I, 35–36: May 16, 1549.   [2] *Ibid.* 36–37.
[3] *Cal. S.P. Dom., Edw. VI*, VI, 396: Apr. [5], 1549.
[4] *Ibid.* 399–400: May ?, 1549.
[5] HMC, *Salisbury MSS.* I, 74.   [6] *Cal. S.P. Scotland*, I, 171–172.
[7] *Scottish correspondence of Mary of Lorraine* (Scot. Hist. Soc., ser. 3, X), 304–305, 310–311: June–July, 1549.

Broughty remained in English hands and under Luttrell's command until the great withdrawal of the late summer of 1549.

The war had dragged on so long and so incessantly that both sides were weary, weak in resources, and were slipping into a war of minor forays accompanied by a good deal of senseless brutality. Thus Arran took the position that Scots serving in the English army should if captured be immediately put to death as traitors, while there is some evidence that both Arran and Wharton had been torturing prisoners in order to gain intelligence. Somerset, outraged, sent his herald through the Scottish lines in May (1549) to warn Arran that unless his orders were revoked, all Scots taken prisoner would be slain, while regretting that he had been forced to such a cruel course.[1] Neither threat was carried out, but brutality and the ill-treatment of prisoners, already general, increased on both sides as a now dreary and senseless conflict drew to a conclusion.

Somerset had been restrained in the size and effectiveness of the force he could spare for Scotland by the erratic but heavy pressure of the French on Boulogne and by the financial weakness of his own government. But the whole of his military planning for the north was completely undermined by the spreading and mounting rebellions at home which, beginning in the spring, reached a point of grave crisis in August and forced a general withdrawal of the border forces in order to deal with a most perilous situation. A valiant effort was made to hold at least Haddington, which had assumed a symbolic significance for both the English and the Scots, precious stores and reinforcements being carried in by Holcroft on the first of August. But Holcroft's long and careful report to Somerset was gloomy indeed. The plague had for a second time struck the garrison and 200 to 300 additional men must be sent in to provide holding strength. Even the veteran Tiberio, with forty dead of plague and forty sick, had warned him that he would simply bring his surviving men out after another month. The English officers thought they could hold for another three weeks, but no longer unless very large forces were sent in—and these were forces which Somerset simply did not have in the black month of August. Holcroft hinted, as well, that it might be prudent to try to come to an agreement with de Thermes, the new French commander-in-chief, who had not moved in force from the precincts of Edinburgh.[2] This careful and forthright

---

[1] *Cal. S.P. Scotland*, I, 175–176: May 19, 1549.

[2] Cotton MSS., Caligula, B, vii, 176: Aug. 2, 1549. Confusion has been occasioned since this and a similar letter from Holcroft (dated July 24) have been bound together in a jumbled order. The letter being cited should probably appear in folio order (as renumbered): 383, 386, 387, 388, 384.

report from a highly trusted field officer persuaded Somerset that Haddington must be abandoned.

The fateful decision to withdraw was reached about a fortnight after Holcroft's report had been received by Somerset. Rutland with 6000 troops, half being mercenary, was ordered to open communications, to force his way into Haddington, and to bring out the garrison and its artillery, after having razed the fortifications. The dragging state of the war, with de Thermes safely and happily ensconced in Edinburgh with his gout and his mistress, is suggested by the fact that what might have been an extremely hazardous operation met with no more than token resistance.[1] Thomas Fisher, writing unhappily to Cecil, put it well when he lamented the abandonment of a stronge position 'hitherto stoutly defended with consumption of treasure and worthy men in plenty'.[2] But this delicate and necessary action, in all but name bringing the war with Scotland to a close, was accomplished between September 14th and 17th. Even in the always turbulent Western March, forces were reduced and border forays took on rather more the normal quality of cattle raids than disciplined warfare. Dacre was using his own funds to pay something to his own troops, while his Italian mercenaries distinguished themselves principally by poaching his deer and driving the inhabitants of Morpeth, where they were quartered, to such terror that they threatened to abandon their homes unless the foreign troops were removed.[3]

English power on the Border was, then, in dissolution in the autumn of 1549, in large part because of the great domestic crisis with which the government was struggling. The process of withdrawal to lightly held border positions was completed when Warwick mustered his strength for the daring *coup d'état* which unseated Somerset and which gave a wholly new direction to English policy. Somerset relinquished a sadly weakened position, but none the less on the day of his fall Broughty, Lauder, Home, Dunglass, Roxburgh, Eyemouth and several lesser strong-points still remained in English control. And Scotland was itself too weak and exhausted to place in execution an ambitious plan to throw the allied forces across the border for an invasion of England. The rivers were in flood and de Thermes nursed his gout in Edinburgh, having no wish to risk his troops in a joint attack with Scottish levies.

[1] Stow, *Annales*, 595–596; Wernham, *Before the Armada*, 176.
[2] *Cal. S.P. Scotland*, I, 179–180. Fisher placed the number in the relieving force at not more than 3500, even country 'tag and rag of all sorts'.
[3] HMC, *12th report*, App. IV: *Rutland MSS*. I, 44–45: Oct. 3 and 14, 1549.

French and Guise though she was, the Queen Dowager complained bitterly to France of the disorders wreaked on Edinburgh by the French troops and their officers. The moment for counter-attack swiftly passed and Mary of Lorraine again lashed out at the want of discipline in the French army which had seriously affected public sentiment and had placed her and her policy in a gravely weakened position. She was not consulted, French intentions were unclear, and a kind of paralysis of will had rendered Scotland quite as impotent as was England.[1]

The war which Somerset had launched with such an overpowering victory had, then, come to a pointless and desultory end. It was from its inception a senseless war attempting by force to impose covenants and a union which reflected Somerset's prescient idealism but not the sentiments of the politically articulate classes of Scotland. It was clear, indeed, that his policy had failed even before the awful expiation of Pinkie. But Somerset sought with frightening stubbornness of purpose to restore a sense of British unity by a policy which in fact all but destroyed it for a century. Surely it should have been clear at least to some of his advisers that the gathering force of a swift and nation-making reformation, whose progress was somewhat delayed by Somerset's intervention, was England's strongest ally to the north of the Tweed. In all, we have reckoned, at least 20,000 of Scottish, French, and English dead were the price of Somerset's mistaken policy. He had in 1547 brilliantly begun a war which could not be won.

Weakness in Scotland in 1549 had as its inevitable corollary a steady deterioration in the relations of England with France, though even in the months of grave domestic crisis English reserves and supplies at Calais and Boulogne were not disastrously drawn down. Paget, Somerset's closest and best adviser, had in January written for the Protector's eyes an unsolicited but none the less valuable statement of his own recommendations. England was at war with Scotland, on the brink of war with France, possessed no allies in Germany, and must reckon with a really unsympathetic emperor. The only prudent recourse in this dangerous situation was to gain a close alliance with the Emperor, even if this should mean a halt to the further reformation of religion. He was also troubled by growing social and economic restlessness in Suffolk, Norfolk, Kent, Sussex, and Wiltshire, which could only be restrained if the nobility and gentry were commanded to restore order. Directly Parliament had voted supplies, Paget strongly recommended that it be dissolved,

[1] Teulet, *Relations*, I, 197–201, 208–211: Nov. 12 and 29, 1549.

postponing the debate on the *Prayer Book*, in order to restrain discussion and to secure the return of the nobility and gentry to their
homes. At the same time, Russell should be dispatched to the west
and Warwick to the north to secure civil order and to restore that
domestic strength on which foreign policy can be built.[1]

This trenchant advice Somerset in part followed, in so far as it
related to foreign affairs, and he was granted at least a short surcease
because the French too were reconsidering their policy *vis-à-vis*
England because of a deep disagreement over the state of their
Scottish alliance. Scottish military weakness, the burdening of the
economy, and the deepening frictions of what was now regarded as a
French occupation force by the population of Edinburgh, all
counselled caution. Even more discouraging was the knowledge,
transmitted in May, that Somerset was seeking a firmer alliance with
Charles V, while in June Paget was sent over to use every persuasion
on the Emperor to secure the inclusion of Boulogne ('The New
Conquest') in the treaty of alliance protecting Calais. Though this
mission failed, Henry could not be sure of its outcome until July,
when the agrarian rebellion in England made it clear that the time
had come for the long-delayed assault on Boulogne. Somerset had
gained no more than time in the negotiations with Charles, save for
the secret permission given for England to recruit as many as five
thousand Saxon mercenaries and five hundred 'Low Germans',
together with licences to purchase equipment for 500 heavy horse,
these troops to be moved into the Boulogne area discreetly through
Guînes and Calais.[2]

There was in this interval of diplomatic feinting and jockeying,
however, considerable military activity on both sides, but all carefully comprehended within the fiction of formal peace. In mid-May
Sir Thomas Cotton, a steady and diligent commander, was named
vice-admiral and entrusted with the bulk of the fleet under instructions to patrol the Channel and to clear the coast and the principal
approaches of French and Scottish vessels. He divided his fleet into
three squadrons beating out from Dover for the Channel, from
Portsmouth for the southern waters, and presumably from Newcastle for the north.[3] In the same season Châtillon, still in command of
French forces before Boulogne, sought unsuccessfully to carry one of
the Boulogne outforts by a surprise attack blended with treasonable

[1] Gammon, *Master of Practises*, 226–228, citing Fitzwilliam MSS. (Northampton
Record Soc.), 'Ntht., Paget Ltr. Book', 5, 7.
[2] *Cal. S.P. Span.* IX, 367: Apr. 19, 1549.
[3] S.P. Dom., Edw. VI, VII, 9, 12; Anderson, *Letters from the archives of Southampton*,
67: May 20, 1549.

agreements with some of the garrison, but was beaten off and was himself wounded. Châtillon had attempted several probing attacks seeking to scale the walls at Bolemberg, losing almost two hundred of his troops. Skirmishing and savage minor engagements continued for several days in late May, until the English command sent special envoys through the lines to inquire whether the attacks had been formally authorized by Henry II, who returned the quite false but saving reply that they had been justly launched as reprisals, but without his knowledge.[1]

The mutually convenient fictions were maintained throughout the spring (1549), while intensified assaults were to become chronic. At the end of May an estimated one thousand French attacked shipping lying in the new mole in the harbour, in a night foray, which could not have been very formidable, since only eight French and two English were counted as killed. Still another effort was made at Boulogne to burn English shipping then provisioning the garrison, by setting in fire boats, while a raid in strength was launched deep into the English pale by a regiment of light horse. There was also now quite certain knowledge from Cobham's intelligence that heavy troop movements were under way towards Boulogne, though it was equally clear that Henry II would hardly dare launch a full-scale attack so long as he could not ferret out the purpose or success of Paget's mission to the Emperor.[2] The evidence of diplomatic failure with the Emperor being wholly clear by July and the equally clear evidence that the English government was faced with serious internal disorders, emboldened France in early August to declare war and simultaneously considerably to increase the pressure on Boulogne.[3] Believing that most of Cotton's fleet lay in Jersey, a strong naval attack was mounted against that commanding outpost, but the engagement went decisively against the French, who sustained very heavy losses.[4] Meanwhile, Henry II, in a gallant royal progress through much of France, went down in person in August to assume command of the large and powerfully equipped army which had been slowly gathering at Montreuil, to augment the forces already on the Boulogne frontiers.

[1] Edward VI, *Chronicle*, 13; *Cal. S.P. Span.* IX, 373, 377, 380: May 8, 22, 28—all the Spanish dispatches being to the Emperor from Renard in Paris, who had recently succeeded St Mauris.

[2] HMC, *Salisbury MSS.*, I, 74; *Cal. S.P. Span.* IX, 390–391: Renard to the Emperor, June 12, 1549; Holinshed, *Chronicles*, III, 909–910.

[3] *A.P.C.* II, 310: Aug. 8, 1549; Harl. MS. 523, #391, f. 47: Somerset to Hoby, Aug. 13, 1549, where the Lord Protector complains of the dishonour of France in levying war during the King's youth.   [4] Edward VI, *Chronicle*, 13.

The English position at Boulogne was formidable in its central fortifications, though the outforts were no more than weakly held and were really indefensible with the resources which the now desperately harried English could provide, and it was now certain that little more could be spared because of searing and uncontrollable rebellions at home. French gold and espionage had also done their work, the commanders at the German (Almain) camp on commanding ground between Boulogne and Ambleteuse surrendering on demand, thereby uncovering the defences of Ambleteuse, Newhaven, and Blackness which all fell with very little resistance.[1] Sir Henry Palmer then thought his position at Bolemberg untenable and gained from the governor (Lord Clinton) permission to withdraw to the central fortifications. Thereupon, in a process of successive uncoverings, all the important outworks were to fall at the first hostile touch. The Council, and most especially Somerset, were furious with Palmer, condemning a commander who 'upon the vain fear and faint-hearted messages of the captain and others of that fort, and without any other apparent or imminent peril', should have been so timid as not to meet his enemies face to face.[2] Palmer was forthwith relieved, Sir John Norton being commanded to replace him. These were shattering and possibly needless losses, though the central bastion, heavily gunned, well garrisoned, and well commanded still stood and English artillery was successful in keeping open the indispensible harbour and its works.[3] Henry II, soon tiring of the slow process of investment and siege now encircling Boulogne and apprehensive because of an outbreak of plague, retired quickly from the scene. Montmorency, in camp near Ambleteuse, wrote to the Queen Dowager in Scotland that the attack had been principally planned to divert the English from Scotland, but it had gone so well that the decision had now been made to carry the city.[4] But France was still uncertain of imperial intentions, with the

[1] The principal outworks, the 'Almain' camp aside, were at Ambleteuse, a coastal town with a small and shallow harbour, Newhaven on the mouth of the Boulogne River, and Blackness and Bolemberg, both being set inland, and the latter forming a very strong natural position. We have found a 1558 (?) map in the Harvard College Library collection to be especially useful. This map also indicates the Tour d'ordre and the forts of Châtillon and d'Outreau. Châtillon was built by Henry II to take a garrison of from 3000–4000 men; the Tour d'ordre was of much earlier date and was not used by either the English or the besieging French.

[2] *Calais Papers*, in *Cal. S.P. For.*, *Edw. VI*, 354; Edward VI, *Chronicle*, 13.

[3] *Vide ibid.* 16–17, for a spirited account of events in the early stages of the siege.

[4] *Foreign correspondence with Marie de Lorraine . . . from the . . . Balcarres papers, 1548–1557*, ed. by Marguerite Wood (Scot. Hist. Soc., ser. 3, VII, Edinburgh, 1925), 55–56.

result that excessive commitments of men and *matériel* were avoided as the French army settled down to the dreary and slow process of siege.

Paget's mission to the Emperor had failed to gain his intervention; the repression of serious rebellion at home was taxing English resources to the full; and as the black summer of 1549 came to a close Warwick and his allies in the Council were preparing to accomplish the ruin of Somerset and the repudiation of his policy. Paget returned to London at the climax of what can only be described as civil strife threatening to slip into civil anarchy. During these dreadful days England literally had no foreign policy, as is witnessed by the fact that for the period July 24th to August 31st, a few unimportant papers aside, no document is to be found in the foreign papers of a power which a few years earlier had been of the first rank amongst European states. But it must be recorded that Boulogne, as well as numerous strong points in Scotland, still remained in English hands on the day when the Duke of Somerset was toppled from power.

X

ADVANCEMENT OF THE COMMONWEALTH AND OF THE REFORMED CHURCH: FIRST PARLIAMENT (SECOND SESSION)

(November 24, 1548–March 14, 1549)

1. THE SECULAR MEASURES

The second session of Parliament, which was to sit for almost four months, was convened when Somerset's prestige was perhaps at its zenith and when his foreign policy still seemed strong and on the whole successful. The memory of his great triumph at Pinkie was still fresh; Shrewsbury had only a few weeks earlier relieved Haddington and had forced the Franco-Scottish allies from the field, while English relations with France on the Calais-Boulogne borders, though strained, were formally correct. Before the session was done, however, Sudeley's machinations at last veered into high treason and the tortuous but compelling evidence had to be laid before Parliament, despite the humiliation and personal distress occasioned for the Lord Protector. But the first reaction had been one of general sympathy for Somerset, resulting if anything in a further enhancement of his reputation for probity and devotion to the welfare of the young sovereign and the commonwealth. This was the period, too, when Somerset was lending powerful approval and support to the Commonwealth Party, whose principal spokesmen were seeking an economic and social reformation which would alleviate burdens and wrongs long suffered by the poorest and most helpless segments of the society. Yet the not wholly explicable fact is that no social or economic legislation of the first importance was enacted during this session, though, as we shall note, an important legislative programme had apparently been under consideration for submission to this Parliament.[1] Somerset seems to have concluded that sweeping legislation for social and economic reform passed by earlier Tudor Parliaments, and still unrepealed, provided him with quite sufficient authority to proceed, as he was doing, to revolutionary courses by

[1] *Vide post*, 426ff.

the means of royal commissions. But it remains puzzling that Somerset did not introduce a 'gathering measure', an omnibus bill, which would lend strength to this policy and give it more explicit authority. As we have suggested, such a measure seems certainly to have been under consideration; it may well have been shelved because the Duke was by no means sure that it could be passed, since he was well aware of the bitter hostility of the nobility and the gentry—and here we really say of the Lords and Commons—to the strong measures he had already undertaken against illegal enclosures, depopulations, and social injustice.

But Somerset did give an important lead to thrusting landlords in 2 and 3 Edward VI, c. 12, in which in effect he placed all of his own tenants under copyhold for their assurance and protection. Even though much of the land on his estates had not in fact been old copyhold or demisable by the custom of the manor, out 'of his charitable and accustomed goodness', and on his petition, the legislation was passed, binding him and his successors, that all such tenures should be written 'in the book or roll' of the manors concerned. The bill was first considered by the Lords and then brought to the Commons on March 5, 1549—the day after its action in the Sudeley case had been completed—gaining enactment on third reading two days later.[1] This remarkable and generous measure tells us a great deal about the character of Somerset, but it had no general significance and the example it meant to set was simply not followed. This measure will be fully considered in the later context of the vigorous programme of agrarian reform which Somerset had undertaken in the summer of 1548.[2]

Also of some social and economic importance was 2 and 3 Edward VI, c. 15, a Commons bill enacted on January 29th. The measure sought to gain greater freedom of trade by laying fines against victuallers who conspired together to sell victuals at agreed prices, and to prohibit artificers and craftsmen from conspiring to agree on the amount of work to be accomplished in a certain period of time or to fix hours of labour. Then, as a sort of after-thought, it was provided that certain skilled craftsmen, among them masons, tile-makers, and glaziers, should lie under no restraints in working in any corporate town though they were not free thereof.

Mention should also be made of 2 and 3 Edward VI, c. 24, which

---

[1] The discussion of the legislative history of this parliamentary session rests, for secular measures, largely on the *Statutes of the Realm*, the *Lords Journal*, and the *Commons Journal*. Since we mean to give clear indications of sources in the text, these sources will not ordinarily be cited in the notes.   [2] *Vide post*, 426ff.

sought to settle a difficult legal technicality which arose when a murderous assault was made in one county and death occurred in another. The legislation held that indictments handed down in the latter county were valid and that trial should proceed there, and further that accessories to murder or felony might be proceeded against in the county where they had become accessories.

These few measures were the only enactments of much secular interest in this session of Parliament, aside from the acts for the attainder of Sir William Sharington (2 and 3 Edward VI, c. 17) and of Thomas Seymour (c. 18), which will be fully considered in later pages.[1] In all, thirty-nine statutes were passed which group themselves in an interesting fashion, suggesting the principal areas of concern of the government and the members:

Economic problems	10
Legal (mostly technical)	5
Constitutional	5
Administrative reform	5
Religion	4
Borough benefits and privileges	3
Social	3
Attainders	2
Military	1
Public weal generally	1
Total	39

The measures passed were usually, of course, those which had been submitted by the Council or which, if they were private bills, enjoyed its approbation. Almost more important, therefore, in revealing the thrust of interest and concern of the articulate classes of the realm are the bills which failed of passage, normally because they were private member bills which did not engage the concern of the Protector and Council. Of these, seventy-eight bills were introduced, nearly all in the Commons, which either failed of passage or which were of such limited concern as not to be considered as statutes of the realm. This group exhibits a very different complexion of interest than the enactments, since forty-four, or more than 56 per cent of the whole, proposed economic, social, or educational reforms of one sort or another. Of these, thirty-five enjoyed no more than a first reading; but there were nineteen which gained a second reading, while twenty-two survived third

[1] *Vide post*, 368–385.

readings and two a fourth. Further, of the whole number, fifteen actually passed the House of Commons and at least three seem to have enjoyed the force of law, though not being counted as statutes because of their limited or private nature. One wishes that we knew more about the contents of certain of these measures which failed of passage, because in them was surely to be found the true texture of the aspirations of the period, which evidently ran just ahead of achievement, even under the benign policy of the Lord Protector.

There do remain, however, two important drafts of bills, probably prepared for this session of Parliament, but never submitted, which reflect the bold and really revolutionary thought of Somerset and his more intimate advisers. Both were almost certainly drafted in the hand of John Hales who, as a commissioner, was with the Protector's full encouragement enforcing with rigour and an almost obsessive zeal the laws against enclosures which had long lain dormant on the statute books. These exploratory drafts of bold and certainly revolutionary social and economic policy may best be separately treated later as part of our discussion of Somerset's courageous but ill-fated effort to correct imbalances and what he regarded as injustices in the English economy.[1]

2. THE MEASURES OF RELIGIOUS REFORMATION

While few secular measures of great importance were enacted into law by the second session of Parliament, momentous decisions were made respecting the worship and faith of England. Both Cranmer and Somerset had moved with great caution and slowness in settling the faith of England, though as we have seen every ordered move had been in the direction of the reformed churches. Moreover, Cranmer's own mind and thought were during the first months of the reign in rapid motion, steadily outrunning the teachings of the church of which he was primate. The spiritual progress of the Church of England had, then, been moderate, but it had been supported as it was thrust forward by a very nearly absolute trial of religious toleration and by a really completely free intellectual environment of discussion and writing. But the time had now arrived for a consolidation, for laying down an arc of definition which it was hoped would include those Englishmen who had been in the process of arriving at personal criteria of faith and the certainly much larger mass of men and women who scarcely thought critically or consecutively about such matters at all, but who were disposed to

[1] *Vide post*, 426ff.

accept the judgement of their superiors in church and state, so long as the comfortable routines and the abiding symbols of an habitual worship were not too violently disturbed.

The first of the spiritual enactments sought to give legal definition to the law and practice of the church with respect to the traditional fast days. The bill was introduced in the Lords on February 4, 1549, and after being considered by a committee comprising Cranmer and the Bishops of Ely, Worcester, and Chichester, was sent on to the Commons, being approved by the Lords on February 16th. So far as our sketchy knowledge of its progress indicates, there was no opposition and the measure was confirmed on its third reading on March 6th. The statute held that though the 'most perfect and clear light of the Gospel' makes it plain that all days and all meats are of equal purity and holiness, none the less certain days of abstinence traditionally observed may induce virtue. Hence the accustomed fish days are to be retained, especially in order that 'the fishers and men using the trade of living by fishing in the sea' may be supported, flesh saved, and scarcity avoided. The enactment was essentially apologetic in its religious reasoning, harshly and honestly secular in stating the prime reasons for the retention of fish days.

In the first session of Parliament a bill had been approved in the Lower House which provided that married men might become priests and hold benefices. This measure was far more limited than a related proposal approved by Convocation a short time earlier by the significant vote of 53 to 22, which would have swept away all canons and statutes against clerical marriages. The bill as approved by Commons was delayed in reaching the Lords where it was read only once before Parliament was prorogued. It is quite clear that the Commons held strong views on the matter, since a similar bill was quickly introduced (December 3rd) in the second session and in the course of the debate was amended in such wise as to permit all priests to marry. Thus re-drafted and extended the measure passed the Lower House on December 20th. There was, however, strong and vocal opposition in the Lords, the bill being delayed, despite pressure from the Commons, until February 11, 1549, when it was given its second reading. In the decisive vote on its third reading (February 19th) eight of the bishops (Bonner, Tunstall, Rugg, Aldrich, Heath, Bush, Day, and Kitchin) cast their votes against the measure and were joined by four of the Lords with known Catholic sympathies (Morley, Dacre, Windsor, and Wharton).

In the discussion of the whole question in Convocation, the strong favourable judgement of Ridley, Taylor (later Bishop of Lincoln),

Dean Benson, and Redman, themselves unmarried, carried great weight. Redman, whose learning and doctrinal conservatism gave his views quite special force, submitted that God's Word does clearly counsel chastity in the priesthood, yet in England the only barrier to clerical marriage was the canons and constitutions of the church. Further, he argued, there was no reason why the King in Parliament might not remove the existing prohibition.[1] The statute itself was essentially apologetic in its reasoning, stating that clerical chastity was preferable, since the priesthood would be 'less intricated and troubled' with the charge of a household. None the less, 'the contrary hath rather been seen, and such uncleanness of living and other great inconveniences, not meet to be rehearsed', have been the fruit of a 'compelled chastity'. Hence all laws and canons heretofore prohibiting the marriage of priests were declared abrogated.

The passage of this act not only served to change the structure of the priesthood but it did violence to the conventions and habitual attitudes of many of the laity, for it cast the clergyman in a new and unfamiliar role. It is possible to argue convincingly that over the longer term its principal benefit was in adding immense genetic strength to the English society, for surely a wholly disproportionate number of the great men and women of the realm have sprung from the rectories and vicarages of the Church of England. And it also brought the church and its ministry into a closer and more organic relation to the life and aspirations of the many parishes across the realm. These forces were already at work even in the short time remaining to Edward VI, for by the onset of the Marian reaction almost exactly 40 per cent of the bishops were married, while the proportion of married clergy ran from about 10 per cent in the conservative north to about 30 per cent in the more forward and more fully reformed counties of Norfolk, Essex, and Middlesex.[2]

There remains for discussion the act 'for the uniformity of service and administration of the sacraments throughout the realm' (2 and 3 Edward VI, c. 1), establishing the first *Book of Common Prayer* as the received and authorized order of worship for the Church of England. The statute must be regarded as one of the most important ever enacted by Parliament and as giving to the Church of England a worship, an habitual order of service, and a doctrinal definition which, with relatively minor revisions, have stood for four centuries and which have moulded a culture as well as a faith. It deserves our full attention.

[1] Burnet, *Reformation*, V, 231, following Camb. C.C.C. MSS., CXIII, 174.
[2] Messenger, *Reformation*, I, 348; Dickens, *English Reformation*, 245.

It may well be one of the cultural and spiritual tragedies of the Reformation that religious controversy and the wish for regional and sectarian symbols of identity forced on the church, Catholic as well as Protestant, the necessity for precise definitions of orthodox modes of worship which reflected the doctrines then being so rigidly defined. It is difficult to recall, or even to believe, that in say 1500 there was in all of Europe no prescribed uniformity of ritual and worship, but rather great variety from diocese to diocese, and in a more limited way even from parish to parish. In England this strongly rooted tradition of liturgical localism had been so far disciplined by reforming, or overly tidy, bishops that only five orders of service survived: those of Bangor, Lincoln, Hereford, York, and most importantly Salisbury (Sarum). Of all these, the Sarum Use by 1500 enjoyed the widest acceptance and prestige. In the Roman Church, as the fracture of the Reformation widened, an inevitable desire for order and discipline led to several attempts to prepare an acceptable rite, of which that of Cardinal Quignon was the most impressive and radical, for he set out to base worship on the most ancient uses and swept away something like two-thirds of the accumulated Saint's Days, while arranging for the reading of most of the Scripture each year. This great work went through scores of editions from 1536 to 1566, but was disliked in orthodox circles and failed to gain acceptance by the Council of Trent. This work was well known to Cranmer, as was the Lutheran order of worship, issued in a series of pamphlets by Luther himself from 1523 to 1537, though no sustained attempt was made to end the diversity of ritual in fact prevailing in Protestant Germany. Before the English reformers, too, was the recently published (1542) *Kirchen Ordnung* compiled by Hermann von Wied, Archbishop of Cologne, who with the active assistance of Bucer, Melanchthon, and Osiander, prepared this authoritative ritual which sought to embrace Zwinglian as well as Lutheran elements of worship.[1]

In England change of ritual had been slow. No important attempt at codification had been made until under Edward VI the service began to be conducted in English and more especially when in 1547 the Act of Parliament was passed establishing communion in both kinds and requiring a substantial mechanical, if not doctrinal, change in the order of the communion service.[2] The reform was codified by the *Order of Communion* (March 8, 1548), prefaced by a

[1] Dixon, *Church of England*, II, 541-542; Procter, Francis, and W. H. Frere, *A new history of the Book of Common Prayer, etc.* (L., 1901, 1914), 20-29; Brightman, F. E., *The English rite, etc.* (2 vols., L., 1915), I, xxviii-xxxviii.   [2] *Vide ante*, 171.

royal proclamation stating that it had been prepared by 'sundry . . . prelates, and other learned men in the Scriptures', though it seems certain that it was principally from Cranmer's own hand. This work made no alterations in the ritual of the mass save for the insertion of English devotions in the middle of the service. But in this same interval the Privy Council had by its own authority abolished the use of candles at Candlemas, ashes on Ash Wednesday, and palms on Palm Sunday, while in October, 1548, it had swept away the use of holy bread, holy water, and creeping to the cross on Good Friday.[1] Thus gradually the structure and form of the service had been changed, the ground being cleared for the codification of these alterations, and their extensions, in the first *Book of Common Prayer*.

In anticipation of doctrinal change and the settling of a reformed worship, Cranmer in early 1548 submitted to certain of the bishops and learned clergy a searching questionnaire covering the whole range of doctrinal issues involved in the central significance of the mass.[2] On the key question, 'What is the oblation and sacrifice of Christ in the mass?', four of the bishops, Ridley, Holbeach, Barlow, and Cranmer himself, returned replies which were Protestant, as did two of the learned clergy, Cox and Taylor. Two others, Holgate and Goodrich, while Protestant in their general sentiments, were on this vital issue still orthodox in their views, as were seven known conservative divines and four of the 'politique' bishops. On still another question of great doctrinal importance, the efficacy of prayers for souls departed, both Cranmer and Ridley replied simply that the practice was 'not convenient'; Cox denounced such masses unequivocally; Holbeach and Goodrich favoured drastic reform of the practice, while all the orthodox bishops of course strongly favoured the retention of such masses.

These frank expressions of divers judgements on the central doctrine of the church, with an undoubted conservative weighting amongst the bishops, must almost certainly have tempered Cranmer's wish for further reformation as he renewed his work on what was to become the first *Book of Common Prayer*. We know that for some years past the Archbishop had been working on a new liturgy and that after the Convocation of 1543 he intended, with Henry VIII's consent, to prepare a simple and common service to replace the five in use in various parts of the realm. His first draft owed something to Quignon's drastic revision, but was based squarely on

[1] Ridley, *Cranmer*, 278–279; Wilkins, *Concilia*, IV, 22.
[2] The text is most conveniently found in Burnet, *Reformation*, V, 197–217, from Lambeth MSS., 1108, f. 6.

the Sarum Use. His second draft, probably prepared in 1545, introduced more radical changes of liturgy, though not of doctrine, and like the first was never formally presented to the King or to the Convocation. But these drafts seem to have been set aside when in 1548 he prepared his final liturgy, drawing most heavily from the Sarum Use, but displaying remaining influences from Quignon, the old Greek liturgies, and various of the Lutheran orders of service.

Cranmer probably first laid his draft before a conference of bishops and theologians convened at Chertsey Abbey on September 23 (1548), the French ambassador reporting a week later that the question of the mass had there been under debate. The meetings were then adjourned to Windsor, where Edward noted that 'a number of bishops and learned men gathered together' to prepare a uniform order of prayer.[1] Both Fuller, a century later, and Burnet (1679) offer lists of the divines present at these conferences, there being an evident confusion between the panel which prepared the *Order of Communion* and that which reviewed the *Prayer Book*. We know almost nothing regarding the debate, though the conservative position was strongly represented by Day and Thirlby amongst the bishops and by at least one of the theologians present. Of the eight Protestants thought to have attended, four (Cranmer, Goodrich, Holbeach, and Ridley) were bishops, while the then views of Skip and Redman are uncertain. Eventually all the members of the panel seem to have accepted the draft, save for Day, though Thirlby was later to oppose it in the House of Lords. It was also almost certainly submitted to all the bishops in October, 1548, in order to gain their support and to speed the passage of the bill imposing a uniform order of service then being drafted for submission to Parliament. But there survives no persuasive evidence that it was ever formally submitted to Convocation.[2]

The enabling Act of Uniformity was introduced first in the House of Commons on December 19, 1548, and on the same day re-delivered to 'Mr Secretary Smith', though debate on the measure seems to have begun even earlier in the Lords, where the principal debate was to occur and where in the bench of bishops almost the whole opposition was concentrated. A few days after the submission

---

[1] Edward VI, *Chronicle*, 10. Gasquet and Bishop (*Edward VI*, 142–146) offer the fullest and most persuasive reconstruction of these meetings, which we here follow.

[2] Gasquet and Bishop, *Edward VI*, 156; Messenger, *Reformation*, I, 374–375; Dickens, *English Reformation*, 218; Ridley, *Cranmer*, 288. The Convocation records were destroyed by fire. One is given pause in the judgement expressed above by the fact that the King, usually most accurate in matters of fact, adduced the support of Convocation for the *Prayer Book* in a letter to the Princess Mary.

of the bill, John Isham wrote to Sir Edward Bellingham in Ireland that all went well in the Parliament which was resolved to set aside all popish traditions and to determine on a godly order of worship. But, he continued, there ' "is great sticking touching the blessed body and blood of Jesus Christ. I trust they will conclude well in it, by the help of the Holy Ghost" ' for ' "part of our bishops that have been most stiff in opinion of the reality of his body, that as He was here on earth should be in the bread, now confess and say that they were not of that opinion. But yet there is hard hold with some to the contrary, who shall relent when it pleaseth God" '.[1]

The bill, ultimately passed with only minor amendments, recalled that there had been divers forms of common prayer as well as differing forms in the administration of the holy communion. But now in order to secure 'a uniform quiet and godly order', the King had appointed Cranmer 'and certain of the most learned and discreet bishops and other learned men' to gather from the practice of the primitive church and from Scripture one convenient form of worship, which to 'his great comfort and quietness of mind' is now set forth as the uniform rite for the whole of the realm. Accordingly, after the Feast of the Pentecost next coming, divine services should be conducted solely as the book prescribes, and any minister refusing to use the book or using any other service, or preaching against the book, shall for the first offence be deprived of his benefice for a year and imprisoned for six months, with complete deprivation and imprisonment for the second offence, and life imprisonment for the third. Penalties were also provided for any who 'in any interludes, plays, songs, rhymes or by other open words' depraved the *Book of Common Prayer*, or who procured the use of any other service or hindered the clergyman in the use of the rite now by law established. A provision was also included that 'any man that understands the Greek, Latin, and Hebrew tongue, or other strange tongue', might read the service in those languages, which might also be employed in university services. And, finally, it was ordered that every parish, at its own charge, must provide prayer books for the conduct of the service, before the prescribed date.[2]

Providentially, rather full and objectively couched minutes survive of the great debate on the bill, or more accurately, on the

---

[1] Froude, *History of England*, V, 145, quoting 'Irish MSS, vol. V, Edw. VI', which we have been unable to find in the Irish papers.

[2] *Statutes of the realm*, IV, i. 37–39; *C.J.* : *L.J.* The price of the book was in June, 1549, set by proclamation: in sheets not more than 2s 2d; bound in forel at not more than 2s 10d; in sheep's leather, 3s 3d; and in calf, 4s (Hughes and Larkin, *Tudor proclamations*, I, 464).

Prayer Book, as informally conducted in the House of Lords.[1] The discussion opened some time after December 14, 1548, and was concluded shortly before the Christmas adjournment of Parliament on December 21st, very possibly two days earlier. One is impressed by the evident freedom of the debate, by the absence of fear amongst those who stated their opposition in unequivocal terms, and by the earnestness of the consideration. Only three laymen spoke at any time during the discussions: Somerset in the role of a fair-minded moderator; Dudley to hasten the process of debate and to press for its conclusion; and Smith, present in his capacity as Secretary, with an ill-tempered, harsh, and utterly secular—an almost contemptuous—impatience with the whole discussion of the central doctrine of Christian belief.

In opening the debate, Somerset proposed in roughly hewn but clear lay language that the essential question was 'whether bread be in the Sacrament after the consecration or not'.[2] The formidable and venerable Tunstall objected to the evasive language of the proposed Prayer Book with respect to the eucharist and made it quite clear that he would lend his support to none save an unequivocal statement of the doctrine of transubstantiation.[3] He sought, indeed, to broaden the debate to include the whole doctrine of the mass, almost immediately involving both Cranmer and Heath in a highly technical and abstruse theological discussion which Somerset had at the outset ruled out of order. But it was Smith who intervened, his interjections throughout the debate being at once rude and intemperate. He now declared it loathsome to contemplate Christ's natural body as present in the sacrament, for His body is manifestly not there.[4] To this Heath rejoined that 'reason will not serve in matters of faith, [and] it is the body that was offered for us . . . it is real'.[5] Cranmer then rose to develop his own position and to expound the doctrinal implications of the language of the *Prayer Book*. The sacrament, he said, was 'the remembrance' of Christ's sacrifice and validates His legacy to us. Those who are unworthy eat but to their own damnation, but the righteous man partakes of His sacrifice, not because He is in the bread and wine but because 'He is in heaven'.[6] Following this simple but Protestant statement,

---

[1] Royal MSS. 17, B, xxxix. The manuscript is printed by Gasquet and Bishop (*Edward VI*, 397–443), whose text we follow with occasional amendments from the manuscript. It is possible that this was a preliminary discussion with the bishops, immediately preceding formal consideration in the Lords.

[2] *Ibid.* 396.   [3] Sturge, Charles, *Cuthbert Tunstal* (L., [1938]), 279.

[4] Dewar, *Sir Thomas Smith*, 38; Harl. MS. 6989, f. 81. Smith was very proud of his intervention in the debate.   [5] Gasquet and Bishop, *Edward VI*, 399.   [6] *Ibid.* 400–401.

Thirlby reminded the Lords that the Book propounded a doctrine 'of the Supper . . . not agreed on among the Bishops, but only in disputation'. For his own part he had never accepted the doctrinal statements with respect to the eucharist as now set forth in the Book. To this Warwick coldly replied 'that it was a perilous word' that Thirlby had spoken, since it fostered discord when it was concord that was sought.[1]

Somerset, who was bending every effort to secure as large an episcopal support for the bill as possible,[2] opened the session on December 17th with a careful and temperate rebuke of Thirlby. He reminded him that the bishops had all been consulted in advance and that though some might not agree, the decision of the majority must be accepted. He recalled, too, that of all the bishops only Day had refused to accept the text of the *Prayer Book*, and that even his cavils had been on relatively minor matters.[3] To this Thirlby replied that he had indeed subscribed to the Book, for it stood with Holy Scripture despite minor imperfections, because he too wished unity in the English church. But he could not agree to the doctrinal implications inherent in the abolition of the elevation and the adoration in the celebration of the mass. In his view, the very fact that there was so much of uncertainty regarding the eucharist made it all the more necessary that doctrine be clearly stated. This quiet but stubborn statement visibly angered Somerset, who declared that 'these vehement sayings sheweth rather a wilfulness and an obstinacy to say he will die in it. To say he will prove it by old doctors, and thereby would persuade men to believe his sayings, when he bringeth no authority in deed'.[4] Bonner came to Thirlby's defence with the blunt statement that the doctrine of the eucharist propounded in the Book had long been condemned as heretical both in England and abroad, again provoking an angry intervention by Somerset.

The Protestant position was ably, though moderately, argued by Cranmer, Ridley, Holbeach, and Goodrich, Ridley's interventions being especially impressive. His argument, presented with great civility, was that 'as Christ took upon him manhood and remaineth God; so is bread made by the Holy Ghost holy and remaineth bread still', just as 'a burning coal is more than a coal for there is fire with it'.[5] Then in a running interchange with Heath, he

[1] Gasquet and Bishop, *Edward VI*, 403.
[2] Constant, G., *The Reformation in England, etc.*, II (N.Y., 1942), 88-89.
[3] Gasquet and Bishop, *Edward VI*, 404.
[4] *Ibid.* 404-406; Shirley, T. F., *Thomas Thirlby, Tudor bishop* (L., 1964), 99-100.
[5] Gasquet and Bishop, *Edward VI*, 415.

maintained that 'the manhood is ever in heaven; his divinity is everywhere present'.[1]

It was Heath who opened the debate on the final day with a long and impressive speech rehearsing the traditional Roman Catholic position on the mass which 'the people that have been commonly called the Church have ... believed'.[2] Both sides, he admitted, grounded their arguments in the Scriptures and doctors, but he accused his Protestant brethren of denying the clear words of Scripture and arguing from tropes and figures. For his part, he would take his stand on the flat assertion that in the mass the elements are the 'body that was wounded with the spear and gushed out blood'.[3] To this Smith rejoined with the tasteless impiety that this was a 'horrible' teaching, for it is worse to 'drink blood than to shed or pour it out', while taunting Heath with what he declared to be the obscurity of his position.[4]

Cranmer and Ridley carried the debate for the Protestant party for most of the final day, though little that was new or helpful was added by either side. A somewhat blasé observer in London could with truth write to a correspondent in the country that 'the bishops sit still ... and are not agreed as yet. ... As for mass, it is in London as it is in the country, some of the old-fashioned and some of the new.'[5] The whole tone of the debate, save for the intemperate interventions of Smith, had been cautious, moderate, and freighted with the sense that a momentous decision was about to be taken with respect to a doctrine which, central though it was, had never found complete unanimity in the Christian church. It is abundantly clear, too, that perhaps as many as half the bishops present were genuinely, almost pathetically, uncertain of what they themselves believed. Hence the quality of the debate was not particularly high, the learning displayed not formidable, and the whole impression left is one of fuzziness and ambiguity of conviction.

On the day that debate was probably ended (December 19th) Smith took the bill at once to the House of Commons where he read it to introduce the discussion.[6] Then, after the Christmas recess, the measure was first formally read in the Lords, on January 7th, and gained its second reading on the 10th. The vote came on January 15, 1549, when, most surprisingly, only two of the temporal peers, Dacre and Derby, cast their votes against this measure which

---

[1] Gasquet and Bishop, *Edward VI*, 416–417.   [2] *Ibid.* 420–421.
[3] *Ibid.* 421–422.   [4] *Ibid.* 422.
[5] HMC, *10th rpt.*, App. IV: *Zachary Lloyd MSS.* 448: [December, 1548].
[6] *C.J.* I, 5.

sought a common ground of worship and of doctrine for the realm. Of the bishops present, ten cast their votes for the measure while eight were recorded as opposed.[1] One misses on the conservative side the procedural skill and the earthy wit and sense of Gardiner, now in prison, who could certainly have presented a more impressive and persuasive case than did his conservative colleagues, who, Tunstall aside, were not famous for their learning. Taking into account what we know of the view of the considerable number of bishops not present, we would agree with Cardinal Gasquet's judgement that of the whole bench thirteen of the bishops almost certainly favoured the Act of Uniformity and the Prayer Book which it established, that ten were as certainly opposed, and that the views of the remaining four should be regarded as uncertain.

This great statute had been fully and freely debated, and, the spiritual peers aside, enjoyed the overwhelming approval of the House of Lords and probably, at least for the formal record, a large majority in the Commons, which had waited impatiently to pass the measure so long under debate in the Lords. The first Act of Uniformity was in a peculiar sense a landmark in the development of parliamentary maturity and in a real sense of a kind of parliamentary sovereignty. The great Reformation statutes of the previous reign, whatever the formal record may say, betray the imperious will and the personal power of a very great sovereign. But the statute of 1549 prescribed the liturgy, and to a large measure the doctrine, of the Church of England by the undoubted and unquestioned authority of Parliament. Instead of reflecting the personal wishes of the Supreme Head of the Church of England, Parliament now 'fully participated in the ultimate exercise of his power, the definition of the true faith'.[2] England was now by law established a Protestant polity and church.

The first *Book of Common Prayer* has been a controversial work from the time of its adoption by Parliament to the present, in large part because readers (and listeners) read more into it than Cranmer

---

[1] Bonner, Tunstall, Heath, Thirlby, Rugg, Aldrich, Skip, and Day. Thirlby had returned from his embassy to the Emperor not many months previously. Somerset expressed to the King his surprise at Thirlby's stalwart opposition, to which Edward is said to have replied, 'Your expectation . . . he might deceive, but not mine. I expected . . . nothing else but he, who has been so long time with the emperor . . . should smell of the Interim.' None the less the government continued to make use of Thirlby's considerable abilities, differentiating between his complete loyalty as a civil servant and his views as a largely inactive and non-resident bishop. (Shirley, *Thirlby*, 101.)

[2] Elton, *Tudor constitution*, 335.

intended. The work was conceived in no sense as a formulary of doctrine, though it does possess doctrinal assumptions, but rather as a liturgical work, a book of worship, which should have no other design than 'to assist the piety of the faithful'.[1] Cranmer sought, indeed, to avoid controversial matters whenever possible in order to gain as wide an acceptance as might be for what he meant to be a universally employed manual of worship and instruction. The preface to the first edition states that the church has fallen away from the ancient and salutary practice of hearing the Bible read each year for the edification of the faithful, and further that the service had been read in Latin to the people, 'which they understood not; so that they have heard with their ears only', while their hearts and minds have found no edification. The service now prescribed had as its principal purpose the reading of the Bible in ordered stages and by excising vain and superstitious matters had been made 'more profitable and commodious' than those lately used. Further, the Book would cure an unfortunate diversity in service from diocese to diocese, so that 'now from henceforth, all the whole realm shall have but one use'.[2]

Though Cranmer and his colleagues had sought to avoid doctrinal controversy, there were none the less fundamentally important doctrinal implications in the Prayer Book, in terms of both what was omitted and what was included. For one thing, and this change violently altered the traditional habits of worship, the medieval 'cult of saints' was almost totally dropped from worship. Even in the first *Book of Homilies* there had been a strong condemnation of the invocation of saints, set in a list of superstitious practices that were to be omitted. Over the years, too, such prayers were quietly dropped from various reformed primers as part of a deliberate and quietly persistent effort to change the structure of worship and of belief. And in the Prayer Book the whole of the traditional calendar of saints was either omitted or rearranged, all traditional prayers to the saints being expunged, save in the service of communion when there was a passing reference to 'the wonderful grace and virtue, declared in all the saints', and especially in the 'most blessed Virgin Mary'. But the rejection of intercession was now complete, for the telling phrase ran: 'Grant this, O father, for Jesus Christ's sake, our only mediator and advocate.' Thus the whole basis and content of worship was shifted by doctrinal assumptions which aligned the

[1] Gasquet and Bishop, *Edward VI*, 184.
[2] *The book of common prayer, etc.* (L., 1549), in *The two liturgies, A.D. 1549, and A.D. 1552, etc.*, ed. by Joseph Ketley (Parker Soc., Cambridge, 1844), 18–19.

Church of England in at least loose association with the reformed churches on the Continent.[1]

The central concern of course was focused on the doctrine and meaning of the mass as it was carefully ordered in the Prayer Book. Here—and the evidence is substantial, because it includes the Prayer Book rebellion in the West—the most revolutionary fact was that the whole of this service and worship was rendered in the English language. Beautiful and haunting though the language was, it without doubt weakened, if it did not destroy, the mystery of the mass for simple men, including a large proportion of the parochial clergy. The content of this change for the conservative layman has been well expressed: 'his indignation was perhaps caused by the fact that he did not wish to have the hidden mystery of the Latin mass replaced by a service in a language which he could understand, and which therefore required a more active mental participation on his part'.[2]

For the more sophisticated, however, it was clear that the doctrinal content of the service of the mass had been only very cautiously shifted towards Continental Protestantism. The central rite, the canon, was, after some personal hesitation, retained by Cranmer even though it had been savagely denounced by Luther as turning the eucharist into a sacrifice. But while retaining the canon, Cranmer altered it in so far as possible in order to destroy the notion of the sacrifice. Particularly, he sought to achieve this by ordering that the recital be spoken or chanted audibly. At the same time, however, Cranmer swept away all of the ceremonies, the sense of mystery, that had long attended and embellished the mass—the washings, crossings, shiftings, and blessings—as well as the ritual which had heretofore characterized the communion of the sick and the burial of the dead. These substantial, and most conspicuous reformations, Cranmer fortified by the specific prohibition of the elevation of the host and of the chalice, which came soon to be regarded symbolically as deeply rooted in the Roman teaching on the mass. The whole of the content of change, then, was doctrinally moderate and ritualistically radical. Change, in the direction of the reformed churches, went only so far as Cranmer thought would be acceptable to men of conservative persuasion or interest, and, perhaps more important, to the great mass of men who were simply inert in matters of faith and worship. Nor does the totality of doctrinal change represent accurately the then far more radical convictions of

[1] White, Helen C., *Tudor books of saints and martyrs* (Madison, Wisconsin, 1963), 89, deals thoughtfully with this matter.   [2] Ridley, J. G., *Cranmer*, 288.

Cranmer himself, as he admitted in the controversy which he was soon to have with Gardiner on the eucharist, and as perceived by Bucer and Fagius, then very close to Cranmer, when they wrote to their Continental brethren that the book was a concession to the 'infirmity of the present age' and an interim design until the nation was ready for further reformation.[1]

When all has been said regarding the content of the Prayer Book, its precise relation to the old faith and the new, still there remains a want of understanding of the significance of this remarkable manual of faith. For even the most astute and sensitive man in 1549 could hardly have apprehended that Parliament had decreed that Sunday after Sunday, in all parishes of the land, men, women, and, more importantly, children, were to listen to the reading of a great literary masterpiece. The Psalms, Gospels, and Epistles were rendered in Coverdale's wholly minor revision of Tyndale's memorable translation of the Bible. But the even greater literary triumph was in the free translation which Cranmer gave to the Collects in the Sarum Use, the Latin original having been tightly aggregated and not always clear in language. The translation is couched in unforgettable phrases, in cadences that are pure poetry, and in the loose and freely flowing, and always idiomatic, style which Cranmer could employ at will. It is translation which in every particular excels as it respects the original text. There is in this style, as well, great nobility, great restraint, and great reverence for the mysteries which it expounds. It has, in Lewis' fine words, 'almost an Augustan shrinking, not from passion, but from what came to be called enthusiasm'.[2] As time was to pass, years of hearing this great poetry spoken—and to hear it is to etch it in memory—this memorable work was to become the spiritual inheritance as it was one of the great works of art of a whole people.

As we have suggested, Cranmer had sought a middle ground, a formulary which in its doctrinal implications did not wholly satisfy his own views, which were in process of change, even on the central doctrine of the mass. And, predictably, it did not from the out-set meet with the approbation of what may after the first Act of

[1] Robinson, *Original letters*, II, 534 ff. See also Dryander's report to Bullinger: 'You will also find something to blame in the matter of the Lord's supper; for the book speaks very obscurely, and however you may try to explain it with candour, you cannot avoid great absurdity. The reason is, that the bishops could not of a long time agree among themselves respecting this article, and it was a long and earnest dispute among them whether transubstantiation should be established or rejected.' (*Ibid.* I, 351: June 5, 1549.)

[2] Lewis, C. S., *English literature in the sixteenth century, etc.* (Oxford, 1954), 220.

Uniformity be fairly described as extremism to the right and to the left. For the time being the conservative bishops, including Stephen Gardiner, were able to adjust their consciences to its prescriptions. But there is abundant evidence that cautious and intemperately conservative country parishes—especially in Devonshire, Cornwall, Dorset, Yorkshire, and parts of Oxfordshire—under clerical leadership, found the Book wholly unacceptable, principally for the presumably irrelevant reason that it was couched in a known tongue. But broadly speaking, in the realm as a whole the mass of men, both lay and clerical, accepted the new liturgy and worshipped without protest and without stirrings of conscience, doubtless in the main because it had been ordered by the King in Parliament.

Far more articulate, and perhaps historically important, was the immediate opposition of radical Protestantism, which, while in general accepting the Book as the law provided, was by no means content with its formulations or with the essentially conservative character of the worship which it prescribed. Above all, Hooper, the intellectual and spiritual leader of advanced Protestantism, simply did not like it and was from the outset bitter in his castigation. 'I am so much offended with that book,' he wrote, 'that if it be not corrected, I neither can nor will communicate with the church in the administration of the [Lord's] supper.' His attack on its doctrinal position with respect to the mass was sustained until the Book was indeed 'corrected'. In still another letter he condemned it as 'very defective and of doubtful construction, and in some respects indeed manifestly impious'.[1] Bucer, enjoying as he did an immense theological reputation in England, also regarded the Book as defective in its treatment of the Lord's Supper, and, as we shall see, later suggested numerous revisions in order to free Anglican worship from what he regarded as popish survivals.[2] The knowledgeable Traheron, a member of Parliament, assured Bullinger that privately Cranmer had accepted Bullinger's own view of the Lord's Supper,[3] but sensed correctly that the Archbishop had thought it unwise too deeply to divide the bishops, with the result that what he regarded as a Lutheran definition of the mass had been accepted.[4] The learned and temperate Dryander, writing at about the same time, criticized the Book for its evidently deliberate obscurity in the great question of the mass, but indicated that this simply reflected the divisions amongst the bishops. But, he submitted, there had none the less been notable progress in the reformation of the Church of

[1] Robinson, *Original letters*, I, 79: Mar. 27, 1550.   [2] *Ibid.* 266, 350–351.
[3] *Ibid.* 323: Dec. 31, 1548.   [4] *Ibid.* 266: Hilles to Bullinger, June 4, 1549.

England, 'where there existed heretofore in the public formularies of doctrine true popery without the name'.[1] This last and respected judgement was not far from the mark. The Church of England was now a Protestant church in the full sense of the term; there were powerful and highly articulate forces which wished its fuller and more radical reform; the *Grundlagen* for Protestantism had been laid and the massing of evangelical pressure was at hand.

[1] Robinson, *Original letters*, I, 351: June 5, 1549.

XI

THE IMPLEMENTATION OF REFORM
(1549)

I. THE VISITATION OF 1548–1549

The first *Book of Common Prayer* came into general use as ordained by statute without many evidences of opposition or disturbance save in those areas which we have noted. It will be remembered that the Act of Uniformity provided no penalties whatsoever for laymen absenting themselves from the service as prescribed by law or, for that matter, attending private or other services. There were, however, in the course of 1548–1549 an unusual number of episcopal visitations designed to apply at least moderate pressure towards reform and to test the acceptance in public worship of the relatively few and mild prescriptions which had been laid down in the first two sessions of Edward's first Parliament. Some comment should be made on at least a sampling of these visitation articles. Thus Cranmer in 1548 ordered a visitation of his own diocese, which differs little in the matters covered from his visitation of the preceding year, save that it lays a far heavier emphasis on the duty of preaching and inquires more strictly regarding the use of English in divine services. His visitors were instructed to make sure that all non-graduate clergy possessed both the Latin and English Bible, as well as the *Paraphrases*, and that some lessons from both the Old and New Testament were read at every service. They were to determine as well whether the clergy were exhorting their parishioners to give to the box for the poor and to remember this charitable obligation in their wills, seeking to gain for the poor the traditional sums which had once been left for masses and pardons. In this same connection, the visitors were to make careful investigation to determine whether trentals and masses were still being said for the dead, with, however, no suggestion of immediate prohibition.[1]

Cranmer's lively, though tolerant, instructions may be compared

---

[1] *Articles to be enquired . . . within the diocese of Canterbury, etc.* (L., 1548), no pagin.; also in Cardwell, *Documentary annals*, I, 49–59.

with those of Wakeman (Gloucester), whose shadowy views on theological questions were as much a mystery to his contemporaries as to us. The inquiries to be made were perfunctory indeed, requiring the visitors to ascertain that prohibited images and shrines had been removed, that lights were limited to the two on the altar, and whether all parishioners had been so taught that they could recite the Lord's Prayer and the Ten Commandments in English.[1] So too, there was little of reforming vigour in the visitation which Rugg, forced to resign his see because of financial irregularities at the close of 1549, ordered for his diocese. His articles added little to the earlier Edwardian visitations, save for an anxious concern regarding civil unquiet in the disturbed county of Norfolk. The visitors were to inquire whether any be known who 'affirm all things to be common, or that there ought to be no magistrates, gentlemen, or rich men, in Christian realms', or who teach that Christians may not take an oath or go to law. Finally, there were to be ferreted out any who held that private persons may make insurrections or force others to give up their goods, or who teach that the magistrate 'may not punish by death notorious malefactors, or use any compulsion or war'.[2] The principal concern here reflected is the security of the state and not the implementation of reform. Rugg might well have argued, indeed, that in Norfolk there was a close and frightening connection between extremist reformed convictions and the dread menace of social revolution.

Far more interesting and searching were visitation articles drawn up shortly after the promulgation of the *Book of Common Prayer*, probably with Cranmer's approbation, which do not appear to have been formally published or carried forward, though both Ridley and Hooper clearly drew on them in subsequent visitations of their own dioceses. The inquiry was specifically concerned with the widespread practice by conservative priests of simulating the Roman mass while technically following the prescribed service. Accordingly, a minister was prohibited from following the Romish practice of kissing the altar, 'washing his fingers at every time in the communion . . . crossing his head with the paten; shifting of the book from one place to another; laying down and licking the chalice . . . holding up his fingers, hands, or thumbs, joined towards his temples; breathing upon the bread or chalice; shewing the sacrament openly before the distribution of the communion;

---

[1] Kennedy, W. P. M., 'Bishop Wakeman's visitation articles for the diocese of Gloucester, 1548', *E.H.R.* XXXIX (1924), 253–254.

[2] *Articles to be inquired of . . . in the byshopricke of Norwyche, etc.* (L., 1549), no pagin.

ringing of sacryng bells', or any other usage not specifically pre-scribed by the Prayer Book.[1] The vivid and detailed recital of what might not be done by the priest in the service of the Eucharist suggests the ingenuity and probably the extent of the evasion of the service as now ordered by the Prayer Book. It was likewise noted that none in the congregation was to be permitted to pray upon beads, while a long and careful list of traditional and superstitious Roman Catholic practices specifically prohibited by one or another statute or royal injunction was set down, including two (holy oil and chrism for the sick) which seem in point of fact to be allowed by the first *Prayer Book*. All this was known to Cranmer, who in the event regarded the first version of the *Book* as interim in character and who before many months had passed was lending his mind to a sweeping revision which would bring English doctrine and worship nearer to the Christian church of antiquity as well as to the reformed churches on the Continent, with which he dreamed of some measure of organic union.

2. REFORM OF THE UNIVERSITIES

Cranmer understood, as all the foreign divines residing in England pointed out, that the effort to preach and teach the reformed faith in the realm was gravely weakened by the want of an educated and preaching clergy. This was the compelling reason, warmly supported by the government, underlying a persistent and on the whole success-ful effort to reform the universities during the Edwardian period and to foster within them stronger centres of both learning and con-viction.[2] The power of visitation, fortified and specified under the Reformation Statutes, was accordingly invoked and the King appointed an eminent and ardently Protestant visiting commission to both the universities, as well as including the chapel royal in Windsor within the competence of the Oxford visitors and Eton College among the duties of the Cambridge visitors.[3]

The universities steeled themselves for this formidable visitation with considerable trepidation for they had thought themselves in danger of at least partial expropriation under the language of the Henrician Chantries Act, though when a survey of the property of

---

[1] *Articles to be followed and observed, etc.* (1549?), in Cardwell, *Documentary annals*, I, 75; also in Frere, *Visitation articles*, II, 192–193.

[2] The discussion of this subject will owe much to the valuable study of Mark H. Curtis, *Oxford and Cambridge in transition, 1558–1642* (Oxford, 1959).

[3] S.P. Dom., Edw. VI, V, 13: Nov. 12, 1548; Rymer, *Foedera*, XV, 178–180.

several of the colleges was ordered in 1546, the King professed to bear in mind that at the universities 'the great number of the youth of this our realm is nourished and educated in the exercise of all kinds of good literature'. Henry VIII had accordingly appointed Matthew Parker, Redman (Master of Trinity), and May to report on collegiate endowments, how the founding statutes were observed, and in general to probe to the heart of their finances. This royal commission was instituted, despite the plea of Cambridge that the universities be permitted to proceed by self-examination and a somewhat hysterical appeal to Catherine Parr to intercede on their behalf, being assured by her that the King's only concern was for the advancement of learning. This appraisal of Henry's motives was evidently wholly correct, for in a memorandum after the commissioners' interview with the King, Parker noted that Henry had observed that 'he had not in his realm so many persons so honestly maintained in living, by so little land and rent'.[1]

But the universities remained frightened and uncertain, observing without doubt that the continuing press of secularization was vesting in lay hands numerous, and rich, ecclesiastical posts which had traditionally been awarded to clergy in the universities.[2] It was known, too, that there were those within the circle of power in London who would purge the religious conservatives in certain of the colleges, particularly at Oxford, by expropriation. Nor could it immediately be known that Somerset was quite as far-seeing and generous in his view of the universities as Henry VIII had in fact been. To those who urged sharp courses in the universities, he is said to have replied, 'If learning decay, which of wild men maketh civil, of blockish and rash persons wise and godly counsellors, of obstinate rebels obedient subjects, and of evil men good and godly Christians; what shall we look for else but barbarism and tumult?' And in a broader sense, he reasoned, if university and college lands were taken, then as easily would all estates be in danger.[3] None the less the colleges remained apprehensive and there were doubtless many instances of prudent concealment of funds, as for example when the notary who normally served Magdalen College, Oxford, in 1548 failed to complete a conveyance for property purchased in Hampshire when the threat of expropriation was believed to be real.[4]

[1] Parker, *Correspondence*, 35–36.
[2] Among others may be mentioned Somerset, who held a deanery, a cathedral treasury, and four prebendaries.
[3] As quoted by Harrison (*Description of Britain*, Bk. II (New Shakspere Soc., ser. 6, pt. i), 88–89). He was a student in Cambridge in 1551.
[4] At Petersfield (VCH, *Hampshire*, III, 117).

The secular strength and bias of the commission was more to be feared by societies which in 1548 were still overwhelmingly clerical in their constitution; the masters were in holy orders, and most of the fellows were at least formally clergy, since under the statutes they must be ordained. Most of the resources flowing in to both universities had assisted, since 1550, in the founding of new colleges and the further strengthening of the old, most of the inns and hostels having disappeared by 1550 as university life became more completely collegiate. There were in 1500 ten colleges in each university, and to this total twelve had been added by 1600, nine before the accession of Elizabeth.[1] Most importantly, the colleges, well before 1548, had begun vigorously to develop instruction supplementary to that traditionally provided by the university, with the result that the tutorial system was fairly shaped by the middle of the century. Further, the colleges were adjusting themselves to the fact that an increasing proportion of their students had no intention of entering the clergy and that parents, whose support lent increasing strength, expected a large measure of direct moral supervision over a student body of a quite different complexion than a college would have known a half century earlier.[2]

The universities were yielding as well—and that rapidly in the age of Edward VI—to the increasingly secular aspirations of what was now a large proportion of their student bodies. The conviction that a formal and sophisticated education was necessary for those who would serve the state, the church, or themselves, was growing, with the result that in the Edwardian era there were as many as nine sons of peers matriculated at Oxford and Cambridge.[3] The great pressure, however, came from the sons of the gentry, who were now crowding in and who, in the judgement of contemporary observers, were not only giving a secular cast to the whole intent and process of education, but were pre-empting scholarships meant for the sons of the poor. The complaint was that 'poor men's children are commonly shut out, and the richer sort received (who in time past thought it dishonour to live as it were upon alms) and yet, being placed, most of them study little other than histories, tables, dice, and trifles'.[4] The classical remonstrance was, of course, that of Latimer, whose grave concern was actually with the secularization

[1] Thompson, Craig R., 'Universities in Tudor England', in Wright, Louis B. and Virginia A. LaMar, *Life and letters in Tudor and Stuart England* (Ithaca, N.Y., 1962), 338.   [2] Curtis, *Oxford and Cambridge*, 39.

[3] Simon, Joan, *Education and society in Tudor England* (Cambridge, 1966), 246.

[4] Harrison, *Description of Britain*, Bk. II (New Shakspere Soc., ser. 6, pt. i), 77.

of education. In his famous Fifth Sermon (1549) he lamented the decline in the number of those who then studied divinity, believing that the sons of the rich were crowding out the poor boys from whom the clergy was principally drawn. He pleaded with the Lords of the Council present in his congregation that as much should be given for divinity exhibitions as had formerly been spent on prayers for the dead and other 'purgatory-matters', for 'there be none now but great men's sons in colleges, and their fathers look not to have them preachers; so every way this office of preaching is pinched at'.[1] Places must be made for the sons of the yeomanry, from which the clergy had long been recruited, for 'Read the chronicles: ye shall find sometime noblemen's sons which have been unpreaching bishops and prelates, but ye shall find none of them learned men'.[2]

The universities had for a generation, somewhat hesitantly and certainly grudgingly, been adapting themselves to these powerful secular demands by the steady reform of their curriculum, which the Edwardian commissioners were to hasten and solidify. Cheke and Smith, both formidable humanists, had been among the early beneficiaries of these reforms, which included the study of Greek and Hebrew, the founding of lectureships in Latin, Greek, rhetoric, and moral philosophy, and clearly fruitful teaching in certain of the colleges in which humanistic learning was well rooted. It is not too much to say that under Edward VI the entire curriculum was re-thought and then shaped on humanistic principles.[3] The new studies, supported and invigorated by tutorials for the fee-paying students, met quite precisely the lay needs of the age, while the abolition of prayers for the dead relieved the colleges of the responsi-bility of prayers for past benefactors and tended to orient scholarly interests and activities in terms of a largely lay education.[4] It is true that the statutory structure of the university curriculum changed much more slowly, but it ceased to have much authority or to rep-resent what actually happened in the colleges or to prescribe the course of study pursued by most students. The college, and not the university, had become the principal instrumentality of education.

The visitation of Oxford was undertaken with some evidences of apprehension by the Council, because of the extremely conservative

[1] Latimer, Hugh, *Works*, ed. by G. E. Corrie (2 vols., Parker Soc., Cambridge, 1844–1845), I, 179.
[2] Latimer, *Works*, I, 102. The Venetian ambassador, Daniel Barbaro, in his report to the Doge and Senate, also indicates his belief that Oxford and Cambridge were not drawing students from as wide a social spectrum as formerly (*Cal. S.P. Ven.* V, 345: May, 1551).
[3] Curtis, *Oxford and Cambridge*, 71.   [4] Simon, *Education and society*, 250.

character of most of its colleges. Nine commissioners were named, Warwick being the titular head, Ridley, Paget, and Petre forming a link with the Cambridge visitation undertaken somewhat earlier in 1549.[1] The visitors were vested with wide powers, including suspension and deprivation for cause, diverting endowments to more fruitful purposes, merging of colleges, reform of the curriculum, and the imposing of an oath of allegiance. They were also instructed to concentrate the study of the arts in New College, of civil law at All Souls, and to gather more strength in the teaching of medicine by assigning the responsibility to a single college.[2]

The inquiry at Oxford was carefully and methodically pursued and the statutes of reform imposed on the university were at once moderate and fruitful. The student was now to devote his first year chiefly to mathematics, his second to dialectics, and his third and fourth to philosophy. Three more years were prescribed for the M.A., with special stress on philosophy, astronomy, and Greek, while the curriculum for students proceeding to degrees in divinity, law, and medicine were thoroughly reformed. The principal difficulties encountered by the commissioners were in their effort to sweep the numerous choristers from the various colleges and to reapply the income so gained, and in dispensing with grammar school instruction in Magdalen College, which was resisted quite as vigorously by the town as by the college. And, finally, with respect to the university constitution, the authority of the Chancellor was greatly enlarged and he was declared to be personally responsible for the administration of the whole *corpus* of the university. These powers, vested in Cox as vice-chancellor (1547–1552), were prudently but firmly exercised in an effort to give a more Protestant complexion to the university, as it were, wearing the Catholics out by patience.[3]

The efforts of the commissioners to reform the colleges were less successful, since the power of deprivation and suspension was moderately employed. The chapel services in the several colleges were given a wholly Protestant order of worship, while all superfluous

[1] S.P. Dom., Edw. VI, VII, 6, 7: May 8, 1549, for the commission, and *ibid*. XIII, 63: October?, 1551, for the later commissioners.

[2] In replying to an inquiry from Bullinger regarding the teaching of medicine at Oxford, Christopher Hales had replied that the instruction could not be compared with that of Paris or the medical faculties of Italy. None the less, he loyally added that Oxford was to be preferred to Cambridge, which 'by reason of the neighbouring fen, is much exposed to fever, as I have experienced more frequently than I could wish'. (Robinson, *Original letters*, I, 190: Dec. 10, 1550.)

[3] Robinson, *Original letters*, II, 468: Stumphius to Bullinger, Nov. 12, 1550. Cox had been, of course, also the senior tutor for the young King (Edward VI, *Chronicle*, 3).

altars and monuments were removed.[1] But little could be done with such conservative strongholds as Exeter and Lincoln, or in such colleges as Balliol and Merton where Catholic sympathizers were in a strong preponderance. New College was also cautiously conservative in the complexion of its fellows, while Henry Cole, the warden, was justly suspected of Roman Catholic sympathy, the visitors being instructed to examine the statutes of the college to discover whether there were sufficient grounds for his deprivation.[2] The moderation with which the commission proceeded is also suggested by the fact that when in 1550 the provostship of Oriel fell vacant, the fellows elected one of their own number, and a conservative, despite the restrained effort of the government to impose an outsider of reformed views.[3] So moderate were the courses of the visitors that even All Souls, itself incidentally a chantry foundation, was neither reformed nor threatened. Many highly placed and senior academic officers of known Catholic views were left undisturbed, but encouragement and support had been lent to younger men of advanced Protestant sentiment, men like Cox, Bentham, and Bickley at Magdalen, or Jewel and William Cole at Corpus, who were rising rapidly in academic prestige and power. Such men, and others like them, were to give to the university a Protestant cast which made it possible for Camden, the great historian, late in his life to say: 'I thank God my life hath been such among men, as I am neither ashamed to live nor fear to die, being secure in Christ my Saviour in whose true religion I was born and bred in the time of King Edward VI.'

Then too, as we have already seen,[4] the appointment of Martyr, with his towering reputation, had tipped the balance at Oxford and had given leadership and confidence into the hands of the younger fellows, so many of whom became Elizabethan Protestant stalwarts. Ulmis could report in 1550 that the Romanists were quiet and subdued at Oxford and that no one any longer appealed to the schoolmen in lectures, but to 'the most ancient fathers . . . and especially the holy scriptures, to which, as to a touchstone, every argument is referred'.[5] But these gains were not so apparent to the sensitive Martyr, who only a few days later confided unhappily to Bucer that the state of the university still left much to be desired, since

[1] Mallet, C. E., *A history of the University of Oxford* (3 vols., L., 1924–1927), II, 88.

[2] HMC, *Salisbury MSS.*, I, 81: Nov., 1550. Cole, under pressure, resigned on Apr. 16, 1551. Cole is chiefly remembered for his sermon in March, 1556, in which, with Cranmer present as a prisoner, he urged that the Archbishop should be burned.

[3] VCH, *Oxfordshire*, III, 122.   [4] *Vide ante*, 191.

[5] Robinson, *Original letters*, II, 412: Ulmis to Gualter, June 1, 1550.

most of the college heads did not really favour the reformed faith, while the statutes imposed by the visitors were furtively evaded.[1]

The strains within the colleges, as relentless, though always moderate, pressure towards Protestantism was applied, must have been great indeed, particularly if, as was so often the case, there was a division of sentiment amongst the fellows. In the case of Magdalen, under pressure both to abandon its grammar school and to reform itself, the divisions became so acrimonious as to bring in the direct intervention of the Privy Council. Magdalen's president since 1535 had been Owen Oglethorpe, who, though he had accepted the Henrician Reformation with what seemed full support, lent increasing sympathy to the old faith as he grew older. His fellows were bitterly divided, a group of about ten of the younger men lending zealous support to the Protestant position and forcing the introduction of the reformed order of worship and indulging in acts of tasteless iconoclasm. The dissident fellows submitted a complaint directly to Somerset that their president was obstructing the reformation of the college in every possible way, which was categorically denied by Oglethorpe and a majority of the fellows.[2] The Council further stirred the controversy by seeking unsuccessfully to secure the appointment of the fervently evangelical William Turner to a fellowship in the college.[3] In 1550 still another attack was launched against Oglethorpe by ten of his fellows, though in a formal defence he denied the charge that he favoured Papists and 'persecuted' those of the reformed faith. The Lord Protector sought personally to quiet this academic tempest, but the Protestant group still contended that Oglethorpe threatened all their efforts to reform and advance the college.[4] The Council was persuaded and, in the one instance of direct intervention in the affairs of a college, ordered Oglethorpe's removal and suggested, to what now appeared to have been a majority of the fellows, the election of the brilliant Cambridge scholar, Walter Haddon, as their president.[5] Oglethorpe, sensing that no further resistance was possible, entered into a private agreement with Haddon by the terms of which he resigned and Haddon's appointment was made by royal mandate.[6]

[1] Camb. C.C.C. MSS., 119, f. 107; printed in Gorham, *Gleanings*, 151–156: June 10, 1550.   [2] S.P. Dom., Edw. VI, V, 12: Nov. 8, 1548.

[3] *Ibid.* XI, 14: Nov. 28, 1550; *ibid.* XIII, 4: Jan. 20, 1551.

[4] Lansdowne MS. 3, #4; *ibid.* 2, #75.   [5] *A.P.C.* IV, 112: Aug. 14, 1552.

[6] S.P. Dom., Edw. VI, XIV, 58: Aug. 6, 1552; Lansdowne MS. 3, #5, #6 (Aug. 11, 1552), #7 (Aug. 29, 1552), #9 (Oct. 12, 1552). It might be added that nine of the reforming group were promptly ejected on the accession of Queen Mary (VCH, *Oxfordshire*, III, 196–197).

Oglethorpe's courageous but perverse resistance seems to have been rooted rather more in his dislike of iconoclasm in his college than in any very deeply held religious conviction. And this must have been true for many older men who watched the destruction of carvings, statues, and stained glass throughout the university on the order of the visitors. But, more importantly, no effort was made to censor the college libraries or to remove papistical materials. In point of fact, the Edwardian period was in the heart of a generation (1530–1556) when there was a notable strengthening of the libraries of the university, especially by the acquisition by gift or by purchase of the great new patristic editions, the pride of humanistic scholarship, then appearing on the Continent.[1] There was also fairly heavy buying in the fields of history, law, and medicine, these acquisitions, mostly folios, compelling the college to jettison bulky and now unused manuscripts of patristic material, now outdated by better and printed texts. Such destruction as there was, then, followed more nearly as a consequence of short-sighted library administration than from Protestant zeal. When in this process of sorting really rare and unpublished Greek and Latin texts were found, there was an intellectual excitement betokening the organic link between Protestant thought and the humanism which had nurtured so many of its leaders.[2] Nor is there substance to the charges frequently made by contemporaries, and often copied by later writers, that the number of students at Oxford declined in this vigorous but turbulent period. In August, 1552, there were 1021 members of the university, of whom 761 were in the colleges and 260 in the halls. This represents a sharp increase of nearly 25 per cent as compared with the total at the accession of Edward VI and was approximately the number enrolled during the reign of Queen Mary.[3]

The visitation of Cambridge was not expected to encounter so many difficulties as had been experienced at Oxford. The temper of the university, and of most of the colleges, had been Protestant for almost a generation, while in this same interval the steady growth in the vitality and distinction of its teaching had made it by the time of Henry VIII's death perhaps the most eminent university in Europe. It is true, however, that difficulties remained. The university found itself in serious financial straits for a generation after 1530, in part because of the disappearance of the regular clergy from the scene,

---

[1] *Oxford college libraries in 1556. Guide to an exhibition held in 1956* (Oxford, 1956), 6–11.   [2] Robinson, *Original letters*, II, 447–448: Ulmis to Bullinger, Feb. 5, 1552.
[3] The three totals employed may in each case include some servants.

but more important because of the strain imposed by inflation on its finances. Though the records are incomplete, it seems too that the number of students taking baccalaureate degrees declined somewhat in the last decade of Henry's reign.[1] But these weaknesses had been far more than over-balanced by the founding of the five Regius professorships in the university in 1540 and the re-founding in 1542 of the decayed monastic Buckingham College as Magdalene and, above all, by the great royal foundation of Trinity College with provision for a master and sixty fellows and scholars. The revenues settled on Trinity possessed a net value of about £1640 p.a., far exceeding that of any other Cambridge college, King's and St John's following with incomes slightly less than £500 p.a.[2]

At the beginning of the Edwardian period, it is not too much to say, Cambridge was graced with more famous names than ever before or since: Ascham, Cheke, Smith, Ridley, Cecil, and Parker being only the most illustrious. There was a weakening of the humanistic resources of the university when the most brilliant of these teachers were co-opted, almost as a body, by the Edwardian government for appointment to high administrative posts, which was to cast a true lustre on government service during these years. Never before, surely, and possibly never since, has a government drawn so much of strength and imagination directly from the universities. Evidences of the decline of instructional vigour at Cambridge came principally from the eloquent pleas of Ascham, Lever, and Latimer, who spoke with heroic exaggeration and from a deep and jealous love for the university.

Thus Ascham, in presenting a petition to Cranmer for favour to the university, in November, 1547, shortly before Parliament was to meet, stressed two weaknesses that should be repaired. The university needed more older scholars, 'by whose example the younger sort might be excited to study, and by whose authority the manners of the rest might be rightly formed and fashioned'. The other weakness was the fact that for the most part only the sons of the rich were being admitted—men who never intended to become true scholars, but who wished instead to prepare themselves for careers in government—thereby creating an environment in the university in which 'good studies' and learning were not easily pursued.[3] Lever stated the case with even more of passion and eloquence. Far more of the monastic wealth, he held, should have been employed for the relief of poverty and the maintenance of learning. Even

---

[1] Mullinger, J. B., *The University of Cambridge* (2 vols., Cambridge, 1873–1874), II, 49–50.   [2] VCH, *Cambridge*, III, 462.   [3] Strype, *Cranmer*, I, 242–243.

though Henry VIII was most generous to Cambridge, the strength
of the university had declined as those studying divinity, mostly
poor boys, had been replaced by the sons of the rich and favoured.
Hence only a small number of 'poor, godly, diligent students' remained, cursed by poverty and weakened by neglect. He accordingly
called upon the government and the rich London merchants to
restore the balance and to train up learned men for the needs of
the church and the good of the whole commonwealth.[1] Lever, and
Ascham too, was of course really complaining, not from concern
for the health and vigour of the university, but because the structure
of life, of aspirations, and of interest had indeed changed in the
universities as secular goals and purposes were creating a new
culture and a new ethic in England.

The visitors appointed for the Cambridge inquiry were all
graduates of the university and all were well known for their devotion to Protestantism and to learning. Ridley and Goodrich were the
only ecclesiastics on the commission; Cheke, Smith, and Paget
represented the lively interest of the Council in the work of the
visitors; May was a learned theologian and Dean of St Paul's, while
Dr Wendy was a physician to the King.[2] The visitors brought with
them new statutes approved, if they had not been drafted, by the
Privy Council itself, for Somerset displayed a keen and persistent
interest in the Cambridge visitation. The statutes to be amended or
replaced were declared to be 'antiquated, semi-barbarous, and
obscure', while those to be drawn were to secure the increase of
learning and virtue and 'to adorn and amplify' the humanities and
the sciences.

These new statutes were ambitious in their scope and resulted in
a recasting of the entire curriculum. Grammar, now widely taught
in schools throughout the realm, was to be dropped from the course
of studies and to be replaced in the first year by instruction in mathematics, and all students were on their admission to have a working
knowledge of both Latin and grammar. Those proceeding towards
the baccalaureate degree were to have instruction in philosophy,
astronomy, perspective, and Greek, while Masters of Arts were to
have studied theology and Hebrew. Public disputations were not
only retained but were to be given additional emphasis. The curri-
cula for professional degrees in law, divinity, and medicine were

[1] Lever, Thomas, *A sermon preached at Pauls Crosse xiii[i] Dec. M.D.L.*, in Arber,
Edward, *English reprints*, #25 (L., 1871), 119-123.
[2] S.P. Dom., Edw. VI, VI, 33, 34: Apr. 9 and 10, 1549; Add. MS. 5804, f. 64b;
Camb. C.C.C. MSS., 106, #176, f. 489.

reformed, the studies and exercises in divinity being especially
expanded and strengthened. All remaining vestiges of popish ceremonies in the service of the colleges were to be eliminated.[1] The
visitors, and the Privy Council, also became involved in a festering
dispute between the officials of the town of Cambridge and the
university, which was settled by an abrupt order of the Council
itself charging the town in no way to interfere with or to oppose the
privileges which had been granted to the university.[2]

The reform of the university having been completed, the visitors
turned to a survey of the several colleges in order to eliminate
popish survivals in their chapels, to review the teaching function,
and to make certain that their statutes conformed with those just
promulgated for the universit. Thus the order of worship was carefully prescribed, and the extremely delicate point of prayers for past
benefactors beautifully handled, for the preacher in his prayer
should intone:

'O Lord, we glorify thee in these thy servants, our benefactors,
departed out of this present life, beseeching thee that, as they for
their time bestowed charitably for our comfort the temporal things
which thou didst give them, so we for our time may faithfully use
the same to the setting forth of thy holy word to thy laud and praise,
and finally that both they and we may ever lastingly reign with thee
in glory.'[3]

The educational tasks of the colleges were enhanced by prescribed
lectures on logic or philosophy, the lecturers to 'explain some Greek
or Latin author who treats concerning polite literature' and to examine the students on the subject matter. Moreover, six lecturers
were to be appointed each year to instruct in logic and in the arts
and sciences. For these exercises the texts were prescribed in detail,
while careful and full injunctions respecting the teaching method,
discipline, and examinations were laid down.[4]

The visitation of Cambridge had gone smoothly, save for one
revolutionary proposal for the creation of a new college, to be called
Edward College, by the merging of Clare Hall and Trinity Hall.
This plan, enjoying the warm support of both Somerset and Smith,
was designed to create a new college, with old and available resources,

---

[1] Lamb, John, *Collection of letters . . . illustrative of the history of the university of
Cambridge, etc.* (L., 1838), 122-146; Harl. MS. 7037, #7, f. 233; *ibid.* 7046, #13,
f. 105.   [2] Lansdowne MS. 3, #16.

[3] Heywood, James, *Early Cambridge university and college statutes, etc.* (L., 1855),
pt. ii, 157-158, 159. For the colleges we have taken the statutes for Clare as typical.

[4] *Ibid.* 161-163.

for training men in civil law and preparing them for service to the state. Smith had been named Professor of Civil Law in 1544 in what proved to be a wholly bootless attempt to bolster a dying discipline. In the course of seven years after his appointment only one student had proceeded LL.D. and only eight had received the baccalaureate degree in law, the attractions of the common law being too great. The plan, therefore, was to devote substantial resources to this somewhat quixotic scheme, which would predictably be bitterly opposed by the fellows of both the halls which were to be merged into the new foundation. Somerset had already asked Gardiner, who had retained his mastership of Trinity Hall, to resign his office and the Hall to the King's use, which had angrily been refused with the comment that Trinity alone could 'breed more civilians than all England did prefer according to their deserts'.[1]

It seems almost certain, incredibly, that Ridley was not fully acquainted with this scheme when he arrived in Cambridge, but pressure was immediately put upon him by Somerset and by Smith, who, unable to leave London, had attached a friend, William Rogers, to the visitation.[2] The usually equable Ridley was outraged, particularly with Smith, but on Somerset's stern instruction to proceed, laboured for two days without success to induce the master and fellows of Clare to agree to a kind of institutional suicide. The commission itself was evidently divided on the merits of the plan, those favouring it suggesting a little maliciously that since Clare was filled with northerners, Ridley, a native of Durham, was partial to them. But in any case the pressure of the commission was wholly without success. Ridley reported to Somerset that only the intervention of the 'King's absolute power' would effect the merger and made it clear, with all respect, that his conscience persuaded him that the step proposed was neither a proper nor a godly action. He wished, indeed, to beseech the King 'to spare Clare College for Latimer's sake'.[3] Rogers, in effect serving Smith as a spy on the commission, reported a few days later that Ridley simply did not want to proceed against Clare and was procrastinating, even refusing to act against the master for the sale of the plate of the Hall.[4] Somerset replied to Ridley on June 10th, making it clear that

[1] Fuller, Thomas, *The history of the University of Cambridge, etc.*, ed. by James Nichols (L., 1840), 180.
[2] S.P. Dom., Edw. VI, VII, 10, 11, 14: May 14, 15, 18, 1549.
[3] *Ibid.* 15, 16, 27: May 18 and June 1, 1549.
[4] *Ibid.* 29: June 9, 1549.

he would not compel the Bishop to proceed against his conscience, but reminding him that the plan for the merger had long been under discussion and that Ridley in his desire for more divinity fellowships would even diminish the scant number being trained in civil law. Surely, he concluded, 'you are not ignorant how necessary a study that study of civil law is to all treaties with foreign princes and strangers, and how few there be . . . at this present to do the King's Majesty service therein'. Ridley's obstinacy in the matter was all too close to that of the fellows of Clare Hall itself.[1] He stood firmly on the position that it would be a great scandal to convert an endowment created for the study of God's Word into one for the study of man's law. Ridley was recalled to London to be questioned and pleaded with, but he simply could not be moved. The commission refused to proceed without him,[2] and the plan was shortly abandoned, having indeed already failed to pass the House of Commons on a third reading.

3. DIFFUSION OF THE REFORMATION UNDER SOMERSET

We have earlier dealt with the evidences of Protestant thought and action in the first months of the reign and have commented on the moderate but persistent shift of the worship and doctrine of the Church of England towards a settlement of religion which was indubitably Protestant. It is of course quite impossible precisely to appraise the extent and the quality of the diffusion of Protestant sentiment during the months of power that remained to Somerset after the Act of Uniformity had established the Prayer Book— principally because the evidence is too fragile and too elusive, though possibly as importantly because the tolerance and magnanimity of the Protector's religious policy provided no martyrs and few intransigent pockets of resistance against which to measure the progress of Protestant conviction. Though the discussion of the great issues both of doctrine and of worship had been sharp and continuous in high places, it none the less remains true that the translation to Protestantism had been accomplished with very little disturbance. We are persuaded that at some unknown and unknowable point in the reign England became predominantly a Protestant nation, but there was no moment of climax or of national decision. It is clear that it was the conspicuous change in ritual—in the

---

[1] S.P. Dom., Edw. VI, VII, 30: June 10, 1549.
[2] *Ibid.* 34: June 15, 1549.

habits of worship—that exercised most men. The use of known English instead of unknown Latin in the communion service, the change in the gestures and actions of the priest in the celebration of the Lord's Supper, and very small matters such as the restraint on the use of candles: these were of the order and the quality of the innovations that really troubled simple men in the thousands of parishes spread across rural England. The ordinary man was simply not concerned, if he knew at all, with the high matters in dispute at Westminster, on which an increasingly Protestant decision was being made, nor can much more be said for the parochial clergy. The parish lent a wonderful spiritual protection to men who did not wish to become deeply involved, and, if it were intellectually homogeneous, stood almost bulwarked in its isolation, save on those rare occasions when a visitation disrupted it for a season. In the words of Lewis, the conscience of the ordinary man was 'much burdened by his own unchastity, profanity, or deficiency in alms-giving, and a religion deeply concerned with the state of the crops and the possibility of making a good end when his time came. But the great controversies were too hard for him'.[1]

And there were many hundreds, more probably some thousands of parish priests as well, who through two decades of swift change in the religious life of the nation either remained inert or took refuge in a frightened and unheroic submission. Most of these men were not much more literate, informed, or, for that matter, interested, than their parishioners. One of them, far more highly educated than most, confessed in 1555 that during the past twenty years he had simply maintained silence, never associating with those who advanced heretical opinions, and taking no position at all.[2] And to take no position at all, which was precisely what most of the parish clergy of England did, was really to yield the whole case to Protestantism which possessed an immensely powerful initiative and which was winning its way in region after region and class after class in the realm.

The power and impetus which Protestantism had gained in England by the year 1549 is eloquently set out in the comments of the refugee divines and scholars, writing to the Protestant leaders on the Continent and if anything likely to be impatient with the moderate course of reform to which Somerset was inclined. Even

---

[1] Lewis, *English literature in the sixteenth century*, 40; *et vide* Powicke's wise and helpful comments on these matters (*Reformation*, 94–95).

[2] Elder, John, *The copie of a letter sent in to Scotlande, etc.* (L., [1555]), F2.

in 1548 the not always accurate Ulmis had written to Bullinger that the Word of God was triumphing in England, that the mass lay 'shaken', and popish practices were principally extirpated. Even more encouragingly, the public preachers in the realm 'for the most part openly and candidly confute... the notion of a carnal partaking' and many had already been won to a Zwinglian view of the sacrament.[1] The far more careful and expert English observer, Traheron, wrote at about the same time that those who were at the summit of power and honour in England were in the main already Zwinglian in their view of the Lord's Supper, save for the conspicuous exceptions of Cranmer, who remained at once inscrutable and lukewarm, and Latimer, the greatest of all English preachers, who 'is slow to decide, and cannot without much difficulty and even timidity renounce an opinion which he has once imbibed'.[2] The always wise and sensitive Dryander, in March, 1549, assured Bullinger that religion was truly established in England, though sensibly no effort was being made to define every difficult point of doctrine but rather to reform and order the public worship. Hence 'many puerilities are still suffered to remain, lest the people should be offended by too great an innovation', but they will in time 'be amended'.[3]

The principal impediment to the more rapid advancement of the Reformation was from the outset of the reign a clergy which was largely incapable of effective preaching even when safely Protestant in senitment. We have seen that early in the Edwardian period rigorous restraints had been imposed on preaching, partly because of growing Protestant radicalism and partly because of clerical ignorance and want of experience. The *Homilies* and now the *Prayer Book* were rapidly remedying this evangelical defect. The already radical Hooper, recently returned from Switzerland, blamed the bishops whose ranks he was shortly to join. The weakness in preaching, he wrote, sprang from the 'maliciousness and wickedness of the bishops', who neither preached nor encouraged others to do so. Hence preaching was mainly in the form of public lectures, of which four were given weekly in Paul's Cross. He was assisting, lecturing in London twice daily 'to so numerous an audience, that the church cannot contain them'.[4] These public sermons, and especially those preached before the King, were carefully arranged,

---

[1] Robinson, *Original letters*, I, 377–378.
[2] *Ibid.* 320: Traheron to Bullinger. The fact is that Latimer simply had no interest in theology.
[3] *Ibid.* 350.
[4] *Ibid.* 66: Hooper to Bullinger, June 25, 1549.

employing the best preachers in the realm and undoubtedly lending great impetus to the rapid spread of advanced Protestant sentiments in the capital.[1]

This device of the set public sermon, usually heavily attended, was being employed not only in London but in other urban communities all over England, while the church waited for the education and training of a preaching clergy in the still feebly nurtured rural parishes which made up most of the realm. Even in the predominantly conservative regions, and hence the more profitably to be examined, ingenious and successful methods were being employed to secure evangelical preaching. Thus the Earl of Derby gained the properties of the chantry college in Manchester on condition that a portion of the income be used for the support of itinerant preachers in the region. Of these the most notable was John Bradford, a Cambridge graduate who had been converted by Latimer's preaching and who was a friend of Bucer. An excellent preacher, Bradford spoke to great crowds in Manchester and at least a dozen other towns in southern Lancashire where by the time of his execution in 1555 he had established permanent and advanced Protestant groups. In this work he was supported by George Marsh, also educated at Cambridge, who was a fervent and most successful preacher not only in London but in numerous market towns in Lancashire.[2]

Even in the conservative and remote reaches of Yorkshire, as Professor Dickens has shown, this same process of powerful, well-appointed, and sustained preaching was doing its effective work under the direction of the moderate reformer, Archbishop Holgate. He not only reformed the statutes and the worship of his own cathedral but gave direct and effective support to preaching in all parts of his diocese. Among others, he appointed to ecclesiastical posts such men as Cottesford, a translator of Zwingli, John Dee, John Jones, Timothy Bright, and the learned and benefice-seeking William Turner, who in June, 1549, wrote to Cecil that Holgate had 'written to me to come to him with all speed'.[3] Holgate, working carefully with the central government, was building up a clerical

---

[1] *Vide*, as an example, notices, usually from Cranmer or Ridley, to Matthew Parker appointing him for public sermons (Camb. C.C.C. MS. 114, ##123, 124, 130, 133).

[2] Leatherbarrow, J. S., *The Lancashire Elizabethan recusants* (Chetham Soc., n.s. 110, Manchester, 1947), 6–8.

[3] Dickens, A. G., *Lollards and Protestants in the diocese of York, 1509–1558* (Oxford, 1959), 194–201; S.P. Dom., Edw. VI, VII, 32, for Turner, who still hoped in vain that Somerset would appoint him to Winchester.

elite of highly educated, gifted, and proven preachers who were
within a few years to win for Protestantism many of the market
towns of the county and to lift the whole level of preaching and the
cure of souls. And this was part of a process now well under way
across the whole face of England, under the care of the bishops if
they were reliably Protestant, by the direction of Cranmer and the
Privy Council if they were not.[1]

This restrained but highly successful evangelical effort was of
course immensely assisted by the establishment of a uniform worship as ordered in the *Prayer Book* and as supported by the *Homilies*
and *Paraphrases*, copies of which were in almost all parish churches
by the close of 1549. And these indispensible and powerful instrumentalities of propaganda were lent rich and effective support by a
veritable flood of publication of vigorous and soundly Protestant
works which were to enjoy wide distribution. As an example, there
were in the interval 1547–1553 seventeen reprintings of one or
another of Tyndale's works, surely the most effective and memorable Protestant writing in England until the Prayer Book was issued.
Possessing a more nearly official standing was the *Primer*, first set
out in 1547, written in beautiful and simple English, and still very
conservative in its doctrinal commitments.[2] Doctrinally still
cautious too, but laying powerful stress on the insular, the deeply
national, character of the Church of England was a 'Form of bidding
of the Common Prayers', apparently, however, never to be published.[3] Also prepared in conjunction with the appearance of the
Prayer Book was a manual of anthems and hymns, the first of a long
and illustrious series of such works which joined music to the worship of the Church of England.[4] More important was a thoroughly
revised edition of the *Homilies* meant to accompany the Prayer
Book, and in at least one printing bound in as an introduction to it.
The preface stated that the King wished all men now to find truth
in the pure and whole Word of God, and that this work was published to aid in overcoming superstition and ignorance, since it
would provide the unlearned clergy with ready and godly sermons

[1] So careful and directly interested were Somerset and the Council in ecclesiastical
appointments that in late 1548 it was reported that a non-resident appointment could be
gained only with the direct approval of the Lord Protector, 'and they say that there are
not four in England that have non-residents' (HMC, *10th rpt.*, App. IV: *Zachary
Lloyd MSS.*, 448: [December, 1548]).

[2] *The primer set furth. etc.* (L., 1547), STC #16048.

[3] Rawlinson MS. 589, printed in *The Crypt* (Ringwood, Hants, 1827), I, 16–18.
Probably 1547.

[4] Royal MSS., App. 74–76 [1547–8].

which were to be read in the appointed order. Thirty-one very short sermons were provided, all extremely effective, well rooted in Scripture, and dealing with matters close to the experience and interests of ordinary men in the simplest and most lucid of language.[1] Also widely distributed, and surely with great and enduring effect, was Marbeck's famous *The Booke of Common Praier Noted*, which set in simple but hauntingly beautiful music those parts of the Prayer Book which could be sung in worship. The work is at once good to the ear and to the eye.[2] Numerous other devotional books drawing from the Prayer Book were quickly prepared, published, and widely distributed.

The ultimate and probably the irrevocable success of the government in making of England a Protestant nation was probably gained by the gradual winning over of the inert mass of men to spiritual acceptance by the very gradual, moderate, and in some ways almost insensible change in the order and spiritual content of worship. This pressure of change, peaceful and unrecorded in large part, may best be studied in the parishes of the realm, though, most unfortunately, relatively few churchwardens' accounts survive from this early period. But even so we must restrict our examination to a relatively small but, one hopes, representative group of parishes. In Cambridgeshire there was almost no recorded resistance to the orderly progress towards Protestantism. There was some slowness in a few parishes in carrying out the prescribed changes in ritual and in acquiring the stipulated books, but in most cases the poverty of the parish was clearly responsible. Only at Brinkley was there deliberate and reasoned opposition from the curate who failed to follow the prescribed order of service in the sacrament of the Eucharist, to remove images as ordered, or to instruct his congregation to cease the use of beads.[3] In adjoining Huntingdonshire, the story was much the same, save that in many parishes the service and the ornaments of the church had by 1550 been reformed well beyond the prescription of the Prayer Book. As a consequence of this reforming zeal upwards of twenty parishes had sold now superfluous church plate by parish agreement. Only at St Neots had there been active resistance when certain gentry of the neighbourhood in 1547 refused to permit images to be removed until the issue had

[1] *Certayne sermons... appoynted*, etc. (1549), STC #13645; and with slight differences as STC 13643, 13644, 13646.
[2] STC #16441 (L., 1550).
[3] VCH, *Cambridge*, II, 170–171.

been decided by the Council.[1] In Buckinghamshire, too, there had been a single case of refusal to take down images, cured by a spell of imprisonment in the Fleet for the recalcitrant persons involved, though in the county as a whole there was a rapid spread of Protestant sentiment amongst the gentry, Lollardy for generations having had a tenacious hold amongst the commoners.[2] So too in Leicestershire the transition to a Protestant service seems to have been carried out without articulate resistance, while churchwardens' accounts suggest that many parishes were reforming the service well beyond the requirements of the law.[3]

In the west, at Exeter, the parish church of St Petrock, where many leading burghers worshipped, celebrated its last obits in 1548 and limed the walls in the next year, while by 1550 all the images had been sold, the altars taken down, and surplus plate in part sold.[4] In Wiltshire there was evidently a slower pace in meeting the requirements of the first Act of Uniformity, though a vigorous visitation of his diocese by Bishop Capon [or Salcot] in 1550 was successful in bringing the county to conformity. But there were still numerous rural parishes which, through inattention or poverty, did not own all the required books as late as 1553.[5] Opposition, though limited to a few parishes under the influence of forthright Catholic gentry, was strong in Oxfordshire in Pyrton hundred and in Watlington, while the formidable and resolutely Catholic Stonor family maintained intact a commitment to conservative worship even under the pressure of the Elizabethan age.[6]

The remarkable achievement of Somerset and Cranmer in settling a reformed church on the realm without resort to the stake or to violent spiritual courses is far clearer and more decisive to us today than it was to these contemporaries. Much remained to be done; the Gospel was not well taught by the clergy; and the implacable resistance of several eminent bishops to the whole settlement did not yield to the mild sanctions beyond which Somerset would not proceed. Those of the reformed party who shared the advanced sentiments of Hooper or most of the refugee clergy were in fact grievously disappointed with the progress towards reformation attained by the time of Somerset's fall from power. Martyr lamented,

[1] VCH, *Hunts*, I, 362–363; *A.P.C.* II, 140.

[2] *Ibid.* 147; VCH, *Bucks*, I, 309.

[3] VCH, *Leics*, I, 369–370; North, Thomas, *A chronicle of the church of S. Martin in Leicester, etc.* (L., 1866), 97, 102.

[4] MacCaffrey, *Exeter*, 190–191.

[5] VCH, *Wilts*, III, 28–30.

[6] VCH, *Oxfordshire*, VIII, 174, 244.

even as the Prayer Book was passing into law, that 'there is nothing more difficult in the world than to found a Church. The stones are generally rough and very unpolished; hence, unless they are rendered plane and smooth by the Spirit, the Word, and examples of holy life, they cannot easily be made to fit each other'.[1] This reveals the mood of those who wished a more radical reformation, and that quickly. And the labourers on the stones of the true church were too few in number and in evangelical competence. Thus Fagius, soon after his arrival in Cranmer's household, estimated, with truly heroic understatement, that there were scarcely ten preachers competent for the labour in hand. The Reformation in England, he felt, stood harassed and endangered from secret and overt Catholics on the one hand and the spreading and zealous heresy of the Anabaptists on the other.[2] These were the dangers also feared by Hooper who was angered by Anabaptist heckling at his own sermons. But above all he feared the inert, the only partially articulate, Catholicism to which he believed 'a great portion of the kingdom' still adhered.[3] These doubts and apprehensions were quite perfectly summed up by Martyr, who, in writing to Bucer, spoke again of the 'most obstinate pertinacity' of the Papists and their friends, who included numerous bishops, doctors, and others of the national leaders of England and who drew many of the people with them. And equally to be feared, he noted with a remarkable sensitivity to the facts, were those in high places who were either 'wholly opposed to religion', or were not of the clergy, or even were cold in their faith. The Lord Protector's government truly and strongly desired a reformation in the realm but was simply without the effective means to secure its purposes.[4]

Fagius, writing once more to Marbach in Strassburg in the summer of 1549, summarized well the estimate of responsible but decidedly evangelical observers of the state of the reformation in England at a moment in time when Somerset's power was ending. All matters seemed to him in a confused and chaotic state. Much remained to be done and the harvest was ready and rich, but there were in fact very few workers. There were too few preachers in England, while most of them did not preach but were content to play the role of gentlemen and to do no more than 'chat in company or at dinner about the Gospel' and to raise artful questions. Many

---

[1] Gorham, *Gleanings*, 74: Martyr to Utenhove, Jan. 15, 1549.
[2] *Ibid.* 78–79: Fagius to John Marbach, Apr. 26, 1549.
[3] Robinson, *Original letters*, I, 65–66: Hooper to Bullinger, June 25, 1549.
[4] *Ibid.* II, 469–472: Martyr to Bucer, Dec. 26, 1548; and see *ibid.* 539.

of the clergy of England, in fact, did no more than 'pass the time of day with Christ, his Gospel, and his church'.[1]

Fagius wrote in late July, 1549, when a stubborn revolt, inspired in large part by religious conservatism, was raging unrepressed in the west of England. He wrote, too, in full knowledge that the bishops of England were deeply divided regarding the nature of true faith and worship, while most of the clergy were inert either as a consequence of ignorance or because their instincts were conservative. And he wrote not much more than two months before Somerset was to be stripped of all power and the English Reformation to be set on a more radical course far more pleasing to Zurich and Strassburg.[2] But Somerset's achievement had in fact been greater and more enduring than was immediately apparent. Eschewing force and violence in religious policy, and after deliberately sweeping away the Henrician apparatus of spiritual intimidation, he had in a climate of free discussion and thought brought the church by ordered and cautious stages across the threshold of Protestantism. He and Cranmer had given the church a formulary of worship and faith expressed in great and compelling beauty which, though revised, was in its essentials to serve men and their needs for centuries to come. He had moved with rare and careful moderation in his religious policy: never ahead of powerful resources of sentiment amongst both clergy and laity; never doing great violence to the past, yet moving steadily towards the ultimate and decisive consensus which was the Elizabethan settlement of religion. We can never know the precise moment when England became a Protestant nation, when the course of reformation became irresistibly Protestant, but the time cannot be far off from the passage, after full and free debate, of the first Act of Uniformity. This is not to say that at the time of Somerset's fall from power the majority of Englishmen were Protestants. They almost certainly were not. But a quantitative estimate is in the event almost without either value or meaning. What counted historically was that Protestantism was by this time deeply and inextricably rooted in London and most other urban centres, and that it had come to hold as well the most prosperous, populous, and advanced regions of southern, southeastern, and eastern England. In the more meaningful terms of its qualitative strength, then, England had become Protestant. Or, to put it another way, the gentry and the merchant aristocracy of England—the classes which in Tudor England possessed together

[1] Hollweg, *Bullingers Hausbuch*, 146.
[2] *Zeitschrift f.d. hist. Theologie*, XL (1870), 426–427.

the ultimate resources of power—had at some time in the course of Edward's reign become predominantly and irreversibly Protestant.[1]

---

[1] One rough measurement of the areas in which Protestantism was deeply rooted is provided by an analysis of the place *where* the Marian martyrs suffered, though it must be remarked that the county in which death occurred was not always the county of origin or that in which the mature career took place. But the compelling fact remains that 85 per cent of those who suffered were from eastern and southeastern England. If those put to death in the Bristol–Gloucester area are added, we account for almost exactly 90 per cent of the executions. See Malden, H. E., 'Notes on the local progress of Protestantism in England in the sixteenth and seventeenth centuries', *Royal Hist. Soc. Trans.*, n.s. II (1885), 61–76, for the data.

Professor Dickens has given us a valuable estimate of the strength of Protestant sentiment as revealed by wills proved in the West Riding and in Nottinghamshire, principally ordering the estates of gentry, prosperous yeomen, and clergy. His data suggest that as early as 1545–1546 something like a fourth of such testators were Protestant in sentiment or at least were alienated from the ancient faith, while amongst these same classes during the years 1549–1550 the proportion of those expressing 'new sentiments' in their testaments of faith had risen to two-thirds. (Dickens, *Lollards and Protestants*, 172, 220; Dickens, *English Reformation*, 192.)

XII

THE ADMINISTRATION OF THE REALM UNDER THE DUKE OF SOMERSET

I. ADMINISTRATION BY PROCLAMATION (1547–1553)

Somerset possessed no genius for administration or little interest in the attention to detail and the absorption with routine matters which are the foundations of successful administration. As we have seen, the Privy Council was vested with the burden of these day-to-day decisions during the whole of the Edwardian era and, happily, it contained a core of members who possessed great administrative gifts and to whom Somerset lent full support and, when required, his attention.[1] None the less the Protector kept ultimate power in his own hands, particularly in matters concerned with foreign affairs. The result was that personal decisions were taken by him quite outside the Council Chamber and occasionally without full disclosure to his colleagues. We have already noted too that Somerset was not easy or relaxed in his relations with other men, and complaints, which cannot be discounted, of an increasing imperiousness, of a growing tendency to lash out at colleagues and subordinates, and of a growing aloofness, mark his tenure of power and account, possibly in large part, for his ultimate ruin. Great though his talents were, magnanimous though his spirit surely was, Somerset had few personal friends and these he had lost before the fateful days of October, 1549. None the less, the Privy Council was a mature, a gifted, and a steadily responsible body in its conduct of administration throughout his tenure. It is not too much to say, indeed, that it came of age during the Edwardian interim, when to a degree it was free of the immense personal authority of the Crown which it had known under Henry VIII and free as well of the paralysing factional divisions which so weakened it under Queen Mary.

The day-to-day administration of the realm and the usual means of implementing policy was effected by the promulgation of pro-

[1] *Vide ante*, 78ff.

clamations weighted with the full authority of the King in Council. This authority, this convenient and immediately applicable tool of policy had enjoyed a rapid and an expanding use under Henry VII, who issued on the average 2·4 proclamations in each regnal year, and more particularly under Henry VIII, who issued just under 6 proclamations yearly, dealing with a wide variety of matters. But the great and mature development of proclamations as an instrument of policy occurred under Edward VI when a total of 113 proclamations were issued, or just short of an average of 19 proclamations in each year of this reign. Further, the great bulk (77) of these proclamations date from the period of Somerset's tenure of power, Northumberland being inexplicably cautious in the use of this means of imposing his policy.[1]

The traditional view that limited the effectiveness of royal proclamations to the enforcement of statute law, the clarification of common law, the formal announcement of a royal action, the enforcement of royal rights under feudal contracts, or the temporary regulation of the realm by an authority derived from the prerogative falls far short of the development of this species of royal authority under Henry VIII and even more significantly under Edward VI. Only about a tenth of the proclamations issued had as their purpose the enforcement of existing statutes and not more than a third laid any claim to authority from statute law.[2] The great majority of them, then, created law at least for the time specified and possessed a kind of legislative character which appears in this reign to have been questioned neither by Parliament nor by the courts.

The early Tudor proclamations tend to be mildly apologetic in tone, as indeed did statute law, appealing for their authority (or necessity) to ancient custom, a quite hazy prescription of God's law, to Parliament, or to the prerogative as the basis for the action being taken, while the general good of the realm is almost invariably cited. The responsibility for enforcement was usually lodged in local or county officials, though on occasion the judges, the Star Chamber, or the Council itself might be charged with the administration. The penalties imposed included a variety of sanctions ranging from fines, forfeitures, imprisonment, and corporal punishment, to death in a few cases.[3]

The range of interest and authority assumed by the Council in its drafting of proclamations covered every aspect of governance

---

[1] Fourteen proclamations were issued in 1550, 15 in 1551, 3 in 1552, and 2 in 1553.

[2] Hughes and Larkin, *Tudor proclamations*, I, xxv–xxvi.

[3] *Ibid.* xxviii–xxix.

and administration, save foreign policy and taxation. If we may classify the 113 proclamations issued in the name of Edward VI, the largest number (33) dealt with political and military matters, while 23 were concerned with economic problems and 18 with technical, monetary, and fiscal decisions, usually connected with the metallic content of the coinage. A considerable number (15) were concerned with religious policy, several indeed possessing distinct legislative content without reference either to the Convocation or to Parliament. The remainder dealt with such matters as enclosures (8), details of administration (6), legal administration (5), and social problems, including provisions for public health (5). There is no evidence whatsoever of any timidity in the employment and expansion of royal power by the use of proclamations under the tenure of the Duke of Somerset.

2. CONCERN FOR PUBLIC ORDER (1547–1549)

One tends to forget how really turbulent the English society was in the first half of the sixteenth century. One forgets, too, that there were still men living during the reign of Edward VI whose memories stretched back to the closing days of the War of the Roses. All the Tudors were in consequence almost obsessively concerned with the preservation of public order, with the strait and sometimes brutal repression of the first symptoms of riot and turbulence. Nor is it too much to say that the whole society lent to the Tudor regime such a large measure of obedience and support because it understood that only by the imposition of order could the state be preserved and strengthened. The most recent instance of the ills that flowed from turbulence out of control was the rising in the north which had been stamped out only after Henry VIII had laid the full power of the state against it. During the reign of Edward VI, when the half mystical, half religious aura of the 'person' of the King was weakened because of his youth, when a religious revolution was under cautious but implacable way, when the economy was gravely dislocated by strains and forces not fully understood, this obsessive fear of disorder was so great as to be the constant preoccupation of the Protector and the Council.

In the task of maintaining order and the rule of law, in moving rapidly and effectively against the first appearances of public disorder, the Edwardian Council, like all Tudor Councils, depended heavily and ultimately wholly on the loyalty and local power of the nobility, and, far more importantly, on the gentry. The gentry were accordingly informed of governmental policy and were called upon to give effect to proclamations and more personal orders from the Council, to inform the government of all instances of turbulence and conspiracy which might endanger public order, and to move instantly and on their own authority in the event of public danger. Hence advancements to knighthood were carefully considered and their distribution was made with the needs of the polity clearly in mind. During the first three years of the reign something like 220 men were dubbed as knights, and a brief analysis of the social and professional status of the group tells us something with respect to the administrative policy and preoccupations of the government. Of this number, 33 were nobles or the sons of nobles, while 34 were soldiers or officers of state. Ten were Lord Mayors of London, mayors of provincial cities, or rich London merchants, while 13 were law officers. But the great mass of these men (119) were local landowners with considerable holdings who were drawn almost wholly from families firmly established in either the upper or the lower gentry. The remaining knights, 11 in all, were of unknown or uncertain status before their elevation in dignity.[1] As might be expected, these knights, wielding considerable territorial authority, were heavily concentrated in the northern counties, along the March borders, and in southwestern England.

This obsessive concern with public order animated the whole of the Council, and in the end the Duke of Somerset undoubtedly fell from power because he was unwilling to apply full and ruthless repression against classes of men which in his view had long been wronged by the society. Somerset's weakness was that he was unable to accept easy and almost instinctive answers to problems which he knew were exceedingly complex and because he always shrank from the application of naked power against those who raised such questions. This his most loyal and understanding colleague, Paget, sensed when in late 1548 he wrote a carefully considered critique of Somerset's policy. The Protector had erred in striving to make all men content and in seeking to offend none. In the late reign, surely, 'all things were too straight, and now they are too loose; then was it dangerous to do or speak though the meaning were not evil, and now every man hath liberty to do and speak at liberty'. The frame of the society, Paget seems to be saying, had been dangerously loosened by an over-indulgence and moderation. Hence England lies at peril in her foreign policy, while at home dissensions are 'now at liberty to burst out, which yet before

[1] Cotton MSS., Claudius, C, iii, ff. 151–178, with additions from scattered sources.

was by fear kept in and constrained'. Hence he urged Somerset to
placate the nobility and gentry, to repeal the tax on sheep which had
offended them, and fully to regain their loyalty so that stern and
effective order might be maintained in the realm.[1]

There was substance in Paget's charges, though it must be emphasized that in these years the Council, the courts of law, the
justices of the peace, and the gentry generally carried forward their
tasks of preserving order and repressing even the evidences of turbulence quite as tightly and effectively as they had under Henry VIII.
Thus an analysis of the fifty-six cases pleaded before the Duchy
Court of Lancaster during the reign attests to a steadily watchful
rigour and an extreme sensitivity in cases where public order might
become involved. The Privy Council intervened directly to secure
the appearance of two husbandmen, tenants of Sir Thomas Langton
of Walton-le-Dale, who had refused to serve with him and 'play
the soldiers', despite his command.[2] The largest number of the
cases were concerned, as one would expect, with the possession of
land, 22 dealing with disputed titles, 3 with trespass, 2 with questions of customary rights, and 1 each with prevention of entry and
forcible entry. There were 6 cases concerned with disputed rights
of advowson and patronage, and 2 dealt with disputed title to goods.
Only 5 cases involving alleged assaults, which could easily provoke
disorder, were tried, while still another group of 3 were cases which
might have threatened the peace. That the danger of turbulence was
by no means confined to the commons is suggested by the fact that
well over half of the total number of plaintiffs and defendants were
members of the gentry and of these more than half were of the
upper gentry.

It is amazing how thorough these trials were, how carefully the
evidence was sifted, particularly when land titles or alleged common
rights in land were at issue, for these cases could easily explode into
violence. Thus at Ditton a complaint was lodged in 1548 that the
property of a minor had been acquired illegally by his guardian who
had conspired with 'divers great men' of the county to drive out the
minor owner 'with force of arms and weapons of war' and who still
retained the property.[3] A few months later, great care was taken in
determining a long and festering dispute between one Robert
Holte, the plaintiff, and certain tenants of the Earl of Derby respect-

[1] Gammon, *Master of practises*, 218–219, citing Fitzwilliam MSS. (Northampton
Record Soc.), 'Ntht., Paget Ltr. Book', 8.
[2] *Pleadings and depositions in the Duchy Court of Lancaster, etc.*, ed. by Henry Fish-
wick (Record Soc. for Lancashire and Cheshire, XL, 1899), 89–90.
[3] *Ibid.* 37.

ing the use of common lands. A royal commission was issued to four justices, three being knights, which twice viewed the land, called the contending parties before it, and examined fifty-three of the older inhabitants of the neighbourhood regarding the facts and, more importantly, the customs with respect to the land in question. Very elaborate, detailed, and conflicting evidence was given respecting the rights of the two parties, while the central question of where the true boundary lay dissolved into a watery confusion because the commissioners could not locate certain tiny streams which ran, or had run, only in extremely wet weather. We do not know what the commission's findings were, but tempers had been cooled, every partisan had had his say, and the justices evidently intended to base their decision squarely on the testimony of the community at large.[1] This and other cases in Lancashire suggest the great care and vigilance taken in the courts of law with all cases that verged on possible turbulence.[2]

To mention, almost at random, a few additional instances of the concern of the central government with such cases, we may note Thomas Seymour's report to Somerset that he had apprehended in the west two Welshmen who had been counterfeiters of coin.[3] At about the same time thirteen persons were tried and fined in Sussex for playing football, always disliked by the Tudors because of the riots in which the games often ended.[4] And in the event of really serious threats to order, direct action was often taken by hiring informers, as when Sir George Harper was sent into Kent in July, 1549, with about £30 to reward informers and to bring in for interrogation by the Council divers suspected persons from Kent and other disturbed counties.[5] The constant vigilance of the Council and of the justices may also be studied in the pardon lists of the Patent Rolls, where, in addition to persons freed from the penalties for a long and sometimes gruesome list of offences, one notes five offenders pardoned for unspecified 'treasons, conspiracies, felonies etc.', one for piracy, another for treasonable words against the royal supremacy, and numerous pardons for counterfeiting.[6]

The Council could be very exacting in its demands for thorough and prompt local action against disturbances or what it tended to

---

[1] *Pleadings in the Duchy Court* (Rec. Soc. for Lancs. and Cheshire, XL), 52–53.
[2] *Ibid.* 94, for another interesting instance.
[3] S.P. Dom., Edw. VI, IV, 46: Aug. 19, 1548.
[4] VCH, *Sussex*, II, 197, citing Ct. R. (PRO), bundle 205, #13.
[5] *A.P.C.* II, 299, 303: July 10 and 25, 1549.
[6] *Cal. Pat. Rolls, Edw. VI*, I, 298, 304, 320; *ibid.* II, 2, 4, 5–6, 244, 246; *ibid.* III, 178; *ibid.* IV, 111, 311, 326; *ibid.* V, 28, 253–254 (the last group being counterfeiting cases).

describe as 'malicious rumors', especially when it was somewhat uncertain of the true nature of the reported offence. In May, 1547, it somewhat brusquely reproved Holgate and the Council of the North for not moving against certain persons in York whom it believed to have used 'very slanderous and naughty words against us' with a seditious intent. They marvelled that they had had no word from the Archbishop concerning these offences and instructed him to proceed with condign punishment against these persons.[1] Some months later the Council brought direct and severe pressures on the cathedral authorities in Exeter to lend full support to the mayor, who was seeking to repress disorder, and to find those who had scattered seditious handbills in the streets.[2] The central government greatly feared such incendiary propaganda, particularly during the frightening days of 1549 when on April 15th it issued a proclamation prohibiting the spreading of scandalous and false rumours regarding the Council, and required the justices to apprehend such inciters, who if found guilty were to be condemned to the galleys.[3] In early July it again sought by proclamation to control or prevent the movement from county to county of vagrants, deserters, and other 'lewd' people who 'stir up rumors, raise up tales, imagine news' and generally disturb the peace and order of the kingdom.[4]

The Council also took most seriously religious brawls and rumours which might precipitate disturbances. Sometimes this preoccupation could seem petty indeed, as in the case of William Croom [or Orran], vicar of Weston in Soyland (near Bridgwater), when they called upon a nearby justice to investigate certain books of prophecy and a parchment roll of English kings since the fall of Troy. The surely bewildered justice (Sir Thomas Dyer) reported that he was sending up the roll but could find no book of prophecies.[5] A few weeks later the Council sought by proclamation to quiet rumours being spread abroad of intended changes in religion and in the ceremonies of the church, which it feared were harmful to civil as well as religious quiet.[6] Such rumours and evidences of religious disquiet reached the Council in a variety of ways, but normally were reported to it, after a preliminary sifting, by the justices of the peace, who bore such a heavy responsibility for public order. Thus when the Prayer Book was introduced, there was a minor disturbance at Glapthorne

[1] Pocock, in *E.H.R.* IX (1894), 542–548.

[2] *A.P.C.* II, App., 534, 538–539: Nov. 26, 1547, and Jan. 3, 1548.

[3] *A proclamation for tale bearers* (April 29, 1549).

[4] Hughes and Larkin, *Tudor proclamations*, I, 469–470: July 8, 1549.

[5] *A.P.C.* II, App., 451, 458: Mar. 10 and 21, 1547.

[6] Hughes and Larkin, *Tudor proclamations*, I, 387–389: May 24, 1547.

(Northants) which the merchant John Johnson reported to the manorial lord, Sir Thomas Brudenell, who in turn laid the facts directly before the Privy Council. Somerset personally read over the reports on the incident, commending both Johnson and Brudenell for their quick and prudent handling of the matter, while instructing the latter to go to Glapthorne to investigate and to commit the ringleaders to prison 'until they be taught to study and apply to quietness and godliness, for such is the obstinacy of many people that without sharpness they will not amend'.[1]

Evidences of serious and fairly widespread civil disquiet appeared in 1548, as a kind of muted prelude to the hot rebellions a year later. This unsettlement was compounded both of religious conservatism and of disquiet provoked by the proclamation of June 1st which promised a thorough inquiry into illegal enclosures and implied that their reformation was at hand.[2] The proclamation promised more of reform than could quickly be accomplished and raised hopes which could not immediately be fulfilled. The Council was seeking—or, more accurately, Somerset was compelling it to seek—to cure disaffection by moderate courses, having some days earlier issued a general pardon to those being held for rebellion in Cornwall in the last months of Henry VIII's reign, save for about thirty ringleaders.[3] The county was in fact still seriously unsettled and this magnanimous act of mercy was probably premature. Even as it was being issued a minor stir occurred amongst the commons of Somerset, which was quickly quieted. There was also a commotion of some sort at Harnham Hill (near Salisbury), while the recently created park enclosures of Lord Stourton and Sir William Herbert were thrown down, which Herbert handled on his own authority when he 'slew and executed many of those rebels'.[4]

Now thoroughly alarmed the Council strictly enjoined sheriffs and justices throughout the realm to man the beacons and to act at once in putting down all unlawful assemblies.[5] Commissioners representing the central government were likewise dispatched into the more restive counties to pacify the commons and to act with full authority if the need should arise. The report of the commissioners sent into Kent, headed by Sir Edward Wotton, twice in earlier years sheriff of the county, is doubtless typical. His journey, Wotton said, would have been in vain had not the King of Arms, in his gorgeous

---

[1] As quoted in Winchester, Barbara, *Tudor family portrait* (L., [1955]), 201.
[2] Hughes and Larkin, *Tudor proclamations*, I, 427–429.
[3] *Ibid.* 425–427: May 17, 1548.   [4] Nichols, *Remains*, II, 225.
[5] S.P. Dom., Edw. VI, IV, 10: May ?, 1548.

and august accoutrements, preceded him into Kent, for on the
first day the commons were rude even to this personification of royal
power. The commissioners had broken up assemblies by their
assurances and had used between £80 and £100 in gifts to poor men
for their journey home. They recommended most sensible conciliatory courses, such as granting a general pardon, giving greater
circulation to the recent proclamation against rumours and tale-
bearing, considering certain grounds of complaint as a petition to
the King, and relieving pressure by recruiting, with conduct money,
those who should better vent their aggressive spirit by service in
Scotland or in Boulogne.[1] Later in the summer a riot occurred at
Enfield against the property of Sir Thomas Wroth, who had for
years been chosen almost automatically as a member of parliament
for Middlesex. This too was skilfully handled when it was determined that the issues in dispute had already been settled by a decree
of the Duchy of Lancaster, four of the rioters being committed to
prison by the Council for a brief season and six more bound over to
good behaviour.[2] The Council likewise dealt directly with a small
stir which occurred in Hampshire, in the region of Botley and
Hamble, when eighteen men were after examination pardoned for
sundry 'treasons, conspiracies, riots, etc.', and their forfeited goods
returned. It is instructive to note that all these rioters were of lowly
social status, thirteen being labourers or husbandmen, and the
remaining miscreants being of equally simple occupations.[3] Thus
the stirs of 1548 had been handled moderately, effectively, and
quickly by the Council and its delegates. And the cases had been
settled, usually in the county where the disturbances had occurred—
the list of prisoners in the Tower, probably prepared in late 1548,
including no offender remaining to be tried for serious offences
against the state.[4] No one in a responsible position in the Edwardian
government, save for the always dour Paget, could possibly have
been prepared for the savage rebellions that broke out in 1549.

3. CONCERN FOR THE SOCIETY (1547–1550)

Like all Tudor governments the Edwardian Privy Council,
especially as inspired by Somerset, was also deeply concerned with
the health and well-being of the society which it ruled. But the

---

[1] HMC, *Salisbury MSS.* I, 54: July 18, 1548.   [2] *A.P.C.* II, 219: Aug. 27, 1548.
[3] *Cal. Pat. Rolls, Edw. VI*, I, 292: Dec. 20, 1548.
[4] S.P. Dom., Edw. VI, V, 10. The list may be dated between December, 1548, and
Whitsun, 1549.

Edwardian intervention to secure what was deemed to be the social good of the realm differs somewhat in that it seems animated more nearly by a moral than by a political purpose. From the wealth of material available only a relatively small sample need be examined of those often quixotic interventions. In the commission granted Sir Richard Sackville as Chancellor of the Court of Augmentations, he was instructed to 'take order for the manumission of villeins'—a reminder that, statute law notwithstanding, there were in various nooks and crannies of the realm men who were technically of unfree status.[1] The amenities of London were enhanced when a cautious licence was issued to one John Dove, a London clothworker, to open 'a tennis play . . . for the recreation of gentlemen, merchants, . . . strangers, and other honest persons'—apprentices, with their justly deserved riotous reputation, alone excepted. This was augmented a few weeks later by two additional licences, one of which also permitted public bowling.[2] Somewhat earlier one of several efforts really to wipe out prostitution in London and its suburbs was made when orders were issued to drive the whores out of the City, while one notorious prostitute with the unforgettable name of 'Founsing Besse' was exhibited through the streets, had her hair cropped, and was pilloried as an example.[3] So too there were persistent, and equally unsuccessful, efforts to control the gypsies, who were feared as vagrants, by inhibiting their incessant movement and by deporting certain of them from Dover to unnamed foreign ports.[4]

Commendable, if sometimes eccentric, efforts to improve the society and to advance knowledge, were also attempted by direct state intervention. In 1550 one Otwell Hollinshed, who employed, it was said, a method of teaching youth which the King thought peculiarly effective, was granted a non-residential canonry and prebendary at Windsor for his support.[5] So too, a physician, Humphrey Cotton, who by long study of his art had learned how 'to cure and heal any [of] our subjects' suffering from divers diseases by the use of baths in Bath, was named keeper of the baths there, one of which should always be free of charge.[6] As an aid to the advancement of knowledge the Dutch publisher, Laurence Torrentinus, employed by the Medici to assemble and print the digests of Roman law, whose work was in press, was by royal order

---

[1] S.P. Dom., Edw. VI, IV, 48: Aug. 24, 1548.
[2] *Cal. Pat. Rolls, Edw. VI*, III, 163, 403; *ibid.* IV, 197; *ibid.* V, 254.
[3] Wriothesley, *Chronicle*, II (Camden Soc., n.s. XX), 4.
[4] *A.P.C.* II, App., 448, 452.   [5] *Cal. Pat. Rolls, Edw. VI*, III, 299,
[6] *Ibid.* III, 309.

given exclusive rights of publication and sale in England for a term
of seven years.[1] So too, the Italian physician Nicholas Encolii was
awarded an annuity of £10 because of his great skill in dissection
and was granted liberty to take the bodies of those hanged for crimes
in Middlesex, Sussex, and Essex in order to teach the art of dissection.[2] The King's love of learning, it was declared, was also
exhibited by the announcement that he had determined to stock his
library at Westminster 'with notable books to be kept there conveniently to his use'. Bartholomew Traheron was appointed keeper
of the collection and was empowered to gather books from the
King's other libraries, provided it be done 'sine alterius damno'.[3]
Fragmentary and necessarily limited as these instances may be, they
may be taken as a fair sample of the steady concern of the central
government with the state of the society and its advancement.

4. REFORM OF ADMINISTRATION (1547-1549)

Some measure of concern was likewise displayed by the Protector's government for administrative reform, or more accurately
for the completion of reforms under way at the time of the late
King's death. Towards the end of 1545 a commission had been
named to study the work of the Court of Augmentations, charged
principally with the administration of the vast monastic properties
expropriated by the Crown, while in the spring of 1546 a larger
commission with expanded instructions was established to review
the work of all the revenue agencies, to recommend reorganization
if needed, and to call in the King's debts. It was speedily apparent
that considerable laxity had overcome both Augmentations and the
Court of General Surveyors, the latter body being responsible for
the administration of the older crown lands. Accordingly in late
1546 the commission concluded that the two courts should be
merged in order to reduce expense, to avoid overlapping, and to
permit tighter auditing and administrative controls. The enabling
legislation had not been passed at the time of Henry's death, but was
enacted by 1 Edward VI, c. 8. The merged court was modelled on
Augmentations, and there was immediately an expansion of field
officials in every county charged with responsibility for all royal
revenues, stricter accounting and control of funds was instituted,

[1] *Cal. Pat. Rolls, Edw. VI*, IV, 106-107. He was a native of Brabant (Hoogewerff,
G. J., 'Laurentius Torrentinus, etc.', *Het Boek*, ser. 2, XV (1926), 273-288, 369-381).
[2] *Cal. Pat. Rolls, Edw. VI*, IV, 261-262.
[3] *Ibid.* III, 74-75.

and centralized authority was vested in the Chancellor.[1] Though only
two of the six revenue courts had been consolidated, they were by
far the most important and came quickly to be regarded in the
merged form as the principal national treasury.[2]

But in the early years of Edward VI, as in the late years of his
father, there remained an absence of close and consistent control
over the court and its functions, with the consequence of inevitable
irregularities, minor frauds, and a leisurely sort of inefficiency. Most
of the difficulty sprang from the fact that for many years officials
charged with the flow of revenue to the Crown were often unwary
enough to indulge in the dangerous practice of using or investing
such sums as were in hand until an approaching audit forced restitution. As we shall note in later pages, those who undertook such
risks were subject to extremely heavy fines, though such offences
were regarded by contemporaries rather more as laxities than as
criminal actions. Fortunately, in Sir Walter Mildmay, Surveyor-
General of the Court of Augmentations, the Crown possessed a
civil servant of complete integrity and great administrative gifts,
who was the driving force for the ambitious reforms undertaken towards the close of the reign. The central problem lay in the administration and sale of crown lands, now greatly increased by the
expropriation of the chantry properties. Better control and audit of
these revenues were established by the appointment of a commission
of seven members, including Mildmay and his brother, Thomas, as
well as the Lord Chamberlain and the Comptroller. They were to
review the letters patent in relation to past as well as current sales
and exchanges of crown lands in order to make certain that the King
had received the full economic value as measured by a capital worth
of twenty times the income.[3]

5. THE COURT OF REQUESTS (1547–1553)

One of the most vehement of the charges brought against Somerset was that he had arrogantly and presumptuously dispensed what
can only be described as royal justice on his own authority and that
he had subverted the Court of Requests to his own purposes, hearing
cases laid before it in the privacy of his own house. As was the case
with most of the reckless and vindictive charges ultimately lodged
against the Protector by Dudley and his followers, there was in

[1] Richardson, W. C., *History of the Court of Augmentations, 1536–1554* (Baton Rouge,
La., 1961), 123–153, on which this paragraph principally rests.   [2] *Ibid.* 160.
[3] S.P. Dom., Edw. VI, II, 30. The document is not dated.

point of fact not much more than a shadowy substance in the allegation. What might have been argued was that during the years when
he was possessed of power he had lent encouragement to the
functioning of the court, had steadily referred cases to it, and had
advanced its reputation as a poor man's court in which cheap, quick,
and summary justice might be found.

Even though the court was of relatively recent origin, its history
and its evolution were quite evidently as shrouded in uncertainty in
the mid-sixteenth century as today. Its authority was conceived as
deriving from the power of dispensing justice inherent in the person
of the king, in a somewhat more immediate and far more personal
sense than was the case for his other courts. In any clear and recog-
nizable form the court cannot be traced back of 1483 when a clerk
of the 'counsell', or court hearing request cases, may have been
appointed, the jurisdiction being denounced in Henry VII's first
parliament, which was rooting out all the Ricardian innovations. In
1493 the jurisdiction of the court was quietly restored by the King,
the court dealing with civil causes in somewhat the same manner as
the refurbished Court of Star Chamber concerned itself with criminal
cases. The court never gained statutory recognition and for some
time seems to have been regarded as a committee of the Council
acting with some informality for the king in the disposition of cases
involving legitimate grievances. It was more formally constituted in
1529 and for the remainder of Henry VIII's reign regarded itself as
a 'poor man's court' in which the litigant could 'have right without
paying any money'.[1]

The court was undoubtedly very active during Somerset's
regime, and after his fall was more carefully defined and its jurisdiction regularized by a royal commission composed of Bedford,
Darcy, Lord Cobham, Ridley, Sir John Mason, Hoby, and two
Masters of Requests, John Lucas and John Cook. This the Council
declared it must do because of 'the great number of suits and requests which be daylie exhibited unto us', which distracted the
Council from 'the great and weighty causes of our estate royal'.
Thereafter the work of the court was to be delegated to the commission, while all private suits 'custumably brought' to the King
or Council were automatically to be referred to the court. It was
further ordered that 'the obstinate and shameless haunters of the
court be banished', while the flow of its business was to be hastened

[1] Pollard, A. F., 'The growth of the Court of Requests', E.H.R. LVI (1941), 301–303;
Leadam, I. S., ed., Select cases in the Court of Requests, A.D. 1497–1569 (Selden Soc.,
XII, L., 1898), x–xiv.

by the appointment of six assistants to aid the masters. The heavy backlog of unheard cases was to be reduced by constant meetings before the customary weekly hearings were resumed, while cases that might be tried before Chancery or by special commissions in the counties were to be referred.[1]

It is undoubtedly true that Somerset looked upon the Court of Requests as a needed and effective court of summary equity and as an important counterpoise of justice for the poor against the mighty. Though Paget warned him that the practice caused great resentment in the Council, he also on rare occasions undoubtedly heard cases privately, thereby reviving a 'royal practice' which had been wholly abandoned a generation earlier. Perhaps even more resented was Somerset's tendency personally to intervene in cases and to render what really amounted to equity judgements quite outside the Court. Probably very early in the reign a petition was lodged with him by Henry Pony, of Smithfield, for the restoration of his brewhouse illegally withheld by one Alice Dacres.[2] In another case he more circumspectly forwarded a petition to the Court, asking that justice be done without any further recourse to him.[3] Nor did Somerset hesitate in the least to offend the powerful, as is witnessed by a brusque letter to Lord Cobham commanding him to cure the complaints of a poor woman against him respecting certain rents. Even though Cobham had proposed a compromise solution through Cecil, the complainant still maintained that Cobham 'did her extreme wrong, being known to all the country', and Somerset had accordingly appointed two referees to investigate the case.[4] With a similar intemperance he called upon Sir William Fermor to assure him of his innocence on a complaint that Fermor unjustly exacted money from the suitor.[5]

In cases more formally lodged with the Court of Requests there is also some evidence not only of Somerset's interest but of actual intervention, though one observes nothing whatsoever of an overweening influence on the masters. In several cases the petitioner addressed his bill directly to Somerset rather than to the King, one case being against a peer and another brought by a village protesting an enclosure. One petitioner refers to Somerset's 'accustomed goodness', and still other bills were addressed to the Protector and

[1] S.P. Dom., Edw. VI, XVIII, 12; Leadam, *Select cases* (Selden Soc., XII), lxxxix–xciii.   [2] S.P. Dom., Edw. VI, II, 26.

[3] Lansdowne MS. 2, #23: Mar. 11, 1548; printed in Ellis, *Original letters*, ser. 3, III, 301–302.   [4] Tytler, *England*, I, 75: Feb. 19, 1548.

[5] HMC, *11th rpt.*, App. VII: *Le Strange papers*, 95: Oct. 4, 1549.

Council. But these instances surely prove nothing more than the comparative informality of the proceedings and the legal naiveté of the petitioners, and all were simply endorsed over to the Court for consideration. Far more important are the occasional cases when it is evident that the Duke was following the action and had written to the defendants ordering them to satisfy the plaintiffs.[1] Some intervention, then, there certainly was, and there almost had to be in a prerogative court from one who held sovereign power. As much as his colleagues seem to have resented Somerset's involvement with Requests, the Council did not hesitate to follow the same practice on occasion long after his fall from power. Thus in March, 1552, they ordered the Court to review the evidence in an old case of counterfeiting and to proceed against the offenders, while in the next year they asked for a judgement in a debt case in order to satisfy the representations of the imperial ambassador.[2]

The procedure of the Court of Requests in this period was not dissimilar to that in the other equity courts. Cases were instituted by petition, cast in legal form and usually signed by a lawyer, and normally addressed to the Crown. The substance of the complaint was set out in detail and it was stated that there was no remedy in common law, that the plaintiff could not afford 'the long track of the common law', or that he could not find remedy in his manorial court. A 'request' was then made for the appearance of the defendant before the court, stress usually being laid on the poverty and humble status of the plaintiff as contrasted with that of the defendant. No case already lost in another court or under consideration in another jurisdiction was accepted. Plaintiffs were in theory, and usually in fact, poor men and women, or royal servants attending the sovereign.

The defendant filed an 'answer' to the complaint, almost invariably urging that the case be heard in a common law or manorial court, followed by specific denial of each of the allegations in the 'request'. If the case was admitted to trial, a writ under the privy seal was issued demanding the presence of the defendant before the Court. If the summons were ignored, a writ of attachment for contempt was issued to the sheriff who could proclaim the defendant a rebel and seize his goods.[3] In this period, as contrasted with the Elizabethan, personal appearance rather than representation by counsel seems normally to have been required unless illness or

[1] As examples: Req. 2/14/32, 2/14/135. Some reference is made to Somerset in a much larger number of cases. As examples: Req. 2/15/88, 2/16/9, 2/17/24, 2/17/79, 2/18/73, 2/18/114.

[2] Lansdowne MS. 160, #87, ff. 283b, 284.   [3] As in Req. 2/15/73.

infirmity of age could be affirmed. Commissions in distant counties, usually composed of justices of the peace, were frequently established either to try cases locally and settle them *in situ* or to take evidence, though the commissions normally required that the case with all the evidence be sent back to Westminster for judgement. The rules of evidence employed by the Court were very broad and informal, private letters, deeds, wills, leases, and other documents being admitted.[1] The Court undoubtedly fulfilled its purpose of offering cheap, quick, and roughly hewn justice to the poor (and sometimes the cantakerous) against the powerful, which of course explains the keen resentment against the Protector for his deep interest in the Court. Among the rich and mighty haled before it were Lord Russell, Sir Humphrey Browne, a judge, Lords Wentworth, Scrope, Sandys, William, Lord Howard, Thomas, Lord Howard, the Countess of Oxford, Sir Francis Leek, and three bishops.

In all, the number of cases tried in the Court of Requests in the Edwardian period totalled about 750, for which the materials are fairly full save for the fact that the verdicts are rarely to be found except in the last years of the reign.[2] On the basis of a random sampling, something like 60 per cent of all the cases tried involve disputes regarding land tenure; upwards of 10 per cent have to do with bonds and contract, and the remainder principally with illegal enclosures, claims with respect to common lands and rents. A brief analysis of a representative group of the cases will perhaps suffice to give some impression of the remarkable range of the pleadings.

In 1547 a plaintiff sued respecting lands which he held in Hertfordshire from the Earl of Shrewsbury, asking that the case be tried by a commission of gentlemen of the shire, since he could not secure a fair hearing in the manorial court.[3] A case involving a claim of stolen goods in Kent, in which wildly contradictory evidence was presented by the opposing parties, had been transferred to Requests by the probably despairing common law courts and was sent back to Kent by Requests to be arbitrated and settled by named local commissioners.[4] Crouchman *v.* Tuke is interesting in that it displays one of Somerset's direct interventions. Crouchman, a London mercer, had lent 100 marks to Charles Tuke who had died, and the claim was lodged against his brother and administrator, George

---

[1] Req. 2/14/14; 2/14/135; 2/15/121; 2/17/58.

[2] Req. 1/9. Leadam has printed two of the cases for this reign (*Select cases*, Selden Soc. XII, 189–195). The cases are to be found in the PRO: Req. 2, Bundles 14–19, and Req. 1/8, 1/9, for the orders and decrees of the court.

[3] Req. 2/14/2: Christopher Hall *v.* John Dean.

[4] Req. 2/14/14: Emma Coveney *v.* Edward Knight and Peter Maplendon.

Tuke. The petition suggests that Somerset had been approached and had ordered the return of the money, which Tuke refused to do. The case was then referred to Sir William Petre and Sir Thomas Smith who could not prevail on Tuke to settle, his claim being that his brother's small estate could not meet both a debt to the Crown and the amount that had been borrowed. The case dragged on for years, for as late as 1552 Requests ordered Tuke to pay the costs thus far sustained by Crouchman and deplored the subtle and obdurate delays of George Tuke.[1]

A few fairly typical cases involving land tenure may be cited, since such litigation occupied so large a proportion of the docket of the Court. In 1 Edward VI Halom lodged a complaint against Cornwall and Zouche, the plaintiff being a tenant of land in Essex on which he paid rent to Cornwall. Zouche had established title to the land in question and now demanded arrears from Halom. When Halom refused to pay, Zouche had seized farm animals from him to the value of the claim, for which Halom had sued him at common law. Zouche, before the Court of Requests, argued that Halom's claim lay against Cornwall who had not enjoyed title to the land.[2] A case involving a claim to copyhold land was referred to local commissioners who certified that the claim was indeed confirmed by the court roll, to which the defendant offered no defence at all, accepting the judgement of the Court.[3] Among several suits prosecuted by quite humble tenants against the mighty during this period may be mentioned Thomas Collett's suit against Lord Windsor, contending, apparently correctly, that Windsor was illegally in possession of his land, and was despoiling it, Windsor being brought before the Council in the course of the proceedings.[4]

The extraordinary variety of the cases brought before the Court of Requests may perhaps be suggested by a few further examples. In 4 Edward VI Henry Forest sued the formidable Sir Ralph Bulmer for his fee of £10 as a surgeon, having, he contended, cured Bulmer's wife of a disease of the mouth described as *morbus Gallicus*, the case hinging on whether Lady Bulmer had or had not been cured.[5] An apprentice was sued by two London merchants for theft of their goods in Antwerp. The court in this case rejected out of hand the defence contention that it did not possess jurisdiction. The defendant had in fact been brought back from Antwerp for trial, was in the Fleet, and the principal evidence was a letter from Sir Thomas

---

[1] Req. 2/14/32: John Crouchman v. George Tuke; Req. 1/9/59.   [2] Req. 2/14/43.
[3] Req. 2/14/68: William and Matthew Bosset v. Christopher Stenham.
[4] Req. 2/15/24.   [5] Req. 2/15/113.

Chamberlain, then governor of the Merchant Adventurers, setting out the facts.[1] William, Lord Howard, found himself before the Court for refusing to pay for clothing and daggers to the value of £20 purchased from the late husband of Katherine Philips. Howard first argued that the Court had no jurisdiction in the case, but then shifted his defence to the contention that he had in fact paid but had lost the receipt. His defence was not accepted and he was ordered by the Court to pay £12 in settlement of the claim.[2] In one of several enclosure cases, the inhabitants of Middleton, Norfolk, presented impressive and sufficient evidence against Osbert Moundeford and Anthony Gibbon that the common lands of the village had been enclosed, many witnesses attesting to the fact that the commons had always been open.[3]

The impression one has in leafing through these cases is that justice was being done, that wrongs inflicted by the powerful against the weak were being righted, and that no case was too small or trifling to engage the full attention of the masters. Somerset was undoubtedly interested in the work of the Court and certainly regarded it as one of the instrumentalities of his social policy. In so far as the formal record shows, his interventions were wholly proper and correct, cases often being referred to the Court after he or other members of the Council had failed in a rough attempt at arbitration. What remains unclear is why most of the cases found their way to Requests rather than to the common law courts or to Chancery, which the usually far richer and more powerful defendants would certainly have preferred. The answer doubtless is that this was the way Somerset wanted such cases tried; he wished a plenary court of equity near at hand to which cases usually involving a quite clear wrong could be referred by the Council. The Court of Requests fitted admirably and constructively into the structure of the social policy to which he was now fully committed.

6. THE NORTHAMPTON CASE (1548–1552)

The moral tone which Somerset was seeking to establish in the governance of England was rudely shaken by a singularly tawdry and vexatious divorce case involving William Parr, a member of the Privy Council, who had been created Marquis of Northampton in the first wholesale bestowal of honours that marked the settlement

---

[1] Req. 2/17/24: Richard Buttell and John Nottyng v. Henry Wyndbourne.
[2] Req. 2/18/73: Katherine Philips v. William, Lord Howard; and Sir Julius Caesar's notes in the case on Lansdowne MS. 125, f. 124.   [3] Req. 2/18/114.

in power of the new government. Parr had held minor official posts under Henry VIII, but was not raised to a position of eminence until 1543, when he was made a privy councillor, following the marriage of his sister Catherine to the King. He was at the beginning a partisan of Somerset's, had been named an assistant executor of the late King's will, and was called to the newly constituted Privy Council in March, 1547.

Northampton had in 1541 married Ann Bourchier, the daughter of Henry, second Earl of Essex, a notable advancement in status for him, since his posts in that year comprised no more than the keepership of a royal park and the stewardship of the manor of Writtle in Essex. He was early separated from his wife against whom he assembled strong proofs of infidelity and adultery. He had made tentative moves towards procuring a divorce late in the reign of Henry VIII, but it was not until the first year of Edward's reign that he petitioned the King for the appointment of a commission of learned men to determine whether he might marry again, his first wife being still alive.[1] In May, 1547, the appeal was taken up by a commission of nine, in which Cranmer, Ridley, and Holbeach were the dominant members. Cranmer took the view that the whole law of marriage was at issue in the case, refusing to proceed despite Northampton's mounting impatience, while a truly vast collection of digests of the works of the fathers and doctors was assembled for the guidance of the commission.[2] Cranmer was also undoubtedly fearful that an easy divorce for so conspicuous a subject would be unsettling in England and would certainly loose the barbed assaults of the Catholics both at home and abroad.

Further, there was known to be a woman in the case, Northampton not deigning to conceal the fact that he wished to marry Elizabeth Brooke, a daughter of Lord Cobham. His patience exhausted by the commission's leisurely investigation, Northampton presented the government and the church with an accomplished fact by secretly marrying her. When this came to the attention of the Council in January, 1548, he was haled before it and admitted the facts, his defence being that his action was in accord with the Word of God, since his first wife was a proved adulteress. The Council, under Somerset's dominance, took the view that to ignore the contempt would 'breed manifold disorders and inconveniences within the realm', and commanded Northampton under pain to separate him-

---

[1] S.P. Dom., Edw. VI, II, 32.
[2] In Lambeth MS. 1108, ff. 144-161, 180, following Burnet, *Reformation*, II, 118–122, and *ibid.* V, 183–184.

self from his second wife and to live apart from her until the case had
been adjudicated by the commission.[1] At the same time, Elizabeth
Brooke was placed in the chaperonage of the Queen Dowager,
Northampton's sister, while the commission, now under heavy
pressure from all sides, at last bestirred itself to make a decision. The
commission's finding was that Scripture clearly held that proved
adultery dissolved a marriage and permitted a re-marriage by the
aggrieved party, though patristic opinion was divided on the issue,
the older fathers inclining to the permission of a divorce in such
cases. The commission's decision, Burnet says, was then laid before
a group of unnamed learned men who also favoured the legalizing
of Northampton's second marriage.[2] Northampton's legal position
in the matter was further buttressed when he secured the passage in
1548 of a private bill in Parliament making any children of the
first marriage illegitimate and of a further act in 1552 which declared the second marriage to be legal.[3] This tangled and unhappy
case alienated Northampton irrevocably from Somerset, one of
whose most bitter enemies he became, and likewise was a factor in
precipitating a really careful and needed review of the law of marriage
to which we will later lend our attention.

[1] A.P.C. II, 164–165: Jan. 28, 1548.
[2] Burnet, Reformation, II, 122; ibid. V, 183–184, for the particulars.
[3] Repealed by one of the first acts of Queen Mary's Parliament. Fortunately, there
were no children by either marriage.

XIII

TREASON AT THE CENTRE OF POWER

I. THE CASE OF THOMAS SEYMOUR (1547–1549)

The first serious fracture in the authority and power of the Lord
Protector came as the consequence of the tangled and muddled
intrigues of his younger brother, Thomas, which taken in their
entirety undoubtedly constituted high treason and were so punished.
Born almost certainly in 1508 Thomas was a few years younger than
his steadier and far more gifted brother, against whom well before
the Edwardian era he exhibited some measure of resentment.
Seymour was employed in rather lowly capacities in the service of
the Crown until in 1536 the marriage of his sister to the King
opened wide the door of preferment. He was speedily granted
considerable estates, after minor diplomatic experience was made a
gentleman of the privy chamber, and in 1537 was knighted. In the
next year the sagacious and ambitious Duke of Norfolk, sensing
that this was a career on which heavy stakes could be laid, suggested
a marriage with his only daughter, the widow of the Duke of Richmond, which was however bitterly and successfully opposed by the
Duke's son, the Earl of Surrey, who detested Seymour as a *parvenu*.
Some years later, on the death of Lord Latimer, Seymour pressed his
suit for the hand of his widow, Catherine Parr, who undoubtedly
would have married him had not the King himself discovered her
abilities and attractions. Seymour from 1538 onwards was almost
constantly employed as a favoured royal servant. He was a junior
member of the embassy dispatched to France in that year, was in the
train of Anne of Cleves as she proceeded from Calais to England,
and served with credit in the war with France. In October, 1544,
Seymour was appointed Admiral of the Fleet, in command of the
squadron screening the southern coast and the Channel against
French attacks, while in the last weeks of Henry's life he was
sworn of the Privy Council.

Seymour was treated with great indulgence by his older brother
in the first months of the new reign. Named an assistant executor in
Henry's will, he was in rapid succession created Baron Sudeley,

appointed once more to the great post of Lord Admiral,[1] and by the first patent of the new reign was named to the Privy Council. But from the beginning he remained savagely jealous of his brother's pre-eminence in the affairs of state, exhibiting, so Sharington was later to testify, great bitterness that he too was not given a special place in 'the parliament house as one of the king his uncles'. From the beginning, too, he was guilty of shocking neglect of his duties as Lord Admiral, refusing to command the fleet in the carefully co-ordinated land and sea assault on Scotland in 1547, and again, in 1548, appointing Clinton in his stead, while he remained at his new seat at Sudeley and in London, nursing his grievances and spinning out his intrigues.[2] He likewise bent to his own purposes the widespread privateering which, once established during the recent French war, could not be rooted out from the southern and western coasts save by the determined efforts of the navy to execute the firm and clear orders from the Council.[3] Instead, Seymour entered into secret pacts with the piratical leaders, and in particular with the notorious Thompson of Calais, under which he received a proportion of the loot and protected pirates taken before the Admiralty Court. Having bought Scilly, Sudeley established there a haven for the piracy which the government was trying desperately to stamp out because of angry and wholly justified complaints from France, the Empire, the Hanse, and English merchants against whom retaliatory measures were being taken.[4]

Early in the reign, too, he had sounded at least some of the Council, and according to the later testimony of John Fowler, a gentleman of the household, the King himself, on the possibility of taking as his wife Anne of Cleves, the Princess Mary, or the Princess Elizabeth, thereby vaulting in one step to greatness of power and status, though he seems to have been warned against this dangerous course and is reported to have concluded, 'I love not to lose my life for a wife. It has been spoken of, but it cannot be'.[5]

These most tentative inquiries proving bootless, Seymour addressed himself with great ardour and secrecy to the courtship of the Queen, with whom, as we have seen, there had been an earlier

---

[1] Rymer, *Foedera*, XV, 127–129: Feb. 17, 1548, for his commission.

[2] Froude, *History of England*, V, 131.

[3] *A.P.C.* II, 130–131: Sept. 25, 1547, ordering every ship putting out to sea to bear the Admiral's licence.

[4] S.P. Dom., Edw. VI, I, 37: Apr. 20, 1547; *ibid.* IV, 8, 40: May 10 and Aug. 9, 1548; Winchester, *Tudor family*, 250, citing from the Johnson MSS. Flemish complaints of losses amounting to £100,000 Flemish; VCH, *Sussex*, II, 147.

[5] S.P. Dom., Edw. VI, VI, 19–22.

attachment. Seymour possessed a strange attraction for many women and the Queen was persuaded to yield, probably in the third month of her widowhood, and a private marriage, for which no official documentation has ever been found, occurred sometime in May, 1547. This rather scandalous affair was conducted with great secrecy, for it raised the fearful possibility, in due time to be laid against Seymour in the articles of indictment, that had his child been born sooner, 'a great doubt' would have arisen 'whether the child born should have been accounted the late king's or yours, whereby a marvellous danger might have ensued to the quiet of the realm'. Seymour first confided the facts to the Duchess of Suffolk, while Catherine urged him not to be so fearful of informing Somerset, suggesting that the best course was first to gain the approval of the King, who was very fond of her, and then of the leading members of the Council for a marriage which in fact had already taken place.[1] In mid-May Seymour had still not dared approach the Protector and Council, appealing to his wife, then in the country, for one of her small pictures which 'shall give me occasion to think on the friendly cheer that I shall receive, when my suit shall be at an end'.[2]

Catherine Parr was an extremely intelligent, equable, and domestic woman with great capacities for love and protective warmth. She was undoubtedly happy in this brief and tragic marriage, though she failed to quiet the bitter temper and the tempestuous, and really mad, ambitions and hatreds of her strange husband. Somerset and the Council in due course learned of the marriage which Seymour was at once too proud and too fearful to acknowledge, the Lord Protector at first reacting with cold rage and then quickly accommodating himself to the facts as they were.[3] But the young King, already dazzled by Seymour's blandishments, offered his congratulations, assuring the couple that 'I will so provide for you both, that hereafter if any grief befall, I shall be a sufficient succour in your godly and praisable enterprises'.[4] But even so Seymour was not content and would not throw off the black rage against his brother. Shortly after she knew she was pregnant Catherine wrote to her husband lamenting his ill treatment, but begging him not 'to unquiet yourself with any of his unfriendly parts, but bear them for the time; as well you can'.[5] Seymour, a little later, complained that

[1] S.P. Dom., Edw. VI, I, 43: May ?, 1547; Ellis, *Original letters*, ser. 1, II, 152; Edward's affection for Catherine is suggested in several letters: Cotton MSS., Nero, C, x, 4; *ibid*. Vespasian, F, iii, 18; Harl. MS. 6986, #9.
[2] S.P. Dom., Edw. VI, I, 41, 42.   [3] Edward VI, *Chronicle*, 6.
[4] Quoted in Strype,*Memorials*, II, i, 208–209.
[5] HMC, *Salisbury MSS*. I, 57.

he could not attain 'justice of those I thought would in all my causes [have] been partial', but was sustained by hearing that 'my little man doth shake his poll' and by the hope that his unborn son (the child was to be a girl) would avenge the wrongs of his father. He was outraged too because his brother wanted him in London to assist with military preparations against France, but intended in fact to join Catherine in the country.[1]

The acid of Seymour's paranoia came in due time to affect Catherine herself, for in a later (though undated) letter she complained of her inability to see or to put certain requests to Somerset, which she blamed on the ill-nature and false promises of the Duchess with whom she had experienced difficulties in the matter of precedence at state functions.[2] For a brief season the pair resided mostly at Sudeley, whose renovation they undertook, in a great household of 120 ladies and gentlemen:

> His house was termed a second court, of right,
> Because there flocked still nobility;
> He spared no cost his lady to delight
> Or to maintain her princely royalty.

Then swiftly and tragically this tortured idyll was over. In early September, 1548, shortly after having given birth to a daughter, Catherine Parr died. The only human force that could possibly have saved Sudeley was gone:

> His climbing high, disdained by his peers,
> Was thought the cause he lived not out his years.[3]

Just a week before Catherine Parr's death, Somerset had written to his brother, as he had so often spoken to him, counselling gentler conduct in his relations with others. He was distressed that Sudeley laid himself open to so many complaints which reached him and which could not be ignored despite the relationship between them. In two minor matters then at issue he urged his brother not to proceed with harsh courses, for 'we would wish rather to hear that all the king's subjects were of you gently and liberally entreated with honour, than that any one should be said to be of you either

---

[1] S.P. Dom., Edw. VI, IV, 14: June 9, 1548.

[2] Dent, Emma, *Annals of Winchcombe and Sudeley* (L., 1877), 163, citing a letter in the Sudeley Castle collection, which I have not seen.

[3] *The legend of Sir Nicholas Throckmorton*, ed. by J. G. Nichols (Roxburghe Club, L., 1874), 17.

injured or extremely handled. Such is the hard affection we do bear towards you'.[1]

But now imprudence mixed with treason overcame Seymour. He had quarrelled violently with the Protector before his wife's death by claiming that Catherine's jewels had descended to her personally and that on her death they became his own property, even appealing to the Princess Mary 'for three or four lines' stating that they had been Catherine's personal rather than state jewels.[2] He had begun as well, and most frantically, a dangerous effort to build a party amongst the nobility, having paid £2000 to Dorset for the presence of the Lady Jane Grey in his household, with a vague intention of marrying her to the King, and using every effort to keep her in his charge after Catherine's death, promising that towards her he would remain 'half father and more'. So too, Sudeley stood opposed to every government measure introduced in Parliament, while he and Dorset were alone amongst the peers in voting against the patent granting Somerset plenary powers until the King attained the age of eighteen.

Far more serious was the fact that shortly after Catherine's death, Seymour had begun to sue for the hand of the Princess Elizabeth, without the Council's permission, and surely with the knowledge that to tamper with the succession to the throne in Tudor England was to cross the line of treason. Further, as a discreet but thorough investigation after his arrest displayed, Seymour had been guilty of quite improper dalliance with the young Princess, when she was still in her fourteenth year and a member of Catherine's household. The not very pleasant facts came out in successive examinations of the Princess' personal servant, Katherine Ashley, a foolish and romantic woman quite enthralled by Seymour's blandishments, and ultimately in the questioning of Elizabeth herself. Probably at Catherine Parr's insistence, Elizabeth had been removed from her household at Chelsea and later, as the full facts came into Somerset's hands, Mrs Ashley was dismissed.[3] It is evident in the quite full, and sometimes earthy, documentation that a proud girl had been seriously embarrassed, that for a season she felt herself without sure or mature counsel, and that very possibly her later wariness in emotional involvements stems from this unpleasant experience of

[1] S.P. Dom., Edw. VI, V, 1: Sept. 1, 1548.

[2] HMC, *Salisbury MSS.*, I, 55: Richard Weston to Sudeley, July 19, 1548; *ibid.* 56: Dec. 17, 1548.

[3] The most important of the documents are in HMC, *Salisbury MSS.* I, 61, 62, 64 (also in *ibid.* XIII (Addenda), 25, 26), 67, 69–70, 72, 73; S.P. Dom., Edw. VI, VI, 6, 19, 20, 21, 22.

her girlhood. But she was tough-fibred and handled herself with great dignity and with an honesty that was always edged with Tudor arrogance. At no time, one can say quite confidently, did the Princess entertain any serious intention of marrying Sudeley, if for no other reason, as she assured Somerset, because she knew the Council would not permit it.[1] With great dignity she assured the Protector that she would do nothing not approved by the Council and stated categorically that, evil reports notwithstanding, she had done nothing with which she or the Council might find fault. She suggested, indeed, that a proclamation might well be issued requiring men to 'refrain their tongues, declaring how the tales be but lies' and that rumours may not be spread concerning the King's sister.[2] Then a few days later, her confidence evidently fully recovered, she moved to the defence of her servant, Katherine Ashley, who, she held, had taken great pains to bring her up in learning and honesty. And, finally, she argued that if her servant were punished or removed men would really believe that she was 'not clear of the deed myself', but was pardoned because of her youth.[3]

In the closing weeks of 1548 Seymour began to act and move with a dangerous, muddled, and erratic recklessness that recalls the inexplicable actions of two other Tudor peers, Surrey and Essex, which catapulted them into treason. He spoke wildly and almost irrationally to numerous peers, as the later depositions showed, always in terms of an insane hatred of his brother and of the power which he wielded. From Dorset, that most stupid of peers, he believed he enjoyed some support as he did from Northampton, the latter bitterly angry because his marriage plans were baulked. He sought as well to build up military strength in the west, where his estate at Sudeley was converted into a depot for the assembly of illicit military supplies. Most of this was at least vaguely known to Somerset and the Council, but the whole involvement in treason was revealed when Sir William Sharington, vice-treasurer of the Bristol mint, was arrested for divers offences, including clipping coins, debasing the currency, and buying up personally and then minting large quantities of church plate.[4] Far more serious was the discovery, after Lacock Abbey, Sharington's great house, was searched by Council agents on January 6, 1549, of an illegal understanding between Seymour and Sharington by whose terms the

[1] S.P. Dom., Edw. VI, VI, 6: Jan. 31, 1549.

[2] Ellis, *Original letters*, ser. 1, II, 157, quoting Lansdowne MS. 1236, #22, f. 33: Feb. 21, [1549].

[3] *Ibid.* f. 35: Mar. 7, [1549].   [4] *Vide post*, 382ff., for a discussion of the case.

Bristol mint had been put at the Admiral's disposal for what could only be regarded as treasonable purposes. Summoned to meet privately with his brother, Seymour arrogantly declined to come until it should be more convenient for him.[1]

The matter was at once laid before the whole Council, which after 'divers conferences', at a meeting on January 17th, at which twenty were present, resolved on measures 'for the stay and repressing of the said Admiral's attempts'. Earlier subversive actions had been borne with, but it was now evident that Sudeley had plotted the overthrow of the Protector and of the Council, had sought to gain control over the person of the King, had with bribes subverted persons close to the King, and had endeavoured without permission to marry the Princess Elizabeth. It was accordingly unanimously voted to lodge him in the Tower until order could be taken.[2] Sudeley was immediately arrested, and within the week such additional persons as Sharington, Fowler, Harrington, described as the Admiral's 'man', and three of Elizabeth's household were also lodged in the Tower for examination, while the grim instruction for an inventory of Sudeley's goods and chattels in various counties went forth.[3]

The Council proceeded with painstaking care on the examination of upwards of twenty persons who supplied testimony, many being of very high estate, somewhat more than a month being devoted to the task. The evidence, gathered into thirty-three formal articles of accusation, was impressive in its bulk and damning in its revelations. We shall shortly deal with the whole body of the findings as couched in the *Articles*, but it may be well to touch here on the evidence that Seymour had sought for treasonable purposes to subvert the young King, gain control of his person, and to alienate him from the Duke of Somerset and the Council, for here we find the most sensitive area of accusation and one, since the King was directly involved, which could not be fully probed. As early as June, 1548, it is certain that John Fowler, in daily and intimate contact with the King, was in Seymour's service and was acting as an intermediary between him and the King, a child of not much more than ten years. Fowler reported that Edward had willed him to write 'declaring his mind and love' for him and had recalled Seymour's promise to aid him

---

[1] S.P. Dom., Edw. VI, VI, 1: Jan. 11, 1549, or possibly a day or two earlier.

[2] *A.P.C.* II, 236–238.

[3] S.P. Dom., Edw. VI, VI, 2, 3, 4: Jan. 18–21, 1549. The imperial ambassador reported on January 27 that Sudeley had conspired to kill the King and the Protector, and somewhat earlier that silver to the value of 200,000 crowns and other property of great value had been found in his house (*Cal. S.P. Span.* IX, 332–333).

if he lacked money. The strict rigour of his upbringing is suggested when Fowler further reported that he did need money, but would name no sum, saying only that he wished to use it for private gifts and would leave the amount to Seymour. The King was then at St James, where Somerset also lodged, though he dined at Westminster. In order to validate the letter the King had written the beginning in his own hand, with the admonition to burn it.[1] A few weeks later Fowler forwarded two scrappy notes in the King's hand, with a covering letter of his own. Edward expressed his affection for his uncle, urged that all letters to Fowler be brought by trustworthy hands, and added that when he needed money he would inform Seymour. Edward himself added that Seymour was to send as a gift for Latimer as much as he thought appropriate.[2] In his own *Declaration* Seymour in effect admitted that he had sought to win the King's affection by secret gifts of this sort, having as he recalled given Cheke £40, half for the King and half for himself, and that he had forwarded £40 with the advice that Latimer be remembered with a gratuity of £20 and that the King keep the remainder for his own uses.

This evidence was greatly expanded in still another deposition made by Fowler.[3] Obviously following the lead of skilled examiners, he indicated that as early as June, 1547, he had been relaying information from the royal household to Seymour and that on instruction he had gained from Edward agreement that the Admiral should marry either Anne of Cleves or the Princess Mary, 'to turn her opinions'. Seymour also used Fowler to present to the King his side in his disputes with the Protector and sought as well the support of Cheke. On many occasions he had instructed Fowler to put the King in remembrance of him and had said that 'if his highness lacked any money to send to him for it and nobody else'. Fowler further testified that Seymour's efforts to ingratiate himself with the King became more intensive after the marriage with Catherine

[1] HMC, *Salisbury MSS.* I, 53: June 26, 1548.
[2] S.P. Dom., Edw. VI, IV, 31: July 19, 1548.
[3] The document is fully printed by Nichols, *Remains*, I, cxv–cxxi. We have combined it for analysis with still another *Confession* of Fowler which may be found in S.P. Dom., Edw. VI, VI, 10. The whole of the evidence given by Fowler seems to me somewhat suspect. He was ingenious but on occasion certainly untruthful, and it seems clear that he was seeking to ingratiate himself with his examiners by successive expansions of his story. But the account is too chatty and circumstantial to be wholly credible. What is certain is that he had for a season Edward's full confidence and was doing Seymour's work for him. Edward, with a remarkable sense of his own involvement, took Cheke quite fully into his confidence and it was probably Cheke who saved him from real embarrassment. The fact is that Edward was frightened and full of a sense of wrong-doing well before Seymour launched into his more dangerous courses.

Parr and added that Edward was furtive in writing and delivering the few notes which he sent to Seymour. Fowler now recalled, or so he testified, gifts from Seymour totalling £188, beginning soon after the King's accession, with smaller additional amounts of which he was uncertain. From these funds, and on the King's instruction, he had given a remembrance of £20 to Cheke, £5 to his French master (Belmain), £5 to his instructor on the virginal, £1 to Barnaby Fitzpatrick, and numerous other small gratuities.

This evidence, which as we have noted does not quite ring true, proves many things about Edward's upbringing and the stern tutelage of the Lord Protector, but it certainly does not of itself prove Sudeley's treason. In minutes set down separately by Paget and Petre for the questioning of Sudeley, we see where the Council was aiming: they wished to know whether the Admiral had conferred with any person, including the King, respecting an alteration of government; whether he had sought any change in the governance of the King's person; whether he had held conversations with the King regarding the marriage of Edward or of his sisters; and whether he had said 'that if he were used as he had been, he would make this the blackest parliament that ever was in England', as other deponents had testified.[1]

Far more damaging, perhaps fatally so, was the King's own signed statement of the facts. Thomas Seymour had come to him 'in the time of the last parliament' [i.e. the first session] and 'desired me to write a thing for him. I asked him what; he said it was none ill thing: it is for the Queen's majesty. I said, if it were good, the Lords [of the Council] would allow it; if it were ill, I would not write it'. Seymour pressed farther and was told by the King that he wished to hear no more of the matter and that Cheke had later told him that his decision was correct. At a later, but unspecified, date Seymour had urged him to take rule into his own hands 'within this two year at least', as other kings had done and that then he could extend favour to 'your men somewhat'. Somerset, Seymour continued, was old 'and I trust will not live long', to which the King said he made the amazing and brutal reply, 'it were better that he should die'. The Admiral then subverted the child by saying, 'Ye are but a very beggarly king now; ye have not to play, or to give to your servants', and then offered to supply him with pocket-money through Fowler. These things the Admiral had urged upon him two or three times, 'and he gave Cheke money, as I bade him; and also to a bookbinder, as Belmain [the French tutor] can tell, and

[1] HMC, *Salisbury MSS.*, I, 65; Haynes, *State papers*, I, 84–86.

to divers others'. Also in a separate deposition, Edward stated that Seymour had on an earlier occasion told him that Somerset would suffer great losses and would possibly be killed in forcing the passage through the Pease during the invasion of Scotland. On Somerset's triumphant return from the north Seymour had told him that he should now begin to rule as other kings did, and that when he retired to Sudeley Seymour had cautioned him not to believe anything said against him.[1]

This was of course damaging as it was incontrovertible evidence and it may be regarded as supplying the last link in the chain of evidence gained by the many depositions so patiently assembled. Proof of treasonable conspiracy had also been gained from Sharington's full and abject confession, so that even before the examinations were complete Somerset had written to Hoby, then abroad, that it was clear that his brother had treasonably sought to take control of the King's person, to move 'plain sedition' in Parliament, and had very nearly accomplished a marriage with the Princess Elizabeth without the consent of the Council.[2]

When the examinations and depositions were considered by the Council on February 22nd, it was unanimously agreed that Seymour 'was sore charged of divers and sundry articles of high treason, great falsehoods and marvellous heinous misdemeanours against the King's Majesty's person and his royal crown'. Some of the Council had examined him on certain of the charges, in which he had dissembled or refused to reply, and it was accordingly agreed that the Lord Chancellor and all the Council, save for Cranmer and Baker who were otherwise engaged, would repair to the Tower and read the articles of accusation, thirty-three in number, to him one after another to see if he could clear himself or offer some excuse.[3] When this was done on the day following, Seymour declined to make any answer unless his accusers were brought before him and unless he was brought to arraignment and trial.[4]

The Council reported these events to the Lord Protector on February 24th and it was at once resolved to lay the case before the King, when the Lord Chancellor would require to know the King's mind and whether the law should proceed against the Admiral, and whether action should be instituted by bill of attainder. In the audience with the King later that day, after each of the Council declared his judgement, Somerset concluded with the fatal words,

---

[1] Haynes, *State papers*, I, 74; Nichols, *Remains*, I, 57–60; HMC, *Salisbury MSS.*, I, 65–66. [2] Harl. MS. 523, #51, f. 79.
[3] *A.P.C.* II, 246–247: Feb. 22, 1549. [4] *Ibid.* 247, 256.

'how sorrowful a case this was unto him', but that 'he did yet rather regard his bounden duty to the King's Majesty and the crown of England than his own son or brother', and hence could not oppose the request of the Lords of the Council. Thereupon the King declared, ' "We do perceive that there is great things which be objected and laid to my Lord Admiral, mine uncle, and they tend to treason, and we perceive that you require but justice to be done. We think it reasonable, and we will well that you proceed according to your request." ' But the Council, determining to proceed by the favoured Tudor instrumentality of a bill of attainder, resolved before the bill was drafted to send a committee from its own number, they being also of the Lords or Commons, to read the articles once more to Seymour in order to see if he had either defence or answer.[1]

The thirty-three articles of accusation were spread in full in the minutes of the Council and form the basis for the bill of attainder drafted in legal form on the 25th of February and laid before Parliament.[2] Though the evidence on which they rest was carefully gathered, it must be said that the *Articles* seem hastily framed, are ill-ordered and repetitive, and form a kind of angry blanket indictment which may however be reduced to four general heads. It was alleged that Sudeley had conspired against the legally constituted authority of the Protector and Council;[3] that he had intended to gather power into his own hands and to this end had sought to gain the favour and control of the King;[4] that he had trifled treasonably with the succession in his own marriage plans;[5] and that he had been guilty of treasonable acts and plans in seeking to carry forward these designs.[6]

Most of these charges have been dealt with in our discussion of the gathering of the evidence against Seymour, but at least a few of the more specific allegations of treasonable actions should be noted. Thus he had sought support among the Council and nobility 'to stick and adhere unto you for the alteration of the state and order of the realm' (art. 4). Those nobles in whom he thought he sensed disaffection, he had urged to 'depart into their countries' and strengthen themselves for his ends (arts. 12–13). He had gathered young gentlemen and yeomen 'to a great multitude' to carry out his purposes (arts. 15–16), having, it was estimated, established some influence over as many as 10,000 men (art. 18). In summary, he had

---

[1] *A.P.C.* II, 257–258: Feb. 24, 1549.
[2] *Ibid.* 248–256; also printed in a satisfactory text in Burnet, *Reformation*, V, 232–241.
[3] Articles ##3, 11.   [4] Articles ##1, 2, 8, 9, 10.
[5] Articles ##19–21.   [6] Articles ##4, 12–18, 22–31, 33.

intended an alteration of the government of the realm (art. 22), as exhibited by very specific actions, including building up pirate strength in the Scilly Isles, plotting with Sharington to finance his nefarious purposes (arts. 23-25), protecting piracy generally for the support of his interest (arts. 26-29), and gathering supplies for the sustenance of a great mass of men in preparation for rebellion (art. 33).

When the Council's committee waited on him in the Tower Sudeley knew beyond peradventure that any hope of protection from his brother or his nephew had vanished and that his trial was at hand. But whether from hopelessness or sheer obduracy he attempted explanation of only three of the charges and refused either to hear or to comment on the remainder. This was the only defence ever offered by Seymour, save for the brief statements some weeks earlier during his preliminary examination. What he said for himself on these three charges deserves careful considera-tion, though it does not seem to exonerate him even with respect to their limited area of accusation. On January 25th when he had been questioned by seven members of the Council regarding the ordering of the King's person, Sudeley contended that he had discussed the matter 'with no creature living' save Rutland, to whom he had said that in view of the King's precocity, he would in two or three years wish for greater liberty of action and that if the King wished him to intervene with the Protector and Council, he would do so.[1] This he amended two days later by saying that on one occasion he had also discussed the proposal with the King himself, but in terms of a more distant future.[2] In this connection Christopher Eyre, Sudeley's keeper in the Tower, had reported to Smith that Seymour had told him that he had thought he had many friends in the Council, but now he knew himself to be mistaken, while further averring that his loyalty to the King and to the succession of Mary and Elizabeth was complete and that he had never contemplated the removal of the King from the charge of the Protector by force.[3] Smith questioned him closely on this point two days later, when Sudeley admitted that he wished the King were in his own house-hold, but had never planned to gain possession of his person without the consent of 'the whole realm'. At the same time he all but admitted that the greater precautions for guarding the King's door at night, introduced by Stanhope, were instituted to prevent his unauthorized access.[4]

[1] HMC, *Salisbury MSS.*, I, #263.
[2] *Ibid.* #267: Jan. 27, 1549.
[3] *Ibid.* #291: Feb. 16, 1549.
[4] *Ibid.* #293: Feb. 18, 1549.

More formally, and finally, Sudeley dealt with these and related matters in his last interrogation by the committee of the Council. Confronted with Fowler's full confession he admitted that about a year previously he had talked with Fowler about the possibility of taking the King by way of a gallery from the royal premises to his own house, but by this had meant no hurt. He also admitted that he had talked with divers persons of the possibility of gaining the King's person by act of parliament, but had changed his mind when it was pointed out that he had agreed to the present arrangement. Confronted with full and impressive evidence, he likewise admitted the secret gifts of money which he had placed through intermediaries in the King's own hands. And he also admitted that he had sought to persuade the King to write the letter to Parliament respecting a change in the government of his person, which he had placed in draft either in Cheke's hands or with the King himself.[1] Beyond this Sudeley never went in his own defence, but even here he had in effect admitted his guilt.

The bill of attainder was introduced in the Lords on February 25th. The record of the examinations and depositions was read, the judges declaring that the offence was manifest treason. The peers on February 27th passed the measure with unanimous voice, the Lord Protector being absent. The *Lords Journal* notes that the peers thought it proper to send the bill at once to the Commons with certain of the ministers who should declare how the Lords had proceeded, and if they chose to proceed in like manner that the Lords would send some of their number to give evidence.[2] The bill declaring Seymour 'adjudged and attainted of high treason'[3] had its first reading in the Lower House on February 28th and its second on March 1st, when a committee was appointed to inform the Lords that 'the evidence shall be heard orderly, as it was before the Lords', and also to require that the Lords who would affirm the evidence 'come hither and declare it viva voce'. On March 4th the Master of the Rolls and others declared it to be the King's pleasure that Sudeley not appear before the Commons, but if further evidence were required the appropriate peers would come down.[4] After some debate a 'marvellous full' house on this same day passed the measure, 'not x or xij at the most giving their nays'.[5]

There was a pause in the momentum of these terrible proceedings for a full five days when the Council must have been debating

[1] S.P. Dom., Edw. VI, VI, 27: Feb. 24, 1549; *A.P.C.* II, 258–260.
[2] *L.J.* I, 346.   [3] *Statutes of the realm*, IV, pt. i, 61–65.
[4] *C.J.* I, 9.   [5] *A.P.C.* II, 260.

whether to carry out the execution of Somerset's brother or not, or more accurately, probably, while Somerset's tortured mind was moving towards a dreadful and reluctant decision. But on March 10th the Council waited upon the King, asking that they might 'proceed to justice' without further troubling him or the Protector 'in this heavy case'. With Somerset beside him the King gave them thanks for their pains and travail for his surety, declaring himself 'willing and commanding them that they should proceed as they required without further molestation' of himself or the Lord Protector.[1] On March 15th the decision was taken and a few days later the execution took place,[2] the King coldly remarking in his *Chronicle* that 'the Lord Sudeley, Admiral of England, was condemned to death and died the March ensuing',[3] one might add with great dignity of carriage and that reckless bravery which had always marked even the most wicked of his actions.

A judgement on the evidence is not difficult, for Sudeley undoubtedly stood guilty of numerous acts that were technically treasonable. Nor can it be denied that he was vicious in character, irresponsible in action, and unfaithful in his discharge of the high offices with which he had been vested. But strangely enough, though the particulars—and few cases have ever been as fully documented—of the charges against him prove treason, one is left unsure whether in their totality his actions really seriously endangered the state. The whole of his plotting was feckless, scarcely concealed, and bizarre, while the weakness of his character and the wildness of his threats and designs made it impossible for him to gather dangerous factions around his leadership. One can only conclude that Seymour was more than a little mad and wonder whether he could not have been safely stowed away in the Tower for the remainder of the reign.

Whatever our judgement may be with respect to Seymour's guilt and the degree of danger which he posed for the state, there can be no doubt whatsoever that the case did grave, perhaps irreparable, damage to Somerset's reputation and position. Men simply could not forget that he bore the ultimate responsibility for his own brother's death, and in any age that is a terrible indictment. Still another wedge had been set in the structure of the Protector's power, still another weakness was exposed which his enemies were

---

[1] *A.P.C. II*, 262: Mar. 10, 1549.

[2] Stow, *Annales*, 596; *Two London chronicles from the collections of John Stow*, ed. by C. L. Kingsford, in *Camden Miscellany*, XII (L., 1910), 17.

[3] Edward VI, *Chronicle*, 10–11.

quick to exploit. Yet the truth is that Somerset was almost helpless once the inquiry into Seymour's activities was launched with the approval which he had to give. The investigation was led by two of the ablest and most ruthless lawyers of England, Rich and Wriothesley, and much of the pressure was supplied by the Earl of Warwick. The proceedings were fair; no torture seems to have been used against any witness; and the judgement of the peers was unanimous. It seems quite clear that Somerset, so far as was possible, withdrew from the whole of the proceedings once it had been set in train, though he alone could and did sign the final warrant for the execution.[1] It was the later recollection of Elizabeth, writing to Queen Mary when she herself stood in danger because of Wyatt's rising, that Somerset had told her 'that if his brother had been suffered to speak with him, he had never suffered; but the persuasions were made to him so great, that he was brought in belief that he could not live safely if the Admiral lived; and that made him give his consent to his death'.[2]

2. THE CASE OF SIR WILLIAM SHARINGTON

As we have noted, it was in part the investigation of the peculations of Sir William Sharington, vice-treasurer of the royal mint at Bristol, which first revealed the whole tangled skein of Seymour's treason. Sharington had held minor offices under Henry VIII which enabled him in 1540 to purchase for £783 the beautiful dissolved abbey at Lacock, in Wiltshire. In 1546 he was given the highly responsible post in the Bristol mint and, being much in favour, was created a Knight of the Bath on the occasion of Edward's coronation. Sharington was a man of considerable, indeed, precocious taste, lavishing on the renovation and decoration of Lacock great care and a personal attention which made it one of the first and certainly one of the most important examples of the Renaissance style of domestic architecture advanced with so much of excitement, and expense, by several of the governing group of this period, including Somerset, Thynne, Sudeley, Warwick, and Smith.[3] Since his own financial resources were limited in early 1547, it was almost certainly the requirements for his expensive work on Lacock which catapulted Sharington into fraud on a really grand scale. He

[1] Pollard, *Somerset*, 198; Read's comment on the case is most perceptive (*Mr. Secretary Cecil*, 54).   [2] Ellis, *Original letters*, ser. 2, II, 256–257.
[3] The development of this school of domestic architecture will be discussed in the second volume of this work.

later confessed that from May to July, 1547, he had pocketed large profits from buying up church plate in the west which he coined into testons that were about two-thirds alloy, despite the stern order of the Council in April to all mints to stop the coinage of this debased currency.

These illegal proceedings were of course well known to workmen in the mint, and the later examination of two of them reveals that there had been widespread gossip in Bristol regarding Sharington's ingenious and highly profitable coinages.[1] The mint records were carefully falsified, enabling him to escape the first audit,[2] though there must have been some suspicion in government circles when Sharington found himself able in 1548 to purchase lands in Wiltshire, Northamptonshire, and Gloucestershire at an outlay of £2808 4s 0d. Thus emboldened, Sharington moved into other ingenious illegalities, defrauding the King (and the realm) of as much as £4000 by using coin clippings and shavings as his own bullion, issuing coins that were under weight, and destroying as well as falsifying the records of his office. These illegalities, on such a reckless scale, made him a perfect victim for blackmail which Thomas Seymour exploited when, as we have seen, he gathered Sharington, much more interested in his new lintels at Lacock than in politics, into his net of treason. These frauds were still being practised as late as January 15, 1549, when the frightened deputy in the mint wrote frantically to Sharington for more silver so the mint could be kept in operation for 'otherwise it may happen to be suspected that more money hath been made than doth appear by the indentures and books of account', though he hoped that the falsified books would stand at least casual audit.[3]

But when the thrust of the investigation of Sudeley's treason exposed the relation with Sharington, the now thoroughly frightened official poured out all that he knew in his second examination by Smith and two other Councillors. He was apparently not really deeply involved in Sudeley's plans and by his evidence added little that was more than corroborating, but the annal of his frauds, fully confessed, suggests an almost incredible laxity in the auditing practices of the age. It was his own estimate that he had gained something like £4000 by his various shifts and thefts, but he could not be sure, since the true records had been destroyed.[4] He stoutly

[1] HMC, *Salisbury MSS.*, I. ##286, 289.
[2] S.P. Dom., Edw. VI, IV, 3: Mar. 24(?), 1548.
[3] HMC, *Salisbury* MSS., I, ##255, 260.
[4] *Ibid.* ##264, 271: Jan. 25 and 29, 1549.

denied, however, that he had in fact coined any money for Sudeley, though there was, it seems certain, an agreement that he would do so when the need arose.[1] The compelling reason for his frauds, as we have suggested, was Lacock, on which he testified he had spent about 2000 marks and which cost him £500 a year to maintain and operate. In outlining his assets, Sharington estimated that there was owed to him £3800, of which £2000 was the debt of Sir William Herbert and £500 of the Lord Protector, while he confessed that his own debts were upwards of £9300, of which he owed £3000 to the King and as much to Sudeley.[2] Sharington appealed to the Protector for mercy and in effect turned state's evidence against Seymour, as the order went out for the inventory and seizure of his property.[3] The appalled and fascinated Council sought in successive examinations to learn more accurately how the gigantic fraud had been accomplished, but the more Sharington confessed— and he was gifted at once in imagination and concealment—the more baffled they must have been. Thus on February 4th he confessed that at the moment when the investigation began he had actually on balance been a creditor of the Lord Admiral to the tune of £2800, but that fearing exposure he had prevailed on Sudeley to give him a promissory note in the amount of £2000, thus belying his earlier testimony.[4] Steady questioning also established a somewhat closer knowledge of Seymour's treasonable intentions than Sharington had earlier confessed, since he admitted that he had told the Admiral that he could on demand advance as much as £4000 from the mint for the support of the contemplated military forces, and as much more as available bullion could provide.[5] This was really all that could be extracted from this ingenious and somehow attractive rogue, who, as the bill of attainder was lodged against him, laid before Shrewsbury and Southampton an abject plea for mercy, even if it should mean imprisonment for life.[6] The bill of attainder, against which oddly enough the Bishop of Norwich voted in the Lords, recited Sharington's offences, or as many of them as could be sifted out, and passed the Lords on February 19th and the Commons on March 6th.[7]

Though no direct assurances seem to have been given to him,

[1] HMC, *Salisbury MSS.*, I, ##272, 273: Jan. 30, 1549.
[2] *Ibid.* XIII (Addenda), 26; Haynes, *State papers*, I, 62–65.
[3] HMC, *Salisbury MSS.*, I, #397; S.P. Dom., Edw. VI, VI, 29.
[4] HMC, *Salisbury MSS.*, I, # 283
[5] *Ibid.* #287: Feb. 11, 1549.
[6] *Ibid.* #295: Feb. 20, 1549.
[7] 2 and 3 Edward VI, c. 17; Edward VI, *Chronicle*, 11.

Sharington's revelations had been helpful to the government in its rooting out of Seymour's treasons. Before the year was out he was pardoned and restored in blood. Within a few months he had sufficiently regained favour to be entrusted with a financial mission by the government and was able, with resources which simply cannot be accounted for in his statements respecting his fraud, to purchase back his lands and his beloved Lacock where, after serving as sheriff of Wiltshire in 1552, he died peacefully in 1553.

XIV

THE FRACTURE IN THE SOCIETY

I. GENERAL COMMENTS ON THE SOCIAL AND ECONOMIC BACKGROUND

We may now turn to the consideration of a rich, somewhat fugitive, and in part controversial body of thought and policy which form the background for the dramatic and shattering events of 1549. In the summer and autumn of that year England was to experience the most serious and widespread rising of the commons since the fourteenth century. This was a revolutionary outburst which thoroughly frightened the dominant political and economic classes of the realm and which led directly and immediately to the forced abdication from power of the Lord Protector, who, with some justice, was thought to be not unsympathetic to those who had vented their discontent, their grievances, and their aspirations in a series of scattered, though, most fortunately, not organically connected risings.

In the present discussion we shall be concerned with what may be described as the pragmatic thought and policy which seems to bear directly on the outbreak of the troubles of 1549, reserving to the concluding volume of this work a consideration of the more sophisticated body of abstruse thought of this decade. It is not too much to say that the main sources for the reforming thought, both social and economic, of the Edwardian period are to be found in the remarkable group of humanist propagandists, directly or indirectly serving Henry VIII as defenders of his religious policy, which in the next generation grew at once more radical and more Protestant and found itself close to the centre of power in the government of the Lord Protector. In some ways, indeed, it may be said that Somerset's brief but fruitful tenure of power was the first European experiment in government by intellectuals.

The first scholar to lend detailed as well as magisterial attention to the revolutionary social and economic developments of the Edwardian era was Professor Tawney, the main lines of whose work still stand. He so suffused himself in the thought and aspirations of the age that he spoke with the vigour and moral force of an Old Testament prophet against the wicked holders of economic power and for the weak and the forlorn. His remains a very great work of history, informed by those moral judgements which somehow in the end are the mark of the giants of our craft.

Tawney, basing his conclusions on sixteenth-century surveys of 118 manors, suggested that something like a fifth of the population of England in our period, roughly defined, were freeholders, or yeomen, who were by this date only loosely linked to the scheme of manorial organization.[1] It is impossible to reckon what proportion of land was held by this class, but, as Professor Tawney did not fully recognize, it was a thrusting class, was in a position to exploit all improvements in farming practices, and was in fact quite as given to forced enclosures and sheep grazing as were its betters. So aggressive and prosperous was the class, in fact, that we have observed that men described as yeomen constituted more than 4 per cent of all purchasers of crown lands in the Edwardian era. Their purchases account for 2·69 per cent of the capital sums laid down for these acquisitions—an amount slightly less than the total afforded by the 'old nobility', slightly more than that expended by the 'new nobility' for the same purpose.[2]

But the great mass of men (Tawney reckons the proportion at 61 per cent) were customary tenants, almost all of whom held by copyhold, though the proportion both of men and of land under this tenure was steadily declining as title by freehold or effective control by leasehold became at once more desirable and more common. The weakness of the position of the copyholder was that ultimately he was protected only by the recorded or remembered custom of his manor, as enforced in the courts, though since the fifteenth century the common law courts had steadily intervened to enforce custom, and we have seen clear evidence that the Edwardian Court of Requests was frequently employed to protect copyhold tenures. The great and usually irrevocable strength of such tenures lay in the fact that any change or abrogation of custom, particularly when enclosures or aggregations of lands were involved, pitted the lord of the manor against the collective and often litigious strength of his copyholders who, Tawney's figures suggest, typically included more than three-fourths of those farming within the ambit of the

[1] Tawney, R. H., *The agrarian problem in the sixteenth century* (L., 1912), 25–33.
[2] *Vide ante*, 107, 118. These proportions would certainly be substantially increased if we could identify precisely those whom we have described as 'others' or 'unknown'.

manor.[1] It should also be stressed that well before 1547 holding by copy was not wholly linked with status, portions of land held by yeomen or even by gentry being by this tenure, thus strengthening the position of far humbler copyholders. Silently at work, too, all over England, was a process of aggregation of estates into larger farming units, quite as marked amongst the gentry as the yeomanry and including numerous enterprising copyholders. This development was bringing larger and more efficient units of cultivation, or of sheep-farming, under control of fewer hands and was introducing social strains frequently and quite wrongly blamed on the enclosure movement.

The process of aggregation, as well as that of enclosure, was hastened through much of the fifteenth century as wool production became more profitable. In Tawney's phrase, 'the movement towards pasture-farming as a special branch of agriculture is one that proceeds gradually for a hundred years, before the demand for wool becomes sufficient to produce the body of capitalistic graziers whose interest came into collision with those of the peasantry'.[2] The demand for land was steadily increasing, profits from the intelligent management of land were rising, and a much closer control over land was being exercised by those who owned or leased their fields. Undoubtedly the chief instrument available for the improvement of land and yield was by enclosures, whether by agreement or purchase, whether the intent was to augment the yield from land by tillage or by grazing. This process had progressed far in the fifteenth century, with undoubted dislocations, depopulation, and suffering amongst the commons in a period when the central government was weak and the moral conscience of the owners of property not especially lively. No less a tribune of the commons of England than Hales thought the enclosure movement, particularly for grazing, was largely over by 1485. More probable it is that this process of change was almost halted by 1517 when the central government undertook seriously to enforce the laws impeding enclosures for pasture, though the really frenetic opposition was not fully to express itself until the reign of Edward VI when for a season moralists were charged with governance.

This view is attested by the careful work of recent investigators. Thus Professor Hoskins suggests that the great majority of the sixty deserted villages of Leicestershire lost their population before 1500, and that very few were abandoned in the mid-sixteenth century, by which time the only way the principal proprietors could

---

[1] Tawney, *Agrarian problem*, 48.   [2] *Ibid.* 115.

enclose was by buying out the considerable number of freeholders within the manor or working out with them the tedious and expensive method of enclosure by agreement.[1] Beresford also suggests, with detailed documentation, that enclosures on a massive scale, leading to wholesale depopulation, took place roughly from 1440 to 1520, with the weighting very heavily in the first half of the interval,[2] save in the extreme north where it continued intermittently through the remainder of the century. The fact undoubtedly is—and we shall have more to say on the point—that the profits to be derived from grazing and the arable uses of land had regained an equilibrium by mid-century, when the steady rise in the export of cloth peaked and began its slow and then disastrous decline. As is so often the fate of moralists, the great preachers and the humanistically inspired laymen, who waxed so hot against enclosures and depopulation, were expressing in classical form the very real fears and sufferings of a generation which was in fact past. England stood in no danger from sheep in 1550.

The immense growth of the cloth industry, which had brought new classes of men to great power and wealth and which had transformed English agriculture, had been so swift, so continuous, and so incredibly profitable to large segments of the population that many years were to pass before its decline after 1550 could be quite comprehended, and it was a decline both relatively and absolutely. It is probable that the export value of woollen cloths doubled between the mid-fifteenth century and the beginning of the sixteenth, doubled once more by the beginning of the last decade of Henry VIII's reign, and continued to increase until it peaked in 1550. This curve of growth is confirmed at least roughly by figures on the number of short cloths exported from London, which rose from 49,214 at the beginning of the sixteenth century, to an average of 102,660 for the triennium 1539–1541, and then peaked at 132,767 for the single year 1550, after which a rapid and irreversible decline set in.[3]

This precocious economic development had in part been sustained by the steady depreciation of the currency, by the sophisticated services supplied by the Antwerp market, by the notable increase of cloth types to meet a varied export demand, and by the

[1] Hoskins, *Essays*, 72, 107.
[2] Beresford, Maurice, *The lost villages of England* (L., [1954]), 166.
[3] Atton, Henry, and H. H. Holland, *The King's customs, etc.* (2 vols., L., 1908–1910), I, 456; Fisher, F. J., 'Commercial trends and policy in sixteenth century England', *Econ. Hist. Rev.* X (1940), 96; Bowden, Peter J., *The wool trade in Tudor and Stuart England* (L., 1962), xvii, 6.

gradual opening up of the central European markets. But the boom was decidedly over in 1551, when the government was compelled for reasons of internal stability to call the currency down and when over-production had in any event come to characterize the industry. The result was a period of sharp depression, marked by the rapid spread of economic distress over the whole realm.

These developments in the economy were watched with great care by the sovereign authority which, as was true throughout the Tudor era, felt wholly free to intervene and to regulate for the public good in matters of detail quite as much as in broad lines of social and economic policy. The regulatory measures ranged over the whole economy and could be minutely specific as well as surprisingly general in their content. A sharp-dealing miller could be placed in heavy bond to require him to exact only normal fees from those who brought corn to him for grinding.[1] Prices of victuals were tightly regulated and the export of bread grains strictly controlled by a government which had to deal not only with a strong inflationary movement but with three bad harvests in the course of the reign. In May, 1547, with a good harvest in prospect, restrictions on the export of grain were lifted by proclamation, only to be tightly resumed when in December prices rose to 6s 8d a quarter for wheat and 5s for rye.[2] Three months later, when there was 'at this present great plenty and abundance of wheat and corn', export restrictions were again lifted, only to be straitly re-imposed on certain foodstuffs in April, 1548, and on all victuals in October of the same year.[3] The embargo on food exports was further tightened in detail in early January, 1549, while on July 2, 1549, with grave civil disorders hindering the harvest in several grain counties, the Council sought to prevent widespread suffering by imposing price regulations on the essential foodstuffs and laying down careful provisions governing their sale.[4] Equally vigilant control was asserted and enforced over the wool and cloth trade throughout the years of Somerset's dominance. The strict monopoly of the Staple's control of wool exports was re-assumed in March, 1547, while the movements, place of trading, and internal administration of the Merchant Adventurers in Flanders were placed under careful control.[5] An ambitious effort was also made to reform the standards of English cloth manufacture by incredibly precise regulations governing

[1] S.P. Dom., Edw. VI, II, 8: Sept. 30, 1547.
[2] Hughes and Larkin, *Tudor proclamations*, I, 386–387, 409.
[3] *Ibid.* 419–420, 423–424, 435–436.
[4] *Ibid.* 439, 464–469, the latter being issued under the authority of 25 Henry VIII, c. 2.
[5] Hughes and Larkin, *Tudor proclamations*, I, 384–385; *A.P.C.* II, App., 545, 556.

shrinking, dyeing, and quality, with instructions for inspection and
the amazing requirement that violators be reported directly to the
Privy Council.[1] At the same time, probably unenforcible, but
valiant, efforts were made by proclamation to put at an end forward
speculation in both raw wool and woollen cloths within the realm.[2]

The care which the government bestowed on the economy,
misguided though it often may have been, is likewise suggested by
the large *corpus* of economic and social measures which were
either passed or considered by Parliament. Though we are treating
these statutory interventions, in the main concerned with agriculture or the wool trade, in their chronological place as part of the
parliamentary history of the reign, it should here be said that of the
118 measures of a public character passed into law by Edward's
two parliaments, 49 (41+ per cent) were directly concerned with
the social and economic needs of the realm. Perhaps as revealing
was the fact that of 279 additional bills introduced in these parliaments, which for a variety of reasons failed to become law, an even
larger proportion (55+ per cent) sought to deal with such matters.
Few governments have ever grappled more manfully with the
problems of the society than did that of the Duke of Somerset; few
have ever been as bold or imaginative in their assault on the in-
equalities and faults of the age; and few indeed have ever wrestled
with as formidable a group of really insoluble weaknesses and ills.

2. THE FISCAL CRISIS, DEBASEMENT, AND INFLATION
(1543–1550)

So accustomed are modern men to the taxing power of the state
that it is difficult quite to comprehend the fact that even in the mid-
sixteenth century the sovereign was expected in normal circumstances to live of his own. Hence parliamentary grants were in-
frequent and irregular, still being regarded as essentially emergency
grants to be levied in time of war, or threatened war, or other unusual national perils. The Tudors depended principally, therefore,
upon the revenue from crown lands, which had increased greatly
in extent and value as lands lost in the anarchical generation of the
War of the Roses were regained, as escheats and attainders added
properties, and as the vast holdings garnered from the monastic
seizure and, under Edward, the chantry endowments, were swept
into royal hands. In the period 1485 to 1540 revenues from crown

[1] Hughes and Larkin, *Tudor proclamations*, I, 453–455: Apr. 17, 1549.
[2] *Ibid.* 457–458, 479–480.

lands had increased more than six times over and stood at something like £200,000 p.a. in 1548 after the chantry lands were seized. This steep rise far more than over-matched a gradual but persistent inflationary process, as well as the rising costs of an increasingly elaborate administrative mechanism, but could not bear the enormous costs of modern warfare in which Henry VIII indulged with such reckless abandon during his last seven years of life. Henry spent upwards of £2,100,000 on his French and Scottish wars, a great sum which was financed from normal revenues, successive parliamentary grants, forced loans, the sale of a large proportion of the monastic lands, and, unfortunately, by debasement of the currency. Moreover, Henry had been driven by his fiscal requirements into the international money market; in 1546 the royal debt, due principally to the Fuggers and at high interest rates, amounted to £152,180, though by the time of his death the sum had been considerably reduced.[1]

Hence fiscal affairs were in serious straits at the moment of Edward's accession and were promptly and irrevocably worsened by prodigal disposal by sale and by gift of crown lands with an income of something more than £41,000 p.a. to satisfy the rapacity of the ruling junta and to help in the payment for a reckless and on the whole completely unsuccessful foreign policy.[2] There were also relatively slight losses from malfeasance, though in general the administration of financial affairs was efficient and honest, and much stricter audits and controls were imposed than in the preceding reign. The chronic fiscal crisis during the reign was in the main caused by the heavy costs of the festering Scottish war and the war on France, which over a period of five years cost the Treasury upwards of £1,356,000 in addition to the heavy normal outlays for defence.[3] This great sum was largely financed by the sale of capital assets (crown lands), further debasement of the coinage, sharp economies in normal royal outlays, and crown borrowing, an essentially weak government unquestionably fearing to lay its full and surely pressing needs before Parliament. The tax imposed on sheep and wool, combined with a tax of 5 per cent on personalty for three years, was levied against bitter opposition principally for

---

[1] Dietz, F. C., *English government finance, 1485–1558* (Univ. of Illinois Studies in the Social Sciences, IX, no. 3, Urbana, 1920), 173. This section on fiscal affairs owes much to this pioneering work.

[2] *Vide ante*, 104 ff. We have seen that about 69 per cent of these resources were from former monastic or chantry lands.

[3] Dietz, F. C., *Finances of Edward VI and Mary* (Smith College Studies in History, III, no. 2, Northampton, Mass., 1918), 81.

general social and economic purposes, and was promptly repealed on Somerset's fall. In all, indeed, the Crown gained no more than £299,000 from parliamentary grants in Edward's entire reign, of which a fair proportion represented collections of taxes levied in Henry's last Parliament. This means that only slightly more than a fifth (22 per cent) of the entire war costs were borne by taxation.

Even after the inglorious conclusion of the war with France in 1550 and the windfall payment by France of £133,333 for the cession of Boulogne, Northumberland was able only slowly to reduce the costs of the military establishment, especially on the Scottish border. Moreover, the net cost of the forces in Ireland alone (£42,000 p.a.) was nearly as much as the outlays for the royal household, which were under careful scrutiny. On occasion, so severe was the fiscal crisis, there was literally no ready money available in any of the revenue courts and the Treasurer had to file orders for payments in turn. Thus in July, 1549, when Somerset wished to pay £100 to Lord Grey for expenses in restoring order in Oxfordshire, he directed the Treasurer of Augmentations that if there was no ready cash, 'we pray you to take some order with such your friends by your bond or otherwise that in no wise he be destitute of the said sum'.[1] Again, in June, 1552, the Treasurer was instructed to draw from arrearages in order to place £1000 in the hands of the wardens on the northern borders.[2] Even the expenses of the household, which, considering the inflation under way, rose only moderately from about £38,800 in 1547–1548 to about £56,800 in 1550–1551, were on occasion difficult to meet, funds being drawn in the critical year 1549 from several sources and then staggered in two or three payments.[3] It was almost certainly this chronic fiscal emergency which forced the Council to the review of the whole problem of revenues and to the administrative reorganization which was under careful consideration in the late months of the reign.[4]

Aside from the sale of capital resources, the principal way in which the government financed its wars and its recurring budgetary deficit was by the disastrous device of severe and repeated debasements of the bullion value of the currency. This was to lead to severe economic dislocations, to a heightened want of confidence in

[1] Richardson, *Augmentations*, 368, quoting Aug. Offic. Treas. Accts., no. 2b, pt. 1.
[2] *A.P.C.* IV, 68, 97, 103, 119, for similar instances. The climax surely came in the summer of 1552 when in August payments on warrants were actually suspended, 'for that his highness is presently in progress and resolved not to be troubled with payments until his return' (*ibid.* 109). [3] *A.P.C.* II, 281–282: May 7, 1549.
[4] S.P. Dom., Edw. VI, VII, 38, 39: June 22, 1549. The later phases of the fiscal problem will be considered in the concluding volume of this study.

governmental policy, and was to constitute one of the chief causes of a pronounced inflation which placed the whole of the economy under severe strain. Nor is it too much to say that this mistaken policy was one of the prime causes for the insurrection which wracked England in 1549 and laid the basis for Warwick's *coup d'état*.

The seductive possibilities of coinage manipulation were by no means new in Europe or in England, and the device had been employed by Henry VIII in his frantic search for funds wherewith to prosecute his wars late in the reign. Thus in the great debasement of 1543-1544, the plan for which was developed chiefly by Wriothesley, the weight of coins was reduced very slightly but the fineness, the true bullion content, was sharply lowered from the ancient standard of 11 oz. 2 dwt. fine to 10 oz. fine, and then in successive stages to 9 oz. (1544), 6 oz. (1545), and 4 oz. (1546), with the result that at the end of the reign Henry's testons (shillings) contained only about one-third silver content. The profits derived at the mint were very great, of the order of £363,000, but the economy was rudely shaken, prices rose swiftly, and in the Low Countries the exchange value of English currency fell from 27s *Flemish* in 1542 to only 21s *Flemish* in 1547. This predictably led to an immediate stimulation of the export trade, especially in cloth, which meant in effect that Henry was paying for his military adventures on the Continent in the coin of English cloth.[1]

During the first two years of the new reign the royal mints continued to issue debased coin struck from the dies of the late King. But under the joint pressure of heavy commitments on the Scottish Border and mounting tension with France, Somerset, despite the warnings of a few in his Council, determined on still further debasement. In June, 1549, Smith laid before the Protector a careful analysis of the fiscal situation with recommendations which might avoid further inflationary courses. The recently voted subsidy should be collected earlier, new sales of crown lands should be made, payments on outstanding debts should be postponed, and further loans raised abroad.[2] These not very original or helpful suggestions were not followed, the government instead ordering the calling in of old coinage and the minting of new issues which were

---

[1] Feavearyear, Albert, *The pound sterling, etc.* (Oxford, 1931; rev. by E. Victor Morgan, *1963*), 54–63; Oman, C. W. C., 'The Tudors and the currency, 1526–1560', *Royal Hist. Soc. Trans.*, n.s. IX (1895), 177–181; Craig, Sir John, *The mint, etc.* (Cambridge, 1953), 106–109 (who estimates the government's profit at about £200,000); de Roover, Raymond, *Gresham on foreign exchange, etc.* (Cambridge, Mass., 1949), 52.

[2] S.P. Dom., Edw. VI, VII, 38.

of increased fineness, in order to make counterfeiting more difficult, but at the same time sharply reduced in weight both gold and silver coins.[1] It seems probable that upwards of £1,000,000 of the new coinage was minted in 1549–1550, accompanied by a sharp rise in prices, while the final debasement carried out by Northumberland in 1550 so lowered values that silver coins had been reduced by about three-fourths of their historical silver content and gold coins by about a quarter.[2] These drastic and irresponsible measures shook public confidence, seriously affected foreign trade, and contributed directly to the spiralling inflation already under way. Northumberland had no other alternative in 1551 than to undertake a bold scheme for the reform of the currency and to order a savage devaluation which further shook the national economy.

Postponing consideration of the lively theoretical discussion of monetary matters provoked by these successive debasements of the coinage,[3] we should at least briefly note a few of the specific contemporary criticisms evoked by the Protector's policy. The author of the famous *Discourse of the Common Weal of this Realm of England*, whom we are inclined to believe was Hales,[4] took a staunchly critical position with respect to governmental policy, arguing that Henry VIII had in the earlier debasements done no more than take an immediate profit from what could be described as a wastage of the capital of the realm. Royal fiat can make any coinage legal in England, but lacks the power to make any other nation accept it at the announced value. Hence so long as England trades abroad, the

[1] This debasement was carried out by successive proclamations, among which were those of Jan. 24, 1549, announcing the new coinage; Jan. 31, 1549, extending the time for calling in old testons; Apr. 1, 1549, resuming payment of the King's debts; Apr. 11, 1549, for the valuation of gold (Hughes and Larkin, *Tudor proclamations*, I, 440–441, 441–443, 445–446, 449–451).   [2] Craig, *The mint*, 111.

[3] Northumberland's fiscal policy will be dealt with in the concluding volume of this work.

[4] The question of authorship has been long in debate. The older view was that Sir Thomas Smith was the author, which, however, was cogently denied by Miss Elizabeth Lamond, in her excellent edition of this work, first published in *1893* (Cambridge) and reissued in 1929, in which she made a strong case for the authorship of John Hales (xvii, xxi, xxviii–xxix). The claims of Smith were once more advanced by Jean-Yves le Branchu in *Écrits notables sur la monnaie, etc.*, I (Paris, 1934), lvii–civ, and by E. Hughes in an article in the *Bulletin of the John Rylands Library*, XXI (1937), 167–175, and more recently, and with considerable vehemence, by Mary Dewar in her *Sir Thomas Smith*, esp. 53–55, and more gently and persuasively in her 'The authorship of the "Discourse of the Commonweal" ' (*Econ. Hist. Rev.*, ser. 2, XIX (1966), 388–400). Internal evidence, undoubted similarities of style, and Miss Lamond's impressive argument dispose this writer to the Hales attribution. But we are by no means certain, and when in citation the author is indicated as [Hales], [Hales ?] is meant. We doubt that the controversy can be resolved.

exchange value of its coinage sets the true measure of its worth.[1] Latimer, reminding his audience that he had spoken honestly and vigorously even before Henry VIII, lashed out at rulers who imposed a debased coinage on their subjects, recalling that even in the Old Testament there were such indignities in the manipulation of coinage, when 'the naughtiness of the silver was the occasion of dearth of all things in the realm' and when poor men were injured by monetary policy.[2] Hales believed, indeed, that the ultimate cause of all the economic ills of the period sprang from the successive coinage debasements. As he puts the argument: 'I think this alteration of the coin to be the first original cause that strangers first sells [sic] their wares dearer to us; and that makes all farmers and tenants, that reareth any commodity, again to sell the same dearer.'[3] Hence it was the ultimate cause that must be attacked, the only possible remedy being to restore the old rate and goodness of the coinage, and this suddenly and with no warning in order to spoil the speculators.[4] Otherwise, as another contemporary put the argument, the social dislocations will worsen as the rich and informed hoard the old coins while the poor will be driven to none but base money.[5]

The mystery of monetary values enthralled as it puzzled men of this decade. But all who wrote were severely critical of the policy of debasement. Croft, when serving as Deputy in Ireland, wrote to the Council pondering why men should not accept a currency at its face value as proclaimed, 'seeing it is for none other use but exchange?' But experience teaches that we esteem only that which reason persuades us to value. And Latimer lashed out in a sermon before the King at what he regarded as a fraud on the realm: 'We have now a pretty little shilling, indeed a very pretty one. I have but one, I think, in my purse, and the last day I had put it away almost for an old groat, and so I trust some will take them.'[6] Preaching again a fortnight later, he recounted that he had been termed a 'seditious fellow' for his jibes at the new coinage. But he was comforted by the reflection that 'Esai the prophet' also condemned debasement and had gone to the root of the matter, which was covetousness, since it was the poor who were ultimately despoiled.[7]

[1] [Hales], *Common weal*, 87–88.   [2] Latimer, *Third sermon*, in *Works*, I, 136–137.
[3] [Hales], *Common weal*, 104.   [4] *Ibid*. 105.
[5] Tawney, R. H., and Eileen Power, *Tudor economic documents, etc.* (3 vols., L., 1924), II, 186–187, quoting Cooper, T., *Chronicle* (1565 ed.).
[6] Latimer, Hugh, *Seven sermons before Edward VI*, ed. by E. Arber (English reprints ser., no. 13, L., 1869), 34–35: Mar. 8, 1549.
[7] *Ibid*. 82–86: Mar. 22, 1549; Latimer, *Works*, I, 137–138.

Hence, all the critics were agreed, there could be no 'patching', no gradual improvement of the coinage, since that would simply mean that the bad money would continue to drive out the good. The only recourse, therefore, Hales maintained, was an immediate and sudden restoration of the coinage. Admittedly there would be strains for a year to two, but all plate in hand could be coined to the restored value, and bullion hoarded by private persons could be coaxed out by a very low mint fee. The important gain would be the restoration of confidence, the rebuilding of the King's credit, and the realization that England's wealth was in the commodities she possessed and produced.[1]

The fiscal straits of the government and the want of confidence induced by debasement likewise affected adversely the effort to maintain a steady and satisfactory rate of exchange in the Antwerp market and to arrange for successive refundings of the royal external debt, amounting to approximately £100,000 *(Flemish)* at the outset of the reign. Dansell, the English fiscal agent in Antwerp, was as early as April,1549, seeking to re-fund the debt with the expectation of paying 14 per cent interest, the general state of European governmental finances in the period being suggested by the fact that Charles V was paying from 15 per cent to 18 per cent for funds.[2] Dansell and Gresham were also trying to protect the English position by buying up available silver bullion at prices which the Council thought too high, hoping that the more pressing current needs for re-funding could be met in part at least by the export of lead and bell-metal. Paget, then in Brussels, thought Dansell had been unjustly censured by the Council, particularly since he had few resources with which to manoeuvre in the money market.[3] An already difficult situation was gravely worsened when civil disorders broke out in the spring, Dansell reporting that he was unable to borrow the £100,000 required for re-funding at 12½ per cent and doubting whether it could be borrowed even at 13 per cent.[4] Further, the pound sterling on the Antwerp exchange had fallen steadily from about 21s 4d in late 1547, and was not to reach its low until June, 1551, when it was valued at 13s 4d. Then gradual recovery of the exchange rate began after the skilled Gresham had been placed in charge in Antwerp, after the devaluations of 1551 had occurred,

[1] [Hales], *Common weal*, 111–114.
[2] *Cal. S.P. For., Edw. VI*, #137: Apr. 20, 1549; S.P. Henry VIII, CCXXIII, 101, for external debt in late 1546.
[3] *Ibid.* ##147, 153, 156, 161, 164, 171.
[4] *Ibid.* #193: July 24, 1549.

and after Gresham's bold scheme for manipulating sterling had begun to have its effects.[1]

Accompanying the fiscal crisis in England, feeding on the successive debasements of the coinage, and mounting rapidly to a climax in 1550 was an inflationary process which had begun in the late fifteenth century all over western Europe. It is broadly accurate to say that the curve of this price rise mounted steeply during the first half of the Edwardian era, as the consequence of the disastrous harvest of 1549, the weakness of the central government, and the economic dislocation following in the train of the final great debasement; it then fell slightly but steadily during the remainder of the reign as the government undertook administrative reforms and subjected the economy to a harsh but effective devaluation of the currency. Though much useful work has been done on the price rise of the sixteenth century, we are still unable fully to assess its causes or its extent. In another place we have indicated our doubts concerning the validity of the price indexes which have in recent years been constructed from data which are incomplete, not widely enough based geographically, and which tend to measure sixteenth-century needs and values in terms which are our own.[2] It may be suggested, indeed, that we have been too much enamoured of the beautiful precision of a statistical method which is in point of fact rooted in faulty and incomplete data. Further, it is disturbing when indexes so constructed fail to demonstrate roughly at least the same rate and direction for all important commodities. Moreover, they seem to lay too heavy an emphasis on undoubted price rises from say 1540 to 1560 which, even as measured by the proposed indexes, suggest price increases not greater than those experienced in Britain or America in the two decades following the Second World War.[3] What is quite clear is that men of the age were aware of the erosion taking place in purchasing power, that real wages were not rising, and that the sharp rise in prices accompanying the debasements from 1543 to 1551 was undoubtedly responsible for widespread disorder, general uncertainty, and almost surely some suffering as several classes of men were driven to and then below the level of subsistence.

Much of the difficulty in which the English society found itself

[1] These matters will be discussed in the concluding volume of this work. It may be said here, however, that when in early 1552 Gresham undertook his mission, the royal debt, mostly to the Fuggers, totalled £123,047, and had been paid down to £45,470 by the close of the year.

[2] Jordan, *Philanthropy in England*, 34–37.

[3] Gould, J. D., 'The price revolution reconsidered', *Econ. Hist. Rev.*, ser. 2, XVII (Dec., 1964), 249–250, has very persuasive and sensible thoughts on these matters.

may certainly be attributed to the swiftness of the price rise over a period of about eight years (1543–1551), to which a relatively unsophisticated economy simply could not adapt itself. In late 1550 a careful observer wrote to Bullinger that a decade earlier a student could live comfortably at Oxford for 20 French crowns a year, but that now 30 crowns would be required as a minimum, while another 10 would permit a man to live comfortably. In these latter days, he added, 'when avarice is every where increasing . . . and this by a divine scourge, every thing has become almost twice as dear'.[1] A flood of testimony from contemporary sources could be presented suggesting that prices seemed to men of the period approximately to have doubled in their memory and that most of the increase had occurred in the past decade. This is also at least roughly confirmed by the proposed indexes, one of which suggests a rise in the prices for consumables of about 2.8 times in the interval 1508 to 1551 and another of about 2.5 times from the 1490s to the 1550s.[2] Something like the same rise seems to have occurred in Lincoln where the average price of the best wheat works out to 7s 4d the quarter in the 1520s and 15s 2d in the 1550s, complicated by a brief but desperate scarcity after the harvests of 1549 and 1551 when authorized prices had to be steeply increased to 24s to bring any wheat into the market, though as scarcity was relieved, wheat fell to about 12s by Michaelmas, 1552.[3]

The causes of this steadily spiralling inflation, the curve of which is remarkably similar on the Continent,[4] are obscure in part because we simply do not have sufficient data of the necessary kind to separate out and assess exceedingly complex historical forces which were at work. The increase in the bullion stores, laid against only slowly rising productivity, has been advanced as a principal factor. Some connection there undoubtedly was, though England was on balance an exporter of bullion for two decades after the monastic spoliation. The leverage against prices was in part surely occasioned by the increasing European stocks of bullion coupled, in all advanced countries, but especially in England, with sharp and successive debasements of the bullion value of the coinage. But prices did not

[1] Robinson, *Original letters*, I, 190: Christopher Hales to Bullinger, Dec. 10, 1550; and see his further complaint a month later to Gualter (*ibid.* 195).

[2] Phelps Brown, E. H., and Sheila V. Hopkins, 'Seven centuries of the prices of consumables, etc.', *Economica*, n.s. XXIII (Nov. 1956), 307 ff.

[3] Hill, J. W. F., *Tudor and Stuart Lincoln* (Cambridge, 1956), 65–66, 222.

[4] Phelps Brown, E. H., and S. V. Hopkins, 'Wage-rates and prices, etc.', *Economica*, n.s. XXIV (Nov., 1957), 290–293, for the remarkably similar movement of prices and wages in France and Alsace.

rise uniformly and simultaneously, the steep increase being in foods, with no more than a gradual rise in industrial products.[1]

Contemporaries tended to place the whole blame for spiralling prices on debasement, and the devaluation undertaken late in the reign suggests strongly that the government was itself so persuaded. There were clamorous and bitter complaints, of which one will perhaps suffice:

> Testons be gone to Oxforde, god be their speede:
> To studie in Brasenose there to proceede.
> ....
> These Testons looke redde: how like you the same?
> Tis atooken of grace: they blushe for shame.
> ....
> We stampe crabs, we stamp testons: which stamping doone.
> We stare uppon Testons now beyond the moone.
> Which stamping of Testons brought it not some skill,
> Our staryng on Testons could iudge them but ill.[2]

But throughout the period of debasement prices simply did not keep pace, the purchasing power of the base coins remaining much higher than the melt value. Put roughly, prices approximately doubled while the debasement was nearly a factor of four. The 'plentifulness of the money and the baseness thereof' was correctly blamed by William Lane for stimulating inflation,[3] but clearly the 'plentifulness' of money was being steadily relieved by the hoarding of older coins against the possibility of even further debasements.[4]

As we have suggested, the steep and damaging inflation of prices was concentrated on foodstuffs, and particularly on the bread grains. Every effort of Parliament, the Council, and local authorities was fixed on the control of these prices, but without marked success. Sir John Mason wrote to Cecil in the worst of the period of scarcity, sceptically wondering whether prices could ever be regulated by the fiat of the sovereign. 'Nature will have her course, etiam si furca expellatur', and for that matter, 'who will keep a cow that may not sell milk for so much as the merchant and he can agree upon'.[5] It

[1] Brenner, Y. S., 'The inflation of prices in early sixteenth century England', *Econ. Hist. Rev.*, ser. 2, XIV (Dec., 1961), 225–226, 230.

[2] Heywood, John, *Works and miscellaneous short poems*, ed. by Burton A. Milligan (Illinois Studies in Language and Literature, vol. 41, Urbana, 1956), 216.

[3] Tawney and Power, *Tudor economic documents*, II, 183.

[4] de Roover, *Gresham*, 85.

[5] *Cal. S.P. For., Edw. VI*, #265; Tytler, *England*, I, 340–342: Dec. 4, 1550.

seems evident that an increased population, combined with the rapid growth of London and other urban centres, was imposing a demand for foodstuffs which a traditional agriculture simply could not meet, at least until a substantial transition from sheep farming to arable had been effected by the close of the century. Surplus labour was on the whole being absorbed by expanding industries which were able without strain rapidly to increase the supply of industrial goods, which accordingly rose only slowly and modestly in cost.[1] It was unskilled agricultural labour which bore the brunt of the price rise, but these classes of men possessed in the soil, in the waste, and in stubbornly defended manorial rights resources, which, though it cannot be statistically demonstrated, none the less bore them through the evil years. But England was to be scarred and battered by fierce stirs and major dislocations as a consequence. This is all too clearly revealed in the examination of quite simple people in Norwich in the aftermath of the great rising there. Here a housewife deposed that at the bakery she had heard many hard words regarding the 'loss of money', while the baker testified that in his shop there was constant talk of high prices and the evils of extortioners. Similar bitter gossip was heard at Sloyly Fair of feared further devaluations, ever-rising prices, and the steadily eroding economic position of poor men and women who were the almost defenceless victims of the inflationary process.[2] There is persuasive evidence that real wages fell by something like 40 per cent between 1500 and 1551, the English society being saved from disaster by the fact that the overwhelming proportion of poor men were still rooted in the land with all the ultimate resilient strength which the land has always lent to those who live close to her—even including a bit of seasonable poaching.[3]

Our uncertainty regarding the causes of the great inflationary movement which set in at about the beginning of the sixteenth century is also greatly heightened by our ignorance of the demographic factors which may very well be of overriding consequence. It is far more than coincidental that the population of England

[1] Brenner, in *Econ. Hist. Rev.*, ser. 2, XIV (Dec., 1961), 232–235; Kerridge, Eric, 'The movement of rent, 1540–1640', *ibid.* VI (Aug., 1953), 28; Gould, 'Price revolution', *ibid.* XVII (Dec., 1964), 266. For the relatively modest rise for cloths in the London market, 1547–1551, see Johnson, A. H., *The history of the worshipful company of the drapers of London* (5 vols., Oxford, 1914–1922), II, 395–396.

[2] Tawney and Power, *Tudor economic documents*, II, 189–191, quoting from the Norwich Municipal Archives, 37b–40.

[3] Knoop, Douglas, and G. P. Jones, *The mediaeval mason, etc.* (Manchester, 1933), Appendix I, Tables I and II; Phelps Brown and Hopkins, in *Economica*, n.s. XXIV, 298–301.

began steadily and quite rapidly to rise simultaneously with prices. As we have suggested, agricultural metho ds of organization were so ossified that they could not keep pace with demand for foodstuffs, while a labour surplus was rapidly created which could not wholly be absorbed by an expanding industrial economy. The demand for goods, and especially foodstuffs, rose rapidly and simply could not be met, particularly during this reign in which one harvest was disastrous and two others slender.

The causes and the extent of the price rise of the sixteenth century are, then, obscure, incredibly complex, and not to be precisely demonstrated in 'indices of prices which are mere statistical artifacts'. But sheep grazing and debasement were the evils on which contemporaries laid the blame, thereby creating 'a traumatic experience' and a malaise not unlike the great depression of our own century.[1]

3. WOOL, SHEEP, AND TRADE

For a full hundred years before our period England enjoyed great prosperity from wool and, as we have seen, radically reorganized its agriculture as more and more formerly arable land was brought under sheep pasture. The demand for English wool, and cloth, seemed insatiable and was greatly stimulated by the fact that wool prices doubled in the century before the accession of Edward VI, whereas grain prices advanced more slowly and erratically.[2] England became, in truth, dangerously dependent on sheep, since through most of the Tudor period approximately 75 per cent of the value of the export trade was in wool and woollen cloth. Further, during the early Tudor era England was moving from a wool-exporting to a cloth-making and exporting economy, with the consequence that her industrial economy was increasingly linked with cloth-making. As we have already noted, the market for English cloth abroad entered a severe depression in 1551 with attendant dislocation in the economy, which was slowly corrected only as wide areas were returned to the plough as the export market failed to revive, while sheep farmers were driven to turn in part to the production of prime mutton for the London and other urban markets. It has been estimated that at about the beginning of our period there may well have been something like 11,000,000 sheep in England, which, if so, suggests that roughly 8,600 square miles of English soil were under sheep

[1] Gould, 'Price revolution', *Econ. Hist. Rev.*, ser. 2, XVII, 266.
[2] Bowden, *Wool trade*, 5.

grazing, if we may assume that no more than two sheep per acre could be carried on average pastures.[1] At the very least we do know that much of the best plough land of England was now steadily under sheep pasture as the country entered into the last decade of a long period of sheep prosperity which had left it most vulnerably exposed.

Flocks were of all sizes, were spread over rich arable as well as marginal pasture lands, and were evidently to be found in considerable numbers in every county in England. The greater profit was to be made from large-scale grazing, which was one of the principal factors underlying the voracious land hunger of the first half of the sixteenth century and the tendency of landowners to aggregate as well as to expand their holdings. Thus in Norfolk and Suffolk, important grazing counties, there were numerous flocks of about 2000 sheep, which seems to be a flock size favoured by many of the gentry. Sir Roger Townshend, in Norfolk, was grazing about 3000 sheep in 1544, but a few years later had increased the number to 4200.[2] In the year when the wool market collapsed, Sir Robert Southwell was grazing almost 10,000 sheep on fourteen different ranges, while three other Norfolk landowners possessed flocks of about 5000.[3] The famed Spencer of Althorp (Northamptonshire) ran flocks in that pasture county of 13,000–14,000 sheep, but this total was almost equalled in Norfolk by Southwell and was exceeded by Sir William Fermor of East Barsham who some years earlier than our period was grazing about 17,000 sheep on twenty-five different properties which he owned, rented, or leased. His nephew and heir, ironically, was killed in Kett's rebellion.[4] The profits from these flocks have been estimated to work out at something like £40 p.a. from a thousand sheep, even though the Norfolk and Suffolk fleeces were recognized to be much inferior to those of Midland sheep, which doubtless accounts for the beginning of the exploitation of the mutton market of London by East Anglian graziers.

As we have indicated, the English wool trade was by the

[1] S.P. Dom., Edw. VI, II, 13. This is a most interesting, and complicated, estimate of the number of sheep, derived in turn from the number of cloths and the amount of wool exported and used in England. It was probably gathered when the tax later imposed on sheep and cloth was being considered. Using an earlier estimate of 38 Henry VIII, the figure was set for 2 Edward VI at 11,089,149. The grazing limit of two sheep per acre for full sustenance on middling pasture land holds for New England and is probably not far off the sixteenth-century figure.

[2] Simpson, Alan, *The wealth of the gentry, 1540–1660* (Chicago, 1961), 183.

[3] Allison, K. J., 'Flock management in the sixteenth and seventeenth centuries', *Econ. Hist. Rev.*, ser. 2, XI (Aug., 1958), 100.

[4] Simpson, *Wealth of the gentry*, 182–183.

beginning of our period in process of completing a transition from
the export of raw wool to the export of finished cloth, something like
85 per cent of the value being in cloths for the interval 1540–1547.[1]
By this date too the export trade was heavily concentrated on
London which was shipping two-thirds of the total value, with
Southampton accounting for no more than 9 per cent, Newcastle
5 per cent, and no other ports with more than 3 per cent of the whole.
The remaining trade in the export of raw wool was by long-estab-
lished law exclusively in the hands of the Staple, which since the
early fifteenth century had been settled in Calais. The Crown depended heavily on the export duty of £2 the sack, often using it as
security for foreign loans and exploiting the monopoly in its diplomatic negotiations.[2] Lying outside the Staple were four northern
counties and a portion of the North Riding which were permitted to
export directly from either Newcastle or Berwick, the trade being
principally in rough wools of marginal quality. But the great days
of the Staple were over as the government lent the full weight of
policy and law to the encouragement of cloth manufacture, as
Spanish wool began to compete, and as the quality of English
fleeces began to deteriorate, almost certainly as a consequence of
pasture over-stocking.

The industry in the sixteenth century developed skills and markets
for two quite different cloths: the woollens (or clothing) which
included such fabrics as broadcloths, kersies, cottons, and friezes,
and the worsteds which were woven from long staple wool carefully combed and then carded. The woollens were very heavy and
found their readiest market in northern and eastern Europe,
whereas the much lighter and finer worsteds were designed for the
Mediterranean and Iberian trade. The woollens had enjoyed a
phenomenal prosperity in the first half of the century, when volume
trebled, and maintained a strong competitive position throughout
the century. But the worsteds were competitive neither in terms of
quality nor price with an expanding Continental cloth industry and
fell into a severe depression until revitalized late in the century by
new blood, better patterns, and more rigorously imposed quality
controls.[3]

[1] Bowden, *Wool trade*, 37; Schanz, Georg, *Englische Handelspolitik gegen Ende des
Mittelalters, etc.* (2 vols., Leipzig, 1881), II, 32–33, presents figures which would suggest
that 91 per cent of the value was in cloth.
[2] S.P. Dom., Edw. VI, II, 13: Oct. ?, 1547; *ibid.* 15, 16, 17, suggest the steady concern of the Crown with the Staple.
[3] The discussion in this paragraph owes much to Bowden's most helpful account
(*Wool trade*, 41–50), and to Schanz (*Englische Handelspolitik, II*, 12–13).

The manufacture of the coarser woollens (kersies) was widespread, but was centred particularly in southwestern England—Devonshire, Dorset, Somerset, and Worcestershire in particular having numerous mills, usually depending on nearby sources of raw wool. More important was the broadcloth industry, now concentrated in such counties as Somerset, Gloucestershire, Worcestershire, Oxfordshire, and, above all, Wiltshire. In 1551, when the Drapers of Worcester were formally incorporated, the trade was at its height with 380 looms in and near Worcester which it was said, surely with heroic exaggeration, gave employment to 8000 workers. Standards of manufacture were not high in the county and the trade suffered considerably as efforts were made to better the quality of the cloth precisely as the export market collapsed.[1] Much of the chalk lands of southern Wiltshire was given over to sheep farming, supplying wool for a thriving cloth industry which also drew fleeces from the great Cotswold grazing region. In the fifteenth century Salisbury had been an important centre for manufacturing and marketing cloth, but the industry had somewhat before our period moved westward to form part of the greatest single concentration in the realm, including Somerset, western Wiltshire, and the Cotswolds.[2] A generation earlier Leland had been most favourably impressed by the activity and prosperity of the small cloth towns of western Wiltshire, and particularly Bradford and Trowbridge, which specialized in white woollens for the export trade and which enjoyed close credit and marketing arrangements with London. Among the greatest clothiers of the region were the Horton family of Ilford, with interests in Bradford and Trowbridge, the Baileys who conducted a successful business for three generations, the Brounckers and the Gerrish families in Melksham, and the famous William Stumpe who had settled his manufacturing in the precincts of Malmesbury Abbey and who shortly afterwards was negotiating with the city of Oxford for Osney Abbey where he planned to give employment to 2000 persons.[3] Stumpe invested heavily in lands in Wiltshire and in the Cotswolds, and when he died in 1552—just past the peak of the clothing boom—left a fortune so great and so liquid that three of his descendants married earls.

Still another centre of cloth-making was to be found in many and scattered towns in Surrey, Sussex, Hampshire, Kent, and Berkshire, specializing in broadcloths and kersies of medium quality, and already by 1550 suffering from the competition of the western and

[1] VCH, *Worcestershire*, II, 285–289.   [2] VCH, *Wiltshire*, IV, 123–141.
[3] *Ibid.* 142–147; *ibid.* VII, 113–114.

southwestern looms. Berkshire and the adjacent Cotswold hills produced wool of very high quality, supplying the numerous mills at such centres as Reading, Colthrop, Wallingford, and above all Newbury where the famous John Winchcombe was one of the most successful and aggressive of the clothiers of the realm in the Edwardian era.[1]

The once famous and prosperous East Anglian region was still an important cloth-producing centre, though only the most efficient looms could compete with the clothiers of western England, until towards the close of the century new methods and tighter controls over quality secured a revival of its earlier reputation and prosperity.[2] Norwich was still an important market centre, but its manufacturing was in the doldrums, the industry in 1550 being concentrated in the smaller towns and villages in the county. In Lincoln the industry had almost disappeared, the Common Council of the city undertaking in 1551 to revive it by making available a disused church and all necessary land on condition that an entrepreneur should make at least twenty cloths a year.[3] Much farther to the north, the industry was at the stage of establishing itself in dozens of small mills supplying both rough woollens and worsteds, while in the remaining region, comprising Lancashire and Westmorland, the available supply of wool was inferior and the cloth made for export was the roughest and heaviest in the realm.[4]

There was great apprehension in England concerning the almost obsessive preoccupation of landowners and renters with laying down soil to pasture, and there was concern as well because of growing competition abroad with English cloth and the first symptoms of the disastrous break in the export cloth market which, as we have seen, occurred in 1551. The government seemed not to regard as necessary any substantial revision of policy with respect to the still burgeoning cloth trade, though it was attacking the organically related problems arising from the ever-increasing dedication of land to sheep farming. But there were complaints and there were apprehensions regarding the state of the industry which a brief sampling of the considerable literature will document.

The clothiers complained in the Star Chamber in April, 1550, that the Merchant Adventurers, expertly versed in the export market, had set a price on cloth which would if maintained cause a loss of £1

[1] VCH, *Berkshire*, I, 388, 389, 390; *ibid*. II, 213; *ibid*. III, 291.

[2] Bowden, *Wool trade*, 53–54.

[3] VCH, *Lincolnshire*, II, 381–382. The effort was unsuccessful, as was usually the case in such undertakings.

[4] Bowden, *Wool trade*, 56.

a cloth.[1] As testimony was taken, however, other clothiers denied the statement, charging that the difficulty lay with 'the multitude of clothiers lately increased'. Quality controls had fallen away so far that 'good making is decayed' and hence prices had fallen. This complaint had also been repeatedly lodged by the Dutch and Flemish merchants, leading to an official protest against the uneven quality of English cloth.[2] The clothiers urged that the apprentice-ship laws respecting cloth-making be more rigorously enforced and a restoration of quality secured. The merchants, for their part, pleaded that prices were set not by them but by the Antwerp market, blaming the 'decay of our money by exchange' as well as the decline of quality for the difficulties in which the trade found itself.[3]

These are no more than premonitions of the severe depression which overcame the industry in 1551 and provoked more reflective consideration of its troubles, one example of which will perhaps suffice. William Cholmeley, a London grocer, writing in 1553, was persuaded that God had specially blessed 'this little corner of the earth', though England had used its resources in a prodigal and wholly irresponsible manner. Thus with the best wool resources in the world the nation was content to export some raw wool and unfinished cloths, rather than fully exploiting its value by the making of such specialized, and labour-using, commodities as caps and dyed cloths. He was particularly indignant that almost the whole of the cloths were exported undyed, giving employment to many thousands in the Low Countries, simply because English dyeing had been so unskilled and irresponsible. If cloths were exported finished, he reckoned that the additional value would pay for all English imports, which had in fact been financed, and that ruinously, by the export of bullion. Admittedly, these skills must be taught at first by foreign workmen induced to come to England, but it must be done since England can no longer afford to depend so completely on 'unwrought' commodities. He blamed particularly the firmly entrenched drapers and clothworkers, who if they were as 'willing to bestow money in the advancing of the public weal as they are in feasting in their halls at the choosing [of] new wardens ... then could they save somewhat toward the compassing of this matter'.

[1] In late 1547, when the export market was in a more flourishing state, the Adven-turers had petitioned the Council to secure dispensation from an Henrician statute fixing maximum prices, so high were prices for cloths in the Antwerp market (*A.P.C.* II, 142–143).

[2] Van der Goes, Aart, *Holland onder de regeering van Keizer Karel den Vijfden, etc.* (Amsterdam, 1791), pt. 3, 114: Oct. 3, 1550.

[3] *A.P.C.* III, 19–20: Apr. 28, 1550.

After experimenting with a Southwark dyer, he expressed himself as certain that the necessary skills could be quickly attained, at a cost not so great as 'one corner' of the hospitals that had been erected in London for the care of the poor, and resulting in far greater sustenance for those now unemployed.[1]

This spirited and interesting critique of English industrial policy was but one of the numerous attacks on the Merchant Adventurers and what was regarded as the tyranny of the great Antwerp market, which had in the past absorbed almost the whole of English cloth exports. The market had been established there in part for the convenience of English merchants and to link easily with the Cologne market, which provided essential facilities for the ultimate distribution of English cloths through Germany and central Europe. During the first half of the sixteenth century Antwerp had become the largest commercial centre in Europe. Even though its congested docks could berth only small vessels, making it necessary for larger ships to unload to barges well downstream, the city had quickly gained great prosperity and, granted large liberties by the Emperor, was remarkably free of restrictions. It had attracted senior members of the largest banking houses in Europe for the financing of trade, while the merchants carrying on business were principally German and English. By the middle of the century there were something like 400 English there, centred on an English house, subject to their own disciplinary regulations, and accorded, as were the Lutherans, an almost complete religious freedom.[2]

In 1543, however, the Emperor increased the heretofore nominal duty on English cloth, thereby precipitating a commercial as well as a diplomatic crisis, since the English maintained that it violated an underlying treaty agreement reached some twenty years earlier which stood unrepealed. Even before Henry VIII's death, some merchants were already leaving Antwerp, and the Netherlanders brought great pressure to bear on the Regent to secure more firmly the privileges of the city.[3] Negotiations respecting English treaty rights were actively pressed by the Lord Protector, the imperial ambassador exhibiting extreme nervousness lest the English should be withdrawn from the city completely.[4] When in early 1548 it

[1] Cholmeley, William, *The request and suite of a true-hearted Englishman . . . in behalf of the dying business'*, in Lansdowne MS. 171, #156, f. 330; also printed in a not very satisfactory text in *Camden Miscellany*, II (1853).

[2] Ramsay, G. D., *English overseas trade during the centuries of emergence, etc.* (L., 1957), 11–18.

[3] Schanz, *Englische Handelspolitik*, I, 105–106, 109.

[4] *Cal. S.P. Span.* IX, 183, 223–224, 229, 250.

became known that Thomas Chamberlain, the English Court Master in Antwerp, had ordered the withdrawal of the whole English community, while imperial merchants were barred from the Calais Staple, matters reached a climax which resulted in imperial concessions in August, 1548, which were gathered in April, 1549, into a restoration for a ten-year period of the treaty rights of 1522.[1] There were, however, other grievances with the city government of Antwerp which led the Merchant Adventurers seriously to consider removing the market for English cloth to Bergen-op-Zoom,[2] and which may well have inspired the young King's dream of establishing in England a free international market.[3]

The fact was that a severe recession was at hand in the cloth trade, probably at least slightly hastened and deepened by the export of goods of poor quality, short weight, and of inferior wool. Further complicating the economic situation, as we have seen, was the progressive debasement of the coinage which stimulated a flood of exports far beyond a now slowly declining demand. Moreover, when Northumberland was at last driven to a partial restoration of the English coinage and when Gresham by his brilliant manipulations lifted dramatically the value of sterling, trade further declined with the result that cloth exports fell by almost 15 per cent in 1551 and another 20 per cent in 1552.[4] The great trade boom in cloth, which had begun in the later Middle Ages, was at an end, while a weak and insecure government found itself face to face with the new phenomenon of urban unemployment on a wide scale. Caught in this deepening depression were scores of London merchants, of whom the well established firm of the Johnsons, active in the Calais Staple since the beginning of the century, was probably stronger than most.[5] Trading and distributing from both London and East Anglian ports, the firm was first weakened by the decline of the Calais Staple market, then gravely hurt by the currency manipulations, which made it extremely difficult to meet its obligations in Antwerp, and then ruined when in desperation the partners tried to recoup their losses by speculative ventures in wine. When the firm failed in April, 1553, it owed at least £8000 to twenty principal creditors.[6]

[1] Schanz, *Englische Handelspolitik*, I, 106.

[2] Smit, H. J., *Bronnen tot de geschiedenis van den Handel met Engeland, etc.*, part 2 (1485–1585), vol. I (Rijkgeschiedkundige Publ. 86, Hague, 1942), 674, 676, 678–683; Tanner MS. 90, ff. 151–152.

[3] Edward VI, *Chronicle*, 168–173.

[4] Ramsay, *English overseas trade*, 22.

[5] Winchester, *Tudor family*, 22–25.   [6] *Ibid.* 277–297.

4. ENCLOSURES (REAL AND IMAGINARY) AND SOCIAL DISCONTENT

We have seen that the English economy had been weakened and rendered very vulnerable by a number of nearly simultaneous developments, not fully understood by the government and in part quite beyond its capacity to control. Successive debasements had by the summer of 1549 severely shaken confidence in the coinage and had created chaos in foreign markets. The economy was further weakened and in certain respects endangered by the sudden spiralling up of an inflationary process long under way. The government's own fiscal affairs were disordered and a relatively small foreign debt remained for years unpaid and could be re-funded only at extremely high interest rates for very short terms. Even graver injury was done to the economy by the weakening and then the collapse of the cloth and wool markets, which had for generations been steadily expanding and which had drawn a dangerously high proportion of English land into sheep grazing with its consequent dislocation to an extremely conservative and inelastic system of agriculture. The ill estate of England from 1549 to 1551 was, then, due to many and exceedingly complex causes, but the bitter complaints and eloquent condemnations centred on sheep and the enclosures of pastures which they had brought in their train. We have seen that in fact the enclosure movement, in so far as its purpose was the laying down of land to pastures, was nearly over more than a generation before our period, but a myth had got itself implanted in the English mind and conscience, with the result that we have many and still moving social tracts and denunciations which bear little relevance to the facts as they were.[1] These tracts of social indignation could be bizarre in their accusations, as for example that enclosures had destroyed 400–500 villages in the Midlands, whereas the official inquiry of 1517 suggests that in the past generation not more than $\frac{1}{2}$ of 1 per cent of the land in twenty-four counties had been enclosed.[2]

The almost certain truth is that from the beginning of the Tudor period to perhaps 1551 the prospering cloth industry, taking the national economy into account, had created far more employment

---

[1] *Vide ante*, 388ff., 402ff.

[2] *Certayne causes gathered together, etc.* (1548?), in *Four supplications* (E.E.T.S., extra ser., XIII), 101; Gay, Edwin F., 'Inclosures in England in the sixteenth century', *Quarterly Journal of Economics*, XVII (1903), 595–597.

than had been destroyed by the spread of grazing. But the difficulty was that labour, then and to a degree now, was not easily mobile and that human beings are not pawns to be shifted about at will. The complaints issue from or are concerned with the Midlands particularly, though it seems quite certain that enclosures had proceeded there more slowly than in some other regions, probably—as Professor Lipson has surmised—because there was relatively little expansion of the cloth industry in the affected area which could absorb *in situ* the labour that had been displaced.[1]

The violent denunciation of enclosures enlivening our period expresses a social sentiment and conscience by no means new in England. Successive statutes, five in all, had been passed protecting tillage land and prohibiting depopulations—the last two as recently as 1534 and 1536. The Tudors were conservative in their social and economic policy, mistrusting change and above all fearing disorder, and these stringent enactments, particularly that of 1517, undoubtedly express the policy which they wished to be followed. These monarchs possessed quite sufficient personal power to drive these laws through Parliament, despite the fact that the enactments ran expressly counter to the self-interest of the gentry and nobility who together comprised most of its membership. But the Tudors did not quite dare rigorously to enforce these laws, save for Wolsey's serious and ill-fated effort, because to have done so would have required the full support of the gentry, as justices of the peace and as commissioners. This was fully sensed by Latimer, one of the most strident of the enemies of enclosures, when he said, 'Let the preacher preach till his tongue be worn to the stumps, nothing is amended. We have good statutes made for the commonwealth, as touching commoners and inclosers, . . . but in the end of the matter there cometh nothing forth'.[2] It was Somerset—high-minded, politically obtuse, and stubborn in his idealism—who ventured on the course of stringent enforcement, not of new laws, but of statutes already enrolled. The landlords fought him with every weapon at their command; the commons rose and the land was torn with social and political strife; but Somerset would not yield even when he was faced with open rebellion in two areas of the realm. There is a ring of credibility in Van der Delft's report: 'I have heard in deep secret that the Protector declared to the Council as his opinion, that the peasants' demands were fair and just; for the poor people who had no land to graze their cattle ought to

---

[1] Lipson, E., *The economic history of England*, I (8th ed., L., 1945), 183.
[2] Latimer, *Works*, I, 101.

retain the commons and the lands that had always been public property, and the noble and the rich ought not to seize and add them to their parks and possessions.'[1] The tragedy is that so far as available evidence indicates, enclosures for grazing were in fact nearly finished by 1520 and were really finished by 1550, when the slow but inexorable return of land to the plough was set in motion by economic forces which we have described. It is not too much to say that Somerset's crusade against enclosures was quixotic and that the venomous opposition launched against him by landowners in and out of his own Council was equally irrelevant. The sheep was no longer the master of England.

An effort has been made to record those enclosures, of whatsoever kind, which were certainly made in an interval of thirteen years (1543–1555) or regarding which litigation occurred during these years, which possibly defines the Edwardian era somewhat too broadly. Though a great deal of time has been expended, it must be stated that the data are certainly incomplete and, as we shall note, are in several respects intractable. In this period of time we have counted only fifty-two enclosures which may be dated with fair certainty, occurring, it is important to observe, in no more than twenty-three of the English counties, and with a heavy concentration in the Midlands and East Anglia. Of the whole number, thirty-five were concluded, begun, or defended in the course of the reign more strictly defined. It should also be observed that we have found only eight counties in which three or more enclosures occurred, with the heaviest concentration in Leicestershire, Northamptonshire, Oxfordshire, and Warwickshire, in which a total of twenty-four have been counted.

It should also be stated that these enclosures were by no means uniform in type and that in a considerable number of instances there is no evidence whatsoever of undue pressure from the principal landowner or of discontent leading to litigation or local disturbances. It is surprising, indeed, that considerably less than half of all these enclosures (twenty-one in all) were in the classical and hated pattern of the conversion of arable, or part arable, land into pasture for sheep or cattle. In twelve instances the principal proprietor was enclosing commons for a variety of purposes, usually for pasture, and it is on the whole these enclosures that seem to have raised the greatest resentment and to have led to riotous protest or litigation. There was also almost automatic resentment when arable

[1] *Cal. S.P. Span.* IX, 395: June 13, 1549. This may well have been related to the imperial envoy by Paget.

or pasture lands were emparked, however legally, by a landowner, usually it appears as a status symbol, the seven cases we have found almost certainly being too low a count. In five instances enclosures were by the agreement of all the parties concerned, a process requiring much time and truly masterly persuasion. The remaining seven cases relate to the enclosure of wasteland, or arable to meadow, and of a variety of lands for unknown purposes. In only twenty-three of these enclosures have we been able to determine the acreage involved, but for these no more than 2762 acres of land was enclosed. Omitted from this reckoning is one huge tract of about 4000 acres of confessedly nearly worthless waste and wet turf. In all, then, if our averages have a sufficient base for statistical projection, the almost valueless Lancashire tract aside, it would seem that not more than 6000 acres of land of all types and for a variety of purposes of exploitation were in fact enclosed in the Edwardian period.[1]

The incredible variety of enclosures and of the problems raised by them may perhaps be further suggested by a brief sampling of a few of the instances. Thus in Barton Hartshorn, Buckinghamshire, the lord of the manor had in about 1550 wrongfully enclosed, it was alleged, about thirty acres of land, thereby denying the commons certain rights of pasture and normal access from the village to the church. The landlord was described in the complaint as of a 'covetous and envious mind' and was said to have wounded one of the tenants in an affray stemming from the enclosure.[2] In the Isle of Ely, where over seventy individual complaints were lodged with the commissioners respecting the enclosure of 329 acres in Ely and Chettisham and 112 in Stuntney, it is evident that most of the resentment related to pre-Edwardian enclosures which deprived the commoners and tenants of rights of pasture after grain had been harvested, overrode copyhold rights, and deprived communities of former rights-of-way. Here—and this must have been frequent—the resentments tended to lie against small and aggressive yeoman

---

[1] Our sources are widespread but certainly incomplete. In all our reading, in secondary works and sources, we have noted down every enclosure reference and have then tried to examine the relevant sources. The records of the Court of Requests have been checked and we believe we have missed relatively few cases where litigation was involved, save for the records of the Court of Star Chamber. What we have not been able to do is to check through the now considerable body of manorial records becoming available in the various county archives where we would suppose more extended information on enclosures, particularly by agreement, should be found. It will be remembered that the only surviving reports of the 1548 commission relate to Warwickshire and Cambridgeshire, and they are incomplete. The more recently published volumes of the Victoria County History, devoting as they do detailed discussion to the economic history of the counties concerned, have been especially useful.

[2] Star Chamber Proc., Phil. & Mary, Bundle 5, #8.

farmers who were aggregating manageable fields from bits and pieces. But only 91 acres of land enclosed (in Downham and Littleport) fall within our period, all being in the classical pattern of arable to sheep grazing.[1] In Dorset, not an open field county and only slightly affected by the enclosure movement, the holdings in Shroton (Iwerne Courtenay) were so small that tenants could not farm them effectively and several had voluntarily returned their copyholds to the lord. By agreements concluded in 1548 the holdings of the remaining tenants were aggregated, the commons of the manor to remain open for pasture for cattle or sheep at specified times.[2] Sir Richard Tyrwhitt, shortly after purchasing Leighton Bromswold, Huntingdonshire, in 1548 enclosed a large field with damage to his tenants, but when complaints were lodged against him by the vicar and others he averred that if the tenants were not content with the cash settlement he had made for their common rights he would return the field, as he did, and 'would himself as he was a true Christian man and knight help to pluck up with his own hands the enclosures'.[3] A less amenable lord of the manor was Sir William Turvile of Croft, Leicestershire, who was haled before the Star Chamber in 1546–1547 on charges of having enclosed a field in which there were common pasture rights, witnesses persuasively repudiating Turvile's claim that he had done no more than repair an ancient enclosure.[4]

We may conclude with a few more instances of Edwardian enclosures, seeking to emphasize their amazing diversity of purpose and result. Among the Privy Councillors, Warwick, Herbert, and Paget were all modest enclosers, Paget having by 1549 consolidated his lands in the manor of West Drayton (Middlesex) in seven closes of 150 acres which he put to pasture, evidently with the consent of the affected tenants, though incomplete enclosures he had made in Great Marlowe (Bucks) were thrown down in the risings of 1549.[5] The gradual process by which most families increased their enclosed holdings within their manors is quite perfectly illustrated at Waterperry (Oxon), where the Curson family had purchased the manor in which many small freeholders and tenants held much of the acreage under arable farming. The Cursons were sheep farmers

[1] VCH, *Cambridge*, IV, 40–42, 91, 95.

[2] Harl. MS. 71, ff. 34–39; VCH, *Dorset*, II, 247–248.

[3] Court of Requests, Edw. VI, Bundle 20, #136.

[4] Hoskins, W. G., *Provincial England. Essays in social and economic history* (L., 1963), 174–178.

[5] Gammon, *Master of practises*, 216, citing Anglesey MSS.; *A.P.C.* III, 414–415; VCH, *Middlesex*, III, 192, 197.

with 400 acres under pasture as early as 1517, but from that point forward they moved very slowly with their acquisitions by purchase, until by 1630 they owned almost the whole of the manor.[1] The related family of Poure in Bletchingdon was more aggressive and ruthless, having in the period 1544–1558 gradually increased their holdings, beyond the demesne lands, from 45 acres to 377 acres for pasture and emparking.[2] In this instance there is clear evidence that rights in common were being overridden, tenants were being turned out on the expiration of leases, and former yeoman farmers were being systematically squeezed out. In Whaddon (Wilts), on the other hand, the principal landowner was permitted by agreement to enclose land then in the use of his tenants in return for equal lands which were enclosed for their benefit.[3] Enclosure by agreement was also gradually made over a long period at Great Alne (Warwick) by the enlightened Sir Robert Throckmorton and his successors, all other rights being protected, with consequent increase in the prosperity of the whole manor, with houses 'newly builded and all the tenants as well and better able to live as before the enclosures and the lordship enriched since'.[4] And finally— though we have not reckoned it as an enclosure—we should mention, as a perfect instance of the sensitivity of the Protector on the question of enclosures, the action taken in disparking Hampton Court Chase, created by lands taken from eleven different parishes late in the reign of Henry VIII when he 'waxed heavy with sickness, age, and corpulences of body' and could not go far to hunt. Accordingly on the complaints of 'many poor men' of damages done to them by the taking of lands and by the depredations of the deer, the Chase was abandoned and the lands thus freed were ordered rented on the terms formerly prevailing.[5]

The evidence seems clearly to indicate that there was very little enclosure under way in England in the Edwardian period and that what there was was undertaken for a variety of reasons, of which grazing was only the principal. It seems probable, too, that most enclosing in the period was done quietly by the consent of all those concerned within the manor, hence never entering into the formal records at all.[6] The most vociferous and bitter complaints arose when the lord of the manor attempted to separate and then enclose his share of the commons, thereby upsetting the whole traditional

---

[1] VCH, *Oxfordshire*, V, 302.
[2] *Ibid.* VI, 58–59, 64–65.
[3] VCH, *Wiltshire*, IV, 47.
[4] VCH, *Warwickshire*, III, 23–24.
[5] *A.P.C.* II, 190–192: May 5, 1548.
[6] Thirsk, Joan, *Tudor enclosures* ([L.], 1959), 8–9.

system of grazing and other common uses which were in law and custom private property rights.[1] The small man, the commoner, could in fact scarcely carry on farming at all without access to the common grazing land. The invasion of these communal rights by the lord of the manor left the small freeholder with clear and enforceable rights, but it left the copyholder with no other remedy than the pleading of the custom of the manor with all the delay and expense which that involved.[2] But such evidence as we have accumulated makes it seem probable that there was very little even of this sort of aggression under way in the Edwardian period; the whole weight of the sovereign and his court was set too squarely against it. The clamour and the restlessness regarding enclosures seem, then, to reflect the memory of past evils and the lively fear of local aggressions which might be set in full tide again when the vigilance of the sovereign was relaxed. It is not too much to say that the rich and eloquent body of protest against enclosures which we find classically expressed in this period bore little relation to the economic realities. But it was none the less incendiary, moving, and memorable in its effect.

5. THE COMMONWEALTH PARTY AND RADICAL THOUGHT

The impetus for social and economic reforms in this middle period of the reign came principally from a group of men, of humanistic background and persuasion, who were generally described as Commonwealth Men. These thinkers were in part governmental officials of the second and third rank; all of them seem to have been advanced Protestants in their religious sentiments; none, oddly enough, was London born[3]; and all of them possessed literary and forensic powers of a very high order. Even more important, this whole group of thinkers and preachers were close to Somerset and lent immensely important literary and propaganda support to the radical social and economic policy to which he was deeply persuaded. We should now treat briefly the pragmatic thought of these men, in so far as it bore directly on decisions of policy, reserving the more theoretical thought of these remarkable humanists to a later consideration.[4]

It should be said at once that the social thought of the Commonwealth Men was in its nature conservative, even though its effect

[1] Tawney, *Agrarian problem*, 237–239.   [2] *Ibid.* 249.
[3] Bindoff, S. T., *Tudor England* (L., 1950, 1951, *1952*), 130–131.
[4] In the concluding volume of this study.

was undoubtedly revolutionary, these men holding in view an ideal, and a very Christian, conception of a state which should be dedicated to the common weal. They all looked back to an imaginary past, just as they looked forward to an ideal future, in which evil and disruptive forces in the society would be fully disciplined. As this social theory was developed by great and powerful preachers like Latimer, Lever, and Becon, the enemies of the commonwealth were declared to be the covetous and avaricious enclosers and pasture farmers, all of whom were sinful and who could be cured only by conviction of sin. This body of thought tended to be abstruse; yet others of the party—men like Forrest, Hogarde, and above all John Hales—not only denounced such evils as sinful, but pressed hard for a definition of state policy which would excise these spreading cancers in the polity which was England. These thinkers insisted that no man lived for himself alone, but that we are dedicated, as we are human beings, to the service of God and the state. As Hales succinctly put the thesis, 'It may not be lawful for every man to use his own as him listeth, but every man must use that he hath to the most benefit of his country'. We must be disciplined in such wise that our actions and aspirations serve not only our own needs but 'profit the commonwealth of [our] country', to which next after God we owe our allegiance.

There was, then, great moral force, a scarcely concealed fanaticism, and profound conviction in the recommendations urged on Somerset by what may be described as the activist wing of the Commonwealth Party. Thus they urged that enclosures and sheep farming be made unprofitable by the use of the taxing power, that the currency be stabilized, and that domestic industry be encouraged by the protection of a wall of tariffs. This thought, then, was intensely pragmatic, even though these men, including Hales, wished to restore an economy and an order of society which sprang from the myth of an ideal past. But in all they set forward they were coolly empirical, this being the first group in England to use statistics effectively in the advancement of their proposals,[1] even though they dealt with figures in a most heroic fashion. They were men with an essentially modern conception of the ambit of sovereignty, who were prepared to use statute law and prerogative power in order to frame, as they thought, a fitter habitation for Christian men.[2] It is no

[1] Ferguson, A. B., 'Renaissance realism in the "Commonwealth" literature of early Tudor England', *Journal of the History of Ideas*, XVI (1955), 287–305.

[2] Tawney, R. H., *Religion and the rise of capitalism, etc.* (N.Y., 1952), 144–145, for his perceptive comments.

14

wonder that they were as hated as they were feared by the nobility and the gentry of England. The sentiments of those who ruled England, of those who were to destroy Somerset, are perfectly expressed in the letter of a frightened and protesting gentleman to Cecil:

'Sir, be plain with my Lord's Grace [Somerset], that under the pretence of simplicity and poverty there may rest much mischief. So do I fear there doth in these men called Common Wealths and their adherents. To declare unto you the state of the gentlemen (I mean as well the greatest as the lowest) I assure you they are in such doubt, that almost they dare touch none of them [the commons], not for that they are afraid of them, but for that some of them have been sent up and come away without punishment, and that Common Wealth called Latimer hath gotten the pardon of others.'[1]

And the hatred and fear of those who ruled England came to be focused on John Hales, who with a truly desperate energy sought to transform and to reform the English society with courses which were in fact revolutionary.

It was to the state, to the sovereign intervention, that the Commonwealth Men looked and to which they so eloquently appealed. Thus one of them called directly on the Protector to remedy the evils of inflation and enclosure and to make sure that the true teachings of the Gospel were followed. Superstition in England has been banished only to be replaced by ambition; land has been taken from the abbeys only to be dedicated to more hateful uses. The wrongs must be righted by Somerset, who 'doth bear the fame, and doth desire the same', whose mind and wishes are good and who may bring great good to England if he rescues the land from the Lord Chancellor, the masters of the mint, the surveyors, the receivers, the lawyers, the sheep masters, and 'such like common wasters' who devour the poor and the substance of the realm.[2] These men lashed out without hesitation at those in and out of the circle of power, as is suggested by Latimer's bitter sermons, preached before the King, against corruption in high places, which resulted in the return from royal officials of considerable sums which had been concealed or withheld from the Crown.[3]

These sentiments were urged with special force in an impressive,

---

[1] S.P. Dom., Edw. VI, VIII, 56: Sir Anthony Aucher to Cecil, Sept. 10, 1549.

[2] *Vox populi, Vox dei* (1547–1548), in Harl. MS. 367, #46, ff. 130–143; printed in *Ballads from manuscripts*, I, ed. by F. J. Furnivall (L., 1868), 124–146.

[3] *A.P.C.* II, 266: Mar. 28, 1549; *ibid.* 409: Mar. 1, 1550.

though unpublished, *Treatise on evils in the realm*, in which, in addition to far-reaching ecclesiastical reforms, the author recommended that direct state controls be laid on land rentals and that all land in tillage twenty years earlier be restored to the plough. Similarly, commons enclosed in the same interval should either be restored to common use or divided equally amongst all inhabitants. The author further insisted that no merchant or artificer enfranchised in a corporate town be permitted to live outside it, and that no merchant, clothworker, or other tradesman should be allowed to carry on an agricultural pursuit lest he injure those who followed husbandry. He would further check the process of aggregating landed estates by forbidding the ownership of multiple farms, while he would protect the whole economy by prohibiting the importation of all articles that could be made in the realm and the export of raw materials, including wool and leather, which might be fabricated within England. Such a programme, he admitted, would require not only the passage of numerous laws but also the acceptance in men's hearts of the ideal of a commonwealth in which they regard more the 'universal profit' of the realm than their own selfish gain.[1]

The Commonwealth Men likewise urged upon the Protector the adoption of a policy carefully designed to secure the restoration of a balance between tillage and grazing, animated by the principle of the general good rather than of private gain. It was argued that the movement for the enclosure of land for sheep grazing had fed on the expectation of greater profit, yet what has been profitable to the individual landowner has been ruinous to the commonwealth. The solution of the problem, Hales maintained, was to make grain farming more profitable by laying governmental restraints on the shipment of unfinished wool and by sharply raising the export customs dues. Every possible action must be taken to lessen the attraction of pastures and to restore a balance in agriculture, which would in turn greatly increase the requirements for labour.[2] The difficulty of the task is suggested by the fact that, in Hales' view, enclosed land under pasture had been worth twice as much per acre as land under tillage.[3] Hence every possible encouragement must be lent to tillage, while the government must not hesitate to move directly, if need be, to lay a direct and discriminatory tax on sheep and cloth— a course which was shortly to be followed. These same sentiments

---

[1] Royal MSS., 17. B. The manuscript is undated, but internal evidence places it in the 1540s, and the general tone late in the decade.

[2] [Hales], *Common weal*, 50, 54–59. [3] *Ibid.* 123–124.

were advanced with particular vigour by an anonymous writer who argued that the imbalance in the English agricultural economy stemmed from the expropriation of the monastic properties, which, he held, created a labour surplus which could be accommodated only by a great increase in tillage. The pressure of population on land is also causing a sharp increase in rents, which the poor simply cannot pay, with the consequence that a whole segment of the population is being pressed below the line of possible self-support. Hence he would urge Parliament to assist in enhancing the land supply by bringing under cultivation great tracts of waste and fen land, would absolutely forbid further conversion of land to pasture, and would sharply increase import duties on all articles which could be made in England. Such measures would be opposed by strong and selfish factions, but Parliament must act in the interests of the commonweal which is England and see to it that the advancement of necessary reforms goes hand in hand with the free preaching of the Gospel.[1]

The Commonwealth Men, it is clear, were moved by an almost obsessive hatred of enclosures, for grazing and sheep had become for them the symbol not of prosperity for the realm but of a threatening ruin. In the train of enclosures, they contended, had come depopulation, a scarcity of the bread grains, and a dislocation of the whole society.[2] From spreading enclosures for pasture have flowed as well, they held, the quickly rising rents which simply barred the poorer classes of men from the agricultural pursuits they have known:

> These raging rents must be looked upon,
> And brought unto the old accustomed rent,
> As they were let at forty years agone;
> Then shall be plenty and most men content.

This desperately needed remedy can be gained only by the direct intervention of the Crown and Parliament; only then will Englishmen be restored:

> Not in thraldom and pinching penury,
> To be as drudges unto their land lords;
> But as yeomen becometh honestly,
> ....

---

[1] *Pyers Plowmans exhortation unto the lordes, knightes, etc.* (n.d.), no pagin. Internal evidence suggests that the pamphlet was written shortly before the passage of the sheep tax in March, 1549.   [2] [Hales], *Common weal*, 15–17.

For what king here will live honorably,
He must then make of England yeomanry.[1]

Enclosures are, then, a creeping, destroying evil which unless summarily checked and in so far as possible rolled back will dissolve the whole society.[2] As a result of their steady extension, 'many of the king's subjects have no ground to live upon . . . and therefore the people still increasing, and their livings diminished, it must needs come to pass that a great part of the people shall be idle and lack livings; and hunger is a bitter thing to bear'.[3]

The charge of widespread and continuing depopulation was persistently made and, so far as we can tell, was universally attributed to the almost completely mythical enclosures of the period. Thus an enemy of England (the French Herald) was made to say in a dialogue that it was wool that had despoiled and depopulated the countryside. The 'clothiers dwell in great farms abroad in the country, having houses with commodities like unto gentlemen', but with all under grass, 'taking thereby away the livings of the poor husbandmen and graziers'.[4] The estimates of such depopulations were wildly, but eloquently, put, ranging upwards from those of Hales and Latimer to a really heroic contention that at least 50,000 ploughs had been put down, with a total loss of sustenance by at least 300,000 persons, who now 'have nothing, but goeth about in England from door to door, and ask their alms for God's sake. And because they will not beg, some of men doth steal, and then they be hanged, and thus the realm doth decay, and by none other ways else, as we do think'.[5] Quite wrong or inaccurate as this whole body of literature was, it was generally accepted and it most certainly formed the moral base for the tragic effort of the Lord Protector to effect what he believed were desperately necessary reforms.

These moralists, who were so profoundly to affect English thought, and the English conscience, were also deeply persuaded that it was excessive grazing that was principally, indeed wholly, responsible for the scarcity of necessaries and for vaulting prices. Thus the poor have been forced down to the level of subsistence:

---

[1] Forrest, William, *The pleasaunt poesye of princelie practise* (1548); text in Tawney and Power, *Tudor economic documents*, III, 43-44. The manuscript, which we have not seen, is among Royal MSS., 17. D. iii; for similar sentiments, see *Vox populi, Vox dei*. S. J. Herrtage points out that Forrest's poem is really a version of E. Colonna's treatise, *De regimine principum, etc.* (*Henry the Eighth*, E.E.T.S., extra ser., no. 32, 1878).

[2] [Hales], *Common weal*, 48. [3] *Ibid.* 48-49.

[4] Coke, John, *The debate betweene the heraldes of Englande and Fraunce, etc.* (L., 1550), I iii[v]. The work was evidently written in 1549.

[5] *Certayne causes*, in *Four supplications*, 102.

> Two pence (in beef) he cannot have served,
> Other in mutton, the price is so high:
> ....
> So goeth he and his to bed hungrily,
> And riseth again with bellies again empty;
> Which turneth to tawny their white English skin,
> Like to the swarthy colored Flanderkin.

Englishmen, this author proudly declared, cannot and will not for long live on roots and herbs, yet they sink into the feebleness born of long hunger:

> Where they were valiant, strong, sturdy and stout,
> To shoot, to wrestle, to do any man's feat,
> To match all nations dwelling here about,

now they are weak, starving, and unable to defend their king and country.[1] The scarcity of victuals is real, is deepening, and, it was alleged, was directly caused by the greed of the sheep masters.[2] The landowners now 'keep the most substance of their lands in their own hands', laying all down to sheep, with the inevitable and unforgivable consequence that foodstuffs have been increasingly scarce, including even eggs and poultry, which were traditionally kept by the cottagers.[3] But now the cottagers and commons have been wholly undone, so great are rentals.

> And where they were wont to uphold a plow
> Now scarce can they find the grass for a cow
> Their children do watch, as hawks for their prey
> Yet can they not get one good meal a day.[4]

A society in which such injustices and needless suffering exist, the author contended, cannot continue for long before dissolution takes place. England must return to the love of God, Englishmen to the love of one man for another.

This dreadful and pervading scarcity, it was maintained, feeds on itself, as sheep and wool continue to form the substance of English wealth and resources. Even the households of the sheep masters,

---

[1] Forrest, *Pleasaunt poesye*, in Tawney and Power, *Tudor economic documents*, III, 40–41.

[2] *Certayne causes*, in *Four supplications*, 95.

[3] *Ibid.* 96.

[4] Churchyard, Thomas, *A myrrour for man*, etc. (L., [c. 1552]), A i[v].

country dwellers, are obliged to buy their foodstuffs.[1] The realm as a consequence of uncontrolled economic folly faces the spectre of starvation for whole classes of men at the first bad harvest. The memory of the oldest living man can recall no such scarcity as now prevails, still another pamphleteer maintained:

Corn hath been as dear here before,
Yet of all other thynges, we had plenty and store,
But nowe, the price of thynges, hath leapt such a leap
That nother food, clothing, nor any other thing is good cheape.[2]

So general and so dangerous is the fact of scarcity and extremely high prices that only the quick and full intervention of the state can restore some measure of safety and rebuild a tolerable society in a land that has been looted and undone by wicked and selfish men.

Hales, the most sophisticated as he was the boldest of these Commonwealth moralists, realized that the economic pressures which had caused a spiralling inflation as well as a physical scarcity of necessaries were far more complex and less readily to be reformed than did most of his party. Thus he saw that many of the gentry were also gravely injured as prices rose, while most of their estates were rented on long-term leases,[3] and that such men had been driven to place all available land under sheep. He laid a heavy blame on debasement of the coinage and understood that the terms of international trade had swung sharply against England.[4] He understood too that while harvests had been good (1546–1548), class after class had been excluded from the market by prices which they simply could not pay. He realized, then, that the deepening economic and social crisis was caused by many factors—in their totality extremely complex. Broadly speaking his recommendations were first to strike down excessive sheep grazing by the use of the taxing power and then to devalue in order to restore the stability, the value, and the honesty of English coinage.[5] These things being done, he would then move to secure the rehabilitation and enlargement of the woollen cloth manufacture. It was towards a sensibly balanced and an equitable economy that Hales was groping his way in economic thinking of great lucidity, inspired by a high sense of civic morality.

But the temper and the zeal of the moralist was strong in Hales, as indeed it was in all the thinkers of the Commonwealth group. He

[1] *Certayne causes*, in *Four supplications*, 101.
[2] Leigh, Valentine, *The pleasaunt playne and pythye pathewaye, etc.* (L., [c. 1549]), A3.
[3] [Hales], *Common weal*, 19–20.   [4] *Ibid.* 33–35.   [5] *Ibid.* 72–80.

summoned England to a commitment to an era of spartan tastes and the conserving of the national resources until all classes of the society had gained protection and some measure of economic security. As his economic thought appealed back largely to an ideal— a mythical—past, so did his social thought. England must renounce luxury and waste if its strength is to be regained. 'I think we were as much dreaded, or more, of our enemies when our gentlemen went simply and our servingmen plainly . . . bearing the heavy sword and buckler on their thighs, instead of . . . light dancing swords and rapiers. And when they rode, carrying good spears in their hands, instead of white rods which they carry now, more like ladies or gentlewomen.'[1] England's economy required that she import many essential commodities, but there were dozens of luxury items which he would either severely limit or altogether prohibit. Twenty years earlier, he averred, there were not a dozen purveyors of imported luxuries in the whole of London, whereas 'now from the Tower to Westminster . . . every street is full of them; and their shops glisters and shine'.[2] All this should be forsworn in a national effort to restore the Commonwealth. The whole foreign trade of the country should be so regulated that its outward commerce is pitched squarely and completely against the essential imports required, such as flax, tar, oil, fish, and the like.[3]

Even though the thought of the Commonwealth Men is often tinctured with a really biting anti-clericalism, it is none the less evident that it was rooted in the soil of medieval Christian thought, modified and sharpened by what can only be described as a rapidly evolving Protestant ethic. Though there had been a careful analysis of the secular causes for the dislocation in the English society and economy, almost every one of the writers who expressed the views of the Commonwealth Party discovered the ultimate cause for the distress of England in the sin of covetousness, which as these writers develop it acquired a particularly sinister significance.[4] Limiting ourselves purposely to the writings of some of the more obscure thinkers who lent support to the Commonwealth Party, we find the sin of covetousness advanced as widespread and as at bottom the cause of England's ills. An anonymous writer in 1547 declared that moral rot became epidemic in the realm when the thirst for gold came to animate all classes:

---

[1] [Hales], *Common weal*, 83.   [2] *Ibid.* 64.   [3] *Ibid.* 68–69.

[4] Varying degrees of stress were laid on the evil of covetousness by twenty-one of the twenty-four writers we have regarded as of or sympathetic to what may be described as the Commonwealth Party.

So ledde they theyr lyves in quiete and reste,
Tyll hourde began hate from east unto weste.
And golde for to growe a lorde of great price,
Whiche chaunged the worlde from vertue to vice.[1]

This avarice has spread to all classes of men and from it have flowed
the forces that have brought England to the point of dissolution. In
even worse verse, another obscure writer complained that covetousness had made all men restless, self-centred, and careless of the
well-being of the state. Land has been put down to pasture, depopulations continue unchecked, good laws are subverted by lawyers
and judges, and hell gapes for those who have thus laid waste the
Commonwealth.[2] These views were indignantly shared by an
anonymous author who declared that insatiable and sinful greed
suffused every class in England. The commonwealth decays because the graziers, the rack-renters, and the sheep growers undermine it to their own evil ends. In London, he charged (quite incorrectly), more is spent for the care of stray dogs than for the poor
of that great city. There can be no recovery in England until those
who possess power apply themselves steadily and forcefully to the
needs of the whole body politic.[3] God is invoked in the 'Prayer for
Landlords' to soften the hearts of those who possess lands, pastures,
and dwelling places, so they will not 'rack and stretch out the rents
. . . nor yet take unreasonable fines . . . after the manner of covetous
worldlings', but rather leave a margin of gain and decency for poor
men who depend upon them.[4]

When this bitter and telling denunciation of covetousness was
tinged with what we can only describe as early Puritanism, as it was
in the writings of Anthony Gilby, it could be a formidable and a
moving force indeed. The faith of the Christian, he reminds us, was
ever marked by a deep and abiding love of our neighbours. Amongst
those who possess wealth in England, Gilby angrily contended,
there were few indeed who exhibited even the rudiments of true
faith. For years past in this commonwealth the whole tendency had
been to make 'the people peasants and slaves', and 'now the commons are so bare and poor that they cry out' against the afflictions
laid upon them.[5] It is simply contrary to our Christian duty and

[1] *A compendious dittie, etc.* ([L., 1547]), A2.
[2] Hogarde, Miles, *A new treatyse, etc.* (L., [1550?]), no pagin.
[3] *The prayse and commendacion of suche as sought comenwelthes* (L., [c. 1548]), no
pagin.   [4] *The primer or book of private prayer* (1553), in *Two liturgies*, 458.
[5] Gilby, Anthony, *A commentary upon the prophet Mycha, etc.* (L., 1551), no pagin.

to common humanity, still another writer contended, when 'thousands of the poor commons can not get so much as one farm nor scant any little house to put their head in'.[1] The bishops and their clergy were bitterly denounced by Gilby for their cold indifference to the wrongs and ills which divided and weakened England, being rather concerned with 'purchasing other men's lands and houses to make their wives ladies and their sons lords'. The landowners, he says, are as a class rapacious and completely covetous, but his most bitter scorn was directed against the merchants, who pretend to be 'gospellers', but who in fact cheat in measure, raise prices, and who when they purchase land seek at once to make slaves of their tenants. 'O you covetous merchants, building your houses in the blood of your brethren.'[2] So ill and desperate was the state of the realm, another author submitted, that only the direct and powerful intervention of the sovereign could preserve the society:

> Of Journeymen and Servyingemen also,
> Withe other divers of our own nation
> That now a roving in others' grounds go,
> To this realm's great depopulation;
> At which the heavens maketh exclamation,
> Burdening your grace by oath that yee have take[n].
> Of this, as you can, redress with speed to make.[3]

And it was quite precisely with 'redress with speed to make' that Somerset, evidently fully sharing the sentiments of the moralist critics whose thought we have been discussing, moved directly in an heroic, but tragic, effort to reform the English society.

6. REMEDIES PROPOSED AND REMEDIES TRIED

All the strains and dislocations which we have sketched, all the wrongs and evils, real and imaginary, which we have noted, were known to Somerset and were eloquently set out by the Commonwealth Party, to which on the whole he listened and by which he was persuaded that strong and immediate sovereign intervention was necessary if Edward's heritage were to be preserved. We have observed that in the second range of governmental service several of the Commonwealth Men had found posts; their views engaged the support of the university intellectuals who had been brought

---

[1] *Pyers Plowmans exhortation*, no pagin.   [2] Gilby, *A commentary*, no pagin.
[3] Forrest, *Pleasaunt poesye*, in Tawney and Power, *Tudor economic documents*, III, 46.

into the service of the state; and they were most persuasively urged upon the government by several of the greatest of the reformed clergy. But these views and these moral judgements, so far as we can tell, had no support whatever in the Privy Council, save for the evidently moderate sympathy of Cranmer. It was, then, Somerset alone who determined on a broad-scale assault on the infinitely complex agrarian problem, which was scarcely well begun before the risings of the summer and the defection of the ruling junta which he had headed swept him from power.

Somerset's attack was levelled explicitly against enclosures for grazing, against the imbalance of English agriculture, against the decay of customary manorial relationships—in brief, against both the wealth and the power of the nobility and the gentry. Yet, violent as was the reaction to his policy, it must be insisted that the policy was at bottom conservative, since it was based on laws long on the statute books and on assumptions regarding the English society to which lip service was paid by all classes of men. The gravest charge which the historian may bring against Somerset is that he may well have excited searing rebellion by the very promise of his social policy and that at the moment of crisis he was unwilling to use summary force against men with whose plight he found himself stirred by sympathy.[1] Somerset was also groping in his policy towards a regulated economy, an economy of proper balance, which was to characterize Elizabethan state interventions, though he was without either the knowledge or the administrative machinery to carry it through effectively.[2] His deep sincerity and his compassion for the poor cannot be doubted, though his stubbornness in seeking to force through a policy for which he had almost no support amongst the dominant political and economic classes betrays an almost incredible want of administrative sensitivity. The famous enclosure investigation was launched at the very moment when agrarian rioting was spreading through Hertfordshire, though, be it said, the serious riotings of 1549 did not break out until it was clear that the Protector could not carry the Parliament, the great landowners, or even his own Council with him. His was the effort, noble in conception, but reckless in its consequences, of one man against impossible and insurmountable odds.[3]

The signal for the launching of this great effort was given when in May, 1548, as we have seen, the royal deer park at Hampton Court

[1] Morris, *The Tudors*, 117.
[2] Nef, J. U., *Industry and government in France and England, 1540–1640* (Phila., 1940), 25–27.   [3] Tawney, *Agrarian problem*, 364.

was disparked and common rights in numerous parishes restored.[1] Not quite a year later, in March, 1549, Somerset gave an unmistakable indication of policy when he caused Parliament to pass a special act securing the protection in perpetuity of copyholders on his own great estates, confirming the title of copyholds let from his own demesne lands, and generally defining and legalizing manorial customs.[2] And shortly afterwards, in June, 1549, the Protector ordered a commission appointed, of which Hales was a member, for the purpose of disforesting and disparking crown lands in Sussex, gained from the attainders of Norfolk and Thomas Seymour, then apportioning them fairly under life tenures and appointing timber for the building of new houses and the repair of old.[3]

The Lord Protector first invoked his prerogative power to warn that long-standing agrarian laws were to be enforced, in a carefully composed proclamation on illegal enclosures, issued in June, 1548. The Council recited 'divers supplications and pitiful complaints' that because of recent enclosures of arable lands 'many have been driven to extreme poverty and compelled to leave the places where they were born'. The consequence has been that where there were formerly numerous households 'bringing forth and nourishing of youth and to the replenishing and fulfilling of his majesty's realms' and serving in its defence, 'now there is nothing kept but sheep or bullocks', that Christian people have by the covetousness of some men been 'eaten up and devoured of brute beasts'. Despite the statutes standing against such enclosures for grazing, the evil continues, the pastures are themselves overstocked and the flocks diseased, while the poor are undone. Hence, due warning was given of an intended 'view and inquiry' of those who have made such enclosures, all persons being commanded to give such information as they possessed.[4] Thus was the realm prepared for the commission on enclosures which was immediately to follow.

Simultaneously, the Protector constituted a royal commission to investigate enclosures in the Midlands area. The plan contemplated other commissions for various parts of the country, but no evidence remains that any others were either fully constituted or effectively active.[5] The Council was evidently unanimously opposed to making

---

[1] *Vide ante*, 415.   [2] *Vide ante*, 306.
[3] *Cal. Pat. Rolls, Edw. VI*, II, 304: June 16, 1549.
[4] Hughes and Larkin, *Tudor proclamations*, I, 427–429: June 1, 1548.
[5] There does, however, seem to have been a presentment in Cambridge in 1548 when commissioners found four almshouses decayed and a tract of land in Jesus Lane illegally enclosed, as well as other small tracts which ought to be in common pasture. In all, 600–700 sheep were being pastured 'to the great hindrance of all the inhabitants of

any public announcement of the commission, but it was none the less launched, with Hales as chairman,[1] to investigate enclosures in the particularly sensitive and important areas of Oxfordshire, Berkshire, Warwickshire, Leicestershire, Buckinghamshire, and Northamptonshire. The commission recited the earlier laws against enclosures which had remained unenforced to the detriment of the state and the suffering of the people. The commissioners were accordingly directed to determine offences against the statutes, while all sheriffs, judges, and others in power were commanded to assist them.[2] They were to proceed under instructions simultaneously handed to them, requiring them to determine how many towns and villages had been destroyed by enclosures since 4 Henry VII, how many houses and people had been vacated, how many ploughs had been laid down, how many parks had been made; to investigate carefully the number of flocks of more than 2000 sheep; and to determine the past history of lands now devoted to pasture.[3]

The work of the commission was most heavily concentrated in the summer of 1548, and then after a lapse, possibly occasioned by Hales' attendance in the second session of Parliament, was resumed again in the summer of 1549, only to be engulfed, and that shortly, in the cataclysm of agrarian insurrections.[4] In each place visited a jury of twelve was empanelled to which a commissioner, usually Hales, set out the instructions under which they served and recited in detail the information that was required. Witnesses were placed under oath and could be sent to ward if they were contumacious. After information had been taken, the commission called offenders before it and of its own authority could forgive past illegalities, order enclosures to be removed, and command land illegally under sheep to be returned to tillage. The initial instructions permitted any two of the commissioners to proceed with the power of the whole, but this was amended in preparation for the resumption of the investigation in 1549, requiring the whole commission to 'proceed together in each place without division of yourselves' in order to lend more weight and authority to its proceedings.[5]

Cambridge'; a farmhouse with thirty acres which had burned two years earlier had not been restored; an access bridge had been pulled down and a road illegally enclosed. (Cooper, C. H., *Annals of Cambridge* (5 vols., Cambridge, 1842–1908), II, 38–40.)

[1] The other members were Sir Francis Russell, Sir Fulke Greville, John Marsh, William Pinnock, and Roger Amys.

[2] The most easily available text is in Strype, *Memorials*, II, ii, 348–351.

[3] S.P. Dom., Edw. VI, VIII, 10; Strype, *Memorials*, II, ii, 359–365.

[4] Tawney, *Agrarian problem*, 366–367.

[5] S.P. Dom., Edw. VI, VIII, 25: July 13, 1549, and *ibid.* 26, 27, 28, 29, all of which are identical save for one slight textual change in #29.

Hales was evidently zealous as well as painstaking in conducting the investigations of the commission, preparing a clear and persuasive explanation which seems to have been read in each area where the proceedings were conducted.[1] He reminded his auditors that there were four good laws against enclosures which had long been ignored to the detriment of the whole commonwealth.[2] So greatly have the commons decayed in consequence that the King must now employ mercenaries for the defence of the realm and impose ever heavier taxes. The intent of the law and of the present commission was to nourish the poor, for they are members of the body politic and if they 'be not provided and cherished ... it cannot be but a great trouble of the body, and a decay of the strength of the realm'.[3] The 'puissance' of the realm includes the poor quite as much as the rich, 'but ... the people of this realm, our native country, is greatly decayed through the greediness of a few men', so that 'where there were in few years [past] ten or twelve thousand people, there be now scarce four thousand', and in many places none at all, so far had depopulation gone. 'Sheep and cattle that were ordained to be eaten of men, hath eaten up the men.' Englishmen have, in fact, been guilty of destroying other Englishmen. Hales continued, making it very clear that the commission had no interest whatsoever in enclosures for tillage or in cases when any man had enclosed his own land on which there were no legal rights of commons. Enclosures for their purposes meant simply: 'when any man hath taken away and enclosed any other men's commons, or hath pulled down houses of husbandry, and converted the lands from tillage to pasture.' He pleaded for the help of the countryside and for the ferreting out of the little tricks and devices by which landlords had sought to evade laws long standing. In their testimony, indeed, all witnesses must bear in mind the state and needs of the whole realm. But, Hales carefully enjoined, it must be the magistrate alone who corrects the evils and illegalities which may be revealed by their testimony. Accordingly, he warned them that they must not 'take upon you to be executors of the statutes; to cut up men's hedges, and to put down their enclosures, ... Be ye not breakers of the law, while ye go about to have vices reformed by the law.'[4]

Hales and his colleagues moved swiftly through the Midland circuit, though it is hardly possible that a thorough and painstaking

[1] Strype, *Memorials*, II, ii, 351–365.
[2] He cites 4 Henry VII, 7 Henry VIII, 25 Henry VIII, and 27 Henry VIII.
[3] Strype, *Memorials*, II, ii, 358–359.
[4] *Ibid.* 362–364. The last line of this exhortation is drawn from the royal instructions to the commission.

survey could have been completed between June 1st, when the commission was issued, and July 22nd, when it gave an interim report to the Protector in which Hales says that most of the Midland area had been covered. He expressed himself as pleased with his reception and as confident that the commons were quiet and tractable: 'If they had Justices of peace and Preachers' minded to further the King's honour, 'all these imaginations and suspicions of civil wars and sedition should be proved to be utterly false'. The people trust Somerset and feel his 'great zeal and love toward them', and they understand the ideal of a state where the universal good of the whole body politic is kept in view. Opposition, then, undoubtedly is from the 'worldlings', yet Somerset's own words are understood and trusted by the commons: 'maugre the Devil, private profit, self-love, money, and such like the Devil's instruments, it shall go forward, and set such a stay in the body of the commonwealth, that all the members shall live in a due . . . harmony, without one having too much, and a great many nothing at all.' Hale's own commission had thus far contented itself with fact-finding and no presentments had been made. But he was disturbed because the commissions for other parts of the realm had not begun their work and he urged on Somerset the high necessity of completing the whole investigation before Parliament was again convened.[1]

Somerset, moving swiftly to lend support to Hales and to bestir the other commissions, in this same month drafted additional sets of instructions for the remaining commissions contemplated and urged that all move immediately to the execution of their task and for the redress of all unlawful enclosures, though it seems likely that most of them were never in fact promulgated.[2] For in August riots broke out in Buckinghamshire, within Hales' circuit, for which the reformer was flatly blamed by Warwick and others in the Council. Hales wrote at once to Warwick from Fladbury to defend his actions, maintaining that the measures contemplated against illegal enclosures were not novel and urging that the realm would remain weak and divided until they were corrected. He enclosed as well a copy of the charge which, as we have noted, he regularly delivered at each place when evidence was taken. He stalwartly concluded that 'it grieved him much . . . that those that seemed to favour God's word

[1] S.P. Dom., Edw. VI, IV, 33: July 22, 1548; in Tytler, *England*, I, 113-117.
[2] S.P. Dom., Edw. VI, VIII, 11. There are four more copies, dated July, but with the day left blank (*ibid.* 12-15), and eight more with both day and month blank (*ibid.* 16-23).

should go about to hinder or speak evil of this thing: whereby the end and fruit of God's word, that is, love and charity to our poor neighbours, should be so set forth and published to the world'.[1] Shortly afterwards, evidently gravely perturbed, Hales wrote to Somerset once more defending his proceedings, holding that the areas through which he had passed were quiet and tractable, and suggesting that it was the papists who were launching rumours against the godly policy which the Protector was seeking to carry forward.

Perhaps in part because of the animus aroused by his activity in the Midlands and probably more importantly because he was a member of the Parliament summoned to meet in November, 1548, Hales seems to have halted for a season the work of the commission and to have undertaken to press his views in Parliament itself. It seems almost certain that he was the author of three bills unsuccessfully introduced in Parliament, or at least prepared for that purpose, the first of which was for the control of food prices, principally by making illegal any speculation in cattle. But far more important were the other measures which express quite perfectly the aspirations and the zealous sentiments of the Commonwealth Party.[2]

The bill to increase tillage argued that excessive and harmful gains had in recent years been derived from the pasturing of sheep and, it was at some point added to the draft, from the feeding of oxen. The consequence has been a scarcity of milch cows and the essential foods derived from them. Scarcity, high prices, and the decline of hospitality have been the consequence, to the great detriment of the realm and the needs of the poor. Hence it should be enacted that any one who (after May 1, 1552, inserted) kept more than 120 sheep should for every additional 50 sheep keep one milch cow and rear one calf for every two cows kept. A heavy fine of 10s

[1] Lansdowne MS. 238, #6, f. 321b; Strype, *Memorials*, II, i, 151.

[2] The two drafts are S.P. Dom., Edw. VI, II, 21 (bill to increase tillage), and *ibid.* V, 22 (monopoly of farms and conversions into pasture). The second is drafted in two hands, one having written the last three pages of a fourteen-plus page document and having inserted some corrections in the earlier pages. Comparison of the hand for II, 21, and most of V, 22, with Hales' known writings (especially *ibid.*, IV, 33; S.P. Dom., Edw. VI, Addenda, IV, 66; and S.P. Dom., Edw. VI, V, 20) most persuasively suggests that Hales was the author. Miss Lamond prints V, 22 (*Common weal*, xlv–lii), ascribing it to Hales. The problem of dating is more uncertain. II, 21, has been tentatively dated November, 1547 by the PRO catalogue, but by no means conclusive internal evidence would suggest that the document was probably prepared about a year later for the second session of Parliament. V, 22, was almost certainly drafted for the same session, though the feast of St Michael the Archangel (Sept. 29, 1548) is described as in the future. Mr M. R. Pickering has given me valued notes on the problem of dating these manuscripts and on their identification.

a month for each milch cow wanting should be imposed, after a survey had been taken in each parish by the parson, the church-wardens, the constable, and other parish officials.

The far more sweeping and important draft of a bill concerning 'monopoly of farms and conversion into pastures' was prefaced in the form of a petition to the King, protesting against the decay of the society, the decline in population, the destruction of villages, and the great scarcity and cost of foodstuffs. The main reason for this dreadful decay, it is argued, has been that great subjects raised to the nobility have forgotten that they should be shepherds to their people and have thought only of themselves, forgetting 'that these honours, estates, and degrees cannot be maintained ... without your poor subjects'. They have instead become graziers and sheep farmers, have pulled down whole villages, and have depleted the country to make runs for their sheep. Hence scarcity, high prices, and instability in the whole society have ensued. It should accord-ingly be enacted that henceforward no person possessing lands worth 100 marks p.a. should employ other lands for his own use exclus-ively, under pain of a fine of £10 a month for lands so used. Nor should any one keep for his own occupation for grazing and pastur-ing any more of his lands than have an accustomed rental value of £100 p.a., under fine of 1s a month per acre for such lands held in pasture. Further, all persons pasturing 1000 sheep or more on their own lands and pastures should for each 1000 place another 200 on common fields. And, finally, it should be enacted that as much of lands formerly held by monasteries and chantries should be main-tained in husbandry and tillage as was so kept thirty years before the date of the act, under a heavy fine of £6 13s 4d a month when there was a violation. Half of the fines imposed should go to the Crown, a quarter to the poor of the affected parish, and the remainder to whoever brought suit.[1]

These were radical and probably unworkable proposals of social and economic policy which were overtly designed to place severe restraints on the use of land of more than a modest value for pur-poses which were judged to be harmful to the society and especially to its poorest and most defenceless members. The proposed legisla-tion was directed squarely and admittedly at the gentry and the nobility, the language of the draft scarcely concealing a bitter animus towards these classes which, however, not only dominated

[1] Hales, though not claiming authorship, discussed the reasons for and the fate of this intended legislation in his *Defence of John Hales*, *etc.* (1549), printed in Lamond ed. (1893) of *Common weal*, lii–lxvii.

Parliament but on whose loyalty and trust Somerset had to base his policy. These were, therefore, politically dangerous proposals, just as they were unrealistic administratively and economically. It is probably for this reason that they were not filed in their full and original form as bills in this session of Parliament. But there was also in these proposals a great deal of idealism and an eloquent concern for the mass of mankind, for the commons, which was in these tolerant and magnanimous years beginning for the first time to assert itself and to find a faint but articulate voice. And Somerset was an over-mighty subject who heard and lent compassionate sympathy to that voice.

It is quite clear that the full weight of Somerset's immense authority was not deployed in the support of these radical proposals, but it was brought to bear to secure the passage of the famous subsidy act (2 and 3 Edward VI, c. 36), a measure freighted with ultimate trouble for the Protector since it singled out sheep for special taxation and was given very sharp teeth indeed. The measure we know had been long under discussion, a memorandum having been drafted months earlier by Hales in which he argued that dearth and high prices in the realm were accounted for by the far too heavy concentration of the national economy on sheep grazing. In order to restore balance in the economy and to provide the Crown with more abundant revenues, he accordingly proposed a tax on sheep, ranging in this preliminary draft from 1d each on sheep in common pastures to 2d each on ewes and lambs on enclosed grazing, and a connected levy of 5s for every cloth exported.[1]

The bill itself, considerably altered from the original recommendation, was first introduced in the Commons on February 1, 1549, and moved to its third reading and passage on March 2nd, having been keenly and bitterly debated. Because of its novel nature and the almost predictable resistance to its enforcement, the preamble—the *apologia*—was unusually long and exhortatory. The heavy outlays in Scotland and the critical need for defence were both stressed. England, it was submitted, must bring herself to readiness against her enemies with full confidence that God will then protect the realm and 'our little shepherd, till years and strength make him better able' to deal with his enemies. Accordingly, in order to subdue the force 'and puissance of our stout foes', it was resolved to levy 'a mass of money' wherewith the King would be well armed and protected. Hence, instead of the usual subsidy, a relief was enacted

[1] S.P. Dom., Edw. VI, V, 20; [Hales], *Common weal*, xlii-xlv. And see S.P. Dom., Edw. VI, II, 13, for further consideration and calculations.

which laid a tax on personal property at the rate of 1s in the pound, to which was conjoined a tax on sheep. Ewes on enclosed lands were to be taxed at 3d per head, wethers and other shear sheep on such lands at 2d, while all sheep on commons or on enclosed arable lands at $1\frac{1}{2}$d, save that men with from 11 to 20 sheep were to pay only 1d per head, and those with fewer than 11 only $\frac{1}{2}$d.

This tax, as well as the relief, was to be paid in three instalments on November 1, 1549, April 20, 1550, and April 20, 1551—a provision offsetting any sheep tax paid against the personal tax levied probably having been accepted in the course of the debate as an amendment to the measure.[1] By the day the first sheep tax was payable, it may here be noted, the summer risings had occurred, Somerset was in the Tower, and the whole concept of the Commonwealth had collapsed.[2] Careful provision was also made in the act for the appointment of commissioners of collection who might put 'honest and discreet persons on oath' in any parish to determine the number and ownership of sheep in every parish and village in the whole realm.

This important and bold legislation was well drafted, was probably enforceable, and was clearly designed to implement a social and economic policy which, while not wholly new, had come to be held by Somerset and his personal advisers with a stubborn tenacity springing from deep moral conviction. It was meant to check and then to retard sheep grazing, which was generally blamed for enclosures, for depopulation, and for the poverty of the commons. It was also a deliberately punitive tax, laying a heavy impost on graziers of large flocks on enclosed pastures. The measure may be regarded as a very early and by no means unsophisticated use of the taxing power to accomplish plotted social ends and purposes. In this respect, indeed, it may be regarded as the precursor of the radical social legislation of the late nineteenth century and of our own time wherewith social ends have been thus achieved. But it was also legislation aimed at an evil largely past, at an economic imbalance already beginning to correct itself. Somerset also incurred from this legislation, which he had driven through a most reluctant Parliament, the deep enmity of particularly powerful classes of men, who, when his hour of weakness came, moved in

[1] Beresford, M. W., 'The poll tax and census of sheep, 1549', *Agric. Hist. Rev.* II (1954), 17.

[2] The tax was repealed in Northumberland's first Parliament by 3 and 4 Edward VI, c. 23, in January, 1550, the anticipated revenues being gained by the inclusion of a subsidy for one year as part of the enactment.

almost instinctively to destroy him. None the less, this strange and complex man remains one of the true architects of the modern world.

Deep resentment and overt opposition among the land-owning classes was mounting against Somerset, and had been expressed both in Parliament and in the Council, well before the risings of 1549 erupted. There is also evidence that discontent amongst the commoners was spreading rapidly in the early months of 1549, as the promise of state intervention and of generous reforms, which at best would have come slowly, failed to secure immediate changes, to relieve both scarcity and high prices, or to alter the attitude and the courses of thrusting landlords. The fact was that the forces now uniting against Somerset were so powerful and so widespread that the tenure of his power was balanced on the fine edge of the little more than nominal support which he could now command from the Council. None the less, he pursued his policy with an almost reckless courage which further separated him and his policy from the dominant political classes. Thus in April, 1549, still another proclamation was issued reciting the letter of the Henrician statutes in force against enclosures and the fact that the recent surveys had shown a hard and flagrant violation of the law. Over great areas what was once tillage land was now under sheep; depopulations had inevitably followed; and houses had been levelled, while 'divers and marvelous crafts' had been employed to frustrate the intent of good laws. Accordingly, the sovereign was now determined to bring the laws against enclosures under full and vigorous enforcement and all his officers and commissioners were admonished to receive complaints and to punish those who had arrogantly stood in contempt of the law.[1]

Even as reports of risings and stirs in numerous counties began to come in, Somerset pressed forward with his policy. In June, Warwick complained bitterly to Cecil that even his park had been entered, enclosures thrown down, and that the tillage plough had trespassed on his fields.[2] Frightened and deeply concerned, Paget, the most forthright of all the Duke's advisers, a few days later, as we have noted in another connection, laid before Somerset an honest and devastating critique of his policy, warning him that the substance of his sovereign power was being rapidly eroded. But the Protector would not be deterred, on the very next day issuing a stringent proclamation in which the commissioners were enjoined to determine

[1] Hughes and Larkin, *Tudor proclamations*, I, 451–453: Apr. 11, 1549.
[2] S.P. Dom., Edw. VI, VII, 35: June 12, 1549.

what illegal enclosures and depopulations had taken place since 4 Henry VII—a full two generations earlier—and generally to assess the amount of land that had been withdrawn from tillage. It was further ordered that a list should be compiled of those persons who kept flocks of more than 2000 sheep, with the ominous instruction to determine 'how many sheep you think have been necessary for the only expenses of such person's household for one year', the commissioners being empowered to call before them in every parish two freeholders, two copyholders or tenants at will, and two farmers in order to elicit the necessary information. Though the commissioners were not empowered to make presentments, it was only too clear that a national survey, on the model of Hales' Midlands inquiry, was intended, while the standing statutes, which were to be enforced, provided ample authority to reverse an economic process which had been under way for at least two centuries.[1] At the same time, a sense of zealous urgency on him, Somerset sought to move the new commissions out into their circuits against common sense and responsible administrative judgement, since agrarian discontent was already being fanned into serious rebellion.[2] Further, as two of the commissioners now named—Sir Thomas Darcy and Sir John Gates—pointed out, these bodies had none save fact-finding powers, with the consequence that 'for lack of present execution of things that shall be before us presented, we are privately in fear lest the people think we do only delay time with them, by which they may be brought into more rage than they are already'. They accordingly submitted that if they were to act at all it would be exceedingly unwise to do so unless they were armed with full powers to overthrow illegal and really objectionable enclosures.[3]

All this was, however, somewhat academic because the great revolts of the summer were at hand and the whole energy of the society was of necessity devoted to their repression. There remained, however, Hales' moving and persuasive *apologia*, the *Defence*, which he composed at Coventry in early September, 1549, before passing as a self-imposed exile to the Continent following Somerset's fall from power. Hales argued that no man had ever sought to improve a commonwealth without incurring the slander of those men who wished no change. This had been his fate.[4] Yet he was not the

---

[1] Hughes and Larkin, *Tudor proclamations*, I, 471–472: July 8, 1549.
[2] S.P. Dom., Edw. VI, VIII, 15–23; *ibid.*, 25–29, on which we have already commented (*vide ante*, 428ff.).   [3] *Ibid.* 24: July 10, 1549.
[4] Hales, *Defence*, lii–liii. We have consulted the manuscript in Lansdowne MS. 238, # 6, f. 292, but have followed Miss Lamond's excellent text (*Common weal*, lii–lxvii).

originator of the enclosure investigation, which sprang from the petition of poor and oppressed men and which enjoyed the support of some who now denounced it. There was no other intention than to strengthen the realm and to relieve the tensions and injustices that plagued the society. Nor could he accept the charge that it was the commission which set off the present stirs which, in fact, rose in counties other than those in which he was carrying on his task. In all his work he found the commons both humble and obedient, though suffering many old wrongs, the real root of disaffection being found in those who endeavoured zealously and corruptly to block the work of the commissioners.[1] Under the instruction of the Protector he had sought no more than full and compelling information on which to act, while the government had pardoned in advance those who had been guilty of illegal enclosures if they would make restitution. The legislation which had been proposed, and which was defeated by rich and selfish men, was designed to do no more than correct the most grievous of existing wrongs. Hales stressed, too, that much of the enclosing for pasture and the consequent depopulation occurred before 1485, with the result that care and slowness were essential if the commonwealth were not to be injured. The commission was therefore working within the narrow limits of the possible, but the whole weight of governmental policy was thrown against a greed and covetousness which had already gravely weakened the fabric of the society. The whole position of the government and, one could add, of the Commonwealth Party was expounded by Hales in one proud and probing sentence: 'Why should we for lucre of a few, which by their doings a man may judge would that there were fewer people then there be, so that they might have more ground for their sheep, make those few that be, less with penury and famine.'[2] Why indeed? This was the question with which Somerset had touched the moral conscience of the realm; this was the question which he sought to resolve by bold, on the whole naive, proposals, but none the less with an answer rooted in morality and a brooding compassion. In so doing he was to forfeit the support of the classes which in their totality represented the structure of power in sixteenth-century England. But the nagging force of the moral questions which he had raised was to persist in English political life until they were resolved by time itself or by decisions of a more sensitively informed national conscience.

---

[1] Hales, *Defence*, lix.   [2] *Ibid.* in *Common weal*, lxv.

XV

THE FRACTURE IN THE POLITY
(THE RISINGS OF 1549)

1. THE BACKGROUND AND THE LESSER STIRS

There was malaise in rural England during the summer months of 1548, occasioned quite as much by the religious changes under way or rumoured as by economic and social discontent, but there was no evidence of serious and spreading disorder, save in the southwestern region. Reports were coming in to the Council of threatened stirs in Kent and in Leicestershire, but these mild disturbances seem to have been no more than evidences of the endemic turbulence of the English society in the Tudor period. No watch was mounted in London until rather late in the summer when by evidently routine orders 300 light horse which had been gathered for the relief of Haddington were set on detached duty in the capital.[1] There were also local disturbances in Warwickshire following Somerset's proclamation establishing the enclosure commission, but these were easily quieted by the local gentry and gained no overt support from the body of the commons of the county.[2]

More serious by far was the chronic disaffection in Cornwall which was focused on an unsavoury adventurer, William Body, who some years earlier had purchased the archdeaconry of Cornwall, but whose title had been vigorously contested in the courts, and who in the last years of Henry VIII's reign had been quite unable to enforce his claims. The conservative sentiments of the region were further exercised by the uncommonly thorough survey made by the Edwardian Chantry Commissioners, though in fact the Commissioners were careful to preserve and to extend the charitable and educational services heretofore borne by a proportion of the chantry endowments. There were also rumours of changes intended in worship and of the Crown's intention to confiscate all church plate, these fears and resentments coming to be centred on the loud and arrogant Body. A tumult broke out in St Keverne parish (as it had

---

[1] Stow, *Annales*, 595.   [2] VCH, *Warwickshire*, II, 441.

in 1497), under the lead of the stipendiary priest there and two yeoman parishioners. A large mob gathered which sought out Body in his house at Helston and there murdered him in a particularly brutal fashion.[1] A brief statement was then read petitioning that all laws be restored to those of the late Henrician years, that this legal 'stand-still' be maintained until the King's twenty-fourth year, and denouncing Body and those like him who accepted the 'new fashions'.

When Sir William Godolphin and the other justices of the peace assembled in Helston, they professed that they were unable either to arrest the murderers or to disperse a now angry and growing crowd which on the next day they estimated numbered 3000 men who were already looting and pilfering. These facts were reported by messenger to distant London, other justices were summoned with their tenants, while several detachments from garrison points in Cornwall and Devonshire added a professional stiffening to the forces being accumulated. By these actions sufficient power was placed under the command of the justices of the peace in the area to arrest the ringleaders, those directly responsible for the murder of Body, and to disperse the mob. Six of those arrested were sent to London for trial,[2] while on May 21st a special commission of oyer and terminer assembled, before which ten of the mob were brought to trial. Nine were found guilty, of whom most, if not all, were in due course executed. Of the six sent to London, only one— the priest, Martin Geoffroy—was in the end tried and executed, while the general pardon with which the Council sought to end this unsavoury and wholly senseless stir, specifically exempted twenty-eight persons. But of these, it seems certain that not more than the ten indicted suffered either death or long imprisonment.[3]

There were, then, no serious risings in 1548, save for the quick and vicious stir in Cornwall, which after a moment of hesitation was well, efficiently, and on the whole humanely handled by resources of authority and order within the region. But the crisis of the following summer, to which we now turn, was very grave indeed, mounting the most serious threat to the stability and sovereign strength of the government that the whole of the sixteenth century was to know, save only for that explosive, though geographically contained, rebell-

---

[1] The Council some months earlier clearly regarded Body as at once intemperate and a breeder of trouble (*A.P.C.* II, App., 536: Dec. 17, 1547).

[2] *Ibid.* 198: May 15, 1548.

[3] In this account of the Cornish stir of 1548 we have principally followed the excellent treatment of A. L. Rowse, *Tudor Cornwall, etc.* (L., [1941]), 253–259, and Frances Rose-Troup, *The western rebellion of 1549, etc.* (L., 1913), 72–92; *Fourth rpt., Dep. Keeper Public Records* (1843), App. II, 217–219, for trials of rebels.

ion which we describe as the Pilgrimage of Grace. It looked in July and August as if the whole of southern England was on the point of social and economic break-up;[1] there were serious stirs in the Midland counties; and in southwestern England and in Norfolk quite separate insurrections, moved in the one instance by religious discontent and in the other by social and economic unrest, were under way which were to require the use of every available, and reliable, military resource of the government to stay and then to repress. In mid-July, indeed, it seemed to the Spanish ambassador, whose views often reflected those of Paget, that sovereign authority in England was on the point of dissolution. Van der Delft thought the disorders sprang mostly from economic rather than religious discontent. All available troops were in the field; great bitterness was being engendered because mercenary troops were being employed against Englishmen; and London was heavily garrisoned with artillery sited to control all the gates of the City.[2]

We have dealt at length with the more formal causes of this searing sweep of rebellion in England,[3] and these at bottom doubtless do explain what occurred, save in Devon and Cornwall where religious conservatism, a general and deep-seated dislike of all change, and a vacuum of power created by the ruin of the Courtenays were also clearly responsible. Enclosures, rack-rents, high prices, physical scarcities, debasement, and the wounding thrust of selfish landlords on the society are all important as causes for this widespread disaffection and malaise. But it seems that the hope inspired by Somerset's policy and his evident sympathy with the lower classes of the society remain the most certain immediate cause of this plague of risings. The hope and expectation was for immediate relief, for an immediate correction of the imbalances in the society, though this Somerset never quite intended and, as we have seen, could not in any case compel the land-owning classes of England to accept. But however true all this may be, it hardly explains why a husbandman or a servant would leave the security of his house to join these ill-disciplined and roving bands of rebels when they passed his door. Deep in the psyche of every such man there must have been a bewildering complexity of human motives, doubtless

[1] Pollard, *History of England*, 32–33.

[2] *Cal. S.P. Span.* IX, 405–406: July 19, 1549.

[3] *Vide ante*, 386–438. It is noteworthy that both Grafton and the *Grey Friars Chronicle* attributed the risings chiefly to enclosures and economic causes. Grafton says that when no improvement followed Somerset's proclamation, the poor 'rashly without orders took upon themselves to redress' their wrongs. (*Grafton's Chronicle*, II, 514; *Grey Friars Chronicle* (Camden Soc. LIII), 59.)

never fully sorted out, but which in the end triggered his action. A nagging wife, too many clamouring children, hatred of a thrusting landlord, bitterness because the tiny obit which he had given for the repose of his mother's soul had been seized, the prospect of easy plunder—all these and many more compelling, but wholly undocumented reasons, inspired men to risk short adventure for the possibility of a hideous death.

We shall, as we proceed, deal first with certain of the more general aspects of the great stirs of 1549, then discuss as fully as the evidence permits the risings and disorders in a considerable number of counties in which the movements were quickly sealed off and suppressed, and then conclude with the true insurrections centred in the southwest and in Norfolk.

It may be here suggested that the revolutionary movement in 1549 failed because it never developed clearly defined objectives or, as was the case in Devon and Cornwall, because the announced objectives were so oddly and conservatively stated that they ran counter to the aspirations of most men in England. The movement failed too because in the whole of England it did not attract the support, and hence was unable to gain the leadership, of any member of the nobility or gentry, save for a very few somewhat eccentric instances in Cornwall and Devon. From fear born of self-interest these classes simply presented a solid front and in the end an impregnable strength against the elements of disorder. The revolutionary movement failed, too, because it was unable to fuse many scattered, so to speak, indigenous, stirs in many counties, the Privy Council consequently being able to seal off Devonshire and Norfolk and then to bring to bear the required military resources for the slaughter of the rebel forces. The suppression of the risings was to be a bloody and an ugly business, the extant sources revealing a deep and bitter cleavage between the gentry of England and the peasantry. The evidence of the hatred of the commons for the gentry—as individuals and as a class—is shocking in its implications respecting the state of the English society, while quite as shocking is the all too eloquently expressed contempt of those who owned the land of England and bore responsibility for the maintenance of order among the lower classes of the society. Latimer and Lever, Somerset and Hales were quite correct in their deep conviction that all was not well with the English society in the mid-sixteenth century.

As early as mid-April, 1549, reports of minor difficulties in several counties began to be laid before the Privy Council. About a month later they had reached such proportions that a carefully drafted proclamation was issued stating that remedy was soon to be taken against illegal enclosures and depopulations, but stating 'that certain numbers of disobedient and seditious persons, assembling themselves together unlawfully in some parts of the realm, have most arrogantly and disloyally ... taken upon them' the royal authority and have overthrown 'pales, hedges, and ditches at their will and pleasure'. The government would in due course bring the law to bear against enclosures, but it would also punish outrageous seditions. Accordingly, all persons were warned against entering into riots, were to report unlawful assemblies and breaking of enclosures to the nearest justice of the peace, while all officers of the Crown were instructed to employ force for breaking up unlawful assemblies and to 'spoil and rifle their houses and goods' at will.[1] At an uncertain date, but probably in June, the government convened a meeting of all justices of the peace who could attend, at which Rich, the Lord Chancellor, expressed the apprehension of the Council and warned them that the peace and the order of the realm depended on their enforcement of the laws and proclamations. The justices, he said, have been slack in enforcing both religious and political order, 'so that in some shires, which be further off, it may appear that the people have never heard of divers of his majesty's proclamations; or, if they have heard, you are content to wink at it, and to neglect it'. Unless they do their duty, and that fully, law will be dissolved, the realm weakened, and the people will become wild and savage for want of curb. Those present were accordingly commanded to repair to their counties and immediately to inform the gentry that laws and proclamations were to be fully enforced and that those who stood in violation would be punished. A little later Rich himself repaired to Essex, where disorderly assemblies had already occurred, and moved with great vigour, and success, in keeping this important and often turbulent shire reasonably peaceful during the critical months of this black summer.[2]

Somerset, and certainly several of his colleagues on the Council, during the early weeks when news of stirs in numerous counties was flowing in, seriously underestimated their gravity and lost precious time in assembling under centralized command forces sufficient for their repression. At first the principal concern seems to have been that spreading disorder would make more difficult Paget's negotiations abroad. Further, there is a feel of authenticity in Van

[1] Hughes and Larkin, *Tudor Proclamations*, I, 461–462: May 23, 1549.
[2] Foxe, *Acts and monuments*, V, 724–725; Coyle, Mary E., *Sir Richard Rich Lord Rich* (unpublished Ph.D. thesis, 1965, Harvard University).

der Delft's report to the Emperor, probably derived from Paget, that the Lord Protector had taken the position in the Council that there was great justice in the demands of the commons.[1] Also, wide publicity was arranged for still another proclamation which promised the speedy reform of unlawful enclosures and depopulations, but which denounced the riots in which those aggrieved took law into their own hands under the persuasion of 'furious and light guides of uproar'. The Council expressed its confidence that such persons had been misled and hence pardoned all save those already in prison as fomenters of such riots and outrages, on condition that they desist from such offences in the future and repair to their homes.[2] This proclamation was promulgated throughout the realm, in London by heralds and trumpeters, while two days later heavier troop concentrations were observed at the gates of the City.[3] A last forlorn effort was made to reduce disorders by persuasion when the Council resolved to send into the troubled regions gifted and trustworthy preachers, who by their godly exhortations might quiet the disturbances and bring the people to a knowledge of their obedience.[4]

Until it was too late, until full-scale insurrections were under way in Norfolk and in the west, Somerset temporized, hoping that the offer of lenient course and speedy reforms would serve to quiet the commotions. He was, indeed, wholly unwilling to use troops, many of the most effective of which were mercenaries, against his fellow-countrymen. His attitude is clearly reflected in Hales' contemplations on the tumults, when he rejected the suggestion that troops be placed in appointed barracks throughout the realm for the suppression of risings. This would be to introduce tyranny in the English society, for such garrison troops would 'take poor men's hens, chickens, pigs, and other provision, and pay nothing for it; except it be an evil turn, as to ravish his wife or daughter for it'. The consequence would be to encourage rebellions born of desperation, for 'the stomachs of Englishmen would never bear that, to suffer such injury and reproaches, as I know such use to do to the subjects of France, in reproach of whom we call them peasants'.[5]

But the tougher and more immediately responsible advisers around Somerset were now persuaded that full-scale force must be used. Paget found himself handicapped in his negotiations with the Emperor by the reports of spreading rebellions and of the inaction

[1] *Cal. S.P. Span.* IX, 395: June 13, 1549.
[2] Hughes and Larkin, *Tudor proclamations*, I, 462–464: June 14, 1549.
[3] *Grey Friars Chronicle* (Camden Soc. LIII), 60.
[4] Strype, *Memorials*, II, i, 262–263.   [5] [Hales], *Common weal*, 94.

of his government. Granvelle had urged on him that the Protector must move 'with the sword of justice in his hand' against the commons, just as the Emperor had on occasion been obliged to do.[1] Sir Thomas Smith, immured at Eton by illness, wrote to Cecil lamenting the paralysis of the government. If Somerset would delegate authority in the shires to strike down tumults, if the gentry and 'grave yeomen householders' in each county were called out, order could soon be restored. The armed might of each shire should stand ready to move 'suddenly in the night' with sixty to one hundred horse to gather in the 'stirrers' before the commons could be roused. Grey, he noted, was moving with the sword in nearby Oxfordshire, and his hangings there were more effective than 'ten thousand proclamations and pardons for the quieting of the people'.[2]

We may now turn to the effective efforts of Lord Grey, and others like him, in containing widespread disaffection in numerous counties, thereby preventing the possibility of a general insurrection which might conceivably have occurred had the two primary centres of rebellion in Devonshire and Norfolk become linked. In commenting on these minor stirs we shall begin with a note on London itself, then move out in a widening arc from the capital. There is almost no evidence of indigenous London support for the agrarian risings, but its artisan classes were hard pressed by scarcities and by high prices, and the floating class of rootless beggars and vagabonds infesting the City were very rightly feared. As we have already observed, small troop concentrations were kept in or near London from April onwards. On July 3rd close watches were set in the capital, while about a fortnight later martial law was declared in the City and trained artillerymen were ordered to mount their pieces at the gates. Before that critical month was finished a day watch had likewise been set at the gates, while the City Companies were ordered to be in readiness for the mustering of the trained bands. It seems probable, too, that the deliberately spaced public hangings in London of convicted rioters from the provinces was intended as a macabre warning, as was the moving out of the famous brass ordnance from the Tower to lend further strength to the defence of the gates. Wide publicity was also given to Cranmer's famous sermon against the rebels, preached at St Paul's before a great concourse of citizens, and then repeated by his chaplain at

[1] *Cal. S.P. For.*, *Edw. VI*, ##185, 189: July 8 and 13, 1549.
[2] S.P. Dom., Edw. VI, VIII, 33: July 19, 1549. Paget might well have mentioned, too, how firmly and successfully Shrewsbury had kept the peace in Derbyshire, Shropshire, and Nottinghamshire, for which Somerset and the Council thanked him on July 19 (Lodge, *Illustrations*, I, 131–132).

Paul's Cross for those who had failed to gain admission. During these nervous days, when only bad news flowed in from the west, the Tower gates were closed, the garrison strengthened, gunners were moved in from the navy, while 2000 horse and 4000 foot were ordered by the Council to be kept about the person of the King.[1]

There was an early disturbance in Essex in the late spring and another in July, which were strenuously suppressed by the local magistrates under the direction of Lord Rich. At least two of the disaffected in the county were hanged in London, one being described as from Rumford, and by mid-July the imperial ambassador reported the county as quiet.[2] Disorders in Kent also broke out in May, but the gentry were gathered immediately and strongly led by Sir Thomas Wyatt and others, who took the ringleaders, of whom two were promptly hanged at Ashford on May 13th and another at Canterbury on the following day. Artillery was lent by the Council to the Kentish magistrates, who mounted it at Canterbury as a further warning, and the county seems to have remained quiet during the difficult weeks of the summer.[3] In Suffolk, too, though many disaffected slipped across the border to join Kett in Norfolk, minor disturbances in May and July were easily suppressed by Sir Anthony Wingfield and other gentry—some of those taken being pilloried at Ipswich, others losing an ear, and at least two being sent to London for trial as ringleaders, one of whom was executed at Tyburn.[4] Wingfield was particularly successful in restoring and then in maintaining order in a critical area, having evidently used money supplied by the Council with great effectiveness in the employment of informers and agents who kept him well apprised of local sentiment. In early August he was given 100 marks for such uses, and a few days later he had made payments totalling £9 6s 8d

---

[1] Wriothesley, *Chronicle*, II (Camden Soc., n.s. XX), 15, 16, 17–19; *Grey Friars Chronicle* (Camden Soc. LIII), 59–60; *A.P.C.*, II, 301–302: July 16, 1549.

[2] Hayward, *Edward VI*, 310; Wriothesley, *Chronicle*, II (Camden Soc., n.s. XX), 15; Holinshed, *Chronicles*, III, 917; *Grey Friars Chronicle* (Camden Soc. LIII), 60; *Cal. S.P. Span.* IX, 405: July 19, 1549; S.P. Dom., Edw. VI, VIII, 61.

[3] *A breviat cronicle, etc.* (Canterbury, [1552]), no pagin.; VCH, *Kent*, III, 300; Edward VI, *Chronicle*, 12; *Grey Friars Chronicle* (Camden Soc. LIII), 60; Holinshed, *Chronicles*, III, 917. Wyatt, a firm admirer of Somerset, was much alarmed by the stirs of 1549 and proposed that a national militia system for internal defence be formed under experienced leaders in each county. Somerset had fallen before the plan could be considered by the Council, but Wyatt proceeded at least to the extent of an informal understanding of how to act in concert with other rich landowners in the county in the event of further emergencies. (Loades, D. M., *Two Tudor conspiracies* (Cambridge, 1965), 49–51.)

[4] VCH, *Suffolk*, II, 182; Hayward, *Edward VI*, 310; Wriothesley, *Chronicle*, II (Camden Soc., n.s. XX), 15; Edward VI, *Chronicle*, 12–13.

to four agents to be used in quieting the county, and about as much for a preacher who was sent out from London to help him with his programme of pacification. He also knew how to use bribes to secure the persons of ringleaders, who were sent on to London for execution, one of whom, a man named Wade, quite miraculously cleared himself of seditious involvement.[1]

In Surrey, also, there was considerable, indeed, endemic, disaffection which gave the Privy Council much concern and which may in part have been occasioned by the lack of strong and locally seated justices of the peace and the want of strong gentry in the county.[2] The Earl of Arundel informed Petre in late June that 'these parts remain as well as may be in a quavering quiet'. But Arundel too was troubled by local weakness, pleading that Sir William Goring be included in the commission of oyer and terminer, since he was much respected by the people for his fair administration of justice.[3] The gentry of the county were commanded to gather and equip as large forces as possible for immediate service. But in Surrey, as in other counties, these levies were not called, principally because the government did not dare trust them, so widespread was disaffection. Riots had to be quelled at Witley Park, where fencing around old commons was thrown down, the grievance stemming from the eviction of an entire parish when Henry VIII created the two parks for Nonsuch Palace.[4] There was also disaffection, if there were not disturbances, in the vicinity of Guildford, while the whole county lay restless under heavy and watchful controls.

Most of the disturbances which we have been describing were evidently minor acts of trespass and riotous assemblies, quickly quieted and broken up. But the stirs in a group of central counties were more serious and were crushed in a most effective, if brutal, fashion. The commons in Buckinghamshire and Berkshire were in an ugly mood during the whole of the summer, but were restrained by a vigilant gentry prodded on by the fearful Privy Council.[5] There was also unrest in Northamptonshire, leading to minor episodes of

[1] *A.P.C.* II, 308, 310, 311, 312, 313, 314, 315, 317. So successful was Wingfield in his methods that one wonders why they were not used in other counties more consistently. £100 was sent into Kent for the pacification of rebels there, but all other efforts were at best sporadic and ill-timed. Had there been more Wingfields in charge in the affected counties, England would not have found herself in such desperate straits by mid-summer.

[2] S.P. Dom., Edw. VI, VIII, 48: Henry Polsted to Cecil.

[3] *Ibid.* VI, VII, 44.

[4] Loseley MSS. (Folger Library), VI, 3: June 30, 1549; VCH, *Surrey*, III, 61; *ibid.* IV, 430.

[5] S.P. Dom., Edw. VI, VIII, 9: July [8?], 1549; Foxe, *Acts and monuments*, V, 738; Dixon, *Church of England*, III, 67.

property damage, but here too there seems to have been no organized violence. In Oxfordshire, however, much more serious rioting occurred. The commons were nearly out of hand in late July, and the Council was gravely alarmed because there was clear evidence that certain of the conservative Catholic clergy were directly involved. Sir John Williams' park at Thame had been forcibly disparked and his deer killed, while there was disaffection in that whole region because of the steady aggregation of lands for sheep pasture by the Dormers, a London merchant family now being absorbed into the gentry. Rycot was also disparked by rioters and its deer killed, while the disorderly commons, who 'slew many sheep', then proceeded to Woodstock where they learned that government forces were moving into the county. Many thereupon deserted, but the remaining force moved towards the Cotswold Hills as far as Chipping Norton. Near here they were hemmed in and dispersed by Lord Grey of Wilton, who with about 1500 troops, of whom many were mercenaries, was on his way to add strength to Russell's forces in the west. But he had been commanded to move first into Berkshire, Buckinghamshire, Northamptonshire, and Oxfordshire 'for appeasing and executing evill disposed persons'. After tracking down the rioters he was able, in the King's succinct account, to 'so abash the rebels that more than half of them ran their ways, and [of the] other[s] that tarried were some slain, some taken, and some hanged'.[1] The rebels dispersed, and with about 200 prisoners in hand, Grey met with the gentry of the shire on July 19th to arrange for selected hangings in the disaffected areas of the county, the heads of the executed rebels then to be mounted in the highest place in their towns 'for the more terror of the said evil people'. Grey submitted that he must press on with his forces to the west, while the sheriff and the gentry with their local forces were to carry out the executions, including two rioters, not yet selected, who were to suffer at Thame. Of the thirteen specifically named, it must be noted that four were country priests and the rest small craftsmen and commoners. Brutal and coldly selective as this summary action was, it seems to have quenched completely what might easily have developed into a serious rising had it gained effective leadership and had it formed a connection with the rebellions even then raging in the west and in Norfolk.[2]

[1] Edward VI, *Chronicle*, 13.
[2] S.P. Dom., Edw. VI, VIII, 9, 32; *Two London chronicles* (Camden Misc. XII), 18; VCH, *Oxfordshire*, I, 444–445; *ibid.* VII, 160; Foxe, *Acts and monuments*, V, 738; Dixon, *Church of England*, III, 67–68.

These Midland stirs were evidently unconnected with another, occurring some weeks earlier in part of Leicestershire and in Rutland, which aroused serious concern and occasioned prompt action by the Council. On June 11th Somerset personally enjoined the Marquis of Dorset and the Earl of Huntingdon to promulgate the proclamation against illegal assemblies in that region, to summon and warn the gentry, and to move against any evidence of disaffection, since 'in most parts of the realm sundry lewd persons have attempted to assemble themselves, and first seeking redress of enclosures, have in some places by seditious priests and other evil people set forth to seek restitution of the old bloody laws'. Further stirs did occur in both counties, and especially in Rutland, where Huntingdon reported that 'there have already divers in the county . . . been condemned, and have suffered for the same', while in the next week several in Leicestershire were to be arraigned. By mid-August, however, both counties had been restored to quiet, the Council thanking Dorset for his constant and 'good diligence' in the King's service.[1]

There is also some evidence of smouldering disaffection, though not of stirs, in Lincolnshire during the course of the spring and summer, as well as some slight aid to Kett's force in Norfolk.[2] The troubles in Cambridgeshire were more serious, though the usually turbulent Isle of Ely lay quiet, perhaps because of outlays for ' "persons who diligently watched at the time of the commotion in Norfolk, lest there should be any rebellion" . . . and on "arms bought" ' for the bishop's account. The enclosure riots in the county were, oddly enough, centred in the city of Cambridge where on July 10th a crowd of about one hundred assembled to pull down enclosures of former commons around the city, and then marched off towards Barnwell Priory, where enclosures had proceeded since the expropriation. This stir was quickly reduced to order and a few of the rioters were probably hanged.[3]

Far more serious were the troubles in the contiguous counties of Wiltshire, Hampshire, and Sussex, which lay athwart the vital lines of communication to the west and likewise dangerously close to the capital itself. The young King, indeed, seems to suggest that the

[1] S.P. Dom., Edw. VI, VII, 31: June 11, 1549; *ibid.* 46: Aug. 19, 1549; Nichols, *Remains*, II, 226–227; VCH, *Rutland*, I, 147, 181, 223; Gay, E. F., 'The Midland revolt, etc.', *Trans. Royal Hist. Soc.*, n.s. XVIII (1904), 195; Edward VI, *Chronicle*, 13–15.

[2] Wriothesley, *Chronicle*, II (Camden Soc., n.s. XX), 13; Holinshed, *Chronicles*, III, 917.

[3] VCH, *Cambridge*, II, 403; *ibid.* III, 14–15; *ibid.* IV, 40.

15

first stirs of 1549 occurred in Wiltshire and that serious difficulty was averted by the quick response of Sir William Herbert, whose park was assailed, who 'did put them down, overrun, and slay them'.[1] Hence during the critical days in the west, when Russell seriously considered falling back on Salisbury, the county remained quiet. The disaffection, never quite breaking out into full turbulence, in Hampshire was more virulent and could never be quite contained, possibly because of the want of strong territorial leadership in the county. As early as May 15th the Lords of the Council warned the sheriffs and justices to stand ready with the full power of the county to repress turbulent and lewd persons who might be affected by the disorders in nearby Wiltshire. Only a few days later the mayor of Southampton and his brethren were advised that divers 'frail persons' in Overton and other places had assembled for riotous purposes, while all the justices were commanded to assemble enough strength to put down any future disorders. It was probably at this time that the park at King's Somborne was opened and the enclosing pale destroyed, while some enclosures were overthrown by night in the neighbourhood of Winchester. There were also disorders near Odiham which were, however, well handled by Sir John Thynne and others of the gentry, Somerset on July 13th commending the actions taken and forwarding a proclamation of the King's free pardon for Thynne's use.[2] It is evident, too, that the central government was by no means content with either the vigilance or the efficiency of the local authorities in Southampton and Winchester, who were bumbling in their efforts and had constantly to be prodded. Thus on July 13th Somerset personally wrote to the mayor of Southampton commanding him to find and hold one 'Friar Wigg' who had lately advocated limitations on the King's power and who was probably a traitor, only to be informed a full ten days later that Wigg had recently been in the town but, being warned, had left and could not be found. Nor, for that matter, could he be found in his former haunts in Winchester.[3]

The immense difficulties in which the government found itself and the complex diversity of the reasons which were causing men to embrace what they must have known were treasonable courses are suggested quite perfectly by the examination and confession of two simple men from northern Hampshire on August 12, 1549.

---

[1] Edward VI, *Chronicle*, 12.   [2] HMC, *Bath MSS.*, IV: *Seymour papers*, 111.
[3] Anderson, *Letters from the archives of Southampton*, 66, 68, 71–72; HMC, *11th rpt.*, Appendix, pt. III: MSS. of the Corporations of Southampton and King's Lynn, 116, 117; VCH, *Hampshire*, IV, 469.

These men, described as servants, had been approached in Winchester some days earlier by a carpenter of that town, John Garnham, who with a man named Flint was undoubtedly planning a stir. Garnham boasted that he and Flint had ready one thousand men in Hampshire and West Sussex, and that they would enjoy the full support of the bishop's own tenants. All was prepared in north Hampshire, where they were waiting for word from Flint in West Sussex. They would finance the stir by plundering all the cathedral clergy, including the Chancellor; they would fortify themselves with two barrels of beer; they would procure horses and carts from sympathetic farmers and, once gathered, would proceed to Salisbury where they would strike off the mayor's head. They had already arranged for a trumpeter and Flint had three pieces of ordnance in mind, which were stored in Selsey Church (in Sussex). They were also in communication with a former priest in Waltham parish, who had urged them to make 'a banner of the five wounds and with a chalice and a host and a priest kneeling to it upon the same banner'. Once they had taken Salisbury, so the reasoning was, all those conscripted into service against the Western Rising would desert from the royal army, and then the 'western men' would follow with all speed, and they would fall on and destroy the army and 'especially the villain Herbert'.[1] This strange blending of local anarchy, unexpressed grievances, the plundering of a cathedral still firmly presided over by a conservative bishop and his chancellor, an evidently casual interest in the banner of the western rebels, a thirst for beer and tavern boastings (at the *Sign of the Crown* in Winchester), a half-formed and dangerously sound strategic sense, and simply a thirsting for violent adventure—all so well expressed in this amazing document—suggest the infinitely complex causes for the rebellions at that moment flaming in the West and in East Anglia.

Firmer and more experienced hands were in control in Sussex, though there had early in the summer been 'a general plague of disturbances there'.[2] Flint, the co-conspirator with Garnham, was evidently quickly clapped into the Tower where as 'a seditious stirrer' he still languished in 1551. But as the rioting broke out in Sussex, the Earl of Arundel was given charge of the county and by

[1] S.P. Dom., Edw. VI, VIII, 41.
[2] Somerset talked personally with men who had been sent up by Bishop Day from Chichester on the charge of having been involved in illegal assemblies. Characteristically, he pardoned them on condition of good behaviour and instructed Day to inform the justices that they were not to be molested for past offences. (HMC, *Bath MSS.*, IV: *Seymour papers*, 111: June 25, 1549.)

blending firmness with humanity was able to restore order without loss of life. He did not put troops in the field against bands of rioters, but rather sent orders to their camps commanding their dispersal and inviting those who had grievances to lay them before him at Arundel Castle. Men did come with complaints, principally against enclosures effected by the gentry, and these grievances the Earl was quick to relieve by personal persuasion.[1]

There remain to be discussed, amongst the lesser disorders, only those experienced in Yorkshire, wholly detached geographically from the counties heretofore mentioned. This stir, narrowly confined but for a moment extremely violent, broke out in the general vicinity of Seamer and was limited to a region on the border between the East and the North Ridings of the county. Foxe, our principal source, wrote that it was caused by a bitter hatred of the course of the Reformation, by rumours of the success of the Western Rising, and by a story current in the area that the King, the nobility, and the gentry, were to be destroyed and the realm to be ruled by four governors to be chosen by a parliament of the commons. To these causes may certainly be added deep local resentment because of the recent chantry expropriation, and the vicious and murderous violence of the ringleaders.

The instigators were a yeoman named Ombler, of East Heslerton, his nephew, Stevenson, and a parish clerk of Seamer named Dale. They met on July 25th, when they decided to 'set forward the stir' at Seamer and East Heslerton, to kill out of hand such of the gentry as might oppose their proceedings, and to fire the beacons, as if to call out the countryside for the defence of the coast. They expected to find their supporters amongst the poor, those unwilling to work, men tempted by the promise of loot, and those who wished the restoration of the ancient religion. Preparations were begun in the parishes of Seamer, on the coast, and Wintringham, but in the latter community the drunken boasting in a tavern by one of the intended participants was reported to neighbouring gentlemen who had time to mount guard. The beacons were fired at two places (Seamer and Staxton), while the leaders with a few followers moved immediately against the household of Matthew White, who with an associate had recently purchased a large tract of chantry lands in Yorkshire. White, his brother-in-law, a visiting York merchant, and a servant of Walter Mildmay, a chantry commissioner in Yorkshire, were seized, carried about a mile from White's house and then stripped and brutally murdered. The rebel group then ranged from parish to parish gathering malcontents and forcing many to join them in what appears to have been an aimless pattern of movement until they numbered perhaps as many as 3000 men. But the gentry of the area were now also aroused and in arms, the feckless Ombler being taken without difficulty on his way to Hunmanby where he hoped to find supporters. Shortly afterwards the remaining leaders were simply plucked off by armed and mounted gentry, the whole lot being sent on to York where they were executed on September 21st. There is no evidence whatever that this stir had attracted any measure of substantial local support. It was simply a murderous foray which collapsed at the first touch of almost automatically organized local resistance.[1]

2. THE RISING IN THE WEST (1549)

We have noted in some detail that much of Cornwall had been unsettled and that there had been occasional turbulence there in the summer of 1548. The riotous events connected with the murder of Archdeacon Body had been handled by the central government with skill and understanding; and in the autumn preachers had been sent into the Duchy in an effort to enlighten as well as to render more tractable a county which still lent a strong and almost instinctive loyalty to the ancient faith, or, perhaps more accurately, to the traditional forms of worship.[2] But the countryside remained deeply unsettled as the chantries fell and as the effective date for the introduction of the service prescribed by the first *Book of Common Prayer* drew near. In the spring of 1549 this discontent was undoubtedly being exploited by conservative clergy, and especially former chantry priests. Riotous demonstrations which broke out in the important market town of Bodmin became serious indeed when direction and some measure of discipline was given to the stir by Humphrey Arundell of Helland, of a family well within the lower ranges of the gentry of the county. Arundell's maternal grandfather

[1] Foxe, *Acts and monuments*, V, 738–741; Holinshed, *Chronicles*, III, 985–987; VCH, *Yorkshire*, II, 485; *ibid.*, III, 415; *The certificates of the commissioners appointed to survey the chantries . . . in the county of York*, ed. by William Page (2 vols., Surtees Soc., XCI, XCII, 1894–1895), I, xvi; Dickens, A. G., 'Some popular reactions to the Edwardian reformation in Yorkshire', *Yorks. Archaeol. Soc. Trans.*, XXXIV (1939), 160–169.
[2] Thus in September, 1548, Dr Tong, a fervent and evangelical preacher, had been paid £33 6s 8d when he was sent to Cornwall (*A.P.C.* II, 220).

had been one of the leaders of the rising of 1497. Attractive in person, with some junior military experience, restless and quarrelsome by nature, and boastful and untruthful, Arundell quickly established his authority, gained control of the Mount, and moved with such dispatch that the sheriff of the county, John Milton, dared not call out the county gentry, in any event partially disaffected. Associated with Arundell in the leadership of the stir were John Winslade of Pelyn, also of the gentry of the county, and his son William. Likewise lending support from the outset were several substantial burghers of Bodmin, including the then mayor, as well as a former mayor of the town. Amongst the leaders too were a few prosperous yeomen, and a considerable number of priests, who spoke for the movement and who almost certainly lent to it a far more religious over-lay than it actually possessed. The Bodmin rebels, restless and ill-armed, determined in a council of war to move on London, there to present their still unformulated demands. They also resolved to be preceded in their march by the consecrated host and a banner signifying the five wounds of Christ. This strange concourse then moved slowly out along the desolate tracks of Bodmin Moor in the general direction of Tavistock. At the same time, a better armed and led detachment was thrusting southwards, capturing Sir Richard Grenville, who had sought to parley with them, and occupying Plymouth, whose castle, however, held out for a season against them.

Meanwhile, and almost certainly quite independently, far more serious trouble had arisen in the small and remote parish of Sampford Courtenay, some five miles northeast of Okehampton, in Devonshire. No more unlikely spot could be imagined for the outbreak of a flaming rebellion, save that its deep isolation had in recent years been profoundly affected by the threat of change reaching down from Westminster. It was then, as it is now, a straggling village of perhaps a score of houses, the parish comprising eighty 'houseling people', stretching along a single street, with its nondescript and singularly ugly church, mostly dating from the late fifteenth century, which was tucked in well below the level of the street and stands in a small and cramped churchyard, scarcely hospitable to scenes of violent action. Yet the Western Rebellion of 1549 began here, and here, where fleeing survivors of the rebel army were hemmed in and cut down, it may be said to have ended. This poor, relatively infertile, and deeply isolated parish had none the less slowly but implacably been affected by the flow of great events. The manor had once been part of the vast Courtenay holdings in Devonshire, but with the attainder of the Marquis of Exeter passed to the Crown which still held the manor and the advowson.[1] It is also certainly important to note that the chantry here was one of the most heavily endowed of the rural chantries of the county, the landed income being £9 10s 8d p.a., with no reprises, and the priest, William Dyscomb, having the whole of the income. The chantry chapel stood about a mile from the church and was reported by the commissioners as possessing ornaments and plate to the value of £6 9s od also one of the highest totals for any rural parish in the county.[2] The chantry lands, all lying in the parish, had of course been recently confiscated, though so far as can be determined they were not sold before the time of Edward VI's death. Other lands in the parish, belonging to a chantry in Okehampton, had, however, been recently sold to John Prideaux, one of the chantry commissioners for Devon and a member of an ambitious gentle family which was aggressively engaged in building a landed fortune.[3]

And there were other changes which profoundly affected this remote rural parish, so evidently overwhelmingly conservative in its way of life and in its faith. A new priest, William Hayes, had recently been installed in the living,[4] about whom little is known save that he was nearly seventy years of age, was not a native of the county, and had expressed himself as personally reluctant to follow the Act of Uniformity, which required him to use the service prescribed by the *Book of Common Prayer* on Whitsunday. So exercised was the community that a local tailor (Thomas Underhill) and a labourer, when informed by Hayes that he must follow the legal service, forbade him to do so and compelled him to celebrate the mass in the accustomed fashion and in the old vestments. This disturbance on June 9th led at once to a riotous assembly, which four of the local justices of the peace and several of the gentry sought to disperse by a

[1] The manor was granted to Lord Clinton on Nov. 16, 1551, who on the next day was licensed to sell it, with other properties, to Sir Richard Sackville. The advowson was retained by the Crown until June 23, 1552, when it was granted as part of an exchange to Sir William Cavendish, Treasurer of the Chamber (*Cal. Pat. Rolls, Edw. VI*, IV, 69).

[2] PRO, Chantry returns, E 301.15, #52.

[3] *Cal. Pat. Rolls, Edw. VI*, II, 259.

[4] The Privy Council was for a season quite incorrectly persuaded that Hayes was one of Mary Tudor's chaplains, and that both Arundell and Hayes were known in the west as 'her men'. Possibly the confusion arose from the fact that Hayes had at one time served Catherine Parr in a clerical capacity. Mary, while also denying any connection with the Norfolk rebellion, indignantly declared that she possessed neither lands nor servants in Devonshire (S.P. Dom., *Edw. VI*, VIII, 30: July 18, 1549; Burnet, *Reformation*, VI, 283–284, for Mary's reply).

parley with the leaders in the course of which one of the gentlemen was seized by a now violent mob and was literally hacked to pieces.[1] News of this tragic event spread rapidly through the county, 'and the common people so well allowed and liked thereof that they clapped their hands for joy: and agreed in one mind to have the same in every [one] of their several parishes'. The now insurgent mob, completely out of hand, fanned out in central and western Devonshire until it joined forces with and absorbed the Cornish rebel forces which were at this moment moving towards Crediton on the main road which then linked Barnstaple with Exeter. A serious rebellion was in progress.[2]

The rebellion grew more serious, too, as it attracted a few more reckless malcontents amongst the gentry and yeomanry, who were immediately accepted as leaders. Among these may be counted Thomas Holmes of Cornwall, a servant to Sir John Arundell, five more men of burgher status from Bodmin and Torrington, Robert Paget, almost certainly a brother of the Edwardian Councillor,[3] and the one member of the upper gentry of the area to become enmeshed in treason, Sir Thomas Pomeroy, a feckless adventurer who had consumed his estates and who was using every device to procure monastic and chantry lands at the moment the rebellion broke out. To these ringleaders must certainly be added a considerable number of country clergy who gave moral support to the rebellion, and at least ten priests who were more directly and fully

---

[1] A later historian of Devon says that of the two local incendiaries in Sampford Courtenay, one 'would have no gentleman; the other no justices of the peace' (Polwhele, Richard, *The history of Devonshire*, I (Exeter, 1797), 254). The murdered gentleman, named Hellier, was buried as an heretic in the churchyard, the body being placed north to south.

[2] Our principal sources for the narrative account of the Western Rising are John Hooker's *The description of the citie of Excester* (L., 1575; Exeter, *1919*), and his *The discourse and discovery of the life of Sir Peter Carewe, etc.* (in *Calendar of the Carew manuscripts . . . at Lambeth, etc.*, vol. I, ed. by J. S. Brewer and William Bullen (L., 1867), lxvii–cxviii), and the Petyt MSS., Inner Temple. We have depended heavily, too, on the narrative on Frances Rose-Troup's admirable history of the rising (*The western rebellion of 1549*) and on the shorter, but brilliant, account of A. L. Rowse (*Tudor Cornwall*). The relevant documents from the Petyt MSS. have been printed by Nicholas Pocock, *Troubles connected with the Prayer Book of 1549, etc.* (Camden Soc., n.s. XXXVII, 1884). We would have used the Pocock text rather than the manuscripts had it not been for Miss Rose-Troup's rather sharp criticism of the accuracy of the transcriptions. In point of fact, a rather close examination leaves one persuaded that Pocock's readings are sufficiently accurate, probably more so than our own.

[3] He was condemned to death, though Russell delayed the execution. Somerset wrote in bitter terms to Russell somewhat later that the matter was 'touching our honour, for as we have been credibly informed divers have not left unspoken that we should consent to [the] death of our own brother and now would wink at' Paget (Petyt MS. 538, xlvi, ff. 451, 456–457).

involved and who implanted on the rising a religious aura which somewhat masks the real complexity of the movement.[1]

During these early days of the rising it seems clear that priests in, or in touch with, the insurgent camps were framing a list of articles, all in the form of demands to be addressed to the central authority in London. At an uncertain date, but perhaps as early as mid-June, a group of eight demands were addressed to the Council, which mentions them in a dispatch to the west dated June 29th, but the number was shortly increased to fifteen. It was to this draft that Cranmer was to make his formal rejoinder and it was probably to this document that Nicholas Udall also made a reply.[2] The articles bear the evident marks of priestly thought and modes of expression, all but one of them being directly or indirectly concerned with statements of religious grievances and aspirations. In Rowse's words, 'they were a complete, a pathetic manifesto of Catholic reaction'.[3] Thus they pleaded for the restoration of the Six Articles, while three of the clauses required the full return to the Roman Catholic celebration of the mass. They wished, too, for the full restoration of the ancient ritual of worship, and that the service prescribed by the Prayer Book be laid aside 'like a Christmas game'. They demanded that Latin should be resumed as the language of the service and that the English Bible be called in, 'since otherwise the clergy could not easily confound heresies'. They further demanded that two outspoken Catholic canons of Exeter Cathedral be returned to their livings, and that Cardinal Pole be called home and added to the King's Council. They asked, as well, that half the expropriated church lands be restored for the support of two chief abbeys to be founded in each county. This was the whole of their demands, save for the curious request that gentlemen should be limited to one servant for every 100 marks of their yearly rentals.

There can be no doubt that the most important of the forces animating the Western Rebellion was fear of religious change. But religious conservatism was by no means the exclusive cause, it seeming more probable that the underlying grievances were social and economic and that the movement was 'captured', to use Pollard's

[1] We have followed Miss Rose-Troup's helpful list of the clergy involved, with a few additions.

[2] Petyt MS. 538, xlvi, f. 432. The most convenient text of the rebel demands may be found in Burnet, *Reformation*, II, 209–210. We shall reserve our consideration of the considerable literature of reply and denunciation to our discussion of Edwardian political thought in the second volume of this work.

[3] Rowse, *Tudor Cornwall*, 271.

apt phrase, by the priestly supporters who were its spokesmen.[1] Devonshire and Cornwall lay far out on the periphery of Tudor England; both counties remained turbulent under both Henry VII and Henry VIII; and both were marginal in terms of economic resources. Further, the structure of power and administration had been severely strained by the sudden and violent disappearance of the Courtenay interest, which Henry VIII recognized full well when in 1539 he sought to plant a huge aggregate of power in the region by the substitution of the Russell interest. The great gift to Lord Russell of monastic lands worth approximately £1000 p.a., while subject to rents to the Crown in the amount of £284 5s 0d p.a., was, significantly, the sole notable exception to the King's policy of selling the expropriated monastic properties at an economic price.[2] Then in the year following, the King created for Russell a new post as Lord President of Devonshire, Cornwall, Dorset, and Somerset, designed to carry great prestige as well as power. This was the Henrician design, but the truth is that it failed to achieve even the elements of its purposes. Russell in fact became ever more absorbed in the tasks of administration in London, while under Edward he was one of the central figures in the ruling junta. His principal residence was never established in the west; he made no more than fleeting visits to the region, and was then rarely outside Exeter. His local prestige and power—and that was what counted in Tudor England—simply did not equal that of such old gentle families as the Edgecombes, the Pollards, the Grenvilles, and the Carews.

There was, then, a power vacuum in Devonshire and Cornwall not wholly filled by a rising gentry which had considerably increased its estates as monastic and chantry properties came on the market. But the Devonshire gentry were relatively poor, with the consequence that of the twenty-five persons who acquired crown lands in the county in the Edwardian period only four were from Devonshire and two from Cornwall, while as many as ten were Londoners and hence almost predictably absentee landlords. Then too, the Devonshire lands sold were usually scattered, there being only eighteen parishes in which there were substantial holdings, the

---

[1] Pollard, *Somerset*, 239. Most contemporary or early commentators considered the underlying causes to be social and economic: *vide Cal. S.P. Ven.*, V, 237–238; *Cal. S.P. Span.* IX, 397; Stow, *Annales*, 596. Stow thought the causes to be both religious and economic; Hooper, however, whose own father was still 'living in ignorance of the true religion' in Somerset, considered the principal causes to spring from the religious conservatism of the region (Robinson, *Original letters*, I, 75).

[2] Youings, Joyce, *Devon monastic lands, etc.* (Devon and Cornwall Rec. Soc., n.s. I, Torquay, 1955), 6–7.

remainder being dispersed in small lots in thirty-nine other parishes of the county. The only really significant holding acquired was by Wriothesley (Southampton), whose estate was principally concentrated in Hampshire and who, so far as can be determined, never saw the two manors which he had purchased. In Cornwall the story is pretty much the same, save for the irony that Sir Thomas and Sir Hugh Pomeroy, both of whom were implicated in the early phases of the Western Rising, were on July 21st at last successful in the purchase of chantry lands, heavily concentrated in their native county. The rebellious ardour of these brothers had cooled in any event and they were now principally concerned with making their peace with the government.[1] We can think of no other county in which the gradual re-distribution of crown lands did less to strengthen the estates and responsibilities of the local, the seated, gentry than Devonshire and Cornwall, while the great Russell grant failed utterly to attain the purposes which the Crown had in mind. The gentry of Devonshire, particularly, were too few, too poor, and themselves in part too disaffected in their true sentiments to put down or to stay a stir which quickly became a serious rebellion.

One anonymous commentator, serving in the royal forces in the west, who was forwarding a copy of the rebel Articles, provides a persuasive estimate of the true complexity of the rising then under way. Though the rebel forces were composed mostly of 'simple and ignorant people, easily deceived', and sturdy vagabonds, who rose in protest against grievances, the movement had already fallen under the control of the priests and the treason now sprang from popery. Hence the Western Rising must be dissociated from stirs in counties like Kent, Essex, Suffolk, and Hampshire which were principally against enclosures and which were checked by the promise of reform and by the efforts of the government to force down both prices and rentals. But in Devonshire the movement was at once violent and treasonable and the priests were able to persuade those in arms that they must either prevail or perish.[2]

It is not certain on precisely what date the Council became even sketchily informed of the rapid deterioration of civil order in Devonshire, but we do know that Somerset hesitated, wishing not to employ main force and also being unwilling to commit large military strength at so distant a point when, as we have seen, there

[1] This discussion is derived from the data more fully analysed in *Excursus* II, *ante*, 103ff. The Pomeroys paid £1982 9s 4d for the purchase.
[2] Text printed by Rose-Troup, *Western rebellion*, 485–492, from the manuscript in Lambeth Palace Library.

were already disorders in the Home Counties and in the Midlands. But there was at hand in court a redoubtable Devonian, Sir Gawen Carew, experienced in military affairs, who, it was hoped, might be able under the King's commission to restore order in the county. Moreover, Sir Peter Carew, a nephew to Sir Gawen, was called to London from his wife's estate in Lincolnshire to go down as well, the Carews bearing together an address to the justices of the peace and the gentry of Devonshire which offered pardon to persons who had refused to receive the *Book of Common Prayer* and to persons now illegally assembled who would return to their duty and allegiance.[1] The Carews hurried at once to Exeter, where many of the refugee gentry of the county had assembled, to learn that the main rebel force was even now encamped at Crediton. It was agreed that the Carews, taking 'a competent company', would immediately press forward to treat with the insurgents and if possible disperse them. However, as the company of horse approached the outskirts of Crediton, they found the highway heavily entrenched and blocked, while barns on either side were packed with armed men in a decidedly belligerent mood. At this critical moment one of the servants in the Carew party foolishly fired one of the barns, with the result that the rebel force panicked and fled the town, leaving behind no one with whom to treat. 'But the fame and rumour of the burning of the barns was so spread throughout the whole country, that the next day the people like a sort of wasps were up in sundry places: among which some took the town of Clyst St Mary', only two miles from Exeter.

The Carews were, however, determined to treat if at all possible, and ventured out again from Exeter with Sir Thomas Denys and Sir Hugh Pollard, only to find fortifications under way at Clyst St Mary, and the mood of the rebels so bellicose that Sir Peter was nearly killed when a gunner had to be restrained by a comrade from firing point blank at him. An agreement was reached, however, under which three of the gentry, but excluding the Carews, were admitted through the rebel lines to a parley which gained no more than a rebel promise to stand quietly if religion were restored to the Henrician Settlement, at least until the King came of age. It was now evident that the rebel leaders could not be persuaded to disperse their bands; Exeter was within a ring of fortifications which could very easily be made siege lines; and there was simply not sufficient local strength amongst the loyal gentry to disperse the rebels by force. On the next morning Sir Peter Carew left for London to inform the

[1] S.P. Dom., Edw. VI, VII, 37: June 20, 1549.

Council of his failure and to recommend that an army be sent, of sufficient strength to quiet the county. To his dismay he was harshly criticized by Somerset for the incident of the barn burning and by Rich for having exceeded the loosely defined powers set out in his commission. But Carew manfully defended himself, perhaps sensing that the Council was steeling itself for the hard decision of levying war on an English county.[1]

Before the return of Carew discussion was clearly well under way in the Council regarding what measure of force should be employed in the southwest. Paget, writing in great alarm from his diplomatic post abroad, urged Somerset to take personal command and to employ the reliable German mercenaries available in England and at Calais, while calling on Sir William Herbert and Lord Shrewsbury to strike southwards from Wales. He recommended as well that exemplary hangings take place as the Lord Protector advanced in martial strength through the affected counties and suggested packing off the more intransigent rebels to service in Boulogne or on the Scottish border. But the decision had in fact already been made to place Russell in command, warrants being issued between June 20th and June 23rd for his expenses, and his orders probably on the 24th. These instructions were, in fact, wholly unsatisfactory and unrealistic, maintaining the pretence that he was to restore order by personal influence and by the assistance of the local justices, and only then should he 'assemble such numbers of men' as might be required to restore order. He was also instructed to see that servants and children were kept in good order, that clothworkers and other artificers be kept employed, and that the service of the Prayer Book be accepted and used. And then, in a different hand, it was added as an afterthought that those spreading rumours should be apprehended and punished as they deserved.[2]

These amazing, these almost irrelevant, instructions were supported by a memorandum addressed on June 26th to the justices of the peace in Devonshire, offering no better advice than that they persuade the ringleaders and their followers to disperse, to remind them what wrongs they did the King and the realm, and that grievances could only be relieved by the legal process. Meanwhile, however, they were to put themselves 'with such of your tenants and servants as you best trust' secretly in readiness to receive the orders of Lord Russell who was 'now in journey towards you'.[3] There is

---

[1] Hooker, *Description of Excester*, 58-65; Hooker, *Life of Sir Peter Carewe* (*Cal. Carew MSS.*), lxxxvi-lxxxviii; Rowse, *Tudor Cornwall*, 266.

[2] S.P. Dom., Edw. VI, VII, 40: June 24, 1549.   [3] *Ibid.* 42: June 26, 1549.

about these documents and about the whole of Somerset's policy in
the days when they were issued an almost dream-like quality, a
feeling that men will somehow yield if they be well instructed, that
evil will be dissipated by good, and that sweet reasonableness must
of its own authority prevail. All that was weak in Somerset's
character was revealed in these dreadful days when he shrank back
from the brutal courses which were now required in southwestern
England and which Lord John Russell, now in motion, was fully
prepared to employ.

Russell, without clear instructions and with relatively small
forces, left London, probably on June 24th, quite uncertain as to
where he would pause to feel out the rebel strength, to treat if
possible, and to gather under his command detached forces then
being assembled. He sent two officers on ahead to reconnoitre the
defensive possibilities of Sherborne, while he was moving in the
direction of Salisbury. His agents gloomily reported that Sherborne
could not easily be defended from attack from the west and that it
offered no domination of principal river courses, which would
permit the rebels to by-pass the town either to the north or to the
south. Consideration had also been given to the region between
Lamport and Bridgwater, extending to the sea, but, while naturally
strong for defence, it did not easily permit the passage of horse.[1]
Pressing on slowly and carefully through Salisbury, Russell then
turned towards Taunton rather than Sherborne, having reached
Hinton St George when Carew sought him out and briefed him on
the strong state of rebel numbers and resolution, before hurrying on
to London to report to the Council on his failure at mediation. The
county of Somerset was quiet and Taunton with its relatively
important road network was to be used as a staging-point for
governmental forces and supplies throughout the rebellion.[2] On

[1] S.P. Dom., Edw. VI, VII, 41: 'The answer ... sent by Mr Dudley and Mr Travers',
c. June 24, 1549.
[2] VCH, Somerset, II, 196. Some weeks earlier, however, a serious stir in and near
Frome had been competently quieted. Sir Richard Fulmerston, Comptroller to Somerset, the Bishop of Bath, Lord Sturton, and other county leaders had dealt swiftly with a
gathering of 200 persons, most of whom were weavers, tinkerers, and other artificers,
who after assembling had thrown down hedges and fences in the neighbourhood.
Fulmerston and his colleagues met at Frome to examine certain of the rioters, who
maintained that they had acted lawfully because they had heard of a proclamation which
authorized their action. The Bishop and others examining told them to submit a list of
their grievances to Lord Stourton, which had since been done by four or five of the ringleaders. There had been other unlawful assemblies in the region and some casting down
of enclosures, as well as much 'lewd and unfitting talk', such as 'why should one man
have all and another nothing'. The disaffected had also threatened that if the justices
of peace sent some of their number to prison, they would be released by a thousand men.

Carew's urging, however, Russell decided to move southwards, by what highway is not clear, and to establish his headquarters and rallying-point at the Carew mansion (Mohun's Ottery), about two-and-one-half miles east of the market town of Honiton and almost a mile off the great road to Salisbury and thence to London. The choice was poor indeed, with only weak defensive terrain to the south and west and served by what are now, and surely were then, no more than deep, narrow, and tortuous farm tracks.[1] But Russell wanted comfort quite as much as defensive strength, and he was in any case not minded to risk an engagement until his reinforcements were in hand.

Meanwhile, Russell had reported to the Council during his stay in Salisbury. Somerset, in the name of the Council, replied on June 29th with further instructions which wavered between force and conciliation. His military counsel was that Russell should move to the evident centre of the rebellious movement at Sampford Courtenay, while protecting his lines of movement towards Exeter.[2] He should show his force, but should first try to persuade the rebellious assemblages to disperse and should quiet evil rumours such as the report that the tax on sheep was to be followed by a levy on pigs and geese, and that the baptism of children was not to be afforded from Sunday to Sunday. If conciliation and offers of pardon failed, he was to hold his cavalry in reserve, site his artillery, and then move in with his hackbutters, killing as many as might be required to capture the ringleaders, causing them to panic and fall back on Sampford Courtenay. Russell would also soon be sent a commission of oyer and terminer to be used if required against the rioters, as well as authority to overthrow illegal enclosures and to control the cost of foodstuffs in the area. The slowness of communication in the period and the danger of distant advice are well demonstrated in this dispatch which, had it been followed literally, would have

---

None the less, Fulmerston and his colleagues felt strong enough to restore and maintain good order and had accordingly determined to meet at Sessions with their own retainers and the honest yeomen and farmers of the area. (HMC, *Bath MSS.* IV: *Seymour papers*, 109–110: May 8, 1549.)

[1] There is now a farmhouse on the site, incorporating the Carew porch, with the initials P.C. on the two sides of the door, the original fireplace and chimney, and at some distance from the front of the house, two elaborate entrance ways wrought in stone.

[2] We have in the Petyt MSS. and in the State Papers remarkably full documentation for the Council's steady communication with Russell. Internal evidence suggests that there was an equal flow of reports and inquiries from Russell to Somerset and the Council. But these documents we have been unable to find. It is wholly possible that they are lost, but we have the uncomfortable feeling that we may have missed them.

thrown the royal army, over very difficult terrain, against Sampford
Courtenay when in fact the rebel main force was a few days later
closing the siege lines around Exeter.[1] Indeed, so ill-informed
was the Council, and so harassed by the stirs in numerous counties,
that late in June the tactically important bridge over the Thames at
Staines was about to be demolished, raising from the town the
protest that to do so would be the 'undoing of all the whole town and
the country thereabouts', and promising to maintain a scouting
force against the possibility of rebellious forces moving in that
direction towards London.[2]

Russell had arrived at Mohun's Ottery at an uncertain date, but
probably between June 30th and July 2nd, since Carew delivered
the Council's instructions of June 29th to him there. Russell in fact
simply sat awaiting the building up of his forces before making any
overt move. He and Carew endeavoured without much success to
augment his strength by local levies and troops from Somerset, but
Russell feared their possible unreliability, which was indeed suggested by a high desertion rate. The Council now promised a
stiffening of mercenaries, but was slow in forwarding them because
of disorders elsewhere, the reluctance of Roman Catholic mercenaries to serve in the west, and because, as Dymock, the chief
recruiting agent, had earlier put it, 'If they should go less in number
than three or four thousand men, they affirm they should be brought
to the butcher's stall'.[3] So fearful was Russell of his position that he
made no move, even of a diversionary sort, to prevent or to relieve
the siege of Exeter, which began on July 3rd. He was in fact dis-
suaded only with great difficulty by Carew from falling back on
Taunton, or even on Salisbury, which had he done so might well
have precipitated a widespread and exceedingly dangerous rising in
the whole of southwestern England.[4] The Council, almost as desperate and surely more harassed than Russell, could do no more as
late as July 10th than order the Bristol mint to sent him £100 for
his immediate recruiting needs, while warning him that it would be
some time—a stir in Buckinghamshire being still in progress—before
they could send him sufficient forces for a direct assault on the
rebels. But they were sending out post-haste 150 Italian hackbutters
and were detaching 300 to 400 horse from Lord Grey's forces
which would be sent to Salisbury as a reserve on which he might

---

[1] Petyt MS. 538, xlvi, ff. 432–434.   [2] S.P. Dom., Edw. VI, VII, 46.
[3] *Cal. S.P. For.*, *Edw. VI*, #144: May 6, 1549.
[4] Hooker, *Description of Excester*, 82; Hooker, *Life of Sir Peter Carewe* (*Cal. Carew MSS.*), 88.

draw. These dispositions being made, the Council would have available—the implication clearly being for only desperate needs— no more than 400 mercenary horse and 1000 German foot. They had, however, commanded Herbert to stand ready with his forces in Gloucestershire and Wiltshire. The only cheerful postscript the Council could add was to include a warrant on the Bristol mint for an additional sum of £500 to meet Russell's needs.[1]

Russell had reported to the Council that he was far too weak to attempt a relief of Exeter, even though it was ill-provisioned, and that before he could move offensively he must have more foot. The Council on July 12 somewhat querulously authorized him to levy 2000 to 4000 foot in the west, they not being 'able to have any foot-men to whom to trust', ordered the Bristol mint to supply his further needs, and suggested that he borrow as well from local merchants. He was to repose his trust only in gentry of Protestant persuasion. They had meant to strengthen him with Grey's heavy striking force, but had to employ him 'upon occasion of a stir here in Buckinghamshire and Oxfordshire by instigation of sundry priests (keep it to yourself)', which they trusted would be speedily repressed so that Grey might continue westward to his relief.[2] Writing a few days later, the misinformed or self-deluded Council took a more sanguine tone, the Oxfordshire stir having been repressed, declaring the realm to be now in obedience save for the southwest and 'some of the light sort remaining tickle, but no great number, namely at and about Norwich', and against these last, they cheerfully concluded, Northampton had been sent.[3]

Meanwhile, the city of Exeter was winning the west for Russell by a brilliant defence against the siege which Arundell locked against it on July 2nd. The balance of religious sentiment in the city was precarious and there was a working-class element with strong sympathy for the rebels, but the merchant oligarchy and the refugee gentry within the walls kept the city firmly under control, while with persuasive skill pointing out that to surrender would mean a general looting and slaughter. It would be presumptuous indeed to recite the annal of this siege, classically and memorably rendered by an eye-witness who happened as well to be an historian.[4] We may, however, point out that the city enjoyed a most resolute leadership, was blessed with reasonably strong natural defences, was stoutly walled and ditched, and possessed a formidable castle overlooking

[1] Petyt MS. 538, xlvi, ff. 435-436.
[2] Vide ante, 447-448; Petyt MS. 538, xlvi, ff. 436-437.
[3] Ibid. f. 438: July 17, 1549.   [4] Hooker, Description of Excester, 56-98.

the city and the surrounding countryside. The rebels were sorely hampered because they possessed no siege guns, though a few light pieces were sited in, and because they were simply not strong enough or sufficiently trained to hope to carry the walls by storm. Arundell, now exercising general command, was also gravely weakened by Russell's very presence at Honiton, against whose possible move he had to detach a considerable portion of his forces. None the less, he maintained fairly effective military discipline over an investing army of perhaps 4000 to 6000 men.[1] But he was thwarted and in the end destroyed because the city, in the final days dangerously short of food, stood firm and intact when Russell at last brought a full five weeks of close investment to an end.

While these stirring and fateful events were in progress within the city, Russell, who thought it even more ill-supplied than it was, still lay at Mohun's Ottery, clamouring for reinforcements, and failing even to throw out strong raiding parties of horse to keep the rebel forces off balance. It seems certain that on July 10th he commanded reliable and professional troops to the number of at least 1350 men, probably quite strong enough to crush the insurrection if he had forced battle on the high ground, level and unbroken, lying midway between Honiton and Exeter. But on July 16th he was demanding large reinforcements of German foot, which the Council was obliged to say could not be spared and who were in any event 'odious to our people . . . in so much as we can hardly move them without quarrel here at hand'.[2] The Council was, however, sending additional

[1] Estimates of the number in the rebel forces, like all sixteenth-century statistics, vary wildly. Hooker, by far the most reliable, sets the size of the investing forces at 2000 (*ibid.* 68), which we have accepted, and to which we would add about 2000 more sent out to counter Russell and to maintain the control of the roads fanning out from the city. Holinshed (*Chronicles*, III, 917) thought the whole rebel force numbered at least 10,000, which was also the figure provided by Hayward (*Edward VI*, 292) and by Foxe (*Acts and monuments*, V, 731). Van der Delft, writing on July 3rd, set the total of rebels under arms at 12,000 (*Cal. S.P. Span.* IX, 397). Froude (*History of England*, V, 183), citing no authority, sets the total at 12,000 men, while Polwhele (*Devonshire*, I, 255) states that Humphrey Arundell commanded 10,000 men.

[2] Russell's force was in the end largely composed of mercenaries. Their employment was relatively recent in England, Henry VIII having made modest use of them, principally on the Continent. But it was Somerset who really first employed them on a considerable scale, mostly for service in the Boulogne area and in Scotland. Mercenary captains and their bands were recruited principally from Germany, Italy, and the Low Countries. As many as 3000 Germans had been employed in Scotland in 1548, while Hoby was raising a force of 2000 in January, 1549, mostly, it should be said, to replace men who had died in the English service in the year just past. It so happened that there were encamped in and near London between 2000 and 3000 seasoned mercenary troops, intended for the Scottish border, when the stirs broke out in the spring of 1549. These bands were employed for the repressing of the risings, together with other foreign troops withdrawn from the Boulogne garrison and from the Border. In Norfolk, the most

mercenary horse and another contingent of Italian hackbutters, while hinting once more that Grey had completed the restoration of order in Buckinghamshire and Oxfordshire and would, presumably, soon be free to join him.[1]

The Council was lending every possible support to Russell and was now reluctantly forced to understand that it had to deal with stirs and illegal assemblies in half of England, with serious insurrections under way in the southwest and in Norfolk. Seeking to regain psychological as well as military control, it issued a spate of half-conciliatory, half-threatening proclamations. On July 8th it offered rewards for the arrest of rumour-mongers and other 'seditious, busy, and disordered' persons whom it denounced for having misled the 'King's true subjects', seeking to differentiate the ringleaders from seduced and otherwise loyal subjects.[2] On the same day another proclamation ordered the enclosure commissions to complete their investigations, with at least the implicit assurance that the commissioners would now be empowered to correct the illegalities which they found and particularly to restore rights of common.[3] This was followed on July 11th by a proclamation declaring forfeit all lands, goods, and chattels of persons who did not immediately make their obedience, alleviated on the day following by still another proclamation formally offering pardon to those who renounced rebellious courses and embraced obedience to the King.[4] This interlocking series of edicts was completed by a proclamation offering pardon to enclosure rioters, but ordering martial law to be applied to persons who engaged in such riotous conduct in the future,[5] and by still another which made subject to martial law

---

effective single crown force consisted of Italian troops stiffened by 1400 German infantry. Further supplies were being recruited in late March, 1549, by John Dymock, operating from Hamburg, who arranged for a supply of 2500 horse and 4000 foot with the Duke of Brunswick and who on May 11, 1549, was loading the first lot on shipboard at Hamburg. These professional mercenary forces were used principally because the government simply did not dare risk the loyalty of shire levies that could have been drawn from affected areas. Moreover, Russell had great difficulty attracting volunteers in the west even when he offered what the Council thought were inflated wages. (For mention of mercenary recruitments and troop movements, *vide Cal. S.P. Span.* IX, 246, 267; *Cal. S.P. Ven.* V, 548; *Zeitschrift des Vereines für hamburgische Geschichte,* V (1866), 32–45, for notices of Courtpenny, a famous mercenary captain; Barthold, F. W., 'Philipp Franz und Johann Philipp, Wild- und Rheingrafen zu Dhaun, etc.', *Historisches Taschenbuch,* n.s. IX (1848), 361; Oman, *Art of war,* 368–369; Strype, *Memorials,* II, i, 165–166; Tytler, *England,* I, 161–164; *A.P.C.* II, App., 556–557; *ibid.* 154, 166–167, 215, 268, 361.) The whole subject deserves detailed study.
[1] Petyt MS. 538, xlvi, ff. 438–439: July 18, 1549.
[2] Hughes and Larkin, *Tudor proclamations,* I, 469–471.   [3] *Ibid.* 471–472.
[4] *Ibid.* 473–474; *ibid.* 474: July 12, 1549.   [5] *Ibid.* 475–476: July 16, 1549.

minor local officials, such as bailiffs and constables, who betrayed their trust and responsibility by leading stirs or by failure to perform their bounden duty.[1]

At least one of these proclamations had been requested by Russell, who continued to wait with his small army at Mohun's Ottery, worried by desertions, and listening credulously to exaggerated reports of the rebel strength before Exeter. On July 18th he had evidently made a doleful report of his position to the Council, demanding a 'main force' before he risked battle or undertook the relief of Exeter. But the Council included far better and more experienced soldiers than Russell and was tiring of his pusillanimity. Somerset replied on July 22nd that the Council was 'sorry to hear from you, as men having experience', any such excuses for failure to act. They were sending him 160 additional mercenary hack-butters, who with others in his force should be mounted with horses taken in the area. It was their estimate, indeed, that with 500 well-led horse—and Russell had many more than that number—he could harry, ambush, cut lines of supply, and otherwise take in hand as many as 5000 rebellious men of indifferent quality. This he must do; more they cannot do, for the main force now entrusted to Warwick must be held for the disorders threatening in Norfolk, Suffolk, Essex, and Kent. Only when these stirs were quieted could Warwick come to his aid. He must move more vigorously in recruiting men from Somerset and Dorset, making it clear that all those who refuse to serve would under the recent proclamations be treated as traitors. Russell, to put it bluntly, was ordered to move towards the suppression of an uncontrolled rebellion, the Council softening somewhat this understandably harsh and peremptory letter by assurance that Grey was moving towards him with 200 horse and that they were sending a naval force to recapture Plymouth.[2]

The fact was that Russell, approaching his sixty-fifth year, had never held an independent command of importance in his life, and simply did not know how to use an army even for scouting or harassing purposes. The Council could not replace him, but Somerset was moving Grey and Herbert towards him with reinforcements, while seeking by all means possible to prod Russell into action. On the 24th both Somerset and Warwick signed the dispatch informing him that Herbert was to join him, he being of 'such courage that he sayeth he is able rather to bring too many than too few' from the

---

[1] Hughes and Larkin, *Tudor proclamations*, I, 476–477: July 22, 1549.
[2] Petyt MS. 538, xlvi, 439–441.

Welsh borders.[1] Now, the Council assured Russell on July 25th, he surely had sufficient forces in hand or promised 'to encounter and subdue the rebels'.[2] But still Russell did not move and, after receiving another evidently querulous letter, the Council once more reiterated its orders. They were themselves not without military experience and had sought only to advise on possible courses of action. If he was having difficulty in recruiting troops in Somerset, two or three judicious hangings of rebels might help to restore loyalty. Nor could they send shot for his ordnance until they were informed of the bore, though for that matter he could easily make moulds and cast his own shot. If the rebels were, as he said, using church goods in order to pay their forces liberally, then he must match the wages paid. And so the patient litany continued setting out the elements of military administration.[3]

At last, on the very day he was forced into action by what developed into a rebel assault against him, Russell was to all intents declared incompetent by Somerset, who was faced with serious rebellion in Norfolk and by the full realization that France would declare war on England within a matter of days. He was amazed that Russell should have called on Herbert for so many foot that he would have 10,000 infantry in the field. Nor did he believe Russell's estimate of rebel strength, for Cornwall and Devon could not possibly put as many as 7000 'tag and rag' in the field against him. Further, of the rebel forces, at least 1000 were besieging Exeter, and as many more were holding strong points already in their hands. In fine, 'the rebels cannot be thought to be in the whole against you past 4000 men, and the most part unarmed'. Against these forces Russell must now muster about as many troops, well armed, and victualled.[4] The Council accordingly urged him—commanded would be the more accurate word—to divide his force and to strike the enemy simultaneously at two places in order to throw them off balance and to exploit his overweening cavalry strength. It would so much be preferred if he would strike now before Herbert brought his reinforcements of 2000 to 3000 foot from Wales and perhaps 2000 from Gloucestershire and Wiltshire. Russell was warned that if he assembled a huge army it would consume his victuals and raise the spectre of wholesale desertions.[5] For this controlled but none the less scathing letter of rebuke Russell scarcely could ever have forgiven Somerset, and it must certainly have had its part in moving

---

[1] Petyt MS. 538, xlvi, f. 442.   [2] Ibid. f. 442.   [3] Ibid. ff. 444–445.
[4] Our count, as of July 28, is 4050, of which the most part were mercenaries.
[5] Petyt MS. 538, xlvi, f. 446.

Russell only a few weeks later to use the main force, which Somerset had so painfully assembled for him, and then taught him how to use, as the principal element of power available to the now disaffected Councillors who had determined to destroy Somerset.

It was probably on July 27th that Russell was at last goaded to throw out a considerable force of horse towards Exeter, the besieged city lying about seventeen miles to the west of Honiton. Finding the main highway blocked, Russell attempted no flanking movement, but instead left the main road on a detour to Ottery St Mary where he camped for the night. He attempted a second foray towards Exeter by still another road, and that also being blocked, fell back on Honiton. The rebels countered by a diversionary action of their own, moving in considerable strength up the main highway as far as Fenny Bridges, about four miles to the west of Honiton, where on July 28th they collided with Russell's outposts. Russell, persuaded by the restive Carews, determined to attack in force in order to clear the highway, and the following morning the royal army was battle-dressed before Coverdale, soon to be Bishop of Exeter, who placed its fortunes in God's hands.

The rebel force lay astride the Otter, which then flowed in four channels, three having bridges, and provided power for several small mills at or near the site. The whole of this level and cramped field of action is now bisected by a main railway line carried on a high fill, while the then highway, the Roman Road from Salisbury to Exeter, ran closer to the scene of the action and to the tiny hamlet on its edge than does the present A-30. Now, too, the small river flows through the site in only three channels, only one of which even in June carries much flow and all of which should in July have been easily fordable for foot and cavalry. The constricted scene of the action is flat and low-lying, and in certain seasons at least must have been wet and probably muddy. In the action that followed, the Carews charged with a shock force to regain the bridges, the assault of the main force following immediately. In this sharp action Sir Gawen Carew was wounded by an arrow, but the bridges were carried and the main rebel force was thrown back in disorder, but did not panic. But while the royal foot were indulging in mild looting, Robert Smyth, leading 250 Cornish reserves, rallied some elements of the rebel main force for a sharp and bloody counterattack along the river flats, which was routed by the main royal force. The rebel army was, however, able to re-group itself and fell back on the troops besieging Exeter. Russell followed for a distance of about three miles and, had he struck with his full power, could almost certainly have raised the siege of Exeter on that day. But he was timorous; he had sustained losses; his ordnance was not in hand; and he told the protesting Carews that he feared diversionary risings to his rear. Russell probably knew as well that Lord Grey with his cavalry and about 300 Italian mercenaries were to join him a few days later. The always careful Hooker tells us that the rebels lost about 300 killed in this short but bloody engagement. Why the rebel leaders, with easily defensible Streteway Hill at their rear, should have committed themselves to pitched battle with mostly professional troops in the constricted and indefensible meadowland at Fenny Bridges remains uncertain.[1]

The overly cautious Russell, his strength really unimpaired by his losses at Fenny Bridges, would have preferred another long wait at Honiton before moving against the rebels investing Exeter with their main force. But the Council had not issued its instructions to Herbert until July 23rd, requiring him to move with such force as he and Russell thought requisite, empowering him to draw military stores and ordnance from Bristol, and setting the rates of pay for his drafts.[2] Herbert's first contingents were not in fact to arrive until after Exeter had been relieved. Meanwhile, the importunities of the Council, now fortified by the advice of the vigorous and experienced Grey, had persuaded Russell to break camp and to move on August 3rd with his main force straight on Exeter. At an uncertain point, but possibly at Alfington, not more than seven miles from Exeter, Russell found his progress blocked by a rebel force of perhaps 2000, well disposed in wings and strongly entrenched. A frontal assault delivered by the royal army broke through, the rebels falling back in fair order to new positions, probably on what is now Aylesbeare Common, a harsh, high, and even now unsettled countryside, where Russell made camp for the night.[3] On the following morning (August 4th) the rebels, strongly reinforced by detachments from Exeter, struck with a frontal assault, which was, however, contained. The rebels fell back, after really heavy losses, on Clyst St Mary, Arundell moving all available forces into action and holding Russell in his lines for the day. But in the early morning of August 5th Russell moved forward in three wings on Clyst St Mary, one of the units falling into an ambush and in retreating losing its

[1] Rose-Troup, *Western rebellion*, 253–260; Hayward, *Edward VI*, 294; Hooker, *Description of Excester*, 83–84.

[2] S.P. Dom., Edw. VI, VIII, 34: July 23, 1549. The draft is roughly drawn with many not very legible amendments.

[3] We follow Hooker in the narrative. The never very reliable Hayward (*Edward VI*, 295) sets the rebel losses in this engagement at 900 dead, surely far too high.

ordnance, which placed sorely needed pieces in rebel hands. Russell was able to rally his army and then attacked again in full force, losing many men in a narrow defile from stones hurled down by probably unarmed rebels, but carrying through to the village which was taken after house-to-house fighting.[1] Russell, as the day closed, moved his army to a better position on Clyst Heath; though still nervous and apprehensive, he allowed himself to be persuaded to slaughter the considerable number of prisoners who had been taken in the heavy fighting of the past two days.[2]

Even after this indefensibly brutal action, Russell felt most insecure during the night when Arundell was moving his remaining artillery and his investing units before Exeter straight across the flank of the royal position in the direction of Topsham. At dawn Russell struck with full strength in order to gain the Topsham road. It was a bitter battle, in which every hedge and every sunken track was desperately defended by the rebel army, but Grey broke through and that night Russell's weary army encamped at Topsham.[3] Arundell, whose losses had been heavy and whose troops were dispirited, but still under discipline, realized full well that his position before Exeter was now wholly untenable. After a council of war it was determined to break off battle and siege, the remaining rebel forces to make their way westwards along the three principal highways fanning out from Exeter.[4] That same morning Russell appeared before the walls of the city, but on the plea of the mayor did not make his formal entry with his army until revictualling had been completed.

Russell, with characteristic indecision laced with timidity of purpose, instead of pressing immediately to complete the grim task of restoring order and destroying enemy units which were now dispersed, without artillery, and with no plan of action, did no more than loll within Exeter for a full ten days, while opportunity slipped from his grasp. Thus, in the worst days of the Norfolk rising, during a period when a French coastal attack was half-expected, Russell stubbornly tied down pointlessly a full third of the military resources of the Crown. He did, of course, reward his western captains, and especially the Carews, with rebel lands, and he did

[1] The action centred on gaining control of a bridge, which still exists, though now disused. For a picture of it, with the formidable concrete structure which has been built alongside, see *Country Life*, Feb. 23, 1967, p. 414.

[2] Hooker, *Description of Excester*, 87–89; Edward VI, *Chronicle*, 13–14.

[3] *Ibid.* 89; Holinshed, *Chronicles*, III, 924–925; Rowse, *Tudor Cornwall*, 278; Hayward, *Edward VI*, 295; Polwhele, *Devonshire*, I, 256.

[4] Rose-Troup, *Western rebellion*, 278–279.

hang a number of rebels in and near Exeter, the most notable of whom was Welsh, the vicar of St Thomas', Exmouth, an undoubted and capable ringleader, though a man of such boisterous and attractive talents that even Hooker shows clear sympathy for him.[1] But it required neither a main force nor Russell's personal presence to perform these ghoulish tasks. Nor would he reduce his strength despite the direct order of the Council. On August 10th the jubilant Council congratulated him on what they knew was a decisive victory, ordering him to dismiss his levies from Dorset and Somerset, who might well be needed for coastal defence and who in any event were not, on Russell's own testimony, wholly reliable 'against the Devonshire men, their neighbours'. Further, they required the immediate return of his mercenary cavalry who were to be sent to France forthwith. And it was pointedly suggested that he should move at once into the countryside to see to it that justices of the peace were restored to authority and the religious services stipulated by law carried forward.[2] Again, on the day following, the Council urged him to reduce his forces for service elsewhere and to move at once into the countryside in order to capture and punish known rebel leaders still in the field.[3]

Once more, and now eight days after the relief of Exeter, Somerset and the Council wrote setting out in specific detail their requirements. Russell's main force simply must be reduced forthwith to help meet the great needs on the Scottish border, the 10,000 to 12,000 men required in Norfolk, and the 8,000 to 10,000 being raised to give the King defensive power against France. Hence they wanted his native foot and his mercenary horse to be sent to London, while with his ample remaining forces he was to complete the task of 'mopping up', 'for if you shall suffer these rebels to breathe, to catch a pride by your somewhat forebearing to follow them, and winning time so to gather strong upon you, you shall not do that with a great number that taken in time you might have done with . . . much fewer'.[4] Russell at last did move out from Exeter on August 16th to complete his necessary but bloody work, but not before he had infuriated Somerset by asking that a protective force of 1000 troops be landed on the southern Devonshire coast, to which the Protector on the 19th replied that such a contingent could by no means be

[1] Hooker, *Description of Excester*, 91.

[2] Petyt MS. 538, xlvi, ff. 447–448.

[3] *Ibid*. f. 451. Somerset, who drafted the dispatch, spoke in troubled terms of Paget's brother, Robert, a known ringleader. His case was difficult, 'yet we have not spared our own brother in matters concerning . . . high treason'. (*Vide ante*, 456.)

[4] Petyt MS. 538, xlvi, f. 452.

spared and concluded by warning him that he must draw his own shipping from the region.[1]

Russell moved with a great force of perhaps as many as 8000 men, Herbert's large contingent having joined him, camping that night at Crediton and then, belatedly, pushing up the Barnstaple road towards Sampford Courtenay where the great insurrection had begun and where Arundell had gathered the remnants of his forces. Early on Sunday morning (August 18th) the scouting forces of both armies collided in a sharp engagement which Grey and Herbert relieved by driving through to the outskirts of Sampford Courtenay, where they found the rebel force strongly and skilfully entrenched. Frontal artillery fire was trained on the rebel line, while the English foot and the Italians delivered well-timed flank attacks from either side. Russell, with the whole of the reserve, then assaulted the rebel line, which now broke. Arundell's force fell back through the town in reasonably good order, though he had lost as many as 500 killed at Sampford Courtenay, and many more were killed or captured as his tattered army now began to disintegrate. Arundell vainly attempted to rally his forces and to gain recruits at Okehampton, but, now under heavy and continuous pressure from the Carews, was captured, with four or five of his principal lieutenants, as he sought to make a final stand at Launceston. Meanwhile, Herbert had been sent with a detached force in pursuit of a rebel remnant of about 1000 men falling back towards Minehead, which was brought to battle near Tiverton, and which was routed, the considerable number of prisoners taken being hanged out of hand. Then, while Russell and Grey moved with the main force to reduce any points of resistance left in Cornwall, Peter Carew and Paulet engaged the last remnants of Arundell's once powerful force in a slaughter, completed by indiscriminate hangings, at King's Weston in Somerset. By the end of August, Russell could report that the great rising of the west was at an end.[2]

The Privy Council, and more particularly Somerset, had followed these events with continuous interest and concern, for as the last pitched battle in the west was taking place at Sampford Courtenay, events in Norfolk were moving to an uncertain climax. The Council was accordingly infinitely relieved when on August 21st it sent

[1] Petyt MS. 538, xlvi, f. 456.
[2] Strype, *Memorials*, II, ii, 422–424 (this is the only text I have found of a letter from Russell to the Council reporting his victory. It may very well be one of the missing series mentioned, *ante*, 463); Holinshed, *Chronicles*, III, 926; Rowse, *Tudor Cornwall*, 280–281, 286; Hooker, *Description of Excester*, 95–96.

congratulations to Russell and asked him to send up Arundell and other principal ringleaders for examination and trial in London.[1] Somerset felt sure enough of his position a few days later to lend encouragement to Hoby, then on a diplomatic mission to the Emperor, assuring him that the west was now quiet and that 'the country cometh daily to my Lord Privy Seal, to crave their pardons, and to be put in some sure hope of grace'. Yorkshire, too, was now quiet, and he had high hope that the Earl of Warwick would soon reduce Norfolk to order; and he could write a week later to say that this was done. But Somerset, idealist and moralist that he was, could not refrain from probing for the causes of this hot wave of rebellion that had swept across the realm. The causes, he confided, were clearly diverse and uncertain in every rebel camp, so 'that it is hard to write what it is; as you know is like to be of people without head and rule, and would have they wot not what'. Some cry out against enclosures, others want their commons back, and still others seem to want that authority which only the gentry have wielded. Save for two or three leaders in the west, he correctly and significantly pointed out, none of the gentry had offered leadership or sympathy to them. Indeed—and on this he had evidently brooded most—'all have conceived a wonderful hate against gentlemen, and take them all as their enemies'.[2]

In fact, Somerset's normal instincts of humanity were quickly restored once opposition in the field had been crushed. He was appalled by the severity with which Sir Anthony Kingston, acting as Russell's provost-marshal, moved through Cornwall and he was equally offended by the wholesale property confiscations and distributions which Russell was making in Devonshire. On August 27th, while again commanding Russell to detach and send on his mercenaries for service at Boulogne, he instructed him to relieve tension and restore quiet in the region by issuing pardons at his discretion, and to hint that a general pardon might soon be forthcoming.[3] About two weeks later, once again patiently demanding the break-up of Russell's large army, he protested that the Lord Privy Seal possessed no authority to seize or distribute lands unless the owners had been attainted of a crime, and that the proclamation under whose authority Russell claimed to proceed was not meant to deny due process of law.[4] Such courses as Russell now followed in

---

[1] Petyt MS. 538, xlvi, f. 458; S.P. Dom., Edw. VI, VIII, 54; *ibid.* 47: Aug. 21, 1549
[2] Harl. MS. 523, #40, ff. 16–20; Strype, *Memorials*, II, ii, 424–425; and see Cotton MSS., Galba, B, xii, ff. 15–19, for a similar analysis.
[3] Petyt MS. 538, xlvi, f. 460.
[4] Hughes and Larkin, *Tudor proclamations*, I, 473–474: July 11, 1549.

the matter could have no other result, he warned, than to breed general despair and throw the multitude of the common people back into rebellion.[1]

The last grisly expiation of rebellion came when in early September Arundell, Pomeroy, and eight others of the surviving ringleaders were sent up to London for examination. They had already been carefully interrogated in the west, in the search for additional rebel captains, and were now sharply questioned, without, however, gaining further useful information. A final decision on these cases was not made until shortly after the Protector's fall, when on November 1 (1549) Pomeroy and four of the other prisoners were released by the Council. One condemned prisoner died shortly afterwards, Arundell and the remaining three of the rebel leaders being executed for high treason on January 27, 1550.[2] There had already been a terrible letting of blood in the west and these almost ritualistic executions came simply as a necessary anti-climax. No one knows how many men were killed in the west, but it may not be far off the mark to risk a guess that rebel losses in battle, by martial law, and by Russell's barbaric slaughter of prisoners may have been approximately 4000 men—a serious demographic loss for an area of somewhat less than 4000 square miles, which was then rather thinly populated. Losses in the royal army may well have totalled something like 400 to 600 men,[3] for in the early stages of these engagements these casualties were considerable. But this casualty ratio of ten to one, fairly well confirmed in at least two engagements, is to be explained not by any want of courage or ill-discipline in a rebel horde which Arundell had almost magically moulded into an army. These troops were simply poorly armed, they were supported by no heavy cavalry and were almost without ordnance. The evidence is clear that in battle a considerable proportion of Arundell's forces were armed with nothing save clubs and stones. That Arundell was able to accomplish his miracle of discipline was due wholly to Russell's almost incredible pusillanimity and a timidity that verges

[1] Petyt MS. 538, xlvi, f. 462.   [2] *Grey Friars Chronicle* (Camden Soc. LIII), 65.
[3] Rose-Troup, the leading authority, estimates total rebel dead, the courts-martial being included, as 5000 and royal losses at 500 (see pages 408–409); both Wriothesley (*Chronicle*, II (Camden Soc., n.s. XX), 20–21) and Stow (*Annales*, 596) set the figure at about 4000. An estimate emanating from London places rebel dead at 5000 (Robinson, *Original letters*, II, 394: Ulmis to Bullinger, August, 1549), while the imperial ambassador accepted a figure of 2000 rebel dead in the fighting around Exeter (*Cal. S.P. Span.* IX, 432: Aug. 13, 1549). By far the most trustworthy contemporary historian estimated that 4000 rebels were slain, though he says many were never counted, while the royal army 'escaped not scot free', especially the mercenary troops, 'who were abhorred of the one party and nothing favoured of the other' (Hooker, *Description of Excester*, 96).

on cowardice. Warwick could not be spared because of grim events in East Anglia; the Protector could scarcely have left London; but one does wonder why Russell was not recalled and Grey, Shrewsbury, or Herbert placed in command early in July.

3. THE RISING IN EAST ANGLIA (1549)

The explosive rising which occurred simultaneously in Norfolk seems in some important respects almost detached from the Western Rising. It occurred in one of the richest agricultural counties in the realm, one of the most populous, and one of the most settled in terms of its institutions and its relations with Westminster. Further, there is no evidence of any communication between the two rebellious areas or of any effort to link the risings; the announced purposes of the two movements were in fact very nearly antithetical. The aspirations of the Norfolk leaders seem to have been almost wholly secular and to have been rooted in social and economic grievances of long standing. The Norfolk rebels, or their articulate leaders, seem, indeed, to have been wholly Protestant in temper, with overtones suggesting sympathy with the more radical and evangelical forces within nascent Anglicanism. Norfolk was also a county which had experienced few enclosures in the Edwardian period, though there was obviously deep and bitter resentment against earlier enclosures, particularly of commons, and a consuming hatred for the great 'sheep gentry' who were still aggregating estates within the shire. How was it, then, that so serious and widespread a rebellion could break out and sweep almost untrammelled across so prosperous, so settled, and so stable a county?

For one thing, it must be said at once that territorial leadership was weak in both Norfolk and Suffolk, just as it was when the test of Russell's authority and prestige came in Devonshire. Rugg, the Bishop of Norwich, was at once incompetent and without moral authority, being forced out of his see for good cause shortly after the rising. Far more importantly, the Duke of Norfolk, who held vast estates in the county and whose personal authority and prestige had long been great, even in proud Norwich, lay in prison, as he had since 1546, under conviction of high treason, while his properties were held by the Crown save as they had been sold. His fall—and the fall of his whole family—had 'created a vacuum in local politics which no other individual or family was sizeable enough to fill'.[1]

[1] Bindoff, S. T., *Ket's rebellion, 1549* (Historical Association, general series, G12, L., 1949), 15. I am greatly indebted to this brilliant essay.

It was perhaps because of the once overweening power and prestige of the Howards that the numerous and rich gentry of the county failed to move quickly and effectively against Kett, leaving almost the whole of the military burden to the central authorities. Professor Bindoff has pointed out that of the fifty-four justices of the peace commissioned in the county, forty-six were local gentry,[1] yet not one of them acted vigorously against Kett; a number of them fled the county; more simply barricaded their doors; and others did nothing until they could join the royal army as it moved into the shire. It is not too much to say that the break-down of local responsibility, of local military power, was quite as complete in Norfolk as in Devonshire. A kind of pervading and spreading paralysis overcame the gentry. It is not easy to explain this provincial weakness, this hollow facade of power and responsibility, for a far larger proportion of Norfolk gentry resided in the county, or on their estates, than in other counties we have studied.[2] Moreover, this class had recently been considerably strengthened by land grants and sales from the Crown, substantial conveyances having been made which involved twenty-two persons: of these one was a noble (Somerset), nine were of the upper gentry, and seven were of the lower gentry. But more important, sixteen of the twenty-two were already residents of Norfolk and, as we have seen, were mostly gentry, who were aggregating their estates. All this should have added to the prestige and responsibility of the Norfolk gentry, should have been a stabilizing factor when the test of disorder came, though, as we have observed, this was by no means the case. The answer may well be that the gentry of Norfolk had for two generations been prosperous, and hated, sheep-farmers on a large scale, whose estates were even now being greatly extended as crown lands came into their hands; they had for too long been concerned with fleeces rather than with arms.[3]

Nor did the 'great trouble' of 1549 break without some warning of existing strains and tensions. Norfolk had long been notable for its large number of small freeholds, most of which were still in arable, often dependent on common pasture rights and hence in direct opposition to the still expanding demand for pasture lands which we have observed among the 'grazing gentry'. This abrasive competition had caused numerous small incidents of fence-breaking in the course of the past two decades, with a clear heightening of

[1] Bindoff, *Ket's rebellion, 1549*, 16.
[2] About 1 in 2·9.
[3] The analysis is based on materials discussed in *Excursus II, ante*, 103ff.

intensity after about 1540 when local mutterings and incendiary ballads were bruited abroad:

> The county gnoffes hob, dick, and hick,
> With club and clooten shoon
> Shall fill the vale of Dussin's Dale
> With slaughtered bodies soon.[1]

There had been a stir at Griston in 1540 in which one John Walker sought unsuccessfully to raise the commons against the gentry, while more recently there had been a fairly serious riot at Rising Chase (near Lynn) when the commons rose, attempting to fortify and victual themselves, but were put down by the gentry of the area, one of whose number was killed.[2] These sentiments were undoubtedly strengthened as they were inflamed by Somerset's enclosure commission, the hopes extended by his proclamation against enclosures, and the generally held conviction, in which there was substance, that the government had embraced a policy lending hope to those who rose with Kett.

The first disturbance in 1549 occurred in the parish of Attleborough and the nearby villages of Eccles and Wilby, where the lord of the manor had recently caused enclosures to be made, thereby depriving the community of common land, probably affecting principally small freeholders and copyholders engaged in corn farming. This was a rich farming area, just to the northeast of Thetford, and one with a fairly dense population, if the comfortably large churches which still dot the landscape offer any certain indication. On the night of June 20th the commoners threw down the hedges, and the rioters responsible returned to their houses without further assembly or movement.[3]

The minor difficulties at Attleborough were almost certainly connected with a more serious stir which occurred near Wymondham,

<hr/>

[1] VCH, Norfolk, II, 494.

[2] Blomefield, Francis, and C. Parkin, Topographical history of... Norfolk (5 vols., Fersfield, 1739-1775; 11 vols., L., 1805-1810), III, 221-222.

[3] Holinshed, Chronicles, III, 963; Blomefield, Norfolk, III, 222; Russell, F. W., Kett's rebellion in Norfolk, etc. (L., 1859), 21-22. Russell's account, which is standard, is almost wholly derived from Nicholas Sotherton's contemporary history of the rising, entitled The Commoyson in No[rfolk] (Harl. MSS., 1576, #94, ff. 564-581). Russell has omitted nothing of importance, and in the main has transcribed verbatim with a high standard of accuracy. We have accordingly decided to follow the printed text. Russell also occasionally draws from Alexander Neville's De furoribus Norfolciensium Ketto duce (L., 1575; translated as Norfolke furies and their foyle. Under Kett, their accursed captaine, etc., L., 1615, 1623), but it seems wiser to cite that work directly when we have employed it.

about six miles to the northeast, on July 6th–7th. As they had for generations, country people over the whole region thronged into Wymondham to gossip, to meet friends, and to watch a play which historically had commemorated the translation of Thomas à Becket. Doubtless inspired by the accounts of some of those who had thrown down hedges at Attleborough, a considerable number of men moved to Morley, to the south and very near Attleborough, where hedges around former commons were thrown down, and then repaired to the north of Wymondham to Hethersett where they levelled certain of the enclosures recently made by an unpopular lawyer-landlord, who was also stripping the former monastic church at Wymondham, which he had recently acquired. This man, with the improbable name of Flowerdew, offered no direct opposition, but diverted attention from his own property with a small distribution of coins and the acceptable suggestion that they move on to overthrow enclosures which Robert Kett had recently raised. Kett they found even more conciliatory than Flowerdew, since he not only undertook to throw down his own hedges but offered himself as the leader of the assembly, which returned to clear the lawyer's lands of enclosures. This riotous company, at first composed of not more than six men, was fed rapidly from country men spending the day at Wymondham; now under Kett's leadership it began to move.[1]

From this amazing beginning, an aimless and probably drunken casting down of hedges was shortly to wax into violent rebellion. It is evident that bitter animus between the Kett family and Flowerdew served as a catalyst, but surely that is not enough to explain Kett's seizure of leadership of a stir which he could probably have quieted. As we have noted, Serj. Flowerdew was disliked by the community in which he was translating himself into a gentleman. But the Ketts —Robert and his brother William—were members of an old and much respected local family of some substance and position. They too were in process of translation from the status of tradesman to lower gentry, for they were now principal landholders in the Wymondham region, strangely enough holding three manors from the Earl of Warwick. Robert alone was reputed to be worth £50 p.a. in lands and we know that he possessed goods valued at about 1000 marks. The family, sometimes known as Knight, was prolific and prosperous, as many as eight of them having been benefactors to divers Norfolk parishes between 1504 and 1618.[2] What moved

[1] Russell, *Kett's rebellion*, 25–30; Neville, *De furoribus*, 21–22, 28; Blomefield, *Norfolk*, III, 223–224.

[2] From unpublished data on the charities of Norfolk, 1480–1660.

Robert Kett to treasonable courses we simply do not know. There
is about this whole tragic story much that reminds one of the way
in which Robert Aske was catapulted into the leadership of the
Northern Rising—it is simply another instance of the incidence of
the wholly unpredictable in human history.[1]

For rather more than a day after Kett had assumed its command,
the mob grew rapidly in numbers as it fed on action, since considerable damage was done to old enclosures in the general area of
Wymondham and Hethersett. The company, now numbering
several hundred men, then moved slowly in the direction of
Norwich, with minor damage done in the vicinity of Cringleford
and at Bowthorpe, three miles due west of Norwich, where Kett
camped on the night of July 9th. On that and the next day rioters
tore down numerous fences on the outskirts of Norwich, which
ironically represented enclosures of commons made for the benefit of
the poor of the city, who thereby gained controlled pasture from
the plots. Already, too, Kett's forces were being rapidly augmented
by sympathizers from the city who slipped away to join him. On
July 9th the apprehensive city officials dispatched a rider to Windsor
to inform the Council that a rising was under way, while other
messengers were sent to ask aid from Sir Roger Townshend and
Sir William Paston, both justices of the peace and members of
powerful county families. At Bowthorpe, too, the sheriff, Sir
Edward Windham, rode out formally to command the unruly and
as yet undisciplined company to disband, and was nearly captured
as he hastily left when he sensed the full ardour of the mob. Kett,
wishing to encamp on Mousehold Heath, about two miles to the
east of the city, and being refused permission to pass through
Norwich, began a wheeling march on July 11th, fording the Wensum
at Hellesdon Bridge, passing through Drayton, and then, removing
hedges as he proceeded, reached his desired, and defensible, site on
July 12th, on high ground well above the level of the city. Here he
encamped, accepted recruits who were soon streaming in, and began
to give organization to and impose discipline on what had heretofore
been an unruly mob.[2] Kett's first considerable augmentation of
power was gained from an insurgent group which, gathering at
Castle Rising, had failed to take Lynn, and had then moved south

[1] Vyse, J. W. M., 'The evidences for Kett's rebellion', *Norfolk Archaeology*, XXVI
(1937), 187; Clayton, Joseph, *Leaders of the people, etc.* (L., 1910), 224; Stow, *Annales*,
597; Blomefield, *Norfolk*, III, 258.
[2] Russell, *Kett's rebellion*, 32–37; Bindoff, *Ket's rebellion*, 3–4; Vyse, in *Norfolk
Archaeology*, XXVI (1937), 188; Blomefield, *Norfolk*, III, 225; Neville, *De furoribus*,
23–24; VCH, *Norfolk*, II, 496.

16

to the Suffolk border before determining to join forces with the rebels on Mousehold Heath. Also joining him was another party which had failed to carry Yarmouth, and which contained a fair number of Suffolk men from the Beccles-Bungay area.[1]

If the gentry of the county were supine and terrorized by this eruption, one must say that the city was for a season simply paralysed. Without the strong natural defences of Exeter, for a time uninstructed by the central government, with few military resources, and with many of the labourers and small tradesmen openly sympathetic with the rebels, the able mayor of the city, Thomas Codd, and the aldermen wisely sought to maintain friendly relations with the rebel forces, while placing the city in a state of defence and employing every effort to keep the insurgents outside the walls. Codd and his brethren first vainly endeavoured to persuade Kett and his followers to disperse. They then consulted with Kett on means for the disciplining of his forces and certainly encouraged Coniers, the vicar of St Martin's Norwich, a strongly evangelical Protestant, to hold services twice daily in the camp. Codd was also probably privy to the journey undertaken by a citizen, Leonard Sotherton, to wait upon the Council in London and to urge that an effort be made to negotiate with Kett on the basis of the articles which the rebel leader and his followers were drafting, with the full knowledge of the mayor and aldermen.

The Council, now gravely concerned with the spread of insurgency in East Anglia, did proceed so far as to send a royal herald to Norwich with Sotherton to offer the King's pardon if the rebels would disperse, but on July 21st Kett rejected the terms. The gates of the city were immediately closed; such guns as were available, including two lent by Sir William Paston, were trained; and the rather feeble musters of the city were called to the walls. Skirmishing at once broke out with the rebels, who proposed a truce on condition of supply from the city. This offer was rejected by the city authorities on July 22nd, but the really helpless position of Codd is suggested by the fact that rebel sympathizers within Norwich had broken into the stores of powder and shot in order to place munitions in Kett's hands. A rebel attempt to storm the city gates was repulsed by bowmen, but a diversionary thrust was successful, doubtless with

---

[1] Bindoff, *Ket's rebellion*, 4; Strype, *Memorials*, II, i, 271–272; Blomefield, *Norfolk*, III, 226. Serious troubles in Suffolk were prevented by the prompt action of leading gentry of the county. The same is true in Essex, where Lord Rich took the lead. Depositions taken at Colchester on August 7th suggest that rebel leaders in Norfolk were attempting with some success to involve Essex (Lansdowne MSS., 2, #25, f. 60).

the help of sympathizers, and the rebel army entered the city. Kett thereupon arrested Codd and several other leading citizens, placing them under mild detention, but continued negotiations with a rich and much respected merchant, Thomas Aldrich, who was in fact at once irascible and courageous.[1]

Shortly after the encampment was made on Mousehold Heath Kett had organized his forces into bands of common geographical origin and had imposed a remarkably quick and effective discipline. He had begun, too, probably in consultation with Codd and with his own lieutenants, to draft a statement of grievances to be laid before the Lord Protector, which would express the roughly hewn aspirations of at least the more articulate amongst his followers. We do not know precisely when these remarkable articles, twenty-seven in number, were formally drafted, but they were in the end signed by Robert Kett, Codd, and Aldrich and were so couched as to derive their authority from named spokesmen from Norwich (though these names are missing), twenty-two of the thirty-three hundreds of Norfolk, and one spokesman, Richard Wright, for the county of Suffolk.[2] The document, in form a petition to the Lord Protector, is arranged in no sensible order, almost as if items were jotted down in an oral discussion, and is concerned with tiny and specific grievances, quite as much as with large and abstruse matters. Several general observations may at once be made concerning the manifesto. Four of the demands refer back to Henry VII as if to an imagined golden past, and restorations were proposed to recover this idealized age. Almost exactly half the grievances related to a variety of agrarian problems, yet there was only one oblique reference in the whole document to enclosures, suggesting that they were, at least in East Anglia, more of a symbol of past wrongs than of present injury. The religious demands were few and scattered, and may be characterized as Protestant in temper with an overlay of evident secularism. Thus it was requested that priests be not permitted to purchase land and that that which they now possessed should be let to laymen. They further demanded that incumbents who did not preach and 'set forth the Word of God' be put out of their livings and competent preachers be installed. They denounced non-residence and also petitioned that all clergymen with livings of £10 p.a. or more either personally or by delegate 'teach poor mens'

[1] Blomefield, *Norfolk*, III, 234–238; Holinshed, *Chronicles*, III, 966, 969; Russell, *Kett's rebellion*, 40.
[2] The articles may be found in Harl. MS. 304, #44, ff. 75–78, and are printed by Russell, *Kett's rebellion*, 48–56.

EDWARD VI: THE YOUNG KING

children of their parish' the catechism and the *Primer*, while also propounding an obscure proposal for the reform of the tithe system. Suffusing many of the demands is an insistence on jealous safeguards for common rights and a clear and evidently bitter dislike of landlords in general and of the gentry in particular. Lords of the manor should possess no rights in common lands, while meadow land and marsh ground should be as they were in 1 Henry VII. They asked for a standard bushel, that the keeping of dovecotes be strictly limited, that copyhold rents be restored to 1 Henry VII, that the fishing and navigation of rivers be completely free to all men, and that lords of the manor be prohibited from purchasing freehold lands and then letting them out as copyhold. They denounced the sale of wardships and the forced marriage of wards, and with great clarity spelled out their most radical demand that no lord or gentleman, if his land was worth £40 p.a. or more, be permitted to raise sheep and cattle save for the uses of his own household.

If it may be said that these somewhat inchoate demands, with one glance of vision, looked back to an imagined and idyllic past, it must at the same time be said that they also looked forward to a day when simple men of small property and power would gain a larger measure of protection and succour from the state. Nearly all of their grievances were in fact to be cured with the passage of time and the firmer intervention of the sovereign power. Nor is it too much to say that Somerset himself had sought by statute, by bills failing of passage, by proclamations, commissions, and private discourse to lend relief or cure to the most substantial of the grievances here propounded. In a true sense this rebellion was engendered by the slowness with which Somerset's programme of social and economic reform was carried forward, and perhaps as well by the half-intuitive sense of humble men that the Protector's policy was foundering because of the obstructing tactics of classes of men who possessed ultimate power in England. These proposals were, of course, doomed because they were conceived in rebellion, and rebellion conjured up for the Tudor mind the anarchy into which England had almost sunk in the period of the War of the Roses. Sympathetic though Somerset may have been to most of these complaints, they were in form and temper demands of rebellious subjects. And it was his appointed task to crush outright rebellion in Norfolk with such few resources as could be spared from the equally formidable necessities in southwestern England.

Surviving sources make it clear that Kett enjoyed widespread and powerful support in Norfolk, and probably in Suffolk as well. We have seen that his camp was governed by spokesmen for twenty-two of the hundreds of the county, and these included the whole of the populous and prosperous northern, eastern, and central portions of the county where freeholds were predominant and the pressure of population on land heavy, while little of his support was gained from the marginal lands of southwestern Norfolk where holdings were large and pastures had long prevailed.[1] In these areas there was on the part of small freeholders, who, as we have seen, were heavily dependent on commons for their pasture needs, a deep-seated dislike and mistrust of the thrusting gentry. This was not new, but Kett had given it eloquent voice. Thus as early as 1540, we are told, John Walker of Griston had boasted that 'if three or four good fellows would ride in the night, with every man a bell, and cry in every town they passed through, "To Swaffham! To Swaffham!" ', by morning 10,000 men would have assembled. Walker's obsession was against the gentry, for he declared it would be a good thing 'if there were only as many gentlemen in Norfolk as there were white bulls'.[2]

Even more interesting, and in some ways perplexing, is the clear evidence that Kett found widespread and strong support amongst the artisans, the small tradesmen, and the semi-skilled workmen in the towns and villages across the two-thirds of Norfolk from which he drew his rural strength. In a probably fair cross-section of the pardon lists one notices that of the forty-nine persons from Norfolk and Suffolk then being released thirty were men with agricultural occupations. But there were also nineteen with clearly urban callings and all of these were either skilled or semi-skilled workmen or small tradesmen.[3] So too, many of those making their way from Suffolk to join Kett at Mousehold Heath were drawn from this same village and urban stratum.[4] The searching interrogations carried on before the mayor and aldermen of Norwich for some months after the rebellion had been quieted also afford much information respecting the widespread and fervent support lent to Kett by the whole community. Here it was testified that Robert Burnham, a parish clerk, had said 'there are too many gentlemen in England by five hundred', while others were accused of remarks suggesting surviving sympathy for Kett and his proposals for reform. A woollen weaver had apparently bitterly castigated Warwick and had said that

[1] Thirsk, *Tudor enclosures*, 14.
[2] Rye, Walter, *A history of Norfolk* (L., 1885), 57, with no source cited.
[3] *Cal. Pat. Rolls, Edw. VI*, III, 31, 147, 328, 330.
[4] Strype, *Memorials*, II, i, 275–276.

Norwich owed him no thanks, while a shoemaker had muttered that the gentry of Norfolk must needs watch 'all the days of their lives'. It was further testified that at Saxlingham the poor had said they were the prey of the gentry, while as late as 1553 threats were still being made openly to tear away again the enclosures around the Norwich commons.[1] These are sentiments after the fact, but they suggest the smouldering discontent from which Kett had drawn his support and the magic of the revolutionary moment when he embodied the half-formed aspirations of wide reaches and many classes in the county of Norfolk. These sentiments also suggest the close interdependence of village and town life in England with the countryside from whence their economic resources were drawn and with which they were closely linked in blood and culture. The evidence from Norfolk simply reinforces Van der Delft's shrewd judgement that there was grave danger that rural discontent might be conjoined with the grievances of labourers and artisans in the towns who were severely afflicted because of the physical scarcity of food-stuffs and mounting prices.[2]

The rebel horde grew apace during most of July, until at least 10,000 men were under Kett's command and dependent on his ingenious plans for feeding his forces by systematic levies upon the gentry and upon Norwich, for which at least in the earlier weeks he gave out receipts for value received.[3] Kett had considerable administrative ability and was able throughout the rising to impose an effective discipline on his camp, being greatly assisted by the two religious services which were held daily, in the English language and in conformity with the new rites. The merchant elite of Norwich were throughout these weeks also able to impose a restraining influence on Kett, though the gentry of the county evidently remained terrorized or were under arrest if they had offered opposition.[4] The remarkable relationship between Norwich and Kett's camp is also suggested by Matthew Parker's effort to quell the rebellion by his preaching. A native of Norwich, the future arch-

---

[1] Tawney and Power, *Tudor economic documents*, I, 47–53.

[2] *Cal. S.P. Span.* IX, 397: July 3, 1549.

[3] Holinshed (*Chronicles*, III, 966) sets 16,000 as his estimate. A modern estimate places the total at perhaps 12,000 (Mackie, J. D., *The earlier Tudors, 1485–1558* (Oxford, 1952), 490). Kett's indictment charges that he had raised 'a multitude of malefactors to the amount of 20,000 persons and upwards', surely an heroic exaggeration (*Fourth rpt., Dep. Keeper Public Records*, App., II, 222). Russell, without strong conviction, thought that as many as 16,000 were encamped at Mousehold at the moment of Kett's greatest strength. In another place (*The charities of rural England, etc.* (L., 1961), 90), we have estimated the total population of Norfolk in 1600 as in the range of 170,000 to 185,000.

[4] HMC, *12th rpt.*, App. IV: *Rutland MSS.* I, 42.

bishop was already a famous scholar at Cambridge and vice-chancellor of the university, when in his sermon to the insurgents he urged them not to loot, to refrain from the pointless shedding of blood, and then sternly enjoined them to return to obedience to the King. There was a dangerous moment as Parker hastily retired from the scene, but the crowd was quieted when Coniers, who, as we have seen, regularly preached to the camp, moved quickly to a service of prayer.[1]

The Council had been kept well informed of the spread of rebellion in Norfolk, had studied the rebel manifesto, and had sought unsuccessfully to secure the dissipation of resistance by a generous offer of royal pardon. But it had not moved with force against the insurgents principally because it was deeply committed in the west and had stripped the London area of reliable troops in order to meet Russell's ever-mounting requirements. But in late July a striking force of about 1800 was assembled, with Italian mercenaries as its principal component, but including the personal followers of several peers and Councillors, as well as numerous gentry drawn from Norfolk and Suffolk. After some hesitation, it was determined that William Parr (Northampton) should be placed in command. The choice was incredibly inept, since Parr had never held an important military command, but was probably dictated by necessity since, the Protector aside, every experienced noble commander was at the time engaged either in the west or on the Scottish border. Perhaps because he had little confidence in Northampton, Somerset carefully ordered him to avoid a battle, to preserve his freedom of movement in the field, and to limit his operations to cutting off the food supply for the rebel camp and seeking to disband the insurgents by negotiations.[2] Every one of these wise instructions Northampton promptly violated, with disastrous results.

Accompanied by Lord Wentworth, Lord Sheffield, Sir Anthony Denny, Sir Ralph Sadler, Sir Thomas Cornwallis, and other of the gentry, Northampton reached the area on July 30th, immediately disregarding his orders by entering Norwich, be it said without serious opposition. Guards were set on the city walls and at the gates. But this same night Kett attacked the city in force, subjecting three of the gates to heavy fire, while hundreds of rebels, protected by this diversion, scaled the walls or slipped in through old breaches, with the aid of sympathizers within the city. Desperate house-to-

[1] Strype, John, *The life and acts of Matthew Parker, etc.* (3 vols., Oxford, 1821), I, 51–54.
[2] Petyt MS. 538, xlvi, f. 452.

house fighting followed in which no quarter was given. The insurgents were finally driven out, but only after heavy losses were
sustained on both sides. On the following day the rebels again
gained access to the city streets, and murderous fighting was resumed in which Northampton lost as many as one hundred killed,
including Lord Sheffield, who, being thrown from his horse, was
brutally clubbed to death. Northampton was, in fact, extremely
fortunate in being able to withdraw his force, now in disorder, from
the city, re-grouping in the field and then ignominiously falling back
on London.[1]

Inevitably, Northampton's withdrawal left the city in a state of
panic, while his bootless occupation had destroyed the delicate
balance in the earlier relations of the city authorities with the rebel
forces. There was some looting, and fires were set which might
have destroyed Norwich had not heavy rains brought them quickly
under control. Kett established a garrison camp in the cathedral
grounds, spread out guards throughout the city, and during the
remainder of his period of power exercised control within the walls.

Meanwhile, the Council, meeting on August 3rd to consider the
harsh realities imposed by Northampton's disaster, resolved to
assemble all possible strength for the reduction of Norfolk and
immediately ordered Shrewsbury to gather his forces and to proceed
towards an area now completely out of royal control.[2] It had at the
outset been Somerset's intention to lead the royal army in person,
but, with consequences incalculable for him and for England, it was
decided instead by him and the Council that Warwick, then in the
north, would be given command.[3] The Earl of Warwick acknowledged his instructions on August 10th, advising at the same
time that Northampton's commission be continued, he 'having
lately by misfortune received discomfort enough, haply this might
give him occasion to think himself utterly discredited, and . . . for
ever discourage him; which, in my opinion, were a great pity'.[4] The
Scottish border and the Boulogne garrisons were ordered to be
dangerously reduced, and on August 15th all the gentry of Essex,

---

[1] Russell, *Kett's rebellion*, 87–98; Holinshed, *Chronicles*, III, 972–974; Somerset
(Petyt MS. 538, xlvi, f. 452) estimated the losses on both sides as 500 killed in this
bloody and feckless enterprise; Blomefield, *Norfolk*, III, 241–244; *Cal. S.P. Span.* IX,
423: Aug. 7, 1549; *Grey Friars Chronicle* (Camden Soc. LIII), 61; *Two London chronicles*
(*Camden Misc.* XIII), 18–19.

[2] Lodge, *Illustrations*, I, 161–162, citing the Howard papers.

[3] Cotton MSS., Vespasian, F, iii, 37, cited by Russell, *Kett's rebellion*, 111–112. So
serious was the situation in the west and so dilatory had Russell been, that Somerset
probably dared not leave London.

[4] S.P. Dom., Edw. VI, VIII, 38.

Suffolk, and Norfolk were required by proclamation to assemble with their retainers for field service.[1] Warwick, as always, now moved with great speed and efficiency, gathering his forces in the Cambridge area. Serving with him were his two sons, Robert and Ambrose, Northampton, Lord Willoughby, Lord Powis, Lord Bray, and the gathered gentry. There were, in addition, the remaining mercenaries in the London area, numbering 1400 troops, with the fire power and experience which his somewhat motley array lacked.[2] The whole force under his command, according to the King's estimate, numbered 6000 foot and 1500 cavalry.[3] Proceeding by rapid marches from Cambridge, to Newmarket, to Thetford, and to Wymondham, Warwick reached Intwood, just three miles to the southwest of Norwich, where on August 23rd he established his field headquarters.

Warwick's plan of action was to treat with the rebels if at all possible, to keep his main force in the field in order to avoid the trap into which Northampton had fallen, to separate the rebels from their supplies and aid from within the city, and loosely to invest the insurgent camp. This last he did with such success that 'they were fain to live three days with water for drink, and eat their meat without bread'.[4] On the day of his arrival, therefore, Warwick sent the King's herald into the city where he was told by the mayor's deputies that many of Kett's forces were within the walls, but they were unarmed and poor and 'weary of their doings', men who would probably surrender if generous terms were advanced. When the herald then went into the rebel camp outside the walls, hundreds of rebels followed him out, joining those on the field, where the herald in Kett's presence rebuked them for their treason while offering pardon if they would lay down their arms. Kett then moved with the herald to another part of the camp, where, unfortunately, one of the herald's guards shot and killed a boy who had made an obscene gesture. Whereupon, the cry went up that the herald, in his traditional garb, was no true herald but wore 'a gay coat, patched together' of popish vestments. Thus the delicate balance of negotiation and pardon was upset and the doom of many men was sealed when Kett was restrained by his own followers as he sought to set

[1] Hughes and Larkin, *Tudor proclamations*, I, 481–482.

[2] Blomefield, *Norfolk*, III, 251; Van der Delft estimated Warwick's force to number 8000–9000 men, while Shrewsbury was in motion with reinforcements (*Cal. S.P. Span.* IX, 432: Aug. 13, 1549). Professor Bindoff suggests that as many as 13,200 troops may have been in the command (*Ket's rebellion*, 6).

[3] Edward VI, *Chronicle*, 15.

[4] Harl. MS. 523, #43, ff. 53–55: Somerset to Hoby, Sept. 1, 1549.

out with the herald for a conference with Warwick.[1] Kett, the propagandist, Kett the brilliant organizer and administrator was, with all his great gifts of leadership, no soldier. At the moment of supreme crisis it was all too clear that his forces were not under military discipline, that he presided over a mob and not an army.

On the next day, August 24th, Warwick determined to strike, leaving his main force in the field while assaulting Norwich from which he was determined to drive all rebel forces. His artillery opened three gates, while his troops stormed in, killing many really unarmed rebels and hanging forty-nine prisoners in the market place by Warwick's command. That night enemy forces again infiltrated into the city and a short but violent street fight broke out, followed by heavy rebel losses and still more hangings. But the battle for Norwich was now really over. Strong defences were mounted, and the rebel army was at last wholly severed from the city from which it had been principally nourished. Then as the steel circle of Warwick's larger investment began to cut off all supplies from rural Norfolk, Kett and his captains realized that they must strike at once, risking all in a pitched battle.

On August 26th Kett, for most uncertain reasons but very possibly because his supply routes were now all severed, broke his high, well-entrenched, and formidable camp on Mousehold, moving his forces to a valley position, not clearly identified, which he was quite unable to entrench before Warwick attacked on the following day.[2] Warwick, pardon again having been rejected, attacked with his German mercenaries and all his cavalry, leaving the English foot as a reserve in the city, moving out against forces as ill-armed as as they were ill-led. It was not so much a battle as a disciplined butchery, from which Kett fled at its close to be captured the following day some eight miles from the scene of the carnage into which he had led so many of the young, the restless, the idealists, and, doubtless, the criminal of the county of Norfolk.[3]

Warwick moved immediately to a 'mopping up' operation in Norwich, hanging several persons against whom complaints had been lodged by responsible persons and then some days later executing nine of Kett's lieutenants. But he withstood the frantic

---

[1] Holinshed, *Chronicles*, III, 977–978; Russell, *Kett's rebellion*, 128–129.

[2] The position is described as at Dussin's Dale. Sotherton seems to suggest that it lay not more than a mile from the Mousehold encampment. Rye's sketch map (*Norfolk Archaeology*, XVI (1905), 91), gives no indication of the site, though it has been most helpful for details on the Mousehold camp.

[3] Russell, *Kett's rebellion*, 146–150, 213–215, quoting Harl. MS. 523, #43, ff. 53–55; Edward VI, *Chronicle*, 16.

pressure of some of the gentry who wished a blood bath and who may well now have been exhibiting a belated martial ferocity to assuage their sense of failure to stamp out the rising in its early phases. Warwick, however, we are told by both Sotherton and Neville, resisted these pressures: 'There must be measure kept, and above all things in punishment men must not exceed'. The wicked deserved to be grievously punished, but the victors should not press too far. Would those who cry out for vengeance 'leave no place for humble petition? none for pardon and mercie? Would they be plowmen themselves, and harrow their owne lands?' Meanwhile, the two principal prisoners, Robert Kett and his brother, were sent to London for trial, and in due course were returned to Norfolk—William to be hanged from the church tower at Wymondham and Robert from the wall of Norwich Castle.[1] On August 29th Warwick and his retinue joined the citizens of Norwich in a service of thanksgiving at St Peter's Mancroft, and then the Earl hurried back to London where he began the conversations and the plotting that were to accomplish the ruin of Somerset.

Meanwhile, in Norfolk the citizenry were beginning the long and expensive repairs and building required to restore Norwich, while throughout the county the gentry were explaining their lassitude during the rebellion or seeking to jockey for position. Sir Thomas Woodhouse tells us that for days the gentry brought in accusations to Warwick, petitioning always for the escheats, though he had himself intervened for one man who had been in Kett's camp no more than two days at the outset. As for himself, he had made no accusations and had asked for no gift though he had lost 2000 sheep, all his bullocks, and most of his corn. His only request, here transmitted to Cecil, was that he be placed on the commission of oyer and terminer, from which he had been excluded, 'that I be not forgotten, for then I shall lose my credit in the county'.[2] The deep fissures and sensitivities of the gentry of the county are even more clearly set out in a long letter from Sir Nicholas LeStrange to Cecil, complaining that Sir Edmund Bedingfield and Sir Roger Townshend, who disliked him because he had refused to sell them adjoining lands, had, so he said, poisoned the mind of Lord Willoughby against him, and had set out rumours charging him with having been a prime mover in the stir at its beginning. This he indignantly denied, since he had been in Hampshire at the time. He

[1] Russell, *Kett's rebellion*, 151, 161–163; *Fourth rpt., Dep. Keeper Publ. Records,* App. II, 222.   [2] S.P. Dom., Edw. VI, VIII, 55(i): Sept. 6, 1549.

had come to London to seek aid from the Council for Norfolk, had tried to help in the dispersing of the rebels, and had then placed himself and his fifty men at Willoughby's disposal. He proudly concluded that his ancestors in Norfolk had for three centuries stood free of such charges, which he held were now brought forward by his personal enemies to secure his undoing.[1] It was no doubt in part to quiet such turmoils and feuds amongst the gentry in several counties that the government called upon all justices of the peace strictly to enforce the laws and proclamations against unlawful assemblies, loitering, and seditious persons, and to quell immediately any further stirs by hanging 'rebels and open traitors to us and to the realm'.[2] A period of black and frightened reaction had set in for which Warwick rather than Somerset was to be the spokesman of the dominant political classes of England which had been severely shaken by the events of the summer.

The losses in Norfolk had been heavy for the whole society of the county and indeed of the nation. Stability of institutions had been rudely shaken, the economy of Norwich had been gravely damaged, and the harvest had not been completed in half the county. More important, perhaps, already festering hatreds of class against class had been worsened and an abyss of local anarchy had suddenly been revealed which could be closed only by the restoration of order by martial law and the period of reaction which followed. The human losses had been heavy, too, particularly on that dreadful day when Kett's poorly armed and ill-led company was systematically slaughtered before the walls of Norwich. The contemporary estimates of the rebel losses range from Holinshed's figure of 3500 to the surely far too high suggestion of 5000 slain on the field of Dussin's Dale. Modern authorities set the figure more cautiously, at from 3000 to 3500 in the battle before Norwich, without usually reckoning the number lost in earlier fighting within Norwich and the toll taken by Warwick's martial law. Our own estimate would be something like 3000 rebels killed in the final engagement, and not far off from 600 in the streets of Norwich and on Warwick's gibbets.[3] Nor did the royal forces go untouched. Northampton lost at least

---

[1] S.P. Dom., Edw. VI, VIII, 60: Sept. 15, 1549. One page of this document seems to be missing.

[2] Ibid. 66. The document is undated, but almost certainly was drafted in early September, 1549. It may have been a draft of an intended proclamation, though never promulgated as such.

[3] Other estimates may be found in: Holinshed, *Chronicles*, III, 982; Stow, *Annales*, 597; Wriothesley, *Chronicle* (Camden Soc., n.s. XX), 21; of modern authorities, the soundest seem to be: Bindoff, *Ket's rebellion*, 6; Blomefield, *Norfolk*, III, 255; Mackie, *Earlier Tudors*, 490; Pollard, *History of England*, 36; VCH, *Norfolk*, II, 498.

one hundred men killed in his fiasco of attempted occupation, and the losses sustained by Warwick were something like 250. Warwick himself records that one of his captains who had served with his 180 foot from the entry of Northampton to the end had lost a third of his command, 'killed at the battle and other skirmishes there'.[1] In all, therefore, the killed in this strange and tragic rising probably fell not far short of 4000 men, only slightly more than our estimate of loss of life in the west. It would seem, taking all the stirs of 1549 in view, that the Venetian diplomatist's estimate of 'the slaughter and destruction of 10,000 or 11,000 natives' was not far off the mark.[2] If so, this represents a not inconsiderable demographic loss, if one reflects that this was the equivalent of something like 150,000 to 165,000 of war dead if translated to the present population of England and Wales.

These losses of men and of treasure, and the weakening of the harmony of reasonable and civilized relations of class to class and man to man were, then, very great. It had meant, too, that English foreign policy was completely paralysed and that the government found itself at war with France as the risings were at their climax. These great eruptions in 1549 were, as we have seen, occasioned by many and exceedingly complex causes. But in both of them, and especially in Norfolk, they sprang from hope and from the belief that ancient wrongs of humble men were about to be righted. The greatest loss, indeed, was precisely here, for Somerset had undoubtedly advanced these hopes and possessed at least a dim, though always thwarted, aspiration for the building in England of a true and a juster commonwealth as a habitation for Christian men. Opposition amongst the dominant classes, those ultimately vested with wealth and power, was already firmly set against him and his policies, well before men gathered at Sampford Courtenay or at Wymondham for unlawful and dangerous purposes. These risings struck the gentry both in Norfolk and in Devon with sheer terror, as the world they knew suddenly lay shattered about them. And Somerset stood alone, helpless and doomed, as these bloody rebellions were at last brought to a close.

[1] S.P. Dom., Edw. VI, VIII, 59: Sept. 14, 1549.   [2] Cal. S.P. Ven. V, 268.

XVI

THE FALL OF SOMERSET

1. BACKGROUND OF FRICTIONS AND CAUSES

It must, then, be said that Somerset's policies and his employment of sovereign power stood discredited in the late summer of 1549. Russell's great force lay in the west and for weeks he had with stubborn insubordination ignored the Protector's orders to make his troops available for other and more urgent uses in Norfolk, along the Scottish border, and for the defence of the English enclaves in France. Warwick, rebellion in Norfolk thoroughly crushed, returned to London, probably on September 14th, and in his person held control of the principal elements of military power, which he was prepared to wield, if need be, to restore a government of 'lords and gentlemen' in the realm. As we shall see, Warwick was also a consummate master of the arts of conspiracy, which he began to employ almost immediately for the staging of a *coup d'état*. At the end of the summer Somerset stood almost alone in the Council. He had made too many enemies: the landlords, the old Catholic order, most of the London merchants, and the Council itself. Further, he had, so to speak, alienated into the hands of Russell, Herbert, and Warwick almost the whole of the military resources of the realm, and this starkly effective power he could not in sufficient time bring back into his own hands. The Protector, certainly the most gifted English soldier of his generation, stood without an army with which to oppose the forces of treason so quickly to enmesh him. These were the immediate circumstances which account for the incredible ease with which Warwick toppled him from power.[1]

But there were other causes and frictions which during the months of his tenure of sovereign power had gravely weakened Somerset's position and credit. His high-minded and cool aloofness which had permitted his colleagues to proceed with the trial and execution of his own brother had seemed to many to be as unnatural as it was

---

[1] For helpful comments on these matters, *vide* Bindoff, *Tudor England*, 157; Dickens, *English Reformation*, 228.

THE FALL OF SOMERSET

indefensible. Sudeley was undoubtedly guilty of high treason and deserved his fate, but it was Somerset who seemed—as he was—directly responsible for a most uncommon and incomprehensible inhumanity. It was this, I think, which marked the beginning of the rapid erosion of his reputation and credit.[1] There was also substance to the charge that his assumption of power ran directly counter to the will of Henry VIII, which became an increasingly sainted document, even though his colleagues on the Council had made this necessary cession of power without any evidence of opposition.

Further, it is important to note that, once Wriothesley had been dismissed, for proper as well as politic cause, Somerset eschewed the exercise of his stated authority either to remove Councillors or to build up within the ruling junta a faction linked to him by personal ties of friendship or obligation. It almost seems, indeed, as if he were contemptuous of the Council and wished to stand alone within it. There was also substance to the complaint that on occasion he exercised judicial competence in the Court of Requests, and, it might have been added, that he was so far increasing its competence that it threatened the jurisdiction of the ancient courts of the realm. There was also considerable truth in the allegation that it was improper as well as illegal for him to affix the King's signature by stamp on important documents, though we are by no means certain that he was in fact guilty of the alleged offence.[2] Probably even more serious, in this age when status and the symbols of status meant so much to men, was the festering grievance of his special seat, his nearly regal dignity in Parliament. Closely connected was the deep resentment, which can be amply documented, because the Protector had early in his tenure adopted, perhaps almost unwittingly, the royal style of address, just as he had offended the French King by addressing him as 'brother'. All this flowed, of course, from his special responsibility for and his jealously guarded right of control over the person of the King, whom he treated with a cold discipline that displayed a total misunderstanding of the nature of an adolescent boy and with a formal respect that scarcely concealed the rigour of the Protector's power. There can be no doubt that Somerset confused his own nature and personality with that of the King, and that he was all too prone to speak as if he were the King, though it must be unequivocally stated that he remained fully aware that the short period of his sovereign capacity was rapidly slipping away and that he wished, as he prayed, that he might hand over to Edward VI at the proper time the full and

[1] Vide ante, 368–382.   [2] Pollard, Somerset, 243.

undamaged substance of regal power. Somerset had many faults and weaknesses; the instinct of treason was not among them.

Nor is it too petty to record that Somerset was also gravely weakened by the temperament and character of his wife, a large (and unanimous) body of evidence suggesting that she was a proud and a difficult woman, as disliked as she was feared by most of those who were intimately associated with the Protector. Somerset remained completely blind to the faults of the Duchess, never intervened to stop her meddling, and seems without any doubt to have been wholly happy with her in a union which produced ten children. It is difficult to analyse Anne Stanhope's faults, in part perhaps because one has an almost intuitive sense that she may well have been maligned. Headstrong, foolish, proud, and ambitious she undoubtedly was, nor did she hesitate on occasion to point out that her lineage was more ancient than that of her husband. She was fiercely protective of Somerset, and she was quite as fiercely protective of her own brood of children, against the claims of Somerset's first brood, who had in effect been disowned by Act of Parliament. She was also almost morbidly jealous of her husband, displaying perhaps the psychological insecurity of the second wife. Yet there was tenderness in her and she remained the close friend of Mary Tudor throughout the reign. For strongly held criticism of her personality and interference it is not necessary, however, to draw from sentiments of Somerset's enemies. His closest colleague, Paget, tersely suggested to Van der Delft in August, 1549, that Somerset's failures and troubles were explained by the fact that 'he has a bad wife'.[1] The loyal but timid Cheke was forced to petition the Duchess abjectly for offence she had taken at some doubtless trivial action of his wife.[2] So too, Sir Thomas Smith felt obliged to make a fuller, though by no means as humiliating, an explanation to the Duchess, who had earlier spoken to him of certain of his faults. It seems that some unnamed informant had sought to persuade her that he was haughty, that he had profited too much and too quickly from the fruits of office, that he did not afford generous hospitality, and that 'my wife doth not go so gorgeously as some would have her. If that be a fault, although she is little, let her bear it. She hath all my money . . .'. And, finally, he had been accused of coldness in religion, which he vehemently denied, and then with a courageous thrust which implied a strong bias of the Duchess for the Commonwealth Party, concluded that not so much could be said for the

---

[1] *Cal. S.P. Span.* IX, 429: Aug. 13, 1549.
[2] Lansdowne MS.2, #34: Jan. 27, 1549.

firmness of faith of 'all these hotlings, when they come where danger is, they shrink; when none is, they can come to kneel upon your grace's carpets, and devise commonwealths as they like; and are angry that other men be not so hasty to run straight as their brains croweth'.[1]

Somerset was also, and somewhat unjustly, accused of enriching himself unduly and wrongly from crown lands during his tenure of power. We have already dealt at length with the outrageous grants which the ruling conciliar junta conferred on themselves, but within the context of this general wrong against the state, the outright grants to Somerset were at once proportionate and on the whole modest.[2] It should be remembered that his father was a rich landowner in his own right and that Somerset before 1547 had inherited lands worth £2400 p.a. from him. Henry VIII had thought highly of his brother-in-law and had, before 1547, vested him with properties yielding something like £2000 p.a. The whole of the grants he took from the Crown during his tenure of office was of the order of £3000 p.a., setting his private income at about £7400 during the period of his Protectorate.[3] These aggregations did, it is true, make him the richest noble in England for a season, but it fell far short in fact of maintaining the standard of living required for the head of state, which was recognized by the grant of an annuity of 8000 marks p.a. payable from the Court of Augmentations quarterly for his expenses 'as Governor and Protector'.[4] The total available income was hence of the order of £12,734 p.a., a certainly sufficient amount,[5] had it not been for his huge outlays on building which, being all too tangible and apparent, beyond any doubt excited keen and bitter criticism amongst all classes of men.[6]

[1] Harl. MS. 6989, f. 141. [#84, f. 81], as rendered by Nichols in *Archaeologia*, xxxviii (1860), 120-127.   [2] *Vide ante*, 63, 116.
[3] The Marquess of Ailesbury sets his income at about £7500 p.a. in this period (*Savernake Forest*, 44). See also Jackson, in *Wilts. Archaeol. and Nat. Hist. Mag.*, XV (1875), 189. The estimate of £7400 p.a. of landed income is probably very close, being based on legal proceedings when Somerset's heir was trying to get his inheritance restored. *Vide* HMC, *Bath MSS.*, IV: *Seymour papers*, 187-188, for the Earl of Hertford's claim as stated Jan. 30, 1580; Egerton MS. 2815 for a reckoning of Somerset's income in the later years of his life.
[4] *Cal. Pat. Rolls, Edw. VI*, I, 184: July 9, 1547.
[5] *Vide* Stone, *Crisis of the aristocracy*, App. XXIII, for details of Somerset's household and personal outlays.
[6] When Sir John Thynne was examined by members of the Council shortly after Somerset's fall from power, three of their eight questions bore on the Protector's building outlays. Thynne could provide no estimate of the amounts expended for this purpose during the past three years, but he believed that the costs were met from his master's own revenues and from the sale of lands. He added that he had often wished that the Duke would put aside his building because he was in debt. (HMC, *Bath MSS.*, IV: *Seymour papers*, 112.)

The Protector's most conspicuous and severely criticized building was in London where in Somerset House he planned and began a great house worthy of a head of state. On his coming to power, Somerset lived in a fairly modest house, granted to him by Henry VIII in 1539, at Chester Place, just outside Temple Bar. But moved by his passion for building and by the strong representations of his Duchess, he determined on an expanded site, including Chester Place, which would quite overmatch the new and pretentious houses already built in the area by his fellow nobles. It was probably in late 1547 that work was begun by the demolition of old London landmarks including the church of St Mary le Strand, a former Inn of Chancery (Chester Inn), several non-descript tenements, and the former London houses of the bishops of Worcester, Llandaff, and Lichfield. The site is roughly that on which Somerset House stands today, but was graced with more extensive grounds, extending to an area of slightly more than six acres which had been literally hewn out of a densely cluttered and populated urban area. These measures doubtless aroused considerable comment and criticism, but nothing when compared with the fact that he also razed much of the fabric of St John of Jerusalem (Clerkenwell), part of the cloister on the north side of St Paul's, and the Charnel House there in order to supply stone and lime for his building needs. As if this were not enough—and every chronicler records the facts in ghoulish detail— the burying-ground in and near the Charnel House was opened and hundreds of cartloads of human bones were removed to be dumped in Finsbury Field where they were covered by city waste.

The vast pile of Somerset House was not yet completed by the time of the Duke's execution, nor could it have been wholly finished even at the time when by constitutional mandate Somerset would have been required to relinquish sovereignty intact to his royal nephew. The demolitions, the desecration of consecrated grounds, the vast outlays visibly being made all aroused criticism ranging from gossip to deep suspicion. As the great, and architecturally important work advanced, it rose as a monument at once to Somerset's consummate taste and to his imprudence as a statesman.[1] And, while this great work, with all its conspicuous outlay, was in progress, Somerset was also engaged in an ambitious programme of

[1] Needham, Raymond, and Alexander Webster, *Somerset House past and present* (N.Y., n.d.), 32–38; Dixon, *Church of England*, III, 124–125; Stow, *Annales*, 596 (as an instance of the criticisms of the chroniclers); Add. MS. 5809, f. 98b, expressing particular resentment that the body of Sir Thomas Mirfin, Lord Mayor of London in 1518, had been removed. We reserve our comments on this important Renaissance building to the concluding volume of this work.

building and renovation at Syon House, the great monastic precincts there having been granted to him by the Crown. This notable and expensive work Somerset lived to complete, the present building being in form and details very close to his design,[1] with its three storeys, architecturally dominated by its four square-angled turrets, and on the east front graced with a long gallery extending a full 130 feet between the two angle turrets.

Nor was this by any means the whole of Somerset's ambitious and extremely expensive building. His birthplace in Wiltshire, Wolf Hall, was, as we have seen, already old and uncomfortable in Sir John Seymour's day. Somerset, continuously adding to his estates in the region, and sharing with his Wiltshire servant and agent, Sir John Thynne, a passion for building, had determined on the construction of a great country house which would grace his extensive land holdings. The site chosen was about three miles to the east of Wolf Hall, between Wilton and Great Bedwyn, on Bedwyn Brail. Well, though certainly not spectacularly, situated between the 500 and 550 foot contours, the site enjoyed a pleasant and extensive view down the Vale of Pewsey.[2] In November, 1548, a prospect was being opened by extensive clearing of undergrowth and the enlargement of several meadows. Somerset had hoped to empark an area of nearly a square mile, but when it was learned that to do so would deprive tenants of Wilton of common pasture rights for 180 cattle, 'to their utter undoing', a much more modest setting was disposed. Thynne was also negotiating with Sir Anthony Hungerford for the purchase of extensive woodlands to the northeast of the site, but some months later the negotiations had settled on the exchange of certain properties. By March, 1549, work was well begun, local stone being tested, clay piled for the burning of bricks, and the plan of the house had been traced. First attention, however, was given to the building of a great conduit, 1000 feet in length, which was consuming a great deal of stone and on which sixty men seem to have been employed for almost a year. The clerk of the works in charge, Bryan Tesh, of Wilton, reported in June, 1549, that the London contractor had been discharged because he had misrepresented the quality of the stone being used, while the French masons sent down from London had been returned because of their drunken habits and the clashes with the neighbours. In late June Somerset was informed that the great conduit was nearly

[1] VCH, *Middlesex*, III, 98.

[2] The site is well shown on the two and one-half inch Ordnance Survey, sheet SU 26, very near 62N/28E. The spring there noted was that designed to serve the house.

completed, grading for the house site was in progress, and stocks of brick were in hand. In the weeks of power and affluence remaining to Somerset, the foundations for the great house were dug and at least partially laid, but an inventory of 2,000,000 bricks, stone for the walls, and other building stone was included when the site was conveyed to Pembroke not long after the Protector's execution. The ruin of the plan was encompassed in the gigantic ruin of his fall and today nothing remains save traces of the foundation and of the conduit, all bleak and overgrown.[1]

These weaknesses and foibles were to be ruthlessly exploited by Somerset's enemies when Dudley's plot was launched against him. They were to exploit, too, the undoubted fact that Somerset had grown more brusque; that his letters and memoranda, as his dispatches to Russell so fully support, tended to be harsh and abrasive; and that he tended not to deal fully or frankly with his colleagues in the Council when he was concerned with military and diplomatic decisions.[2] All this rankled most grievously in War- wick's breast, though his earlier relations with Somerset had been easy and friendly. But from the spring of 1548 onwards Warwick tended to be much out of London, spending a great deal of his time at Dudley Castle. There was scarcely concealed rage and hatred against the Protector in Warwick's letter to Cecil in July, 1548, protesting Somerset's refusal to remove a justice in order to appoint Warwick's nominee, Gosnold. 'Thus from one degree to another,' he wrote, 'this matter has been tossed smally to my poor credit or estimation.' He was sure he had 'base friends' who rejoiced that he was thus used. It was clear that he must now 'shape my garments after my cloth[?]'. And then he bluntly and ominously concluded— and the warning was meant for Somerset—that 'if they work me no more displeasure, I shall be the better willing to forgive them'.[3] But a far deeper bitterness, and an evident hatred, was engendered by Somerset's very personal and stubborn insistence on pressing forward with the work of Hales' commission and by his determination to enforce the dormant statutes against enclosures and depopula-

[1] The Marquess of Ailesbury, *Savernake Forest*, 48–49; Add. MS. 34,566, ff. 3 and 5, for the negotiations with Hungerford; Jackson, in *Wilts. Archaeol. and Nat. Hist. Mag.* XV (1875), 179–186; private information kindly supplied by the Marquess of Ailesbury; field notes.

[2] Somerset's imperious nature grew with power and age. As early as 1544 he had lashed out bitterly at Russell in a minor misunderstanding regarding a land grant from the Crown (HMC, *Bath MSS.* IV: *Seymour papers*, 97–98); his tone in requiring in- formation could be peremptory (*ibid.* 97, 101, 104); and he could be scathing even in his relations with Thynne, his closest confidant and friend (*ibid.* 108, 114–115).

[3] S.P. Dom., Edw. VI, IV, 26: July 7, 1548.

tions. Thus Warwick was furious when his own park was ploughed and when other trespassers were committed on his lands,[1] and he became the most outspoken of those in the Council who protested against the Protector's social policy. The risings which followed, which Dudley played so important a role in repressing, signalled the ruin of Somerset's policy and gave focus as well as sufficient cause for conciliar discontent, to which Warwick, 'the subtlest intriguer in English history', gave direction and organization.[2] A recently discovered source also suggests that Warwick was deeply aggrieved because Somerset failed to come to his assistance before Norwich, either in person or with additional supplies. Warwick returned to London in mid-September, his army principally still in the field, and, it must be remembered, he returned a hero. And immediately, this prickly man was further angered because Somerset refused the reversion of two minor posts to Warwick's son, Sir Ambrose, who had served with credit in Norfolk, granting them instead to Thomas Fisher, one of his own secretaries.[3] Further, this account, by one favourably disposed to Somerset, suggests that the Duke behaved coldly towards Warwick on his return, and that 'there was no request that he made . . . but he had a repulse and went without it'.[4] Almost immediately, while the King lay at Hampton Court and while Somerset enjoyed a few days of hunting in Hampshire, Dudley forged and then closed the ring of conspiracy around the Lord Protector.

Warwick alone of all the Council possessed sufficient courage and ruthlessness to foment a conspiracy from the grievances so many of his colleagues harboured against Somerset. Old and bitter grievances they were. Herbert had been violently opposed to the enclosure commission and was outraged when he too found his recently formed park ploughed. Russell, of a more amiable quality of mind, had been deeply offended by Somerset's deserved strictures on his command in the west and was now at last coming up towards London in slow stages. Northampton was still embittered by the Protector's refusal to help him with his marital difficulties, while Dorset had been closely connected with Thomas Seymour and still resented the lapse of the plan to marry his daughter (Lady Jane) to the King. More ominous was the fact that almost immediately after

[1] S.P. Dom., Edw. VI, VII, 35: June 18, 1549.   [2] Pollard, *Somerset*, 244–245.
[3] Malkiewicz, A. J. A., 'An eye-witness's account of the *coup d'état* of October 1549', *E.H.R.* LXX (1955), ff. 7a–7b. The manuscript, here well edited, is in Add. MS. 48,126, ff. 6a–16a. The editor suggests that it was written *c.* 1561 by an unknown person who had possibly served Somerset in a secretarial capacity.
[4] Malkiewicz, in *E.H.R.* LXX (1955), f. 8a.

his return to London, Warwick had begun discussions with those of the Privy Council who were known to be Roman Catholic in faith or sentiment. This was fully known by the Princess Mary who in September informed the imperial envoy that there was serious friction in the Council and that Warwick, Southampton, Arundel, and Paulet had approached her to determine whether she would lend her support to an impeachment of the Lord Protector, to which she had sensibly replied that she had no intention of intervening in governmental affairs.[1] Warwick's courtship of Southampton, Arundel, and St John must have proceeded fairly openly, since on September 15th Van der Delft reported that the divisions in the Council were well known, and especially the ill-will between Warwick and Somerset.[2] The Emperor was seriously concerned because of these reports, since any serious disturbance would almost certainly result in a coastal attack by France, and he warned Mary to stand clear of any involvement and instructed his ambassador to show 'no passion against the Protector'.[3] A few days later, in an almost hysterical dispatch, Van der Delft reported that Paget had informed him that the Protector was in an extremely difficult position and, now aware of conspiratorial courses against him, could scarcely see two Councillors speaking together without immediate suspicion. Further, Warwick had called on him to warn that 'Ambassador Hoby is entirely devoted to the Protector, and his creature', while throwing out the veiled hint that the time was at hand for the Emperor to come forward as the 'father' of the young King.[4]

Among all his colleagues in the Council, only Paget was sufficiently honest and courageous to deal frankly with Somerset and to warn him of the accumulation of grievance and hatred which he was building up within the governing junta. As we know, the two men stood in a rather special relationship, and between them there was a personal understanding stretching back to the last hours of Henry VIII's life.[5] But these warnings and this blunt advice should for other reasons have been seriously considered by Somerset, since Paget was beyond doubt the ablest as he was the most perceptive of all the Council. And he was devoted to England even more tenaciously than to the Lord Protector, which gave great force to all his policy recommendations just as they did to his frank criticism of Edward Seymour.

[1] *Cal. S.P. Span.* IX, 445–446.   [2] *Ibid.* 448.
[3] *Ibid.* 450: Sept. 17, 1549.   [4] *Ibid.* 454–455: Sept. 23, 1549.
[5] *Vide ante*, 51–53, 57–62.

As early as January, 1548, Paget had given Somerset a New Year's token in the form of short but pithy counsel. The Protector should render justice without favour and take care to appoint only 'assured and staid men' as officers of state under him. He should liberally reward the worthy servants of the Crown, and he should take fees and rewards from none save the King. Be affable to the good, Paget continued, and severe to the evil, and above all the Protector should follow the advice rendered to him in Council and make sure that those about him as ministers of state were without corruption.[1] These are of course conventional sentiments, and were so expressed, suggesting strongly, however, that during the first year of his tenure of power Somerset had met the high standards and expectations of the wisest of his Councillors.

But not so Paget's advice to the Duke written after a meeting of the Council on May 8, 1549, in which Paget thought his manner had been both boorish and unfitting. Paget says that he dared be frank because he loved the Protector. So rough and sharp had Somerset become in Council that men feared to speak their minds, 'though it were never so necessary; for you know it; which in the end will be dangerous unto you'. He had tried to speak freely and honestly, but on occasion Somerset 'nips me so sharply', which he had borne because he knew his mind and nature. But not so other men, who if they 'shall be snapped, God knows what loss you shall have by it'. His colleagues were troubled by his temper in Council, as was exhibited that very morning when Sir Richard Lee was so severely handled that he 'came to my chamber weeping' and 'seemed almost out of his wits'. Paget suggested, indeed, that neither Henry VIII nor Wolsey dealt so severely with those who did not agree with them in Council. Somerset had of late grown choleric. This should not be the mood or mien even of monarchs, but most surely, 'a subject in great authority, as your Grace is, using such fashion, is like to fall into great danger and peril of his own person, beside that to the commonweal'. Paget begged for a gentler manner and that on those occasions when the whole Council opposed him he learn to follow advice. He closed by reminding Somerset that he sought no more than the King's honour 'and your own surety and preservation'.[2] This remarkable document opens for us a perfect insight into the arrogance that was growing in Somerset's mien, into the reasons why the confidence of men seeking to work with him was eroding, and why at the end so few of his associates stood with him. Among those who did stand faithful was

[1] Strype, *Memorials*, II, i, 35.   [2] S.P. Dom., Edw. VI, VII, 5: May 8, 1549.

Paget, surely a minister of singular courage, honesty, and perceptivity. But try as he might Somerset could not overcome the quick temper, the sharp tongue, and the abrasive nature which so tragically weakened the greatness of the man.

While abroad on his embassy to the Emperor in the summer of 1549, Paget, brooding on the risings that were now sweeping England and on Somerset's stubbornly held social and economic policy, and deeply concerned by the ruin of English foreign policy, wrote even more fully and frankly to the Lord Protector. Once more he reminded Somerset of the special relation between them and of the compact they had reached in the gallery at Westminster while Henry VIII was dying. But the Protector had ignored his advice and had gravely weakened his power by his steady sympathy and unwise efforts to help the poor. It is indeed a great 'pity, . . . that your too much gentleness should be an occasion of so great an evil as is now chanced in England by these rebels'. He would remind the Protector that every society is cemented together by law and by religion, and when either is weak or lacking, 'farewell all just society, farewell kings, government, justice and all other virtues'. And just this dissolution was now occurring in England. The old religion had been forbidden before the new was firmly planted, while in stir after stir the very fabric of law had been severely damaged. 'Would to God, that at the first stir you had followed the matter hotly, and caused justice to have been administered in solemn fashion to the terror of others, and then to have granted a pardon.' But Somerset had in effect in advance given pardons for violence, while making it all too clear that his sympathies ran with the needs and the demands of the poor. Somerset had sought to do too much and that far too quickly. Indeed, and here Paget was correct, all the agitation regarding enclosures relates to old rather than present wrongs. These men now in revolt have with their fathers before them lived quietly for sixty years with the enclosures now being thrown down. Hence what a now unruly commons seeks is liberty, or rather a liberty to overthrow all law and order. Paget had warned Somerset repeatedly of all this and so had the Council: 'I know in the matter of the commons, every man in the Council have misliked your proceedings, and wished it otherwise.' Somerset knows that he is absolutely loyal and that he has lent him an unflinching support. But he must now urge most strongly that the realm be restored to an absolute obedience, and only then should reforms be attempted. This, Paget almost says, must be done, and that quickly, for the sources of Somerset's power were rapidly being exhausted. In this remarkable disquisition, dour and blunt as it is, is to be found an exact delineation of the fatal flaws in Somerset's greatness as a statesman. He was proud, he was arrogant, he was incapable of working with others in the Council chamber, and he was vested with a vision of the society not shared, and on the whole feared, by colleagues like Paget whose feet were firmly planted on the solid earth of effective power.[1]

Once more, and almost at the point of greatest crisis in the risings of 1549, Paget's mind and brooding concern were at least partially revealed in a letter to Petre, written from Bruges. Paget is concerned for Somerset not only because of his policies but because he leans too heavily on Thynne, whom he regarded as at once covetous and dishonest. He prays, in fact, 'that the covetous disposition of that man do my Lord's Grace no hurt. There is no one thing whereof his Grace hath need to take such heed as of that man's proceedings, . . .' He plainly suggested that England's prestige abroad could not be restored until the realm was brought to full obedience, and this could not be done until '*new fantasies*' and innovations of reform were halted. Then there follows an important suggestion that Paget as early as July 22nd knew or sensed that discussions were already under way in the Council for some *coup* which would either limit the Protector's power or even exclude him from authority. This he forthrightly condemned, for '*to alter the state of a realm would ask ten years' deliberation*' and England, he trusts, will be warned by its own past against the dangers of 'war abroad and war among ourselves'.[2] At the very least, it is clear that by late July the disquiet and fear in the Privy Council was giving way to at least casual and exploratory discussions which had as their intention the limitation of the Protector's power. We know that by early September these discussions were fairly open and serious. A wave of reaction and fear, among the governing classes and in the Council, created the perfect opportunity for Warwick, the consummate conspirator, returning with a victorious army behind him. And Warwick, once his essentially careful mind had considered the risk and estimated his resources, was not one to delay action.

---

[1] There are two versions of this important document. We have followed S.P. Dom., Edw. VI, VIII, 4, which is probably the original. The version in Cotton MSS., Titus, F, iii, ff. 277–279, is accurate save for minor differences, but is in a later hand. The letter is printed in fairly full form by Strype (*Memorials*, II, ii, 429–437).

[2] Tytler, *England*, I, 190–192: July 22, 1549. The dispatch was addressed to Petre or, in the event of his absence, to Sir Thomas Smith (*Cal. S.P. For.*, *Edw. VI*, #192).

2. THE COUP D'ÉTAT (SEPTEMBER–OCTOBER, 1549)

We have spoken of the coldness and the friction which characterized the relations of Somerset and Warwick following on the
Earl's triumphant return to London in the middle of September.
The known fact that Warwick was frequently with Wriothesley,
and to a lesser extent with Arundel, also could suggest nothing
else to Somerset than that there was plotting in progress and that in
his machinations Warwick was overtly bidding for Roman Catholic
support. But there was no open breach and Somerset's movements,
in so far as we can trace them, display no hint of real alarm until
September 25th when in a letter to Russell on western matters he
concluded with the cryptic (and prophetic) addendum that 'we
look for you and Sir William Herbert, at the farthest about the 8th
day of the next month, about which time we would gladly have you
here for matters of importance'.[1] This is evidently not still another
of the earlier series of letters, commanding Russell to return with
most of his force for military needs in Norfolk, now happily past,
but is without much doubt the first of other, and far more urgent,
letters in which the Protector sought to enlist Russell's support in
the crisis which he now sensed was about to break.

Somerset knew full well that, save for about 500 household
troops, he possessed no power and that in a true sense he stood
helpless between Warwick's as yet not fully discharged army and
the strong forces in the west commanded by a peer whom he had
probably alienated, and who at the least no longer answered his
dispatches. Accordingly, on Septembr 30th a proclamation was
drafted and promulgated, commanding that all troops in the realm,
having been paid, should immediately proceed towards their
appointed commands, whether on the Scottish border or elsewhere,
and, most specifically, that such troops should immediately 'avoid
and depart forth of [from] the city of London and the suburbs of
the same', where many hundreds of Warwick's troops in fact were.
And on the next day, we believe, Somerset drew, but did not issue
until October 5th, a proclamation which in the name of the King
commanded 'all his loving subjects' to repair, fully arrayed, to
Hampton Court for the defence of his royal person and of the Lord
Protector, 'against whom certain [ones] hath attempted a most
dangerous conspiracy'.[2] Despite these precautionary measures,

---

[1] Petyt MS. 538, xlvi, f. 466.
[2] Hughes and Larkin, *Tudor proclamations*, I, 483; S.P. Dom., Edw. VI, IX, 1, 2.

Somerset was conducting his affairs normally on the following day (October 2nd) when Paulet (or a near colleague) laid before him the needs of many poor soldiers, as yet unpaid, for whom a considerable sum was assigned on the 3rd,[1] though Somerset quickly expressed his regret for the action since he was now persuaded that Warwick meant to employ them against him.[2] Hoby was later to express the view that all the preparations being made against the Protector proceeded 'by the onlie malice of the Erle of Warwicke',[3] who had now engaged the support of so many of his colleagues that 'every lord and counsellor went through the city weaponed, and had their servants likewise weaponed, attending upon them in new liveries, to the great wondering of many' of the citizenry of London.[4] By this date (October 3rd) there was already in the City a suspicious concentration of at least eleven of the original executors of Henry VIII's will,[5] and when news reached him that the London Lords, as we shall call the Warwick group, had twice dined together in private conference, Somerset would have been naive indeed had he not concluded that a conspiracy was now fully formed against him. With him and the King at Hampton Court there were of the Council Cranmer, Paget, Cecil, Sir Thomas Smith, and Petre, as well as Somerset's closest friend, Sir John Thynne, The focal centre for the deliberations of the London Council was at first Warwick's house at Ely Place, though after Paulet was successful in gaining control of the Tower, Warwick withdrew into the fastnesses of the City, lodging in the house of Sir John York, the master of the Southwark mint.[6] Hayward may well have been accurate when he tells us that these steady London discussions, before action was taken, were principally between Warwick and the two Catholic peers, Southampton and Arundel, 'which often held the greatest part of the night', for Dudley thought it necessary to his plans to enlist the sympathy and support of those alarmed by the progress of the Reformation under Somerset.[7]

Weak though his position was, Somerset thought himself obliged by the force being deployed against him to issue on October 5th the proclamation calling to his aid a general array which, as we

[1] *A.P.C.* II, 328-329.   [2] Malkiewicz, in *E.H.R.* LXX (1955), f. 9b.

[3] Hoby, Sir Thomas, *The travels and life of Sir Thomas Hoby, etc.*, ed. by Edgar Powell (Camden Miscellany, X, 1902), 21.

[4] Holinshed, *Chronicles*, III, 1014.

[5] They were Warwick, Southampton, North, Paulet, the two Wottons, Rich, Southwell, Arundel, and Sir Edmund Peckham.

[6] *Grafton's Chronicle*, II, 522; *Two London chronicles* (Camden Misc. XII), 19.

[7] Hayward, *Edward VI*, 309.

have observed, had been readied some days earlier. He was now deeply committed and spent the whole of the day calling for assistance from whatever quarter.[1] Two couriers had already been dispatched to Russell and Herbert, but now a formal command was issued summoning them both, with their forces, to repair to Hampton Court to ensure the safety of the King and as an assurance 'of your private good affections towards us'. Herbert, being nearer, could reach the Court sooner, and that he was to do, presumably by post, his forces to follow him.[2] At the same time a warrant was placed in the hands of Somerset's brother, Sir Henry Seymour, requiring him to raise forces of horse and foot and to repair 'with all expedition' to join the Protector in putting down a conspiracy against the Crown.[3] On this same day, too, Somerset issued orders to his servant, Golding, to take under his charge the 'things, servants, and ordinary power' of the Earl of Oxford, and to assemble the forces thus requisitioned for such military service as the Protector might require for the King's uses.[4] Guards were set that night at Hampton Court, the small force of about 500 household troops presumably being the only well armed and disciplined men in hand, while Somerset sent agents into the City to try to determine the extent and the nature of the conspiracy which he had now to meet.

Early on the morning of Saturday, October 6th, unidentified agents returned to Hampton Court to report that there was in the streets of London considerable military movement, especially of horse. The whole court was at once aroused, men were placed under arms, entrenchments were begun and the gates fortified. Somerset, preparing for a sudden sortie of horse, addressed the court, informing the household that Warwick and certain other lords were resolved to throw him down and to make Mary Regent. He reminded them, too, of the machinations of Richard III and de-

---

[1] Somerset could undoubtedly have waged civil war had he been so disposed. Russell and Herbert both informed the Council that Hampshire and Wiltshire were deeply aroused. Typical of what was happening, at least in southern England, is revealed by the account of a Kentish gentleman, John Eason, who some months later recalled that on receipt of Somerset's call for troops, 'I took 352 men furnished to serve the king, and as we were coming towards Windsor, for that I heard divers tales by the way to discourage my men, I animated them, declaring unto them that I would bring them to the king'. He continues that 'I was sure that my Lord Protector . . . could be no traitor', and he could but conclude that the power gathering in London was to be employed against the King. Therefore he 'marched forward and coming by the way I heard that the Lord Protector had yielded, so I paid my men their wages from my own money and distributed my victuals among them, and then returned home'. (S.P. Dom., Edw. VI, X, 18: John Eason to Cecil, July 24, 1550.)   [2] S.P. Dom. Edw. VI, IX, 5.
[3] *Ibid.* 3 (signed with the King's stamp and in form from the King).   [4] *Ibid.* 4.

clared to them that the thrust of the conspiracy ran against the King rather than himself. He accordingly pledged his own life to the defence of the King, stating that 'I myself will be one of the first that will die in the gate, if they come in by any forcible manner into the court'.[1] During the course of the day, so the imperial ambassador recorded, as many as 4000 'peasants' answered this general summons for aid, whom Somerset divided into companies and assigned to quarters. These volunteers, whatever their number, would have been completely untrained and were probably in the main unarmed. Late in the afternoon, Somerset, still preparing to defend Hampton Court, sent away his wife who, we are told, was rudely handled both by courtiers and by the gathering commons, 'who put all this trouble down to her'.[2]

But, professional soldier that he was, Somerset knew that the quality of the assembling force was useless for his needs and that Hampton Court was in fact naturally indefensible. His position was hopeless, unless the nobility and great gentry, with their re-tainers, instantly heeded his call, or unless Russell and Herbert had decided to lend him their support. Accordingly, still another appeal was drafted in the King's name, informing both Russell and Herbert of the heinous conspiracy forming against the Protector by untruthful men who had not hesitated to spread the rumour abroad that he had sold Boulogne and had withheld the wages of troops being disbanded, when in fact nothing had been done without the approval of the Council. Hence they were commanded to repair at once to the Court for his defence.[3] These orders were supplemented by a private dispatch signed by Somerset and to be delivered by his son, Sir Edward Seymour. This angrily denounced to Russell those who had raised against him a conspiracy supported only by deliberate lies, such as that he was already under arrest, that he was resolved to free Gardiner and Bonner, and was de-termined to restore the old religion. This is the treatment he had received from those who should regard him with 'favour and love', and he called on Russell to join him at Windsor[4] for the defence of the King and the realm with 'such forces and power as you may'.[5]

In the course of this day, too, Somerset instructed Petre, who had joined him not more than two days earlier, to make the first attempt

---

[1] Malkiewicz, in *E.H.R.* LXX (1955), f. 10b.
[2] *Cal. S.P. Span.* IX, 459: Oct. 8, 1549.   [3] S.P. Dom., Edw. VI, IX, 8, 9.
[4] This suggests that this dispatch was sent late on October 6th, since the decision to remove the King to Windsor was not taken until evening on that day.
[5] S.P. Dom., Edw. VI, IX, 6, 7.

at parley by waiting on the London Lords in order to determine the reasons for their unauthorized meetings there, to warn them that they were risking the possible offence of treason, and to feel out the strength and intent of the conspiracy. For whatever reason—and persuasion, self-interest, and outright fear all suggest themselves— Petre never returned from this mission, casting his lot, however reluctantly, with the London Lords.[1] That night Somerset, realizing that his position at Hampton Court was indefensible, reached his decision to remove the King and such forces as he had to the stronger natural defences of Windsor Castle, which would also place him at least a few miles more distant from the London Lords and closer to possible help from Russell and Herbert. As the King put it so tersely in his *Chronicle*, 'that night, with all the people, at nine or ten o'clock at night, I went to Windsor, and there was watch and ward kept every night'.[2] We know from later evidence that this was in fact a frightening experience for the still very young King, and it was one for which he never forgave Somerset. Not fully informed by his aloof uncle, not certain of his own role in what was occurring, slightly ill with one of his periodic colds, and probably sound asleep when he was routed from his bed, the royal child was handled more like a piece of infinitely valuable baggage than the fledgling Tudor monarch that he was.

Meanwhile, on this same critical day, the Council in London, which now numbered sixteen, if Petre be included, was busily concerned with propaganda efforts and in securing its own position with the always somewhat unpredictable and fiercely independent government of the City. Hence a pronouncement was issued stating that the King's person was in danger from the falsehoods and treasons of the Duke, promising to 'let the people know the truth', and requiring all subjects to be in readiness to repair to them for the King's service.[3] Very full, and piously defensive, notes were kept of still another meeting of the London Lords at Ely House, evidently to be employed as occasion required for propaganda purposes. Somerset was wholly blamed for the recent 'great slaughter and effusion of blood'. He had ignored their advice and had persisted in his fantasies. So too, on his own authority he had abandoned Haddington and had placed Boulogne in great danger. They had resolved on this day to repair to Hampton Court, accompanied only by an ordinary number of servants, in order to 'bring things into

[1] Emmison, F. G., *Tudor secretary. Sir William Petre, etc.* (L., 1961), 75–76.
[2] Edward VI, *Chronicle*, 17; *Cal. S.P. Span.*, IX, 457.
[3] S.P. Dom., Edw. VI, IX, 10: Oct. 6, 1549.

frame again'; but even as they prepared to mount, news came that Somerset was raising the commons and that they might be destroyed if they proceeded. Somerset had deliberately appealed to the commons against them and other nobles and gentry. Libels setting out his lies had appeared in London, and he was raising up horse against them. Hence they had resolved to stay in London; they had determined to warn the country not to obey Somerset's orders; and they had taken the precaution of securing the Tower and of calling certain nobles and gentry to join them.[1] Later in the day the London Lords called the Lord Mayor and aldermen before them, when the Council's case was sketched for them by Rich, who had just joined his colleagues, and probably by other members of the junta. We do not have an authentic version of Rich's presentation, that printed by Hayward being an invention. But we may fairly assume that the charges which we have just noted were set out as the explanation of their position. The City officials present agreed to mount a strong watch, but pointed out that they could not meet a demand for military aid without the consent of the Common Council before which they proposed promptly to lay the Lords' demands and in their presence.[2]

The Common Council was convened to hear the demands of the Lords on the following day and again on October 9th. The Lords had now stated their requirements at 2000 men and the watching of the City, while to the great embarrassment of this thoroughly representative body, a counter-demand from the Lord Protector at Windsor for 1000 troops for the repression of conspiracy could not be ignored. The Recorder, Brooke, laid both claims before the members, recommending that the City lend its support to the London Lords, since the Protector had abused the King and the realm and must be relieved of his custody of the King's person. But at the same time he suggested that no more than 500 troops be supplied for the needs of the Lords.

The Common Council, quite as much as the Lord Mayor and aldermen, were of course under direct and overweening pressure from the London Lords. But there was evidently strong resistance to Brooke's proposal. In fact, the assembly stood mute until 'a wise and good citizen', George Stadlow, rose to point out that it was good to think of things now past in order to avoid danger to come.

---

[1] *A.P.C.* II, 330–332.

[2] Stow, *Annales*, 597; Hayward, *Edward VI*, 304–305, for the unreliable text; Foxe, *Acts and monuments*, VI, 288–289 (who follows in part the later and more formal accusation lodged against Somerset, *vide post*, 522–523); *Grafton's Chronicle*, II, 522–523; Holinshed, *Chronicles*, III, 1017–1018.

He reminded his fellow citizens of the chronicler Fabyan's account of the wars of Henry III with the barons of that age, when, as now, the Lords required the aid of London for the common good. Aid was given and the Lords won the war and captured the King. In due time, however, the King and his son were released, full pardon being granted to the City by act of Parliament. But what followed? The City's liberties were revoked, strangers were set over it, and the goods of the citizens lay at the mercy of a king who had neither forgotten nor forgiven. 'Such it is to enter into the wrath of a prince.' Therefore he presented that aid should be extended to the King, 'whose voice we ought to hearken unto', rather than to the Lords. His advice was that the City join with the Lords to petition the King to hear the complaints now lodged against Somerset, to see if they may be 'justly alleged and proved'. Moved by this eloquent and sensible speech, displaying as it did an almost overt scepticism towards the allegations against Somerset, the meeting was evidently adjourned without decision. But on the next day pressure was again applied on the Common Council by the Lords, who felt it necessary to offer assurance that no alterations whatsoever in religion were intended, but 'only the preservation and enforcement of the laws as they stood'. Then on October 9th or 10th, when the crisis was approaching resolution, the Common Council at last voted to supply 500 men, or if that proved insufficient, 1000, who were to be placed under the orders of the Lords of the Council.[1]

There was considerable and devoted sentiment in the City favouring Somerset in this struggle for power, and there were more who, at once prudent in instinct and unsure as to the issues, held a position well and skilfully expounded by Stadlow. But the Lords held the Tower, were martialling their own retainers, were in a position to exact some measure of support from the City, and held under command the fragments of Warwick's army still in and near the capital. They were evidently playing for time until they gained a commitment from Russell and Herbert, whose power was decisive.

Every available resource of propaganda was now employed by Somerset and his partisans to gain further support from the unde-clared, particularly in London, though the time remaining was in fact much too short for very effective measures. It was probably on

[1] Harl. MS. 1759, #43, ff. 174b, 253 (for Stadlow's speech); Hargrave MS. 134 ('Acts of Common Council'), ff. 109, 109b; Stow, *Annales*, 597; *A.P.C.* II, 337-338: Oct. 8, 1549, and signed by 17 members; Foxe, *Acts and monuments*, VI, 289-290; Hayward, *Edward VI*, 306; *Grafton's Chronicle*, II, 523; Holinshed, *Chronicles*, III, 1018.

October 7th that letters were drawn up over the King's signature, appealing to the nobility to perform their sworn and bounden duty to lend immediate support to the Duke, though we find no evidence that they were in fact distributed.[1] Quickly drafted handbills were also drawn, and circulated in London and in the region around Windsor, which stated the Protector's case in somewhat hysterical terms. The people must remember their due obedience and not be deceived by 'the painted eloquence of . . . crafty traitors'. The Lords opposing Somerset are those who have undone the King's subjects. Now fearing Somerset's intention to redress the wrongs of the people in the next Parliament, these men seek to destroy him and then in due course the King. The people must stick fast in their allegiance to the King, for these Lords are those who have 'come up but late from the dunghill; a sort . . . more meet to keep swine than to occupy' the offices which they hold.[2] The people must rise with their full power to defend the legal government and the godly purposes of the Lord Protector. This is particularly so for the poor commons, who had their 'pardon this year by the mercy of the king and the goodness of the Lord Protector; for whom let us fight'.[3]

These hasty and incendiary propaganda efforts did not, however, distract Somerset from a serious and now sustained effort to find some basis of accommodation with the London Lords. These negotiations for a settlement were pursued with measured caution by both sides because both Somerset and Warwick well understood that England might easily be plunged into a dreadful and ruinous civil war. Somerset, in a letter to the London Lords, protested because Petre, sent by those of the Council at Windsor with a messenger, had been, as he supposed, forcibly detained. He was 'right sorry' that the Lords thus proceeded with violence, for he stood ready to parley 'if any reasonable conditions and offers will take place', or if he could know what was required of him. He assured them that they would find him reasonable if the safety of the King could be assured and an 'effusion of Christian blood avoided'.[4] This carefully composed and wholly conciliatory document can only mean that even before he had received final word from Russell and Herbert, Somerset sensed that the forces against him were overweening in their strength and that surrender of his power would be required unless he were prepared to embrace civil war. But he was still levying archers in the region lying about Windsor on this same

[1] S.P. Dom., Edw. VI, IX, 13.
[2] Ibid. 11: Oct. 7, 1549.　　　　[3] Ibid. 12: Oct. ?, 1549.
[4] Ibid. 16: Oct. 7, 1549.

17

day,[1] and he seems to have moved with a small force as far as Kingston, until a gentleman of the Privy Chamber, sent on to see if the Tower could be gained in the King's name, returned with the dread news that it had been seized for the Lords.[2]

The London Lords, after considering the message brought by Petre, and probably Somerset's letter as well, replied on this same day (October 7th) in an important dispatch which they formally addressed to the King. They expressed themselves as grieved that efforts were being made to cause the King to doubt their fidelity, for they had consulted together for no other purpose than to safeguard him and his realm. They had long sought to advise Somerset, but he has 'refused to hear reason', and they would reason with him again were it not that he had drawn force about himself. It was only for the redress of these ills that they remained in London and had caused Petre to remain with them.[3]

Probably simultaneously, and with more helpful informality, the Lords likewise replied directly to Somerset's conciliatory message with a dispatch which was in form addressed to the members of the Council then at Windsor. They maintained that Somerset had misrepresented the purpose of their London meetings, for their sole concern had been only the safety of the King's person and the good estate of his realm. If Somerset had only heeded their advice, all matters could have been resolved without domestic disturbance. But since the Duke had raised force against them they had no other choice than to assemble and to take action. If Somerset would agree to absent himself from the King, be ordered by justice and reason, and disperse his armed forces, they would in their turn act as good subjects and Councillors. They pointed out that they 'be almost the whole Council', and they clearly intimated that if those few of their colleagues at Windsor failed to agree with them, force ('a stir') would be the inevitable consequence.[4] This was of course a complete misrepresentation of what had happened, the assurances given to Somerset were purposely vague, and it was clear that they were demanding his deposition from the seat of power. The 'force' of England in fact lay, and this they knew, not in Somer-

[1] S.P. Dom., Edw. VI, IX, 15: Oct. 7, 1549.

[2] Malkiewicz, in *E.H.R.* LXX (1955), ff. 11a–11b; S.P. Dom., Edw. VI, IX, 14, on the taking over of the Tower.

[3] S.P. Dom., Edw. VI, IX, 17: Oct. 7, 1549; two copies in *ibid.* 18, 19; *A.P.C.* II, 333–334. The original is in part certainly in Southampton's hand, and the remainder probably in Petre's (Emmison, *Petre*, 77). It is signed by 16 members of the Council.

[4] S.P. Dom., Edw. VI, IX, 22: Oct. 7, 1549; Cotton MSS., Caligula, B, vii, 404; this too was signed by 16 members of the Council (*A.P.C.* II, 335–336). At the end of this message, they plead with Cranmer and Paget to embrace their position.

set's undisciplined and largely unarmed commons, but with them and with Russell and Herbert.

While now committed to negotiation, albeit on their own terms, the London Lords none the less took effective action on October 7th–8th to increase their already formidable strength and to weaken the title as well as the credit of the Lord Protector. They sent Cheyney and Nicholas Wotton to the Spanish ambassador to explain their actions, blaming all on Somerset 'who had been moved by ambition to manage affairs for his own private profit and according to his will'. They had no other recourse than to take matters into their own hands, and they assured Van der Delft (by no means correctly) that all the nobility had assembled in London for their support, save for Derby who would arrive on the morrow. From their account and from other sources Van der Delft reckoned they could put 5000 horse and large forces of infantry in the field.[1] The Lords were also proclaiming Somerset a traitor throughout London, and before a proclamation of treason was formally drafted, sent communications to all sheriffs and justices of the peace, declaring that the Duke was gathering forces to accomplish his treasonable designs and forbidding any assembly of force unless directly ordered in writing by the Privy Council.[2]

And then on the 8th a long and important justification of their action was published by the Lords, in the august form of a proclamation, though legally, of course, they were without capacity to issue such a document without the express consent of the King and the Protector therein denounced. The Lords recalled the quiet estate of the realm at the moment of Henry's death and the domestic calamities and the foreign humiliations which had followed. The 'only root and chief cause of all these evils' had been the government of the Protector. He had enriched himself, had built sumptuously while wars were under way with Scotland and France, had overturned Henry VIII's will, and had ignored the advice of his Council. It was to relieve England of these perils that the Lords resolved to meet in London and had sought to persuade the Duke to live 'within reasonable limits, and to rule by advice'. This had been their sole purpose, to which Somerset had reacted by the levying of force, the spreading of rumours of conspiracy and treason, and by measures to maintain his treasonable power by force of arms if need be. To buttress these designs he had used the King, 'of tender age', wrongfully as the instrumentality of his evil purpose.

[1] *Cal. S.P. Span.* IX, 457–459: Oct. 8, 1549.
[2] S.P. Dom., Edw. VI, IX, 20, 28; *Grey Friars Chronicle* (Camden Soc. LIII), 64.

Hence they commanded that no assistance of any sort be lent to Somerset and that obedience be given only to commands, proclamations, and orders issuing from them.[1]

The final, and the completely decisive, addition of power to the position of the London Lords came when on this same day (October 8th) Russell and Herbert at last replied to Somerset's repeated petitions for their aid in quelling what he denounced as conspiracy. It will be recalled that two months earlier the stream of letters and commands to Russell, first to reduce his forces in the west and then to return with them, had simply been ignored. There may have been replies from Russell, but if so they have been lost. But it is surely clear that for the past month Russell and Herbert had stayed in the west with an army which was the strongest single military entity in the realm and had then begun a slow movement towards London with sufficient forces to save or destroy Somerset. It would seem almost certain that Warwick had been in communication with them and it is probable that he had private assurances of their support when his disaffection gave way to conspiracy at some date very near to mid-September. But, if so, there remains no written evidence that has been found until the shattering decision was made known to Somerset on October 8th, when Russell and Herbert had reached Andover, a scant forty miles from Windsor, rendering the Protector's position there wholly untenable in the event of an attack launched by Warwick from London and by Russell from Hampshire. Russell, justly but scathingly denounced by Somerset during the Western Rising for his inertia and over-caution, now had his complete revenge. In the coldest of language Russell and Herbert indicated that they had had assurances from London that the Lords there meant no injury to the King. The present crisis sprang only from a private quarrel between Somerset and the Lords of London, which had moved them to 'levy as great a power as we may' in order to secure the safety of the King and of the realm. They accordingly urged Somerset to conform himself, to make sure that his private causes did not result in the undoing of the realm. They prayed God that this quarrel should not go to battle, for with the Tudor spectre of the War of the Roses in mind, they warned him that if 'the hands of the nobility be once polluted each with others blood', the quarrel once begun would never end until the realm was reduced to anarchy.

[1] *A proclamation conteinyng the trouth of the Duke of Somersets euel government* (L., [1549]; STC 7828). The document was signed by 19 members of the Council, the full number of which stood at 29 at this date. This manifesto bears a close resemblance in the points made, or alleged, to the articles finally gathered in somewhat unfinished form (*vide post*, 522–523).

It is for this reason that Somerset's proclamation calling out 'the commons we mislike very much', as did the gentry in the counties where they had been.[1]

This grim dispatch was almost certainly not yet in Somerset's hands on October 8th when two additional overtures of negotiation were made from Windsor to London. The first was in form from the King to the Lords, lamenting the imminent danger in which he lay unless the present 'uproars' be brought to an end. They have in the past served him well, as has his uncle, 'and by God's grace may by your good advices serve us full well here after'. All men have their faults, and if they intend 'with cruelty to purge' the faults of his uncle, 'Which of you . . . shall be able [again] to stand before us'? He wishes the quarrel healed and to that end sends Philip Hoby to await their answer.[2]

With this, or at least on the same day, went the decisive commitments from Somerset and those of the Council with him at Windsor, ensuring the realm against the terrible rage of civil war. Cranmer, Paget, and Smith assured the London Lords of their loyalty to the King and the realm and that the Lord Protector would yield his office on honourable terms. Somerset in turn gave his assurances that he would be bound by the negotiated terms of any two of the London Council whom the Lords might appoint with two whom he would appoint from Windsor. At the same time, Somerset wrote a moving personal letter to Warwick reminding him of their friendship from the days of their youth, wondering how it could so quickly be destroyed by 'rumors and bruits, or persuasion of others'. All this, truly a complete yielding, was eloquently underscored by Smith in a private letter to Petre, urging him to seek a settlement, since he is 'no seeker of extremity nor blood, but of moderation in all things'. He cannot believe that the Lords will require with blood that which they can gain with persuasion and honour. 'I pray you join with us . . . that things may be brought to moderation.' He lamented his own case, for he cannot leave the King and Somerset, for from the Protector he has had all, even though 'I have misliked also some things that you and the rest of my Lords there did mislike'. But now all men must strive for moderation and an honourable resolution lest the realm bear in one year the double tragedy of two civil wars.[3]

The momentum of events now became more rapid as Somerset

[1] Petyt MS. 538, xlvi, f. 470; S.P. Dom., Edw. VI, IX, 23: Oct. 8, 1549.

[2] S.P. Dom., Edw. VI, IX, 24: Oct. 8, 1549; Harl. MS. 353, #23, f. 76.

[3] Ibid. 26; Cotton MSS., Caligula, B, vii, 407; Stow, Annales, 598; S.P. Dom., Edw. VI, IX, 27, for the documentation of this paragraph.

had few counters with which even to negotiate terms. But not so with the timorous John Russell who on October 9th must have puzzled the London Council by writing them that he had fallen back a day's march from Andover to Wilton. He explained that in the Andover region 'the countreys every way were in a roar that no man wist what to do'. The gentry had been commanded to present themselves at Windsor and the commons were stirred and ready to send 5000–6000 men to Somerset's relief, had it not been for their (Russell and Herbert both signed the letter) restraining presence. They cannot believe the Duke will take the field, but if he should they have deprived him of possible support from Hampshire, Wiltshire, Somersetshire, Gloucestershire, and the west. They do not understand why the London Lords have not kept in close communication with them, Somerset having so few of the Councillors with him. They have made themselves so strong that they can restore communication by force if need be. They now wished to know what proclamations to issue and when and with what force they should move up to close on Windsor, if that were required.[1]

But, as we have seen, events were outrunning Russell's communications: for on this day the London Lords, now numbering twenty-two, forwarded letters, amounting to instructions, to the King, the Windsor Councillors, and individually to Cranmer and Paget. The tone towards Somerset was coldly hostile, since the charges against him now were principally that he had severed them from the King's presence and had through his entire tenure of power broken the express terms of the will positing power in the whole body of the Council. They demanded that he submit himself to law as a subject and they charged those of the Council at Windsor to see that the King was not removed from Windsor, and that they should associate themselves with the London Council so that 'things may soon be quickly and moderately compounded'.[2]

These letters had been brought from London by Hoby, trusted as he was by both factions. He addressed Somerset and his followers, pleading that their London colleagues were not men of blood, for they say on their honour that 'they do not intend, nor will hurt . . . the person of my Lord the Duke, nor of none of you all, nor take away any of his lands or goods'. Nor did they forget that Somerset was the King's uncle. They were resolved only 'to give order for the protectorship, which hath not been so well ordered as they think

[1] S.P. Dom., Edw. VI, IX, 31: Oct. 9, 1549.
[2] Ibid. 37; A.P.C. II, 337–342, 343; Cotton MSS., Caligula, B, vii, 408.

it should have been' and to see the realm better administered for the King. Then turning to Somerset, Hoby bade him not to be afraid, for 'I will lose this my neck, if you have any hurt'. Then, we are told, all present fell on their knees as the dreadful tension lifted when the Duke indicated his willingness to yield on the terms thus offered.[1] We are told, too, by an observer then at court, that Hoby secretly placed in William Howard's hands the informal articles of accusation gathered against Somerset, which as they were read by the court circle further weakened the credit and authority of the Lord Protector, who now stood defenceless.[2]

Even as Somerset's power, or perhaps more accurately, his will, for resistance crumbled, the London Lords thought it wise to send to the Princesses Mary and Elizabeth their version, not unmarred by falsehood, of what was occurring. As a group they had long been troubled by the Duke's pride and ambition and by his unwillingness to take advice. In the Council he treated all who spoke in opposition with complete contempt. They had at the outset planned nothing more than to dine together and to arrange to treat with him, to which Somerset reacted by seizing the Tower (wholly untrue), raising the commons around Hampton Court, and alleging that they meant to destroy the King and to install Mary as Regent. Hence they had no other choice than to arm themselves, to gain the support of the City, to take over the Tower, and to secure the person of the King from his 'cruel and greedy hands', which they hoped could be accomplished without bloodshed.[3] At the same time, they dispatched to Rutland, commanding such forces as remained on the northern border, a copy of their 'proclamation' of the 'detestable treasons and manifold outrageous doings' of the Duke. Since the safety of the King was obviously endangered, they continued, all the Council, 'one or two only excepted', were even now consulting on necessary measures to be taken. Somerset might in the end attempt to stir the realm on its frontiers and Rutland was accordingly ordered to take his instructions only from the Privy Council.[4]

---

[1] Harl. MS. 353, #23, f. 77, printed in Tytler, *England*, I, 238–240. This is evidently the gist of a memorandum kept by Smith.

[2] Malkiewicz, in *E.H.R.* LXX (1955), ff. 13b–14a; Edward VI, *Chronicle*, 17–18. Howard (later Baron Howard of Effingham) was a trusted professional soldier. The King's account most decidedly suggests that the articles were in fact circulated at court (*vide post*, 522–523). [3] S.P. Dom., Edw. VI, IX, 33: Oct. 9, 1549.

[4] HMC, *12th rpt.*, App. IV: *Rutland MSS.*, IV, 191–192. Rutland replied five days later from Berwick, after the crisis had passed, indicating that he would use his best efforts to preserve order, but reminding the Council that his garrison in Scotland and on the border had been stripped of troops and that he urgently needed 1000 more English soldiers (*ibid.* 193).

It seems probable that Hoby returned to London in the early morning of October 10th, bearing a brief declaration from Cranmer, Smith, and Paget which in effect stated that they accepted the authority of the London Lords and suggested that at least some of the Lords should come to Windsor forthwith, since the question of the residence and protection of the King must now be settled on known terms.[1] Meanwhile, in London the Council, as we may now describe the London Lords, were taking formal and cautious steps to avoid a spontaneous rising when the necessary action of arresting and detaining Somerset was taken—a step which they really postponed for almost two days because of their understandable apprehension. Hence they drafted still another proclamation, never formally promulgated, against those who in divers places, but especially in London, were still issuing 'vile false and traitorous bills, papers and books' against those who stood ready to deliver the person of the King from the Duke's custody, a reward of 100 crowns being offered for information leading to the conviction of such treasonable persons.[2]

The Lords now felt sufficiently strong to move decisively into the vacuum of power created by Somerset's capitulation, particularly since they knew that Russell had again reversed direction and was at the moment of their action probably once more in or near Andover. They accordingly wrote to Paget thanking him for his efforts to secure the safety of the King's person and indicated that they now intended to take Somerset into custody and to hold Smith, Cecil, Thynne, and Whalley until further decision could be reached.[3] The Lords, in this same meeting, understanding that by the 'diligent travail' of Cranmer and Paget the King was once more attended and guarded by his own servants of the household, ordered Sir Anthony Wingfield, Sir Anthony St Leger, and Sir John Williams to prepare to go to Windsor with the force necessary to take the person of the Duke and to hold under house arrest Sir Michael Stanhope and Edward Wolf, in addition to those just mentioned.[4] Wingfield's departure was, however, delayed, while Hoby made still another journey out to Windsor to make certain that the set piece of the surrender was fully arranged. Hoby, who had handled the whole of the negotiations with superb skill, read brief letters in the Chamber

[1] Cotton MSS., Caligula, B, vii, 412.
[2] S.P. Dom., Edw. VI, IX, 40: Oct. 10(?), 1549; *A proclamacion concernyng the deuisers of certain vile letters, etc.* (s. sh. fol.; STC 7829). This document was signed by 22 of the Council.
[3] Cotton MSS., Caligula, B, vii, 410: Oct. 10, 1549.
[4] *A.P.C.* II, 342–343: Oct. 10, 1549.

of Presence in which Somerset was declared a traitor, while at the same time the Lords again gave sufficient assurances respecting the safety of his person.

Paget and all the retinue accepted the terms forthwith, there being in them nothing really new, and according to one account Somerset was at once placed in the custody of twelve yeomen of the guard.[1] Early the next day (October 11th) Wingfield with 500 horse made the ceremonial journey, and with Cranmer and Paget, reported back that day to the still nervous Council that he had arrested Somerset, who was being held under strong guard at Windsor until further orders should arrive. With him at Windsor were his eldest son and his younger brother, who were also to be held for the time being. The King Wingfield had found quite safe, though troubled with 'a great rheum', doubtless caused in part by the night ride from Hampton Court to Windsor. Provision had been made for him at Richmond, though the royal physicians would have preferred London or Hampton. The King in any event wished to leave Windsor where he said he felt in prison, since there were no galleries or gardens in which he could walk, and in a merry mood had inquired when he should see the London Lords.[2] Perhaps, too, everyone save the King himself had in this bruising test of strength forgotten that the morrow was the royal birthday.

The Council moved carefully while quarters in the Tower were being prepared for Somerset. A very full meeting of that body was held at Windsor—twenty-four in all, with Cranmer and Paget in attendance—at which Smith, Stanhope, Thynne, Wolf, and William Grey were examined cursorily, as friends of the Duke and as 'the principal instruments and councillors that he did use both at this time and otherwise also in the affairs of his ill government'. They were forthwith ordered to the Tower, while in the same action Smith was declared deprived of his office and his place in the Council.[3] On October 14th Somerset was take from Windsor to the Tower by Wingfield and perhaps 300 horse, riding through the City 'betwixt the Earls of Southampton and of Huntingdon'. They were joined by the Lord Mayor, the sheriffs, and the Recorder, with aldermen or their deputies guarding the line of march with armed men drawn from their respective wards.[4] Then the Tower gates closed against a

[1] Malkiewicz, in *E.H.R.* LXX (1955), f. 14b; Harl. MS. 353, #23, f. 77; Ellis, *Original letters*, ser. 1, II, 174-175.
[2] S.P. Dom., Edw VI, IX, 42: Oct. 11, 1549.   [3] *A.P.C.* II, 343: Oct. 13, 1549.
[4] Stow, *Annales*, 600 (Stow seems to have been an eye-witness to the event); *A.P.C.* II, 344: Oct. 14, 1549; S.P. Dom., Edw. VI, IX, 45; Holinshed, *Chronicles*, III, 1018–1019; *Two London chronicles* (Camden Misc. XII), 19–20.

man who had sought to do much—perhaps too much—alone, and who at the end found himself completely alone, the hostage of his enemies. The Privy Council, now fully vested with power, felt secure enough to rescind the order that had gone out to 'sundry gentlemen' in each county to join them against the forces gathered by the Duke to advance his 'rebellious proceedings',[1] and to prepare for the English ambassadors abroad a highly coloured and distorted account of the *coup d'état* that had occurred.[2]

Somerset was to emerge from prison and was in due season to regain his seat in the Privy Council and to recover most of his estates before the final cataclysm overcame him. But he was never again to hold the reins of sovereignty or to be able to dispose policy. We shall reserve our final comments on the man and his character to a later place, but some few conclusions may here be ventured. His enemies had brought him down with an incredible ease because when the issue was drawn Somerset refused to expose the young King and the realm to the awful peril of civil war. The commons who at his first call poured in to Hampton Court to lend him support were after a moment of indecision sent home and no further call to arms was made by him. Somerset fell because he no longer enjoyed the support of the Privy Council, which in its turn stood as the embodiment of the governing classes of England and as the artifact of Henry VIII's will. In all that body, so far as the sources disclose, only Cranmer, Paget, and Smith failed to betray him. And Cranmer was without political interest or influence; Paget, though bound by honour to the Duke, had, as we have seen, been scathing in his strictures on Somerset's policy; while Smith was scarcely within the inner precincts of power.

We have in the course of this study commented fully on the successive erosions of Somerset's power and credit. He had by his actions and the gradual unfolding of his social and economic views almost completely alienated the classes which possessed political and economic power in the realm, even before the great rebellions of 1549 frightened all those who wished for stable government. All this had united the Council against him in a conspiracy which would have been treasonable had it not been so easily and so brilliantly successful. The vague and inchoate articles of complaint lodged against the Protector, which he was obliged to endorse before he regained his liberty, accused Somerset of many faults and wrongs. But of the twenty-nine articles, it is significant that nine were

[1] Cotton MSS., Titus, B, ii, 24, f. 50.   [2] S.P. Dom., Edw. VI, IX, 41.

concerned with his enclosure policy and the undoubted sympathy which he bore for the poor, the helpless, and the wronged in the rural society of mid-sixteenth century England.[1] There were as many which condemned him, as irrelevantly as incorrectly, for his conduct as he measured the extent of the conspiracy brought against him and which he in the end decided not to oppose with force or arms. These articles were no more than a crude propaganda piece, a thin and tawdry fabric with which to clothe conspiracy. But six of their number do strike to the root of Somerset's real faults as a leader of men. These are the articles which charge him with shortness of temper, an overweening mien, and an unmovable stubbornness when his own policy was questioned by his colleagues. Somerset possessed a high view of human nature; he sought to build an England which would have provided a fitter habitation for Christian men; and he wanted neither courage nor resolution as he sought to translate his vision into social reality. He was without administrative ability, he was naive in his judgement of men and events, and he was on occasion reckless and improvident in his uses of power. All this is true, but the Duke of Somerset remains none the less a very great man whose magnanimity and high idealism were never to be forgotten as Englishmen spoke in quiet corners, in the fields, and on the sea of the age of the 'Good Duke'.

---

[1] The best text for this document is probably that to be found in Stow, *Annales*, 601–602. Foxe renders it with variants in 20 articles and Holinshed follows him. Hayward prints an evidently defective version which Burnet also follows. There is a transcript of the document in Add. MSS. 9069, f. 43b. It seems in form to be a loose and rather random gathering of notes by the London Lords, never codified or refined, which were rather casually laid before Somerset for his submission while negotiations for his release were about to begin.

INDEX

Hayward, John: estimates by, 254, 260, 286

Heath, Bishop Nicholas, 20, 130, 309, 315, 316–317

Hellesdon Bridge (Norfolk), 481

Helmingham (Suffolk), 223–224

Helston (Cornwall), 440

Henry II, King of France: Order of the Garter for, 96; accession of, 236; foreign policy of, 236–237, 246–247, 264, 272, 280–286, 291, 293–294, 296; and Boulogne, 302, 303

Henry III, King of England, 512

Henry VII, King of England, 111, 121, 360, 429, 458, 483, 484

Henry VIII, King of England: nature of Henrician Reformation, 17–25; Protestant strength at close of reign of, 27–33; speech of, to Parliament (1545), 31; the will of, 54–57, 58, 59; attainders under, 111; and the universities, 326–327; debts of, 392; and coinage, 394; see also 103, 113, 125, 312, 333–334, 348–349, 350, 352, 358, 360, 415, 439, 458, 495, 497, 498, 502, 507, 515, 522

Herbert, Sir William, first Earl of Pembroke, Baron Herbert of Cardiff: rise of, 74, 100–101, 116; Privy Councillor, 80, 83, 88; military activities of, 461, 465, 468, 469, 471, 474, 477, 501, 506, 508, 509, 513, 515, 516, 518; see also 53, 56, 63, 128, 355, 384, 414, 451

Hereford, Bishop of, 139, 214

Hereford, Viscount, see Devereux, Walter

Herefordshire: lands in, 109, 117

Heresbach, Conrad, 240–241

heresy, convictions for, 228–229

Hertford, Earl of, see Seymour, Edward

Hertford Castle, 51–52

Hertfordshire: lands in, 101, 109, 117; Reformation in, 185, 186; riots in, 427

Heslerton, East (Yorks), 452

Hethersett (Norfolk): stir at, 480–481

Hever Castle, 240

Hickman, Anthony, 153

Hilles, Richard, 125–126

Hilsey, Bishop John, 20

Hinton St George (Somerset), 462

Hoby, Sir Philip: ambassador to Emperor, 282; negotiations of, 502, 507, 517–520; see also 64, 84, 129

Hoby, Sir Thomas, 129, 195, 360

Hogarde, Miles, 417

Holbeach, Bishop Henry, 20, 130, 312, 313, 316, 366

Holcroft, Sir Thomas, 274, 280, 284, 285, 297–299

Holgate, Archbishop Robert, 20, 47, 130, 174–175, 223, 312, 341, 354

Holinshed, Raphael: estimates by, 257, 260, 492

Hollinshed, Otwell, 357

Holmes, Thomas, 456

Holte, Robert, 352–353

Holy Island, 244, 266, 287

Home Castle, 261, 299

Homilies, The, see Book of Homilies

Honiton (Devon), 463, 466, 470, 471

Hooker, John, 471

Hooper, Bishop John: and reformation of clergy, 133–134; and Utenhove, 198; and Bullinger, 202; and Bonner, 217; see also 18, 20, 73, 135, 154, 229, 322, 325, 340, 344

Horsey, Sir Jasper, 40

Horton (family), 405

Hoskins, Professor W. G., 389–390

Howard, Henry, Earl of Surrey, 49–50, 81, 93, 95

Howard, Thomas, third Duke of Norfolk, 37, 38, 46, 47, 49–50, 55, 81, 90, 95, 368, 477–478

Howard, William Lord, Baron Howard of Effingham, 363, 365, 519

Hume, John, 227

Hungerford, Sir Anthony, 499

Hunmanby (Yorks), 453

Hunning, William, 87

Hunsdon (Herts), 39, 206

Huntingdon, Earl of, see Hastings, Francis

Huntingdonshire: lands in, 108, 109, 116, 117; M.P. for, 168; Reformation in, 343–344

St Johnston, 246

St Keverne (Cornwall): rising in, 440

St Leger, Sir Anthony, 64, 520

St Mary le Strand, 498

St Mauris, John de, 235, 237, 247, 293, 294, 302

St Michael, Order of, 272

St Neots (Hunts), 149–150, 343

St Paul's Cathedral (London): Reformation in, 148, 163, 165; disorders in, 188–189, 227; services in, 215, 216, 260

Salcot, Bishop, 20, 130, 344

Salisbury (Wilts), 23, 152, 186, 405, 450, 451, 461, 462, 465

Sampford Courtenay (Devon): rising at, 454–456, 463, 464, 493; battle at, 474

Sampson, Bishop Richard, 130

Sandon (Herts), 224

Sandys of the Vyne, Thomas, second Lord, 96, 97, 363

Sarum Use, 311, 313, 321

Savernake Forest (Wilts), 33

Saxlingham (Norfolk), 486

Schmalkaldic War, see Germany, Protestant princes of

Schmutz, Alexander, 204

schools, founding of, 114–115

Scilly Isles, 369, 379

Scoloker, Anthony, 142

Scory, Bishop John, 20

Scotland: army sent against (1544), 45, 46; included in treaty with France, 231–232; at centre of French foreign policy, 236; Reformation in, 241; deterioration of relations with (1543–1547), 241–246; English failure to isolate, 246–250; preparations for invasion of, 250–253; invasion of, 253–263; occupation of, 263–268; English party in, rebuilt, 263–264, 271; French intervention in, 264–265, 268–282; English command in, 265–266; Harrison's proposal for English union with, 269–270; English Border raids on, 273, 274; siege of English strong points in, 283–291; English replacements in (May

1549), 296–297; decision to withdraw from, 298–299

Scotland, Marches of, 93, 96, 244, 251, 265, 296, 299; see also Conyers, John; Dacre, William; Grey, William; Manners, Henry; Seymour, Edward; Wharton, Thomas

Scottish Estates, 242, 283

Scrope, John, eighth Baron Scrope, 90, 92, 363

Seamer (Yorks), 452

Secretary of State: office of, 86–87

Sedbergh (Yorks): school at, 115

Selsey (Sussex), 451

Selve, Odet de, 76, 235, 295

Seton, John, 221

Seymour (family), 33, 74

Seymour, Anne, Duchess of Somerset, 46, 142, 206, 496–497, 509

Seymour, Edward, Viscount Beauchamp of Hache (cr. 1536), Earl of Hertford (cr. 1537), Duke of Somerset (cr. 1547): lineage of, 33–34, 74; rise of (1539–1547), 36, 45–48; marriages and children of, 46, 496–497; and Gardiner, 47–48; Van der Delft's estimate of, 48, 61, 69, 76–77; and Paget, 50–54, 57, 60, 286, 300, 351–352, 502–507; and Henry VIII's will, 55, 58; religious views of, 56, 125–130, 139, 166, 181, 219; settlement of power on, 57–65, 72–77; and Wriothesley, 71; Privy Councillor, 80, 82, 88; and Grey of Wilton, 91–92; in Scottish campaign, 93, 150, 234–235, 242–243, 255–259, 262; and Herbert, 101; estates of, 116, 122; policy of toleration of, 126–127; 174; and William Turner, 135, 332, 341; and radical Protestantism, 145–154 et passim; foreign policy of, 168; concern of, for the society, 177, 356–358; and religious refugees, 197; friendship of, for Princess Mary, 206–207; dependence of, on Emperor, 237–239; prepares invasion of Scotland, 250–253; proclamation to Scotland, 252–253; invasion of Scotland, 253–263;